FAIT[...]
NEW [...]
WITH [...] PSALMS

prepared by

H. Eddie Fox World Director World Methodist Evangelism, The World Methodist Council and Executive Director The World Methodist Evangelism Institute, www.worldmethodist.org	**George E. Morris** The Dan and Lil Hankey Senior Professor World Evangelism The World Methodist Council and Former Senior Pastor First United Methodist Church Peoria, Illinois, USA

I pray that the sharing of your faith
may become effective when you perceive
all the good that we may do for Christ.

(Philemon 6)

World Evangelism
World Methodist Council

The Foundation
for Evangelism

Cokesbury
Nashville

National indigenous Methodist Churches, in cooperation with
World Methodist Evangelism,
have published the
"Basics of Christian Conversion and the Essentials for Leading a Person to Christ"
in the following languages:

Bengali	Indonesian	Shangaan
Bulgarian	Kannada	Slovakian
Czech	Kimeru	Sotho
Chinese	Korean	Spanish
Estonian	Latvian	Swahili
French	Marathi	Tamil
Gujarati	Northern	Telugu
Haitian	Sotho	Tongan
Hausa	Polish	Urdu
Hindi	Portuguese	Xhosa
Iban	Punjab	Yoruba
Igbo	Russian	Zulu
	Samoan	

Additional languages in process:
Akan, Cebuano, Ewe, Fijian, Ga, Hungarian, Iloknao, Lithuanian,
Macedonian, Ndebele, Norwegian, Nyungne, Romanian, Serbian, Shona, Swedish,
Tagalog, Tonga (Zimbabwe), Xitswa, Vietnamese

ISBN 978-0-687-64279-3

08 09 10 11 12 13 14 15 — 10 9 8 7 6 5 4 3 2 1

MANUFACTURED IN CHINA

Presented To

_By_

 FAITH
UNITED METHODIST CHURCH
7431 East 91st Street
Tulsa, OK 74133
918.252.1679

Date

PREFACE

This *Faith-Sharing New Testament with the Psalms* was designed to provide as clear a statement as possible of the basics of Christian conversion and discipleship. It is intended to be used by those persons who desire to be grounded in the Christian faith and to gracefully share that faith with others. This New Testament is offered as an appropriate tool for use in leading persons to accept Christ Jesus as Lord and Savior.

We gratefully acknowledge the inspired dreams and gifts of two deeply committed Christian Laypersons, Jack and Phyllis Jones of Georgia. They envisioned a Faith-Sharer's New Testament suitable to train and encourage Christians everywhere to witness to their faith. This dream inspired their outstanding church leader, Bishop Richard C. Looney, Resident Bishop of the South Georgia Area of The United Methodist Church, to pursue the development of this *Faith-Sharing New Testament*. He called the people of his area, where John Wesley had served as a missionary, to share the good news of Christ with friends, relatives, associates, neighbors, and strangers. The first edition of the *Faith-Sharing New Testament* was produced for the South Georgia area of The United Methodist Church.

As this material was being developed further, we field tested it in Brazil, Kenya, Russia, Estonia, and in the United States of America. We have taught the concepts expressed in this *Faith-Sharing New Testament* for many years in countries all around the world and throughout North America.

To make this model for learning and witnessing easier to use, we have placed biblical passages beneath each question and answer. We have attempted to keep the answers short and to the point. Since it is impossible in a brief statement to provide all the information that faith-sharers need, persons using this material as a basis for their preparation for witnessing are encouraged to take advantage of the revised and expanded resources in the *Faith-Sharing* textbook and the *Faith-Sharing* videotape, authored by us and published by Discipleship Resources.

The materials offered in the *Faith-Sharing New Testament* are plain truths and essentials confirmed by Scripture. In interpreting the Christian faith, we strongly affirm the importance of church teaching throughout history, Christian experience, and reason. However we believe that Scripture is primary and contains all that is necessary for faith and practice. Users of this resource are reminded that this is not the only way to share faith. As we stated above, this is a "tool" for those who are eager to learn the essentials of the faith and how to share their faith with others. Moreover, this "*graceful* pattern" for sharing faith should not be treated as an end unto itself, but the beginning of a lifelong process of faithful discipleship and witnessing. The use of these introductory materials should *not* take the place of Scripture. We stress, instead, the importance of using the *Holy Bible* as the *primary* source of one's learning and testimony.

We have a vision that Christians around the world will share the incredible good news of Jesus Christ. It is our deep prayer that persons will have a sense of competence and confidence in sharing the Christian faith through the power of the Holy Spirit. Our prayer for faith-sharers is the same as that of the apostle Paul. Writing to his dear friend and co-worker Philemon, Paul said: "I pray that the sharing of your faith may become effective when you perceive all the good that we may do for Christ" (Philemon 6).

H. Eddie Fox

George E. Morris

BASICS
OF
CHRISTIAN CONVERSION
AND
DISCIPLESHIP

1. What is a Christian?

A Christian is a person who believes that the living God is revealed in and through Jesus Christ, who accepts Jesus Christ as Lord and Savior, who lives in obedient communion with God through the power of the Holy Spirit, and who takes his or her place in the community of Christ's church.

Acts 11:26 John1:1–5, 14–18
John 14:8–11 Hebrews 1:1–3

2. Who is Jesus Christ?

The word *Christ* comes from the Greek word that means "anointed" and is comparable to the Hebrew word *Messiah*. Jesus is the Christ because in Christ "all the fullness of God was pleased to dwell," and through Christ "God was pleased to reconcile to himself all things" (Colossians 1:19–20). The people of God in the Old Testament looked forward to a promised Messiah who would establish the reign of justice, love, and peace for the whole world. Jesus is that Messiah.

Acts 3:13–19 Acts 10:36–43
Acts 4:11–12 Colossians 1:15–20
John 1:1–5, 14–18 John 14:8–11

3. Who is the Holy Spirit?

The Holy Spirit proceeds from and is one in being with God the Father and the Son, Jesus Christ. The Holy Spirit convinces the world of sin, of righteousness, and of judgment. The Spirit leads human beings through faithful response to the gospel into the fellowship of the church. The Spirit comforts, sustains, and empowers believers and guides them in their pursuit of truth.

John 3:1–10	Romans 8:1–17
John 4:1–30	Acts 1:6–8; 2:1–13, 32–39
John 14:14–29	1 Corinthians 3:16; 12:13
John 15:26–27	1 Thessalonians 5:19
John 16:12–15	John 20:19–23

(Note: Various names are used for the Holy Spirit—for example, Advocate, Comforter, Spirit of Truth, Holy Ghost, Spirit, Spirit of God, Spirit of Christ.)

4. What is the invitation to Christian discipleship?

All people are invited by God to repent, to trust and follow Jesus Christ, to learn from his words and deeds, and to share in his mission, through the power of the Holy Spirit and in company with other Christians.

Mark 1:16–20; 3:13–15	Revelation 3:20
John 20:21–22	Matthew 11:28–30
Acts 1:8	

5. What is the mission of Jesus Christ?

To proclaim the good news of the kingdom of God, to call people to "see" the kingdom, to repent, to "enter" the kingdom, and to live obediently in the kingdom.

Mark 1:14–15
John 3:1–21

6. What is the kingdom of God?

The kingdom of God is God's active and sovereign reign over all creation, over all that God has made. It is a new order of things where antagonisms between peoples, nations, sexes, races, and generations are overcome and a new environment of justice, love, freedom, and peace prevails. Only those persons who turn from their sin and accept Jesus Christ as Savior and Lord can fully "see" and enter" the kingdom of God. In the end, God's reign will be acknowledged by all when God judges the whole human race through Christ.

Luke 11:1–4   Revelation 4:11
1 Corinthians 15:24–28   Matthew 25:31–46;
Mark 1:14–15   13:24–33
Philippians 2:5–11

7.   What is sin?

Sin is the condition of estrangement from God that affects the whole human race and results in rebellion against God and God's kingdom. This rebellion leads to bondage. Sins are specific actions, words, or thoughts that arise from our sinful condition and deny the presence, purpose, and reign of God.

Romans 3:9–18, 23; 7:13–20
Psalm 51:1–5

(Note: Various words for "sin" are used in the Bible—for example, *offense, injustice, failure, godlessness, missing the mark,* and the like.)

8.   What are the effects of sin?

Sin corrupts our relationship with God, with one another, with ourselves, and with the whole creation. The primary result of sin is bondage. Thus sin is more than a transgression; it is bondage. It not only alienates us from God, but it also brings us into captivity. It is more than an outward act or habit; it is a deep-seated inward condition. It is not only a "contagious disease," but it is also a cumulative process related to the social and cosmic dimensions of the world. It pollutes not only us, but also every aspect of our existence and infects the very structures of human life and society as well.

Mark 7:21–23   James 4:1–17
Romans 6:23   1 John 1:8–10; 3:4; 5:17

9. What is the good news (gospel/evangel)?

The good news is that God has acted decisively and uniquely in Jesus Christ to deal with our sinful condition. God has acted to save us by offering us love, grace, forgiveness, acceptance, and new life in Christ.

John 3:16–17
Acts 10:36–43
2 Corinthians 5:17

10. What is grace?

Grace is God's sovereign love and unmerited favor to all. It is initiated by God and freely given to undeserving and ungodly people.

Matthew 11:28–30   Romans 5:6–8
Luke 15   Ephesians 2:4–9
John 3:16–17

11. What is salvation?

Salvation is the forgiveness of our sin, deliverance from bondage, and the gift of new life in Christ. It is a process that begins now, gives victory over sin and death, and is completed with God in heaven.

Mark 2:1–5; 10:28–31, 45
Romans 5:15–21
2 Corinthians 5:18–21

12. What is Christian conversion?

It is the change that God works in us as we respond to God's grace in repentance and faith. Repentance and faith are the necessary responses to Jesus and his message of the kingdom. Through repentance and faith, the saving initiative of God is translated into human experience.

> Acts 26:18; 9:1–22
> Ephesians 4:22–24

(Note that Paul's conversion should not be taken as the only model for Christian conversion. Many people experience a more gradual process. See *Faith-Sharing,* chapter 4.)

13. What is repentance?

Repentance is turning away from sin and toward God. It is the turning of one's total life toward the total will of God. It is a response to God's initiative and grace.

> Psalm 51:1–14
> Luke 3:1–14; 15:17–20

14. What is Christian faith?

Christian faith is a centered, personal, relational response to God that involves trust and obedience. Faith in Jesus Christ is trusting that through him alone, God gives us eternal life.

> Acts 16:29–31   James 2:14–26
> Ephesians 2:4–10   2 Corinthians 4:3–7

(Note: See *Faith-Sharing,* chapter 3.)

15. What has Jesus done to make salvation possible?

Jesus came to reveal God to humankind and to offer God's grace. To achieve this, Jesus shared our human life and death. He died on a cruel cross, but God brought him back from

death, thereby conquering death and sin and opening the
kingdom of God to all who repent and believe.

> John 3:16–17   Colossians 2:11–15
> Romans 8:31–39   Philippians 2:5
> 2 Corinthians 5:14–18; 8:9

16. What is the new birth?

New birth, regeneration, and *conversion* are terms used to
describe the process, in both its instantaneous and its gradual aspects, by which we are brought by God from the state
of sin into new life in Jesus Christ, and in which we grow
through the inspiration and workings of the Holy Spirit
within us. To be born again is to see and to enter the kingdom of God.

> John 3:1–8; 14–17
> Ephesians 2:1–5

17. How are we put right with God?

We are put right (that is, justified) when we accept God's
forgiveness of our sin in Christ Jesus and when we, through
the grace of God, become God's children. God restores us
to a right relationship. God does this on the basis of what
Jesus Christ has done for us in his death and resurrection
and on the basis of our faith. We are put right when God
forgives our sin, accepts us, and declares us to be God's
children.

> Romans 5:1–2; 8:1
> 1 Corinthians 1:26–31

(Note: See also Scripture passages under questions 15
and 16)

18. How do we become God's holy people?

We become God's holy people (that is, we are sanctified) through the power and the work of the Holy Spirit in our lives. As we are made new from within, we are transformed by God's patient love into the likeness of Christ. We are given the power to do the will of God, and therefore we grow up into Christian maturity both individually and corporately.

> Romans 12:1–21
> Ephesians 3:14–21; 4:12–16
> 1 Peter 2:9–10

19. How can we know we are saved?

Assurance of salvation is given to us in the Bible, by the inner witness of the Holy Spirit, by the evidence in our words and deeds, and through the inspiration, support, and encouragement of our brothers and sisters in the fellowship of the church.

> John 10:27–30   2 Timothy 2:11–13
> Romans 8:14–17, 31–39   Hebrews 10:23–25
> Galatians 5:19–23   1 John 1:5–2:6

(Note: The Bible does not encourage us to rely solely on our feelings.)

20. What are the marks of persons who are right with God?

They show the fruit of the Spirit: love, joy, peace, patience, kindness, goodness, faithfulness, gentleness, and self-control. But the greatest of all marks is love.

> 1 Corinthians 12:31–13:13
> Galatians 5:22–26
> 1 John 3:11–24

21. What is the church of Jesus Christ?

The church of Jesus Christ is a worldwide community of all those who have been called into being by God and who live under the lordship of Jesus Christ. It is a redeemed and redeeming fellowship in which the gospel is proclaimed and the sacraments are offered. Under the guidance of the Holy Spirit, the church seeks to provide opportunities for worship, growth in faith, and witness to the world. Methodists share a common heritage with all Christians everywhere who claim Jesus Christ as Lord and Savior. Every church is a local outpost of the worldwide community of believers.

> Matthew 16:13–20   Romans 1:6
> John 17:18–23   1 Corinthians 1:9; 12:12–31

22. What is a local Methodist, United Methodist, or other congregation in the Wesleyan tradition?

A local church is a community of people who have accepted Jesus Christ as Lord of their lives. It is a place where the gospel is preached and where the sacraments are celebrated. The function of the local church, under the guidance of the Holy Spirit and in accordance with Scripture, is to help people to know Jesus Christ personally as Lord and Savior and to live their daily lives in the light of their relationship with God. Local Methodist/Wesleyan congregations have an evangelistic, nurturing, serving, and witnessing responsibility for their membership, surrounding area, and the entire world.

> Matthew 26:26–30;   Acts 1:6–8
>   28:16–20   1 Corinthians 11:17–26
> Mark 14:22–26   Ephesians 4:7–16
> Luke 22:14–23

23. What are the distinctive features of the Methodist / Wesleyan movement?

Its message has been summarized as:

All need to be saved.
All may be saved.
All may know that they are saved.
All may be saved to the utmost.

Traditional features of the people called Methodist include:

• the importance of blending knowledge with vital piety, a quickened mind with a warmed evangelical heart;

• the importance of shared leadership (lay and clergy) in the life and mission of the church;

• the importance of blending personal commitment with social responsibility; Methodists have always held that the purpose of Christian conversion is not only to get one's soul ready for heaven, but also to taste the first fruit of heaven through a life of justice, love, and mercy in this world;

• the importance of hymn singing in worship and in teaching Christian truth;

• the importance of blending, preaching, and testifying with sacramental worship (the Lord's Supper and baptism);

• the importance of expressing gratitude for God's grace by rendering unselfish service;

• the development of congregations into smaller groups for instruction, pastoral care, and fellowship;

• the importance of blending *ardor* with *order* in matters of faith and practice;

• the importance of a connectional system that links local congregations to districts, to conferences, and to the world-wide fellowship.

24. Who is welcome as a member of Methodist, United Methodist, or other congregations in the Wesleyan tradition?

All people who confess Jesus Christ as Lord and Savior and who accept the challenge to serve him in the life of the church and the world are welcome as full members. If not already baptized, those seeking membership will be baptized before being received as full members.

PRAYER LIST

THE
FAITH-SHARING
NEW TESTAMENT
WITH THE PSALMS

THE
FAITH-SHARING
NEW TESTAMENT
WITH THE PSALMS

New Revised Standard Version

Cokesbury
Nashville

BOOKS OF
THE NEW TESTAMENT
AND PSALMS

TO THE READER

This preface is addressed to you by the Committee of translators, who wish to explain, as briefly as possible, the origin and character of our work. The publication of our revision is yet another step in the long, continual process of making the Bible available in the form of the English language that is most widely current in our day. To summarize in a single sentence: the New Revised Standard Version of the Bible is an authorized revision of the Revised Standard Version, published in 1952, which was a revision of the American Standard Version, published in 1901, which, in turn, embodied earlier revisions of the King James Version, published in 1611.

In the course of time, the King James Version came to be regarded as "the Authorized Version." With good reason it has been termed "the noblest monument of English prose," and it has entered, as no other book has, into the making of the personal character and the public institutions of the English-speaking peoples. We owe to it an incalculable debt.

Yet the King James Version has serious defects. By the middle of the nineteenth century, the development of biblical studies and the discovery of many biblical manuscripts more ancient than those on which the King James Version was based made it apparent that these defects were so many as to call for revision. The task was begun, by authority of the Church of England, in 1870. The (British) Revised Version of the Bible was published in 1881–1885; and the American Standard Version, its variant embodying the preferences of the American scholars associated with the work, was published, as was mentioned above, in 1901. In 1928 the copyright of the latter was acquired by the International Council of Religious Education and thus passed into the ownership of the churches of the United States and Canada that were associated in this Council through their boards of education and publication.

The Council appointed a committee of scholars to have charge of the text of the American Standard Version and to undertake inquiry concerning the need for further revision. After studying the questions whether or not revision should be undertaken, and if so, what its nature and extent should be, in 1937 the Council authorized a revision. The scholars who served as members of the Committee worked in two sections, one dealing with the Old Testament and one with the New Testament. In 1946 the Revised Standard Version of the New Testament was published. The publication of the Revised Standard Version of the Bible, containing the Old and New Testaments, took place on September 30, 1952. A translation of the Apocryphal/Deuterocanonical Books of the Old Testament followed in 1957. In 1977 this collection was issued in an expanded edition, containing three additional texts received by Eastern Orthodox communions (3 and 4 Maccabees and Psalm 151). Thereafter the Revised Standard Version gained the distinction of being officially authorized for use by all major Christian churches: Protestant, Anglican, Roman Catholic, and Eastern Orthodox.

The Revised Standard Version Bible Committee is a continuing body, comprising about thirty members, both men and women. Ecumenical in representation, it includes scholars affiliated with various Protestant denominations, as well as several Roman Catholic members, an Eastern Orthodox member, and a Jewish member who serves in the Old Testament section. For a period of time the Committee included several members from Canada and from England.

Because no translation of the Bible is perfect or is acceptable to all groups of readers, and because discoveries of older manuscripts and further investigation of linguistic features of the text continue to become available, renderings of the Bible have proliferated. During the years following the publication of the Revised Standard Version, twenty-six other English translations and revisions of the Bible were produced by committees and by individual scholars — not to mention twenty-five other translations and revisions of the New Testament alone. One of the latter was the second edition of the RSV New Testament, issued in 1971, twenty-five years after its initial publication.

Following the publication of the RSV Old Testament in 1952, significant advances were made in the discovery and interpretation of documents in Semitic languages related to Hebrew. In addition to the information that had become available in the late 1940s from the Dead Sea texts of Isaiah and Habakkuk, subsequent acquisitions from the same area brought to light many other early copies of all the books of the Hebrew Scriptures (except Esther), though most of these copies are fragmentary. During the same period early Greek manuscript copies of books of the New Testament also became available.

In order to take these discoveries into account, along with recent studies of documents in Semitic languages related to Hebrew, in 1974 the Policies Committee of the Revised Standard Version, which is a standing committee of the National Council of the Churches of Christ in the U.S.A., authorized the preparation of a revision of the entire RSV Bible.

For the Old Testament the Committee has made use of the Biblia Hebraica Stuttgartensia (1977; ed. sec. emendata, 1983). This is an edition of the Hebrew and Aramaic text as current early in the Christian era and fixed by Jewish scholars (the "Masoretes") of the sixth to the ninth centuries. The vowel signs, which were added by the Masoretes, are accepted in the main, but where a more probable and convincing reading can be obtained by assuming different vowels, this has been done. No notes are given in such cases, because the vowel points are less ancient and reliable than the consonants. When an alternative reading given by the Masoretes is translated in a footnote, this is identified by the words "Another reading is."

Departures from the consonantal text of the best manuscripts have been made only where it seems clear that errors in copying had been made before the text was standardized. Most of the corrections adopted are based on the ancient versions (translations into Greek, Aramaic, Syriac, and Latin), which were made prior to the time of the work of the Masoretes and which therefore may reflect earlier forms of the Hebrew text. In such instances a footnote specifies the version or versions from which the correction has been derived and also gives a translation of the Masoretic Text. Where it was deemed appropriate to do so, information is supplied in footnotes from subsidiary Jewish traditions concerning other textual readings (the Tiqqune Sopherim, "emendations of the scribes"). These are identified in the footnotes as "Ancient Heb tradition."

Occasionally it is evident that the text has suffered in transmission and that none of the versions provides a satisfactory restoration. Here we can only follow the best judgment of competent scholars as to the most probable reconstruction of the original text. Such reconstructions are indicated in footnotes by the abbreviation Cn ("Correction"), and a translation of the Masoretic Text is added.

For the Apocryphal/Deuterocanonical Books of the Old Testament the Committee has made use of a number of texts. For most of these books the basic Greek text from which the present translation was made is the edition of the Septuagint prepared by Alfred Rahlfs and published by the Württemberg Bible Society (Stuttgart, 1935). For several of the books the more recently published individual volumes of the Göttingen Septuagint project were utilized. For the book of Tobit it was decided to follow the form of the Greek text found in codex Sinaiticus (supported as it is by evidence from Qumran); where this text is defective, it was supplemented and corrected by other Greek manuscripts. For the three Additions to Daniel (namely, Susanna, the Prayer of Azariah and the Song of the Three Jews, and Bel and the Dragon) the Committee continued to use the Greek version attributed to Theodotion (the so-called "Theodotion-Daniel"). In translating Ecclesiasticus (Sirach), while constant reference was made to the Hebrew fragments of a large portion of this book (those discovered at Qumran and Masada as well as those recovered from the Cairo Geniza), the Committee generally followed the Greek text (including verse numbers) published by Joseph Ziegler in the Göttingen Septuagint (1965). But in many places the Committee has translated the Hebrew text when this provides a reading that is clearly superior to the Greek; the Syriac and Latin versions were also consulted throughout and occasionally adopted. The basic text adopted in rendering 2 Esdras is the Latin version given in Biblia Sacra, edited by Robert Weber (Stuttgart, 1971). This was supplemented by consulting the Latin text as edited by R. L. Bensly (1895) and by Bruno Violet (1910), as well as by taking into account the several Oriental versions of 2 Esdras, namely, the Syriac, Ethiopic, Arabic (two forms, referred to as Arabic 1 and Arabic 2), Armenian, and Georgian versions. Finally, since the Additions to the Book of Esther are disjointed and quite unintelligible as they stand in most editions of the Apocrypha, we have provided them with their original context by translating the whole of the Greek version of Esther from Robert Hanhart's Göttingen edition (1983).

For the New Testament the Committee has based its work on the most recent edition of The Greek New Testament, prepared by an interconfessional and international committee and published by the United Bible Societies (1966; 3rd ed. corrected, 1983; information concerning changes to be introduced into the critical apparatus of the forthcoming 4th edition was available to the Committee). As in that edition, double brackets are used to enclose a few passages that are generally regarded to be later additions to the text, but which we have retained because of their evident antiquity and their importance in the textual tradition. Only in very rare instances have we replaced the text or the punctuation of the Bible Societies' edition by an alternative that seemed to us to be superior. Here and there in the footnotes the phrase, "Other ancient authorities read," identifies alternative readings preserved by Greek manuscripts and early versions. In both Testaments, alternative renderings of the text are indicated by the word "Or."

As for the style of English adopted for the present revision, among the mandates given to the Committee in 1980 by the Division of Education and Ministry of the National Council of Churches of Christ (which now holds the copyright of the RSV Bible) was the directive to continue in the tradition of the King James Bible, but to introduce such changes as are warranted on the basis of accuracy, clarity, euphony, and current English usage. Within the constraints set by the original texts and by the mandates of the Division, the Committee has followed the maxim, "As literal as possible, as free as necessary." As a consequence, the New Revised Standard Version (NRSV) remains essentially a literal translation. Paraphrastic renderings have been adopted only sparingly, and then chiefly to compensate for a deficiency in the English language — the lack of a common gender third person singular pronoun.

During the almost half a century since the publication of the RSV, many in the churches have become sensitive to the danger of linguistic sexism arising from the inherent bias of the English language towards the masculine gender, a bias that in the case of the Bible has often restricted or obscured the meaning of the original text. The mandates from the Division specified that, in references to men and women, masculine-oriented language should be eliminated as far as this can be done without altering passages that reflect the historical situation of ancient patriarchal culture. As can be appreciated, more than once the Committee found that the several mandates stood in tension and even in conflict. The various concerns had to be balanced case by case in order to provide a faithful and acceptable rendering without using contrived English. Only very occasionally has the pronoun "he" or "him" been retained in passages where the reference may have been to a woman as well as to a man; for example, in several legal texts in Leviticus and Deuteronomy. In such instances of formal, legal language, the options of either putting the passage in the plural or of introducing additional nouns to avoid masculine pronouns in English seemed to the Committee to obscure the historic structure and literary character of the original. In the vast majority of cases, however, inclusiveness has been attained by simple rephrasing or by introducing plural forms when this does not distort the meaning of the passage. Of course, in narrative and in parable no attempt was made to generalize the sex of individual persons.

Another aspect of style will be detected by readers who compare the more stately English rendering of the Old Testament with the less formal rendering adopted for the New Testament. For example, the traditional distinction between shall and will in English has been retained in the Old Testament as appropriate in rendering a document that embodies what may be termed the classic form of Hebrew, while in the New Testament the abandonment of such distinctions in the usage of the future tense in English reflects the more colloquial nature of the koine Greek used by most New Testament authors except when they are quoting the Old Testament.

Careful readers will notice that here and there in the Old Testament the word LORD (or in certain cases GOD) is printed in capital letters. This represents the traditional manner in English versions of rendering the Divine Name, the "Tetragrammaton" (see the notes on Exodus 3.14, 15), following the precedent of the ancient Greek and Latin translators and the long established practice in the reading of the Hebrew Scriptures in the synagogue. While it is almost if not quite certain that the Name was originally pronounced "Yahweh," this pronunciation was not indicated when the Masoretes added vowel sounds to the consonantal Hebrew text. To the four consonants YHWH of the Name, which had come to be regarded as too sacred to be pronounced, they attached vowel signs indicating that in its place should be read the Hebrew word Adonai meaning "Lord" (or Elohim meaning "God"). Ancient Greek translators employed the word Kyrios ("Lord") for the Name. The Vulgate likewise used the Latin word Dominus ("Lord"). The form "Jehovah" is of late medieval origin; it is a combination of the consonants of the Divine Name and the vowels attached to it by the Masoretes but belonging to an entirely different word. Although the American Standard Version (1901) had used "Jehovah" to render the Tetragrammaton (the sound of Y being represented by J and the sound of W by V, as in Latin), for two reasons the Committees that produced the RSV and the NRSV returned to the more familiar usage of the King James Version. (1) The word "Jehovah" does not accurately represent any form of the Name ever used in Hebrew. (2) The use of any proper name for the one and only God, as though there were other gods from whom the true God had to be distinguished, began to be discontinued in Judaism before the Christian era and is inappropriate for the universal faith of the Christian Church.

It will be seen that in the Psalms and in other prayers addressed to God the archaic second person singular pronouns (thee, thou, thine) and verb forms (art, hast, hadst) are no longer used. Although some readers may regret this change, it should be pointed out that in the original languages neither the Old Testament nor the New makes any linguistic distinction between addressing a human being and addressing the Deity. Furthermore, in the tradition of the King James Version one will not expect to find the use of capital letters for pronouns that refer to the Deity — such capitalization is an unnecessary innovation that has only recently been introduced into a few English translations of the Bible. Finally, we have left to the discretion of the licensed publishers such matters as section headings, cross-references, and clues to the pronunciation of proper names.

This new version seeks to preserve all that is best in the English Bible as it has been known and used through the years. It is intended for use in public reading and congregational worship, as well as in private study, instruction, and meditation. We have resisted the temptation to introduce terms and phrases that merely reflect current moods, and have tried to put the message of the Scriptures in simple, enduring words and expressions that are worthy to stand in the great tradition of the King James Bible and its predecessors.

In traditional Judaism and Christianity, the Bible has been more than a historical document to be preserved or a classic of literature to be cherished and admired; it is recognized as the unique record of God's dealings with people over the ages. The Old Testament sets forth the call of a special people to enter into covenant relation with the God of justice and steadfast love and to bring God's law to the nations. The New Testament records the life and work of Jesus Christ, the one in whom "the Word became flesh," as well as describes the rise and spread of the early Christian Church. The Bible carries its full message, not to those who regard it simply as a noble literary heritage of the past or who wish to use it to enhance political purposes and advance otherwise desirable goals, but to all persons and communities who read it so that they may discern and understand what God is saying to them. That message must not be disguised in phrases that are no longer clear, or hidden under words that have changed or lost their meaning; it must be presented in language that is direct and plain and meaningful to people today. It is the hope and prayer of the translators that this version of the Bible may continue to hold a large place in congregational life and to speak to all readers, young and old alike, helping them to understand and believe and respond to its message.

For the Committee,
BRUCE M. METZGER

The Gospel According to

MATTHEW

1 An account of the geneal-ogy[a] of Jesus the Messiah,[b] the son of David, the son of Abraham.

2 Abraham was the father of Isaac, and Isaac the father of Jacob, and Jacob the father of Judah and his brothers, ³and Judah the father of Perez and Zerah by Tamar, and Perez the father of Hezron, and Hezron the father of Aram, ⁴and Aram the father of Aminadab, and Aminadab the father of Nahshon, and Nahshon the father of Salmon, ⁵and Salmon the father of Boaz by Rahab, and Boaz the father of Obed by Ruth, and Obed the father of Jesse, ⁶and Jesse the father of King David.

And David was the father of Solomon by the wife of Uriah, ⁷and Solomon the father of Rehoboam, and Rehoboam the father of Abijah, and Abijah the father of Asaph,[c] ⁸and Asaph[c] the father of Jehoshaphat, and Jehoshaphat the father of Joram, and Joram the father of Uzziah, ⁹and Uzziah the father of Jotham, and Jotham the father of Ahaz, and Ahaz the father of Hezekiah, ¹⁰and Hezekiah the father of Manasseh, and Manasseh the father of Amos,[d] and Amos[d] the father of Josiah, ¹¹and Josiah the father of Jechoniah and his brothers, at the time of the deportation to Babylon.

12 And after the deportation to Babylon: Jechoniah was the father of Salathiel, and Salathiel the father of Zerubbabel, ¹³and Zerubbabel the father of Abiud, and Abiud the father of Eliakim, and Eliakim the father of Azor, ¹⁴and Azor the father of Zadok, and Zadok the father of Achim, and Achim the father of Eliud, ¹⁵and Eliud the father of Eleazar, and Eleazar the father of Matthan, and Matthan the father of Jacob, ¹⁶and Jacob the father of Joseph the husband of Mary, of whom Jesus was born, who is called the Messiah.[e]

17 So all the generations from Abraham to David are fourteen generations; and from David to the deportation to Babylon, fourteen generations; and from the deportation to Babylon to the Messiah,[e] fourteen generations.

18 Now the birth of Jesus the Messiah[b] took place in this way. When his mother Mary had been engaged to Joseph, but before they lived together, she was found to be with child from the Holy Spirit. ¹⁹Her husband Joseph, being a righteous man and unwilling to expose her to public

[a]Or *birth* [b]Or *Jesus Christ* [c]Other ancient authorities read *Asa* [d]Other ancient authorities read *Amon* [e]Or *the Christ*

disgrace, planned to dismiss her quietly. [20]But just when he had resolved to do this, an angel of the Lord appeared to him in a dream and said, "Joseph, son of David, do not be afraid to take Mary as your wife, for the child conceived in her is from the Holy Spirit. [21]She will bear a son, and you are to name him Jesus, for he will save his people from their sins." [22]All this took place to fulfill what had been spoken by the Lord through the prophet:

[23] "Look, the virgin shall
      conceive and bear a son,
      and they shall name him
            Emmanuel,"

which means, "God is with us." [24]When Joseph awoke from sleep, he did as the angel of the Lord commanded him; he took her as his wife, [25]but had no marital relations with her until she had borne a son;[a] and he named him Jesus.

2 In the time of King Herod, after Jesus was born in Bethlehem of Judea, wise men[b] from the East came to Jerusalem, [2]asking, "Where is the child who has been born king of the Jews? For we observed his star at its rising,[c] and have come to pay him homage." [3]When King Herod heard this, he was frightened, and all Jerusalem with him; [4]and calling together all the chief priests and scribes of the people, he inquired of them where the Messiah[d] was to be born. [5]They told him, "In Bethlehem of Judea; for so it has been written by the prophet:

[6] 'And you, Bethlehem, in
      the land of Judah,
   are by no means least
      among the rulers of
            Judah;
   for from you shall come a
      ruler
   who is to shepherd[e] my
      people Israel.'"

7 Then Herod secretly called for the wise men[f] and learned from them the exact time when the star had appeared. [8]Then he sent them to Bethlehem, saying, "Go and search diligently for the child; and when you have found him, bring me word so that I may also go and pay him homage." [9]When they had heard the king, they set out; and there, ahead of them, went the star that they had seen at its rising,[g] until it stopped over the place where the child was. [10]When they saw that the star had stopped,[h] they were overwhelmed with joy. [11]On entering the house, they saw the child with Mary his mother; and they knelt down and paid him homage. Then, opening their treasure chests, they offered him gifts of gold, frankincense, and myrrh. [12]And having been warned in a dream not to return to Herod, they left for their own country by another road.

13 Now after they had left, an angel of the Lord appeared to Joseph in a dream and said, "Get up, take the child and his mother, and flee to Egypt, and remain

[a]Other ancient authorities read *her firstborn son* [b]Or *astrologers;* Gk *magi* [c]Or *in the East* [d]Or *the Christ* [e]Or *rule* [f]Or *astrologers;* Gk *magi* [g]Or *in the East* [h]Gk *saw the star*

there until I tell you; for Herod is about to search for the child, to destroy him." [14]Then Joseph[a] got up, took the child and his mother by night, and went to Egypt, [15]and remained there until the death of Herod. This was to fulfill what had been spoken by the Lord through the prophet, "Out of Egypt I have called my son."

16 When Herod saw that he had been tricked by the wise men, he was infuriated, and he sent and killed all the children in and around Bethlehem who were two years old or under, according to the time that he had learned from the wise men. [17]Then was fulfilled what had been spoken through the prophet Jeremiah:

[18] "A voice was heard in
    Ramah,
    wailing and loud
        lamentation,
    Rachel weeping for her
        children;
    she refused to be
        consoled, because
    they are no more."

19 When Herod died, an angel of the Lord suddenly appeared in a dream to Joseph in Egypt and said, [20]"Get up, take the child and his mother, and go to the land of Israel, for those who were seeking the child's life are dead." [21]Then Joseph[a] got up, took the child and his mother, and went to the land of Israel. [22]But when he heard that Archelaus was ruling over Judea in place of his father Herod, he was afraid to go there. And after being warned in a dream, he went away to the district of Galilee. [23]There he made his home in a town called Nazareth, so that what had been spoken through the prophets might be fulfilled, "He will be called a Nazorean."

3 In those days John the Baptist appeared in the wilderness of Judea, proclaiming, [2]"Repent, for the kingdom of heaven has come near."[b] [3]This is the one of whom the prophet Isaiah spoke when he said,

    "The voice of one crying
        out in the wilderness:
    Prepare the way of the Lord,
        make his paths
        straight.'"

[4]Now John wore clothing of camel's hair with a leather belt around his waist, and his food was locusts and wild honey. [5]Then the people of Jerusalem and all Judea were going out to him, and all the region along the Jordan, [6]and they were baptized by him in the river Jordan, confessing their sins.

7 But when he saw many Pharisees and Sadducees coming for baptism, he said to them, "You brood of vipers! Who warned you to flee from the wrath to come? [8]Bear fruit worthy of repentance. [9]Do not presume to say to yourselves, 'We have Abraham as our ancestor'; for I tell you, God is able from these stones to raise up children to Abraham. [10]Even now the ax is lying at the root of the trees; every tree therefore that does not

[a]Gk he [b]Or is at hand

bear good fruit is cut down and thrown into the fire.

11 "I baptize you with[a] water for repentance, but one who is more powerful than I is coming after me; I am not worthy to carry his sandals. He will baptize you with the Holy Spirit and fire. [12]His winnowing fork is in his hand, and he will clear his threshing floor and will gather his wheat into the granary; but the chaff he will burn with unquenchable fire."

13 Then Jesus came from Galilee to John at the Jordan, to be baptized by him. [14]John would have prevented him, saying, "I need to be baptized by you, and do you come to me?" [15]But Jesus answered him, "Let it be so now; for it is proper for us in this way to fulfill all righteousness." Then he consented. [16]And when Jesus had been baptized, just as he came up from the water, suddenly the heavens were opened to him and he saw the Spirit of God descending like a dove and alighting on him. [17]And a voice from heaven said, "This is my Son, the Beloved,[b] with whom I am well pleased."

4 Then Jesus was led up by the Spirit into the wilderness to be tempted by the devil. [2]He fasted forty days and forty nights, and afterwards he was famished. [3]The tempter came and said to him, "If you are the Son of God, command these stones to become loaves of bread." [4]But he answered, "It is written,

One does not live by bread
    alone,
but by every word that
    comes from the mouth
    of God.'"

5 Then the devil took him to the holy city and placed him on the pinnacle of the temple, [6]saying to him, "If you are the Son of God, throw yourself down; for it is written,

'He will command his
    angels concerning you,'
and 'On their hands they
    will bear you up,
so that you will not dash
    your foot against a
    stone.'"

[7]Jesus said to him, "Again it is written, 'Do not put the Lord your God to the test.'"

8 Again, the devil took him to a very high mountain and showed him all the kingdoms of the world and their splendor; [9]and he said to him, "All these I will give you, if you will fall down and worship me." [10]Jesus said to him, "Away with you, Satan! for it is written,

'Worship the Lord your
    God,
    and serve only him.'"

[11]Then the devil left him, and suddenly angels came and waited on him.

12 Now when Jesus[c] heard that John had been arrested, he withdrew to Galilee. [13]He left Nazareth and made his home in Capernaum by the sea, in the ter-

[a]Or in [b]Or my beloved Son [c]Gk he

ritory of Zebulun and Naphtali, [14]so that what had been spoken through the prophet Isaiah might be fulfilled:

[15] "Land of Zebulun, land of
    Naphtali,
    on the road by the sea,
    across the Jordan,
    Galilee of the Gentiles—
[16] the people who sat in darkness
    have seen a great light,
    and for those who sat in the
    region and shadow
    of death
    light has dawned."

[17]From that time Jesus began to proclaim, "Repent, for the kingdom of heaven has come near."[a]

[18] As he walked by the Sea of Galilee, he saw two brothers, Simon, who is called Peter, and Andrew his brother, casting a net into the sea—for they were fishermen. [19]And he said to them, "Follow me, and I will make you fish for people." [20]Immediately they left their nets and followed him. [21]As he went from there, he saw two other brothers, James son of Zebedee and his brother John, in the boat with their father Zebedee, mending their nets, and he called them. [22]Immediately they left the boat and their father, and followed him.

[23] Jesus[b] went throughout Galilee, teaching in their synagogues and proclaiming the good news[c] of the kingdom and curing every disease and every sickness among the people. [24]So his fame spread throughout all Syria, and they brought to him all the sick, those who were afflicted with various diseases and pains, demoniacs, epileptics, and paralytics, and he cured them. [25]And great crowds followed him from Galilee, the Decapolis, Jerusalem, Judea, and from beyond the Jordan.

5 When Jesus[b] saw the crowds, he went up the mountain; and after he sat down, his disciples came to him. [2]Then he began to speak, and taught them, saying:

[3] "Blessed are the poor in spirit, for theirs is the kingdom of heaven.

[4] "Blessed are those who mourn, for they will be comforted.

[5] "Blessed are the meek, for they will inherit the earth.

[6] "Blessed are those who hunger and thirst for righteousness, for they will be filled.

[7] "Blessed are the merciful, for they will receive mercy.

[8] "Blessed are the pure in heart, for they will see God.

[9] "Blessed are the peacemakers, for they will be called children of God.

[10] "Blessed are those who are persecuted for righteousness' sake, for theirs is the kingdom of heaven.

[11] "Blessed are you when people revile you and persecute you and utter all kinds of evil against you falsely[d] on my account. [12]Rejoice and be glad, for your reward is great in heaven,

[a]Or *is at hand* [b]Gk *He* [c]Gk *gospel* [d]Other ancient authorities lack *falsely*

5

for in the same way they persecuted the prophets who were before you.

13 "You are the salt of the earth; but if salt has lost its taste, how can its saltiness be restored? It is no longer good for anything, but is thrown out and trampled under foot.

14 "You are the light of the world. A city built on a hill cannot be hid. [15]No one after lighting a lamp puts it under the bushel basket, but on the lampstand, and it gives light to all in the house. [16]In the same way, let your light shine before others, so that they may see your good works and give glory to your Father in heaven.

17 "Do not think that I have come to abolish the law or the prophets; I have come not to abolish but to fulfill. [18]For truly I tell you, until heaven and earth pass away, not one letter,[a] not one stroke of a letter, will pass from the law until all is accomplished. [19]Therefore, whoever breaks[b] one of the least of these commandments, and teaches others to do the same, will be called least in the kingdom of heaven; but whoever does them and teaches them will be called great in the kingdom of heaven. [20]For I tell you, unless your righteousness exceeds that of the scribes and Pharisees, you will never enter the kingdom of heaven.

21 "You have heard that it was said to those of ancient times, 'You shall not murder'; and 'whoever murders shall be liable to judgment.' [22]But I say to you that if you are angry with a brother or sister,[c] you will be liable to judgment; and if you insult[d] a brother or sister,[e] you will be liable to the council; and if you say, 'You fool,' you will be liable to the hell[f] of fire. [23]So when you are offering your gift at the altar, if you remember that your brother or sister[g] has something against you, [24]leave your gift there before the altar and go; first be reconciled to your brother or sister,[g] and then come and offer your gift. [25]Come to terms quickly with your accuser while you are on the way to court[h] with him, or your accuser may hand you over to the judge, and the judge to the guard, and you will be thrown into prison. [26]Truly I tell you, you will never get out until you have paid the last penny.

27 "You have heard that it was said, 'You shall not commit adultery.' [28]But I say to you that everyone who looks at a woman with lust has already committed adultery with her in his heart. [29]If your right eye causes you to sin, tear it out and throw it away; it is better for you to lose one of your members than for your whole body to be thrown into hell.[f] [30] And if your right hand causes you to sin, cut it off and throw it away; it is better for you to lose one of your members than for your whole body to go into hell.[f]

[a]Gk one iota y [b]Or annuls [c]Gk a brother; other ancient authorities add without cause [d]Gk say Raca to (an obscure term of abuse) [e] Gk a brother [f] Gk Gehenna [g] Gk your brother [h]Gk lacks to court

31 "It was also said, 'Whoever divorces his wife, let him give her a certificate of divorce.' [32]But I say to you that anyone who divorces his wife, except on the ground of unchastity, causes her to commit adultery; and whoever marries a divorced woman commits adultery.

33 "Again, you have heard that it was said to those of ancient times, 'You shall not swear falsely, but carry out the vows you have made to the Lord.' [34]But I say to you, Do not swear at all, either by heaven, for it is the throne of God, [35]or by the earth, for it is his footstool, or by Jerusalem, for it is the city of the great King. [36]And do not swear by your head, for you cannot make one hair white or black. [37]Let your word be 'Yes, Yes' or 'No, No'; anything more than this comes from the evil one.[a]

38 "You have heard that it was said, 'An eye for an eye and a tooth for a tooth.' [39]But I say to you, Do not resist an evildoer. But if anyone strikes you on the right cheek, turn the other also; [40]and if anyone wants to sue you and take your coat, give your cloak as well; [41]and if anyone forces you to go one mile, go also the second mile. [42]Give to everyone who begs from you, and do not refuse anyone who wants to borrow from you.

43 "You have heard that it was said, 'You shall love your neighbor and hate your enemy.' [44]But I say to you, Love your enemies and pray for those who persecute you, [45]so that you may be children of your Father in heaven; for he makes his sun rise on the evil and on the good, and sends rain on the righteous and on the unrighteous. [46]For if you love those who love you, what reward do you have? Do not even the tax collectors do the same? [47]And if you greet only your brothers and sisters,[b] what more are you doing than others? Do not even the Gentiles do the same? [48]Be perfect, therefore, as your heavenly Father is perfect.

6 "Beware of practicing your piety before others in order to be seen by them; for then you have no reward from your Father in heaven.

2 "So whenever you give alms, do not sound a trumpet before you, as the hypocrites do in the synagogues and in the streets, so that they may be praised by others. Truly I tell you, they have received their reward. [3]But when you give alms, do not let your left hand know what your right hand is doing, [4]so that your alms may be done in secret; and your Father who sees in secret will reward you.[c]

5 "And whenever you pray, do not be like the hypocrites; for they love to stand and pray in the synagogues and at the street corners, so that they may be seen by others. Truly I tell you, they have received their reward. [6]But whenever you pray, go into your room and shut the door and pray to your Father who is in secret; and your Father who sees in secret will reward you.[c]

[a]Or *evil* [b] Gk *your brothers* [c] Other ancient authorities add *openly*

7 "When you are praying, do not heap up empty phrases as the Gentiles do; for they think that they will be heard because of their many words. [8]Do not be like them, for your Father knows what you need before you ask him.

9 "Pray then in this way:

Our Father in heaven,
    hallowed be your name.
[10]   Your kingdom come.
    Your will be done,
    on earth as it is in
    heaven.
[11]   Give us this day our
    daily bread.[a]
[12] And forgive us our debts,
    as we also have
    forgiven our debtors.
[13]   And do not bring us to
    the time of trial,[b]
    but rescue us from the
    evil one.[c]

[14] For if you forgive others their trespasses, your heavenly Father will also forgive you; [15]but if you do not forgive others, neither will your Father forgive your trespasses.

16 "And whenever you fast, do not look dismal, like the hypocrites, for they disfigure their faces so as to show others that they are fasting. Truly I tell you, they have received their reward. [17]But when you fast, put oil on your head and wash your face, [18]so that your fasting may be seen not by others but by your Father who is in secret; and your Father who sees in secret will reward you.[d]

19 "Do not store up for yourselves treasures on earth, where moth and rust[e] consume and where thieves break in and steal; [20]but store up for yourselves treasures in heaven, where neither moth nor rust[e] consumes and where thieves do not break in and steal. [21]For where your treasure is, there your heart will be also.

22 "The eye is the lamp of the body. So, if your eye is healthy, your whole body will be full of light; [23]but if your eye is unhealthy, your whole body will be full of darkness. If then the light in you is darkness, how great is the darkness!

24 "No one can serve two masters; for a slave will either hate the one and love the other, or be devoted to the one and despise the other. You cannot serve God and wealth.[f]

25 "Therefore I tell you, do not worry about your life, what you will eat or what you will drink,[g] or about your body, what you will wear. Is not life more than food, and the body more than clothing? [26]Look at the birds of the air; they neither sow nor reap nor gather into barns, and yet your heavenly Father feeds them. Are you not of more value than they? [27]And can any of you by worrying add a single hour to your span of life?[h] [28]And why do you worry about clothing? Consider the lilies of the field, how

---

[a]Or *our bread for tomorrow* [b]Or *us into temptation* [c]Or *from evil.* Other ancient authorities add, in some form, *For the kingdom and the power and the glory are yours forever. Amen.* [d]Other ancient authorities add *openly* [e]Gk *eating* [f]Gk *mammon* [g]Other ancient authorities lack *or what you will drink* [h]Or *add one cubit to your height*

they grow; they neither toil nor spin, ²⁹yet I tell you, even Solomon in all his glory was not clothed like one of these. ³⁰But if God so clothes the grass of the field, which is alive today and tomorrow is thrown into the oven, will he not much more clothe you—you of little faith? ³¹Therefore do not worry, saying, 'What will we eat?' or 'What will we drink?' or 'What will we wear?' ³²For it is the Gentiles who strive for all these things; and indeed your heavenly Father knows that you need all these things. ³³But strive first for the kingdom of God[a] and his[b] righteousness, and all these things will be given to you as well.

34 "So do not worry about tomorrow, for tomorrow will bring worries of its own. Today's trouble is enough for today.

7 "Do not judge, so that you may not be judged. ²For with the judgment you make you will be judged, and the measure you give will be the measure you get. ³Why do you see the speck in your neighbor's[c] eye, but do not notice the log in your own eye? ⁴Or how can you say to your neighbor,[d] 'Let me take the speck out of your eye,' while the log is in your own eye? ⁵You hypocrite, first take the log out of your own eye, and then you will see clearly to take the speck out of your neighbor's[c] eye.

6 "Do not give what is holy to dogs; and do not throw your pearls before swine, or they will trample them under foot and turn and maul you.

7 "Ask, and it will be given you; search, and you will find; knock, and the door will be opened for you. ⁸For everyone who asks receives, and everyone who searches finds, and for everyone who knocks, the door will be opened. ⁹Is there anyone among you who, if your child asks for bread, will give a stone? ¹⁰Or if the child asks for a fish, will give a snake? ¹¹If you then, who are evil, know how to give good gifts to your children, how much more will your Father in heaven give good things to those who ask him!

12 "In everything do to others as you would have them do to you; for this is the law and the prophets.

13 "Enter through the narrow gate; for the gate is wide and the road is easy[e] that leads to destruction, and there are many who take it. ¹⁴For the gate is narrow and the road is hard that leads to life, and there are few who find it.

15 "Beware of false prophets, who come to you in sheep's clothing but inwardly are ravenous wolves. ¹⁶You will know them by their fruits. Are grapes gathered from thorns, or figs from thistles? ¹⁷In the same way, every good tree bears good fruit, but the bad tree bears bad fruit. ¹⁸A good tree cannot bear bad fruit, nor can a bad tree bear good fruit. ¹⁹Every tree that does not bear good fruit is cut down and

---

[a]Other ancient authorities lack *of God* [b]Or *its* [c]Gk *brother's* [d]Gk *brother* [e]Other ancient authorities read *for the road is wide and easy*

thrown into the fire. [20]Thus you will know them by their fruits.

21 "Not everyone who says to me, 'Lord, Lord,' will enter the kingdom of heaven, but only the one who does the will of my Father in heaven. [22]On that day many will say to me, 'Lord, Lord, did we not prophesy in your name, and cast out demons in your name, and do many deeds of power in your name?' [23]Then I will declare to them, 'I never knew you; go away from me, you evildoers.'

24 "Everyone then who hears these words of mine and acts on them will be like a wise man who built his house on rock. [25]The rain fell, the floods came, and the winds blew and beat on that house, but it did not fall, because it had been founded on rock. [26]And everyone who hears these words of mine and does not act on them will be like a foolish man who built his house on sand. [27]The rain fell, and the floods came, and the winds blew and beat against that house, and it fell—and great was its fall!"

28 Now when Jesus had finished saying these things, the crowds were astounded at his teaching, [29]for he taught them as one having authority, and not as their scribes.

8 When Jesus[a] had come down from the mountain, great crowds followed him; [2]and there was a leper[b] who came to him and knelt before him, saying, "Lord, if you choose, you can make me clean." [3]He stretched out his hand and touched him, saying, "I do choose. Be made clean!" Immediately his leprosy was cleansed. [4]Then Jesus said to him, "See that you say nothing to anyone; but go, show yourself to the priest, and offer the gift that Moses commanded, as a testimony to them."

5 When he entered Capernaum, a centurion came to him, appealing to him [6]and saying, "Lord, my servant is lying at home paralyzed, in terrible distress." [7]And he said to him, "I will come and cure him." [8]The centurion answered, "Lord, I am not worthy to have you come under my roof; but only speak the word, and my servant will be healed. [9]For I also am a man under authority, with soldiers under me; and I say to one, 'Go,' and he goes, and to another, 'Come,' and he comes, and to my slave, 'Do this,' and the slave does it." [10]When Jesus heard him, he was amazed and said to those who followed him, "Truly I tell you, in no one in[c] Israel have I found such faith. [11]I tell you, many will come from east and west and will eat with Abraham and Isaac and Jacob in the kingdom of heaven, [12]while the heirs of the kingdom will be thrown into the outer darkness, where there will be weeping and gnashing of teeth." [13]And to the centurion Jesus said, "Go; let it be done for you according to your

---

[a]Gk *he* [b]The terms *leper* and *leprosy* can refer to several diseases [c]Other ancient authorities read *Truly I tell you, not even*

faith." And the servant was healed in that hour.

14 When Jesus entered Peter's house, he saw his mother-in-law lying in bed with a fever; [15]he touched her hand, and the fever left her, and she got up and began to serve him. [16]That evening they brought to him many who were possessed with demons; and he cast out the spirits with a word, and cured all who were sick. [17]This was to fulfill what had been spoken through the prophet Isaiah, "He took our infirmities and bore our diseases."

18 Now when Jesus saw great crowds around him, he gave orders to go over to the other side. [19]A scribe then approached and said, "Teacher, I will follow you wherever you go." [20]And Jesus said to him, "Foxes have holes, and birds of the air have nests; but the Son of Man has nowhere to lay his head." [21]Another of his disciples said to him, "Lord, first let me go and bury my father." [22]But Jesus said to him, "Follow me, and let the dead bury their own dead."

23 And when he got into the boat, his disciples followed him. [24]A windstorm arose on the sea, so great that the boat was being swamped by the waves; but he was asleep. [25]And they went and woke him up, saying, "Lord, save us! We are perishing!" [26]And he said to them, "Why are you afraid, you of little faith?" Then he got up and rebuked the winds and the sea; and there was a dead calm. [27]They were amazed, say-ing, "What sort of man is this, that even the winds and the sea obey him?"

28 When he came to the other side, to the country of the Gadarenes,[a] two demoniacs com-ing out of the tombs met him. They were so fierce that no one could pass that way. [29]Suddenly they shouted, "What have you to do with us, Son of God? Have you come here to torment us before the time?" [30]Now a large herd of swine was feeding at some distance from them. [31]The demons begged him, "If you cast us out, send us into the herd of swine." [32]And he said to them, "Go!" So they came out and entered the swine; and suddenly, the whole herd rushed down the steep bank into the sea and per-ished in the water. [33]The swine-herds ran off, and on going into the town, they told the whole story about what had happened to the demoniacs. [34]Then the whole town came out to meet Jesus; and when they saw him, they begged him to leave their neighborhood. [1]And after getting

9 into a boat he crossed the sea and came to his own town.

2 And just then some people were carrying a paralyzed man lying on a bed. When Jesus saw their faith, he said to the paralyt-ic, "Take heart, son; your sins are for-given." [3]Then some of the scribes said to themselves, "This man is blaspheming." [4]But Jesus,

---

[a]Other ancient authorities read *Gergesenes;* others, *Gerasenes*

perceiving their thoughts, said, "Why do you think evil in your hearts? [5]For which is easier, to say, 'Your sins are forgiven,' or to say, 'Stand up and walk'? [6]But so that you may know that the Son of Man has authority on earth to forgive sins"—he then said to the paralytic—"Stand up, take your bed and go to your home." [7]And he stood up and went to his home. [8]When the crowds saw it, they were filled with awe, and they glorified God, who had given such authority to human beings.

9 As Jesus was walking along, he saw a man called Matthew sitting at the tax booth; and he said to him, "Follow me." And he got up and followed him.

10 And as he sat at dinner[a] in the house, many tax collectors and sinners came and were sitting[b] with him and his disciples. [11]When the Pharisees saw this, they said to his disciples, "Why does your teacher eat with tax collectors and sinners?" [12]But when he heard this, he said, "Those who are well have no need of a physician, but those who are sick. [13]Go and learn what this means, 'I desire mercy, not sacrifice.' For I have come to call not the righteous but sinners."

14 Then the disciples of John came to him, saying, "Why do we and the Pharisees fast often,[c] but your disciples do not fast?" [15]And Jesus said to them, "The wedding guests cannot mourn as long as the bridegroom is with them, can they? The days will come when the bridegroom is taken away from them, and then they will fast. [16]No one sews a piece of unshrunk cloth on an old cloak, for the patch pulls away from the cloak, and a worse tear is made. [17]Neither is new wine put into old wineskins; otherwise, the skins burst, and the wine is spilled, and the skins are destroyed; but new wine is put into fresh wineskins, and so both are preserved."

18 While he was saying these things to them, suddenly a leader of the synagogue[d] came in and knelt before him, saying, "My daughter has just died; but come and lay your hand on her, and she will live." [19]And Jesus got up and followed him, with his disciples. [20]Then suddenly a woman who had been suffering from hemorrhages for twelve years came up behind him and touched the fringe of his cloak, [21]for she said to herself, "If I only touch his cloak, I will be made well." [22]Jesus turned, and seeing her he said, "Take heart, daughter; your faith has made you well." And instantly the woman was made well. [23]When Jesus came to the leader's house and saw the flute players and the crowd making a commotion, [24]he said, "Go away; for the girl is not dead but sleeping." And they laughed at him. [25]But when the crowd had been put outside, he went in and took

---

[a]Gk *reclined* [b]Gk *were reclining* [c]Other ancient authorities lack *often* [d]Gk lacks *of the synagogue*

her by the hand, and the girl got up. 26And the report of this spread throughout that district.

27 As Jesus went on from there, two blind men followed him, crying loudly, "Have mercy on us, Son of David!" 28When he entered the house, the blind men came to him; and Jesus said to them, "Do you believe that I am able to do this?" They said to him, "Yes, Lord." 29Then he touched their eyes and said, "According to your faith let it be done to you." 30And their eyes were opened. Then Jesus sternly ordered them, "See that no one knows of this." 31But they went away and spread the news about him throughout that district.

32 After they had gone away, a demoniac who was mute was brought to him. 33And when the demon had been cast out, the one who had been mute spoke; and the crowds were amazed and said, "Never has anything like this been seen in Israel." 34But the Pharisees said, "By the ruler of the demons he casts out the demons."a

35 Then Jesus went about all the cities and villages, teaching in their synagogues, and proclaiming the good news of the kingdom, and curing every disease and every sickness. 36When he saw the crowds, he had compassion for them, because they were harassed and helpless, like sheep without a shepherd. 37Then he said to his disciples, "The harvest is plentiful, but the laborers are few; 38therefore ask the Lord of the harvest to send out laborers into his harvest."

10 Then Jesusb summoned his twelve disciples and gave them authority over unclean spirits, to cast them out, and to cure every disease and every sickness. 2These are the names of the twelve apostles: first, Simon, also known as Peter, and his brother Andrew; James son of Zebedee, and his brother John; 3Philip and Bartholomew; Thomas and Matthew the tax collector; James son of Alphaeus, and Thaddaeus;c 4Simon the Cananaean, and Judas Iscariot, the one who betrayed him.

5 These twelve Jesus sent out with the following instructions: "Go nowhere among the Gentiles, and enter no town of the Samaritans, 6but go rather to the lost sheep of the house of Israel. 7As you go, proclaim the good news, 'The kingdom of heaven has come near.'d 8Cure the sick, raise the dead, cleanse the lepers,e cast out demons. You received without payment; give without payment. 9Take no gold, or silver, or copper in your belts, 10no bag for your journey, or two tunics, or sandals, or a staff; for laborers deserve their food. 11Whatever town or village you enter, find out who in it is worthy, and stay there until you leave. 12As you enter the house,

aOther ancient authorities lack this verse bGk he cOther ancient authorities read Lebbaeus, or Lebbaeus called Thaddaeus dOr is at hand eThe term leper and leprosy can refer to several diseases

greet it. ¹³If the house is worthy, let your peace come upon it; but if it is not worthy, let your peace return to you. ¹⁴If anyone will not welcome you or listen to your words, shake off the dust from your feet as you leave that house or town. ¹⁵Truly I tell you, it will be more tolerable for the land of Sodom and Gomorrah on the day of judgment than for that town.

16 "See, I am sending you out like sheep into the midst of wolves; so be wise as serpents and innocent as doves. ¹⁷Beware of them, for they will hand you over to councils and flog you in their synagogues; ¹⁸and you will be dragged before governors and kings because of me, as a testimony to them and the Gentiles. ¹⁹When they hand you over, do not worry about how you are to speak or what you are to say; for what you are to say will be given to you at that time; ²⁰for it is not you who speak, but the Spirit of your Father speaking through you. ²¹Brother will betray brother to death, and a father his child, and children will rise against parents and have them put to death; ²²and you will be hated by all because of my name. But the one who endures to the end will be saved. ²³When they persecute you in one town, flee to the next; for truly I tell you, you will not have gone through all the towns of Israel before the Son of Man comes.

24 "A disciple is not above the teacher, nor a slave above the master; ²⁵it is enough for the disciple to be like the teacher, and the slave like the master. If they have called the master of the house Beelzebul, how much more will they malign those of his household!

26 "So have no fear of them; for nothing is covered up that will not be uncovered, and nothing secret that will not become known. ²⁷What I say to you in the dark, tell in the light; and what you hear whispered, proclaim from the housetops. ²⁸Do not fear those who kill the body but cannot kill the soul; rather fear him who can destroy both soul and body in hell.^a ²⁹Are not two sparrows sold for a penny? Yet not one of them will fall to the ground apart from your Father. ³⁰And even the hairs of your head are all counted. ³¹So do not be afraid; you are of more value than many sparrows.

32 "Everyone therefore who acknowledges me before others, I also will acknowledge before my Father in heaven; ³³but whoever denies me before others, I also will deny before my Father in heaven.

34 "Do not think that I have come to bring peace to the earth; I have not come to bring peace, but a sword.

³⁵ For I have come to set a
        man against his father,
    and a daughter against her
        mother,
    and a daughter-in-law
        against her
        mother-in-law;

^aGk *Gehenna*

36   and one's foes will be
        members of one's
        own household.
37Whoever loves father or mother more than me is not worthy of me; and whoever loves son or daughter more than me is not worthy of me; 38and whoever does not take up the cross and follow me is not worthy of me. 39Those who find their life will lose it, and those who lose their life for my sake will find it.

40 "Whoever welcomes you welcomes me, and whoever welcomes me welcomes the one who sent me. 41Whoever welcomes a prophet in the name of a prophet will receive a prophet's reward; and whoever welcomes a righteous person in the name of a righteous person will receive the reward of the righteous; 42and whoever gives even a cup of cold water to one of these little ones in the name of a disciple—truly I tell you, none of these will lose their reward."

11 Now when Jesus had finished instructing his twelve disciples, he went on from there to teach and proclaim his message in their cities.

2 When John heard in prison what the Messiah[a] was doing, he sent word by his[b] disciples 3and said to him, "Are you the one who is to come, or are we to wait for another?" 4Jesus answered them, "Go and tell John what you hear and see: 5the blind receive their sight, the lame walk, the lepers[c] are cleansed, the deaf hear, the dead are raised, and the poor have good news brought to them. 6And blessed is anyone who takes no offense at me."

7 As they went away, Jesus began to speak to the crowds about John: "What did you go out into the wilderness to look at? A reed shaken by the wind? 8What then did you go out to see? Someone[d] dressed in soft robes? Look, those who wear soft robes are in royal palaces. 9What then did you go out to see? A prophet?[e] Yes, I tell you, and more than a prophet. 10This is the one about whom it is written,

'See, I am sending my
        messenger ahead of you,
who will prepare your
        way before you.'

11Truly I tell you, among those born of women no one has arisen greater than John the Baptist; yet the least in the kingdom of heaven is greater than he. 12 From the days of John the Baptist until now the kingdom of heaven has suffered violence,[f] and the violent take it by force. 13For all the prophets and the law prophesied until John came; 14and if you are willing to accept it, he is Elijah who is to come. 15Let anyone with ears[g] listen!

16 "But to what will I compare this generation? It is like children sitting in the marketplaces and calling to one another,

[a]Or the Christ [b]Other ancient authorities read two of his [c]The term leper and leprosy can refer to several diseases [d]Or Why then did you go out? To see someone [e]Other ancient authorities read Why then did you go out? To see a prophet? [f]Or has been coming violently [g]Other ancient authorities add to hear

17 'We played the flute for
you, and you did not
dance;
we wailed, and you did
not mourn.'
18For John came neither eating
nor drinking, and they say, 'He
has a demon'; 19the Son of Man
came eating and drinking, and
they say, 'Look, a glutton and a
drunkard, a friend of tax collectors and sinners!' Yet wisdom is
vindicated by her deeds."[a]

20 Then he began to reproach
the cities in which most of his
deeds of power had been done,
because they did not repent.
21"Woe to you, Chorazin! Woe to
you, Bethsaida! For if the deeds
of power done in you had been
done in Tyre and Sidon, they
would have repented long ago in
sackcloth and ashes. 22But I tell
you, on the day of judgment it
will be more tolerable for Tyre
and Sidon than for you. 23And
you, Capernaum,
will you be exalted to
heaven? No, you will be
brought down to Hades.
For if the deeds of power done in
you had been done in Sodom, it
would have remained until this
day. 24But I tell you that on the
day of judgment it will be more
tolerable for the land of Sodom
than for you."

25 At that time Jesus said, "I
thank[b] you, Father, Lord of heav-
en and earth, because you have
hidden these things from the
wise and the intelligent and have
revealed them to infants; 26yes ,

Father, for such was your gra-
cious will.[c] 27All things have
been handed over to me by my
Father; and no one knows the
Son except the Father, and no
one knows the Father except the
Son and anyone to whom the
Son chooses to reveal him.

28 "Come to me, all you that
are weary and are carrying heavy
burdens, and I will give you rest.
29Take my yoke upon you, and
learn from me; for I am gentle
and humble in heart, and you
will find rest for your souls. 30For
my yoke is easy, and my burden
is light."

12 At that time Jesus went
through the grainfields on
the sabbath; his disciples were
hungry, and they began to pluck
heads of grain and to eat. 2When
the Pharisees saw it, they said to
him, "Look, your disciples are
doing what is not lawful to do on
the sabbath." 3He said to them,
"Have you not read what David
did when he and his companions
were hungry? 4He entered the
house of God and ate the bread of
the Presence, which it was not
lawful for him or his companions
to eat, but only for the priests.
5Or have you not read in the law
that on the sabbath the priests
in the temple break the sabbath and yet are guiltless? 6I tell
you, something greater than the
temple is here. 7But if you
had known what this means, desire mercy and not sacrifice,' you

[a]Other ancient authorities read *children* [b]Or *praise*
[c]Or *for so it was well-pleasing in your sight*

would not have condemned the guiltless. [8]For the Son of Man is lord of the sabbath."

9 He left that place and entered their synagogue; [10]a man was there with a withered hand, and they asked him, "Is it lawful to cure on the sabbath?" so that they might accuse him. [11]He said to them, "Suppose one of you has only one sheep and it falls into a pit on the sabbath; will you not lay hold of it and lift it out? [12]How much more valuable is a human being than a sheep! So it is lawful to do good on the sabbath." [13]Then he said to the man, "Stretch out your hand." He stretched it out, and it was restored, as sound as the other. [14]But the Pharisees went out and conspired against him, how to destroy him.

15 When Jesus became aware of this, he departed. Many crowds[a] followed him, and he cured all of them, [16]and he ordered them not to make him known. [17]This was to fulfill what had been spoken through the prophet Isaiah:

[18] "Here is my servant, whom
I have chosen,
my beloved, with whom
my soul is well
pleased.
I will put my Spirit upon
him,
and he will proclaim
justice to the
Gentiles.
[19] He will not wrangle or cry
aloud,
nor will anyone hear his
voice in the streets.
[20] He will not break a bruised
reed
or quench a smoldering
wick
until he brings justice to
victory.
[21] And in his name the
Gentiles will hope."

22 Then they brought to him a demoniac who was blind and mute; and he cured him, so that the one who had been mute could speak and see. [23]All the crowds were amazed and said, "Can this be the Son of David?" [24]But when the Pharisees heard it, they said, "It is only by Beelzebul, the ruler of the demons, that this fellow casts out the demons." [25]He knew what they were thinking and said to them, "Every kingdom divided against itself is laid waste, and no city or house divided against itself will stand. [26]If Satan casts out Satan, he is divided against himself; how then will his kingdom stand? [27]If I cast out demons by Beelzebul, by whom do your own exorcists[b] cast them out? Therefore they will be your judges. [28]But if it is by the Spirit of God that I cast out demons, then the kingdom of God has come to you. [29]Or how can one enter a strong man's house and plunder his property, without first tying up the strong man? Then indeed the house can be plundered. [30]Whoever is not with me is against me, and whoever does not gather with me scatters.

[a]Other ancient authorities lack *crowds* [b]Gk *sons*

[31]Therefore I tell you, people will be forgiven for every sin and blasphemy, but blasphemy against the Spirit will not be forgiven. [32]Whoever speaks a word against the Son of Man will be forgiven, but whoever speaks against the Holy Spirit will not be forgiven, either in this age or in the age to come.

33 "Either make the tree good, and its fruit good; or make the tree bad, and its fruit bad; for the tree is known by its fruit. [34]You brood of vipers! How can you speak good things, when you are evil? For out of the abundance of the heart the mouth speaks. [35]The good person brings good things out of a good treasure, and the evil person brings evil things out of an evil treasure. [36]I tell you, on the day of judgment you will have to give an account for every careless word you utter; [37]for by your words you will be justified, and by your words you will be condemned."

38 Then some of the scribes and Pharisees said to him, "Teacher, we wish to see a sign from you." [39]But he answered them, "An evil and adulterous generation asks for a sign, but no sign will be given to it except the sign of the prophet Jonah. [40]For just as Jonah was three days and three nights in the belly of the sea monster, so for three days and three nights the Son of Man will be in the heart of the earth. [41]The people of Nineveh will rise up at the judgment with this generation and condemn it, because they repented at the proclamation of Jonah, and see, something greater than Jonah is here! [42]The queen of the South will rise up at the judgment with this generation and condemn it, because she came from the ends of the earth to listen to the wisdom of Solomon, and see, something greater than Solomon is here!

43 "When the unclean spirit has gone out of a person, it wanders through waterless regions looking for a resting place, but it finds none. [44]Then it says, 'I will return to my house from which I came.' When it comes, it finds it empty, swept, and put in order. [45]Then it goes and brings along seven other spirits more evil than itself, and they enter and live there; and the last state of that person is worse than the first. So will it be also with this evil generation."

46 While he was still speaking to the crowds, his mother and his brothers were standing outside, wanting to speak to him. [47]Someone told him, "Look, your mother and your brothers are standing outside, wanting to speak to you."[a] [48]But to the one who had told him this, Jesus[b] replied, "Who is my mother, and who are my brothers?" [49]And pointing to his disciples, he said, "Here are my mother and my brothers! [50]For whoever does the will of my Father in heaven is my brother and sister and mother."

[a]Other ancient authorities lack verse 47 [b]Gk he

13 That same day Jesus went out of the house and sat beside the sea. ²Such great crowds gathered around him that he got into a boat and sat there, while the whole crowd stood on the beach. ³And he told them many things in parables, saying: "Listen! A sower went out to sow. ⁴And as he sowed, some seeds fell on the path, and the birds came and ate them up. ⁵Other seeds fell on rocky ground, where they did not have much soil, and they sprang up quickly, since they had no depth of soil. ⁶But when the sun rose, they were scorched; and since they had no root, they withered away. ⁷Other seeds fell among thorns, and the thorns grew up and choked them. ⁸Other seeds fell on good soil and brought forth grain, some a hundredfold, some sixty, some thirty. ⁹Let anyone with ears*ᵃ* listen!"

10 Then the disciples came and asked him, "Why do you speak to them in parables?" ¹¹He answered, "To you it has been given to know the secrets*ᵇ* of the kingdom of heaven, but to them it has not been given. ¹²For to those who have, more will be given, and they will have an abundance; but from those who have nothing, even what they have will be taken away. ¹³The reason I speak to them in parables is that 'seeing they do not perceive, and hearing they do not listen, nor do they understand.' ¹⁴With them indeed is fulfilled the prophecy of Isaiah that says:

'You will indeed listen,
    but never understand,
and you will indeed look,
    but never perceive.
¹⁵ For this people's heart has
        grown dull,
    and their ears are hard
        of hearing,
    and they have shut
        their eyes;
    so that they might not
        look with their eyes,
    and listen with their ears,
    and understand with their
        heart and turn—
    and I would heal them.'
¹⁶But blessed are your eyes, for they see, and your ears, for they hear. ¹⁷Truly I tell you, many prophets and righteous people longed to see what you see, but did not see it, and to hear what you hear, but did not hear it.

18 "Hear then the parable of the sower. ¹⁹When anyone hears the word of the kingdom and does not understand it, the evil one comes and snatches away what is sown in the heart; this is what was sown on the path. ²⁰As for what was sown on rocky ground, this is the one who hears the word and immediately receives it with joy; ²¹yet such a person has no root, but endures only for a while, and when trouble or persecution arises on account of the word, that person immediately falls away.*ᶜ* ²²As for what was sown among thorns, this is the one who hears the word, but the cares of the world

---

*ᵃOther ancient authorities add *to hear* *ᵇOr *mysteries*
*ᶜGk *stumbles*

and the lure of wealth choke the word, and it yields nothing. ²³But as for what was sown on good soil, this is the one who hears the word and understands it, who indeed bears fruit and yields, in one case a hundredfold, in another sixty, and in another thirty."

24 He put before them another parable: "The kingdom of heaven may be compared to someone who sowed good seed in his field; ²⁵but while everybody was asleep, an enemy came and sowed weeds among the wheat, and then went away. ²⁶So when the plants came up and bore grain, then the weeds appeared as well. ²⁷And the slaves of the householder came and said to him, 'Master, did you not sow good seed in your field? Where, then, did these weeds come from?' ²⁸He answered, 'An enemy has done this.' The slaves said to him, 'Then do you want us to go and gather them?' ²⁹But he replied, 'No; for in gathering the weeds you would uproot the wheat along with them. ³⁰Let both of them grow together until the harvest; and at harvest time I will tell the reapers, Collect the weeds first and bind them in bundles to be burned, but gather the wheat into my barn.'"

31 He put before them another parable: "The kingdom of heaven is like a mustard seed that someone took and sowed in his field; ³²it is the smallest of all the seeds, but when it has grown it is the greatest of shrubs and becomes a tree, so that the birds of the air come and make nests in its branches."

33 He told them another parable: "The kingdom of heaven is like yeast that a woman took and mixed in with[a] three measures of flour until all of it was leavened."

34 Jesus told the crowds all these things in parables; without a parable he told them nothing. ³⁵This was to fulfill what had been spoken through the prophet:[b]

"I will open my mouth to
    speak in parables;
I will proclaim what has
    been hidden from the
    foundation of the
    world."[c]

36 Then he left the crowds and went into the house. And his disciples approached him, saying, "Explain to us the parable of the weeds of the field." ³⁷He answered, "The one who sows the good seed is the Son of Man; ³⁸the field is the world, and the good seed are the children of the kingdom; the weeds are the children of the evil one, ³⁹and the enemy who sowed them is the devil; the harvest is the end of the age, and the reapers are angels. ⁴⁰Just as the weeds are collected and burned up with fire, so will it be at the end of the age. ⁴¹The Son of Man will send his angels, and they will collect out of his kingdom all causes of sin and all evildoers, ⁴²and they will throw them into the furnace

[a]Gk hid in [b]Other ancient authorities read the prophet Isaiah [c]Other ancient authrioties lack of the world

of fire, where there will be weeping and gnashing of teeth. [43]Then the righteous will shine like the sun in the kingdom of their Father. Let anyone with ears[a] listen!

44 "The kingdom of heaven is like treasure hidden in a field, which someone found and hid; then in his joy he goes and sells all that he has and buys that field.

45 "Again, the kingdom of heaven is like a merchant in search of fine pearls; [46] on finding one pearl of great value, he went and sold all that he had and bought it.

47 "Again, the kingdom of heaven is like a net that was thrown into the sea and caught fish of every kind; [48]when it was full, they drew it ashore, sat down, and put the good into baskets but threw out the bad. [49]So it will be at the end of the age. The angels will come out and separate the evil from the righteous [50]and throw them into the furnace of fire, where there will be weeping and gnashing of teeth.

51 "Have you understood all this?" They answered, "Yes." [52]And he said to them, "Therefore every scribe who has been trained for the kingdom of heaven is like the master of a household who brings out of his treasure what is new and what is old." [53]When Jesus had finished these parables, he left that place.

54 He came to his hometown and began to teach the people[b] in their synagogue, so that they were astounded and said, "Where did this man get this wisdom and these deeds of power? [55]Is not this the carpenter's son? Is not his mother called Mary? And are not his brothers James and Joseph and Simon and Judas? [56]And are not all his sisters with us? Where then did this man get all this?" [57]And they took offense at him. But Jesus said to them, "Prophets are not without honor except in their own country and in their own house." [58]And he did not do many deeds of power there, because of their unbelief.

14 At that time Herod the ruler[c] heard reports about Jesus; [2]and he said to his servants, "This is John the Baptist; he has been raised from the dead, and for this reason these powers are at work in him." [3]For Herod had arrested John, bound him, and put him in prison on account of Herodias, his brother Philip's wife,[d] [4]because John had been telling him, "It is not lawful for you to have her." [5]Though Herod[e] wanted to put him to death, he feared the crowd, because they regarded him as a prophet. [6]But when Herod's birthday came, the daughter of Herodias danced before the company, and she pleased Herod [7]so much that he promised on oath to grant her whatever she might ask. [8]Prompted by her mother, she

[a]Other ancient authorities add to hear [b]Gk them [c]Gk tetrarch [d]Other ancient authorities read his brother's wife [e]Gk he

said, "Give me the head of John the Baptist here on a platter." [9]The king was grieved, yet out of regard for his oaths and for the guests, he commanded it to be given; [10]he sent and had John beheaded in the prison. [11]The head was brought on a platter and given to the girl, who brought it to her mother. [12]His disciples came and took the body and buried it; then they went and told Jesus.

13 Now when Jesus heard this, he withdrew from there in a boat to a deserted place by himself. But when the crowds heard it, they followed him on foot from the towns. [14]When he went ashore, he saw a great crowd; and he had compassion for them and cured their sick. [15]When it was evening, the disciples came to him and said, "This is a deserted place, and the hour is now late; send the crowds away so that they may go into the villages and buy food for themselves." [16]Jesus said to them, "They need not go away; you give them something to eat." [17]They replied, "We have nothing here but five loaves and two fish." [18]And he said, "Bring them here to me." [19]Then he ordered the crowds to sit down on the grass. Taking the five loaves and the two fish, he looked up to heaven, and blessed and broke the loaves, and gave them to the disciples, and the disciples gave them to the crowds. [20]And all ate and were filled; and they took up what was left over of the broken pieces, twelve baskets full. [21]And those who ate were about five thousand men, besides women and children.

22 Immediately he made the disciples get into the boat and go on ahead to the other side, while he dismissed the crowds. [23]And after he had dismissed the crowds, he went up the mountain by himself to pray. When evening came, he was there alone, [24]but by this time the boat, battered by the waves, was far from the land,[a] for the wind was against them. [25]And early in the morning he came walking toward them on the sea. [26]But when the disciples saw him walking on the sea, they were terrified, saying, "It is a ghost!" And they cried out in fear. [27]But immediately Jesus spoke to them and said, "Take heart, it is I; do not be afraid."

28 Peter answered him, "Lord, if it is you, command me to come to you on the water." [29]He said, "Come." So Peter got out of the boat, started walking on the water, and came toward Jesus. [30]But when he noticed the strong wind,[b] he became frightened, and beginning to sink, he cried out, "Lord, save me!" [31]Jesus immediately reached out his hand and caught him, saying to him, "You of little faith, why did you doubt?" [32]When they got into the boat, the wind ceased. [33]And those in the boat worshiped him, saying, "Truly you are the Son of God."

[a]Other ancient authorities read *was out on the sea*
[b]Other ancient authorities read *the wind*

34 When they had crossed over, they came to land at Gennesaret. [35]After the people of that place recognized him, they sent word throughout the region and brought all who were sick to him, [36]and begged him that they might touch even the fringe of his cloak; and all who touched it were healed.

15 Then Pharisees and scribes came to Jesus from Jerusalem and said, [2]"Why do your disciples break the tradition of the elders? For they do not wash their hands before they eat." [3]He answered them, "And why do you break the commandment of God for the sake of your tradition? [4]For God said,[a] 'Honor your father and your mother,' and, 'Whoever speaks evil of father or mother must surely die.' [5]But you say that whoever tells father or mother, 'Whatever support you might have had from me is given to God,'[b] then that person need not honor the father.[c] [6]So, for the sake of your tradition, you make void the word[d] of God. [7]You hypocrites! Isaiah prophesied rightly about you when he said:

8   'This people honors me
        with their lips,
     but their hearts are far
        from me;
9   in vain do they worship
        me,
     teaching human precepts
        as doctrines.'"

10 Then he called the crowd to him and said to them, "Listen and understand: [11]it is not what goes into the mouth that defiles a person, but it is what comes out of the mouth that defiles." [12]Then the disciples approached and said to him, "Do you know that the Pharisees took offense when they heard what you said?" [13]He answered, "Every plant that my heavenly Father has not planted will be uprooted. [14]Let them alone; they are blind guides of the blind.[e] And if one blind person guides another, both will fall into a pit." [15]But Peter said to him, "Explain this parable to us." [16]Then he said, "Are you also still without understanding? [17]Do you not see that whatever goes into the mouth enters the stomach, and goes out into the sewer? [18]But what comes out of the mouth proceeds from the heart, and this is what defiles. [19]For out of the heart come evil intentions, murder, adultery, fornication, theft, false witness, slander. [20]These are what defile a person, but to eat with unwashed hands does not defile."

21 Jesus left that place and went away to the district of Tyre and Sidon. [22]Just then a Canaanite woman from that region came out and started shouting, "Have mercy on me, Lord, Son of David; my daughter is tormented by a demon." [23]But he did not answer her at all. And his disciples came and urged him, saying, "Send her away, for

---

[a]Other ancient authorities read *commanded, saying* [b]Or *is an offering* [c]Other ancient authorities add *or the mother* [d]Other ancient authorities read *law;* others, *commandment* [e]Other ancient authorities lack *of the blind*

she keeps shouting after us." [24]He answered, "I was sent only to the lost sheep of the house of Israel." [25]But she came and knelt before him, saying, "Lord, help me." [26]He answered, "It is not fair to take the children's food and throw it to the dogs." [27]She said, "Yes, Lord, yet even the dogs eat the crumbs that fall from their masters' table." [28]Then Jesus answered her, "Woman, great is your faith! Let it be done for you as you wish." And her daughter was healed instantly.

29 After Jesus had left that place, he passed along the Sea of Galilee, and he went up the mountain, where he sat down. [30]Great crowds came to him, bringing with them the lame, the maimed, the blind, the mute, and many others. They put them at his feet, and he cured them, [31]so that the crowd was amazed when they saw the mute speaking, the maimed whole, the lame walking, and the blind seeing. And they praised the God of Israel.

32 Then Jesus called his disciples to him and said, "I have compassion for the crowd, because they have been with me now for three days and have nothing to eat; and I do not want to send them away hungry, for they might faint on the way." [33]The disciples said to him, "Where are we to get enough bread in the desert to feed so great a crowd?" [34]Jesus asked them, "How many loaves have you?" They said, "Seven, and a few small fish." [35]Then ordering the crowd to sit down on the ground, [36]he took the seven loaves and the fish; and after giving thanks he broke them and gave them to the disciples, and the disciples gave them to the crowds. [37]And all of them ate and were filled; and they took up the broken pieces left over, seven baskets full. [38]Those who had eaten were four thousand men, besides women and children. [39]After sending away the crowds, he got into the boat and went to the region of Magadan.[a]

16 The Pharisees and Sadducees came, and to test Jesus[b] they asked him to show them a sign from heaven. [2]He answered them, "When it is evening, you say, 'It will be fair weather, for the sky is red.' [3]And in the morning, 'It will be stormy today, for the sky is red and threatening.' You know how to interpret the appearance of the sky, but you cannot interpret the signs of the times.[c] [4]An evil and adulterous generation asks for a sign, but no sign will be given to it except the sign of Jonah." Then he left them and went away.

5 When the disciples reached the other side, they had forgotten to bring any bread. [6]Jesus said to them, "Watch out, and beware of the yeast of the Pharisees and Sadducees." [7]They said to one another, "It is because we have brought no bread." [8]And becoming aware of it, Jesus said, "You of

[a]Other ancient authorities read *Magdala or Magdalan* [b]Gk *him* [c]Other ancient authorities lack[2] *When it is . . . of the times*

little faith, why are you talking about having no bread? ⁹Do you still not perceive? Do you not remember the five loaves for the five thousand, and how many baskets you gathered? ¹⁰Or the seven loaves for the four thousand, and how many baskets you gathered? ¹¹How could you fail to perceive that I was not speaking about bread? Beware of the yeast of the Pharisees and Sadducees!" ¹²Then they understood that he had not told them to beware of the yeast of bread, but of the teaching of the Pharisees and Sadducees.

13 Now when Jesus came into the district of Caesarea Philippi, he asked his disciples, "Who do people say that the Son of Man is?" ¹⁴And they said, "Some say John the Baptist, but others Elijah, and still others Jeremiah or one of the prophets." ¹⁵He said to them, "But who do you say that I am?" ¹⁶Simon Peter answered, "You are the Messiah,ᵃ the Son of the living God." ¹⁷And Jesus answered him, "Blessed are you, Simon son of Jonah! For flesh and blood has not revealed this to you, but my Father in heaven. ¹⁸And I tell you, you are Peter,ᵇ and on this rockᶜ I will build my church, and the gates of Hades will not prevail against it. ¹⁹I will give you the keys of the kingdom of heaven, and whatever you bind on earth will be bound in heaven, and whatever you loose on earth will be loosed in heaven." ²⁰Then he sternly ordered the disciples not to tell anyone that he wasᵈ the Messiah.ᵃ

21 From that time on, Jesus began to show his disciples that he must go to Jerusalem and undergo great suffering at the hands of the elders and chief priests and scribes, and be killed, and on the third day be raised. ²²And Peter took him aside and began to rebuke him, saying, "God forbid it, Lord! This must never happen to you." ²³But he turned and said to Peter, "Get behind me, Satan! You are a stumbling block to me; for you are setting your mind not on divine things but on human things."

24 Then Jesus told his disciples, "If any want to become my followers, let them deny themselves and take up their cross and follow me. ²⁵For those who want to save their life will lose it, and those who lose their life for my sake will find it. ²⁶For what will it profit them if they gain the whole world but forfeit their life? Or what will they give in return for their life?

27 "For the Son of Man is to come with his angels in the glory of his Father, and then he will repay everyone for what has been done. ²⁸Truly I tell you, there are some standing here who will not taste death before they see the Son of Man coming in his kingdom."

17 Six days later, Jesus took with him Peter and James and his brother John and led them

ᵃOr the Christ ᵇGk Petros ᶜGk petra ᵈOther ancient authorities add Jesus

up a high mountain, by themselves. ²And he was transfigured before them, and his face shone like the sun, and his clothes became dazzling white. ³Suddenly there appeared to them Moses and Elijah, talking with him. ⁴Then Peter said to Jesus, "Lord, it is good for us to be here; if you wish, I*ᵃ* will make three dwellings*ᵇ* here, one for you, one for Moses, and one for Elijah." ⁵While he was still speaking, suddenly a bright cloud overshadowed them, and from the cloud a voice said, "This is my Son, the Beloved;*ᶜ* with him I am well pleased; listen to him!" ⁶When the disciples heard this, they fell to the ground and were overcome by fear. ⁷But Jesus came and touched them, saying, "Get up and do not be afraid." ⁸And when they looked up, they saw no one except Jesus himself alone.

9 As they were coming down the mountain, Jesus ordered them, "Tell no one about the vision until after the Son of Man has been raised from the dead." ¹⁰And the disciples asked him, "Why, then, do the scribes say that Elijah must come first?" ¹¹He replied, "Elijah is indeed coming and will restore all things; ¹²but I tell you that Elijah has already come, and they did not recognize him, but they did to him whatever they pleased. So also the Son of Man is about to suffer at their hands." ¹³Then the disciples understood that he was speaking to them about John the Baptist.

14 When they came to the crowd, a man came to him, knelt before him, ¹⁵and said, "Lord, have mercy on my son, for he is an epileptic and he suffers terribly; he often falls into the fire and often into the water. ¹⁶And I brought him to your disciples, but they could not cure him." ¹⁷Jesus answered, "You faithless and perverse generation, how much longer must I be with you? How much longer must I put up with you? Bring him here to me." ¹⁸And Jesus rebuked the demon,*ᵈ* and it*ᵉ* came out of him, and the boy was cured instantly. ¹⁹Then the disciples came to Jesus privately and said, "Why could we not cast it out?" ²⁰He said to them, "Because of your little faith. For truly I tell you, if you have faith the size of a*ᶠ* mustard seed, you will say to this mountain, 'Move from here to there,' and it will move; and nothing will be impossible for you."*ᵍ*

22 As they were gathering*ʰ* in Galilee, Jesus said to them, "The Son of Man is going to be betrayed into human hands, ²³and they will kill him, and on the third day he will be raised." And they were greatly distressed.

24 When they reached Capernaum, the collectors of the temple tax*ⁱ* came to Peter and said, "Does your teacher not pay

ᵃOther ancient authorities read we ᵇOr tents ᶜOr my beloved Son ᵈGk it or him ᵉGk the demon ᶠGk faith as a grain of ᵍOther ancient authorities add verse 21, But this kind does not come out except by prayer and fasting ʰOther ancient authorities read living ⁱGk didrachma

the temple tax?" [25]He said, "Yes, he does." And when he came home, Jesus spoke of it first, asking, "What do you think, Simon? From whom do kings of the earth take toll or tribute? From their children or from others?" [26]When Peter[a] said, "From others," Jesus said to him, "Then the children are free. [27]However, so that we do not give offense to them, go to the sea and cast a hook; take the first fish that comes up; and when you open its mouth, you will find a coin;[b] take that and give it to them for you and me."

18 At that time the disciples came to Jesus and asked, "Who is the greatest in the kingdom of heaven?" [2]He called a child, whom he put among them, [3]and said, "Truly I tell you, unless you change and become like children, you will never enter the kingdom of heaven. [4]Whoever becomes humble like this child is the greatest in the kingdom of heaven. [5]Whoever welcomes one such child in my name welcomes me.

[6]"If any of you put a stumbling block before one of these little ones who believe in me, it would be better for you if a great millstone were fastened around your neck and you were drowned in the depth of the sea. [7]Woe to the world because of stumbling blocks! Occasions for stumbling are bound to come, but woe to the one by whom the stumbling block comes!

[8]"If your hand or your foot causes you to stumble, cut it off and throw it away; it is better for you to enter life maimed or lame than to have two hands or two feet and to be thrown into the eternal fire. [9]And if your eye causes you to stumble, tear it out and throw it away; it is better for you to enter life with one eye than to have two eyes and to be thrown into the hell[c] of fire.

[10]"Take care that you do not despise one of these little ones; for, I tell you, in heaven their angels continually see the face of my Father in heaven[d] [12]What do you think? If a shepherd has a hundred sheep, and one of them has gone astray, does he not leave the ninety-nine on the mountains and go in search of the one that went astray? [13]And if he finds it, truly I tell you, he rejoices over it more than over the ninety-nine that never went astray. [14]So it is not the will of your[e] Father in heaven that one of these little ones should be lost.

[15]"If another member of the church[f] sins against you,[g] go and point out the fault when the two of you are alone. If the member listens to you, you have regained that one.[h] [16]But if you are not listened to, take one or two others along with you, so that every word may be confirmed by the evidence of two or three witnesses.

---

[a]Gk *he* [b]Gk *stater;* the stater was worth two didrachmas; [c]Gk *Gehenna* [d]Other ancient authorities add verse 11, *For the Son of Man came to save the lost* [e]Other ancient authorities read *my* [f]Gk *If your brother* [g]Other ancient authorities lack *against you* [h]Gk *the brother*

17If the member refuses to listen to them, tell it to the church; and if the offender refuses to listen even to the church, let such a one be to you as a Gentile and a tax collector. 18Truly I tell you, whatever you bind on earth will be bound in heaven, and whatever you loose on earth will be loosed in heaven. 19Again, truly I tell you, if two of you agree on earth about anything you ask, it will be done for you by my Father in heaven. 20For where two or three are gathered in my name, I am there among them."

21 Then Peter came and said to him, "Lord, if another member of the church*a* sins against me, how often should I forgive? As many as seven times?" 22Jesus said to him, "Not seven times, but, I tell you, seventy-seven*b* times.

23 "For this reason the kingdom of heaven may be compared to a king who wished to settle accounts with his slaves. 24When he began the reckoning, one who owed him ten thousand talents*c* was brought to him; 25and, as he could not pay, his lord ordered him to be sold, together with his wife and children and all his possessions, and payment to be made. 26So the slave fell on his knees before him, saying, 'Have patience with me, and I will pay you everything.' 27And out of pity for him, the lord of that slave released him and forgave him the debt. 28But that same slave, as he went out, came upon one of his fellow slaves who owed him a hundred denarii;*d* and seizing him by the throat, he said, 'Pay what you owe.' 29Then his fellow slave fell down and pleaded with him, 'Have patience with me, and I will pay you.' 30But he refused; then he went and threw him into prison until he would pay the debt. 31When his fellow slaves saw what had happened, they were greatly distressed, and they went and reported to their lord all that had taken place. 32Then his lord summoned him and said to him, 'You wicked slave! I forgave you all that debt because you pleaded with me. 33Should you not have had mercy on your fellow slave, as I had mercy on you?' 34And in anger his lord handed him over to be tortured until he would pay his entire debt. 35So my heavenly Father will also do to every one of you, if you do not forgive your brother or sister*e* from your heart."

19 When Jesus had finished saying these things, he left Galilee and went to the region of Judea beyond the Jordan. 2Large crowds followed him, and he cured them there.

3 Some Pharisees came to him, and to test him they asked, "Is it lawful for a man to divorce his wife for any cause?" 4He answered, "Have you not read that the one who made them at the

---

*a*Gk *if my brother* *b*Or *seventy times seven* *c*A talent was worth more than fifteen years' wages of a laborer *d*The denarius was the usual day's wage for a laborer *e*Gk *brother*

beginning 'made them male and female,' [5]and said, 'For this reason a man shall leave his father and mother and be joined to his wife, and the two shall become one flesh'? [6]So they are no longer two, but one flesh. Therefore what God has joined together, let no one separate." [7]They said to him, "Why then did Moses command us to give a certificate of dismissal and to divorce her?" [8]He said to them, "It was because you were so hard-hearted that Moses allowed you to divorce your wives, but from the beginning it was not so. [9]And I say to you, whoever divorces his wife, except for unchastity, and marries another commits adultery."[a]

10 His disciples said to him, "If such is the case of a man with his wife, it is better not to marry." [11]But he said to them, "Not everyone can accept this teaching, but only those to whom it is given. [12]For there are eunuchs who have been so from birth, and there are eunuchs who have been made eunuchs by others, and there are eunuchs who have made themselves eunuchs for the sake of the kingdom of heaven. Let anyone accept this who can."

13 Then little children were being brought to him in order that he might lay his hands on them and pray. The disciples spoke sternly to those who brought them; [14]but Jesus said, "Let the little children come to me, and do not stop them; for it is to such as these that the kingdom of heaven belongs." [15]And

he laid his hands on them and went on his way.

16 Then someone came to him and said, "Teacher, what good deed must I do to have eternal life?" [17]And he said to him, "Why do you ask me about what is good? There is only one who is good. If you wish to enter into life, keep the commandments." [18]He said to him, "Which ones?" And Jesus said, "You shall not murder; You shall not commit adultery; You shall not steal; You shall not bear false witness; [19]Honor your father and mother; also, You shall love your neighbor as yourself." [20]The young man said to him, "I have kept all these;[b] what do I still lack?" [21]Jesus said to him, "If you wish to be perfect, go, sell your possessions, and give the money[c] to the poor, and you will have treasure in heaven; then come, follow me." [22]When the young man heard this word, he went away grieving, for he had many possessions.

23 Then Jesus said to his disciples, "Truly I tell you, it will be hard for a rich person to enter the kingdom of heaven. [24]Again I tell you, it is easier for a camel to go through the eye of a needle than for someone who is rich to enter the kingdom of God." [25]When the disciples heard this, they were greatly astounded and said, "Then who can be saved?" [26]But

---

[a]Other ancient authorities read *except on the ground of unchastity, causes her to commit adultery;* others add at the end of the verse *and he who marries a divorced woman commits adultery* [b]Other ancient authorities add *from my youth* [c]Gk lacks *the money*

Jesus looked at them and said, "For mortals it is impossible, but for God all things are possible."

27 Then Peter said in reply, "Look, we have left everything and followed you. What then will we have?" [28]Jesus said to them, "Truly I tell you, at the renewal of all things, when the Son of Man is seated on the throne of his glory, you who have followed me will also sit on twelve thrones, judging the twelve tribes of Israel. [29]And everyone who has left houses or brothers or sisters or father or mother or children or fields, for my name's sake, will receive a hundredfold[a], and will inherit eternal life. [30]But many who are first will be last, and the last will be first.

20 "For the kingdom of heaven is like a landowner who went out early in the morning to hire laborers for his vineyard. [2]After agreeing with the laborers for the usual daily wage,[b] he sent them into his vineyard. [3]When he went out about nine o'clock, he saw others standing idle in the marketplace; [4]and he said to them, 'You also go into the vineyard, and I will pay you whatever is right.' So they went. [5]When he went out again about noon and about three o'clock, he did the same. [6]And about five o'clock he went out and found others standing around; and he said to them, 'Why are you standing here idle all day?' [7]They said to him, 'Because no one has hired us.' He said to them, 'You also go into the

vineyard.' [8]When evening came, the owner of the vineyard said to his manager, 'Call the laborers and give them their pay, beginning with the last and then going to the first.' [9]When those hired about five o'clock came, each of them received the usual daily wage.[b] [10]Now when the first came, they thought they would receive more; but each of them also received the usual daily wage.[b] [11]And when they received it, they grumbled against the landowner, [12]saying, 'These last worked only one hour, and you have made them equal to us who have borne the burden of the day and the scorching heat.' [13]But he replied to one of them, 'Friend, I am doing you no wrong; did you not agree with me for the usual daily wage?[b] [14]Take what belongs to you and go; I choose to give to this last the same as I give to you. [15]Am I not allowed to do what I choose with what belongs to me? Or are you envious because I am generous?[c] [16]So the last will be first, and the first will be last."[d]

17 While Jesus was going up to Jerusalem, he took the twelve disciples aside by themselves, and said to them on the way, [18]"See, we are going up to Jerusalem, and the Son of Man will be handed over to the chief priests and scribes, and they will condemn him to death; [19]then they

[a]Other ancient authorities read *manifold* [b]Gk *a denarius* [c]Gk *is your eye evil because I am good?* [d]Other ancient authorities add *for many are called but few are chosen*

will hand him over to the Gentiles to be mocked and flogged and crucified; and on the third day he will be raised."

20 Then the mother of the sons of Zebedee came to him with her sons, and kneeling before him, she asked a favor of him. ²¹And he said to her, "What do you want?" She said to him, "Declare that these two sons of mine will sit, one at your right hand and one at your left, in your kingdom." ²²But Jesus answered, "You do not know what you are asking. Are you able to drink the cup that I am about to drink?"^a They said to him, "We are able." ²³He said to them, "You will indeed drink my cup, but to sit at my right hand and at my left, this is not mine to grant, but it is for those for whom it has been prepared by my Father."

24 When the ten heard it, they were angry with the two brothers. ²⁵But Jesus called them to him and said, "You know that the rulers of the Gentiles lord it over them, and their great ones are tyrants over them. ²⁶It will not be so among you; but whoever wishes to be great among you must be your servant, ²⁷and whoever wishes to be first among you must be your slave; ²⁸just as the Son of Man came not to be served but to serve, and to give his life a ransom for many."

29 As they were leaving Jericho, a large crowd followed him. ³⁰There were two blind men sitting by the roadside. When they heard that Jesus was passing by, they shouted, "Lord,^b have

mercy on us, Son of David!" ³¹The crowd sternly ordered them to be quiet; but they shouted even more loudly, "Have mercy on us, Lord, Son of David!" ³²Jesus stood still and called them, saying, "What do you want me to do for you?" ³³They said to him, "Lord, let our eyes be opened." ³⁴Moved with compassion, Jesus touched their eyes. Immediately they regained their sight and followed him.

21 When they had come near Jerusalem and had reached Bethphage, at the Mount of Olives, Jesus sent two disciples, ²saying to them, "Go into the village ahead of you, and immediately you will find a donkey tied, and a colt with her; untie them and bring them to me. ³If anyone says anything to you, just say this, 'The Lord needs them.' And he will send them immediately.^c ⁴This took place to fulfill what had been spoken through the prophet, saying,

5   "Tell the daughter of Zion,
       Look, your king is coming
            to you,
       humble, and mounted on
            a donkey,
            and on a colt, the foal
            of a donkey."

⁶The disciples went and did as Jesus had directed them; ⁷they brought the donkey and the colt, and put their cloaks on them, and

---

^aOther ancient authorities add *or to be baptized with the baptism that I am baptized with?* ^bOther ancient authorities lack *Lord* ^cOr *'The Lord needs them and will send them back immediately.'*

he sat on them. [8]A very large crowd[a] spread their cloaks on the road, and others cut branches from the trees and spread them on the road. [9]The crowds that went ahead of him and that followed were shouting,

"Hosanna to the Son
of David!
Blessed is the one who
comes in the name of
the Lord!
Hosanna in the highest
heaven!"

[10]When he entered Jerusalem, the whole city was in turmoil, asking, "Who is this?" [11]The crowds were saying, "This is the prophet Jesus from Nazareth in Galilee." [12]Then Jesus entered the temple[b] and drove out all who were selling and buying in the temple, and he overturned the tables of the money changers and the seats of those who sold doves. [13]He said to them, "It is written,

'My house shall be called a
house of prayer';
but you are making it a
den of robbers.'"

[14] The blind and the lame came to him in the temple, and he cured them. [15]But when the chief priests and the scribes saw the amazing things that he did, and heard[c] the children crying out in the temple, "Hosanna to the Son of David," they became angry [16]and said to him, "Do you hear what these are saying?" Jesus said to them, "Yes; have you never read,

'Out of the mouths of
infants and nursing
babies

you have prepared praise
for yourself'?"

[17]He left them, went out of the city to Bethany, and spent the night there.

[18] In the morning, when he returned to the city, he was hungry. [19]And seeing a fig tree by the side of the road, he went to it and found nothing at all on it but leaves. Then he said to it, "May no fruit ever come from you again!" And the fig tree withered at once. [20]When the disciples saw it, they were amazed, saying, "How did the fig tree wither at once?" [21]Jesus answered them, "Truly I tell you, if you have faith and do not doubt, not only will you do what has been done to the fig tree, but even if you say to this mountain, 'Be lifted up and thrown into the sea,' it will be done. [22]Whatever you ask for in prayer with faith, you will receive."

[23] When he entered the temple, the chief priests and the elders of the people came to him as he was teaching, and said, "By what authority are you doing these things, and who gave you this authority?" [24]Jesus said to them, "I will also ask you one question; if you tell me the answer, then I will also tell you by what authority I do these things. [25]Did the baptism of John come from heaven, or was it of human origin?" And they argued with one another, "If we say, 'From heaven,' he will say to us,

[a]Or *Most of the crowd* [b]Other ancient authorities add *of God* [c]Gk lacks *heard*

'Why then did you not believe him?' [26]But if we say, 'Of human origin,' we are afraid of the crowd; for all regard John as a prophet." [27]So they answered Jesus, "We do not know." And he said to them, "Neither will I tell you by what authority I am doing these things.

28 "What do you think? A man had two sons; he went to the first and said, 'Son, go and work in the vineyard today.' [29]He answered, 'I will not'; but later he changed his mind and went. [30]The father[a] went to the second and said the same; and he answered, 'I go, sir'; but he did not go. [31]Which of the two did the will of his father?" They said, "The first." Jesus said to them, "Truly I tell you, the tax collectors and the prostitutes are going into the kingdom of God ahead of you. [32]For John came to you in the way of righteousness and you did not believe him, but the tax collectors and the prostitutes believed him; and even after you saw it, you did not change your minds and believe him.

33 "Listen to another parable. There was a landowner who planted a vineyard, put a fence around it, dug a wine press in it, and built a watchtower. Then he leased it to tenants and went to another country. [34]When the harvest time had come, he sent his slaves to the tenants to collect his produce. [35]But the tenants seized his slaves and beat one, killed another, and stoned another. [36]Again he sent other slaves, more than the first; and they treated them in the same way. [37]Finally he sent his son to them, saying, 'They will respect my son.' [38]But when the tenants saw the son, they said to themselves, 'This is the heir; come, let us kill him and get his inheritance.' [39]So they seized him, threw him out of the vineyard, and killed him. [40]Now when the owner of the vineyard comes, what will he do to those tenants?" [41]They said to him, "He will put those wretches to a miserable death, and lease the vineyard to other tenants who will give him the produce at the harvest time."

42 Jesus said to them, "Have you never read in the scriptures:

'The stone that the builders
    rejected
has become the
    cornerstone;[b]
this was the Lord's doing,
and it is amazing in our
    eyes'?

[43]Therefore I tell you, the kingdom of God will be taken away from you and given to a people that produces the fruits of the kingdom.[c] [44]The one who falls on this stone will be broken to pieces; and it will crush anyone on whom it falls."[d]

45 When the chief priests and the Pharisees heard his parables, they realized that he was speaking about them. [46]They wanted to arrest him, but they feared the crowds, because they regarded him as a prophet.

---

[a]Gk He [b]Or keystone [c]Gk the fruits of it [d]Other ancient authorities lack verse 44

22 Once more Jesus spoke to them in parables, saying: [2]"The kingdom of heaven may be compared to a king who gave a wedding banquet for his son. [3]He sent his slaves to call those who had been invited to the wedding banquet, but they would not come. [4]Again he sent other slaves, saying, 'Tell those who have been invited: Look, I have prepared my dinner, my oxen and my fat calves have been slaughtered, and everything is ready; come to the wedding banquet.' [5]But they made light of it and went away, one to his farm, another to his business, [6]while the rest seized his slaves, mistreated them, and killed them. [7]The king was enraged. He sent his troops, destroyed those murderers, and burned their city. [8]Then he said to his slaves, 'The wedding is ready, but those invited were not worthy. [9]Go therefore into the main streets, and invite everyone you find to the wedding banquet.' [10]Those slaves went out into the streets and gathered all whom they found, both good and bad; so the wedding hall was filled with guests.

[11]"But when the king came in to see the guests, he noticed a man there who was not wearing a wedding robe, [12]and he said to him, 'Friend, how did you get in here without a wedding robe?' And he was speechless. [13]Then the king said to the attendants, 'Bind him hand and foot, and throw him into the outer darkness, where there will be weeping and gnashing of teeth.' [14]For many are called, but few are chosen."

[15]Then the Pharisees went and plotted to entrap him in what he said. [16]So they sent their disciples to him, along with the Herodians, saying, "Teacher, we know that you are sincere, and teach the way of God in accordance with truth, and show deference to no one; for you do not regard people with partiality. [17]Tell us, then, what you think. Is it lawful to pay taxes to the emperor, or not?" [18]But Jesus, aware of their malice, said, "Why are you putting me to the test, you hypocrites? [19]Show me the coin used for the tax." And they brought him a denarius. [20]Then he said to them, "Whose head is this, and whose title?" [21]They answered, "The emperor's." Then he said to them, "Give therefore to the emperor the things that are the emperor's, and to God the things that are God's." [22]When they heard this, they were amazed; and they left him and went away.

[23]The same day some Sadducees came to him, saying there is no resurrection;[a] and they asked him a question, saying, [24]"Teacher, Moses said, 'If a man dies childless, his brother shall marry the widow, and raise up children for his brother.' [25]Now there were seven brothers among us; the first married, and died childless, leaving the widow to his brother. [26]The sec-

---

[a]Other ancient authorities read *who say that there is no resurrection*

ond did the same, so also the third, down to the seventh. [27]Last of all, the woman herself died. [28]In the resurrection, then, whose wife of the seven will she be? For all of them had married her."

29 Jesus answered them, "You are wrong, because you know neither the scriptures nor the power of God. [30]For in the resurrection they neither marry nor are given in marriage, but are like angels[a] in heaven. [31]And as for the resurrection of the dead, have you not read what was said to you by God, [32]'I am the God of Abraham, the God of Isaac, and the God of Jacob'? He is God not of the dead, but of the living." [33]And when the crowd heard it, they were astounded at his teaching.

34 When the Pharisees heard that he had silenced the Sadducees, they gathered together, [35]and one of them, a lawyer, asked him a question to test him. [36]"Teacher, which commandment in the law is the greatest?" [37]He said to him, "'You shall love the Lord your God with all your heart, and with all your soul, and with all your mind.' [38]This is the greatest and first commandment. [39]And a second is like it: 'You shall love your neighbor as yourself.' [40]On these two commandments hang all the law and the prophets."

41 Now while the Pharisees were gathered together, Jesus asked them this question: [42]"What do you think of the Messiah?[b] Whose son is he?"

They said to him, "The son of David." [43]He said to them, "How is it then that David by the Spirit[c] calls him Lord, saying,

[44]   'The Lord said to my Lord,
       "Sit at my right hand,
       until I put your enemies
           under your feet"'?

[45]If David thus calls him Lord, how can he be his son?" [46]No one was able to give him an answer, nor from that day did anyone dare to ask him any more questions.

23 Then Jesus said to the crowds and to his disciples, [2]"The scribes and the Pharisees sit on Moses' seat; [3]therefore, do whatever they teach you and follow it; but do not do as they do, for they do not practice what they teach. [4]They tie up heavy burdens, hard to bear,[d] and lay them on the shoulders of others; but they themselves are unwilling to lift a finger to move them. [5]They do all their deeds to be seen by others; for they make their phylacteries broad and their fringes long. [6]They love to have the place of honor at banquets and the best seats in the synagogues, [7]and to be greeted with respect in the marketplaces, and to have people call them rabbi. [8]But you are not to be called rabbi, for you have one teacher, and you are all students.[e] [9]And call no one your father on earth, for you have one

[a]Other ancient authorities add *of God* [b]Or *Christ* [c]Gk *in spirit* [d]Other ancient authorities lack *hard to bear* [e]Gk *brothers*

Father—the one in heaven. [10]Nor are you to be called instructors, for you have one instructor, the Messiah.[a] [11]The greatest among you will be your servant. [12]All who exalt themselves will be humbled, and all who humble themselves will be exalted.

13 "But woe to you, scribes and Pharisees, hypocrites! For you lock people out of the kingdom of heaven. For you do not go in yourselves, and when others are going in, you stop them.[b] [14] [15]Woe to you, scribes and Pharisees, hypocrites! For you cross sea and land to make a single convert, and you make the new convert twice as much a child of hell[c] as yourselves.

16 "Woe to you, blind guides, who say, 'Whoever swears by the sanctuary is bound by nothing, but whoever swears by the gold of the sanctuary is bound by the oath.' [17]You blind fools! For which is greater, the gold or the sanctuary that has made the gold sacred? [18]And you say, 'Whoever swears by the altar is bound by nothing, but whoever swears by the gift that is on the altar is bound by the oath.' [19]How blind you are! For which is greater, the gift or the altar that makes the gift sacred? [20]So whoever swears by the altar, swears by it and by everything on it; [21]and whoever swears by the sanctuary, swears by it and by the one who dwells in it; [22]and whoever swears by heaven, swears by the throne of God and by the one who is seated upon it.

23 "Woe to you, scribes and Pharisees, hypocrites! For you tithe mint, dill, and cummin, and have neglected the weightier matters of the law: justice and mercy and faith. It is these you ought to have practiced without neglecting the others. [24]You blind guides! You strain out a gnat but swallow a camel!

25 "Woe to you, scribes and Pharisees, hypocrites! For you clean the outside of the cup and of the plate, but inside they are full of greed and self-indulgence. [26]You blind Pharisee! First clean the inside of the cup,[d] so that the outside also may become clean.

27 "Woe to you, scribes and Pharisees, hypocrites! For you are like whitewashed tombs, which on the outside look beautiful, but inside they are full of the bones of the dead and of all kinds of filth. [28]So you also on the outside look righteous to others, but inside you are full of hypocrisy and lawlessness.

29 "Woe to you, scribes and Pharisees, hypocrites! For you build the tombs of the prophets and decorate the graves of the righteous, [30]and you say, 'If we had lived in the days of our ancestors, we would not have taken part with them in shedding the blood of the prophets.' [31]Thus you testify against your-

[a]*Or the Christ* [b]Other authorities add here (or after verse 12) verse 14, *Woe to you, scribes and Pharisees, hypocrites! For you devour widows' houses and for the sake of appearance you make long prayers; therefore you will receive the greater condemnation* [c]Gk *Gehenna* [d]Other ancient authorities add *and of the plate*

selves that you are descendants of those who murdered the prophets. [32]Fill up, then, the measure of your ancestors. [33]You snakes, you brood of vipers! How can you escape being sentenced to hell?[a] [34]Therefore I send you prophets, sages, and scribes, some of whom you will kill and crucify, and some you will flog in your synagogues and pursue from town to town, [35]so that upon you may come all the righteous blood shed on earth, from the blood of righteous Abel to the blood of Zechariah son of Barachiah, whom you murdered between the sanctuary and the altar. [36]Truly I tell you, all this will come upon this generation.

37 "Jerusalem, Jerusalem, the city that kills the prophets and stones those who are sent to it! How often have I desired to gather your children together as a hen gathers her brood under her wings, and you were not willing! [38]See, your house is left to you, desolate.[b] [39]For I tell you, you will not see me again until you say, 'Blessed is the one who comes in the name of the Lord.'"

24 As Jesus came out of the temple and was going away, his disciples came to point out to him the buildings of the temple. [2]Then he asked them, "You see all these, do you not? Truly I tell you, not one stone will be left here upon another; all will be thrown down."

3 When he was sitting on the Mount of Olives, the disciples came to him privately, saying, "Tell us, when will this be, and what will be the sign of your coming and of the end of the age?" [4]Jesus answered them, "Beware that no one leads you astray. [5]For many will come in my name, saying, 'I am the Messiah!'[c] and they will lead many astray. [6]And you will hear of wars and rumors of wars; see that you are not alarmed; for this must take place, but the end is not yet. [7]For nation will rise against nation, and kingdom against kingdom, and there will be famines[d] and earthquakes in various places: [8]all this is but the beginning of the birth pangs.

9 "Then they will hand you over to be tortured and will put you to death, and you will be hated by all nations because of my name. [10]Then many will fall away,[e] and they will betray one another and hate one another. [11]And many false prophets will arise and lead many astray. [12]And because of the increase of lawlessness, the love of many will grow cold. [13]But the one who endures to the end will be saved. [14]And this good news[f] of the kingdom will be proclaimed throughout the world, as a testimony to all the nations; and then the end will come.

15 "So when you see the desolating sacrilege standing in the holy place, as was spoken of by

[a]Gk Gehenna [b]Other ancient authorities lack desolate [c]Or the Christ [d]Other ancient authorities add and pestilences [e]Or stumble [f]Or gospel

the prophet Daniel (let the reader understand), [16]then those in Judea must flee to the mountains; [17]the one on the housetop must not go down to take what is in the house; [18]the one in the field must not turn back to get a coat. [19]Woe to those who are pregnant and to those who are nursing infants in those days! [20]Pray that your flight may not be in winter or on a sabbath. [21]For at that time there will be great suffering, such as has not been from the beginning of the world until now, no, and never will be. [22]And if those days had not been cut short, no one would be saved; but for the sake of the elect those days will be cut short. [23]Then if anyone says to you, 'Look! Here is the Messiah!'[a] or 'There he is!'—do not believe it. [24]For false messiahs[b] and false prophets will appear and produce great signs and omens, to lead astray, if possible, even the elect. [25]Take note, I have told you beforehand. [26]So , if they say to you, 'Look! He is in the wilderness,' do not go out. If they say, 'Look! He is in the inner rooms,' do not believe it. [27]For as the lightning comes from the east and flashes as far as the west, so will be the coming of the Son of Man. [28]Wherever the corpse is, there the vultures will gather.

[29] "Immediately after the suffering of those days

> the sun will be darkened,
> and the moon will not
> give its light;
> the stars will fall from
> heaven,

and the powers of
heaven will be shaken.
[30]Then the sign of the Son of Man will appear in heaven, and then all the tribes of the earth will mourn, and they will see 'the Son of Man coming on the clouds of heaven' with power and great glory. [31]And he will send out his angels with a loud trumpet call, and they will gather his elect from the four winds, from one end of heaven to the other.

[32] "From the fig tree learn its lesson: as soon as its branch becomes tender and puts forth its leaves, you know that summer is near. [33]So also, when you see all these things, you know that he[c] is near, at the very gates. [34]Truly I tell you, this generation will not pass away until all these things have taken place. [35]Heaven and earth will pass away, but my words will not pass away.

[36] "But about that day and hour no one knows, neither the angels of heaven, nor the Son,[d] but only the Father. [37]For as the days of Noah were, so will be the coming of the Son of Man. [38]For as in those days before the flood they were eating and drinking, marrying and giving in marriage, until the day Noah entered the ark, [39]and they knew nothing until the flood came and swept them all away, so too will be the coming of the Son of Man. [40]Then two will be in the field; one will be taken and one will be

---

[a]Or *the Christ* [b]Or *christs* [c]Or *it* [d]Other ancient authorities lack *nor the Son*

left. [41]Two women will be grinding meal together; one will be taken and one will be left. [42]Keep awake therefore, for you do not know on what day[a] your Lord is coming. [43]But understand this: if the owner of the house had known in what part of the night the thief was coming, he would have stayed awake and would not have let his house be broken into. [44]Therefore you also must be ready, for the Son of Man is coming at an unexpected hour.

45 "Who then is the faithful and wise slave, whom his master has put in charge of his household, to give the other slaves[b] their allowance of food at the proper time? [46]Blessed is that slave whom his master will find at work when he arrives. [47]Truly I tell you, he will put that one in charge of all his possessions. [48]But if that wicked slave says to himself, 'My master is delayed,' [49]and he begins to beat his fellow slaves, and eats and drinks with drunkards, [50]the master of that slave will come on a day when he does not expect him and at an hour that he does not know. [51]He will cut him in pieces[c] and put him with the hypocrites, where there will be weeping and gnashing of teeth.

25 "Then the kingdom of heaven will be like this. Ten bridesmaids[d] took their lamps and went to meet the bridegroom.[e] [2]Five of them were foolish, and five were wise. [3]When the foolish took their lamps, they took no oil with them; [4]but the wise took flasks of oil with their lamps. [5]As the bridegroom was delayed, all of them became drowsy and slept. [6]But at midnight there was a shout, 'Look! Here is the bridegroom! Come out to meet him.' [7]Then all those bridesmaids[d] got up and trimmed their lamps. [8]The foolish said to the wise, 'Give us some of your oil, for our lamps are going out.' [9]But the wise replied, 'No! there will not be enough for you and for us; you had better go to the dealers and buy some for yourselves.' [10]And while they went to buy it, the bridegroom came, and those who were ready went with him into the wedding banquet; and the door was shut. [11]Later the other bridesmaids[d] came also, saying, 'Lord, lord, open to us.' [12]But he replied, 'Truly I tell you, I do not know you.' [13]Keep awake therefore, for you know neither the day nor the hour.[f]

14 "For it is as if a man, going on a journey, summoned his slaves and entrusted his property to them; [15]to one he gave five talents,[g] to another two, to another one, to each according to his ability. Then he went away. [16]The one who had received the five talents went off at once and traded with them, and made five more talents. [17]In the same way, the one who had the two talents made two more talents. [18]But the

---

[a]Other ancient authorities read *at what hour* [b]Gk *to give them* [c]Or *cut him off* [d]Gk *virgins* [e]Other ancient authorities add *and the bride* [f]Other ancient authorities add *in which the Son of Man is coming* [g]A talent was worth more than fifteen years' wages of a laborer

one who had received the one talent went off and dug a hole in the ground and hid his master's money. [19]After a long time the master of those slaves came and settled accounts with them. [20]Then the one who had received the five talents came forward, bringing five more talents, saying, 'Master, you handed over to me five talents; see, I have made five more talents.' [21]His master said to him, 'Well done, good and trustworthy slave; you have been trustworthy in a few things, I will put you in charge of many things; enter into the joy of your master.' [22]And the one with the two talents also came forward, saying, 'Master, you handed over to me two talents; see, I have made two more talents.' [23]His master said to him, 'Well done, good and trustworthy slave; you have been trustworthy in a few things, I will put you in charge of many things; enter into the joy of your master.' [24]Then the one who had received the one talent also came forward, saying, 'Master, I knew that you were a harsh man, reaping where you did not sow, and gathering where you did not scatter seed; [25]so I was afraid, and I went and hid your talent in the ground. Here you have what is yours.' [26]But his master replied, 'You wicked and lazy slave! You knew, did you, that I reap where *I did* not sow, and gather where I did not scatter? [27]Then you ought to have invested my money with the bankers, and on my return I would have received what was my own with interest. [28]So take the talent from him, and give it to the one with the ten talents. [29]For to all those who have, more will be given, and they will have an abundance; but from those who have nothing, even what they have will be taken away. [30]As for this worthless slave, throw him into the outer darkness, where there will be weeping and gnashing of teeth.'

31 "When the Son of Man comes in his glory, and all the angels with him, then he will sit on the throne of his glory. [32]All the nations will be gathered before him, and he will separate people one from another as a shepherd separates the sheep from the goats, [33]and he will put the sheep at his right hand and the goats at the left. [34]Then the king will say to those at his right hand, 'Come, you that are blessed by my Father, inherit the kingdom prepared for you from the foundation of the world; [35]for I was hungry and you gave me food, I was thirsty and you gave me something to drink, I was a stranger and you welcomed me, [36]I was naked and you gave me clothing, I was sick and you took care of me, I was in prison and you visited me.' [37]Then the righteous will answer him, 'Lord, when was it that we saw you hungry and gave you food, or thirsty and gave you something to drink? [38]And when was it that we saw you a stranger and welcomed you, or naked and gave you clothing? [39]And when was it

that we saw you sick or in prison and visited you?' [40]And the king will answer them, 'Truly I tell you, just as you did it to one of the least of these who are members of my family,[a] you did it to me.' [41]Then he will say to those at his left hand, 'You that are accursed, depart from me into the eternal fire prepared for the devil and his angels; [42]for I was hungry and you gave me no food, I was thirsty and you gave me nothing to drink, [43]I was a stranger and you did not welcome me, naked and you did not give me clothing, sick and in prison and you did not visit me.' [44]Then they also will answer, 'Lord, when was it that we saw you hungry or thirsty or a stranger or naked or sick or in prison, and did not take care of you?' [45]Then he will answer them, 'Truly I tell you, just as you did not do it to one of the least of these, you did not do it to me.' [46]And these will go away into eternal punishment, but the righteous into eternal life."

26 When Jesus had finished saying all these things, he said to his disciples, [2]"You know that after two days the Passover is coming, and the Son of Man will be handed over to be crucified."

3 Then the chief priests and the elders of the people gathered in the palace of the high priest, who was called Caiaphas, [4]and they conspired to arrest Jesus by stealth and kill him. [5]But they said, "Not during the festival, or there may be a riot among the people."

6 Now while Jesus was at Bethany in the house of Simon the leper,[b] [7]a woman came to him with an alabaster jar of very costly ointment, and she poured it on his head as he sat at the table. [8]But when the disciples saw it, they were angry and said, "Why this waste? [9]For this ointment could have been sold for a large sum, and the money given to the poor." [10]But Jesus, aware of this, said to them, "Why do you trouble the woman? She has performed a good service for me. [11]For you always have the poor with you, but you will not always have me. [12]By pouring this ointment on my body she has prepared me for burial. [13]Truly I tell you, wherever this good news[c] is proclaimed in the whole world, what she has done will be told in remembrance of her."

14 Then one of the twelve, who was called Judas Iscariot, went to the chief priests [15]and said, "What will you give me if I betray him to you?" They paid him thirty pieces of silver. [16]And from that moment he began to look for an opportunity to betray him.

17 On the first day of Unleavened Bread the disciples came to Jesus, saying, "Where do you want us to make the preparations for you to eat the Passover?" [18]He said, "Go into the city to a certain man, and say to him,

[a]Gk these my brothers [b]The terms leper and leprosy can refer to several diseases [c]Or gospel

'The Teacher says, My time is near; I will keep the Passover at your house with my disciples.'" [19]So the disciples did as Jesus had directed them, and they prepared the Passover meal.

20 When it was evening, he took his place with the twelve;[a] [21]and while they were eating, he said, "Truly I tell you, one of you will betray me." [22]And they became greatly distressed and began to say to him one after another, "Surely not I, Lord?" [23]He answered, "The one who has dipped his hand into the bowl with me will betray me. [24]The Son of Man goes as it is written of him, but woe to that one by whom the Son of Man is betrayed! It would have been better for that one not to have been born." [25]Judas, who betrayed him, said, "Surely not I, Rabbi?" He replied, "You have said so."

26 While they were eating, Jesus took a loaf of bread, and after blessing it he broke it, gave it to the disciples, and said, "Take, eat; this is my body." [27]Then he took a cup, and after giving thanks he gave it to them, saying, "Drink from it, all of you; [28]for this is my blood of the[b] covenant, which is poured out for many for the forgiveness of sins. [29]I tell you, I will never again drink of this fruit of the vine until that day when I drink it new with you in my Father's kingdom."

30 When they had sung the hymn, they went out to the Mount of Olives.

31 Then Jesus said to them, "You will all become deserters because of me this night; for it is written,

'I will strike the shepherd,
   and the sheep of the
      flock will be
      scattered.'

[32]But after I am raised up, I will go ahead of you to Galilee." [33]Peter said to him, "Though all become deserters because of you, I will never desert you." [34]Jesus said to him, "Truly I tell you, this very night, before the cock crows, you will deny me three times." [35]Peter said to him, "Even though I must die with you, I will not deny you." And so said all the disciples.

36 Then Jesus went with them to a place called Gethsemane; and he said to his disciples, "Sit here while I go over there and pray." [37]He took with him Peter and the two sons of Zebedee, and began to be grieved and agitated. [38]Then he said to them, "I am deeply grieved, even to death; remain here, and stay awake with me." [39]And going a little farther, he threw himself on the ground and prayed, "My Father, if it is possible, let this cup pass from me; yet not what I want but what you want." [40]Then he came to the disciples and found them sleeping; and he said to Peter, "So, could you not stay awake with me one hour? [41]Stay awake and pray that you may not come

---

[a]Other ancient authorities add *disciples* [b]Other ancient authorities add *new*

into the time of trial;[a] the spirit indeed is willing, but the flesh is weak." [42]Again he went away for the second time and prayed, "My Father, if this cannot pass unless I drink it, your will be done." [43]Again he came and found them sleeping, for their eyes were heavy. [44]So leaving them again, he went away and prayed for the third time, saying the same words. [45]Then he came to the disciples and said to them, "Are you still sleeping and taking your rest? See, the hour is at hand, and the Son of Man is betrayed into the hands of sinners. [46]Get up, let us be going. See, my betrayer is at hand."

[47]While he was still speaking, Judas, one of the twelve, arrived; with him was a large crowd with swords and clubs, from the chief priests and the elders of the people. [48]Now the betrayer had given them a sign, saying, "The one I will kiss is the man; arrest him." [49]At once he came up to Jesus and said, "Greetings, Rabbi!" and kissed him. [50]Jesus said to him, "Friend, do what you are here to do." Then they came and laid hands on Jesus and arrested him. [51]Suddenly, one of those with Jesus put his hand on his sword, drew it, and struck the slave of the high priest, cutting off his ear. [52]Then Jesus said to him, "Put your sword back into its place; for all who take the sword will perish by the sword. [53]Do you think that I cannot appeal to my Father, and he will at once send me more than twelve legions of angels? [54]But how then would the scriptures be

fulfilled, which say it must happen in this way?" [55]At that hour Jesus said to the crowds, "Have you come out with swords and clubs to arrest me as though I were a bandit? Day after day I sat in the temple teaching, and you did not arrest me. [56]But all this has taken place, so that the scriptures of the prophets may be fulfilled." Then all the disciples deserted him and fled.

57 Those who had arrested Jesus took him to Caiaphas the high priest, in whose house the scribes and the elders had gathered. [58]But Peter was following him at a distance, as far as the courtyard of the high priest; and going inside, he sat with the guards in order to see how this would end. [59]Now the chief priests and the whole council were looking for false testimony against Jesus so that they might put him to death, [60]but they found none, though many false witnesses came forward. At last two came forward [61]and said, "This fellow said, 'I am able to destroy the temple of God and to build it in three days.'" [62]The high priest stood up and said, "Have you no answer? What is it that they testify against you?" [63]But Jesus was silent. Then the high priest said to him, "I put you under oath before the living God, tell us if you are the Messiah,[b] the Son of God." [64]Jesus said to him, "You have said so. But I tell you,

[a]Or *into temptation* [b]Or *Christ*

From now on you will
 see the Son of Man
seated at the right hand
 of Power
and coming on the
 clouds of heaven."

[65]Then the high priest tore his clothes and said, "He has blasphemed! Why do we still need witnesses? You have now heard his blasphemy. [66]What is your verdict?" They answered, "He deserves death." [67]Then they spat in his face and struck him; and some slapped him, [68]saying, "Prophesy to us, you Messiah! Who is it that struck you?"

69 Now Peter was sitting outside in the courtyard. A servant-girl came to him and said, "You also were with Jesus the Galilean." [70]But he denied it before all of them, saying, "I do not know what you are talking about." [71]When he went out to the porch, another servant-girl saw him, and she said to the bystanders, "This man was with Jesus of Nazareth."[a] [72]Again he denied it with an oath, "I do not know the man." [73]After a little while the bystanders came up and said to Peter, "Certainly you are also one of them, for your accent betrays you." [74]Then he began to curse, and he swore an oath, "I do not know the man!" At that moment the cock crowed. [75]Then Peter remembered what Jesus had said: "Before the cock crows, you will deny me three times." And he went out and wept bitterly.

27 When morning came, all the chief priests and the elders of the people conferred together against Jesus in order to bring about his death. [2]They bound him, led him away, and handed him over to Pilate the governor.

3 When Judas, his betrayer, saw that Jesus[b] was condemned, he repented and brought back the thirty pieces of silver to the chief priests and the elders. [4]He said, "I have sinned by betraying innocent[c] blood." But they said, "What is that to us? See to it yourself." [5]Throwing down the pieces of silver in the temple, he departed; and he went and hanged himself. [6]But the chief priests, taking the pieces of silver, said, "It is not lawful to put them into the treasury, since they are blood money." [7]After conferring together, they used them to buy the potter's field as a place to bury foreigners. [8]For this reason that field has been called the Field of Blood to this day. [9]Then was fulfilled what had been spoken through the prophet Jeremiah,[d] "And they took[e] the thirty pieces of silver, the price of the one on whom a price had been set,[f] on whom some of the people of Israel had set a price, [10]and they gave[g] them for the potter's field, as the Lord commanded me."

11 Now Jesus stood before the governor; and the governor asked him, "Are you the King of the Jews?" Jesus said, "You say so."

a Gk *the Nazorean* *b* Gk *he* *c* Other ancient authorities read *righteous* *d* Other ancient authorities read *Zechariah* or *Isaiah* *e* Or *I took* *f* Or *the price of the precious One* *g* Other ancient authorities read *I gave*

[12]But when he was accused by the chief priests and elders, he did not answer. [13]Then Pilate said to him, "Do you not hear how many accusations they make against you?" [14]But he gave him no answer, not even to a single charge, so that the governor was greatly amazed.

15 Now at the festival the governor was accustomed to release a prisoner for the crowd, anyone whom they wanted. [16]At that time they had a notorious prisoner, called Jesus[a] Barabbas. [17]So after they had gathered, Pilate said to them, "Whom do you want me to release for you, Jesus[a] Barabbas or Jesus[a] who is called the Messiah?"[b] [18]For he realized that it was out of jealousy that they had handed him over. [19]While he was sitting on the judgment seat, his wife sent word to him, "Have nothing to do with that innocent man, for today I have suffered a great deal because of a dream about him." [20]Now the chief priests and the elders persuaded the crowds to ask for Barabbas and to have Jesus killed. [21]The governor again said to them, "Which of the two do you want me to release for you?" And they said, "Barabbas." [22]Pilate said to them, "Then what should I do with Jesus who is called the Messiah?"[b] All of them said, "Let him be crucified!" [23]Then he asked, "Why, what evil has he done?" But they shouted all the more, "Let him be crucified!"

24 So when Pilate saw that he could do nothing, but rather that a riot was beginning, he took some water and washed his hands before the crowd, saying, "I am innocent of this man's blood;[c] see to it yourselves." [25]Then the people as a whole answered, "His blood be on us and on our children!" [26]So he released Barabbas for them; and after flogging Jesus, he handed him over to be crucified.

27 Then the soldiers of the governor took Jesus into the governor's headquarters,[d] and they gathered the whole cohort around him. [28]They stripped him and put a scarlet robe on him, [29]and after twisting some thorns into a crown, they put it on his head. They put a reed in his right hand and knelt before him and mocked him, saying, "Hail, King of the Jews!" [30]They spat on him, and took the reed and struck him on the head. [31]After mocking him, they stripped him of the robe and put his own clothes on him. Then they led him away to crucify him. [32]As they went out, they came upon a man from Cyrene named Simon; they compelled this man to carry his cross. [33]And when they came to a place called Golgotha (which means Place of a Skull), [34]they offered him wine to drink, mixed with gall; but when he tasted it, he would not drink it. [35]And when they had crucified him, they divided his clothes among themselves by

[a]Other ancient authorities lack *Jesus* [b]Or *the Christ* [c]Other ancient authorities read *this righteous blood*, or *this righteous man's blood* [d]Gk *the praetorium*

casting lots;[a] 36then they sat down there and kept watch over him. 37Over his head they put the charge against him, which read, "This is Jesus, the King of the Jews."

38 Then two bandits were crucified with him, one on his right and one on his left. 39Those who passed by derided him,[b] shaking their heads 40and saying, "You who would destroy the temple and build it in three days, save yourself! If you are the Son of God, come down from the cross." 41In the same way the chief priests also, along with the scribes and elders, were mocking him, saying, 42"He saved others;[c] he cannot save himself.[c] He is the King of Israel; let him come down from the cross now, and we will believe in him. 43He trusts in God; let God deliver him now, if he wants to; for he said, 'I am God's Son.'" 44The bandits who were crucified with him also taunted him in the same way.

45 From noon on, darkness came over the whole land[d] until three in the afternoon. 46And about three o'clock Jesus cried with a loud voice, "Eli, Eli, lema sabachthani?" that is, "My God, my God, why have you forsaken me?" 47When some of the bystanders heard it, they said, "This man is calling for Elijah." 48At once one of them ran and got a sponge, filled it with sour wine, put it on a stick, and gave it to him to drink. 49But the others said, "Wait, let us see whether Elijah will come to save him."[e]

50Then Jesus cried again with a loud voice and breathed his last.[f] 51At that moment the curtain of the temple was torn in two, from top to bottom. The earth shook, and the rocks were split. 52The tombs also were opened, and many bodies of the saints who had fallen asleep were raised. 53After his resurrection they came out of the tombs and entered the holy city and appeared to many. 54Now when the centurion and those with him, who were keeping watch over Jesus, saw the earthquake and what took place, they were terrified and said, "Truly this man was God's Son!"[g]

55 Many women were also there, looking on from a distance; they had followed Jesus from Galilee and had provided for him. 56Among them were Mary Magdalene, and Mary the mother of James and Joseph, and the mother of the sons of Zebedee.

57 When it was evening, there came a rich man from Arimathea, named Joseph, who was also a disciple of Jesus. 58He went to Pilate and asked for the body of Jesus; then Pilate ordered it to be given to him. 59So Joseph took the body and wrapped it in a clean linen cloth 60and laid it in his own new tomb, which he had

---

[a]Other ancient authorities add *in order that what had been spoken through the prophet might be fulfilled, "They divided my clothes among themselves, and for my clothing they cast lots."* [b]Or *blasphemed* [c]Or *is he unable to save himself?* [d]Or *earth* [e]Other ancient authorities add *And another took a spear and pierced his side, and out came water and blood* [f]Or *gave up his spirit* [g]Or *a son of God*

hewn in the rock. He then rolled a great stone to the door of the tomb and went away. [61]Mary Magdalene and the other Mary were there, sitting opposite the tomb.

62 The next day, that is, after the day of Preparation, the chief priests and the Pharisees gathered before Pilate [63]and said, "Sir, we remember what that impostor said while he was still alive, 'After three days I will rise again.' [64]Therefore command the tomb to be made secure until the third day; otherwise his disciples may go and steal him away, and tell the people, 'He has been raised from the dead,' and the last deception would be worse than the first." [65]Pilate said to them, "You have a guard[a] of soldiers; go, make it as secure as you can."[b] [66]So they went with the guard and made the tomb secure by sealing the stone.

28 After the sabbath, as the first day of the week was dawning, Mary Magdalene and the other Mary went to see the tomb. [2]And suddenly there was a great earthquake; for an angel of the Lord, descending from heaven, came and rolled back the stone and *sat on it.* [3]*His* appearance was like lightning, and his clothing white as snow. [4]For fear of him the guards shook and became like dead men. [5]But the angel said to the women, "Do not be afraid; I know that you are looking for Jesus who was crucified. [6]He is not here; for he has been raised, as he said. Come, see the place where he[c] lay. [7]Then go quickly and tell his disciples, 'He has been raised from the dead,[d] and indeed he is going ahead of you to Galilee; there you will see him.' This is my message for you." [8]So they left the tomb quickly with fear and great joy, and ran to tell his disciples. [9]Suddenly Jesus met them and said, "Greetings!" And they came to him, took hold of his feet, and worshiped him. [10]Then Jesus said to them, "Do not be afraid; go and tell my brothers to go to Galilee; there they will see me."

11 While they were going, some of the guard went into the city and told the chief priests everything that had happened. [12]After the priests[e] had assembled with the elders, they devised a plan to give a large sum of money to the soldiers, [13]telling them, "You must say, 'His disciples came by night and stole him away while we were asleep.' [14]If this comes to the governor's ears, we will satisfy him and keep you out of trouble." [15]So they took the money and did as they were directed. And this story is still told among the Jews to this day.

16 Now the eleven disciples *went* to Galilee, to the mountain to which Jesus *had directed* them. [17]When they saw him, they worshiped him; but some doubted. [18]And Jesus came and said to them, "All authority in heaven

[a]Or Take a guard [b]Gk you know how [c]Other ancient authorities read the Lord [d]Other ancient authorities lack from the dead [e]Gk they

and on earth has been given to me. ¹⁹Go therefore and make disciples of all nations, baptizing them in the name of the Father and of the Son and of the Holy Spirit, ²⁰and teaching them to obey everything that I have commanded you. And remember, I am with you always, to the end of the age."ᵃ

ᵃOther ancient authorities add Amen

The Gospel According to

MARK

1 The beginning of the good newsᵃ of Jesus Christ, the Son of God.ᵇ

2 As it is written in the prophet Isaiah,ᶜ

"See, I am sending my
    messenger ahead of
    you,ᵈ
who will prepare your way;
3   the voice of one crying out
        in the wilderness:
'Prepare the way of the
    Lord,
make his paths straight,'"

⁴John the baptizer appearedᵉ in the wilderness, proclaiming a baptism of repentance for the forgiveness of sins. ⁵And people from the whole Judean countryside and all the people of Jerusalem were going out to him, and were baptized by him in the river Jordan, confessing their sins. ⁶Now John was clothed with camel's hair, with a leather belt around his waist, and he ate locusts and wild honey. ⁷He proclaimed, "The one who is more powerful than I is coming after me; I am not worthy to stoop down and untie the thong of his sandals. ⁸I have baptized you withᶠ water; but he will baptize you withᶠ the Holy Spirit."

9 In those days Jesus came from Nazareth of Galilee and was baptized by John in the Jordan. ¹⁰And just as he was coming up out of the water, he saw the heavens torn apart and the Spirit descending like a dove on him. ¹¹And a voice came from heaven, "You are my Son, the Beloved;ᵍ with you I am well pleased."

12 And the Spirit immediately drove him out into the wilderness. ¹³He was in the wilderness forty days, tempted by Satan; and he was with the wild beasts; and the angels waited on him.

14 Now after John was arrested, Jesus came to Galilee, proclaiming the good newsᵃ of God,ʰ

ᵃOr gospel ᵇOther ancient authorities lack the Son of God ᶜOther ancient authorities read in the prophets ᵈGk before your face ᵉOther ancient authorities read John was baptizing ᶠOr in ᵍOr my beloved Son ʰOther ancient authorities read of the kingdom

[15]and saying, "The time is fulfilled, and the kingdom of God has come near;[a] repent, and believe in the good news."

16 As Jesus passed along the Sea of Galilee, he saw Simon and his brother Andrew casting a net into the sea—for they were fishermen. [17]And Jesus said to them, "Follow me and I will make you fish for people." [18]And immediately they left their nets and followed him. [19]As he went a little farther, he saw James son of Zebedee and his brother John, who were in their boat mending the nets. [20]Immediately he called them; and they left their father Zebedee in the boat with the hired men, and followed him.

21 They went to Capernaum; and when the sabbath came, he entered the synagogue and taught. [22]They were astounded at his teaching, for he taught them as one having authority, and not as the scribes. [23]Just then there was in their synagogue a man with an unclean spirit, [24]and he cried out, "What have you to do with us, Jesus of Nazareth? Have you come to destroy us? I know who you are, the Holy One of God." [25]But Jesus rebuked him, saying, "Be silent, and come out of him!" [26]And the unclean spirit, convulsing him and crying with a loud voice, came out of him. [27]They were all amazed, and they kept on asking one another, "What is this? A new teaching—with authority! He[b] commands even the unclean spirits, and they obey him." [28]At once his fame began to spread throughout the surrounding region of Galilee.

29 As soon as they[c] left the synagogue, they entered the house of Simon and Andrew, with James and John. [30]Now Simon's mother-in-law was in bed with a fever, and they told him about her at once. [31]He came and took her by the hand and lifted her up. Then the fever left her, and she began to serve them.

32 That evening, at sundown, they brought to him all who were sick or possessed with demons. [33]And the whole city was gathered around the door. [34]And he cured many who were sick with various diseases, and cast out many demons; and he would not permit the demons to speak, because they knew him.

35 In the morning, while it was still very dark, he got up and went out to a deserted place, and there he prayed. [36]And Simon and his companions hunted for him. [37]When they found him, they said to him, "Everyone is searching for you." [38]He answered, "Let us go on to the neighboring towns, so that I may proclaim the message there also; for that is what I came out to do." [39]And he went throughout Galilee, proclaiming the message in their synagogues and casting out demons.

40 A leper[d] came to him beg-

[a]Or is at hand [b]Or A new teaching! With authority he [c]Other ancient authorities read he [d]The terms leper and leprosy can refer to several diseases

ging him, and kneeling[a] he said to him, "If you choose, you can make me clean." [41]Moved with pity,[b] Jesus[c] stretched out his hand and touched him, and said to him, "I do choose. Be made clean!" [42]Immediately the leprosy left him, and he was made clean. [43]After sternly warning him he sent him away at once, [44]saying to him, "See that you say nothing to anyone; but go, show yourself to the priest, and offer for your cleansing what Moses commanded, as a testimony to them." [45]But he went out and began to proclaim it freely, and to spread the word, so that Jesus[c] could no longer go into a town openly, but stayed out in the country; and people came to him from every quarter.

2 When he returned to Capernaum after some days, it was reported that he was at home. [2]So many gathered around that there was no longer room for them, not even in front of the door; and he was speaking the word to them. [3]Then some people[d] came, bringing to him a paralyzed man, carried by four of them. [4]And when they could not bring him to Jesus because of the crowd, they removed the roof above him; and after having dug through it, they let down the mat on which the paralytic lay. [5]When Jesus saw their faith, he said to the paralytic, "Son, your sins are forgiven." [6]Now some of the scribes were sitting there, questioning in their hearts, [7]"Why does this fellow speak in

this way? It is blasphemy! Who can forgive sins but God alone?" [8]At once Jesus perceived in his spirit that they were discussing these questions among themselves; and he said to them, "Why do you raise such questions in your hearts? [9]Which is easier, to say to the paralytic, 'Your sins are forgiven,' or to say, 'Stand up and take your mat and walk'? [10]But so that you may know that the Son of Man has authority on earth to forgive sins"—he said to the paralytic—[11]"I say to you, stand up, take your mat and go to your home." [12]And he stood up, and immediately took the mat and went out before all of them; so that they were all amazed and glorified God, saying, "We have never seen anything like this!"

[13] Jesus[e] went out again beside the sea; the whole crowd gathered around him, and he taught them. [14]As he was walking along, he saw Levi son of Alphaeus sitting at the tax booth, and he said to him, "Follow me." And he got up and followed him.

[15] And as he sat at dinner[f] in Levi's[g] house, many tax collectors and sinners were also sitting[h] with Jesus and his disciples—for there were many who followed him. [16]When the scribes of[i] the Pharisees saw that he was eating with sinners and tax collectors,

[a]Other ancient authorities lack *kneeling* [b]Other ancient authorities read *anger* [c]Gk *he* [d]Gk *they* [e]Gk *He* [f]Gk *reclined* [g]Gk *his* [h]Gk *reclining* [i]Other ancient authorities read *and*

they said to his disciples, "Why does he eat[a] with tax collectors and sinners?" [17]When Jesus heard this, he said to them, "Those who are well have no need of a physician, but those who are sick; I have come to call not the righteous but sinners."

18 Now John's disciples and the Pharisees were fasting; and people[b] came and said to him, "Why do John's disciples and the disciples of the Pharisees fast, but your disciples do not fast?" [19]Jesus said to them, "The wedding guests cannot fast while the bridegroom is with them, can they? As long as they have the bridegroom with them, they cannot fast. [20]The days will come when the bridegroom is taken away from them, and then they will fast on that day.

21 "No one sews a piece of unshrunk cloth on an old cloak; otherwise, the patch pulls away from it, the new from the old, and a worse tear is made. [22]And no one puts new wine into old wineskins; otherwise, the wine will burst the skins, and the wine is lost, and so are the skins; but one puts new wine into fresh wineskins."[c]

23 One sabbath he was going through the grainfields; and as they made their way his disciples began to pluck heads of grain. [24]The Pharisees said to him, "Look, why are they doing what is not lawful on the sabbath?" [25]And he said to them, "Have you never read what David did when he and his com-panions were hungry and in need of food? [26]He entered the house of God, when Abiathar was high priest, and ate the bread of the Presence, which it is not lawful for any but the priests to eat, and he gave some to his com-panions." [27]Then he said to them, "The sabbath was made for humankind, and not humankind for the sabbath; [28]so the Son of Man is lord even of the sabbath."

3 Again he entered the syna-gogue, and a man was there who had a withered hand. [2]They watched him to see whether he would cure him on the sabbath, so that they might accuse him. [3]And he said to the man who had the withered hand, "Come forward." [4]Then he said to them, "Is it lawful to do good or to do harm on the sabbath, to save life or to kill?" But they were silent. [5]He looked around at them with anger; he was grieved at their hardness of heart and said to the man, "Stretch out your hand." He stretched it out, and his hand was restored. [6]The Pharisees went out and immediately con-spired with the Herodians against him, how to destroy him.

7 Jesus departed with his dis-ciples to the sea, and a great mul-titude from Galilee followed him; [8]hearing all that he was doing, they came to him in great numbers from Judea, Jerusalem, Idumea, beyond the Jordan, and

[a]Other ancient authorities add *and drink.* [b]Gk *they* [c]Other ancient authorities lack *but one puts new wine into fresh wineskins*

the region around Tyre and Sidon. [9]He told his disciples to have a boat ready for him because of the crowd, so that they would not crush him; [10]for he had cured many, so that all who had diseases pressed upon him to touch him. [11]Whenever the unclean spirits saw him, they fell down before him and shouted, "You are the Son of God!" [12]But he sternly ordered them not to make him known.

13 He went up the mountain and called to him those whom he wanted, and they came to him. [14]And he appointed twelve, whom he also named apostles,[a] to be with him, and to be sent out to proclaim the message, [15]and to have authority to cast out demons. [16]So he appointed the twelve:[b] Simon (to whom he gave the name Peter); [17]James son of Zebedee and John the brother of James (to whom he gave the name Boanerges, that is, Sons of Thunder); [18]and Andrew, and Philip, and Bartholomew, and Matthew, and Thomas, and James son of Alphaeus, and Thaddaeus, and Simon the Cananaean, [19]and Judas Iscariot, who betrayed him.

Then he went home; [20]and the crowd came together again, so that they could not even eat. [21]When his family heard it, they went out to restrain him, for people were saying, "He has gone out of his mind." [22]And the scribes who came down from Jerusalem said, "He has Beelzebul, and by the ruler of the demons he casts out demons." [23]And he called them to him, and spoke to them in parables, "How can Satan cast out Satan? [24]If a kingdom is divided against itself, that kingdom cannot stand. [25]And if a house is divided against itself, that house will not be able to stand. [26]And if Satan has risen up against himself and is divided, he cannot stand, but his end has come. [27]But no one can enter a strong man's house and plunder his property without first tying up the strong man; then indeed the house can be plundered.

28 "Truly I tell you, people will be forgiven for their sins and whatever blasphemies they utter; [29]but whoever blasphemes against the Holy Spirit can never have forgiveness, but is guilty of an eternal sin"— [30]for they had said, "He has an unclean spirit."

31 Then his mother and his brothers came; and standing outside, they sent to him and called him. [32]A crowd was sitting around him; and they said to him, "Your mother and your brothers and sisters[c] are outside, asking for you." [33]And he replied, "Who are my mother and my brothers?" [34]And looking at those who sat around him, he said, "Here are my mother and my brothers! [35]Whoever does the will of God is my brother and sister and mother."

[a]Other ancient authorities lack *whom he also named apostles* [b]Other ancient authorities lack *So he appointed the twelve* [c]Other ancient authorities lack *and sisters*

4 Again he began to teach beside the sea. Such a very large crowd gathered around him that he got into a boat on the sea and sat there, while the whole crowd was beside the sea on the land. ²He began to teach them many things in parables, and in his teaching he said to them: ³"Listen! A sower went out to sow. ⁴And as he sowed, some seed fell on the path, and the birds came and ate it up. ⁵Other seed fell on rocky ground, where it did not have much soil, and it sprang up quickly, since it had no depth of soil. ⁶And when the sun rose, it was scorched; and since it had no root, it withered away. ⁷Other seed fell among thorns, and the thorns grew up and choked it, and it yielded no grain. ⁸Other seed fell into good soil and brought forth grain, growing up and increasing and yielding thirty and sixty and a hundredfold." ⁹And he said, "Let anyone with ears to hear listen!"

10 When he was alone, those who were around him along with the twelve asked him about the parables. ¹¹And he said to them, "To you has been given the secret[a] of the kingdom of God, but for those outside, everything comes in parables; ¹²in order that

'they may indeed look, but
  not perceive,
and may indeed listen,
  but not understand;
so that they may not turn
  again and be forgiven.'"

13 And he said to them, "Do you not understand this parable? Then how will you understand all the parables? ¹⁴The sower sows the word. ¹⁵These are the ones on the path where the word is sown: when they hear, Satan immediately comes and takes away the word that is sown in them. ¹⁶And these are the ones sown on rocky ground: when they hear the word, they immediately receive it with joy. ¹⁷But they have no root, and endure only for a while; then, when trouble or persecution arises on account of the word, immediately they fall away.[b] ¹⁸And others are those sown among the thorns: these are the ones who hear the word, ¹⁹but the cares of the world, and the lure of wealth, and the desire for other things come in and choke the word, and it yields nothing. ²⁰And these are the ones sown on the good soil: they hear the word and accept it and bear fruit, thirty and sixty and a hundredfold."

21 He said to them, "Is a lamp brought in to be put under the bushel basket, or under the bed, and not on the lampstand? ²²For there is nothing hidden, except to be disclosed; nor is anything secret, except to come to light. ²³Let anyone with ears to hear listen!" ²⁴And he said to them, "Pay attention to what you hear; the measure you give will be the measure you get, and still more will be given you. ²⁵For to those who have, more will be given; and from those who have nothing,

---

ᵃOr mystery ᵇOr stumble

even what they have will be taken away."

26 He also said, "The kingdom of God is as if someone would scatter seed on the ground, ²⁷and would sleep and rise night and day, and the seed would sprout and grow, he does not know how. ²⁸The earth produces of itself, first the stalk, then the head, then the full grain in the head. ²⁹But when the grain is ripe, at once he goes in with his sickle, because the harvest has come."

30 He also said, "With what can we compare the kingdom of God, or what parable will we use for it? ³¹It is like a mustard seed, which, when sown upon the ground, is the smallest of all the seeds on earth; ³²yet when it is sown it grows up and becomes the greatest of all shrubs, and puts forth large branches, so that the birds of the air can make nests in its shade."

33 With many such parables he spoke the word to them, as they were able to hear it; ³⁴he did not speak to them except in parables, but he explained everything in private to his disciples.

35 On that day, when evening had come, he said to them, "Let us go across to the other side." ³⁶And leaving the crowd behind, they took him with them in the boat, just as he was. Other boats were with him. ³⁷A great windstorm arose, and the waves beat into the boat, so that the boat was already being swamped. ³⁸But he was in the stern, asleep on the cushion; and they woke him up and said to him, "Teacher, do you not care that we are perishing?" ³⁹He woke up and rebuked the wind, and said to the sea, "Peace! Be still!" Then the wind ceased, and there was a dead calm. ⁴⁰He said to them, "Why are you afraid? Have you still no faith?" ⁴¹And they were filled with great awe and said to one another, "Who then is this, that even the wind and the sea obey him?"

5 They came to the other side of the sea, to the country of the Gerasenes.[a] ²And when he had stepped out of the boat, immediately a man out of the tombs with an unclean spirit met him. ³He lived among the tombs; and no one could restrain him any more, even with a chain; ⁴for he had often been restrained with shackles and chains, but the chains he wrenched apart, and the shackles he broke in pieces; and no one had the strength to subdue him. ⁵Night and day among the tombs and on the mountains he was always howling and bruising himself with stones. ⁶When he saw Jesus from a distance, he ran and bowed down before him; ⁷and he shouted at the top of his voice, "What have you to do with me, Jesus, Son of the Most High God? I adjure you by God, do not torment me." ⁸For he had said to him, "Come out of the man, you unclean spirit!" ⁹Then Jesus[b] asked him, "What is your name?"

[a]Other ancient authorities read *Gergesenes*; others, *Gadarenes* [b]Gk *he*

He replied, "My name is Legion; for we are many." [10]He begged him earnestly not to send them out of the country. [11]Now there on the hillside a great herd of swine was feeding; [12]and the unclean spirits[a] begged him, "Send us into the swine; let us enter them." [13]So he gave them permission. And the unclean spirits came out and entered the swine; and the herd, numbering about two thousand, rushed down the steep bank into the sea, and were drowned in the sea.

14 The swineherds ran off and told it in the city and in the country. Then people came to see what it was that had happened. [15]They came to Jesus and saw the demoniac sitting there, clothed and in his right mind, the very man who had had the legion; and they were afraid. [16]Those who had seen what had happened to the demoniac and to the swine reported it. [17]Then they began to beg Jesus[b] to leave their neighborhood. [18]As he was getting into the boat, the man who had been possessed by demons begged him that he might be with him. [19]But Jesus[b] refused, and said to him, "Go home to your friends, and tell them how much the Lord has done for you, and what mercy he has shown you." [20]And he went away and began to proclaim in the Decapolis how much Jesus had done for him; and everyone was amazed.

21 When Jesus had crossed again in the boat[c] to the other side, a great crowd gathered around him; and he was by the sea. [22]Then one of the leaders of the synagogue named Jairus came and, when he saw him, fell at his feet [23]and begged him repeatedly, "My little daughter is at the point of death. Come and lay your hands on her, so that she may be made well, and live." [24]So he went with him.

And a large crowd followed him and pressed in on him. [25]Now there was a woman who had been suffering from hemorrhages for twelve years. [26]She had endured much under many physicians, and had spent all that she had; and she was no better, but rather grew worse. [27]She had heard about Jesus, and came up behind him in the crowd and touched his cloak, [28]for she said, "If I but touch his clothes, I will be made well." [29]Immediately her hemorrhage stopped; and she felt in her body that she was healed of her disease. [30]Immediately aware that power had gone forth from him, Jesus turned about in the crowd and said, "Who touched my clothes?" [31]And his disciples said to him, "You see the crowd pressing in on you; how can you say, 'Who touched me?'" [32]He looked all around to see who had done it. [33]But the woman, knowing what had happened to her, came in fear and trembling, fell down before him, and told him the whole truth. [34]He said to her, "Daughter,

[a]Gk *they* [b]Gk *him* [c]Other ancient authorities lack *in the boat*

your faith has made you well; go in peace, and be healed of your disease."

35 While he was still speaking, some people came from the leader's house to say, "Your daughter is dead. Why trouble the teacher any further?" [36]But overhearing[a] what they said, Jesus said to the leader of the synagogue, "Do not fear, only believe." [37]He allowed no one to follow him except Peter, James, and John, the brother of James. [38]When they came to the house of the leader of the synagogue, he saw a commotion, people weeping and wailing loudly. [39]When he had entered, he said to them, "Why do you make a commotion and weep? The child is not dead but sleeping." [40]And they laughed at him. Then he put them all outside, and took the child's father and mother and those who were with him, and went in where the child was. [41]He took her by the hand and said to her, "Talitha cum," which means, "Little girl, get up!" [42]And immediately the girl got up and began to walk about (she was twelve years of age). At this they were overcome with amazement. [43]He strictly ordered them that no one should know this, and told them to give her something to eat.

6 He left that place and came to his hometown, and his disciples followed him. [2]On the sabbath he began to teach in the synagogue, and many who heard him were astounded. They said, "Where did this man get all this? What is this wisdom that has been given to him? What deeds of power are being done by his hands! [3]Is not this the carpenter, the son of Mary[b] and brother of James and Joses and Judas and Simon, and are not his sisters here with us?" And they took offense[c] at him. [4]Then Jesus said to them, "Prophets are not without honor, except in their hometown, and among their own kin, and in their own house." [5]And he could do no deed of power there, except that he laid his hands on a few sick people and cured them. [6]And he was amazed at their unbelief.

Then he went about among the villages teaching. [7]He called the twelve and began to send them out two by two, and gave them authority over the unclean spirits. [8]He ordered them to take nothing for their journey except a staff; no bread, no bag, no money in their belts; [9]but to wear sandals and not to put on two tunics. [10]He said to them, "Wherever you enter a house, stay there until you leave the place. [11]If any place will not welcome you and they refuse to hear you, as you leave, shake off the dust that is on your feet as a testimony against them." [12]So they went out and proclaimed that all should repent. [13]They cast out many demons, and anointed with oil many who were sick and cured them.

[a]Or *ignoring;* other ancient authorities read *hearing*
[b]Other ancient authorities read *son of the carpenter and of Mary* [c]Or *stumbled*

14 King Herod heard of it, for Jesus'[a] name had become known. Some were[b] saying, "John the baptizer has been raised from the dead; and for this reason these powers are at work in him." [15]But others said, "It is Elijah." And others said, "It is a prophet, like one of the prophets of old." [16]But when Herod heard of it, he said, "John, whom I beheaded, has been raised."

17 For Herod himself had sent men who arrested John, bound him, and put him in prison on account of Herodias, his brother Philip's wife, because Herod[c] had married her. [18]For John had been telling Herod, "It is not lawful for you to have your brother's wife." [19]And Herodias had a grudge against him, and wanted to kill him. But she could not, [20]for Herod feared John, knowing that he was a righteous and holy man, and he protected him. When he heard him, he was greatly perplexed;[d] and yet he liked to listen to him. [21]But an opportunity came when Herod on his birthday gave a banquet for his courtiers and officers and for the leaders of Galilee. [22]When his daughter Herodias[e] came in and danced, she pleased Herod and his guests; and the king said to the girl, "Ask me for whatever you wish, and I will give it." [23]And he solemnly swore to her, "Whatever you ask me, I will give you, even half of my kingdom." [24]She went out and said to her mother, "What should I ask for?" She replied, "The head of John the baptizer." [25]Immediately she rushed back to the king and requested, "I want you to give me at once the head of John the Baptist on a platter." [26]The king was deeply grieved; yet out of regard for his oaths and for the guests, he did not want to refuse her. [27]Immediately the king sent a soldier of the guard with orders to bring John's[a] head. He went and beheaded him in the prison, [28]brought his head on a platter, and gave it to the girl. Then the girl gave it to her mother. [29]When his disciples heard about it, they came and took his body, and laid it in a tomb.

30 The apostles gathered around Jesus, and told him all that they had done and taught. [31]He said to them, "Come away to a deserted place all by yourselves and rest a while." For many were coming and going, and they had no leisure even to eat. [32]And they went away in the boat to a deserted place by themselves. [33]Now many saw them going and recognized them, and they hurried there on foot from all the towns and arrived ahead of them. [34]As he went ashore, he saw a great crowd; and he had compassion for them, because they were like sheep without a shepherd; and he began to teach them many things. [35]When it grew late, his disciples came to him and said,

[a]Gk *his* [b]Other ancient authorities read *He was* [c]Gk *he*
[d]Other ancient authorities read *he did many things*
[e]Other ancient authorities read *the daughter of Herodias herself*

"This is a deserted place, and the hour is now very late; ³⁶send them away so that they may go into the surrounding country and villages and buy something for themselves to eat." ³⁷But he answered them, "You give them something to eat." They said to him, "Are we to go and buy two hundred denarii*a* worth of bread, and give it to them to eat?" ³⁸And he said to them, "How many loaves have you? Go and see." When they had found out, they said, "Five, and two fish." ³⁹Then he ordered them to get all the people to sit down in groups on the green grass. ⁴⁰So they sat down in groups of hundreds and of fifties. ⁴¹Taking the five loaves and the two fish, he looked up to heaven, and blessed and broke the loaves, and gave them to his disciples to set before the people; and he divided the two fish among them all. ⁴²And all ate and were filled; ⁴³and they took up twelve baskets full of broken pieces and of the fish. ⁴⁴Those who had eaten the loaves numbered five thousand men.

45 Immediately he made his disciples get into the boat and go on ahead to the other side, to Bethsaida, while he dismissed the crowd. ⁴⁶After saying farewell to them, he went up on the mountain to pray.

47 When evening came, the boat was out on the sea, and he was alone on the land. ⁴⁸When he saw that they were straining at the oars against an adverse wind, he came towards them early in the morning, walking on the sea.

He intended to pass them by. ⁴⁹But when they saw him walking on the sea, they thought it was a ghost and cried out; ⁵⁰for they all saw him and were terrified. But immediately he spoke to them and said, "Take heart, it is I; do not be afraid." ⁵¹Then he got into the boat with them and the wind ceased. And they were utterly astounded, ⁵²for they did not understand about the loaves, but their hearts were hardened.

53 When they had crossed over, they came to land at Gennesaret and moored the boat. ⁵⁴When they got out of the boat, people at once recognized him, ⁵⁵and rushed about that whole region and began to bring the sick on mats to wherever they heard he was. ⁵⁶And wherever he went, into villages or cities or farms, they laid the sick in the marketplaces, and begged him that they might touch even the fringe of his cloak; and all who touched it were healed.

7 Now when the Pharisees and some of the scribes who had come from Jerusalem gathered around him, ²they noticed that some of his disciples were eating with defiled hands, that is, without washing them. ³(For the Pharisees, and all the Jews, do not eat unless they thoroughly wash their hands,*b* thus observing the tradition of the elders; ⁴and they do not eat anything from the market unless they wash

*a*The denarius was the usual day's wage for a laborer
*b*Meaning of Gk uncertain

it;[a] and there are also many other traditions that they observe, the washing of cups, pots, and bronze kettles.[b]) [5]So the Pharisees and the scribes asked him, "Why do your disciples not live[c] according to the tradition of the elders, but eat with defiled hands?" [6]He said to them, "Isaiah prophesied rightly about you hypocrites, as it is written,

'This people honors me
        with their lips,
    but their hearts are far
        from me;
[7]   in vain do they worship
        me,
    teaching human precepts
        as doctrines.'

[8]You abandon the commandment of God and hold to human tradition."

[9] Then he said to them, "You have a fine way of rejecting the commandment of God in order to keep your tradition! [10]For Moses said, 'Honor your father and your mother'; and, 'Whoever speaks evil of father or mother must surely die.' [11]But you say that if anyone tells father or mother, 'Whatever support you might have had from me is Corban' (that is, an offering to God[d])— [12]then you no longer permit doing anything for a father or a mother, [13]thus making void the word of God through your tradition that you have handed on. And you do many things like this."

[14] Then he called the crowd again and said to them, "Listen to me, all of you, and understand: [15]there is nothing outside a person that by going in can defile, but the things that come out are what defile."[e]

[17] When he had left the crowd and entered the house, his disciples asked him about the parable. [18]He said to them, "Then do you also fail to understand? Do you not see that whatever goes into a person from outside cannot defile, [19]since it enters, not the heart but the stomach, and goes out into the sewer?" (Thus he declared all foods clean.) [20]And he said, "It is what comes out of a person that defiles. [21]For it is from within, from the human heart, that evil intentions come: fornication, theft, murder, [22]adultery, avarice, wickedness, deceit, licentiousness, envy, slander, pride, folly. [23]All these evil things come from within, and they defile a person."

[24] From there he set out and went away to the region of Tyre.[f] He entered a house and did not want anyone to know he was there. Yet he could not escape notice, [25]but a woman whose little daughter had an unclean spirit immediately heard about him, and she came and bowed down at his feet. [26]Now the woman was a Gentile, of Syrophoenician origin. She begged him to cast the demon out of her daughter. [27]He

[a]Other ancient authorities read *and when they come from the marketplace, they do not eat unless they purify themselves* [b]Other ancient authorities add *and beds* [c]Gk *walk* [d]Gk lacks *to God* [e]Other ancient authorities add verse 16, *"Let anyone with ears to hear listen"* [f]Other ancient authorities add *and Sidon*

said to her, "Let the children be fed first, for it is not fair to take the children's food and throw it to the dogs." [28]But she answered him, "Sir,[a] even the dogs under the table eat the children's crumbs." [29]Then he said to her, "For saying that, you may go— the demon has left your daughter." [30]So she went home, found the child lying on the bed, and the demon gone.

31 Then he returned from the region of Tyre, and went by way of Sidon towards the Sea of Galilee, in the region of the Decapolis. [32]They brought to him a deaf man who had an impediment in his speech; and they begged him to lay his hand on him. [33]He took him aside in private, away from the crowd, and put his fingers into his ears, and he spat and touched his tongue. [34]Then looking up to heaven, he sighed and said to him, "Ephphatha," that is, "Be opened." [35]And immediately his ears were opened, his tongue was released, and he spoke plainly. [36]Then Jesus[b] ordered them to tell no one; but the more he ordered them, the more zealously they proclaimed it. [37]They were astounded beyond measure, saying, "He has done everything well; he even makes the deaf to hear and the mute to speak."

8 In those days when there was again a great crowd without anything to eat, he called his disciples and said to them, [2]"I have compassion for the crowd, because they have been with me now for three days and have nothing to eat. [3]If I send them away hungry to their homes, they will faint on the way—and some of them have come from a great distance." [4]His disciples replied, "How can one feed these people with bread here in the desert?" [5]He asked them, "How many loaves do you have?" They said, "Seven." [6]Then he ordered the crowd to sit down on the ground; and he took the seven loaves, and after giving thanks he broke them and gave them to his disciples to distribute; and they distributed them to the crowd. [7]They had also a few small fish; and after blessing them, he ordered that these too should be distributed. [8]They ate and were filled; and they took up the broken pieces left over, seven baskets full. [9]Now there were about four thousand people. And he sent them away. [10]And immediately he got into the boat with his disciples and went to the district of Dalmanutha.[c]

11 The Pharisees came and began to argue with him, asking him for a sign from heaven, to test him. [12]And he sighed deeply in his spirit and said, "Why does this generation ask for a sign? Truly I tell you, no sign will be given to this generation." [13]And he left them, and getting into the boat again, he went across to the other side.

14 Now the disciples[d] had for-

[a]Or *Lord;* other ancient authorities prefix *Yes* [b]Gk *he* [c]Other ancient authorities read *Mageda* or *Magdala* [d]Gk *they*

gotten to bring any bread; and they had only one loaf with them in the boat. [15]And he cautioned them, saying, "Watch out—beware of the yeast of the Pharisees and the yeast of Herod."[a] [16]They said to one another, "It is because we have no bread." [17]And becoming aware of it, Jesus said to them, "Why are you talking about having no bread? Do you still not perceive or understand? Are your hearts hardened? [18]Do you have eyes, and fail to see? Do you have ears, and fail to hear? And do you not remember? [19]When I broke the five loaves for the five thousand, how many baskets full of broken pieces did you collect?" They said to him, "Twelve." [20]"And the seven for the four thousand, how many baskets full of broken pieces did you collect?" And they said to him, "Seven." [21]Then he said to them, "Do you not yet understand?"

22 They came to Bethsaida. Some people[b] brought a blind man to him and begged him to touch him. [23]He took the blind man by the hand and led him out of the village; and when he had put saliva on his eyes and laid his hands on him, he asked him, "Can you see anything?" [24]And the man[c] looked up and said, "I can see people, but they look like trees, walking." [25]Then Jesus[c] laid his hands on his eyes again; and he looked intently and his sight was restored, and he saw everything clearly. [26]Then he sent him away to his home, saying, "Do not even go into the village."[d]

27 Jesus went on with his disciples to the villages of Caesarea Philippi; and on the way he asked his disciples, "Who do people say that I am?" [28]And they answered him, "John the Baptist; and others, Elijah; and still others, one of the prophets." [29]He asked them, "But who do you say that I am?" Peter answered him, "You are the Messiah."[e] [30]And he sternly ordered them not to tell anyone about him.

31 Then he began to teach them that the Son of Man must undergo great suffering, and be rejected by the elders, the chief priests, and the scribes, and be killed, and after three days rise again. [32]He said all this quite openly. And Peter took him aside and began to rebuke him. [33]But turning and looking at his disciples, he rebuked Peter and said, "Get behind me, Satan! For you are setting your mind not on divine things but on human things."

34 He called the crowd with his disciples, and said to them, "If any want to become my followers, let them deny themselves and take up their cross and follow me. [35]For those who want to save their life will lose it, and those who lose their life for my

---

[a]Other ancient authorities read *the Herodians* [b]Gk *They* [c]Gk *he* [d]Other ancient authorities add *or tell anyone in the village* [e]Or *the Christ*

sake, and for the sake of the gospel,[a] will save it. [36]For what will it profit them to gain the whole world and forfeit their life? [37]Indeed, what can they give in return for their life? [38]Those who are ashamed of me and of my words[b] in this adulterous and sinful generation, of them the Son of Man will also be ashamed when he comes in the glory of his Father with the holy angels."

9 And he said to them, "Truly I tell you, there are some standing here who will not taste death until they see that the kingdom of God has come with[c] power."

2 Six days later, Jesus took with him Peter and James and John, and led them up a high mountain apart, by themselves. And he was transfigured before them, [3]and his clothes became dazzling white, such as no one[d] on earth could bleach them. [4]And there appeared to them Elijah with Moses, who were talking with Jesus. [5]Then Peter said to Jesus, "Rabbi, it is good for us to be here; let us make three dwellings,[e] one for you, one for Moses, and one for Elijah." [6]He did not know what to say, for they were terrified. [7]Then a cloud overshadowed them, and from the cloud there came a voice, "This is my Son, the Beloved;[f] listen to him!" [8]Suddenly when they looked around, they saw no one with them any more, but only Jesus.

9 As they were coming down the mountain, he ordered them to tell no one about what they had seen, until after the Son of Man had risen from the dead. [10]So they kept the matter to themselves, questioning what this rising from the dead could mean. [11]Then they asked him, "Why do the scribes say that Elijah must come first?" [12]He said to them, "Elijah is indeed coming first to restore all things. How then is it written about the Son of Man, that he is to go through many sufferings and be treated with contempt? [13]But I tell you that Elijah has come, and they did to him whatever they pleased, as it is written about him."

14 When they came to the disciples, they saw a great crowd around them, and some scribes arguing with them. [15]When the whole crowd saw him, they were immediately overcome with awe, and they ran forward to greet him. [16]He asked them, "What are you arguing about with them?" [17]Someone from the crowd answered him, "Teacher, I brought you my son; he has a spirit that makes him unable to speak; [18]and whenever it seizes him, it dashes him down; and he foams and grinds his teeth and becomes rigid; and I asked your disciples to cast it out, but they could not do so." [19]He answered them, "You faithless generation,

[a]Other ancient authorities read *lose their life for the sake of the gospel* [b]Other ancient authorities read *and of mine* [c]Or *in* [d]Gk *no fuller* [e]Or *tents* [f]Or *my beloved Son*

how much longer must I be among you? How much longer must I put up with you? Bring him to me." [20]And they brought the boy[a] to him. When the spirit saw him, immediately it convulsed the boy,[a] and he fell on the ground and rolled about, foaming at the mouth. [21]Jesus[b] asked the father, "How long has this been happening to him?" And he said, "From childhood. [22]It has often cast him into the fire and into the water, to destroy him; but if you are able to do anything, have pity on us and help us." [23]Jesus said to him, "If you are able!—All things can be done for the one who believes." [24]Immediately the father of the child cried out,[c] "I believe; help my unbelief!" [25]When Jesus saw that a crowd came running together, he rebuked the unclean spirit, saying to it, "You spirit that keeps this boy from speaking and hearing, I command you, come out of him, and never enter him again!" [26]After crying out and convulsing him terribly, it came out, and the boy was like a corpse, so that most of them said, "He is dead." [27]But Jesus took him by the hand and lifted him up, and he was able to stand. [28]When he had entered the house, his disciples asked him privately, "Why could we not cast it out?" [29]He said to them, "This kind can come out only through prayer."[d]

30 They went on from there and passed through Galilee. He did not want anyone to know it; [31]for he was teaching his disciples, saying to them, "The Son of Man is to be betrayed into human hands, and they will kill him, and three days after being killed, he will rise again." [32]But they did not understand what he was saying and were afraid to ask him.

33 Then they came to Capernaum; and when he was in the house he asked them, "What were you arguing about on the way?" [34]But they were silent, for on the way they had argued with one another who was the greatest. [35]He sat down, called the twelve, and said to them, "Whoever wants to be first must be last of all and servant of all." [36]Then he took a little child and put it among them; and taking it in his arms, he said to them, [37]"Whoever welcomes one such child in my name welcomes me, and whoever welcomes me welcomes not me but the one who sent me."

38 John said to him, "Teacher, we saw someone[e] casting out demons in your name, and we tried to stop him, because he was not following us." [39]But Jesus said, "Do not stop him; for no one who does a deed of power in my name will be able soon afterward to speak evil of me. [40]Whoever is not against us is for us. [41]For truly I tell you, whoever gives you a cup of water to drink because you bear the name of Christ will by no means lose the reward.

---

[a]Gk *him* [b]Gk *He* [c]Other ancient authorities add *with tears* [d]Other ancient authorities add *and fasting* [e]Other ancient authorities add *who does not follow us*

42 "If any of you put a stumbling block before one of these little ones who believe in me,[a] it would be better for you if a great millstone were hung around your neck and you were thrown into the sea. [43]If your hand causes you to stumble, cut it off; it is better for you to enter life maimed than to have two hands and to go to hell,[b] to the unquenchable fire.[c] [45]And if your foot causes you to stumble, cut it off; it is better for you to enter life lame than to have two feet and to be thrown into hell.[b,c] [47]And if your eye causes you to stumble, tear it out; for it is better for you to enter the kingdom of God with one eye than to have two eyes and to be thrown into hell,[b] [48]where their worm never dies, and the fire is never quenched.

49 "For everyone will be salted with fire.[d] [50]Salt is good; but if salt has lost its saltiness, how can you season it?[e] Have salt in yourselves, and be at peace with one another."

10 He left that place and went to the region of Judea and[f] beyond the Jordan. And crowds again gathered around him; and, as was his custom, he again taught them.

2 Some Pharisees came, and to test him they asked, "Is it lawful for a man to divorce his wife?" [3]He answered them, "What did Moses command you?" [4]They said, "Moses allowed a man to write a certificate of dismissal and to divorce her." [5]But Jesus said to them, "Because of your hardness of heart he wrote this

commandment for you. [6]But from the beginning of creation, 'God made them male and female.' [7]'For this reason a man shall leave his father and mother and be joined to his wife,[g] [8]and the two shall become one flesh.' So they are no longer two, but one flesh. [9]Therefore what God has joined together, let no one separate."

10 Then in the house the disciples asked him again about this matter. [11]He said to them, "Whoever divorces his wife and marries another commits adultery against her; [12]and if she divorces her husband and marries another, she commits adultery."

13 People were bringing little children to him in order that he might touch them; and the disciples spoke sternly to them. [14]But when Jesus saw this, he was indignant and said to them, "Let the little children come to me; do not stop them; for it is to such as these that the kingdom of God belongs. [15]Truly I tell you, whoever does not receive the kingdom of God as a little child will never enter it." [16]And he took them up in his arms, laid his hands on them, and blessed them.

17 As he was setting out on a journey, a man ran up and knelt before him, and asked him, "Good Teacher, what must I do to inherit

[a]Other ancient authorities lack *in me* [b]Gk *Gehenna* [c]Verses 44 and 46 (which are identical with verse 48) are lacking in the best ancient authorities [d]Other ancient authorities either add or substitute *and every sacrifice will be salted with salt* [e]Or *how can you restore its saltiness?* [f]Other ancient authorities lack *and* [g]Other ancient authorities lack *and be joined to his wife*

eternal life?" [18]Jesus said to him, "Why do you call me good? No one is good but God alone. [19]You know the commandments: 'You shall not murder; You shall not commit adultery; You shall not steal; You shall not bear false witness; You shall not defraud; Honor your father and mother.'" [20]He said to him, "Teacher, I have kept all these since my youth." [21]Jesus, looking at him, loved him and said, "You lack one thing; go, sell what you own, and give the money[a] to the poor, and you will have treasure in heaven; then come, follow me." [22]When he heard this, he was shocked and went away grieving, for he had many possessions.

[23] Then Jesus looked around and said to his disciples, "How hard it will be for those who have wealth to enter the kingdom of God!" [24]And the disciples were perplexed at these words. But Jesus said to them again, "Children, how hard it is[b] to enter the kingdom of God! [25]It is easier for a camel to go through the eye of a needle than for someone who is rich to enter the kingdom of God." [26]They were greatly astounded and said to one another,[c] "Then who can be saved?" [27]Jesus looked at them and said, "For mortals it is impossible, but not for God; for God all things are possible."

[28] Peter began to say to him, "Look, we have left everything and followed you." [29]Jesus said, "Truly I tell you, there is no one who has left house or brothers or sisters or mother or father or children or fields, for my sake and for the sake of the good news,[d] [30]who will not receive a hundredfold now in this age—houses, brothers and sisters, mothers and children, and fields, with persecutions—and in the age to come eternal life. [31]But many who are first will be last, and the last will be first."

[32] They were on the road, going up to Jerusalem, and Jesus was walking ahead of them; they were amazed, and those who followed were afraid. He took the twelve aside again and began to tell them what was to happen to him, [33]saying, "See, we are going up to Jerusalem, and the Son of Man will be handed over to the chief priests and the scribes, and they will condemn him to death; then they will hand him over to the Gentiles; [34]they will mock him, and spit upon him, and flog him, and kill him; and after three days he will rise again."

[35] James and John, the sons of Zebedee, came forward to him and said to him, "Teacher, we want you to do for us whatever we ask of you." [36]And he said to them, "What is it you want me to do for you?" [37]And they said to him, "Grant us to sit, one at your right hand and one at your left, in your glory." [38]But Jesus said to them, "You do not know what you are asking. Are you able to drink the cup that I drink, or be

[a]Or lacks the money [b]Other ancient authorities add for those who trust in riches [c]Other ancient authorities read to him [d]Or gospel

baptized with the baptism that I am baptized with?" [39]They replied, "We are able." Then Jesus said to them, "The cup that I drink you will drink; and with the baptism with which I am baptized, you will be baptized; [40]but to sit at my right hand or at my left is not mine to grant, but it is for those for whom it has been prepared."

[41] When the ten heard this, they began to be angry with James and John. [42]So Jesus called them and said to them, "You know that among the Gentiles those whom they recognize as their rulers lord it over them, and their great ones are tyrants over them. [43]But it is not so among you; but whoever wishes to become great among you must be your servant, [44]and whoever wishes to be first among you must be slave of all. [45]For the Son of Man came not to be served but to serve, and to give his life a ransom for many."

[46] They came to Jericho. As he and his disciples and a large crowd were leaving Jericho, Bartimaeus son of Timaeus, a blind beggar, was sitting by the roadside. [47]When he heard that it was Jesus of Nazareth, he began to shout out and say, "Jesus, Son of David, have mercy on me!" [48]Many sternly ordered him to be quiet, but he cried out even more loudly, "Son of David, have mercy on me!" [49]Jesus stood still and said, "Call him here." And they called the blind man, saying to him, "Take heart; get up, he is calling you." [50]So throwing off his cloak, he sprang up and came to Jesus. [51]Then Jesus said to him, "What do you want me to do for you?" The blind man said to him, "My teacher,[a] let me see again." [52]Jesus said to him, "Go; your faith has made you well." Immediately he regained his sight and followed him on the way.

11 When they were approaching Jerusalem, at Bethphage and Bethany, near the Mount of Olives, he sent two of his disciples [2]and said to them, "Go into the village ahead of you, and immediately as you enter it, you will find tied there a colt that has never been ridden; untie it and bring it. [3]If anyone says to you, 'Why are you doing this?' just say this, 'The Lord needs it and will send it back here immediately.'" [4]They went away and found a colt tied near a door, outside in the street. As they were untying it, [5]some of the bystanders said to them, "What are you doing, untying the colt?" [6]They told them what Jesus had said; and they allowed them to take it. [7]Then they brought the colt to Jesus and threw their cloaks on it; and he sat on it. [8]Many people spread their cloaks on the road, and others spread leafy branches that they had cut in the fields. [9]Then those who went ahead and those who followed were shouting,

"Hosanna!
Blessed is the one who
comes in the name of
the Lord!

[a]Aramaic *Rabbouni*

[10] Blessed is the coming
    kingdom of our
    ancestor David!
Hosanna in the highest
    heaven!"

11 Then he entered Jerusalem and went into the temple; and when he had looked around at everything, as it was already late, he went out to Bethany with the twelve.

12 On the following day, when they came from Bethany, he was hungry. [13]Seeing in the distance a fig tree in leaf, he went to see whether perhaps he would find anything on it. When he came to it, he found nothing but leaves, for it was not the season for figs. [14]He said to it, "May no one ever eat fruit from you again." And his disciples heard it.

15 Then they came to Jerusalem. And he entered the temple and began to drive out those who were selling and those who were buying in the temple, and he overturned the tables of the money changers and the seats of those who sold doves; [16]and he would not allow anyone to carry anything through the temple. [17]He was teaching and saying, "Is it not written,

'My house shall be called a
    house of prayer for
    all the nations'?
But you have made it a
    den of robbers."

[18]And when the chief priests and the scribes heard it, they kept looking for a way to kill him; for they were afraid of him, because the whole crowd was spellbound by his teaching. [19]And when evening came, Jesus and his disciples[a] went out of the city.

20 In the morning as they passed by, they saw the fig tree withered away to its roots. [21]Then Peter remembered and said to him, "Rabbi, look! The fig tree that you cursed has withered." [22]Jesus answered them, "Have[b] faith in God. [23]Truly I tell you, if you say to this mountain, 'Be taken up and thrown into the sea,' and if you do not doubt in your heart, but believe that what you say will come to pass, it will be done for you. [24]So I tell you, whatever you ask for in prayer, believe that you have received[c] it, and it will be yours.

25 "Whenever you stand praying, forgive, if you have anything against anyone; so that your Father in heaven may also forgive you your trespasses."[d]

27 Again they came to Jerusalem. As he was walking in the temple, the chief priests, the scribes, and the elders came to him [28]and said, "By what authority are you doing these things? Who gave you this authority to do them?" [29]Jesus said to them, "I will ask you one question; answer me, and I will tell you by what authority I do these things. [30]Did the baptism of John come from heaven, or was it of human

[a]Gk *they:* other ancient authorities read *he* [b]Other ancient authorities read *"If you have* [c]Other ancient authorities read *are receiving* [d]Other ancient authorities add verse 26, *"But if you do not forgive, neither will your Father in heaven forgive your trespasses."*

origin? Answer me." [31]They argued with one another, "If we say, 'From heaven,' he will say, 'Why then did you not believe him?' [32]But shall we say, 'Of human origin'?"—they were afraid of the crowd, for all regarded John as truly a prophet. [33]So they answered Jesus, "We do not know." And Jesus said to them, "Neither will I tell you by what authority I am doing these things."

12 Then he began to speak to them in parables. "A man planted a vineyard, put a fence around it, dug a pit for the wine press, and built a watchtower; then he leased it to tenants and went to another country. [2]When the season came, he sent a slave to the tenants to collect from them his share of the produce of the vineyard. [3]But they seized him, and beat him, and sent him away empty-handed. [4]And again he sent another slave to them; this one they beat over the head and insulted. [5]Then he sent another, and that one they killed. And so it was with many others; some they beat, and others they killed. [6]He had still one other, a beloved son. Finally he sent him to them, saying, 'They will respect my son.' [7]But those tenants said to one another, 'This is the heir; come, let us kill him, and the inheritance will be ours.' [8]So they seized him, killed him, and threw him out of the vineyard. [9]What then will the owner of the vineyard do? He will come and destroy the tenants and give the vineyard to others. [10]Have you not read this scripture:

> 'The stone that the builders rejected
> has become the cornerstone;[a]
[11] this was the Lord's doing,
> and it is amazing in our eyes'?"

12 When they realized that he had told this parable against them, they wanted to arrest him, but they feared the crowd. So they left him and went away.

13 Then they sent to him some Pharisees and some Herodians to trap him in what he said. [14]And they came and said to him, "Teacher, we know that you are sincere, and show deference to no one; for you do not regard people with partiality, but teach the way of God in accordance with truth. Is it lawful to pay taxes to the emperor, or not? [15]Should we pay them, or should we not?" But knowing their hypocrisy, he said to them, "Why are you putting me to the test? Bring me a denarius and let me see it." [16]And they brought one. Then he said to them, "Whose head is this, and whose title?" They answered, "The emperor's." [17]Jesus said to them, "Give to the emperor the things that are the emperor's, and to God the things that are God's." And they were utterly amazed at him.

18 Some Sadducees, who say there is no resurrection, came to him and asked him a question, saying, [19]"Teacher, Moses wrote for us that 'if a man's brother dies,

[a]Or *keystone*

leaving a wife but no child, the man[a] shall marry the widow and raise up children for his brother.' 20There were seven brothers; the first married and, when he died, left no children; 21and the second married her[b] and died, leaving no children; and the third likewise; 22none of the seven left children. Last of all the woman herself died. 23In the resurrection[c] whose wife will she be? For the seven had married her."

24 Jesus said to them, "Is not this the reason you are wrong, that you know neither the scriptures nor the power of God? 25For when they rise from the dead, they neither marry nor are given in marriage, but are like angels in heaven. 26And as for the dead being raised, have you not read in the book of Moses, in the story about the bush, how God said to him, 'I am the God of Abraham, the God of Isaac, and the God of Jacob'? 27He is God not of the dead, but of the living; you are quite wrong."

28 One of the scribes came near and heard them disputing with one another, and seeing that he answered them well, he asked him, "Which commandment is the first of all?" 29Jesus answered, "The first is, 'Hear, O Israel: the Lord our God, the Lord is one; 30you shall love the Lord your God with all your heart, and with all your soul, and with all your mind, and with all your strength.' 31The second is this, 'You shall love your neighbor as yourself.' There is no other com-

mandment greater than these." 32Then the scribe said to him, "You are right, Teacher; you have truly said that 'he is one, and besides him there is no other'; 33and 'to love him with all the heart, and with all the understanding, and with all the strength,' and 'to love one's neighbor as oneself,'—this is much more important than all whole burnt offerings and sacrifices." 34When Jesus saw that he answered wisely, he said to him, "You are not far from the kingdom of God." After that no one dared to ask him any question.

35 While Jesus was teaching in the temple, he said, "How can the scribes say that the Messiah[d] is the son of David? 36David himself, by the Holy Spirit, declared,

'The Lord said to my Lord,
  "Sit at my right hand,
    until I put your enemies
      under your feet."'

37David himself calls him Lord; so how can he be his son?" And the large crowd was listening to him with delight.

38 As he taught, he said, "Beware of the scribes, who like to walk around in long robes, and to be greeted with respect in the marketplaces, 39and to have the best seats in the synagogues and places of honor at banquets! 40They devour widows' houses and for the sake of appearance say long prayers. They will receive the greater condemnation."

[a]Gk *his brother* [b]Gk *her* [c]Other ancient authorities add *when they rise* [d]Or *the Christ*

41 He sat down opposite the treasury, and watched the crowd putting money into the treasury. Many rich people put in large sums. [42]A poor widow came and put in two small copper coins, which are worth a penny. [43]Then he called his disciples and said to them, "Truly I tell you, this poor widow has put in more than all those who are contributing to the treasury. [44]For all of them have contributed out of their abundance; but she out of her poverty has put in everything she had, all she had to live on."

13 As he came out of the temple, one of his disciples said to him, "Look, Teacher, what large stones and what large buildings!" [2]Then Jesus asked him, "Do you see these great buildings? Not one stone will be left here upon another; all will be thrown down."

3 When he was sitting on the Mount of Olives opposite the temple, Peter, James, John, and Andrew asked him privately, [4]"Tell us, when will this be, and what will be the sign that all these things are about to be accomplished?" [5]Then Jesus began to say to them, "Beware that no one leads you astray. [6]Many will come in my name and say, 'I am he!'[a] and they will lead many astray. [7]When you hear of wars and rumors of wars, do not be alarmed; this must take place, but the end is still to come. [8]For nation will rise against nation, and kingdom against kingdom; there will be earthquakes in various places; there will be famines. This is but the beginning of the birth pangs.

9 "As for yourselves, beware; for they will hand you over to councils; and you will be beaten in synagogues; and you will stand before governors and kings because of me, as a testimony to them. [10]And the good news[b] must first be proclaimed to all nations. [11]When they bring you to trial and hand you over, do not worry beforehand about what you are to say; but say whatever is given you at that time, for it is not you who speak, but the Holy Spirit. [12]Brother will betray brother to death, and a father his child, and children will rise against parents and have them put to death; [13]and you will be hated by all because of my name. But the one who endures to the end will be saved.

14 "But when you see the desolating sacrilege set up where it ought not to be (let the reader understand), then those in Judea must flee to the mountains; [15]the one on the housetop must not go down or enter the house to take anything away; [16]the one in the field must not turn back to get a coat. [17]Woe to those who are pregnant and to those who are nursing infants in those days! [18]Pray that it may not be in winter. [19]For in those days there will be suffering, such as has not been from the beginning of the creation that

[a]Gk I am [b]Gk gospel

God created until now, no, and never will be. ²⁰And if the Lord had not cut short those days, no one would be saved; but for the sake of the elect, whom he chose, he has cut short those days. ²¹And if anyone says to you at that time, 'Look! Here is the Messiah!'ᵃ or 'Look! There he is!'—do not believe it. ²²False messiahsᵇ and false prophets will appear and produce signs and omens, to lead astray, if possible, the elect. ²³But be alert; I have already told you everything.

24 "But in those days, after that suffering,

the sun will be darkened,
and the moon will not
give its light,
25   and the stars will be falling
from heaven,
and the powers in the
heavens will be shaken.

²⁶Then they will see 'the Son of Man coming in clouds' with great power and glory. ²⁷Then he will send out the angels, and gather his elect from the four winds, from the ends of the earth to the ends of heaven.

28 "From the fig tree learn its lesson: as soon as its branch becomes tender and puts forth its leaves, you know that summer is near. ²⁹So also, when you see these things taking place, you know that heᶜ is near, at the very gates. ³⁰Truly I tell you, this generation will not pass away until all these things have taken place. ³¹Heaven and earth will pass away, but my words will not pass away.

32 "But about that day or hour no one knows, neither the angels in heaven, nor the Son, but only the Father. ³³Beware, keep alert;ᵈ for you do not know when the time will come. ³⁴It is like a man going on a journey, when he leaves home and puts his slaves in charge, each with his work, and commands the doorkeeper to be on the watch. ³⁵Therefore, keep awake—for you do not know when the master of the house will come, in the evening, or at midnight, or at cockcrow, or at dawn, ³⁶or else he may find you asleep when he comes suddenly. ³⁷And what I say to you I say to all: Keep awake."

14 It was two days before the Passover and the festival of Unleavened Bread. The chief priests and the scribes were looking for a way to arrest Jesus by stealth and kill him; ²for they said, "Not during the festival, or there may be a riot among the people."

3 While he was at Bethany in the house of Simon the leper,ᶠ as he sat at the table, a woman came with an alabaster jar of very costly ointment of nard, and she broke open the jar and poured the ointment on his head. ⁴But some were there who said to one another in anger, "Why was the ointment wasted in this way? ⁵For this ointment could have been sold for more than three hundred

---

ᵃOr *the Christ* ᵇOr *christs* ᶜOr *it* ᵈOther ancient authorities add *and pray* ᵉGk *him* ᶠThe terms *leper* and *leprosy* can refer to several diseases

denarii,[a] and the money given to the poor." And they scolded her. [6]But Jesus said, "Let her alone; why do you trouble her? She has performed a good service for me. [7]For you always have the poor with you, and you can show kindness to them whenever you wish; but you will not always have me. [8]She has done what she could; she has anointed my body beforehand for its burial. [9]Truly I tell you, wherever the good news[b] is proclaimed in the whole world, what she has done will be told in remembrance of her."

[10] Then Judas Iscariot, who was one of the twelve, went to the chief priests in order to betray him to them. [11]When they heard it, they were greatly pleased, and promised to give him money. So he began to look for an opportunity to betray him.

[12] On the first day of Unleavened Bread, when the Passover lamb is sacrificed, his disciples said to him, "Where do you want us to go and make the preparations for you to eat the Passover?" [13]So he sent two of his disciples, saying to them, "Go into the city, and a man carrying a jar of water will meet you; follow him, [14]and wherever he enters, say to the owner of the house, 'The Teacher asks, Where is my guest room where I may eat the Passover with my disciples?' [15]He will show you a large room upstairs, furnished and ready. Make preparations for us there." [16]So the disciples set out and went to the city, and found every-thing as he had told them; and they prepared the Passover meal.

[17] When it was evening, he came with the twelve. [18]And when they had taken their places and were eating, Jesus said, "Truly I tell you, one of you will betray me, one who is eating with me." [19]They began to be distressed and to say to him one after another, "Surely, not I?" [20]He said to them, "It is one of the twelve, one who is dipping bread[c] into the bowl[d] with me. [21]For the Son of Man goes as it is written of him, but woe to that one by whom the Son of Man is betrayed! It would have been better for that one not to have been born."

[22] While they were eating, he took a loaf of bread, and after blessing it he broke it, gave it to them, and said, "Take; this is my body." [23]Then he took a cup, and after giving thanks he gave it to them, and all of them drank from it. [24]He said to them, "This is my blood of the[e] covenant, which is poured out for many. [25]Truly I tell you, I will never again drink of the fruit of the vine until that day when I drink it new in the kingdom of God."

[26] When they had sung the hymn, they went out to the Mount of Olives. [27]And Jesus said to them, "You will all become deserters; for it is written,

---

[a]The denarius was the usual day's wage for a laborer [b]Or gospel [c]Gk lacks bread [d]Other ancient authorities read same bowl [e]Other ancient authorities add new

'I will strike the shepherd,
and the sheep will be
scattered.'

[28]But after I am raised up, I will
go before you to Galilee." [29]Peter
said to him, "Even though all
become deserters, I will not."
[30]Jesus said to him, "Truly I tell
you, this day, this very night
before the cock crows twice, you
will deny me three times." [31]But
he said vehemently, "Even
though I must die with you, I will
not deny you." And all of them
said the same.

32 They went to a place called
Gethsemane; and he said to his
disciples, "Sit here while I pray."
[33]He took with him Peter and
James and John, and began to be
distressed and agitated. [34]And
said to them, "I am deeply
grieved, even to death; remain
here, and keep awake." [35]And
going a little farther, he threw
himself on the ground and
prayed that, if it were possible,
the hour might pass from him.
[36]He said, "Abba[a], Father, for you
all things are possible; remove
this cup from me; yet, not what I
want, but what you want." [37]He
came and found them sleeping;
and he said to Peter, "Simon, are
you asleep? Could you not keep
awake one hour? [38]Keep awake
and pray that you may not come
into the time of trial;[b] the spirit
indeed is willing, but the flesh is
weak." [39]And again he went
away and prayed, saying the
same words. [40]And once more he
came and found them sleeping,
for their eyes were very heavy;
and they did not know what to
say to him. [41]He came a third
time and said to them, "Are you
still sleeping and taking your
rest? Enough! The hour has
come; the Son of Man is betrayed
into the hands of sinners. [42]Get
up, let us be going. See, my
betrayer is at hand."

43 Immediately, while he was
still speaking, Judas, one of the
twelve, arrived; and with him
there was a crowd with swords
and clubs, from the chief priests,
the scribes, and the elders. [44]Now
the betrayer had given them a
sign, saying, "The one I will kiss
is the man; arrest him and lead
him away under guard." [45]So
when he came, he went up to
him at once and said, "Rabbi!"
and kissed him. [46]Then they laid
hands on him and arrested him.
[47]But one of those who stood
near drew his sword and struck
the slave of the high priest, cutting off his ear. [48]Then Jesus said
to them, "Have you come out
with swords and clubs to arrest
me as though I were a bandit?
[49]Day after day I was with you in
the temple teaching, and you did
not arrest me. But let the scriptures be fulfilled." [50]All of them
deserted him and fled.

51 A certain young man was
following him, wearing nothing
but a linen cloth. They caught
hold of him, [52]but he left the
linen cloth and ran off naked.

53 They took Jesus to the high
priest; and all the chief priests,

[a]Aramaic for *Father* [b]Or *into temptation*

the elders, and the scribes were assembled. ⁵⁴Peter had followed him at a distance, right into the courtyard of the high priest; and he was sitting with the guards, warming himself at the fire. ⁵⁵Now the chief priests and the whole council were looking for testimony against Jesus to put him to death; but they found none. ⁵⁶For many gave false testimony against him, and their testimony did not agree. ⁵⁷Some stood up and gave false testimony against him, saying, ⁵⁸"We heard him say, 'I will destroy this temple that is made with hands, and in three days I will build another, not made with hands.'" ⁵⁹But even on this point their testimony did not agree. ⁶⁰Then the high priest stood up before them and asked Jesus, "Have you no answer? What is it that they testify against you?" ⁶¹But he was silent and did not answer. Again the high priest asked him, "Are you the Messiah,ᵃ the Son of the Blessed One?" ⁶²Jesus said, "I am; and

'you will see the Son of
　　　Man
seated at the right hand of
　　　the Power,'
and 'coming with the
　　　clouds of heaven.'"

⁶³Then the high priest tore his clothes and said, "Why do we still need witnesses? ⁶⁴You have heard his blasphemy! What is your decision?" All of them condemned him as deserving death. ⁶⁵Some began to spit on him, to blindfold him, and to strike him, saying to

him, "Prophesy!" The guards also took him over and beat him.

66 While Peter was below in the courtyard, one of the servant-girls of the high priest came by. ⁶⁷When she saw Peter warming himself, she stared at him and said, "You also were with Jesus, the man from Nazareth." ⁶⁸But he denied it, saying, "I do not know or understand what you are talking about." And he went out into the forecourt.ᵇ Then the cock crowed.ᶜ ⁶⁹And the servant-girl, on seeing him, began again to say to the bystanders, "This man is one of them." ⁷⁰But again he denied it. Then after a little while the bystanders again said to Peter, "Certainly you are one of them; for you are a Galilean." ⁷¹But he began to curse, and he swore an oath, "I do not know this man you are talking about." ⁷²At that moment the cock crowed for the second time. Then Peter remembered that Jesus had said to him, "Before the cock crows twice, you will deny me three times." And he broke down and wept.

15 As soon as it was morning, the chief priests held a consultation with the elders and scribes and the whole council. They bound Jesus, led him away, and handed him over to Pilate. ²Pilate asked him, "Are you the King of the Jews?" He answered him, "You say so." ³Then the chief priests accused him of many

ᵃOr *the Christ* ᵇOr *gateway* ᶜOther ancient authorities lack *Then the cock crowed* things. ⁴Pilate asked him again, "Have you no answer? See how many charges they bring against you." ⁵But Jesus made no further reply, so that Pilate was amazed.

6 Now at the festival he used to release a prisoner for them, anyone for whom they asked. ⁷Now a man called Barabbas was in prison with the rebels who had committed murder during the insurrection. ⁸So the crowd came and began to ask Pilate to do for them according to his custom. ⁹Then he answered them, "Do you want me to release for you the King of the Jews?" ¹⁰For he realized that it was out of jealousy that the chief priests had handed him over. ¹¹But the chief priests stirred up the crowd to have him release Barabbas for them instead. ¹²Pilate spoke to them again, "Then what do you wish me to do*ᵃ* with the man you call*ᵇ* the King of the Jews?" ¹³They shouted back, "Crucify him!" ¹⁴Pilate asked them, "Why, what evil has he done?" But they shouted all the more, "Crucify him!" ¹⁵So Pilate, wishing to satisfy the crowd, released Barabbas for them; and after flogging Jesus, he handed him over to be crucified.

16 Then the soldiers led him into the courtyard of the palace (that is, the governor's headquarters*ᶜ*); and they called together the whole cohort. ¹⁷And they clothed him in a purple cloak; and after twisting some thorns into a crown, they put it on him. ¹⁸And they began saluting him, "Hail, King of the Jews!" ¹⁹They struck his head with a reed, spat upon him, and knelt down in homage to him. ²⁰After mocking him, they stripped him of the purple cloak and put his own clothes on him. Then they led him out to crucify him.

21 They compelled a passerby, who was coming in from the country, to carry his cross; it was Simon of Cyrene, the father of Alexander and Rufus. ²²Then they brought Jesus*ᵈ* to the place called Golgotha (which means the place of a skull). ²³And they offered him wine mixed with myrrh; but he did not take it. ²⁴And they crucified him, and divided his clothes among them, casting lots to decide what each should take.

25 It was nine o'clock in the morning when they crucified him. ²⁶The inscription of the charge against him read, "The King of the Jews." ²⁷And with him they crucified two bandits, one on his right and one on his left.*ᵉ* ²⁹Those who passed by derided*ᶠ* him, shaking their heads and saying, "Aha! You who would destroy the temple and build it in three days, ³⁰save yourself, and come down from the cross!" ³¹In the same way the chief priests, along with the scribes, were also mocking him among themselves and saying,

---

*ᵃ*Other ancient authorities read *what should I do* *ᵇ*Other ancient authorities lack *the man you call* *ᶜ*Gk *the praetorium* *ᵈ*Gk *him* *ᵉ*Other ancient authorities add verse 28, *And the scripture was fulfilled that says, "And he was counted among the lawless."* *ᶠ*Or blasphemed

"He saved others; he cannot save himself. [32]Let the Messiah,[a] the King of Israel, come down from the cross now, so that we may see and believe." Those who were crucified with him also taunted him.

33 When it was noon, darkness came over the whole land[b] until three in the afternoon. [34]At three o'clock Jesus cried out with a loud voice, "Eloi, Eloi, lema sabachthani?" which means, "My God, my God, why have you forsaken me?"[c] [35]When some of the bystanders heard it, they said, "Listen, he is calling for Elijah." [36]And someone ran, filled a sponge with sour wine, put it on a stick, and gave it to him to drink, saying, "Wait, let us see whether Elijah will come to take him down." [37]Then Jesus gave a loud cry and breathed his last. [38]And the curtain of the temple was torn in two, from top to bottom. [39]Now when the centurion, who stood facing him, saw that in this way he[d] breathed his last, he said, "Truly this man was God's Son!"[e]

40 There were also women looking on from a distance; among them were Mary Magdalene, and Mary the mother of James the younger and of Joses, and Salome. [41]These used to follow him and provided for him when he was in Galilee; and there were many other women who had come up with him to Jerusalem.

42 When evening had come, and since it was the day of Preparation, that is, the day before the sabbath, [43]Joseph of Arimathea, a respected member of the council, who was also himself waiting expectantly for the kingdom of God, went boldly to Pilate and asked for the body of Jesus. [44]Then Pilate wondered if he were already dead; and summoning the centurion, he asked him whether he had been dead for some time. [45]When he learned from the centurion that he was dead, he granted the body to Joseph. [46]Then Joseph[f] bought a linen cloth, and taking down the body,[g] wrapped it in the linen cloth, and laid it in a tomb that had been hewn out of the rock. He then rolled a stone against the door of the tomb. [47]Mary Magdalene and Mary the mother of Joses saw where the body was laid.

16 When the sabbath was over, Mary Magdalene, and Mary the mother of James, and Salome bought spices, so that they might go and anoint him. [2]And very early on the first day of the week, when the sun had risen, they went to the tomb. [3]They had been saying to one another, "Who will roll away the stone for us from the entrance to the tomb?" [4]When they looked up, they saw that the stone, which was very large, had already been rolled back. [5]As they entered the tomb, they saw a young man, dressed in a white robe, sitting on the right side; and

[a]Or *the Christ* [b]Or *earth* [c]Other ancient authorities read *made me a reproach* [d]Other ancient authorities add *cried out and* [e]Or *a son of God* [f]Gk *he* [g]Gk *it*

they were alarmed. [6]But he said to them, "Do not be alarmed; you are looking for Jesus of Nazareth, who was crucified. He has been raised; he is not here. Look, there is the place they laid him. [7]But go, tell his disciples and Peter that he is going ahead of you to Galilee; there you will see him, just as he told you." [8]So they went out and fled from the tomb, for terror and amazement had seized them; and they said nothing to anyone, for they were afraid.[a]

THE SHORTER ENDING OF MARK

[[And all that had been commanded them they told briefly to those around Peter. And afterward Jesus himself sent out through them, from east to west, the sacred and imperishable proclamation of eternal salvation.[b]]]

THE LONGER ENDING OF MARK

9 [[Now after he rose early on the first day of the week, he appeared first to Mary Magdalene, from whom he had cast out seven demons. [10]She went out and told those who had been with him, while they were mourning and weeping. [11]But when they heard that he was alive and had been seen by her, they would not believe it.

12 After this he appeared in another form to two of them, as they were walking into the country. [13]And they went back and told the rest, but they did not believe them.

14 Later he appeared to the eleven themselves as they were sitting at the table; and he upbraided them for their lack of faith and stubbornness, because they had not believed those who saw him after he had risen.[c] [15]And he said to them, "Go into all the world and proclaim the good news[d] to the whole creation. [16]The one who believes and is baptized will be saved; but the one who does not believe will be condemned. [17]And these signs will accompany those who believe: by using my name they will cast out demons; they will speak in new tongues; [18]they will pick up snakes in their hands,[e] and if they drink any deadly thing, it will not hurt them; they will lay their hands on the sick, and they will recover."

19 So then the Lord Jesus, after he had spoken to them, was

[a]Some of the most ancient authorities bring the book to a close at the end of verse 8. One authority concludes the book with the shorter ending; others include the shorter ending and then continue with verses 9-20. In most authorities verses 9-20 follow immediately after verse 8, though in some of these authorities the passage is marked as being doubtful. [b]Other ancient authorities add *Amen* [c]Other ancient authorities add, in whole or in part, *And they excused themselves, saying, "This age of lawlessness and unbelief is under Satan, who does not allow the truth and power of God to prevail over the unclean things of the spirits. Therefore reveal your righteosuensss now"—thus they spoke to Christ. And Christ replied to them, "The term of years of Satan's power has been fulfilled, but other terrible things draw near. And for those who have sinned I was handed over to death, that they may return to the truth and sin no more, that they may inherit the spiritual and imperishable glory of righteousness that is in heaven."* [d]*Or gospel* [e]Other ancient authorities lack *in their hands*

taken up into heaven and sat down at the right hand of God. ²⁰And they went out and proclaimed the good news everywhere, while the Lord worked

with them and confirmed the message by the signs that accompanied it.[a]]]

[a]Other ancient authorities add *Amen*

The Gospel According to

LUKE

1 Since many have undertaken to set down an orderly account of the events that have been fulfilled among us, ²just as they were handed on to us by those who from the beginning were eyewitnesses and servants of the word, ³I too decided, after investigating everything carefully from the very first,[a] to write an orderly account for you, most excellent Theophilus, ⁴so that you may know the truth concerning the things about which you have been instructed.

5 In the days of King Herod of Judea, there was a priest named Zechariah, who belonged to the priestly order of Abijah. His wife was a descendant of Aaron, and her name was Elizabeth. ⁶Both of them were righteous before God, living blamelessly according to all the commandments and regulations of the Lord. ⁷But they had no children, because Elizabeth was barren, and both were getting on in years.

8 Once when he was serving as

priest before God and his section was on duty, ⁹he was chosen by lot, according to the custom of the priesthood, to enter the sanctuary of the Lord and offer incense. ¹⁰Now at the time of the incense offering, the whole assembly of the people was praying outside. ¹¹Then there appeared to him an angel of the Lord, standing at the right side of the altar of incense. ¹²When Zechariah saw him, he was terrified; and fear overwhelmed him. ¹³But the angel said to him, "Do not be afraid, Zechariah, for your prayer has been heard. Your wife Elizabeth will bear you a son, and you will name him John. ¹⁴You will have joy and gladness, and many will rejoice at his birth, ¹⁵for he will be great in the sight of the Lord. He must never drink wine or strong drink; even before his birth he will be filled with the Holy Spirit. ¹⁶He will turn many of the people of Israel to the Lord their God. ¹⁷With the

[a]Or *for a long time*

spirit and power of Elijah he will go before him, to turn the hearts of parents to their children, and the disobedient to the wisdom of the righteous, to make ready a people prepared for the Lord." [18]Zechariah said to the angel, "How will I know that this is so? For I am an old man, and my wife is getting on in years." [19]The angel replied, "I am Gabriel. I stand in the presence of God, and I have been sent to speak to you and to bring you this good news. [20]But now, because you did not believe my words, which will be fulfilled in their time, you will become mute, unable to speak, until the day these things occur."

21 Meanwhile the people were waiting for Zechariah, and wondered at his delay in the sanctuary. [22]When he did come out, he could not speak to them, and they realized that he had seen a vision in the sanctuary. He kept motioning to them and remained unable to speak. [23]When his time of service was ended, he went to his home.

24 After those days his wife Elizabeth conceived, and for five months she remained in seclusion. She said, [25]"This is what the Lord has done for me when he looked favorably on me and took away the disgrace I have endured among my people."

26 In the sixth month the angel Gabriel was sent by God to a town in Galilee called Nazareth, [27]to a virgin engaged to a man whose name was Joseph, of the house of David. The vir-

gin's name was Mary. [28]And he came to her and said, "Greetings, favored one! The Lord is with you."[a] [29]But she was much perplexed by his words and pondered what sort of greeting this might be. [30]The angel said to her, "Do not be afraid, Mary, for you have found favor with God. [31]And now, you will conceive in your womb and bear a son, and you will name him Jesus. [32]He will be great, and will be called the Son of the Most High, and the Lord God will give to him the throne of his ancestor David. [33]He will reign over the house of Jacob forever, and of his kingdom there will be no end." [34]Mary said to the angel, "How can this be, since I am a virgin?"[b] [35]The angel said to her, "The Holy Spirit will come upon you, and the power of the Most High will overshadow you; therefore the child to be born[c] will be holy; he will be called Son of God. [36]And now, your relative Elizabeth in her old age has also conceived a son; and this is the sixth month for her who was said to be barren. [37]For nothing will be impossible with God." [38]Then Mary said, "Here am I, the servant of the Lord; let it be with me according to your word." Then the angel departed from her.

39 In those days Mary set out and went with haste to a Judean town in the hill country,

---

[a]Other ancient authorities add *Blessed are you among women* [b]Gk *I do not know a man* [c]Other ancient authorities add *of you*

⁴⁰where she entered the house of Zechariah and greeted Elizabeth. ⁴¹When Elizabeth heard Mary's greeting, the child leaped in her womb. And Elizabeth was filled with the Holy Spirit ⁴²and exclaimed with a loud cry, "Blessed are you among women, and blessed is the fruit of your womb. ⁴³And why has this happened to me, that the mother of my Lord comes to me? ⁴⁴For as soon as I heard the sound of your greeting, the child in my womb leaped for joy. ⁴⁵And blessed is she who believed that there would be*a* a fulfillment of what was spoken to her by the Lord."

46 And Mary*b* said,

"My soul magnifies the Lord,

47 and my spirit rejoices in God my Savior,

48 for he has looked with favor on the lowliness of his servant.

Surely, from now on all generations will call me blessed;

49 for the Mighty One has done great things for me,

and holy is his name.

50 His mercy is for those who fear him from generation to generation.

51 He has shown strength with his arm;

he has scattered the proud in the thoughts of their hearts.

52 He has brought down the powerful from their thrones,

and lifted up the lowly;

53 he has filled the hungry with good things,

and sent the rich away empty.

54 He has helped his servant Israel,

in remembrance of his mercy,

55 according to the promise he made to our ancestors,

to Abraham and to his descendants forever."

56 And Mary remained with her about three months and then returned to her home.

57 Now the time came for Elizabeth to give birth, and she bore a son. ⁵⁸Her neighbors and relatives heard that the Lord had shown his great mercy to her, and they rejoiced with her.

59 On the eighth day they came to circumcise the child, and they were going to name him Zechariah after his father. ⁶⁰But his mother said, "No; he is to be called John." ⁶¹They said to her, "None of your relatives has this name." ⁶²Then they began motioning to his father to find out what name he wanted to give him. ⁶³He asked for a writing tablet and wrote, "His name is John." And all of them were amazed. ⁶⁴Immediately his mouth was opened and his tongue freed,

*a*Or believed, for there will be *b*Other ancient authorities read Elizabeth

and he began to speak, praising God. 65Fear came over all their neighbors, and all these things were talked about throughout the entire hill country of Judea. 66All who heard them pondered them and said, "What then will this child become?" For, indeed, the hand of the Lord was with him.

67 Then his father Zechariah was filled with the Holy Spirit and spoke this prophecy:

68 "Blessed be the Lord God
of Israel,
for he has looked
favorably on his
people and redeemed
them.
69 He has raised up a mighty
savior[a] for us
in the house of his
servant David,
70 as he spoke through the
mouth of his holy
prophets from of old,
71 that we would be saved
from our enemies
and from the hand of
all who hate us.
72 Thus he has shown the
mercy promised to
our ancestors,
and has remembered his
holy covenant,
73 the oath that he swore to
our ancestor Abraham,
to grant us 74that we,
being rescued from
the hands of our
enemies,
might serve him without
fear, 75in holiness
and righteousness
before him all our days.

76 And you, child, will be
called the prophet of
the Most High;
for you will go before the
Lord to prepare his
ways,
77 to give knowledge of
salvation to his people
by the forgiveness
of their sins.
78 By the tender mercy of our
God,
the dawn from on high
will break upon[b] us,
79 to give light to those who
sit in darkness and in
the shadow of death,
to guide our feet into the
way of peace."

80 The child grew and became strong in spirit, and he was in the wilderness until the day he appeared publicly to Israel.

2 In those days a decree went out from Emperor Augustus that all the world should be registered. 2This was the first registration and was taken while Quirinius was governor of Syria. 3All went to their own towns to be registered. 4Joseph also went from the town of Nazareth in Galilee to Judea, to the city of David called Bethlehem, because he was descended from the house and family of David. 5He went to be registered with Mary, to whom he was engaged and who was expecting a child. 6While they were there, the time

---

[a]Gk *a horn of salvation* [b]Other ancient authorities read *has broken upon*

came for her to deliver her child. [7]And she gave birth to her first-born son and wrapped him in bands of cloth, and laid him in a manger, because there was no place for them in the inn.

8 In that region there were shepherds living in the fields, keeping watch over their flock by night. [9]Then an angel of the Lord stood before them, and the glory of the Lord shone around them, and they were terrified. [10]But the angel said to them, "Do not be afraid; for see—I am bringing you good news of great joy for all the people: [11]to you is born this day in the city of David a Savior, who is the Messiah,[a] the Lord. [12]This will be a sign for you: you will find a child wrapped in bands of cloth and lying in a manger." [13]And suddenly there was with the angel a multitude of the heavenly host,[b] praising God and saying,

[14]   "Glory to God in the
      highest heaven,
  and on earth peace
      among those whom
      he favors!"[c]

15 When the angels had left them and gone into heaven, the shepherds said to one another, "Let us go now to Bethlehem and see this thing that has taken place, which the Lord has made known to us." [16]So they went with haste and found Mary and Joseph, and the child lying in the manger. [17]When they saw this, they made known what had been told them about this child; [18]and all who heard it were amazed at what the shepherds told them.

[19]But Mary treasured all these words and pondered them in her heart. [20]The shepherds returned, glorifying and praising God for all they had heard and seen, as it had been told them.

21 After eight days had passed, it was time to circumcise the child; and he was called Jesus, the name given by the angel before he was conceived in the womb.

22 When the time came for their purification according to the law of Moses, they brought him up to Jerusalem to present him to the Lord [23](as it is written in the law of the Lord, "Every firstborn male shall be designated as holy to the Lord"), [24]and they offered a sacrifice according to what is stated in the law of the Lord, "a pair of turtledoves or two young pigeons."

25 Now there was a man in Jerusalem whose name was Simeon;[d] this man was righteous and devout, looking forward to the consolation of Israel, and the Holy Spirit rested on him. [26]It had been revealed to him by the Holy Spirit that he would not see death before he had seen the Lord's Messiah.[e] [27]Guided by the Spirit, Simeon[f] came into the temple; and when the parents brought in the child Jesus, to do for him what was customary under the law, [28]Simeon[g] took him in his arms and praised God, saying,

---

[a] Or *the Christ* [b] Gk *army* [c] Other ancient authorities read *peace, goodwill among people* [d] Gk *Symeon* [e] Or *the Lord's Christ* [f] Gk *In the Spirit, he* [g] Gk *he*

29 "Master, now you are
    dismissing your
      servant[a] in peace,
    according to your word;
30 for my eyes have seen your
    salvation,
31 which you have prepared
    in the presence of all
      peoples,
32 a light for revelation to the
      Gentiles
    and for glory to your
      people Israel."

33 And the child's father and mother were amazed at what was being said about him. 34Then Simeon blessed them and said to his mother Mary, "This child is destined for the falling and the rising of many in Israel, and to be a sign that will be opposed 35so that the inner thoughts of many will be revealed—and a sword will pierce your own soul too."

36 There was also a prophet, Anna[b] the daughter of Phanuel, of the tribe of Asher. She was of a great age, having lived with her husband seven years after her marriage, 37then as a widow to the age of eighty-four. She never left the temple but worshiped there with fasting and prayer night and day. 38At that moment she came, and began to praise God and to speak about the child[c] to all who were looking for the redemption of Jerusalem.

39 When they had finished everything required by the law of the Lord, they returned to Galilee, to their own town of Nazareth. 40The child grew and became strong, filled with wisdom; and the favor of God was upon him.

41 Now every year his parents went to Jerusalem for the festival of the Passover. 42And when he was twelve years old, they went up as usual for the festival. 43When the festival was ended and they started to return, the boy Jesus stayed behind in Jerusalem, but his parents did not know it. 44Assuming that he was in the group of travelers, they went a day's journey. Then they started to look for him among their relatives and friends. 45When they did not find him, they returned to Jerusalem to search for him. 46After three days they found him in the temple, sitting among the teachers, listening to them and asking them questions. 47And all who heard him were amazed at his understanding and his answers. 48When his parents[d] saw him they were astonished; and his mother said to him, "Child, why have you treated us like this? Look, your father and I have been searching for you in great anxiety." 49He said to them, "Why were you searching for me? Did you not know that I must be in my Father's house?"[e] 50But they did not understand what he said to them. 51Then he went down with them and came to Nazareth, and was obedient to them. His mother treasured all these things in her heart.

[a]Gk slave [b]Gk Hanna [c]Gk him [d]Gk they [e]Or be about my Father's interests?

52 And Jesus increased in wisdom and in years,[a] and in divine and human favor.

3 In the fifteenth year of the reign of Emperor Tiberius, when Pontius Pilate was governor of Judea, and Herod was ruler[b] of Galilee, and his brother Philip ruler[b] of the region of Ituraea and Trachonitis, and Lysanias ruler[b] of Abilene, [2]during the high priesthood of Annas and Caiaphas, the word of God came to John son of Zechariah in the wilderness. [3]He went into all the region around the Jordan, proclaiming a baptism of repentance for the forgiveness of sins, [4]as it is written in the book of the words of the prophet Isaiah,

"The voice of one crying
out in the wilderness:
'Prepare the way of the
Lord,
make his paths straight.
5 Every valley shall be filled,
and every mountain and
hill shall be made low,
and the crooked shall be
made straight,
and the rough ways
made smooth;
6 and all flesh shall see the
salvation of God.'"

7 John said to the crowds that came out to be baptized by him, "You brood of vipers! Who warned you to flee from the wrath to come? [8]Bear fruits worthy of repentance. Do not begin to say to yourselves, 'We have Abraham as our ancestor'; for I tell you, God is able from these stones to raise up children to Abraham. [9]Even now the ax is lying at the root of the trees; every tree therefore that does not bear good fruit is cut down and thrown into the fire."

10 And the crowds asked him, "What then should we do?" [11]In reply he said to them, "Whoever has two coats must share with anyone who has none; and whoever has food must do likewise." [12]Even tax collectors came to be baptized, and they asked him, "Teacher, what should we do?" [13]He said to them, "Collect no more than the amount prescribed for you." [14]Soldiers also asked him, "And we, what should we do?" He said to them, "Do not extort money from anyone by threats or false accusation, and be satisfied with your wages."

15 As the people were filled with expectation, and all were questioning in their hearts concerning John, whether he might be the Messiah,[c] [16]John answered all of them by saying, "I baptize you with water; but one who is more powerful than I is coming; I am not worthy to untie the thong of his sandals. He will baptize you with[d] the Holy Spirit and fire. [17]His winnowing fork is in his hand, to clear his threshing floor and to gather the wheat into his granary; but the chaff he will burn with unquenchable fire."

18 So, with many other exhortations, he proclaimed the good news to the people. [19]But Herod

[a]Or in stature [b]Gk tetrarch [c]Or the Christ [d]Or in

the ruler, who had been rebuked by him because of Herodias, his brother's wife, and because of all the evil things that Herod had done, [20]added to them all by shutting up John in prison.

21 Now when all the people were baptized, and when Jesus also had been baptized and was praying, the heaven was opened, [22]and the Holy Spirit descended upon him in bodily form like a dove. And a voice came from heaven, "You are my Son, the Beloved;[a] with you I am well pleased."[b]

23 Jesus was about thirty years old when he began his work. He was the son (as was thought) of Joseph son of Heli, [24]son of Matthat, son of Levi, son of Melchi, son of Jannai, son of Joseph, [25]son of Mattathias, son of Amos, son of Nahum, son of Esli, son of Naggai, [26]son of Maath, son of Mattathias, son of Semein, son of Josech, son of Joda, [27]son of Joanan, son of Rhesa, son of Zerubbabel, son of Shealtiel,[c] son of Neri, [28]son of Melchi, son of Addi, son of Cosam, son of Elmadam, son of Er, [29]son of Joshua, son of Eliezer, son of Jorim, son of Matthat, son of Levi, [30]son of Simeon, son of Judah, son of Joseph, son of Jonam, son of Eliakim, [31]son of Melea, son of Menna, son of Mattatha, son of Nathan, son of David, [32]son of Jesse, son of Obed, son of Boaz, son of Sala,[d] son of Nahshon, [33]son of Amminadab, son of Admin, son of Arni,[e] son of Hezron, son of Perez, son of Judah, [34]son of Jacob, son of Isaac, son of Abraham, son of Terah, son of Nahor, [35]son of Serug, son of Reu, son of Peleg, son of Eber, son of Shelah, [36]son of Cainan, son of Arphaxad, son of Shem, son of Noah, son of Lamech, [37]son of Methuselah, son of Enoch, son of Jared, son of Mahalaleel, son of Cainan, [38]son of Enos, son of Seth, son of Adam, son of God.

4 Jesus, full of the Holy Spirit, returned from the Jordan and was led by the Spirit in the wilderness, [2]where for forty days he was tempted by the devil. He ate nothing at all during those days, and when they were over, he was famished. [3]The devil said to him, "If you are the Son of God, command this stone to become a loaf of bread." [4]Jesus answered him, "It is written, 'One does not live by bread alone.'"

5 Then the devil[f] led him up and showed him in an instant all the kingdoms of the world. [6]And the devil[f] said to him, "To you I will give their glory and all this authority; for it has been given over to me, and I give it to anyone I please. [7]If you, then, will worship me, it will all be yours." [8]Jesus answered him, "It is written,

[a]Or my beloved Son [b]Other ancient authorities read You are my Son, today I have begotten you [c]Gk Salathiel [d]Other ancient authorities read Salmon [e]Other ancient authorities read Amminadab, son of Aram; others vary widely [f]Gk he

'Worship the Lord your
　　　God,
　　and serve only him.'"

9 Then the devil took him to Jerusalem, and placed him on the pinnacle of the temple, saying to him, "If you are the Son of God, throw yourself down from here, [10]for it is written,

'He will command his
　　angels concerning you,
　to protect you,'

[11]and

'On their hands they will
　　bear you up,
　so that you will not dash
　　your foot against a
　　stone.'"

[12]Jesus answered him, "It is said, 'Do not put the Lord your God to the test.'" [13]When the devil had finished every test, he departed from him until an opportune time.

[14]Then Jesus, filled with the power of the Spirit, returned to Galilee, and a report about him spread through all the surrounding country. [15]He began to teach in their synagogues and was praised by everyone.

16 When he came to Nazareth, where he had been brought up, he went to the synagogue on the sabbath day, as was his custom. He stood up to read, [17]and the scroll of the prophet Isaiah was given to him. He unrolled the scroll and found the place where it was written:

[18]　"The Spirit of the Lord is
　　upon me,
　because he has anointed
　　me

to bring good news to
　　the poor.
He has sent me to proclaim
　　release to the captives
and recovery of sight to
　　the blind,
to let the oppressed go free,
[19] to proclaim the year of the
　　Lord's favor."

[20]And he rolled up the scroll, gave it back to the attendant, and sat down. The eyes of all in the synagogue were fixed on him. [21]Then he began to say to them, "Today this scripture has been fulfilled in your hearing." [22]All spoke well of him and were amazed at the gracious words that came from his mouth. They said, "Is not this Joseph's son?" [23]He said to them, "Doubtless you will quote to me this proverb, 'Doctor, cure yourself!' And you will say, 'Do here also in your hometown the things that we have heard you did at Capernaum.'" [24]And he said, "Truly I tell you, no prophet is accepted in the prophet's hometown. [25]But the truth is, there were many widows in Israel in the time of Elijah, when the heaven was shut up three years and six months, and a severe famine over all the land; [26]yet Elijah was sent to none of them except to a widow at Zarephath in Sidon. [27]There were also many lepers[a] in Israel in the time of the prophet Elisha, and none of them was cleansed

_____

[a]The terms _leper_ and _leprosy_ can refer to several diseases

except Naaman the Syrian." [28]When they heard this, all in the synagogue were filled with rage. [29]They got up, drove him out of the town, and led him to the brow of the hill on which their town was built, so that they might hurl him off the cliff. [30]But he passed through the midst of them and went on his way.

31 He went down to Capernaum, a city in Galilee, and was teaching them on the sabbath. [32]They were astounded at his teaching, because he spoke with authority. [33]In the synagogue there was a man who had the spirit of an unclean demon, and he cried out with a loud voice, [34]"Let us alone! What have you to do with us, Jesus of Nazareth? Have you come to destroy us? I know who you are, the Holy One of God." [35]But Jesus rebuked him, saying, "Be silent, and come out of him!" When the demon had thrown him down before them, he came out of him without having done him any harm. [36]They were all amazed and kept saying to one another, "What kind of utterance is this? For with authority and power he commands the unclean spirits, and out they come!" [37]And a report about him began to reach every place in the region.

38 After leaving the synagogue he entered Simon's house. Now Simon's mother-in-law was suffering from a high fever, and they asked him about her. [39]Then he stood over her and rebuked the fever, and it left her.

Immediately she got up and began to serve them.

40 As the sun was setting, all those who had any who were sick with various kinds of diseases brought them to him; and he laid his hands on each of them and cured them. [41]Demons also came out of many, shouting, "You are the Son of God!" But he rebuked them and would not allow them to speak, because they knew that he was the Messiah.[a]

42 At daybreak he departed and went into a deserted place. And the crowds were looking for him; and when they reached him, they wanted to prevent him from leaving them. [43]But he said to them, "I must proclaim the good news of the kingdom of God to the other cities also; for I was sent for this purpose." [44]So he continued proclaiming the message in the synagogues of Judea.[b]

5 Once while Jesus[c] was standing beside the lake of Gennesaret, and the crowd was pressing in on him to hear the word of God, [2]he saw two boats there at the shore of the lake; the fishermen had gone out of them and were washing their nets. [3]He got into one of the boats, the one belonging to Simon, and asked him to put out a little way from the shore. Then he sat down and taught the crowds from the boat. [4]When he had finished speaking, he said to Simon, "Put out into the deep water and let down your

[a]Or the Christ [b]Other ancient authorities read Galilee [c]Gk he

nets for a catch." [5]Simon answered, "Master, we have worked all night long but have caught nothing. Yet if you say so, I will let down the nets." [6]When they had done this, they caught so many fish that their nets were beginning to break. [7]So they signaled their partners in the other boat to come and help them. And they came and filled both boats, so that they began to sink. [8]But when Simon Peter saw it, he fell down at Jesus' knees, saying, "Go away from me, Lord, for I am a sinful man!" [9]For he and all who were with him were amazed at the catch of fish that they had taken; [10]and so also were James and John, sons of Zebedee, who were partners with Simon. Then Jesus said to Simon, "Do not be afraid; from now on you will be catching people." [11]When they had brought their boats to shore, they left everything and followed him.

12 Once, when he was in one of the cities, there was a man covered with leprosy.[a] When he saw Jesus, he bowed with his face to the ground and begged him, "Lord, if you choose, you can make me clean." [13]Then Jesus[b] stretched out his hand, touched him, and said, "I do choose. Be made clean." Immediately the leprosy[a] left him. [14]And he ordered him to tell no one. "Go," he said, "and show yourself to the priest, and, as Moses commanded, make an offering for your cleansing, for a testimony to them." [15]But now

more than ever the word about Jesus[c] spread abroad; many crowds would gather to hear him and to be cured of their diseases. [16]But he would withdraw to deserted places and pray.

17 One day, while he was teaching, Pharisees and teachers of the law were sitting near by (they had come from every village of Galilee and Judea and from Jerusalem); and the power of the Lord was with him to heal.[d] [18]Just then some men came, carrying a paralyzed man on a bed. They were trying to bring him in and lay him before Jesus;[c] [19]but finding no way to bring him in because of the crowd,[e] they went up on the roof and let him down with his bed through the tiles into the middle of the crowd[e] in front of Jesus. [20]When he saw their faith, he said, "Friend,[f] your sins are forgiven you." [21]Then the scribes and the Pharisees began to question, "Who is this who is speaking blasphemies? Who can forgive sins but God alone?" [22]When Jesus perceived their questionings, he answered them, "Why do you raise such questions in your hearts? [23]Which is easier, to say, 'Your sins are forgiven you,' or to say, 'Stand up and walk'? [24]But so that you may know that the Son of Man has authority on earth to forgive sins"—he said to the one who was paralyzed—"I

[a]The terms *leper* and *leprosy* can refer to several diseases [b]Gk *he* [c]Gk *him* [d]Other ancient authorities read *was present to heal them* [e]Gk *into the midst* [f]Gk *Man*

say to you, stand up and take your bed and go to your home." [25]Immediately he stood up before them, took what he had been lying on, and went to his home, glorifying God. [26]Amazement seized all of them, and they glorified God and were filled with awe, saying, "We have seen strange things today."

27 After this he went out and saw a tax collector named Levi, sitting at the tax booth; and he said to him, "Follow me." [28]And he got up, left everything, and followed him.

29 Then Levi gave a great banquet for him in his house; and there was a large crowd of tax collectors and others sitting at the table[a] with them. [30]The Pharisees and their scribes were complaining to his disciples, saying, "Why do you eat and drink with tax collectors and sinners?" [31]Jesus answered, "Those who are well have no need of a physician, but those who are sick; [32]I have come to call not the righteous but sinners to repentance."

33 Then they said to him, "John's disciples, like the disciples of the Pharisees, frequently fast and pray, but your disciples eat and drink." [34]Jesus said to them, "You cannot make wedding guests fast while the bridegroom is with them, can you? [35]The days will come when the bridegroom will be taken away from them, and then they will fast in those days." [36]He also told them a parable: "No one tears a piece from a new garment and sews it on an old garment; otherwise the new will be torn, and the piece from the new will not match the old. [37]And no one puts new wine into old wineskins; otherwise the new wine will burst the skins and will be spilled, and the skins will be destroyed. [38]But new wine must be put into fresh wineskins. [39]And no one after drinking old wine desires new wine, but says, 'The old is good.'"[b]

6 One sabbath[c] while Jesus[d] was going through the grainfields, his disciples plucked some heads of grain, rubbed them in their hands, and ate them. [2]But some of the Pharisees said, "Why are you doing what is not lawful[e] on the sabbath?" [3]Jesus answered, "Have you not read what David did when he and his companions were hungry? [4]He entered the house of God and took and ate the bread of the Presence, which it is not lawful for any but the priests to eat, and gave some to his companions?" [5]Then he said to them, "The Son of Man is lord of the sabbath."

6 On another sabbath he entered the synagogue and taught, and there was a man there whose right hand was withered. [7]The scribes and the Pharisees watched him to see whether he would cure on the sabbath, so that they might find

[a]Gk *reclining* [b]Other ancient authorities read *better;* others lack verse 39 [c]Other ancient authorities read *On the second first sabbath* [d]Gk *he* [e]Other ancient authorities add *to do*

an accusation against him. 8Even though he knew what they were thinking, he said to the man who had the withered hand, "Come and stand here." He got up and stood there. 9Then Jesus said to them, "I ask you, is it lawful to do good or to do harm on the sabbath, to save life or to destroy it?" 10After looking around at all of them, he said to him, "Stretch out your hand." He did so, and his hand was restored. 11But they were filled with fury and discussed with one another what they might do to Jesus.

12 Now during those days he went out to the mountain to pray; and he spent the night in prayer to God. 13And when day came, he called his disciples and chose twelve of them, whom he also named apostles: 14Simon, whom he named Peter, and his brother Andrew, and James, and John, and Philip, and Bartholomew, 15and Matthew, and Thomas, and James son of Alphaeus, and Simon, who was called the Zealot, 16and Judas son of James, and Judas Iscariot, who became a traitor.

17 He came down with them and stood on a level place, with a great crowd of his disciples and a great multitude of people from all Judea, Jerusalem, and the coast of Tyre and Sidon. 18They had come to hear him and to be healed of their diseases; and those who were troubled with unclean spirits were cured. 19And all in the crowd were trying to touch him, for power came out from him and healed all of them.

20 Then he looked up at his disciples and said:
"Blessed are you who are poor,
for yours is the kingdom of God.
21 "Blessed are you who are hungry now,
for you will be filled.
"Blessed are you who weep now,
for you will laugh.
22"Blessed are you when people hate you, and when they exclude you, revile you, and defame you[a] on account of the Son of Man. 23Rejoice in that day and leap for joy, for surely your reward is great in heaven; for that is what their ancestors did to the prophets.
24 "But woe to you who are rich,
for you have received your consolation.
25 "Woe to you who are full now,
for you will be hungry.
"Woe to you who are laughing now,
for you will mourn and weep.
26 "Woe to you when all speak well of you, for that is what their ancestors did to the false prophets.

27 "But I say to you that listen, Love your enemies, do good to those who hate you, 28bless those who curse you, pray for those who

[a]Gk cast out your name as evil

abuse you. [29]If anyone strikes you on the cheek, offer the other also; and from anyone who takes away your coat do not withhold even your shirt. [30]Give to everyone who begs from you; and if anyone takes away your goods, do not ask for them again. [31]Do to others as you would have them do to you.

[32] "If you love those who love you, what credit is that to you? For even sinners love those who love them. [33]If you do good to those who do good to you, what credit is that to you? For even sinners do the same. [34]If you lend to those from whom you hope to receive, what credit is that to you? Even sinners lend to sinners, to receive as much again. [35]But love your enemies, do good, and lend, expecting nothing in return.[a] Your reward will be great, and you will be children of the Most High; for he is kind to the ungrateful and the wicked. [36]Be merciful, just as your Father is merciful.

[37] "Do not judge, and you will not be judged; do not condemn, and you will not be condemned. Forgive, and you will be forgiven; [38]give, and it will be given to you. A good measure, pressed down, shaken together, running over, will be put into your lap; for the measure you give will be the measure you get back."

[39] He also told them a parable: "Can a blind person guide a blind person? Will not both fall into a pit? [40]A disciple is not above the teacher, but everyone who is fully qualified will be like the teacher. [41]Why do you see the speck in your neighbor's[b] eye, but do not notice the log in your own eye? [42]Or how can you say to your neighbor,[c] 'Friend,[c] let me take out the speck in your eye,' when you yourself do not see the log in your own eye? You hypocrite, first take the log out of your own eye, and then you will see clearly to take the speck out of your neighbor's[b] eye.

[43] "No good tree bears bad fruit, nor again does a bad tree bear good fruit; [44]for each tree is known by its own fruit. Figs are not gathered from thorns, nor are grapes picked from a bramble bush. [45]The good person out of the good treasure of the heart produces good, and the evil person out of evil treasure produces evil; for it is out of the abundance of the heart that the mouth speaks.

[46] "Why do you call me 'Lord, Lord,' and do not do what I tell you? [47]I will show you what someone is like who comes to me, hears my words, and acts on them. [48]That one is like a man building a house, who dug deeply and laid the foundation on rock; when a flood arose, the river burst against that house but could not shake it, because it had been well built.[d] [49]But the one who hears and does not act is like a man who built a house on

[a]Other ancient authorities read *despairing of no one* [b]Gk *brother's* [c]Gk *brother* [d]Other ancient authorities read *founded upon the rock*

the ground without a foundation. When the river burst against it, immediately it fell, and great was the ruin of that house."

7 After Jesus[a] had finished all his sayings in the hearing of the people, he entered Capernaum. [2]A centurion there had a slave whom he valued highly, and who was ill and close to death. [3]When he heard about Jesus, he sent some Jewish elders to him, asking him to come and heal his slave. [4]When they came to Jesus, they appealed to him earnestly, saying, "He is worthy of having you do this for him, [5]for he loves our people, and it is he who built our synagogue for us." [6]And Jesus went with them, but when he was not far from the house, the centurion sent friends to say to him, "Lord, do not trouble yourself, for I am not worthy to have you come under my roof; [7]therefore I did not presume to come to you. But only speak the word, and let my servant be healed. [8]For I also am a man set under authority, with soldiers under me; and I say to one, 'Go,' and he goes, and to another, 'Come,' and he comes, and to my slave, 'Do this,' and the slave does it." [9]When Jesus heard this he was amazed at him, and turning to the crowd that followed him, he said, "I tell you, not even in Israel have I found such faith." [10]When those who had been sent returned to the house, they found the slave in good health.

11 Soon afterwards[b] he went to a town called Nain, and his disciples and a large crowd went with him. [12]As he approached the gate of the town, a man who had died was being carried out. He was his mother's only son, and she was a widow; and with her was a large crowd from the town. [13]When the Lord saw her, he had compassion for her and said to her, "Do not weep." [14]Then he came forward and touched the bier, and the bearers stood still. And he said, "Young man, I say to you, rise!" [15]The dead man sat up and began to speak, and Jesus[a] gave him to his mother. [16]Fear seized all of them; and they glorified God, saying, "A great prophet has risen among us!" and "God has looked favorably on his people!" [17]This word about him spread throughout Judea and all the surrounding country.

18 The disciples of John reported all these things to him. So John summoned two of his disciples [19]and sent them to the Lord to ask, "Are you the one who is to come, or are we to wait for another?" [20]When the men had come to him, they said, "John the Baptist has sent us to you to ask, 'Are you the one who is to come, or are we to wait for another?'" [21]Jesus[c] had just then cured many people of diseases, plagues, and evil spirits, and had given sight to many who were blind. [22]And he answered them, "Go and tell John what you have

[a]Gk *he* [b]Other ancient authorities read *Next day* [c]Gk *He*

seen and heard: the blind receive their sight, the lame walk, the lepers[a] are cleansed, the deaf hear, the dead are raised, the poor have good news brought to them. [23]And blessed is anyone who takes no offense at me."

24 When John's messengers had gone, Jesus[b] began to speak to the crowds about John:[c] "What did you go out into the wilderness to look at? A reed shaken by the wind? [25]What then did you go out to see? Someone[d] dressed in soft robes? Look, those who put on fine clothing and live in luxury are in royal palaces. [26]What then did you go out to see? A prophet? Yes, I tell you, and more than a prophet. [27]This is the one about whom it is written,

'See, I am sending my
        messenger ahead of
        you,
who will prepare your way
        before you.'

[28]I tell you, among those born of women no one is greater than John; yet the least in the kingdom of God is greater than he." [29](And all the people who heard this, including the tax collectors, acknowledged the justice of God,[e] because they had been baptized with John's baptism. [30]But by refusing to be baptized by him, the Pharisees and the lawyers rejected God's purpose for themselves.)

31 "To what then will I compare the people of this generation, and what are they like? [32]They are like children sitting in the marketplace and calling to one another,

'We played the flute for
        you, and you did not
        dance;
we wailed, and you did
        not weep.'

[33]For John the Baptist has come eating no bread and drinking no wine, and you say, 'He has a demon'; [34]the Son of Man has come eating and drinking, and you say, 'Look, a glutton and a drunkard, a friend of tax collectors and sinners!' [35]Nevertheless, wisdom is vindicated by all her children."

36 One of the Pharisees asked Jesus[c] to eat with him, and he went into the Pharisee's house and took his place at the table. [37]And a woman in the city, who was a sinner, having learned that he was eating in the Pharisee's house, brought an alabaster jar of ointment. [38]She stood behind him at his feet, weeping, and began to bathe his feet with her tears and to dry them with her hair. Then she continued kissing his feet and anointing them with the ointment. [39]Now when the Pharisee who had invited him saw it, he said to himself, "If this man were a prophet, he would have known who and what kind of woman this is who is touching him—that she is a sinner." [40]Jesus spoke up and said to him, "Simon, I have something to say to you." "Teacher," he replied, "Speak." [41]A certain creditor had

---

[a]The terms *leper* and *leprosy* can refer to several diseases [b]Gk *he* [c]Gk *him* [d]Or *Why then did you go out? To see someone* [e]Or *praised God*

two debtors; one owed five hundred denarii,[a] and the other fifty. 42When they could not pay, he canceled the debts for both of them. Now which of them will love him more?" 43Simon answered, "I suppose the one for whom he canceled the greater debt." And Jesus said to him, "You have judged rightly." 44Then turning toward the woman, he said to Simon, "Do you see this woman? I entered your house; you gave me no water for my feet, but she has bathed my feet with her tears and dried them with her hair. 45You gave me no kiss, but from the time I came in she has not stopped kissing my feet. 46You did not anoint my head with oil, but she has anointed my feet with ointment. 47Therefore, I tell you, her sins, which were many, have been forgiven; hence she has shown great love. But the one to whom little is forgiven, loves little." 48Then he said to her, "Your sins are forgiven." 49But those who were at the table with him began to say among themselves, "Who is this who even forgives sins?" 50And he said to the woman, "Your faith has saved you; go in peace."

8 Soon afterwards he went on through cities and villages, proclaiming and bringing the good news of the kingdom of God. The twelve were with him, 2as well as some women who had been cured of evil spirits and infirmities: Mary, called Magdalene, from whom seven demons

had gone out, 3and Joanna, the wife of Herod's steward Chuza, and Susanna, and many others, who provided for them[b] out of their resources.

4 When a great crowd gathered and people from town after town came to him, he said in a parable: 5"A sower went out to sow his seed; and as he sowed, some fell on the path and was trampled on, and the birds of the air ate it up. 6Some fell on the rock; and as it grew up, it withered for lack of moisture. 7Some fell among thorns, and the thorns grew with it and choked it. 8Some fell into good soil, and when it grew, it produced a hundredfold." As he said this, he called out, "Let anyone with ears to hear listen!"

9 Then his disciples asked him what this parable meant. 10He said, "To you it has been given to know the secrets[c] of the kingdom of God; but to others I speak[d] in parables, so that

'looking they may not
perceive,
and listening they may
not understand.'

11 "Now the parable is this: The seed is the word of God. 12The ones on the path are those who have heard; then the devil comes and takes away the word from their hearts, so that they may not believe and be saved. 13The ones on the rock are those who, when they hear the word,

[a]The denarius was the usual day's wages for a laborer [b]Other ancient authorities read him [c]Or mysteries [d]Gk lacks I speak

receive it with joy. But these have no root; they believe only for a while and in a time of testing fall away. ¹⁴As for what fell among the thorns, these are the ones who hear; but as they go on their way, they are choked by the cares and riches and pleasures of life, and their fruit does not mature. ¹⁵But as for that in the good soil, these are the ones who, when they hear the word, hold it fast in an honest and good heart, and bear fruit with patient endurance.

16 "No one after lighting a lamp hides it under a jar, or puts it under a bed, but puts it on a lampstand, so that those who enter may see the light. ¹⁷For nothing is hidden that will not be disclosed, nor is anything secret that will not become known and come to light. ¹⁸Then pay attention to how you listen; for to those who have, more will be given; and from those who do not have, even what they seem to have will be taken away."

19 Then his mother and his brothers came to him, but they could not reach him because of the crowd. ²⁰And he was told, "Your mother and your brothers are standing outside, wanting to see you." ²¹But he said to them, "My mother and my brothers are those who hear the word of God and do it."

22 One day he got into a boat with his disciples, and he said to them, "Let us go across to the other side of the lake." So they put out, ²³and while they were sailing he fell asleep. A windstorm swept down on the lake, and the boat was filling with water, and they were in danger. ²⁴They went to him and woke him up, shouting, "Master, Master, we are perishing!" And he woke up and rebuked the wind and the raging waves; they ceased, and there was a calm. ²⁵He said to them, "Where is your faith?" They were afraid and amazed, and said to one another, "Who then is this, that he commands even the winds and the water, and they obey him?"

26 Then they arrived at the country of the Gerasenes,ᵃ which is opposite Galilee. ²⁷As he stepped out on land, a man of the city who had demons met him. For a long time he had wornᵇ no clothes, and he did not live in a house but in the tombs. ²⁸When he saw Jesus, he fell down before him and shouted at the top of his voice, "What have you to do with me, Jesus, Son of the Most High God? I beg you, do not torment me"— ²⁹for Jesusᶜ had commanded the unclean spirit to come out of the man. (For many times it had seized him; he was kept under guard and bound with chains and shackles, but he would break the bonds and be driven by the demon into the wilds.) ³⁰Jesus then asked him, "What is your name?" He said, "Legion"; for many demons had

---

ᵃOther ancient authorities read *Gadarenes;* others, *Gergesenes* ᵇOther ancient authorities read *a man of the city who had had demons for a long time met him. He wore* ᶜGk *he*

entered him. [31]They begged him not to order them to go back into the abyss.

32 Now there on the hillside a large herd of swine was feeding; and the demons[a] begged Jesus[b] to let them enter these. So he gave them permission. [33]Then the demons came out of the man and entered the swine, and the herd rushed down the steep bank into the lake and was drowned.

34 When the swineherds saw what had happened, they ran off and told it in the city and in the country. [35]Then people came out to see what had happened, and when they came to Jesus, they found the man from whom the demons had gone sitting at the feet of Jesus, clothed and in his right mind. And they were afraid. [36]Those who had seen it told them how the one who had been possessed by demons had been healed. [37]Then all the people of the surrounding country of the Gerasenes[c] asked Jesus[b] to leave them; for they were seized with great fear. So he got into the boat and returned. [38]The man from whom the demons had gone begged that he might be with him; but Jesus[d] sent him away, saying, [39]"Return to your home, and declare how much God has done for you." So he went away, proclaiming throughout the city how much Jesus had done for him.

40 Now when Jesus returned, the crowd welcomed him, for they were all waiting for him. [41]Just then there came a man named Jairus, a leader of the synagogue.

He fell at Jesus' feet and begged him to come to his house, [42]for he had an only daughter, about twelve years old, who was dying.

As he went, the crowds pressed in on him. [43]Now there was a woman who had been suffering from hemorrhages for twelve years; and though she had spent all she had on physicians,[e] no one could cure her. [44]She came up behind him and touched the fringe of his clothes, and immediately her hemorrhage stopped. [45]Then Jesus asked, "Who touched me?" When all denied it, Peter[f] said, "Master, the crowds surround you and press in on you." [46]But Jesus said, "Someone touched me; for I noticed that power had gone out from me." [47]When the woman saw that she could not remain hidden, she came trembling; and falling down before him, she declared in the presence of all the people why she had touched him, and how she had been immediately healed. [48]He said to her, "Daughter, your faith has made you well; go in peace."

49 While he was still speaking, someone came from the leader's house to say, "Your daughter is dead; do not trouble the teacher any longer." [50]When Jesus heard this, he replied, "Do not fear. Only believe, and she will be saved." [51]When he came

[a]Gk *they* [b]Gk *him* [c]Other ancient authorities read *Gadarenes;* others, *Gergesenes* [d]Gk *he* [e]Other ancient authorities lack *and though she had spent all she had on physicians* [f]Other ancient authorities add *and those who were with him*

to the house, he did not allow anyone to enter with him, except Peter, John, and James, and the child's father and mother. [52]They were all weeping and wailing for her; but he said, "Do not weep; for she is not dead but sleeping." [53]And they laughed at him, knowing that she was dead. [54]But he took her by the hand and called out, "Child, get up!" [55]Her spirit returned, and she got up at once. Then he directed them to give her something to eat. [56]Her parents were astounded; but he ordered them to tell no one what had happened.

9 Then Jesus[a] called the twelve together and gave them power and authority over all demons and to cure diseases, [2]and he sent them out to proclaim the kingdom of God and to heal. [3]He said to them, "Take nothing for your journey, no staff, nor bag, nor bread, nor money—not even an extra tunic. [4]Whatever house you enter, stay there, and leave from there. [5]Wherever they do not welcome you, as you are leaving that town shake the dust off your feet as a testimony against them." [6]They departed and went through the villages, bringing the good news and curing diseases everywhere.

7 Now Herod the ruler[b] heard about all that had taken place, and he was perplexed, because it was said by some that John had been raised from the dead, [8]by some that Elijah had appeared, and by others that one of the ancient prophets had arisen. [9]Herod said, "John I beheaded; but who is this about whom I hear such things?" And he tried to see him.

10 On their return the apostles told Jesus[c] all they had done. He took them with him and withdrew privately to a city called Bethsaida. [11]When the crowds found out about it, they followed him; and he welcomed them, and spoke to them about the kingdom of God, and healed those who needed to be cured.

12 The day was drawing to a close, and the twelve came to him and said, "Send the crowd away, so that they may go into the surrounding villages and countryside, to lodge and get provisions; for we are here in a deserted place." [13]But he said to them, "You give them something to eat." They said, "We have no more than five loaves and two fish—unless we are to go and buy food for all these people." [14]For there were about five thousand men. And he said to his disciples, "Make them sit down in groups of about fifty each." [15]They did so and made them all sit down. [16]And taking the five loaves and the two fish, he looked up to heaven, and blessed and broke them, and gave them to the disciples to set before the crowd. [17]And all ate and were filled. What was left over was gathered up, twelve baskets of broken pieces.

[a]Gk *he* [b]Gk *tetarch* [c]Gk *him*

18 Once when Jesus[a] was praying alone, with only the disciples near him, he asked them, "Who do the crowds say that I am?" [19]They answered, "John the Baptist; but others, Elijah; and still others, that one of the ancient prophets has arisen." [20]He said to them, "But who do you say that I am?" Peter answered, "The Messiah[b] of God."

21 He sternly ordered and commanded them not to tell anyone, [22]saying, "The Son of Man must undergo great suffering, and be rejected by the elders, chief priests, and scribes, and be killed, and on the third day be raised."

23 Then he said to them all, "If any want to become my followers, let them deny themselves and take up their cross daily and follow me. [24]For those who want to save their life will lose it, and those who lose their life for my sake will save it. [25]What does it profit them if they gain the whole world, but lose or forfeit themselves? [26]Those who are ashamed of me and of my words, of them the Son of Man will be ashamed when he comes in his glory and the glory of the Father and of the holy angels. [27]But truly I tell you, there are some standing here who will not taste death before they see the kingdom of God."

28 Now about eight days after these sayings Jesus[a] took with him Peter and John and James, and went up on the mountain to pray. [29]And while he was praying, the appearance of his face changed, and his clothes became dazzling white. [30]Suddenly they saw two men, Moses and Elijah, talking to him. [31]They appeared in glory and were speaking of his departure, which he was about to accomplish at Jerusalem. [32]Now Peter and his companions were weighed down with sleep; but since they had stayed awake,[c] they saw his glory and the two men who stood with him. [33]Just as they were leaving him, Peter said to Jesus, "Master, it is good for us to be here; let us make three dwellings,[d] one for you, one for Moses, and one for Elijah"—not knowing what he said. [34]While he was saying this, a cloud came and overshadowed them; and they were terrified as they entered the cloud. [35]Then from the cloud came a voice that said, "This is my Son, my Chosen;[e] listen to him!" [36]When the voice had spoken, Jesus was found alone. And they kept silent and in those days told no one any of the things they had seen.

37 On the next day, when they had come down from the mountain, a great crowd met him. [38]Just then a man from the crowd shouted, "Teacher, I beg you to look at my son; he is my only child. [39]Suddenly a spirit seizes him, and all at once he[f] shrieks. It convulses him until he foams at the mouth; it mauls him and will scarcely leave him. [40]I begged your

[a]Gk he [b]Or The Christ [c]Or but when they were fully awake [d]Or tents [e]Other ancient authorities read my Beloved [f]Or it

disciples to cast it out, but they could not." [41]Jesus answered, "You faithless and perverse generation, how much longer must I be with you and bear with you? Bring your son here." [42]While he was coming, the demon dashed him to the ground in convulsions. But Jesus rebuked the unclean spirit, healed the boy, and gave him back to his father. [43]And all were astounded at the greatness of God.

While everyone was amazed at all that he was doing, he said to his disciples, [44]"Let these words sink into your ears: The Son of Man is going to be betrayed into human hands." [45]But they did not understand this saying; its meaning was concealed from them, so that they could not perceive it. And they were afraid to ask him about this saying.

46 An argument arose among them as to which one of them was the greatest. [47]But Jesus, aware of their inner thoughts, took a little child and put it by his side, [48]and said to them, "Whoever welcomes this child in my name welcomes me, and whoever welcomes me welcomes the one who sent me; for the least among all of you is the greatest."

49 John answered, "Master, we saw someone casting out demons in your name, and we tried to stop him, because he does not follow with us." [50]But Jesus said to him, "Do not stop him; for whoever is not against you is for you."

51 When the days drew near for him to be taken up, he set his face to go to Jerusalem. [52]And he sent messengers ahead of him. On their way they entered a village of the Samaritans to make ready for him; [53]but they did not receive him, because his face was set toward Jerusalem. [54]When his disciples James and John saw it, they said, "Lord, do you want us to command fire to come down from heaven and consume them?"[a] [55]But he turned and rebuked them. [56]Then[b] they went on to another village.

57 As they were going along the road, someone said to him, "I will follow you wherever you go." [58]And Jesus said to him, "Foxes have holes, and birds of the air have nests; but the Son of Man has nowhere to lay his head." [59]To another he said, "Follow me." But he said, "Lord, first let me go and bury my father." [60]But Jesus[c] said to him, "Let the dead bury their own dead; but as for you, go and proclaim the kingdom of God." [61]Another said, "I will follow you, Lord; but let me first say farewell to those at my home." [62]Jesus said to him, "No one who puts a hand to the plow and looks back is fit for the kingdom of God."

10 After this the Lord appointed seventy[d] others and sent them on ahead of him in pairs to every town and place

---

[a]Other ancient authorities add *as Elijah did* [b]Other ancient authorities read *rebuked them, and said, "You do not know what spirit you are of,* [56]*for the Son of Man has not come to destroy the lives of human beings but to save them."* [c]Gk *he* [d]Other ancient authorities read *seventy-two*

where he himself intended to go. ²He said to them, "The harvest is plentiful, but the laborers are few; therefore ask the Lord of the harvest to send out laborers into his harvest. ³Go on your way. See, I am sending you out like lambs into the midst of wolves. ⁴Carry no purse, no bag, no sandals; and greet no one on the road. ⁵Whatever house you enter, first say, 'Peace to this house!' ⁶And if anyone is there who shares in peace, your peace will rest on that person; but if not, it will return to you. ⁷Remain in the same house, eating and drinking whatever they provide, for the laborer deserves to be paid. Do not move about from house to house. ⁸Whenever you enter a town and its people welcome you, eat what is set before you; ⁹cure the sick who are there, and say to them, 'The kingdom of God has come near to you.'ᵃ ¹⁰But whenever you enter a town and they do not welcome you, go out into its streets and say, ¹¹'Even the dust of your town that clings to our feet, we wipe off in protest against you. Yet know this: the kingdom of God has come near.'ᵇ ¹²I tell you, on that day it will be more tolerable for Sodom than for that town.

13 "Woe to you, Chorazin! Woe to you, Bethsaida! For if the deeds of power done in you had been done in Tyre and Sidon, they would have repented long ago, sitting in sackcloth and ashes. ¹⁴But at the judgment it will be more tolerable for Tyre and Sidon than for you. ¹⁵And you, Capernaum,

> will you be exalted to
> heaven?
> No, you will be brought
> down to Hades.

16 "Whoever listens to you listens to me, and whoever rejects you rejects me, and whoever rejects me rejects the one who sent me."

17 The seventyᶜ returned with joy, saying, "Lord, in your name even the demons submit to us!" ¹⁸He said to them, "I watched Satan fall from heaven like a flash of lightning. ¹⁹See, I have given you authority to tread on snakes and scorpions, and over all the power of the enemy; and nothing will hurt you. ²⁰Nevertheless, do not rejoice at this, that the spirits submit to you, but rejoice that your names are written in heaven."

21 At that same hour Jesusᵈ rejoiced in the Holy Spiritᵉ and said, "I thankᶠ you, Father, Lord of heaven and earth, because you have hidden these things from the wise and the intelligent and have revealed them to infants; yes, Father, for such was your gracious will.ᵍ ²²All things have been handed over to me by my Father; and no one knows who the Son is except the Father, or who the Father is except the Son and anyone to whom the Son chooses to reveal him."

ᵃOr *is at hand for you* ᵇOr *is at hand* ᶜOther ancient authorities read *seventy-two* ᵈGk *he* ᵉOther authorities read *in the spirit* ᶠOr *praise* ᵍOr *for so it was well-pleasing in your sight*

23 Then turning to the disciples, Jesus said to them privately, "Blessed are the eyes that see what you see! 24For I tell you that many prophets and kings desired to see what you see, but did not see it, and to hear what you hear, but did not hear it."

25 Just then a lawyer stood up to test Jesus.[a] "Teacher," he said, "what must I do to inherit eternal life?" 26He said to him, "What is written in the law? What do you read there?" 27He answered, "You shall love the Lord your God with all your heart, and with all your soul, and with all your strength, and with all your mind; and your neighbor as yourself." 28And he said to him, "You have given the right answer; do this, and you will live."

29 But wanting to justify himself, he asked Jesus, "And who is my neighbor?" 30Jesus replied, "A man was going down from Jerusalem to Jericho, and fell into the hands of robbers, who stripped him, beat him, and went away, leaving him half dead. 31Now by chance a priest was going down that road; and when he saw him, he passed by on the other side. 32So likewise a Levite, when he came to the place and saw him, passed by on the other side. 33But a Samaritan while traveling came near him; and when he saw him, he was moved with pity. 34He went to him and bandaged his wounds, having poured oil and wine on them. Then he put him on his own animal, brought him to an inn, and took care of him. 35The next day he took out two denarii,[b] gave them to the innkeeper, and said, 'Take care of him; and when I come back, I will repay you whatever more you spend.' 36Which of these three, do you think, was a neighbor to the man who fell into the hands of the robbers?" 37He said, "The one who showed him mercy." Jesus said to him, "Go and do likewise."

38 Now as they went on their way, he entered a certain village, where a woman named Martha welcomed him into her home. 39She had a sister named Mary, who sat at the Lord's feet and listened to what he was saying. 40But Martha was distracted by her many tasks; so she came to him and asked, "Lord, do you not care that my sister has left me to do all the work by myself? Tell her then to help me." 41But the Lord answered her, "Martha, Martha, you are worried and distracted by many things; 42there is need of only one thing.[c] Mary has chosen the better part, which will not be taken away from her."

11 He was praying in a certain place, and after he had finished, one of his disciples said to him, "Lord, teach us to pray, as John taught his disciples." 2He said to them, "When you pray, say:

---

[a]Gk him [b]The denarius was the usual day's wage for a laborer [c]Other ancient authorities read *few things are necessary, or only one*

Father,[a] hallowed be your
name.
Your kingdom come.[b]

3 Give us each day our
daily bread.[c]

4 And forgive us our sins,
for we ourselves
forgive everyone
indebted to us.
And do not bring us to
the time of trial."[d]

5 And he said to them, "Suppose one of you has a friend, and you go to him at midnight and say to him, 'Friend, lend me three loaves of bread; [6]for a friend of mine has arrived, and I have nothing to set before him.' [7]And he answers from within, 'Do not bother me; the door has already been locked, and my children are with me in bed; I cannot get up and give you anything.' [8]I tell you, even though he will not get up and give him anything because he is his friend, at least because of his persistence he will get up and give him whatever he needs.

9 "So I say to you, Ask, and it will be given you; search, and you will find; knock, and the door will be opened for you. [10]For everyone who asks receives, and everyone who searches finds, and for everyone who knocks, the door will be opened. [11]Is there anyone among you who, if your child asks for[e] a fish, will give a snake instead of a fish? [12]Or if the child asks for an egg, will give a scorpion? [13]If you then, who are evil, know how to give good gifts to your children, how much more will the heavenly Father give the Holy Spirit[f] to those who ask him!"

14 Now he was casting out a demon that was mute; when the demon had gone out, the one who had been mute spoke, and the crowds were amazed. [15]But some of them said, "He casts out demons by Beelzebul, the ruler of the demons." [16]Others, to test him, kept demanding from him a sign from heaven. [17]But he knew what they were thinking and said to them, "Every kingdom divided against itself becomes a desert, and house falls on house. [18]If Satan also is divided against himself, how will his kingdom stand? —for you say that I cast out the demons by Beelzebul. [19]Now if I cast out the demons by Beelzebul, by whom do your exorcists[g] cast them out? Therefore they will be your judges. [20]But if it is by the finger of God that I cast out the demons, then the kingdom of God has come to you. [21]When a strong man, fully armed, guards his castle, his property is safe. [22]But when one stronger than he attacks him and overpowers him, he takes away his armor in which he trusted and divides his plun-

[a]Other ancient authorities read *Our Father in heaven* [b]A few ancient authorities read *Your Holy Spirit come upon us and cleanse us.* Other ancient authorities add *Your will be done, on earth as in heaven* [c]Or *our bread for tomorrow* [d]Or *us into temptation.* Other ancient authorities add *but rescue us from the evil one (or from evil)* [e]Other ancient authorities add *bread, will give a stone; or if your child asks for* [f]Other ancient authorities read *the Father give the Holy Spirit from heaven* [g]Gk *sons*

der. [23]Whoever is not with me is against me, and whoever does not gather with me scatters.

24 "When the unclean spirit has gone out of a person, it wanders through waterless regions looking for a resting place, but not finding any, it says, 'I will return to my house from which I came.' [25]When it comes, it finds it swept and put in order. [26]Then it goes and brings seven other spirits more evil than itself, and they enter and live there; and the last state of that person is worse than the first."

27 While he was saying this, a woman in the crowd raised her voice and said to him, "Blessed is the womb that bore you and the breasts that nursed you!" [28]But he said, "Blessed rather are those who hear the word of God and obey it!"

29 When the crowds were increasing, he began to say, "This generation is an evil generation; it asks for a sign, but no sign will be given to it except the sign of Jonah. [30]For just as Jonah became a sign to the people of Nineveh, so the Son of Man will be to this generation. [31]The queen of the South will rise at the judgment with the people of this generation and condemn them, because she came from the ends of the earth to listen to the wisdom of Solomon, and see, something greater than Solomon is here! [32]The people of Nineveh will rise up at the judgment with this generation and condemn it, because they repented at the proclama-

tion of Jonah, and see, something greater than Jonah is here!

33 "No one after lighting a lamp puts it in a cellar,[a] but on the lampstand so that those who enter may see the light. [34]Your eye is the lamp of your body. If your eye is healthy, your whole body is full of light; but if it is not healthy, your body is full of darkness. [35]Therefore consider whether the light in you is not darkness. [36]If then your whole body is full of light, with no part of it in darkness, it will be as full of light as when a lamp gives you light with its rays."

37 While he was speaking, a Pharisee invited him to dine with him; so he went in and took his place at the table. [38]The Pharisee was amazed to see that he did not first wash before dinner. [39]Then the Lord said to him, "Now you Pharisees clean the outside of the cup and of the dish, but inside you are full of greed and wickedness. [40]You fools! Did not the one who made the outside make the inside also? [41]So give for alms those things that are within; and see, everything will be clean for you.

42 "But woe to you Pharisees! For you tithe mint and rue and herbs of all kinds, and neglect justice and the love of God; it is these you ought to have practiced, without neglecting the others. [43]Woe to you Pharisees! For you love to have the seat of honor

[a]Other ancient authorities add *or under the bushel basket*

103

in the synagogues and to be greeted with respect in the marketplaces. 44Woe to you! For you are like unmarked graves, and people walk over them without realizing it."

45 One of the lawyers answered him, "Teacher, when you say these things, you insult us too." 46And he said, "Woe also to you lawyers! For you load people with burdens hard to bear, and you yourselves do not lift a finger to ease them. 47Woe to you! For you build the tombs of the prophets whom your ancestors killed. 48So you are witnesses and approve of the deeds of your ancestors; for they killed them, and you build their tombs. 49Therefore also the Wisdom of God said, 'I will send them prophets and apostles, some of whom they will kill and persecute,' 50so that this generation may be charged with the blood of all the prophets shed since the foundation of the world, 51from the blood of Abel to the blood of Zechariah, who perished between the altar and the sanctuary. Yes, I tell you, it will be charged against this generation. 52Woe to you lawyers! For you have taken away the key of knowledge; you did not enter yourselves, and you hindered those who were entering."

53 When he went outside, the scribes and the Pharisees began to be very hostile toward him and to cross-examine him about many things, 54lying in wait for him, to catch him in something he might say.

12 Meanwhile, when the crowd gathered by the thousands, so that they trampled on one another, he began to speak first to his disciples, "Beware of the yeast of the Pharisees, that is, their hypocrisy. 2Nothing is covered up that will not be uncovered, and nothing secret that will not become known. 3Therefore whatever you have said in the dark will be heard in the light, and what you have whispered behind closed doors will be proclaimed from the housetops.

4 "I tell you, my friends, do not fear those who kill the body, and after that can do nothing more. 5But I will warn you whom to fear: fear him who, after he has killed, has authority[a] to cast into hell.[b] Yes, I tell you, fear him! 6Are not five sparrows sold for two pennies? Yet not one of them is forgotten in God's sight. 7But even the hairs of your head are all counted. Do not be afraid; you are of more value than many sparrows.

8 "And I tell you, everyone who acknowledges me before others, the Son of Man also will acknowledge before the angels of God; 9but whoever denies me before others will be denied before the angels of God. 10And everyone who speaks a word against the Son of Man will be forgiven; but whoever blasphemes against the Holy Spirit will not be forgiven. 11When they bring you before the synagogues,

[a]Or *power* [b]Gk *Gehenna*

the rulers, and the authorities, do not worry about how[a] you are to defend yourselves or what you are to say; [12]for the Holy Spirit will teach you at that very hour what you ought to say."

13 Someone in the crowd said to him, "Teacher, tell my brother to divide the family inheritance with me." [14]But he said to him, "Friend, who set me to be a judge or arbitrator over you?" [15]And he said to them, "Take care! Be on your guard against all kinds of greed; for one's life does not consist in the abundance of possessions." [16]Then he told them a parable: "The land of a rich man produced abundantly. [17]And he thought to himself, 'What should I do, for I have no place to store my crops?' [18]Then he said, 'I will do this: I will pull down my barns and build larger ones, and there I will store all my grain and my goods. [19]And I will say to my soul, 'Soul, you have ample goods laid up for many years; relax, eat, drink, be merry.' [20]But God said to him, 'You fool! This very night your life is being demanded of you. And the things you have prepared, whose will they be?' [21]So it is with those who store up treasures for themselves but are not rich toward God."

22 He said to his disciples, "Therefore I tell you, do not worry about your life, what you will eat, or about your body, what you will wear. [23]For life is more than food, and the body more than clothing. [24]Consider the ravens: they neither sow nor reap, they have neither storehouse nor barn, and yet God feeds them. Of how much more value are you than the birds! [25]And can any of you by worrying add a single hour to your span of life?[b] [26]If then you are not able to do so small a thing as that, why do you worry about the rest? [27]Consider the lilies, how they grow: they neither toil nor spin;[c] yet I tell you, even Solomon in all his glory was not clothed like one of these. [28]But if God so clothes the grass of the field, which is alive today and tomorrow is thrown into the oven, how much more will he clothe you—you of little faith! [29]And do not keep striving for what you are to eat and what you are to drink, and do not keep worrying. [30]For it is the nations of the world that strive after all these things, and your Father knows that you need them. [31]Instead, strive for his[d] kingdom, and these things will be given to you as well.

32 "Do not be afraid, little flock, for it is your Father's good pleasure to give you the kingdom. [33]Sell your possessions, and give alms. Make purses for yourselves that do not wear out, an unfailing treasure in heaven, where no thief comes near and no moth destroys. [34]For where your treasure is, there your heart will be also.

35 "Be dressed for action and have your lamps lit; [36]be like those

---

[a]Other ancient authorities add *or what* [b]Or *add a cubit to your stature* [c]Other ancient authorities read *Consider the lilies; they neither spin nor weave* [d]Other ancient authorities read *God's*

who are waiting for their master to return from the wedding banquet, so that they may open the door for him as soon as he comes and knocks. [37]Blessed are those slaves whom the master finds alert when he comes; truly I tell you, he will fasten his belt and have them sit down to eat, and he will come and serve them. [38]If he comes during the middle of the night, or near dawn, and finds them so, blessed are those slaves.

39 "But know this: if the owner of the house had known at what hour the thief was coming, he would[a] not have let his house be broken into. [40]You also must be ready, for the Son of Man is coming at an unexpected hour."

41 Peter said, "Lord, are you telling this parable for us or for everyone?" [42]And the Lord said, "Who then is the faithful and prudent manager whom his master will put in charge of his slaves, to give them their allowance of food at the proper time? [43]Blessed is that slave whom his master will find at work when he arrives. [44]Truly I tell you, he will put that one in charge of all his possessions. [45]But if that slave says to himself, 'My master is delayed in coming,' and if he begins to beat the other slaves, men and women, and to eat and drink and get drunk, [46]the master of that slave will come on a day when he does not expect him and at an hour that he does not know, and will cut him in pieces,[b] and put him with the unfaithful. [47]That slave who knew what his master wanted, but did not prepare himself or do what was wanted, will receive a severe beating. [48]But the one who did not know and did what deserved a beating will receive a light beating. From everyone to whom much has been given, much will be required; and from the one to whom much has been entrusted, even more will be demanded.

49 "I came to bring fire to the earth, and how I wish it were already kindled! [50]I have a baptism with which to be baptized, and what stress I am under until it is completed! [51]Do you think that I have come to bring peace to the earth? No, I tell you, but rather division! [52]From now on five in one household will be divided, three against two and two against three; [53]they will be divided:

> father against son
> and son against father,
> mother against daughter
> and daughter against
>   mother,
> mother-in-law against
>   her daughter-in-law
> and daughter-in-law against
>   mother-in-law."

54 He also said to the crowds, "When you see a cloud rising in the west, you immediately say, 'It is going to rain'; and so it happens. [55]And when you see the south wind blowing, you say, 'There will be scorching heat'; and

---

[a]Other ancient authorities add *would have watched* and [b]Or *cut him off*

it happens. [56]You hypocrites! You know how to interpret the appearance of earth and sky, but why do you not know how to interpret the present time?

57 "And why do you not judge for yourselves what is right? [58]Thus, when you go with your accuser before a magistrate, on the way make an effort to settle the case,[a] or you may be dragged before the judge, and the judge hand you over to the officer, and the officer throw you in prison. [59]I tell you, you will never get out until you have paid the very last penny."

13 At that very time there were some present who told him about the Galileans whose blood Pilate had mingled with their sacrifices. [2]He asked them, "Do you think that because these Galileans suffered in this way they were worse sinners than all other Galileans? [3]No, I tell you; but unless you repent, you will all perish as they did. [4]Or those eighteen who were killed when the tower of Siloam fell on them—do you think that they were worse offenders than all the others living in Jerusalem? [5]No, I tell you; but unless you repent, you will all perish just as they did."

6 Then he told this parable: "A man had a fig tree planted in his vineyard; and he came looking for fruit on it and found none. [7]So he said to the gardener, 'See here! For three years I have come looking for fruit on this fig tree, and still I find none. Cut it down!

Why should it be wasting the soil?' [8]He replied, 'Sir, let it alone for one more year, until I dig around it and put manure on it. [9]If it bears fruit next year, well and good; but if not, you can cut it down.'"

10 Now he was teaching in one of the synagogues on the sabbath. [11]And just then there appeared a woman with a spirit that had crippled her for eighteen years. She was bent over and was quite unable to stand up straight. [12]When Jesus saw her, he called her over and said, "Woman, you are set free from your ailment." [13]When he laid his hands on her, immediately she stood up straight and began praising God. [14]But the leader of the synagogue, indignant because Jesus had cured on the sabbath, kept saying to the crowd, "There are six days on which work ought to be done; come on those days and be cured, and not on the sabbath day." [15]But the Lord answered him and said, "You hypocrites! Does not each of you on the sabbath untie his ox or his donkey from the manger, and lead it away to give it water? [16]And ought not this woman, a daughter of Abraham whom Satan bound for eighteen long years, be set free from this bondage on the sabbath day?" [17]When he said this, all his opponents were put to shame; and the entire crowd was rejoicing at all the wonderful things that he was doing.

[a]Gk settle with him

18 He said therefore, "What is the kingdom of God like? And to what should I compare it? ¹⁹It is like a mustard seed that someone took and sowed in the garden; it grew and became a tree, and the birds of the air made nests in its branches."

20 And again he said, "To what should I compare the kingdom of God? ²¹It is like yeast that a woman took and mixed in with^a three measures of flour until all of it was leavened."

22 Jesus^b went through one town and village after another, teaching as he made his way to Jerusalem. ²³Someone asked him, "Lord, will only a few be saved?" He said to them, ²⁴"Strive to enter through the narrow door; for many, I tell you, will try to enter and will not be able. ²⁵When once the owner of the house has got up and shut the door, and you begin to stand outside and to knock at the door, saying, 'Lord, open to us,' then in reply he will say to you, 'I do not know where you come from.' ²⁶Then you will begin to say, 'We ate and drank with you, and you taught in our streets.' ²⁷But he will say, 'I do not know where you come from; go away from me, all you evildoers!' ²⁸There will be weeping and gnashing of teeth when you see Abraham and Isaac and Jacob and all the prophets in the kingdom of God, and you yourselves thrown out. ²⁹Then people will come from east and west, from north and south, and will eat in the king-

dom of God. ³⁰Indeed, some are last who will be first, and some are first who will be last."

31 At that very hour some Pharisees came and said to him, "Get away from here, for Herod wants to kill you." ³²He said to them, "Go and tell that fox for me,^c 'Listen, I am casting out demons and performing cures today and tomorrow, and on the third day I finish my work. ³³Yet today, tomorrow, and the next day I must be on my way, because it is impossible for a prophet to be killed outside of Jerusalem.' ³⁴Jerusalem, Jerusalem, the city that kills the prophets and stones those who are sent to it! How often have I desired to gather your children together as a hen gathers her brood under her wings, and you were not willing! ³⁵See, your house is left to you. And I tell you, you will not see me until the time comes when^d you say, 'Blessed is the one who comes in the name of the Lord.'"

14 On one occasion when Jesus^e was going to the house of a leader of the Pharisees to eat a meal on the sabbath, they were watching him closely. ²Just then, in front of him, there was a man who had dropsy. ³And Jesus asked the lawyers and Pharisees, "Is it lawful to cure people on the sabbath, or not?" ⁴But they were silent. So Jesus^e took him and healed him, and sent him away. ⁵Then he said to them, "If one of

^aGk *hid in* ^bGk *He* ^cGk lacks *for me* ^dOther ancient authorities lack *the time comes when* ^eGk *he*

108

you has a child[a] or an ox that has fallen into a well, will you not immediately pull it out on a sabbath day?" 6And they could not reply to this.

7 When he noticed how the guests chose the places of honor, he told them a parable. 8"When you are invited by someone to a wedding banquet, do not sit down at the place of honor, in case someone more distinguished than you has been invited by your host; 9and the host who invited both of you may come and say to you, 'Give this person your place,' and then in disgrace you would start to take the lowest place. 10But when you are invited, go and sit down at the lowest place, so that when your host comes, he may say to you, 'Friend, move up higher'; then you will be honored in the presence of all who sit at the table with you. 11For all who exalt themselves will be humbled, and those who humble themselves will be exalted."

12 He said also to the one who had invited him, "When you give a luncheon or a dinner, do not invite your friends or your brothers or your relatives or rich neighbors, in case they may invite you in return, and you would be repaid. 13But when you give a banquet, invite the poor, the crippled, the lame, and the blind. 14And you will be blessed, because they cannot repay you, for you will be repaid at the resurrection of the righteous."

15 One of the dinner guests, on hearing this, said to him,

"Blessed is anyone who will eat bread in the kingdom of God!" 16Then Jesus[b] said to him, "Someone gave a great dinner and invited many. 17At the time for the dinner he sent his slave to say to those who had been invited, 'Come; for everything is ready now.' 18But they all alike began to make excuses. The first said to him, 'I have bought a piece of land, and I must go out and see it; please accept my regrets.' 19Another said, 'I have bought five yoke of oxen, and I am going to try them out; please accept my regrets.' 20Another said, 'I have just been married, and therefore I cannot come.' 21So the slave returned and reported this to his master. Then the owner of the house became angry and said to his slave, 'Go out at once into the streets and lanes of the town and bring in the poor, the crippled, the blind, and the lame.' 22And the slave said, 'Sir, what you ordered has been done, and there is still room.' 23Then the master said to the slave, 'Go out into the roads and lanes, and compel people to come in, so that my house may be filled. 24For I tell you,[c] none of those who were invited will taste my dinner.'"

25 Now large crowds were traveling with him; and he turned and said to them, 26"Whoever comes to me and does not hate father and mother, wife and

[a]Other ancient authorities read *a donkey* [b]Gk *he* [c]The Greek word for *you* here is plural

109

children, brothers and sisters, yes, and even life itself, cannot be my disciple. [27]Whoever does not carry the cross and follow me cannot be my disciple. [28]For which of you, intending to build a tower, does not first sit down and estimate the cost, to see whether he has enough to complete it? [29]Otherwise, when he has laid a foundation and is not able to finish, all who see it will begin to ridicule him, [30]saying, 'This fellow began to build and was not able to finish.' [31]Or what king, going out to wage war against another king, will not sit down first and consider whether he is able with ten thousand to oppose the one who comes against him with twenty thousand? [32]If he cannot, then, while the other is still far away, he sends a delegation and asks for the terms of peace. [33]So therefore, none of you can become my disciple if you do not give up all your possessions.

34 "Salt is good; but if salt has lost its taste, how can its saltiness be restored?[a] [35]It is fit neither for the soil nor for the manure pile; they throw it away. Let anyone with ears to hear listen!"

15 Now all the tax collectors and sinners were coming near to listen to him. [2]And the Pharisees and the scribes were grumbling and saying, "This fellow welcomes sinners and eats with them."

3 So he told them this parable: [4]"Which one of you, having a hundred sheep and losing one of them, does not leave the ninety-nine in the wilderness and go after the one that is lost until he finds it? [5]When he has found it, he lays it on his shoulders and rejoices. [6]And when he comes home, he calls together his friends and neighbors, saying to them, 'Rejoice with me, for I have found my sheep that was lost.' [7]Just so, I tell you, there will be more joy in heaven over one sinner who repents than over ninety-nine righteous persons who need no repentance.

8 "Or what woman having ten silver coins,[b] if she loses one of them, does not light a lamp, sweep the house, and search carefully until she finds it? [9]When she has found it, she calls together her friends and neighbors, saying, 'Rejoice with me, for I have found the coin that I had lost.' [10]Just so, I tell you, there is joy in the presence of the angels of God over one sinner who repents."

11 Then Jesus[c] said, "There was a man who had two sons. [12]The younger of them said to his father, 'Father, give me the share of the property that will belong to me.' So he divided his property between them. [13]A few days later the younger son gathered all he had and traveled to a distant country, and there he squandered his property in dissolute living. [14]When he had spent everything, a severe famine took place throughout that country, and

[a]Or how can it be used for seasoning? [b]Gk drachmas, each worth about a day's wage for a laborer [c]Gk he

he began to be in need. [15]So he went and hired himself out to one of the citizens of that country, who sent him to his fields to feed the pigs. [16]He would gladly have filled himself with[a] the pods that the pigs were eating; and no one gave him anything. [17]But when he came to himself he said, 'How many of my father's hired hands have bread enough and to spare, but here I am dying of hunger! [18]I will get up and go to my father, and I will say to him, "Father, I have sinned against heaven and before you; [19]I am no longer worthy to be called your son; treat me like one of your hired hands."' [20]So he set off and went to his father. But while he was still far off, his father saw him and was filled with compassion; he ran and put his arms around him and kissed him. [21]Then the son said to him, 'Father, I have sinned against heaven and before you; I am no longer worthy to be called your son.'[b] [22]But the father said to his slaves, 'Quickly, bring out a robe—the best one—and put it on him; put a ring on his finger and sandals on his feet. [23]And get the fatted calf and kill it, and let us eat and celebrate; [24]for this son of mine was dead and is alive again; he was lost and is found!' And they began to celebrate.

[25] "Now his elder son was in the field; and when he came and approached the house, he heard music and dancing. [26]He called one of the slaves and asked what was going on. [27]He replied, 'Your brother has come, and your father has killed the fatted calf, because he has got him back safe and sound.' [28]Then he became angry and refused to go in. His father came out and began to plead with him. [29]But he answered his father, 'Listen! For all these years I have been working like a slave for you, and I have never disobeyed your command; yet you have never given me even a young goat so that I might celebrate with my friends. [30]But when this son of yours came back, who has devoured your property with prostitutes, you killed the fatted calf for him!' [31]Then the father said to him, 'Son, you are always with me, and all that is mine is yours. [32]But we had to celebrate and rejoice, because this brother of yours was dead and has come to life; he was lost and has been found.'"

16

Then Jesus[c] said to the disciples, "There was a rich man who had a manager, and charges were brought to him that this man was squandering his property. [2]So he summoned him and said to him, 'What is this that I hear about you? Give me an accounting of your management, because you cannot be my manager any longer.' [3]Then the manager said to himself, 'What will I do, now that my master is taking the position away from me? I am not strong enough

---

[a]Other ancient authorities read *filled his stomach with*
[b]Other ancient authorities add *Treat me like one of your hired servants* [c]Gk *he*

to dig, and I am ashamed to beg. ⁴I have decided what to do so that, when I am dismissed as manager, people may welcome me into their homes.' ⁵So , summoning his master's debtors one by one, he asked the first, 'How much do you owe my master?' ⁶He answered, 'A hundred jugs of olive oil.' He said to him, 'Take your bill, sit down quickly, and make it fifty.' ⁷Then he asked another, 'And how much do you owe?' He replied, 'A hundred containers of wheat.' He said to him, 'Take your bill and make it eighty.' ⁸And his master commended the dishonest manager because he had acted shrewdly; for the children of this age are more shrewd in dealing with their own generation than are the children of light. ⁹And I tell you, make friends for yourselves by means of dishonest wealthᵃ so that when it is gone, they may welcome you into the eternal homes.ᵇ

10 "Whoever is faithful in a very little is faithful also in much; and whoever is dishonest in a very little is dishonest also in much. ¹¹If then you have not been faithful with the dishonest wealth,ᵃ who will entrust to you the true riches? ¹²And if you have not been faithful with what belongs to another, who will give you what is your own? ¹³No slave can serve two masters; for a slave will either hate the one and love the other, or be devoted to the one and despise the other. You cannot serve God and wealth."ᵃ

14 The Pharisees, who were lovers of money, heard all this, and they ridiculed him. ¹⁵So he said to them, "You are those who justify yourselves in the sight of others; but God knows your hearts; for what is prized by human beings is an abomination in the sight of God.

16 "The law and the prophets were in effect until John came; since then the good news of the kingdom of God is proclaimed, and everyone tries to enter it by force.ᶜ ¹⁷But it is easier for heaven and earth to pass away, than for one stroke of a letter in the law to be dropped.

18 "Anyone who divorces his wife and marries another commits adultery, and whoever marries a woman divorced from her husband commits adultery.

19 "There was a rich man who was dressed in purple and fine linen and who feasted sumptuously every day. ²⁰And at his gate lay a poor man named Lazarus, covered with sores, ²¹who longed to satisfy his hunger with what fell from the rich man's table; even the dogs would come and lick his sores. ²²The poor man died and was carried away by the angels to be with Abraham.ᵈ The rich man also died and was buried. ²³In Hades, where he was being tormented, he looked up and saw Abraham far away with Lazarus by his side.ᵉ ²⁴He called out, 'Father Abraham, have mercy

ᵃGk mammon ᵇGk tents ᶜOr everyone is strongly urged to enter it ᵈGk to Abraham's bosom ᵉGk in his bosom

on me, and send Lazarus to dip the tip of his finger in water and cool my tongue; for I am in agony in these flames.' [25]But Abraham said, 'Child, remember that during your lifetime you received your good things, and Lazarus in like manner evil things; but now he is comforted here, and you are in agony. [26]Besides all this, between you and us a great chasm has been fixed, so that those who might want to pass from here to you cannot do so, and no one can cross from there to us.' [27]He said, 'Then, father, I beg you to send him to my father's house— [28]for I have five brothers—that he may warn them, so that they will not also come into this place of torment.' [29]Abraham replied, 'They have Moses and the prophets; they should listen to them.' [30]He said, 'No, father Abraham; but if someone goes to them from the dead, they will repent.' [31]He said to him, 'If they do not listen to Moses and the prophets, neither will they be convinced even if someone rises from the dead.'"

17 Jesus[a] said to his disciples, "Occasions for stumbling are bound to come, but woe to anyone by whom they come! [2]It would be better for you if a millstone were hung around your neck and you were thrown into the sea than for you to cause one of these little ones to stumble. [3]Be on your guard! If another disciple[b] sins, you must rebuke the offender, and if there is repentance, you must forgive. [4]And if

the same person sins against you seven times a day, and turns back to you seven times and says, 'I repent,' you must forgive."

5 The apostles said to the Lord, "Increase our faith!" [6]The Lord replied, "If you had faith the size of a[c] mustard seed, you could say to this mulberry tree, 'Be uprooted and planted in the sea,' and it would obey you.

7 "Who among you would say to your slave who has just come in from plowing or tending sheep in the field, 'Come here at once and take your place at the table'? [8]Would you not rather say to him, 'Prepare supper for me, put on your apron and serve me while I eat and drink; later you may eat and drink'? [9]Do you thank the slave for doing what was commanded? [10]So you also, when you have done all that you were ordered to do, say, 'We are worthless slaves; we have done only what we ought to have done!'"

11 On the way to Jerusalem Jesus[d] was going through the region between Samaria and Galilee. [12]As he entered a village, ten lepers[e] approached him. Keeping their distance, [13]they called out, saying, "Jesus, Master, have mercy on us!" [14]When he saw them, he said to them, "Go and show yourselves to the priests." And as they went, they were made clean. [15]Then one of them, when he saw that he was healed, turned back, praising God

---

[a]Gk He [b]Gk your brother [c]Gk faith as a grain of [d]Gk he [e]The terms leper and leprosy can refer to several diseases

with a loud voice. [16]He prostrated himself at Jesus'[a] feet and thanked him. And he was a Samaritan. [17]Then Jesus asked, "Were not ten made clean? But the other nine, where are they? [18]Was none of them found to return and give praise to God except this foreigner?" [19]Then he said to him, "Get up and go on your way; your faith has made you well."

20 Once Jesus was asked by the Pharisees when the kingdom of God was coming, and he answered, "The kingdom of God is not coming with things that can be observed; [21]nor will they say, 'Look, here it is!' or 'There it is!' For, in fact, the kingdom of God is among[b] you."

22 Then he said to the disciples, "The days are coming when you will long to see one of the days of the Son of Man, and you will not see it. [23]They will say to you, 'Look there!' or 'Look here!' Do not go, do not set off in pursuit. [24]For as the lightning flashes and lights up the sky from one side to the other, so will the Son of Man be in his day.[c] [25]But first he must endure much suffering and be rejected by this generation. [26]Just as it was in the days of Noah, so too it will be in the days of the Son of Man. [27]They were eating and drinking, and marrying and being given in marriage, until the day Noah entered the ark, and the flood came and destroyed all of them. [28]Likewise, just as it was in the days of Lot: they were eating and drinking, buying and selling, planting and building, [29]but on the day that Lot left Sodom, it rained fire and sulfur from heaven and destroyed all of them [30]—it will be like that on the day that the Son of Man is revealed. [31]On that day, anyone on the housetop who has belongings in the house must not come down to take them away; and likewise anyone in the field must not turn back. [32]Remember Lot's wife. [33]Those who try to make their life secure will lose it, but those who lose their life will keep it. [34]I tell you, on that night there will be two in one bed; one will be taken and the other left. [35]There will be two women grinding meal together; one will be taken and the other left."[d] [37]Then they asked him, "Where, Lord?" He said to them, "Where the corpse is, there the vultures will gather."

18

Then Jesus[e] told them a parable about their need to pray always and not to lose heart. [2]He said, "In a certain city there was a judge who neither feared God nor had respect for people. [3]In that city there was a widow who kept coming to him and saying, 'Grant me justice against my opponent.' [4]For a while he refused; but later he said to himself, 'Though I have no fear of God and no respect for anyone, [5]yet because this widow keeps bothering me, I will grant her justice, so that she may not wear me

---

[a]Gk *his* [b]Or *within* [c]Other ancient authorities lack *in his day* [d]Other ancient authorities add verse 36, *"Two will be in the field; one will be taken and the other left."* [e]Gk *he*

out by continually coming.'"[a] [6]And the Lord said, "Listen to what the unjust judge says. [7]And will not God grant justice to his chosen ones who cry to him day and night? Will he delay long in helping them? [8]I tell you, he will quickly grant justice to them. And yet, when the Son of Man comes, will he find faith on earth?"

[9] He also told this parable to some who trusted in themselves that they were righteous and regarded others with contempt: [10]"Two men went up to the temple to pray, one a Pharisee and the other a tax collector. [11]The Pharisee, standing by himself, was praying thus, 'God, I thank you that I am not like other people: thieves, rogues, adulterers, or even like this tax collector. [12]I fast twice a week; I give a tenth of all my income.' [13]But the tax collector, standing far off, would not even look up to heaven, but was beating his breast and saying, 'God, be merciful to me, a sinner!' [14]I tell you, this man went down to his home justified rather than the other; for all who exalt themselves will be humbled, but all who humble themselves will be exalted."

[15] People were bringing even infants to him that he might touch them; and when the disciples saw it, they sternly ordered them not to do it. [16]But Jesus called for them and said, "Let the little children come to me, and do not stop them; for it is to such as these that the kingdom of God belongs. [17]Truly I tell you, whoever does not receive the kingdom of God as a little child will never enter it."

[18] A certain ruler asked him, "Good Teacher, what must I do to inherit eternal life?" [19]Jesus said to him, "Why do you call me good? No one is good but God alone. [20]You know the commandments: 'You shall not commit adultery; You shall not murder; You shall not steal; You shall not bear false witness; Honor your father and mother.'" [21]He replied, "I have kept all these since my youth." [22]When Jesus heard this, he said to him, "There is still one thing lacking. Sell all that you own and distribute the money[b] to the poor, and you will have treasure in heaven; then come, follow me." [23]But when he heard this, he became sad; for he was very rich. [24]Jesus looked at him and said, "How hard it is for those who have wealth to enter the kingdom of God! [25]Indeed, it is easier for a camel to go through the eye of a needle than for someone who is rich to enter the kingdom of God."

[26] Those who heard it said, "Then who can be saved?" [27]He replied, "What is impossible for mortals is possible for God."

[28] Then Peter said, "Look, we have left our homes and followed you." [29]And he said to them, "Truly I tell you, there is no one who has left house or wife or brothers or parents or children, for the sake of the kingdom of God,

---

[a]Or *so that she may not finally come and slap me in the face* [b]Gk lacks *the money*

[30]who will not get back very much more in this age, and in the age to come eternal life."

31 Then he took the twelve aside and said to them, "See, we are going up to Jerusalem, and everything that is written about the Son of Man by the prophets will be accomplished. [32]For he will be handed over to the Gentiles; and he will be mocked and insulted and spat upon. [33]After they have flogged him, they will kill him, and on the third day he will rise again." [34]But they understood nothing about all these things; in fact, what he said was hidden from them, and they did not grasp what was said.

35 As he approached Jericho, a blind man was sitting by the roadside begging. [36]When he heard a crowd going by, he asked what was happening. [37]They told him, "Jesus of Nazareth[a] is passing by." [38]Then he shouted, "Jesus, Son of David, have mercy on me!" [39]Those who were in front sternly ordered him to be quiet; but he shouted even more loudly, "Son of David, have mercy on me!" [40]Jesus stood still and ordered the man to be brought to him; and when he came near, he asked him, [41]"What do you want me to do for you?" He said, "Lord, let me see again." [42]Jesus said to him, "Receive your sight; your faith has saved you." [43]Immediately he regained his sight and followed him, glorifying God; and all the people, when they saw it, praised God.

19 He entered Jericho and was passing through it. [2]A man was there named Zacchaeus; he was a chief tax collector and was rich. [3]He was trying to see who Jesus was, but on account of the crowd he could not, because he was short in stature. [4]So he ran ahead and climbed a sycamore tree to see him, because he was going to pass that way. [5]When Jesus came to the place, he looked up and said to him, "Zacchaeus, hurry and come down; for I must stay at your house today." [6]So he hurried down and was happy to welcome him. [7]All who saw it began to grumble and said, "He has gone to be the guest of one who is a sinner." [8]Zacchaeus stood there and said to the Lord, "Look, half of my possessions, Lord, I will give to the poor; and if I have defrauded anyone of anything, I will pay back four times as much." [9]Then Jesus said to him, "Today salvation has come to this house, because he too is a son of Abraham. [10]For the Son of Man came to seek out and to save the lost."

11 As they were listening to this, he went on to tell a parable, because he was near Jerusalem, and because they supposed that the kingdom of God was to appear immediately. [12]So he said, "A nobleman went to a distant country to get royal power for himself and then return. [13]He summoned ten of his slaves, and

[a]Gk the Nazorean

116

gave them ten pounds,[a] and said to them, 'Do business with these until I come back.' [14]But the citizens of his country hated him and sent a delegation after him, saying, 'We do not want this man to rule over us.' [15]When he returned, having received royal power, he ordered these slaves, to whom he had given the money, to be summoned so that he might find out what they had gained by trading. [16]The first came forward and said, 'Lord, your pound has made ten more pounds.' [17]He said to him, 'Well done, good slave! Because you have been trustworthy in a very small thing, take charge of ten cities.' [18]Then the second came, saying, 'Lord, your pound has made five pounds.' [19]He said to him, 'And you, rule over five cities.' [20]Then the other came, saying, 'Lord, here is your pound. I wrapped it up in a piece of cloth, [21]for I was afraid of you, because you are a harsh man; you take what you did not deposit, and reap what you did not sow.' [22]He said to him, 'I will judge you by your own words, you wicked slave! You knew, did you, that I was a harsh man, taking what I did not deposit and reaping what I did not sow? [23]Why then did you not put my money into the bank? Then when I returned, I could have collected it with interest.' [24]He said to the bystanders, 'Take the pound from him and give it to the one who has ten pounds.' [25](And they said to him, 'Lord, he has ten pounds!') [26]'I tell you, to all those who have, more will be given; but from those who have nothing, even what they have will be taken away. [27]But as for these enemies of mine who did not want me to be king over them—bring them here and slaughter them in my presence.'"

28 After he had said this, he went on ahead, going up to Jerusalem.

29 When he had come near Bethphage and Bethany, at the place called the Mount of Olives, he sent two of the disciples, [30]saying, "Go into the village ahead of you, and as you enter it you will find tied there a colt that has never been ridden. Untie it and bring it here. [31]If anyone asks you, 'Why are you untying it?' just say this, 'The Lord needs it.'" [32]So those who were sent departed and found it as he had told them. [33]As they were untying the colt, its owners asked them, "Why are you untying the colt?" [34]They said, "The Lord needs it." [35]Then they brought it to Jesus; and after throwing their cloaks on the colt, they set Jesus on it. [36]As he rode along, people kept spreading their cloaks on the road. [37]As he was now approaching the path down from the Mount of Olives, the whole multitude of the disciples began to praise God joyfully with a loud voice for all the deeds of power that they had seen, [38]saying,

[a]The mina, rendered here by *pound*, was about three months' wages for a laborer

"Blessed is the king
who comes in the name
of the Lord!
Peace in heaven,
and glory in the highest
heaven!"

39Some of the Pharisees in the crowd said to him, "Teacher, order your disciples to stop." 40He answered, "I tell you, if these were silent, the stones would shout out."

41 As he came near and saw the city, he wept over it, 42saying, "If you, even you, had only recognized on this day the things that make for peace! But now they are hidden from your eyes. 43Indeed, the days will come upon you, when your enemies will set up ramparts around you and surround you, and hem you in on every side. 44They will crush you to the ground, you and your children within you, and they will not leave within you one stone upon another; because you did not recognize the time of your visitation from God."a

45 Then he entered the temple and began to drive out those who were selling things there; 46and he said, "It is written,

'My house shall be a house
of prayer';

but you have made it a
den of robbers."

47 Every day he was teaching in the temple. The chief priests, the scribes, and the leaders of the people kept looking for a way to kill him; 48but they did not find anything they could do, for all the people were spellbound by what they heard.

20 One day, as he was teaching the people in the temple and telling the good news, the chief priests and the scribes came with the elders 2and said to him, "Tell us, by what authority are you doing these things? Who is it who gave you this authority?" 3He answered them, "I will also ask you a question, and you tell me: 4Did the baptism of John come from heaven, or was it of human origin?" 5They discussed it with one another, saying, "If we say, 'From heaven,' he will say, 'Why did you not believe him?' 6But if we say, 'Of human origin,' all the people will stone us; for they are convinced that John was a prophet." 7So they answered that they did not know where it came from. 8Then Jesus said to them, "Neither will I tell you by what authority I am doing these things."

9 He began to tell the people this parable: "A man planted a vineyard, and leased it to tenants, and went to another country for a long time. 10When the season came, he sent a slave to the tenants in order that they might give him his share of the produce of the vineyard; but the tenants beat him and sent him away empty-handed. 11Next he sent another slave; that one also they beat and insulted and sent away empty-handed. 12And he sent still a third; this one also they wounded and threw out. 13Then the owner of the vineyard

a Gk lacks *from God*

said, 'What shall I do? I will send my beloved son; perhaps they will respect him.' [14]But when the tenants saw him, they discussed it among themselves and said, 'This is the heir; let us kill him so that the inheritance may be ours.' [15]So they threw him out of the vineyard and killed him. What then will the owner of the vineyard do to them? [16]He will come and destroy those tenants and give the vineyard to others." When they heard this, they said, "Heaven forbid!" [17]But he looked at them and said, "What then does this text mean:

'The stone that the builders rejected
has become the cornerstone'[a]?

[18]Everyone who falls on that stone will be broken to pieces; and it will crush anyone on whom it falls." [19]When the scribes and chief priests realized that he had told this parable against them, they wanted to lay hands on him at that very hour, but they feared the people.

20 So they watched him and sent spies who pretended to be honest, in order to trap him by what he said, so as to hand him over to the jurisdiction and authority of the governor. [21]So they asked him, "Teacher, we know that you are right in what you say and teach, and you show deference to no one, but teach the way of God in accordance with truth. [22]Is it lawful for us to pay taxes to the emperor, or not?" [23]But he perceived their crafti-

ness and said to them, [24]"Show me a denarius. Whose head and whose title does it bear?" They said, "The emperor's." [25]He said to them, "Then give to the emperor the things that are the emperor's, and to God the things that are God's." [26]And they were not able in the presence of the people to trap him by what he said; and being amazed by his answer, they became silent.

27 Some Sadducees, those who say there is no resurrection, came to him [28]and asked him a question, "Teacher, Moses wrote for us that if a man's brother dies, leaving a wife but no children, the man[b] shall marry the widow and raise up children for his brother. [29]Now there were seven brothers; the first married, and died childless; [30]then the second [31]and the third married her, and so in the same way all seven died childless. [32]Finally the woman also died. [33]In the resurrection, therefore, whose wife will the woman be? For the seven had married her."

34 Jesus said to them, "Those who belong to this age marry and are given in marriage; [35]but those who are considered worthy of a place in that age and in the resurrection from the dead neither marry nor are given in marriage. [36]Indeed they cannot die anymore, because they are like angels and are children of God, being children of the resurrection. [37]And the fact that the dead

[a]Or keystone [b]Gk his brother

119

are raised Moses himself showed, in the story about the bush, where he speaks of the Lord as the God of Abraham, the God of Isaac, and the God of Jacob. 38Now he is God not of the dead, but of the living; for to him all of them are alive." 39Then some of the scribes answered, "Teacher, you have spoken well." 40For they no longer dared to ask him another question.

41 Then he said to them, "How can they say that the Messiah*a* is David's son? 42For David himself says in the book of Psalms,

'The Lord said to my Lord,
  "Sit at my right hand,
43   until I make your enemies
      your footstool."'

44David thus calls him Lord; so how can he be his son?"

45 In the hearing of all the people he said to the*b* disciples, 46"Beware of the scribes, who like to walk around in long robes, and love to be greeted with respect in the marketplaces, and to have the best seats in the synagogues and places of honor at banquets. 47They devour widows' houses and for the sake of appearance say long prayers. They will receive the greater condemnation."

21 He looked up and saw rich people putting their gifts into the treasury; 2he also saw a poor widow put in two small copper coins. 3He said, "Truly I tell you, this poor widow has put in more than all of them; 4for all of them have contributed out of

their abundance, but she out of her poverty has put in all she had to live on."

5 When some were speaking about the temple, how it was adorned with beautiful stones and gifts dedicated to God, he said, 6"As for these things that you see, the days will come when not one stone will be left upon another; all will be thrown down."

7 They asked him, "Teacher, when will this be, and what will be the sign that this is about to take place?" 8And he said, "Beware that you are not led astray; for many will come in my name and say, 'I am he!'*c* and, 'The time is near!'*d* Do not go after them.

9 "When you hear of wars and insurrections, do not be terrified; for these things must take place first, but the end will not follow immediately." 10Then he said to them, "Nation will rise against nation, and kingdom against kingdom; 11there will be great earthquakes, and in various places famines and plagues; and there will be dreadful portents and great signs from heaven.

12 "But before all this occurs, they will arrest you and persecute you; they will hand you over to synagogues and prisons, and you will be brought before kings and governors because of my name. 13This will give you an opportunity to testify. 14So make

---

*a*Or the Christ *b*Other ancient authorities read his *c*Gk I am *d*Or at hand up your minds not to prepare your defense in advance; [15]for I will give you words*a* and a wisdom that none of your opponents will be able to withstand or contradict. [16]You will be betrayed even by parents and brothers, by relatives and friends; and they will put some of you to death. [17]You will be hated by all because of my name. [18]But not a hair of your head will perish. [19]By your endurance you will gain your souls.

20 "When you see Jerusalem surrounded by armies, then know that its desolation has come near.*b* [21]Then those in Judea must flee to the mountains, and those inside the city must leave it, and those out in the country must not enter it; [22]for these are days of vengeance, as a fulfillment of all that is written. [23]Woe to those who are pregnant and to those who are nursing infants in those days! For there will be great distress on the earth and wrath against this people; [24]they will fall by the edge of the sword and be taken away as captives among all nations; and Jerusalem will be trampled on by the Gentiles, until the times of the Gentiles are fulfilled.

25 "There will be signs in the sun, the moon, and the stars, and on the earth distress among nations confused by the roaring of the sea and the waves. [26]People will faint from fear and foreboding of what is coming upon the world, for the powers of the heavens will be shaken. [27]Then they will see 'the Son of Man coming in a cloud' with power and great glory. [28]Now when these things begin to take place, stand up and raise your heads, because your redemption is drawing near."

29 Then he told them a parable: "Look at the fig tree and all the trees; [30]as soon as they sprout leaves you can see for yourselves and know that summer is already near. [31]So also, when you see these things taking place, you know that the kingdom of God is near. [32]Truly I tell you, this generation will not pass away until all things have taken place. [33]Heaven and earth will pass away, but my words will not pass away.

34 "Be on guard so that your hearts are not weighed down with dissipation and drunkenness and the worries of this life, and that day catch you unexpectedly, [35]like a trap. For it will come upon all who live on the face of the whole earth. [36]Be alert at all times, praying that you may have the strength to escape all these things that will take place, and to stand before the Son of Man."

37 Every day he was teaching in the temple, and at night he would go out and spend the night on the Mount of Olives, as it was called. [38]And all the people would get up early in the morning to listen to him in the temple.

22 Now the festival of Unleavened Bread, which is called the Passover, was near.

*a*Gk *a mouth* *b*Or *is at hand*

[2]The chief priests and the scribes were looking for a way to put Jesus[a] to death, for they were afraid of the people.

3 Then Satan entered into Judas called Iscariot, who was one of the twelve; [4]he went away and conferred with the chief priests and officers of the temple police about how he might betray him to them. [5]They were greatly pleased and agreed to give him money. [6]So he consented and began to look for an opportunity to betray him to them when no crowd was present.

7 Then came the day of Unleavened Bread, on which the Passover lamb had to be sacrificed. [8]So Jesus[b] sent Peter and John, saying, "Go and prepare the Passover meal for us that we may eat it." [9]They asked him, "Where do you want us to make preparations for it?" [10]"Listen," he said to them, "when you have entered the city, a man carrying a jar of water will meet you; follow him into the house he enters [11]and say to the owner of the house, 'The teacher asks you, "Where is the guest room, where I may eat the Passover with my disciples?"' [12]He will show you a large room upstairs, already furnished. Make preparations for us there." [13]So they went and found everything as he had told them; and they prepared the Passover meal.

14 When the hour came, he took his place at the table, and the apostles with him. [15]He said to them, "I have eagerly desired to eat this Passover with you before I suffer; [16]for I tell you, I will not eat[c] it until it is fulfilled in the kingdom of God." [17]Then he took a cup, and after giving thanks he said, "Take this and divide it among yourselves; [18]for I tell you that from now on I will not drink of the fruit of the vine until the kingdom of God comes." [19]Then he took a loaf of bread, and when he had given thanks, he broke it and gave it to them, saying, "This is my body, which is given for you. Do this in remembrance of me." [20]And he did the same with the cup after supper, saying, "This cup that is poured out for you is the new covenant in my blood.[d] [21]But see, the one who betrays me is with me, and his hand is on the table. [22]For the Son of Man is going as it has been determined, but woe to that one by whom he is betrayed!" [23]Then they began to ask one another, which one of them it could be who would do this.

24 A dispute also arose among them as to which one of them was to be regarded as the greatest. [25]But he said to them, "The kings of the Gentiles lord it over them; and those in authority over them are called benefactors. [26]But not so with you; rather the greatest among you must become like the youngest, and the leader like one who serves. [27]For who is greater, the one who is at the table or the one who serves? Is it

[a]Gk him [b]Gk he [c]Other ancient authorities read *never eat it again* [d]Other ancient authorities lack, in whole or in part, verses 19b-20 (*which is given . . . in my blood*)

not the one at the table? But I am among you as one who serves.

28 "You are those who have stood by me in my trials; 29and I confer on you, just as my Father has conferred on me, a kingdom, 30so that you may eat and drink at my table in my kingdom, and you will sit on thrones judging the twelve tribes of Israel.

31 "Simon, Simon, listen! Satan has demanded[a] to sift all of you like wheat, 32but I have prayed for you that your own faith may not fail; and you, when once you have turned back, strengthen your brothers." 33And he said to him, "Lord, I am ready to go with you to prison and to death!" 34Jesus[b] said, "I tell you, Peter, the cock will not crow this day, until you have denied three times that you know me."

35 He said to them, "When I sent you out without a purse, bag, or sandals, did you lack anything?" They said, "No, not a thing." 36He said to them, "But now, the one who has a purse must take it, and likewise a bag. And the one who has no sword must sell his cloak and buy one. 37For I tell you, this scripture must be fulfilled in me, 'And he was counted among the lawless'; and indeed what is written about me is being fulfilled." 38They said, "Lord, look, here are two swords." He replied, "It is enough."

39 He came out and went, as was his custom, to the Mount of Olives; and the disciples followed him. 40When he reached the place, he said to them, "Pray that you may not come into the time of trial."[c] 41Then he withdrew from them about a stone's throw, knelt down, and prayed, 42"Father, if you are willing, remove this cup from me; yet, not my will but yours be done." [[43Then an angel from heaven appeared to him and gave him strength. 44In his anguish he prayed more earnestly, and his sweat became like great drops of blood falling down on the ground.]][d] 45When he got up from prayer, he came to the disciples and found them sleeping because of grief, 46and he said to them, "Why are you sleeping? Get up and pray that you may not come into the time of trial."[c]

47 While he was still speaking, suddenly a crowd came, and the one called Judas, one of the twelve, was leading them. He approached Jesus to kiss him; 48but Jesus said to him, "Judas, is it with a kiss that you are betraying the Son of Man?" 49When those who were around him saw what was coming, they asked, "Lord, should we strike with the sword?" 50Then one of them struck the slave of the high priest and cut off his right ear. 51But Jesus said, "No more of this!" And he touched his ear and healed him. 52Then Jesus said to the chief priests, the officers of the temple police, and the elders who had come for him, "Have you come out with swords and clubs

---

[a] Or *has obtained permission* [b] Gk *He* [c] Or *into tempta-tion* [d] Other ancient authorities lack verses 43 and 44

as if I were a bandit? ⁵³When I was with you day after day in the temple, you did not lay hands on me. But this is your hour, and the power of darkness!"

54 Then they seized him and led him away, bringing him into the high priest's house. But Peter was following at a distance. ⁵⁵When they had kindled a fire in the middle of the courtyard and sat down together, Peter sat among them. ⁵⁶Then a servant-girl, seeing him in the firelight, stared at him and said, "This man also was with him." ⁵⁷But he denied it, saying, "Woman, I do not know him." ⁵⁸A little later someone else, on seeing him, said, "You also are one of them." But Peter said, "Man, I am not!" ⁵⁹Then about an hour later still another kept insisting, "Surely this man also was with him; for he is a Galilean." ⁶⁰But Peter said, "Man, I do not know what you are talking about!" At that moment, while he was still speaking, the cock crowed. ⁶¹The Lord turned and looked at Peter. Then Peter remembered the word of the Lord, how he had said to him, "Before the cock crows today, you will deny me three times." ⁶²And he went out and wept bitterly.

63 Now the men who were holding Jesus began to mock him and beat him; ⁶⁴they also blindfolded him and kept asking him, "Prophesy! Who is it that struck you?" ⁶⁵They kept heaping many other insults on him.

66 When day came, the assembly of the elders of the peo-ple, both chief priests and scribes, gathered together, and they brought him to their council. ⁶⁷They said, "If you are the Messiah,ᵃ tell us." He replied, "If I tell you, you will not believe; ⁶⁸and if I question you, you will not answer. ⁶⁹But from now on the Son of Man will be seated at the right hand of the power of God." ⁷⁰All of them asked, "Are you, then, the Son of God?" He said to them, "You say that I am." ⁷¹Then they said, "What further testimony do we need? We have heard it ourselves from his own lips!"

23 Then the assembly rose as a body and brought Jesusᵇ before Pilate. ²They began to accuse him, saying, "We found this man perverting our nation, forbidding us to pay taxes to the emperor, and saying that he himself is the Messiah, a king."ᶜ ³Then Pilate asked him, "Are you the king of the Jews?" He answered, "You say so." ⁴Then Pilate said to the chief priests and the crowds, "I find no basis for an accusation against this man." ⁵But they were insistent and said, "He stirs up the people by teaching throughout all Judea, from Galilee where he began even to this place."

6 When Pilate heard this, he asked whether the man was a Galilean. ⁷And when he learned that he was under Herod's jurisdiction, he sent him off to Herod, who was himself in Jerusalem at

---

ᵃOr the Christ ᵇGk him ᶜOr is an anointed king

that time. [8]When Herod saw Jesus, he was very glad, for he had been wanting to see him for a long time, because he had heard about him and was hoping to see him perform some sign. [9]He questioned him at some length, but Jesus[a] gave him no answer. [10]The chief priests and the scribes stood by, vehemently accusing him. [11]Even Herod with his soldiers treated him with contempt and mocked him; then he put an elegant robe on him, and sent him back to Pilate. [12]That same day Herod and Pilate became friends with each other; before this they had been enemies.

[13] Pilate then called together the chief priests, the leaders, and the people, [14]and said to them, "You brought me this man as one who was perverting the people; and here I have examined him in your presence and have not found this man guilty of any of your charges against him. [15]Neither has Herod, for he sent him back to us. Indeed, he has done nothing to deserve death. [16]I will therefore have him flogged and release him."[b]

[18] Then they all shouted out together, "Away with this fellow! Release Barabbas for us!" [19](This was a man who had been put in prison for an insurrection that had taken place in the city, and for murder.) [20]Pilate, wanting to release Jesus, addressed them again; [21]but they kept shouting, "Crucify, crucify him!" [22]A third time he said to them, "Why, what evil has he done? I have found in him no ground for the sentence of death; I will therefore have him flogged and then release him." [23]But they kept urgently demanding with loud shouts that he should be crucified; and their voices prevailed. [24]So Pilate gave his verdict that their demand should be granted. [25]He released the man they asked for, the one who had been put in prison for insurrection and murder, and he handed Jesus over as they wished.

[26] As they led him away, they seized a man, Simon of Cyrene, who was coming from the country, and they laid the cross on him, and made him carry it behind Jesus. [27]A great number of the people followed him, and among them were women who were beating their breasts and wailing for him. [28]But Jesus turned to them and said, "Daughters of Jerusalem, do not weep for me, but weep for yourselves and for your children. [29]For the days are surely coming when they will say, 'Blessed are the barren, and the wombs that never bore, and the breasts that never nursed.' [30]Then they will begin to say to the mountains, 'Fall on us'; and to the hills, 'Cover us.' [31]For if they do this when the wood is green, what will happen when it is dry?"

[32] Two others also, who were criminals, were led away to be put to death with him. [33]When they

---

[a]Gk *he* [b]Here, or after verse 19, other ancient authorities add verse 17, *Now he was obliged to release someone for them at the festival*

came to the place that is called The Skull, they crucified Jesus[a] there with the criminals, one on his right and one on his left. [[[34]Then Jesus said, "Father, forgive them; for they do not know what they are doing."]] [b] And they cast lots to divide his clothing. [35]And the people stood by, watching; but the leaders scoffed at him, saying, "He saved others; let him save himself if he is the Messiah[c] of God, his chosen one!" [36]The soldiers also mocked him, coming up and offering him sour wine, [37]and saying, "If you are the King of the Jews, save yourself!" [38]There was also an inscription over him,[d] "This is the King of the Jews."

[39] One of the criminals who were hanged there kept deriding[e] him and saying, "Are you not the Messiah?[c] Save yourself and us!" [40]But the other rebuked him, saying, "Do you not fear God, since you are under the same sentence of condemnation? [41]And we indeed have been condemned justly, for we are getting what we deserve for our deeds, but this man has done nothing wrong." [42]Then he said, "Jesus, remember me when you come into[f] your kingdom." [43]He replied, "Truly I tell you, today you will be with me in Paradise."

[44] It was now about noon, and *darkness came over the whole* land[g] until three in the afternoon, [45]while the sun's light failed;[h] and the curtain of the temple was torn in two. [46]Then Jesus, crying with a loud voice, said, "Father, into your hands I commend my spirit." Having said this, he breathed his last. [47]When the centurion saw what had taken place, he praised God and said, "Certainly this man was innocent."[i] [48]And when all the crowds who had gathered there for this spectacle saw what had taken place, they returned home, beating their breasts. [49]But all his acquaintances, including the women who had followed him from Galilee, stood at a distance, watching these things.

[50] Now there was a good and righteous man named Joseph, who, though a member of the council, [51]had not agreed to their plan and action. He came from the Jewish town of Arimathea, and he was waiting expectantly for the kingdom of God. [52]This man went to Pilate and asked for the body of Jesus. [53]Then he took it down, wrapped it in a linen cloth, and laid it in a rock-hewn tomb where no one had ever been laid. [54]It was the day of Preparation, and the sabbath was beginning.[j] [55]The women who had come with him from Galilee followed, and they saw the tomb and how his body was laid. [56]Then they returned, and prepared spices and ointments.

On the sabbath they rested according to the commandment.

---

[a]Gk *him* [b]Other ancient authorities lack the sentence *Then Jesus . . . what they are doing* [c]Or *the Christ* [d]Other ancient authorities add *written in Greek and Latin and Hebrew* (that is, *Aramaic*) [e]Or *blaspheming* [f]Other ancient authorities read *in* [g]Or *earth* [h]Or *the sun was eclipsed.* Other ancient authorities read *the sun was darkened* [i]Or *righteous* [j]Gk *was dawing*

24 But on the first day of the week, at early dawn, they came to the tomb, taking the spices that they had prepared. ²They found the stone rolled away from the tomb, ³but when they went in, they did not find the body.ᵃ ⁴While they were perplexed about this, suddenly two men in dazzling clothes stood beside them. ⁵The womenᵇ were terrified and bowed their faces to the ground, but the menᶜ said to them, "Why do you look for the living among the dead? He is not here, but has risen.ᵈ ⁶Remember how he told you, while he was still in Galilee, ⁷that the Son of Man must be handed over to sinners, and be crucified, and on the third day rise again." ⁸Then they remembered his words, ⁹and returning from the tomb, they told all this to the eleven and to all the rest. ¹⁰Now it was Mary Magdalene, Joanna, Mary the mother of James, and the other women with them who told this to the apostles. ¹¹But these words seemed to them an idle tale, and they did not believe them. ¹²But Peter got up and ran to the tomb; stooping and looking in, he saw the linen cloths by themselves; then he went home, amazed at what had happened.ᵉ

13 Now on that same day two of them were going to a village called Emmaus, about seven milesᶠ from Jerusalem, ¹⁴and talking with each other about all these things that had happened. ¹⁵While they were talking and discussing, Jesus himself came near and went with them, ¹⁶but their eyes were kept from recognizing him. ¹⁷And he said to them, "What are you discussing with each other while you walk along?" They stood still, looking sad.ᵍ ¹⁸Then one of them, whose name was Cleopas, answered him, "Are you the only stranger in Jerusalem who does not know the things that have taken place there in these days?" ¹⁹He asked them, "What things?" They replied, "The things about Jesus of Nazareth,ʰ who was a prophet mighty in deed and word before God and all the people, ²⁰and how our chief priests and leaders handed him over to be condemned to death and crucified him. ²¹But we had hoped that he was the one to redeem Israel.ⁱ Yes, and besides all this, it is now the third day since these things took place. ²²Moreover, some women of our group astounded us. They were at the tomb early this morning, ²³and when they did not find his body there, they came back and told us that they had indeed seen a vision of angels who said that he was alive. ²⁴Some of those who were with us went to the tomb and found it just as the women had said; but they did not see him." ²⁵Then he said to them,

ᵃOther ancient authorities add *of the Lord Jesus* ᵇGk *They* ᶜGk *but they* ᵈOther ancient authorities lack *He is not here, but has risen* ᵉOther ancient authorities lack verse 12 ᶠGk *sixty stadia;* other ancient authorities read *a hundred sixty stadia* ᵍOther ancient authorities read *walk along, looking sad?"* ʰOther ancient authorities read *Jesus the Nazorean* ⁱOr *to set Israel free*

"Oh, how foolish you are, and how slow of heart to believe all that the prophets have declared! [26]Was it not necessary that the Messiah[a] should suffer these things and then enter into his glory?" [27]Then beginning with Moses and all the prophets, he interpreted to them the things about himself in all the scriptures.

28 As they came near the village to which they were going, he walked ahead as if he were going on. [29]But they urged him strongly, saying, "Stay with us, because it is almost evening and the day is now nearly over." So he went in to stay with them. [30]When he was at the table with them, he took bread, blessed and broke it, and gave it to them. [31]Then their eyes were opened, and they recognized him; and he vanished from their sight. [32]They said to each other, "Were not our hearts burning within us[b] while he was talking to us on the road, while he was opening the scriptures to us?" [33]That same hour they got up and returned to Jerusalem; and they found the eleven and their companions gathered together. [34]They were saying, "The Lord has risen indeed, and he has appeared to Simon!" [35]Then they told what had happened on the road, and how he had been made known to them in the breaking of the bread.

36 While they were talking about this, Jesus himself stood among them and said to them, "Peace be with you."[c] [37]They were startled and terrified, and thought that they were seeing a ghost. [38]He said to them, "Why are you frightened, and why do doubts arise in your hearts? [39]Look at my hands and my feet; see that it is I myself. Touch me and see; for a ghost does not have flesh and bones as you see that I have." [40]And when he had said this, he showed them his hands and his feet.[d] [41]While in their joy they were disbelieving and still wondering, he said to them, "Have you anything here to eat?" [42]They gave him a piece of broiled fish, [43]and he took it and ate in their presence.

44 Then he said to them, "These are my words that I spoke to you while I was still with you—that everything written about me in the law of Moses, the prophets, and the psalms must be fulfilled." [45]Then he opened their minds to understand the scriptures, [46]and he said to them, "Thus it is written, that the Messiah[a] is to suffer and to rise from the dead on the third day, [47]and that repentance and forgiveness of sins is to be proclaimed in his name to all nations,[e] beginning from Jerusalem. [48]You are witnesses of these things. [49]And see, I am sending upon you what my Father promised; so stay here in the city until you have been clothed with power from on high."

[a]Or *the Christ* [b]Other ancient authorities lack *within us* [c]Other ancient authorities lack *and said to them, "Peace be wih you."* [d]Other ancient authorities lack verse 40 [e]Or *nations. Beginning from Jerusalem you are witnesses*

50 Then he led them out as far as Bethany, and, lifting up his hands, he blessed them. 51While he was blessing them, he withdrew from them and was carried up into heaven.[a] 52And they worshiped him, and[b] returned to Jerusalem with great joy; 53and they were continually in the temple blessing God.[c]

[a]Other ancient authorities lack *and was carried up into heaven* [b]Other ancient authorities lack *worshiped him, and* [c]Other ancient authorities add *Amen*

The Gospel According to

JOHN

1 In the beginning was the Word, and the Word was with God, and the Word was God. 2He was in the beginning with God. 3All things came into being through him, and without him not one thing came into being. What has come into being 4in him was life,[a] and the life was the light of all people. 5The light shines in the darkness, and the darkness did not overcome it.

6 There was a man sent from God, whose name was John. 7He came as a witness to testify to the light, so that all might believe through him. 8He himself was not the light, but he came to testify to the light. 9The true light, which enlightens everyone, was coming into the world.[b]

10 He was in the world, and the world came into being through him; yet the world did not know him. 11He came to what was his own,[c] and his own people did not accept him. 12But to all who received him, who believed in his name, he gave power to become children of God, 13who were born, not of blood or of the will of the flesh or of the will of man, but of God.

14 And the Word became flesh and lived among us, and we have seen his glory, the glory as of a father's only son,[d] full of grace and truth. 15(John testified to him and cried out, "This was he of whom I said, 'He who comes after me ranks ahead of me because he was before me.'") 16From his fullness we have all received, grace upon grace. 17The law indeed was given through Moses; grace and truth came through Jesus Christ. 18No one has ever seen God. It is God the only Son,[e] who is close to the Father's heart,[f] who has made him known.

[a]Or 3*through him. And without him not one thing came into being that has come into being* 4*In him was life* [b]*He was the true light that enlightens everyone coming into the world* [c]Or *to his own home* [d]Or *the Father's only Son* [e]Other ancient authorities read *It is an only Son, God,* or *It is the only Son* [f]Gk *bosom*

19 This is the testimony given by John when the Jews sent priests and Levites from Jerusalem to ask him, "Who are you?" 20He confessed and did not deny it, but confessed, "I am not the Messiah."*a* 21And they asked him, "What then? Are you Elijah?" He said, "I am not." "Are you the prophet?" He answered, "No." 22Then they said to him, "Who are you? Let us have an answer for those who sent us. What do you say about yourself?" 23He said,

"I am the voice of one
　　crying out in the
　　wilderness,
'Make straight the way of
　　the Lord,'"

as the prophet Isaiah said.

24 Now they had been sent from the Pharisees. 25They asked him, "Why then are you baptizing if you are neither the Messiah,*a* nor Elijah, nor the prophet?" 26John answered them, "I baptize with water. Among you stands one whom you do not know, 27the one who is coming after me; I am not worthy to untie the thong of his sandal." 28This took place in Bethany across the Jordan where John was baptizing.

29 The next day he saw Jesus coming toward him and declared, "Here is the Lamb of God who takes away the sin of the world! 30This is he of whom I said, 'After me comes a man who ranks ahead of me because he was before me.' 31I myself did not know him; but I came baptizing with water for this reason, that

he might be revealed to Israel." 32And John testified, "I saw the Spirit descending from heaven like a dove, and it remained on him. 33I myself did not know him, but the one who sent me to baptize with water said to me, 'He on whom you see the Spirit descend and remain is the one who baptizes with the Holy Spirit.' 34And I myself have seen and have testified that this is the Son of God."*b*

35 The next day John again was standing with two of his disciples, 36and as he watched Jesus walk by, he exclaimed, "Look, here is the Lamb of God!" 37The two disciples heard him say this, and they followed Jesus. 38When Jesus turned and saw them following, he said to them, "What are you looking for?" They said to him, "Rabbi" (which translated means Teacher), "where are you staying?" 39He said to them, "Come and see." They came and saw where he was staying, and they remained with him that day. It was about four o'clock in the afternoon. 40One of the two who heard John speak and followed him was Andrew, Simon Peter's brother. 41He first found his brother Simon and said to him, "We have found the Messiah" (which is translated Anointed*c*). 42He brought Simon*d* to Jesus, who looked at him and said, "You are Simon son of John. You are to be called Cephas" (which is translated Peter*e*).

---

*a*Or *the Christ* *b*Other ancient authorities read *is God's chosen one* *c*Or *Christ* *d*Gk *him* *e*From the word for *rock* in Aramaic (*kepha*) and Greek (*petra*), respectively

43 The next day Jesus decided to go to Galilee. He found Philip and said to him, "Follow me." [44]Now Philip was from Bethsaida, the city of Andrew and Peter. [45]Philip found Nathanael and said to him, "We have found him about whom Moses in the law and also the prophets wrote, Jesus son of Joseph from Nazareth." [46]Nathanael said to him, "Can anything good come out of Nazareth?" Philip said to him, "Come and see." [47]When Jesus saw Nathanael coming toward him, he said of him, "Here is truly an Israelite in whom there is no deceit!" [48]Nathanael asked him, "Where did you get to know me?" Jesus answered, "I saw you under the fig tree before Philip called you." [49]Nathanael replied, "Rabbi, you are the Son of God! You are the King of Israel!" [50]Jesus answered, "Do you believe because I told you that I saw you under the fig tree? You will see greater things than these." [51]And he said to him, "Very truly, I tell you,[a] you will see heaven opened and the angels of God ascending and descending upon the Son of Man."

2 On the third day there was a wedding in Cana of Galilee, and the mother of Jesus was there. [2]Jesus and his disciples had also been invited to the wedding. [3]When the wine gave out, the mother of Jesus said to him, "They have no wine." [4]And Jesus said to her, "Woman, what concern is that to you and to me? My hour has not yet come." [5]His mother said to the servants, "Do whatever he tells you." [6]Now standing there were six stone water jars for the Jewish rites of purification, each holding twenty or thirty gallons. [7]Jesus said to them, "Fill the jars with water." And they filled them up to the brim. [8]He said to them, "Now draw some out, and take it to the chief steward." So they took it. [9]When the steward tasted the water that had become wine, and did not know where it came from (though the servants who had drawn the water knew), the steward called the bridegroom [10]and said to him, "Everyone serves the good wine first, and then the inferior wine after the guests have become drunk. But you have kept the good wine until now." [11]Jesus did this, the first of his signs, in Cana of Galilee, and revealed his glory; and his disciples believed in him.

12 After this he went down to Capernaum with his mother, his brothers, and his disciples; and they remained there a few days.

13 The Passover of the Jews was near, and Jesus went up to Jerusalem. [14]In the temple he found people selling cattle, sheep, and doves, and the money changers seated at their tables. [15]Making a whip of cords, he drove all of them out of the temple, both the sheep and the cattle. He also poured out the coins of the money changers and

---

[a]Both instances of the Greek word for *you* in this verse are plural

overturned their tables. ¹⁶He told those who were selling the doves, "Take these things out of here! Stop making my Father's house a marketplace!" ¹⁷His disciples remembered that it was written, "Zeal for your house will consume me." ¹⁸The Jews then said to him, "What sign can you show us for doing this?" ¹⁹Jesus answered them, "Destroy this temple, and in three days I will raise it up." ²⁰The Jews then said, "This temple has been under construction for forty-six years, and will you raise it up in three days?" ²¹But he was speaking of the temple of his body. ²²After he was raised from the dead, his disciples remembered that he had said this; and they believed the scripture and the word that Jesus had spoken.

23 When he was in Jerusalem during the Passover festival, many believed in his name because they saw the signs that he was doing. ²⁴But Jesus on his part would not entrust himself to them, because he knew all people ²⁵and needed no one to testify about anyone; for he himself knew what was in everyone.

3 Now there was a Pharisee named Nicodemus, a leader of the Jews. ²He came to Jesus*ᵃ* by night and said to him, "Rabbi, we know that you are a teacher who has come from God; for no one can do these signs that you do apart from the presence of God." ³Jesus answered him, "Very truly, I tell you, no one can see the kingdom of God without being born from above."*ᵇ* ⁴Nicodemus said to him, "How can anyone be born after having grown old? Can one enter a second time into the mother's womb and be born?" ⁵Jesus answered, "Very truly, I tell you, no one can enter the kingdom of God without being born of water and Spirit. ⁶What is born of the flesh is flesh, and what is born of the Spirit is spirit.*ᶜ* ⁷Do not be astonished that I said to you, 'You*ᵈ* must be born from above.'*ᵉ* ⁸The wind blows where it chooses, and you hear the sound of it, but you do not know where it comes from or where it goes. So it is with everyone who is born of the Spirit." ⁹Nicodemus said to him, "How can these things be?" ¹⁰Jesus answered him, "Are you a teacher of Israel, and yet you do not understand these things?

11 "Very truly, I tell you, we speak of what we know and testify to what we have seen; yet you*ᶠ* do not receive our testimony. ¹²If I have told you about earthly things and you do not believe, how can you believe if I tell you about heavenly things? ¹³No one has ascended into heaven except the one who descended from heaven, the Son of Man.*ᵍ* ¹⁴And just as Moses lifted up the serpent in the wilderness, so must the Son of Man be lifted up, ¹⁵that whoever believes in him may have eternal life.*ʰ*

---

*ᵃ*Gk *him* *ᵇ*Or *born anew* *ᶜ*The same Greek word means both *wind* and *spirit* *ᵈ*The Greek word for *you* here is plural *ᵉ*Or *anew* *ᶠ*The Greek word for *you* here and in verse 12 is plural *ᵍ*Other ancient authorities add *who is in heaven* *ʰ*Some interpreters hold that the quotation concludes with verse 15

16 "For God so loved the world that he gave his only Son, so that everyone who believes in him may not perish but may have eternal life.

17 "Indeed, God did not send the Son into the world to condemn the world, but in order that the world might be saved through him. [18]Those who believe in him are not condemned; but those who do not believe are condemned already, because they have not believed in the name of the only Son of God. [19]And this is the judgment, that the light has come into the world, and people loved darkness rather than light because their deeds were evil. [20]For all who do evil hate the light and do not come to the light, so that their deeds may not be exposed. [21]But those who do what is true come to the light, so that it may be clearly seen that their deeds have been done in God."

22 After this Jesus and his disciples went into the Judean countryside, and he spent some time there with them and baptized. [23]John also was baptizing at Aenon near Salim because water was abundant there; and people kept coming and were being baptized [24]—John, of course, had not yet been thrown into prison.

25 Now a discussion about purification arose between John's disciples and a Jew.[a] [26]They came to John and said to him, "Rabbi, the one who was with you across the Jordan, to whom you testi-

fied, here he is baptizing, and all are going to him." [27]John answered, "No one can receive anything except what has been given from heaven. [28]You yourselves are my witnesses that I said, 'I am not the Messiah,[b] but I have been sent ahead of him.' [29]He who has the bride is the bridegroom. The friend of the bridegroom, who stands and hears him, rejoices greatly at the bridegroom's voice. For this reason my joy has been fulfilled. [30]He must increase, but I must decrease."[c]

31 The one who comes from above is above all; the one who is of the earth belongs to the earth and speaks about earthly things. The one who comes from heaven is above all. [32]He testifies to what he has seen and heard, yet no one accepts his testimony. [33]Whoever has accepted his testimony has certified[d] this, that God is true. [34]He whom God has sent speaks the words of God, for he gives the Spirit without measure. [35]The Father loves the Son and has placed all things in his hands. [36]Whoever believes in the Son has eternal life; whoever disobeys the Son will not see life, but must endure God's wrath.

4 Now when Jesus[e] learned that the Pharisees had heard, "Jesus is making and baptizing more disciples than John" [2]—although it was not Jesus himself but his disciples who baptized—

[a]Other ancient authorities read *the Jews* [b]Or *the Christ* [c]Some interpreters hold that the quotation continues through verse 36 [d]Gk *set a seal to* [e]Other ancient authorities read *the Lord*

[3]he left Judea and started back to Galilee. [4]But he had to go through Samaria. [5]So he came to a Samaritan city called Sychar, near the plot of ground that Jacob had given to his son Joseph. [6]Jacob's well was there, and Jesus, tired out by his journey, was sitting by the well. It was about noon.

7 A Samaritan woman came to draw water, and Jesus said to her, "Give me a drink." [8](His disciples had gone to the city to buy food.) [9]The Samaritan woman said to him, "How is it that you, a Jew, ask a drink of me, a woman of Samaria?" (Jews do not share things in common with Samaritans.)[a] [10]Jesus answered her, "If you knew the gift of God, and who it is that is saying to you, 'Give me a drink,' you would have asked him, and he would have given you living water." [11]The woman said to him, "Sir, you have no bucket, and the well is deep. Where do you get that living water? [12]Are you greater than our ancestor Jacob, who gave us the well, and with his sons and his flocks drank from it?" [13]Jesus said to her, "Everyone who drinks of this water will be thirsty again, [14]but those who drink of the water that I will give them will never be thirsty. The water that I will give will become in them a spring of water gushing up to eternal life." [15]The woman said to him, "Sir, give me this water, so that I may never be thirsty or have to keep coming here to draw water."

16 Jesus said to her, "Go, call your husband, and come back." [17]The woman answered him, "I have no husband." Jesus said to her, "You are right in saying, 'I have no husband'; [18]for you have had five husbands, and the one you have now is not your husband. What you have said is true!" [19]The woman said to him, "Sir, I see that you are a prophet. [20]Our ancestors worshiped on this mountain, but you[b] say that the place where people must worship is in Jerusalem." [21]Jesus said to her, "Woman , believe me, the hour is coming when you will worship the Father neither on this mountain nor in Jerusalem. [22]You worship what you do not know; we worship what we know, for salvation is from the Jews. [23]But the hour is coming, and is now here, when the true worshipers will worship the Father in spirit and truth, for the Father seeks such as these to worship him. [24]God is spirit, and those who worship him must worship in spirit and truth." [25]The woman said to him, "I know that Messiah is coming" (who is called Christ). "When he comes, he will proclaim all things to us." [26]Jesus said to her, "I am he,[c] the one who is speaking to you."

27 Just then his disciples came. They were astonished that he was speaking with a woman,

---

[a]Other ancient authorities lack this sentence [b]The Greek word for *you* here and in verses 21 and 22 is plural [c]Gk *I am*

but no one said, "What do you want?" or, "Why are you speaking with her?" [28]Then the woman left her water jar and went back to the city. She said to the people, [29]"Come and see a man who told me everything I have ever done! He cannot be the Messiah,[a] can he?" [30]They left the city and were on their way to him.

31 Meanwhile the disciples were urging him, "Rabbi, eat something." [32]But he said to them, "I have food to eat that you do not know about." [33]So the disciples said to one another, "Surely no one has brought him something to eat?" [34]Jesus said to them, "My food is to do the will of him who sent me and to complete his work. [35]Do you not say, 'Four months more, then comes the harvest'? But I tell you, look around you, and see how the fields are ripe for harvesting. [36]The reaper is already receiving[b] wages and is gathering fruit for eternal life, so that sower and reaper may rejoice together. [37]For here the saying holds true, 'One sows and another reaps.' [38]I sent you to reap that for which you did not labor. Others have labored, and you have entered into their labor."

39 Many Samaritans from that city believed in him because of the woman's testimony, "He told me everything I have ever done." [40]So when the Samaritans came to him, they asked him to stay with them; and he stayed there two days. [41]And many more believed because of his word. [42]They said to the woman, "It is no longer because of what you said that we believe, for we have heard for ourselves, and we know that this is truly the Savior of the world."

43 When the two days were over, he went from that place to Galilee [44](for Jesus himself had testified that a prophet has no honor in the prophet's own country). [45]When he came to Galilee, the Galileans welcomed him, since they had seen all that he had done in Jerusalem at the festival; for they too had gone to the festival.

46 Then he came again to Cana in Galilee where he had changed the water into wine. Now there was a royal official whose son lay ill in Capernaum. [47]When he heard that Jesus had come from Judea to Galilee, he went and begged him to come down and heal his son, for he was at the point of death. [48]Then Jesus said to him, "Unless you[c] see signs and wonders you will not believe." [49]The official said to him, "Sir, come down before my little boy dies." [50]Jesus said to him, "Go; your son will live." The man believed the word that Jesus spoke to him and started on his way. [51]As he was going down, his slaves met him and told him that his child was alive. [52]So he asked them the hour when he began to recover, and they said to him, "Yesterday at one in the

[a]Or the Christ [b]Or[35] . . . the fields are already ripe for harvesting [36]The reaper is receiving [c]Both instances of the Greek word for you in this verse are plural

afternoon the fever left him." [53]The father realized that this was the hour when Jesus had said to him, "Your son will live." So he himself believed, along with his whole household. [54]Now this was the second sign that Jesus did after coming from Judea to Galilee.

5 After this there was a festival of the Jews, and Jesus went up to Jerusalem.

2 Now in Jerusalem by the Sheep Gate there is a pool, called in Hebrew[a] Beth-zatha,[b] which has five porticoes. [3]In these lay many invalids—blind, lame, and paralyzed.[c] [5]One man was there who had been ill for thirty-eight years. [6]When Jesus saw him lying there and knew that he had been there a long time, he said to him, "Do you want to be made well?" [7]The sick man answered him, "Sir, I have no one to put me into the pool when the water is stirred up; and while I am making my way, someone else steps down ahead of me." [8]Jesus said to him, "Stand up, take your mat and walk." [9]At once the man was made well, and he took up his mat and began to walk.

Now that day was a sabbath. [10]So the Jews said to the man who had been cured, "It is the sabbath; it is not lawful for you to carry your mat." [11]But he answered them, "The man who made me well said to me, 'Take up your mat and walk.'" [12]They asked him, "Who is the man who said to you, 'Take it up and walk'?" [13]Now the man who had been healed did not know who it was, for Jesus had disappeared in[d] the crowd that was there. [14]Later Jesus found him in the temple and said to him, "See, you have been made well! Do not sin any more, so that nothing worse happens to you." [15]The man went away and told the Jews that it was Jesus who had made him well. [16]Therefore the Jews started persecuting Jesus, because he was doing such things on the sabbath. [17]But Jesus answered them, "My Father is still working, and I also am working." [18]For this reason the Jews were seeking all the more to kill him, because he was not only breaking the sabbath, but was also calling God his own Father, thereby making himself equal to God.

19 Jesus said to them, "Very truly, I tell you, the Son can do nothing on his own, but only what he sees the Father[e] doing; for whatever the Father does, the Son does likewise. [20]The Father loves the Son and shows him all that he himself is doing; and he will show him greater works than these, so that you will be astonished. [21]Indeed, just as the Father raises the dead and gives them life, so also the Son gives life to whomever he wishes. [22]The

[a]That is, Aramaic [b]Other ancient authorities read Bethesda, others Bethsaida [c]Other ancient authorities add, wholly or in part, waiting for the stirring of the water, [d]for an angel of the Lord went down at certain seasons into the pool, and stirred up the water; whoever stepped in first after the stirring of the water was made well from whatever disease that person had. [d]Or had left because of [e]Gk that one

Father judges no one but has given all judgment to the Son, [23]so that all may honor the Son just as they honor the Father. Anyone who does not honor the Son does not honor the Father who sent him. [24]Very truly, I tell you, anyone who hears my word and believes him who sent me has eternal life, and does not come under judgment, but has passed from death to life.

25 "Very truly, I tell you, the hour is coming, and is now here, when the dead will hear the voice of the Son of God, and those who hear will live. [26]For just as the Father has life in himself, so he has granted the Son also to have life in himself; [27]and he has given him authority to execute judgment, because he is the Son of Man. [28]Do not be astonished at this; for the hour is coming when all who are in their graves will hear his voice [29]and will come out—those who have done good, to the resurrection of life, and those who have done evil, to the resurrection of condemnation.

30 "I can do nothing on my own. As I hear, I judge; and my *judgment is just, because I seek* to do not my own will but the will of him who sent me.

31 "If I testify about myself, my testimony is not true. [32]There is another who testifies on my behalf, and I know that his testimony to me is true. [33]You sent messengers to John, and he testified to the truth. [34]Not that I accept such human testimony, but I say these things so that you may be saved. [35]He was a burning and shining lamp, and you were willing to rejoice for a while in his light. [36]But I have a testimony greater than John's. The works that the Father has given me to complete, the very works that I am doing, testify on my behalf that the Father has sent me. [37]And the Father who sent me has himself testified on my behalf. You have never heard his voice or seen his form, [38]and you do not have his word abiding in you, because you do not believe him whom he has sent.

39 "You search the scriptures because you think that in them you have eternal life; and it is they that testify on my behalf. [40]Yet you refuse to come to me to have life. [41]I do not accept glory from human beings. [42]But I know that you do not have the love of God in[a] you. [43]I have come in my Father's name, and you do not accept me; if another comes in his own name, you will accept him. [44]How can you believe when you accept glory from one another and do not seek the glory that comes from the one who alone is God? [45]Do not think that I will accuse you before the Father; your accuser is Moses, on whom you have set your hope. [46]If you believed Moses, you would believe me, for he wrote about me. [47]But if you do not believe what he wrote, how will you believe what I say?"

[a]Or *among*

6 After this Jesus went to the other side of the Sea of Galilee, also called the Sea of Tiberias.[a] [2] A large crowd kept following him, because they saw the signs that he was doing for the sick. [3] Jesus went up the mountain and sat down there with his disciples. [4] Now the Passover, the festival of the Jews, was near. [5] When he looked up and saw a large crowd coming toward him, Jesus said to Philip, "Where are we to buy bread for these people to eat?" [6] He said this to test him, for he himself knew what he was going to do. [7] Philip answered him, "Six months' wages[b] would not buy enough bread for each of them to get a little." [8] One of his disciples, Andrew, Simon Peter's brother, said to him, [9] "There is a boy here who has five barley loaves and two fish. But what are they among so many people?" [10] Jesus said, "Make the people sit down." Now there was a great deal of grass in the place; so they[c] sat down, about five thousand in all. [11] Then Jesus took the loaves, and when he had given thanks, he distributed them to those who were seated; so also the fish, as much as they wanted. [12] When they were satisfied, he told his disciples, "Gather up the fragments left over, so that nothing may be lost." [13] So they gathered them up, and from the fragments of the five barley loaves, left by those who had eaten, they filled twelve baskets. [14] When the people saw the sign that he had done, they began to say, "This is indeed the prophet who is to come into the world."

[15] When Jesus realized that they were about to come and take him by force to make him king, he withdrew again to the mountain by himself.

[16] When evening came, his disciples went down to the sea, [17] got into a boat, and started across the sea to Capernaum. It was now dark, and Jesus had not yet come to them. [18] The sea became rough because a strong wind was blowing. [19] When they had rowed about three or four miles,[d] they saw Jesus walking on the sea and coming near the boat, and they were terrified. [20] But he said to them, "It is I;[e] do not be afraid." [21] Then they wanted to take him into the boat, and immediately the boat reached the land toward which they were going.

[22] The next day the crowd that had stayed on the other side of the sea saw that there had been only one boat there. They also saw that Jesus had not got into the boat with his disciples, but that his disciples had gone away alone. [23] Then some boats from Tiberias came near the place where they had eaten the bread after the Lord had given thanks.[f] [24] So when the crowd saw that neither Jesus nor his disciples were there, they themselves got

---

[a] Gk of Galilee of Tiberius [b] Gk Two hundred denarii; the denarius was the usual day's wage for a laborer [c] Gk the men [d] Gk about twenty-five or thirty stadia [e] Gk I am [f] Other ancient authorities lack after the Lord had given thanks

into the boats and went to Capernaum looking for Jesus.

25 When they found him on the other side of the sea, they said to him, "Rabbi, when did you come here?" [26]Jesus answered them, "Very truly, I tell you, you are looking for me, not because you saw signs, but because you ate your fill of the loaves. [27]Do not work for the food that perishes, but for the food that endures for eternal life, which the Son of Man will give you. For it is on him that God the Father has set his seal." [28]Then they said to him, "What must we do to perform the works of God?" [29]Jesus answered them, "This is the work of God, that you believe in him whom he has sent." [30]So they said to him, "What sign are you going to give us then, so that we may see it and believe you? What work are you performing? [31]Our ancestors ate the manna in the wilderness; as it is written, 'He gave them bread from heaven to eat.'" [32]Then Jesus said to them, "Very truly, I tell you, it was not Moses who gave you the bread from heaven, but it is my Father who gives you the true bread from heaven. [33]For the bread of God is that which[a] comes down from heaven and gives life to the world." [34]They said to him, "Sir, give us this bread always."

35 Jesus said to them, "I am the bread of life. Whoever comes to me will never be hungry, and whoever believes in me will never be thirsty. [36]But I said to you that you have seen me and yet do not believe. [37]Everything that the Father gives me will come to me, and anyone who comes to me I will never drive away; [38]for I have come down from heaven, not to do my own will, but the will of him who sent me. [39]And this is the will of him who sent me, that I should lose nothing of all that he has given me, but raise it up on the last day. [40]This is indeed the will of my Father, that all who see the Son and believe in him may have eternal life; and I will raise them up on the last day."

41 Then the Jews began to complain about him because he said, "I am the bread that came down from heaven." [42]They were saying, "Is not this Jesus, the son of Joseph, whose father and mother we know? How can he now say, 'I have come down from heaven'?" [43]Jesus answered them, "Do not complain among yourselves. [44]No one can come to me unless drawn by the Father who sent me; and I will raise that person up on the last day. [45]It is written in the prophets, 'And they shall all be taught by God.' Everyone who has heard and learned from the Father comes to me. [46]Not that anyone has seen the Father except the one who is from God; he has seen the Father. [47]Very truly, I tell you, whoever believes has eternal life. [48]I am the bread of life. [49]Your ancestors ate the manna in the wilderness, and they died. [50]This is the bread

[a]Or *he who*

that comes down from heaven, so that one may eat of it and not die. [51]I am the living bread that came down from heaven. Whoever eats of this bread will live forever; and the bread that I will give for the life of the world is my flesh."

52 The Jews then disputed among themselves, saying, "How can this man give us his flesh to eat?" [53]So Jesus said to them, "Very truly, I tell you, unless you eat the flesh of the Son of Man and drink his blood, you have no life in you. [54]Those who eat my flesh and drink my blood have eternal life, and I will raise them up on the last day; [55]for my flesh is true food and my blood is true drink. [56]Those who eat my flesh and drink my blood abide in me, and I in them. [57]Just as the living Father sent me, and I live because of the Father, so whoever eats me will live because of me. [58]This is the bread that came down from heaven, not like that which your ancestors ate, and they died. But the one who eats this bread will live forever." [59]He said these things while he was teaching in the synagogue at Capernaum.

60 When many of his disciples heard it, they said, "This teaching is difficult; who can accept it?" [61]But Jesus, being aware that his disciples were complaining about it, said to them, "Does this offend you? [62]Then what if you were to see the Son of Man ascending to where he was before? [63]It is the spirit that gives life; the flesh is useless. The words that I have

spoken to you are spirit and life. [64]But among you there are some who do not believe." For Jesus knew from the first who were the ones that did not believe, and who was the one that would betray him. [65]And he said, "For this reason I have told you that no one can come to me unless it is granted by the Father."

66 Because of this many of his disciples turned back and no longer went about with him. [67]So Jesus asked the twelve, "Do you also wish to go away?" [68]Simon Peter answered him, "Lord, to whom can we go? You have the words of eternal life. [69]We have come to believe and know that you are the Holy One of God."[a] [70]Jesus answered them, "Did I not choose you, the twelve? Yet one of you is a devil." [71]He was speaking of Judas son of Simon Iscariot,[b] for he, though one of the twelve, was going to betray him.

7 After this Jesus went about in Galilee. He did not wish[c] to go about in Judea because the Jews were looking for an opportunity to kill him. [2]Now the Jewish festival of Booths[d] was near. [3]So his brothers said to him, "Leave here and go to Judea so that your disciples also may see the works you are doing; [4]for no one who wants[e] to be widely

[a]Other ancient authorities read the Christ, the Son of the living God [b]Other ancient authorities read Judas Iscariot son of Simon; others, Judas son of Simon from Karyot (Kerioth) [c]Other ancient authorities read was not at liberty [d]Or Tabernacles [e]Other ancient authorities read wants it

known acts in secret. If you do these things, show yourself to the world." [5](For not even his brothers believed in him.) [6]Jesus said to them, "My time has not yet come, but your time is always here. [7]The world cannot hate you, but it hates me because I testify against it that its works are evil. [8]Go to the festival yourselves. I am not[a] going to this festival, for my time has not yet fully come." [9]After saying this, he remained in Galilee.

[10] But after his brothers had gone to the festival, then he also went, not publicly but as it were[b] in secret. [11]The Jews were looking for him at the festival and saying, "Where is he?" [12]And there was considerable complaining about him among the crowds. While some were saying, "He is a good man," others were saying, "No, he is deceiving the crowd." [13]Yet no one would speak openly about him for fear of the Jews.

[14] About the middle of the festival Jesus went up into the temple and began to teach. [15]The Jews were astonished at it, saying, "How does this man have such learning,[c] when he has never been taught?" [16]Then Jesus answered them, "My teaching is not mine but his who sent me. [17]Anyone who resolves to do the will of God will know whether the teaching is from God or whether I am speaking on my own. [18]Those who speak on their own seek their own glory; but the one who seeks the glory of him who sent him is true, and there is nothing false in him.

[19] "Did not Moses give you the law? Yet none of you keeps the law. Why are you looking for an opportunity to kill me?" [20]The crowd answered, "You have a demon! Who is trying to kill you?" [21]Jesus answered them, "I performed one work, and all of you are astonished. [22]Moses gave you circumcision (it is, of course, not from Moses, but from the patriarchs), and you circumcise a man on the sabbath. [23]If a man receives circumcision on the sabbath in order that the law of Moses may not be broken, are you angry with me because I healed a man's whole body on the sabbath? [24]Do not judge by appearances, but judge with right judgment."

[25] Now some of the people of Jerusalem were saying, "Is not this the man whom they are trying to kill? [26]And here he is, speaking openly, but they say nothing to him! Can it be that the authorities really know that this is the Messiah?[d] [27]Yet we know where this man is from; but when the Messiah[d] comes, no one will know where he is from." [28]Then Jesus cried out as he was teaching in the temple, "You know me, and you know where I am from. I have not come on my own. But the one who sent me is true, and you do not know him.

---

[a]Other ancient authorities add *yet* [b]Other ancient authorities lack *as it were* [c]Or *this man know his letters* [d]Or *the Christ*

[29]I know him, because I am from him, and he sent me." [30]Then they tried to arrest him, but no one laid hands on him, because his hour had not yet come. [31]Yet many in the crowd believed in him and were saying, "When the Messiah comes, will he do more signs than this man has done?"[a]

32 The Pharisees heard the crowd muttering such things about him, and the chief priests and Pharisees sent temple police to arrest him. [33]Jesus then said, "I will be with you a little while longer, and then I am going to him who sent me. [34]You will search for me, but you will not find me; and where I am, you cannot come." [35]The Jews said to one another, "Where does this man intend to go that we will not find him? Does he intend to go to the Dispersion among the Greeks and teach the Greeks? [36]What does he mean by saying, 'You will search for me and you will not find me' and 'Where I am, you cannot come'?"

37 On the last day of the festival, the great day, while Jesus was standing there, he cried out, "Let anyone who is thirsty come to me, [38]and let the one who believes in me drink. As[b] the scripture has said, 'Out of the believer's heart[c] shall flow rivers of living water.'" [39]Now he said this about the Spirit, which believers in him were to receive; for as yet there was no Spirit,[d] because Jesus was not yet glorified.

40 When they heard these words, some in the crowd said, "This is really the prophet." [41]Others said, "This is the Messiah."[e] But some asked, "Surely the Messiah does not come from Galilee, does he? [42]Has not the scripture said that the Messiah is descended from David and comes from Bethlehem, the village where David lived?" [43]So there was a division in the crowd because of him. [44]Some of them wanted to arrest him, but no one laid hands on him.

45 Then the temple police went back to the chief priests and Pharisees, who asked them, "Why did you not arrest him?" [46]The police answered, "Never has anyone spoken like this!" [47]Then the Pharisees replied, "Surely you have not been deceived too, have you? [48]Has any one of the authorities or of the Pharisees believed in him? [49]But this crowd, which does not know the law—they are accursed." [50]Nicodemus, who had gone to Jesus[f] before, and who was one of them, asked, [51]"Our law does not judge people without first giving them a hearing to find out what they are doing, does it?" [52]They replied, "Surely you are not also from Galilee, are you? Search and you will see that no prophet is to arise from Galilee."

[a]Other ancient authorities read *is doing* [b]Or *come to me and drink* [38]*The one who believes in me, as* [c]Gk *out of his belly* [d]Other ancient authorities read *for as yet the Spirit* (others, *Holy Spirit*) *had not been given* [e]Gk Or *the Christ* [f]Gk *him*

[[[53]Then each of them went home, [8] [1]while Jesus went to the Mount of Olives. [2]Early in the morning he came again to the temple. All the people came to him and he sat down and began to teach them. [3]The scribes and the Pharisees brought a woman who had been caught in adultery; and making her stand before all of them, [4]they said to him, "Teacher, this woman was caught in the very act of committing adultery. [5]Now in the law Moses commanded us to stone such women. Now what do you say?" [6]They said this to test him, so that they might have some charge to bring against him. Jesus bent down and wrote with his finger on the ground. [7]When they kept on questioning him, he straightened up and said to them, "Let anyone among you who is without sin be the first to throw a stone at her." [8]And once again he bent down and wrote on the ground.[a] [9]When they heard it, they went away, one by one, beginning with the elders; and Jesus was left alone with the woman standing before him. [10]Jesus straightened up and said to her, "Woman, where are they? Has no one condemned you?" [11]She said, "No one, sir."[b] And Jesus said, "Neither do I condemn you. Go your way, and from now on do not sin again."]][c]

[12] Again Jesus spoke to them, saying, "I am the light of the world. Whoever follows me will never walk in darkness but will have the light of life." [13]Then the Pharisees said to him, "You are testifying on your own behalf; your testimony is not valid." [14]Jesus answered, "Even if I testify on my own behalf, my testimony is valid because I know where I have come from and where I am going, but you do not know where I come from or where I am going. [15]You judge by human standards;[d] I judge no one. [16]Yet even if I do judge, my judgment is valid; for it is not I alone who judge, but I and the Father[e] who sent me. [17]In your law it is written that the testimony of two witnesses is valid. [18]I testify on my own behalf, and the Father who sent me testifies on my behalf." [19]Then they said to him, "Where is your Father?" Jesus answered, "You know neither me nor my Father. If you knew me, you would know my Father also." [20]He spoke these words while he was teaching in the treasury of the temple, but no one arrested him, because his hour had not yet come.

[21] Again he said to them, "I am going away, and you will search for me, but you will die in your sin. Where I am going, you cannot come." [22]Then the Jews said, "Is he going to kill himself? Is that what he means by saying,

[a]Other ancient authorities add *the sins of each of them*
[b]Or *Lord* [c]The most ancient authorities lack 7.53—8.11; other authorities add the passage here or after 7.36 or after 21.25 or after Luke 21.38, with variations of text; some mark the passage as doubtful. [d]Gk *according to the flesh* [e]Other ancient authorities read *he*

'Where I am going, you cannot come'?" [23]He said to them, "You are from below, I am from above; you are of this world, I am not of this world. [24]I told you that you would die in your sins, for you will die in your sins unless you believe that I am he."[a] [25]They said to him, "Who are you?" Jesus said to them, "Why do I speak to you at all?[b] [26]I have much to say about you and much to condemn; but the one who sent me is true, and I declare to the world what I have heard from him." [27]They did not understand that he was speaking to them about the Father. [28]So Jesus said, "When you have lifted up the Son of Man, then you will realize that I am he,[a] and that I do nothing on my own, but I speak these things as the Father instructed me. [29]And the one who sent me is with me; he has not left me alone, for I always do what is pleasing to him." [30]As he was saying these things, many believed in him.

31 Then Jesus said to the Jews who had believed in him, "If you continue in my word, you are truly my disciples; [32]and you will know the truth, and the truth will make you free." [33]They answered him, "We are descendants of Abraham and have never been slaves to anyone. What do you mean by saying, 'You will be made free'?"

34 Jesus answered them, "Very truly, I tell you, everyone who commits sin is a slave to sin. [35]The slave does not have a permanent place in the household; the son has a place there forever. [36]So if the Son makes you free, you will be free indeed. [37]I know that you are descendants of Abraham; yet you look for an opportunity to kill me, because there is no place in you for my word. [38]I declare what I have seen in the Father's presence; as for you, you should do what you have heard from the Father."[c]

39 They answered him, "Abraham is our father." Jesus said to them, "If you were Abraham's children, you would be doing[d] what Abraham did, [40]but now you are trying to kill me, a man who has told you the truth that I heard from God. This is not what Abraham did. [41]You are indeed doing what your father does." They said to him, "We are not illegitimate children; we have one father, God himself." [42]Jesus said to them, "If God were your Father, you would love me, for I came from God and now I am here. I did not come on my own, but he sent me. [43]Why do you not understand what I say? It is because you cannot accept my word. [44]You are from your father the devil, and you choose to do your father's desires. He was a murderer from the beginning and does not stand in the truth, because there is no truth in him. When he lies, he speaks according to his own nature, for

[a]Gk I am [b]Or What I have told you from the beginning [c]Other ancient authorities read you do what you have heard from your father [d]Other ancient authorities read If you are Abraham's children, then do

he is a liar and the father of lies. [45]But because I tell the truth, you do not believe me. [46]Which of you convicts me of sin? If I tell the truth, why do you not believe me? [47]Whoever is from God hears the words of God. The reason you do not hear them is that you are not from God."

[48] The Jews answered him, "Are we not right in saying that you are a Samaritan and have a demon?" [49]Jesus answered, "I do not have a demon; but I honor my Father, and you dishonor me. [50]Yet I do not seek my own glory; there is one who seeks it and he is the judge. [51]Very truly, I tell you, whoever keeps my word will never see death." [52]The Jews said to him, "Now we know that you have a demon. Abraham died, and so did the prophets; yet you say, 'Whoever keeps my word will never taste death.' [53]Are you greater than our father Abraham, who died? The prophets also died. Who do you claim to be?" [54]Jesus answered, "If I glorify myself, my glory is nothing. It is my Father who glorifies me, he of whom you say, 'He is our God,' [55]though you do not know him. But I know him; if I would say that I do not know him, I would be a liar like you. But I do know him and I keep his word. [56]Your ancestor Abraham rejoiced that he would see my day; he saw it and was glad." [57]Then the Jews said to him, "You are not yet fifty years old, and have you seen Abraham?"[a] [58]Jesus said to them, "Very truly,

I tell you, before Abraham was, I am." [59]So they picked up stones to throw at him, but Jesus hid himself and went out of the temple.

9 As he walked along, he saw a man blind from birth. [2]His disciples asked him, "Rabbi, who sinned, this man or his parents, that he was born blind?" [3]Jesus answered, "Neither this man nor his parents sinned; he was born blind so that God's works might be revealed in him. [4]We[b] must work the works of him who sent me[c] while it is day; night is coming when no one can work. [5]As long as I am in the world, I am the light of the world." [6]When he had said this, he spat on the ground and made mud with the saliva and spread the mud on the man's eyes, [7]saying to him, "Go, wash in the pool of Siloam" (which means Sent). Then he went and washed and came back able to see. [8]The neighbors and those who had seen him before as a beggar began to ask, "Is this not the man who used to sit and beg?" [9] Some were saying, "It is he." Others were saying, "No, but it is someone like him." He kept saying, "I am the man." [10]But they kept asking him, "Then how were your eyes opened?" [11]He answered, "The man called Jesus made mud, spread it on my eyes, and said to me, 'Go to Siloam and wash.' Then I went and washed

[a]Other ancient authorities read *has Abraham seen you?* [b]Other ancient authorities read *I* [c]Other ancient authorities read *us*

and received my sight." [12]They said to him, "Where is he?" He said, "I do not know."

13 They brought to the Pharisees the man who had formerly been blind. [14]Now it was a sabbath day when Jesus made the mud and opened his eyes. [15]Then the Pharisees also began to ask him how he had received his sight. He said to them, "He put mud on my eyes. Then I washed, and now I see." [16]Some of the Pharisees said, "This man is not from God, for he does not observe the sabbath." But others said, "How can a man who is a sinner perform such signs?" And they were divided. [17]So they said again to the blind man, "What do you say about him? It was your eyes he opened." He said, "He is a prophet."

18 The Jews did not believe that he had been blind and had received his sight until they called the parents of the man who had received his sight [19]and asked them, "Is this your son, who you say was born blind? How then does he now see?" [20]His parents answered, "We know that this is our son, and that he was born blind; [21]but we do not know how it is that now he sees, nor do we know who opened his eyes. Ask him; he is of age. He will speak for himself." [22]His parents said this because they were afraid of the Jews; for the Jews had already agreed that anyone who confessed Jesus[a] to be the Messiah[b] would be put out of the syna-gogue. [23]Therefore his parents said, "He is of age; ask him."

24 So for the second time they called the man who had been blind, and they said to him, "Give glory to God! We know that this man is a sinner." [25]He answered, "I do not know whether he is a sinner. One thing I do know, that though I was blind, now I see." [26]They said to him, "What did he do to you? How did he open your eyes?" [27]He answered them, "I have told you already, and you would not listen. Why do you want to hear it again? Do you also want to become his disciples?" [28]Then they reviled him, saying, "You are his disciple, but we are disciples of Moses. [29]We know that God has spoken to Moses, but as for this man, we do not know where he comes from." [30]The man answered, "Here is an astonishing thing! You do not know where he comes from, and yet he opened my eyes. [31]We know that God does not listen to sinners, but he does listen to one who worships him and obeys his will. [32]Never since the world began has it been heard that anyone opened the eyes of a person born blind. [33]If this man were not from God, he could do nothing." [34]They answered him, "You were born entirely in sins, and are you trying to teach us?" And they drove him out.

35 Jesus heard that they had driven him out, and when he found him, he said, "Do you be-

---

[a]Gk *him* [b]Or *the Christ*

lieve in the Son of Man?"[a] [36]He answered, "And who is he, sir?[b] Tell me, so that I may believe in him." [37]Jesus said to him, "You have seen him, and the one speaking with you is he." [38]He said, "Lord,[b] I believe." And he worshiped him. [39]Jesus said, "I came into this world for judgment so that those who do not see may see, and those who do see may become blind." [40]Some of the Pharisees near him heard this and said to him, "Surely we are not blind, are we?" [41]Jesus said to them, "If you were blind, you would not have sin. But now that you say, 'We see,' your sin remains.

10

[1]"Very truly, I tell you, anyone who does not enter the sheepfold by the gate but climbs in by another way is a thief and a bandit. [2]The one who enters by the gate is the shepherd of the sheep. [3]The gatekeeper opens the gate for him, and the sheep hear his voice. He calls his own sheep by name and leads them out. [4]When he has brought out all his own, he goes ahead of them, and the sheep follow him because they know his voice. [5]They will not follow a stranger, but they will run from him because they do not know the voice of strangers." [6]Jesus used this figure of speech with them, but they did not understand what he was saying to them.

[7]So again Jesus said to them, "Very truly, I tell you, I am the gate for the sheep. [8]All who came before me are thieves and bandits; but the sheep did not listen to them. [9]I am the gate. Whoever enters by me will be saved, and will come in and go out and find pasture. [10]The thief comes only to steal and kill and destroy. I came that they may have life, and have it abundantly.

[11]"I am the good shepherd. The good shepherd lays down his life for the sheep. [12]The hired hand, who is not the shepherd and does not own the sheep, sees the wolf coming and leaves the sheep and runs away—and the wolf snatches them and scatters them. [13]The hired hand runs away because a hired hand does not care for the sheep. [14]I am the good shepherd. I know my own and my own know me, [15]just as the Father knows me and I know the Father. And I lay down my life for the sheep. [16]I have other sheep that do not belong to this fold. I must bring them also, and they will listen to my voice. So there will be one flock, one shepherd. [17]For this reason the Father loves me, because I lay down my life in order to take it up again. [18]No one takes[c] it from me, but I lay it down of my own accord. I have power to lay it down, and I have power to take it up again. I have received this command from my Father."

[19]Again the Jews were divided because of these words. [20]Many of them were saying, "He has a demon and is out of his mind.

---

[a]Other ancient authorities read *the Son of God* [b]*Sir* and *Lord* translate the same Greek word [c]Other ancient authorities read *has taken*

Why listen to him?" [21]Others were saying, "These are not the words of one who has a demon. Can a demon open the eyes of the blind?"

22 At that time the festival of the Dedication took place in Jerusalem. It was winter, [23]and Jesus was walking in the temple, in the portico of Solomon. [24]So the Jews gathered around him and said to him, "How long will you keep us in suspense? If you are the Messiah,[a] tell us plainly." [25]Jesus answered, "I have told you, and you do not believe. The works that I do in my Father's name testify to me; [26]but you do not believe, because you do not belong to my sheep. [27]My sheep hear my voice. I know them, and they follow me. [28]I give them eternal life, and they will never perish. No one will snatch them out of my hand. [29]What my Father has given me is greater than all else, and no one can snatch it out of the Father's hand.[b] [30]The Father and I are one."

31 The Jews took up stones again to stone him. [32]Jesus replied, "I have shown you many good works from the Father. For which of these are you going to stone me?" [33]The Jews answered, "It is not for a good work that we are going to stone you, but for blasphemy, because you, though only a human being, are making yourself God." [34]Jesus answered, "Is it not written in your law,[c] 'I said, you are gods'? [35]If those to whom the word of God came were called 'gods'—and the

scripture cannot be annulled— [36]can you say that the one whom the Father has sanctified and sent into the world is blaspheming because I said, 'I am God's Son'? [37]If I am not doing the works of my Father, then do not believe me. [38]But if I do them, even though you do not believe me, believe the works, so that you may know and understand[d] that the Father is in me and I am in the Father." [39]Then they tried to arrest him again, but he escaped from their hands.

40 He went away again across the Jordan to the place where John had been baptizing earlier, and he remained there. [41]Many came to him, and they were saying, "John performed no sign, but everything that John said about this man was true." [42]And many believed in him there.

11 Now a certain man was ill, Lazarus of Bethany, the village of Mary and her sister Martha. [2]Mary was the one who anointed the Lord with perfume and wiped his feet with her hair; her brother Lazarus was ill. [3]So the sisters sent a message to Jesus,[e] "Lord, he whom you love is ill." [4]But when Jesus heard it, he said, "This illness does not lead to death; rather it is for God's glory, so that the Son of God may be glorified through it."

[a]Or *the Christ* [b]Other ancient authorities read *My Father who has given them to me is greater than all, and no one can snatch them out of the Father's hand* [c]Other ancient authorities read *in the law* [d]Other ancient authorities lack *and understand;* others read *and believe* [e]Gk *him*

[5]Accordingly, though Jesus loved Martha and her sister and Lazarus, [6]after having heard that Lazarus[a] was ill, he stayed two days longer in the place where he was.

[7] Then after this he said to the disciples, "Let us go to Judea again." [8]The disciples said to him, "Rabbi, the Jews were just now trying to stone you, and are you going there again?" [9]Jesus answered, "Are there not twelve hours of daylight? Those who walk during the day do not stumble, because they see the light of this world. [10]But those who walk at night stumble, because the light is not in them." [11]After saying this, he told them, "Our friend Lazarus has fallen asleep, but I am going there to awaken him." [12]The disciples said to him, "Lord, if he has fallen asleep, he will be all right." [13]Jesus, however, had been speaking about his death, but they thought that he was referring merely to sleep. [14]Then Jesus told them plainly, "Lazarus is dead. [15]For your sake I am glad I was not there, so that you may believe. But let us go to him." [16]Thomas, who was called the Twin,[b] said to his fellow disciples, "Let us also go, that we may die with him."

[17] When Jesus arrived, he found that Lazarus[a] had already been in the tomb four days. [18]Now Bethany was near Jerusalem, some two miles[c] away, [19]and many of the Jews had come to Martha and Mary to console them about their brother. [20]When Martha heard that Jesus was coming, she went and met him, while Mary stayed at home. [21]Martha said to Jesus, "Lord, if you had been here, my brother would not have died. [22]But even now I know that God will give you whatever you ask of him." [23]Jesus said to her, "Your brother will rise again." [24]Martha said to him, "I know that he will rise again in the resurrection on the last day." [25]Jesus said to her, "I am the resurrection and the life.[d] Those who believe in me, even though they die, will live, [26]and everyone who lives and believes in me will never die. Do you believe this?" [27]She said to him, "Yes, Lord, I believe that you are the Messiah,[e] the Son of God, the one coming into the world."

[28] When she had said this, she went back and called her sister Mary, and told her privately, "The Teacher is here and is calling for you." [29]And when she heard it, she got up quickly and went to him. [30]Now Jesus had not yet come to the village, but was still at the place where Martha had met him. [31]The Jews who were with her in the house, consoling her, saw Mary get up quickly and go out. They followed her because they thought that she was going to the tomb to weep there. [32]When Mary came where Jesus was and saw him, she knelt at his feet and said to him, "Lord, if you had been here, my brother would not have died." [33]When Jesus saw her

---

[a]Gk he [b]Gk *Didymus* [c]Gk *fifteen stadia* [d]Other ancient authorities lack *and the life* [e]Or *the Christ*

weeping, and the Jews who came with her also weeping, he was greatly disturbed in spirit and deeply moved. 34He said, "Where have you laid him?" They said to him, "Lord, come and see." 35Jesus began to weep. 36So the Jews said, "See how he loved him!" 37But some of them said, "Could not he who opened the eyes of the blind man have kept this man from dying?"

38 Then Jesus, again greatly disturbed, came to the tomb. It was a cave, and a stone was lying against it. 39Jesus said, "Take away the stone." Martha , the sister of the dead man, said to him, "Lord, already there is a stench because he has been dead four days." 40Jesus said to her, "Did I not tell you that if you believed, you would see the glory of God?" 41So they took away the stone. And Jesus looked upward and said, "Father, I thank you for having heard me. 42I knew that you always hear me, but I have said this for the sake of the crowd standing here, so that they may believe that you sent me." 43When he had said this, he cried with a loud voice, "Lazarus, come out!" 44The dead man came out, his hands and feet bound with strips of cloth, and his face wrapped in a cloth. Jesus said to them, "Unbind him, and let him go."

45 Many of the Jews therefore, who had come with Mary and had seen what Jesus did, believed in him. 46But some of them went to the Pharisees and told them what he had done. 47So the chief priests and the Pharisees called a meeting of the council, and said, "What are we to do? This man is performing many signs. 48If we let him go on like this, everyone will believe in him, and the Romans will come and destroy both our holy place*a* and our nation." 49But one of them, Caiaphas, who was high priest that year, said to them, "You know nothing at all! 50You do not understand that it is better for you to have one man die for the people than to have the whole nation destroyed." 51He did not say this on his own, but being high priest that year he prophesied that Jesus was about to die for the nation, 52and not for the nation only, but to gather into one the dispersed children of God. 53So from that day on they planned to put him to death.

54 Jesus therefore no longer walked about openly among the Jews, but went from there to a town called Ephraim in the region near the wilderness; and he remained there with the disciples.

55 Now the Passover of the Jews was near, and many went up from the country to Jerusalem before the Passover to purify themselves. 56They were looking for Jesus and were asking one another as they stood in the temple, "What do you think? Surely he will not come to the festival, will he?" 57Now the chief priests and the Pharisees had given orders

a Or our temple; Greek our place

that anyone who knew where Jesus[a] was should let them know, so that they might arrest him.

12 Six days before the Passover Jesus came to Bethany, the home of Lazarus, whom he had raised from the dead. [2]There they gave a dinner for him. Martha served, and Lazarus was one of those at the table with him. [3]Mary took a pound of costly perfume made of pure nard, anointed Jesus' feet, and wiped them[b] with her hair. The house was filled with the fragrance of the perfume. [4]But Judas Iscariot, one of his disciples (the one who was about to betray him), said, [5]"Why was this perfume not sold for three hundred denarii[c] and the money given to the poor?" [6](He said this not because he cared about the poor, but because he was a thief; he kept the common purse and used to steal what was put into it.) [7]Jesus said, "Leave her alone. She bought it[d] so that she might keep it for the day of my burial. [8]You always have the poor with you, but you do not always have me."

9 When the great crowd of the Jews learned that he was there, they came not only because of Jesus but also to see Lazarus, whom he had raised from the dead. [10]So the chief priests planned to put Lazarus to death as well, [11]since it was on account of him that many of the Jews were deserting and were believing in Jesus.

12 The next day the great crowd that had come to the festival heard that Jesus was coming to Jerusalem. [13]So they took branches of palm trees and went out to meet him, shouting,

"Hosanna!
Blessed is the one who
    comes in the name of
    the Lord—
the King of Israel!"

[14]Jesus found a young donkey and sat on it; as it is written:
[15]   "Do not be afraid, daughter
        of Zion.
    Look, your king is coming,
        sitting on a donkey's colt!"

[16]His disciples did not understand these things at first; but when Jesus was glorified, then they remembered that these things had been written of him and had been done to him. [17]So the crowd that had been with him when he called Lazarus out of the tomb and raised him from the dead continued to testify.[e] [18]It was also because they heard that he had performed this sign that the crowd went to meet him. [19]The Pharisees then said to one another, "You see, you can do nothing. Look, the world has gone after him!"

20 Now among those who went up to worship at the festival were some Greeks. [21]They came to Philip, who was from Bethsaida in Galilee, and said to him, "Sir, we wish to see Jesus." [22]Philip went and told Andrew; then Andrew and Philip went and

[a]Gk he [b]Gk his feet [c]Three hundred denarii would be nearly a year's wages for a laborer [d]Gk lacks She bought it [e]Other ancient authorities read with him began to testify that he had called . . . from the dead

told Jesus. [23]Jesus answered them, "The hour has come for the Son of Man to be glorified. [24]Very truly, I tell you, unless a grain of wheat falls into the earth and dies, it remains just a single grain; but if it dies, it bears much fruit. [25]Those who love their life lose it, and those who hate their life in this world will keep it for eternal life. [26]Whoever serves me must follow me, and where I am, there will my servant be also. Whoever serves me, the Father will honor.

[27] "Now my soul is troubled. And what should I say—'Father, save me from this hour'? No, it is for this reason that I have come to this hour. [28]Father, glorify your name." Then a voice came from heaven, "I have glorified it, and I will glorify it again." [29]The crowd standing there heard it and said that it was thunder. Others said, "An angel has spoken to him." [30]Jesus answered, "This voice has come for your sake, not for mine. [31]Now is the judgment of this world; now the ruler of this world will be driven out. [32]And I, when I am lifted up from the earth, will draw all people[a] to myself." [33]He said this to indicate the kind of death he was to die. [34]The crowd answered him, "We have heard from the law that the Messiah[b] remains forever. How can you say that the Son of Man must be lifted up? Who is this Son of Man?" [35]Jesus said to them, "The light is with you for a little longer. Walk while you have the light, so that the darkness may not overtake you.

If you walk in the darkness, you do not know where you are going. [36]While you have the light, believe in the light, so that you may become children of light."

After Jesus had said this, he departed and hid from them. [37]Although he had performed so many signs in their presence, they did not believe in him. [38]This was to fulfill the word spoken by the prophet Isaiah:

"Lord, who has believed
        our message,
and to whom has
        the arm of the Lord been
        revealed?"

[39]And so they could not believe, because Isaiah also said,

[40] "He has blinded their eyes
        and hardened their heart,
    so that they might not look
        with their eyes,
    and understand with their
        heart and turn—
    and I would heal them."

[41]Isaiah said this because[c] he saw his glory and spoke about him. [42]Nevertheless many, even of the authorities, believed in him. But because of the Pharisees they did not confess it, for fear that they would be put out of the synagogue; [43]for they loved human glory more than the glory that comes from God.

[44] Then Jesus cried aloud: "Whoever believes in me believes not in me but in him who sent me. [45]And whoever sees me sees him who sent me. [46]I have come as

[a]Other ancient authorities read *all things* [b]Or *the Christ* [c]Other ancient witnesses read *when*

light into the world, so that everyone who believes in me should not remain in the darkness. [47]I do not judge anyone who hears my words and does not keep them, for I came not to judge the world, but to save the world. [48]The one who rejects me and does not receive my word has a judge; on the last day the word that I have spoken will serve as judge, [49]for I have not spoken on my own, but the Father who sent me has himself given me a commandment about what to say and what to speak. [50]And I know that his commandment is eternal life. What I speak, therefore, I speak just as the Father has told me."

13

Now before the festival of the Passover, Jesus knew that his hour had come to depart from this world and go to the Father. Having loved his own who were in the world, he loved them to the end. [2]The devil had already put it into the heart of Judas son of Simon Iscariot to betray him. And during supper [3]Jesus, knowing that the Father had given all things into his hands, and that he had come from God and was going to God, [4]got up from the table,[a] took off his outer robe, and tied a towel around himself. [5]Then he poured water into a basin and began to wash the disciples' feet and to wipe them with the towel that was tied around him. [6]He came to Simon Peter, who said to him, "Lord, are you going to wash my feet?" [7]Jesus answered, "You do

not know now what I am doing, but later you will understand." [8]Peter said to him, "You will never wash my feet." Jesus answered, "Unless I wash you, you have no share with me." [9]Simon Peter said to him, "Lord, not my feet only but also my hands and my head!" [10]Jesus said to him, "One who has bathed does not need to wash, except for the feet,[b] but is entirely clean. And you[c] are clean, though not all of you." [11]For he knew who was to betray him; for this reason he said, "Not all of you are clean."

12 After he had washed their feet, had put on his robe, and had returned to the table, he said to them, "Do you know what I have done to you? [13]You call me Teacher and Lord—and you are right, for that is what I am. [14]So if I, your Lord and Teacher, have washed your feet, you also ought to wash one another's feet. [15]For I have set you an example, that you also should do as I have done to you. [16]Very truly, I tell you, servants[d] are not greater than their master, nor are messengers greater than the one who sent them. [17]If you know these things, you are blessed if you do them. [18]I am not speaking of all of you; I know whom I have chosen. But it is to fulfill the scripture, 'The one who ate my bread[e] has lifted his heel against me.' [19]I tell you this now, before it occurs, so

[a]Gk *from supper* [b]Other ancient authorities lack *except for the feet* [c]The Greek word for *you* here is plural [d]Gk *slaves* [e]Other ancient authorities read *ate bread with me*

that when it does occur, you may believe that I am he.[a] [20]Very truly, I tell you, whoever receives one whom I send receives me; and whoever receives me receives him who sent me."

21 After saying this Jesus was troubled in spirit, and declared, "Very truly, I tell you, one of you will betray me." [22]The disciples looked at one another, uncertain of whom he was speaking. [23]One of his disciples—the one whom Jesus loved—was reclining next to him; [24]Simon Peter therefore motioned to him to ask Jesus of whom he was speaking. [25]So while reclining next to Jesus, he asked him, "Lord, who is it?" [26]Jesus answered, "It is the one to whom I give this piece of bread when I have dipped it in the dish."[b] So when he had dipped the piece of bread, he gave it to Judas son of Simon Iscariot.[c] [27]After he received the piece of bread,[d] Satan entered into him. Jesus said to him, "Do quickly what you are going to do." [28]Now no one at the table knew why he said this to him. [29]Some thought that, because Judas had the common purse, Jesus was telling him, "Buy what we need for the festival"; or, that he should give something to the poor. [30]So, after receiving the piece of bread, he immediately went out. And it was night.

31 When he had gone out, Jesus said, "Now the Son of Man has been glorified, and God has been glorified in him. [32]If God has been glorified in him,[e] God will also glorify him in himself and will glorify him at once. [33]Little children, I am with you only a little longer. You will look for me; and as I said to the Jews so now I say to you, 'Where I am going, you cannot come.' [34]I give you a new commandment, that you love one another. Just as I have loved you, you also should love one another. [35]By this everyone will know that you are my disciples, if you have love for one another."

36 Simon Peter said to him, "Lord, where are you going?" Jesus answered, "Where I am going, you cannot follow me now; but you will follow afterward." [37]Peter said to him, "Lord, why can I not follow you now? I will lay down my life for you." [38]Jesus answered, "Will you lay down your life for me? Very truly, I tell you, before the cock crows, you will have denied me three times.

14 "Do not let your hearts be troubled. Believe[f] in God, believe also in me. [2]In my Father's house there are many dwelling places. If it were not so, would I have told you that I go to prepare a place for you?[g] [3]And if I go and prepare a place for you, I will come again and will take you to myself, so that where I am,

[a]Gk I am [b]Gk dipped it [c]Other ancient authorities read Judas Iscariot son of Simon; others, Judas son of Simon from Karyot (Kerioth) [d]Other ancient authorities lack If God has been glorified in him [f]Or You believe [g]Or If it were not so, I would have told you; for I go to prepare a place for you

there you may be also. [4]And you know the way to the place where I am going."[a] [5]Thomas said to him, "Lord, we do not know where you are going. How can we know the way?" [6]Jesus said to him, "I am the way, and the truth, and the life. No one comes to the Father except through me. [7]If you know me, you will know[b] my Father also. From now on you do know him and have seen him."

8 Philip said to him, "Lord, show us the Father, and we will be satisfied." [9]Jesus said to him, "Have I been with you all this time, Philip, and you still do not know me? Whoever has seen me has seen the Father. How can you say, 'Show us the Father'? [10]Do you not believe that I am in the Father and the Father is in me? The words that I say to you I do not speak on my own; but the Father who dwells in me does his works. [11]Believe me that I am in the Father and the Father is in me; but if you do not, then believe me because of the works themselves. [12]Very truly, I tell you, the one who believes in me will also do the works that I do and, in fact, will do greater works than these, because I am going to the Father. [13]I will do whatever you ask in my name, so that the Father may be glorified in the Son. [14]If in my name you ask me[c] for anything, I will do it.

15 "If you love me, you will keep[d] my commandments. [16]And I will ask the Father, and he will give you another Advocate,[e] to be with you forever. [17]This is the Spirit of truth, whom the world cannot receive, because it neither sees him nor knows him. You know him, because he abides with you, and he will be in[f] you.

18 "I will not leave you orphaned; I am coming to you. [19]In a little while the world will no longer see me, but you will see me; because I live, you also will live. [20]On that day you will know that I am in my Father, and you in me, and I in you. [21]They who have my commandments and keep them are those who love me; and those who love me will be loved by my Father, and I will love them and reveal myself to them." [22]Judas (not Iscariot) said to him, "Lord, how is it that you will reveal yourself to us, and not to the world?" [23]Jesus answered him, "Those who love me will keep my word, and my Father will love them, and we will come to them and make our home with them. [24]Whoever does not love me does not keep my words; and the word that you hear is not mine, but is from the Father who sent me.

25 "I have said these things to you while I am still with you. [26]But the Advocate,[e] the Holy Spirit, whom the Father will send in my name, will teach you everything, and remind you of all that I have said to you. [27]Peace I leave with you; my peace I give

---

[a]Other ancient authorities read *Where I am going you know, and the way you know* [b]Other ancient authorities read *If you had known me, you would have known* [c]Other ancient authorities lack *me* [d]Other ancient authorities read *me, keep* [e]Or *Helper* [f]Or *among*

to you. I do not give to you as the world gives. Do not let your hearts be troubled, and do not let them be afraid. ²⁸You heard me say to you, 'I am going away, and I am coming to you.' If you loved me, you would rejoice that I am going to the Father, because the Father is greater than I. ²⁹And now I have told you this before it occurs, so that when it does occur, you may believe. ³⁰I will no longer talk much with you, for the ruler of this world is coming. He has no power over me; ³¹but I do as the Father has commanded me, so that the world may know that I love the Father. Rise, let us be on our way.

15 "I am the true vine, and my Father is the vinegrower. ²He removes every branch in me that bears no fruit. Every branch that bears fruit he prunes[a] to make it bear more fruit. ³You have already been cleansed[a] by the word that I have spoken to you. ⁴Abide in me as I abide in you. Just as the branch cannot bear fruit by itself unless it abides in the vine, neither can you unless you abide in me. ⁵I am the vine, you are the branches. Those who abide in me and I in them bear much fruit, because apart from me you can do nothing. ⁶Whoever does not abide in me is thrown away like a branch and withers; such branches are gathered, thrown into the fire, and burned. ⁷If you abide in me, and my words abide in you, ask for whatever you wish, and it will be done for you. ⁸My Father

is glorified by this, that you bear much fruit and become[b] my disciples. ⁹As the Father has loved me, so I have loved you; abide in my love. ¹⁰If you keep my commandments, you will abide in my love, just as I have kept my Father's commandments and abide in his love. ¹¹I have said these things to you so that my joy may be in you, and that your joy may be complete.

12 "This is my commandment, that you love one another as I have loved you. ¹³No one has greater love than this, to lay down one's life for one's friends. ¹⁴You are my friends if you do what I command you. ¹⁵ I do not call you servants[c] any longer, because the servant[d] does not know what the master is doing; but I have called you friends, because I have made known to you everything that I have heard from my Father. ¹⁶You did not choose me but I chose you. And I appointed you to go and bear fruit, fruit that will last, so that the Father will give you whatever you ask him in my name. ¹⁷I am giving you these commands so that you may love one another.

18 "If the world hates you, be aware that it hated me before it hated you. ¹⁹If you belonged to the world,[e] the world would love you as its own. Because you do not belong to the world, but I have chosen you out of the world—therefore the world hates

---

[a] The same Greek root refers to pruning and cleansing [b] Or be [c] Gk slaves [d] Gk slave [e] Gk were of the world

you. [20]Remember the word that I said to you, 'Servants[a] are not greater than their master.' If they persecuted me, they will persecute you; if they kept my word, they will keep yours also. [21]But they will do all these things to you on account of my name, because they do not know him who sent me. [22]If I had not come and spoken to them, they would not have sin; but now they have no excuse for their sin. [23]Whoever hates me hates my Father also. [24]If I had not done among them the works that no one else did, they would not have sin. But now they have seen and hated both me and my Father. [25]It was to fulfill the word that is written in their law, 'They hated me without a cause.'

26 "When the Advocate[b] comes, whom I will send to you from the Father, the Spirit of truth who comes from the Father, he will testify on my behalf. [27]You also are to testify because you have been with me from the beginning.

16 "I have said these things to you to keep you from stumbling. [2]They will put you out of the synagogues. Indeed, an hour is coming when those who kill you will think that by doing so they are offering worship to God. [3]And they will do this because they have not known the Father or me. [4]But I have said these things to you so that when their hour comes you may remember that I told you about them.

"I did not say these things to you from the beginning, because I was with you. [5]But now I am going to him who sent me; yet none of you asks me, 'Where are you going?' [6]But because I have said these things to you, sorrow has filled your hearts. [7]Nevertheless I tell you the truth: it is to your advantage that I go away, for if I do not go away, the Advocate[b] will not come to you; but if I go, I will send him to you. [8]And when he comes, he will prove the world wrong about[c] sin and righteousness and judgment: [9]about sin, because they do not believe in me; [10]about righteousness, because I am going to the Father and you will see me no longer; [11]about judgment, because the ruler of this world has been condemned.

12 "I still have many things to say to you, but you cannot bear them now. [13]When the Spirit of truth comes, he will guide you into all the truth; for he will not speak on his own, but will speak whatever he hears, and he will declare to you the things that are to come. [14]He will glorify me, because he will take what is mine and declare it to you. [15]All that the Father has is mine. For this reason I said that he will take what is mine and declare it to you.

16 "A little while, and you will no longer see me, and again a little while, and you will see me." [17]Then some of his disciples said to one another, "What does

---

[a]Gk Slaves [b]Or Helper [c]Or convict the world of

he mean by saying to us, 'A little while, and you will no longer see me, and again a little while, and you will see me'; and 'Because I am going to the Father'?" [18]They said, "What does he mean by this 'a little while'? We do not know what he is talking about." [19]Jesus knew that they wanted to ask him, so he said to them, "Are you discussing among yourselves what I meant when I said, 'A little while, and you will no longer see me, and again a little while, and you will see me'? [20]Very truly, I tell you, you will weep and mourn, but the world will rejoice; you will have pain, but your pain will turn into joy. [21]When a woman is in labor, she has pain, because her hour has come. But when her child is born, she no longer remembers the anguish because of the joy of having brought a human being into the world. [22]So you have pain now; but I will see you again, and your hearts will rejoice, and no one will take your joy from you. [23]On that day you will ask nothing of me.[a] Very truly, I tell you, if you ask anything of the Father in my name, he will give it to you.[b] [24]Until now you have not asked for anything in my name. Ask and you will receive, so that your joy may be complete.

[25] "I have said these things to you in figures of speech. The hour is coming when I will no longer speak to you in figures, but will tell you plainly of the Father. [26]On that day you will ask in my name. I do not say to you that I will ask the Father on your behalf; [27]for the Father himself loves you, because you have loved me and have believed that I came from God.[c] [28]I came from the Father and have come into the world; again, I am leaving the world and am going to the Father."

29 His disciples said, "Yes, now you are speaking plainly, not in any figure of speech! [30]Now we know that you know all things, and do not need to have anyone question you; by this we believe that you came from God." [31]Jesus answered them, "Do you now believe? [32]The hour is coming, indeed it has come, when you will be scattered, each one to his home, and you will leave me alone. Yet I am not alone because the Father is with me. [33]I have said this to you, so that in me you may have peace. In the world you face persecution. But take courage; I have conquered the world!"

17 After Jesus had spoken these words, he looked up to heaven and said, "Father, the hour has come; glorify your Son so that the Son may glorify you, [2]since you have given him authority over all people,[d] to give eternal life to all whom you have given him. [3]And this is eternal life, that they may know you, the only true God, and Jesus Christ whom you have sent. [4]I glorified you on earth by finishing the work

[a]Or *will ask me no question* [b]Other ancient authorities read *Father, he will give it to you in my name* [c]Other ancient authorities read *the Father* [d]Gk *flesh*

that you gave me to do. [5]So now, Father, glorify me in your own presence with the glory that I had in your presence before the world existed.

6 "I have made your name known to those whom you gave me from the world. They were yours, and you gave them to me, and they have kept your word. [7]Now they know that everything you have given me is from you; [8]for the words that you gave to me I have given to them, and they have received them and know in truth that I came from you; and they have believed that you sent me. [9]I am asking on their behalf; I am not asking on behalf of the world, but on behalf of those whom you gave me, because they are yours. [10]All mine are yours, and yours are mine; and I have been glorified in them. [11]And now I am no longer in the world, but they are in the world, and I am coming to you. Holy Father, protect them in your name that you have given me, so that they may be one, as we are one. [12]While I was with them, I protected them in your name that[a] you have given me. I guarded them, and not one of them was lost except the one destined to be lost,[b] so that the scripture might be fulfilled. [13]But now I am coming to you, and I speak these things in the world so that they may have my joy made complete in themselves.[c] [14]I have given them your word, and the world has hated them because they do not belong to the world,

just as I do not belong to the world. [15]I am not asking you to take them out of the world, but I ask you to protect them from the evil one.[d] [16]They do not belong to the world, just as I do not belong to the world. [17]Sanctify them in the truth; your word is truth. [18]As you have sent me into the world, so I have sent them into the world. [19]And for their sakes I sanctify myself, so that they also may be sanctified in truth.

20 "I ask not only on behalf of these, but also on behalf of those who will believe in me through their word, [21]that they may all be one. As you, Father, are in me and I am in you, may they also be in us,[e] so that the world may believe that you have sent me. [22]The glory that you have given me I have given them, so that they may be one, as we are one, [23]I in them and you in me, that they may become completely one, so that the world may know that you have sent me and have loved them even as you have loved me. [24]Father, I desire that those also, whom you have given me, may be with me where I am, to see my glory, which you have given me because you loved me before the foundation of the world.

25 "Righteous Father, the world does not know you, but I know you; and these know that you have sent me. [26]I made your name known to them, and I will

[a]Other ancient authorities read *protected in your name those whom* [b]Gk *except the son of destruction* [c]Or *among themselves* [d]Or *from evil* [e]Other ancient authorities read *be one in us*

make it known, so that the love with which you have loved me may be in them, and I in them."

18 After Jesus had spoken these words, he went out with his disciples across the Kidron valley to a place where there was a garden, which he and his disciples entered. ²Now Judas, who betrayed him, also knew the place, because Jesus often met there with his disciples. ³So Judas brought a detachment of soldiers together with police from the chief priests and the Pharisees, and they came there with lanterns and torches and weapons. ⁴Then Jesus, knowing all that was to happen to him, came forward and asked them, "Whom are you looking for?" ⁵They answered, "Jesus of Nazareth."ᵃ Jesus replied, "I am he."ᵇ Judas, who betrayed him, was standing with them. ⁶When Jesusᶜ said to them, "I am he,"ᵇ they stepped back and fell to the ground. ⁷Again he asked them, "Whom are you looking for?" And they said, "Jesus of Nazareth."ᵃ ⁸Jesus answered, "I told you that I am he.ᵇ So if you are looking for me, let these men go." ⁹This was to fulfill the word that he had spoken, "I did not lose a single one of those whom you gave me." ¹⁰Then Simon Peter, who had a sword, drew it, struck the high priest's slave, and cut off his right ear. The slave's name was Malchus. ¹¹Jesus said to Peter, "Put your sword back into its sheath. Am I not to drink the cup that the Father has given me?"

12 So the soldiers, their officer, and the Jewish police arrested Jesus and bound him. ¹³First they took him to Annas, who was the father-in-law of Caiaphas, the high priest that year. ¹⁴Caiaphas was the one who had advised the Jews that it was better to have one person die for the people.

15 Simon Peter and another disciple followed Jesus. Since that disciple was known to the high priest, he went with Jesus into the courtyard of the high priest, ¹⁶but Peter was standing outside at the gate. So the other disciple, who was known to the high priest, went out, spoke to the woman who guarded the gate, and brought Peter in. ¹⁷The woman said to Peter, "You are not also one of this man's disciples, are you?" He said, "I am not." ¹⁸Now the slaves and the police had made a charcoal fire because it was cold, and they were standing around it and warming themselves. Peter also was standing with them and warming himself.

19 Then the high priest questioned Jesus about his disciples and about his teaching. ²⁰Jesus answered, "I have spoken openly to the world; I have always taught in synagogues and in the temple, where all the Jews come together. I have said nothing in secret. ²¹Why do you ask me? Ask those who heard what I said to them; they know what I said."

ᵃGk the Nazorean ᵇGk I am ᶜGk he

[22]When he had said this, one of the police standing nearby struck Jesus on the face, saying, "Is that how you answer the high priest?" [23]Jesus answered, "If I have spoken wrongly, testify to the wrong. But if I have spoken rightly, why do you strike me?" [24]Then Annas sent him bound to Caiaphas the high priest.

25 Now Simon Peter was standing and warming himself. They asked him, "You are not also one of his disciples, are you?" He denied it and said, "I am not." [26]One of the slaves of the high priest, a relative of the man whose ear Peter had cut off, asked, "Did I not see you in the garden with him?" [27]Again Peter denied it, and at that moment the cock crowed.

28 Then they took Jesus from Caiaphas to Pilate's headquarters.[a] It was early in the morning. They themselves did not enter the headquarters,[a] so as to avoid ritual defilement and to be able to eat the Passover. [29]So Pilate went out to them and said, "What accusation do you bring against this man?" [30]They answered, "If this man were not a criminal, we would not have handed him over to you." [31]Pilate said to them, "Take him yourselves and judge him according to your law." The Jews replied, "We are not permitted to put anyone to death." [32](This was to fulfill what Jesus had said when he indicated the kind of death he was to die.)

33 Then Pilate entered the headquarters again, summoned Jesus, and asked him, "Are you the King of the Jews?" [34]Jesus answered, "Do you ask this on your own, or did others tell you about me?" [35]Pilate replied, "I am not a Jew, am I? Your own nation and the chief priests have handed you over to me. What have you done?" [36]Jesus answered, "My kingdom is not from this world. If my kingdom were from this world, my followers would be fighting to keep me from being handed over to the Jews. But as it is, my kingdom is not from here." [37]Pilate asked him, "So you are a king?" Jesus answered, "You say that I am a king. For this I was born, and for this I came into the world, to testify to the truth. Everyone who belongs to the truth listens to my voice." [38]Pilate asked him, "What is truth?"

After he had said this, he went out to the Jews again and told them, "I find no case against him. [39]But you have a custom that I release someone for you at the Passover. Do you want me to release for you the King of the Jews?" [40]They shouted in reply, "Not this man, but Barabbas!" Now Barabbas was a bandit.

19 Then Pilate took Jesus and had him flogged. [2]And the soldiers wove a crown of thorns and put it on his head, and they dressed him in a purple robe. [3]They kept coming up to him, saying, "Hail, King of the Jews!" and striking him on the face. [4]Pilate went out again and said to

[a]Gk the praetorium

them, "Look, I am bringing him out to you to let you know that I find no case against him." [5]So Jesus came out, wearing the crown of thorns and the purple robe. Pilate said to them, "Here is the man!" [6]When the chief priests and the police saw him, they shouted, "Crucify him! Crucify him!" Pilate said to them, "Take him yourselves and crucify him; I find no case against him." [7]The Jews answered him, "We have a law, and according to that law he ought to die because he has claimed to be the Son of God."

8 Now when Pilate heard this, he was more afraid than ever. [9]He entered his headquarters[a] again and asked Jesus, "Where are you from?" But Jesus gave him no answer. [10]Pilate therefore said to him, "Do you refuse to speak to me? Do you not know that I have power to release you, and power to crucify you?" [11]Jesus answered him, "You would have no power over me unless it had been given you from above; therefore the one who handed me over to you is guilty of a greater sin." [12]From then on Pilate tried to release him, but the Jews cried out, "If you release this man, you are no friend of the emperor. Everyone who claims to be a king sets himself against the emperor."

13 When Pilate heard these words, he brought Jesus outside and sat[b] on the judge's bench at a place called The Stone Pavement, or in Hebrew[c] Gabbatha. [14]Now it was the day of Preparation for the Passover; and it was about noon. He said to the Jews, "Here is your King!" [15]They cried out, "Away with him! Away with him! Crucify him!" Pilate asked them, "Shall I crucify your King?" The chief priests answered, "We have no king but the emperor." [16]Then he handed him over to them to be crucified.

So they took Jesus; [17]and carrying the cross by himself, he went out to what is called The Place of the Skull, which in Hebrew[c] is called Golgotha. [18]There they crucified him, and with him two others, one on either side, with Jesus between them. [19]Pilate also had an inscription written and put on the cross. It read, "Jesus of Nazareth,[d] the King of the Jews." [20]Many of the Jews read this inscription, because the place where Jesus was crucified was near the city; and it was written in Hebrew,[c] in Latin, and in Greek. [21]Then the chief priests of the Jews said to Pilate, "Do not write, 'The King of the Jews,' but, 'This man said, I am King of the Jews.'" [22]Pilate answered, "What I have written I have written." [23]When the soldiers had crucified Jesus, they took his clothes and divided them into four parts, one for each soldier. They also took his tunic; now the tunic was seamless, woven in one piece from the top. [24]So they said to one another, "Let us not tear it, but cast lots for it to see who will

[a]Gk *the praetorium* [b]Or *seated him* [c]That is, *Aramaic* [d]Gk *the Nazorean*

get it." This was to fulfill what the scripture says,

"They divided my clothes
    among themselves,
and for my clothing they
    cast lots."

25And that is what the soldiers did. Meanwhile, standing near the cross of Jesus were his mother, and his mother's sister, Mary the wife of Clopas, and Mary Magdalene. 26When Jesus saw his mother and the disciple whom he loved standing beside her, he said to his mother, "Woman, here is your son." 27Then he said to the disciple, "Here is your mother." And from that hour the disciple took her into his own home.

28 After this, when Jesus knew that all was now finished, he said (in order to fulfill the scripture), "I am thirsty." 29A jar full of sour wine was standing there. So they put a sponge full of the wine on a branch of hyssop and held it to his mouth. 30When Jesus had received the wine, he said, "It is finished." Then he bowed his head and gave up his spirit.

31 Since it was the day of Preparation, the Jews did not want the bodies left on the cross during the sabbath, especially because that sabbath was a day of great solemnity. So they asked Pilate to have the legs of the crucified men broken and the bodies removed. 32Then the soldiers came and broke the legs of the first and of the other who had been crucified with him. 33But when they came to Jesus and saw that he was already dead, they

did not break his legs. 34Instead, one of the soldiers pierced his side with a spear, and at once blood and water came out. 35(He who saw this has testified so that you also may believe. His testimony is true, and he knows*a* that he tells the truth.) 36These things occurred so that the scripture might be fulfilled, "None of his bones shall be broken." 37And again another passage of scripture says, "They will look on the one whom they have pierced."

38 After these things, Joseph of Arimathea, who was a disciple of Jesus, though a secret one because of his fear of the Jews, asked Pilate to let him take away the body of Jesus. Pilate gave him permission; so he came and removed his body. 39Nicodemus, who had at first come to Jesus by night, also came, bringing a mixture of myrrh and aloes, weighing about a hundred pounds. 40They took the body of Jesus and wrapped it with the spices in linen cloths, according to the burial custom of the Jews. 41Now there was a garden in the place where he was crucified, and in the garden there was a new tomb in which no one had ever been laid. 42And so, because it was the Jewish day of Preparation, and the tomb was nearby, they laid Jesus there.

20 Early on the first day of the week, while it was still dark, Mary Magdalene came to the tomb and saw that the stone

*a*Or *there is one who knows*

had been removed from the tomb. [2]So she ran and went to Simon Peter and the other disciple, the one whom Jesus loved, and said to them, "They have taken the Lord out of the tomb, and we do not know where they have laid him." [3]Then Peter and the other disciple set out and went toward the tomb. [4]The two were running together, but the other disciple outran Peter and reached the tomb first. [5]He bent down to look in and saw the linen wrappings lying there, but he did not go in. [6]Then Simon Peter came, following him, and went into the tomb. He saw the linen wrappings lying there, [7]and the cloth that had been on Jesus' head, not lying with the linen wrappings but rolled up in a place by itself. [8]Then the other disciple, who reached the tomb first, also went in, and he saw and believed; [9]for as yet they did not understand the scripture, that he must rise from the dead. [10]Then the disciples returned to their homes.

11 But Mary stood weeping outside the tomb. As she wept, she bent over to look[a] into the tomb; [12]and she saw two angels in white, sitting where the body of Jesus had been lying, one at the head and the other at the feet. [13]They said to her, "Woman, why are you weeping?" She said to them, "They have taken away my Lord, and I do not know where they have laid him." [14]When she had said this, she turned around and saw Jesus standing there, but she did not know that it was Jesus. [15]Jesus said to her, "Woman, why are you weeping? Whom are you looking for?" Supposing him to be the gardener, she said to him, "Sir, if you have carried him away, tell me where you have laid him, and I will take him away." [16]Jesus said to her, "Mary!" She turned and said to him in Hebrew,[b] "Rabbouni!" (which means Teacher). [17]Jesus said to her, "Do not hold on to me, because I have not yet ascended to the Father. But go to my brothers and say to them, 'I am ascending to my Father and your Father, to my God and your God.'" [18]Mary Magdalene went and announced to the disciples, "I have seen the Lord"; and she told them that he had said these things to her.

19 When it was evening on that day, the first day of the week, and the doors of the house where the disciples had met were locked for fear of the Jews, Jesus came and stood among them and said, "Peace be with you." [20]After he said this, he showed them his hands and his side. Then the disciples rejoiced when they saw the Lord. [21]Jesus said to them again, "Peace be with you. As the Father has sent me, so I send you." [22]When he had said this, he breathed on them and said to them, "Receive the Holy Spirit. [23]If you forgive the sins of any, they are forgiven them; if you retain the sins of any, they are retained."

[a]Gk lacks *to look* [b]That is, *Aramaic*

24 But Thomas (who was the Twin[a]), one of the twelve, was not with them when Jesus came. [25]So the other disciples told him, "We have seen the Lord." But he said to them, "Unless I see the mark of the nails in his hands, and put my finger in the mark of the nails and my hand in his side, I will not believe."

26 A week later his disciples were again in the house, and Thomas was with them. Although the doors were shut, Jesus came and stood among them and said, "Peace be with you." [27]Then he said to Thomas, "Put your finger here and see my hands. Reach out your hand and put it in my side. Do not doubt but believe." [28]Thomas answered him, "My Lord and my God!" [29]Jesus said to him, "Have you believed because you have seen me? Blessed are those who have not seen and yet have come to believe."

30 Now Jesus did many other signs in the presence of his disciples, which are not written in this book. [31]But these are written so that you may come to believe[b] that Jesus is the Messiah,[c] the Son of God, and that through believing you may have life in his name.

21 After these things Jesus showed himself again to the disciples by the Sea of Tiberias; and he showed himself in this way. [2]Gathered there together were Simon Peter, Thomas called the Twin,[a] Nathanael of Cana in Galilee, the sons of Zebedee, and two others of his disciples. [3]Simon Peter said to them, "I am going fishing." They said to him, "We will go with you." They went out and got into the boat, but that night they caught nothing.

4 Just after daybreak, Jesus stood on the beach; but the disciples did not know that it was Jesus. [5]Jesus said to them, "Children, you have no fish, have you?" They answered him, "No." [6]He said to them, "Cast the net to the right side of the boat, and you will find some." So they cast it, and now they were not able to haul it in because there were so many fish. [7]That disciple whom Jesus loved said to Peter, "It is the Lord!" When Simon Peter heard that it was the Lord, he put on some clothes, for he was naked, and jumped into the sea. [8]But the other disciples came in the boat, dragging the net full of fish, for they were not far from the land, only about a hundred yards[d] off.

9 When they had gone ashore, they saw a charcoal fire there, with fish on it, and bread. [10]Jesus said to them, "Bring some of the fish that you have just caught." [11]So Simon Peter went aboard and hauled the net ashore, full of large fish, a hundred fifty-three of them; and though there were so many, the net was not torn. [12]Jesus said to them, "Come and have breakfast." Now none of the disciples dared to ask him, "Who

[a]Gk *Didymus* [b]Other ancient authorities read *may continue to believe* [c]Or *the Christ* [d]Gk *two hundred cubits*

are you?" because they knew it was the Lord. [13]Jesus came and took the bread and gave it to them, and did the same with the fish. [14]This was now the third time that Jesus appeared to the disciples after he was raised from the dead.

15 When they had finished breakfast, Jesus said to Simon Peter, "Simon son of John, do you love me more than these?" He said to him, "Yes, Lord; you know that I love you." Jesus said to him, "Feed my lambs." [16]A second time he said to him, "Simon son of John, do you love me?" He said to him, "Yes, Lord; you know that I love you." Jesus said to him, "Tend my sheep." [17]He said to him the third time, "Simon son of John, do you love me?" Peter felt hurt because he said to him the third time, "Do you love me?" And he said to him, "Lord, you know everything; you know that I love you." Jesus said to him, "Feed my sheep. [18]Very truly, I tell you, when you were younger, you used to fasten your own belt and to go wherever you wished. But when you grow old, you will stretch out your hands, and someone else will fasten a belt around you and take you where you do not wish to go." [19](He said this to indicate the kind of death by which he would glorify God.) After this he said to him, "Follow me."

20 Peter turned and saw the disciple whom Jesus loved following them; he was the one who had reclined next to Jesus at the supper and had said, "Lord, who is it that is going to betray you?" [21]When Peter saw him, he said to Jesus, "Lord, what about him?" [22]Jesus said to him, "If it is my will that he remain until I come, what is that to you? Follow me!" [23]So the rumor spread in the community[a] that this disciple would not die. Yet Jesus did not say to him that he would not die, but, "If it is my will that he remain until I come, what is that to you?"[b]

24 This is the disciple who is testifying to these things and has written them, and we know that his testimony is true. [25]But there are also many other things that Jesus did; if every one of them were written down, I suppose that the world itself could not contain the books that would be written.

[a]Gk *among the brothers* [b]Other ancient authorities lack *what is that to you*

The
ACTS
of the Apostles

1 In the first book, Theophilus, I wrote about all that Jesus did and taught from the beginning [2]until the day when he was taken up to heaven, after giving instructions through the Holy Spirit to the apostles whom he had chosen. [3]After his suffering he presented himself alive to them by many convincing proofs, appearing to them during forty days and speaking about the kingdom of God. [4]While staying[a] with them, he ordered them not to leave Jerusalem, but to wait there for the promise of the Father. "This," he said, "is what you have heard from me; [5]for John baptized with water, but you will be baptized with[b] the Holy Spirit not many days from now."

6 So when they had come together, they asked him, "Lord, is this the time when you will restore the kingdom to Israel?" [7]He replied, "It is not for you to know the times or periods that the Father has set by his own authority. [8]But you will receive power when the Holy Spirit has come upon you; and you will be my witnesses in Jerusalem, in all Judea and Samaria, and to the ends of the earth." [9]When he had said this, as they were watching, he was lifted up, and a cloud took him out of their sight. [10]While he was going and they were gazing up toward heaven, suddenly two men in white robes stood by them. [11]They said, "Men of Galilee, why do you stand looking up toward heaven? This Jesus, who has been taken up from you into heaven, will come in the same way as you saw him go into heaven."

12 Then they returned to Jerusalem from the mount called Olivet, which is near Jerusalem, a sabbath day's journey away. [13]When they had entered the city, they went to the room upstairs where they were staying, Peter, and John, and James, and Andrew, Philip and Thomas, Bartholomew and Matthew, James son of Alphaeus, and Simon the Zealot, and Judas son of[c] James. [14]All these were constantly devoting themselves to prayer, together with certain women, including Mary the mother of Jesus, as well as his brothers.

15 In those days Peter stood up among the believers[d] (together the crowd numbered about one hundred twenty persons) and said, [16]"Friends,[e] the scripture had to be fulfilled, which the Holy Spirit through David foretold

[a]Or eating [b]Or by [c]Or the brother of [d]Gk brothers [e]Gk Men, brothers

167

concerning Judas, who became a guide for those who arrested Jesus— [17]for he was numbered among us and was allotted his share in this ministry." [18](Now this man acquired a field with the reward of his wickedness; and falling headlong,[a] he burst open in the middle and all his bowels gushed out. [19]This became known to all the residents of Jerusalem, so that the field was called in their language Hakeldama, that is, Field of Blood.) [20]"For it is written in the book of Psalms,

'Let his homestead become
    desolate,
and let there be no one
    to live in it';

and

'Let another take his
    position of overseer.'

[21]So one of the men who have accompanied us during all the time that the Lord Jesus went in and out among us, [22]beginning from the baptism of John until the day when he was taken up from us—one of these must become a witness with us to his resurrection." [23]So they proposed two, Joseph called Barsabbas, who was also known as Justus, and Matthias. [24]Then they prayed and said, "Lord, you know everyone's heart. Show us which one of these two you have chosen [25]to take the place[b] in this ministry and apostleship from which Judas turned aside to go to his own place." [26]And they cast lots for them, and the lot fell on Matthias; and he was added to the eleven apostles.

The Coming of the Holy Spirit

2 When the day of Pentecost had come, they were all together in one place. [2]And suddenly from heaven there came a sound like the rush of a violent wind, and it filled the entire house where they were sitting. [3]Divided tongues, as of fire, appeared among them, and a tongue rested on each of them. [4]All of them were filled with the Holy Spirit and began to speak in other languages, as the Spirit gave them ability.

[5]Now there were devout Jews from every nation under heaven living in Jerusalem. [6]And at this sound the crowd gathered and was bewildered, because each one heard them speaking in the native language of each. [7]Amazed and astonished, they asked, "Are not all these who are speaking Galileans? [8]And how is it that we hear, each of us, in our own native language? [9]Parthians, Medes, Elamites, and residents of Mesopotamia, Judea and Cappadocia, Pontus and Asia, [10]Phrygia and Pamphylia, Egypt and the parts of Libya belonging to Cyrene, and visitors from Rome, both Jews and proselytes, [11]Cretans and Arabs—in our own languages we hear them speaking about God's deeds of power." [12]All were amazed and perplexed, saying to one another, "What does this mean?" [13]But others sneered and said, "They are filled with new wine."

---

[a]Or *swelling up* [b]Other ancient authorities read *the share*

14 But Peter, standing with the eleven, raised his voice and addressed them, "Men of Judea and all who live in Jerusalem, let this be known to you, and listen to what I say. ¹⁵Indeed, these are not drunk, as you suppose, for it is only nine o'clock in the morning. ¹⁶No, this is what was spoken through the prophet Joel:

17 'In the last days it will be,
        God declares,
    that I will pour out my
        Spirit upon all flesh,
    and your sons and your
        daughters shall
        prophesy,
    and your young men shall
        see visions,
    and your old men shall
        dream dreams.
18 Even upon my slaves, both
        men and women,
    in those days I will pour
        out my Spirit;
    and they shall prophesy.
19 And I will show portents in
        the heaven above
    and signs on the earth
        below,
    blood, and fire, and
        smoky mist.
20 The sun shall be turned to
        darkness
    and the moon to blood,
        before the coming of
        the Lord's great and
        glorious day.
21 Then everyone who calls
        on the name of the
        Lord shall be saved.'

22 "You that are Israelites,ᵃ listen to what I have to say: Jesus of Nazareth,ᵇ a man attested to you by God with deeds of power, wonders, and signs that God did through him among you, as you yourselves know— ²³this man, handed over to you according to the definite plan and foreknowledge of God, you crucified and killed by the hands of those outside the law. ²⁴But God raised him up, having freed him from death,ᶜ because it was impossible for him to be held in its power. ²⁵For David says concerning him,

    'I saw the Lord always
        before me,
    for he is at my right
        hand so that I will
        not be shaken;
26 therefore my heart was
        glad, and my tongue
        rejoiced;
    moreover my flesh will
        live in hope.
27 For you will not abandon
        my soul to Hades,
    or let your Holy One
        experience corruption.
28 You have made known to
        me the ways of life;
    you will make me full of
        gladness with your
        presence.'

29 "Fellow Israelites,ᵈ I may say to you confidently of our ancestor David that he both died and was buried, and his tomb is with us to this day. ³⁰Since he was a prophet, he knew that God had sworn with an oath to him that he would put one of his descendants on his throne. ³¹Foreseeing

ᵃGk Men, Israelites ᵇGk the Nazorean ᶜGk the pains of death ᵈGk Men, brothers

this, David[a] spoke of the resurrection of the Messiah,[b] saying,

'He was not abandoned to
    Hades,
nor did his flesh
    experience
    corruption.'

[32]This Jesus God raised up, and of that all of us are witnesses. [33]Being therefore exalted at[c] the right hand of God, and having received from the Father the promise of the Holy Spirit, he has poured out this that you both see and hear. [34]For David did not ascend into the heavens, but he himself says,

'The Lord said to my Lord,
    "Sit at my right hand,
[35]   until I make your
            enemies your
            footstool."'

[36]Therefore let the entire house of Israel know with certainty that God has made him both Lord and Messiah,[d] this Jesus whom you crucified."

[37] Now when they heard this, they were cut to the heart and said to Peter and to the other apostles, "Brothers, what should we do?" [38]Peter said to them, "Repent, and be baptized every one of you in the name of Jesus Christ so that your sins may be forgiven; and you will receive the gift of the Holy Spirit. [39]For the promise is for you, for your children, and for all who are far away, everyone whom the Lord our God calls to him." [40]And he testified with many other arguments and exhorted them, saying, "Save yourselves from this corrupt generation." [41]So those who welcomed his message were baptized, and that day about three thousand persons were added. [42]They devoted themselves to the apostles' teaching and fellowship, to the breaking of bread and the prayers.

43 Awe came upon everyone, because many wonders and signs were being done by the apostles. [44]All who believed were together and had all things in common; [45]they would sell their possessions and goods and distribute the proceeds[e] to all, as any had need. [46]Day by day, as they spent much time together in the temple, they broke bread at home[f] and ate their food with glad and generous[g] hearts, [47]praising God and having the goodwill of all the people. And day by day the Lord added to their number those who were being saved.

3 One day Peter and John were going up to the temple at the hour of prayer, at three o'clock in the afternoon. [2]And a man lame from birth was being carried in. People would lay him daily at the gate of the temple called the Beautiful Gate so that he could ask for alms from those entering the temple. [3]When he saw Peter and John about to go into the temple, he asked them for alms. [4]Peter looked intently at him, as did John, and said, "Look at us." [5]And he fixed his attention on them, expecting to receive

[a]Gk *he* [b]Or *the Christ* [c]Or *by* [d]Or *Christ* [e]Gk *them* [f]Or *from house to house* [g]Or *sincere*

something from them. ⁶But Peter said, "I have no silver or gold, but what I have I give you; in the name of Jesus Christ of Nazareth,ᵃ stand up and walk." ⁷And he took him by the right hand and raised him up; and immediately his feet and ankles were made strong. ⁸Jumping up, he stood and began to walk, and he entered the temple with them, walking and leaping and praising God. ⁹All the people saw him walking and praising God, ¹⁰and they recognized him as the one who used to sit and ask for alms at the Beautiful Gate of the temple; and they were filled with wonder and amazement at what had happened to him.

11 While he clung to Peter and John, all the people ran together to them in the portico called Solomon's Portico, utterly astonished. ¹²When Peter saw it, he addressed the people, "You Israelites,ᵇ why do you wonder at this, or why do you stare at us, as though by our own power or piety we had made him walk? ¹³The God of Abraham, the God of Isaac, and the God of Jacob, the God of our ancestors has glorified his servantᶜ Jesus, whom you handed over and rejected in the presence of Pilate, though he had decided to release him. ¹⁴But you rejected the Holy and Righteous One and asked to have a murderer given to you, ¹⁵and you killed the Author of life, whom God raised from the dead. To this we are witnesses. ¹⁶And by faith in his name, his name itself has made this man strong, whom you see and know; and the faith that is through Jesusᵈ has given him this perfect health in the presence of all of you.

17 "And now, friends,ᵉ I know that you acted in ignorance, as did also your rulers. ¹⁸In this way God fulfilled what he had foretold through all the prophets, that his Messiahᶠ would suffer. ¹⁹Repent therefore, and turn to God so that your sins may be wiped out, ²⁰so that times of refreshing may come from the presence of the Lord, and that he may send the Messiahᵍ appointed for you, that is, Jesus, ²¹who must remain in heaven until the time of universal restoration that God announced long ago through his holy prophets. ²²Moses said, 'The Lord your God will raise up for you from your own people a prophet like me. You must listen to whatever he tells you. ²³And it will be that everyone who does not listen to that prophet will be utterly rooted out of the people.' ²⁴And all the prophets, as many as have spoken, from Samuel and those after him, also predicted these days. ²⁵You are the descendants of the prophets and of the covenant that God gave to your ancestors, saying to Abraham, 'And in your descendants all the families of the earth shall be blessed.' ²⁶When God raised up his servant,ᶜ he sent him

---

ᵃGk *the Nazorean* ᵇGk *Men, Israelites* ᶜOr *child* ᵈGk *him* ᵉGk *brothers* ᶠOr *his Christ* ᵍOr *the Christ*

first to you, to bless you by turning each of you from your wicked ways."

4 While Peter and John[a] were speaking to the people, the priests, the captain of the temple, and the Sadducees came to them, [2]much annoyed because they were teaching the people and proclaiming that in Jesus there is the resurrection of the dead. [3]So they arrested them and put them in custody until the next day, for it was already evening. [4]But many of those who heard the word believed; and they numbered about five thousand.

[5]The next day their rulers, elders, and scribes assembled in Jerusalem, [6]with Annas the high priest, Caiaphas, John,[b] and Alexander, and all who were of the high-priestly family. [7]When they had made the prisoners[c] stand in their midst, they inquired, "By what power or by what name did you do this?" [8]Then Peter, filled with the Holy Spirit, said to them, "Rulers of the people and elders, [9]if we are questioned today because of a good deed done to someone who was sick and are asked how this man has been healed, [10]let it be known to all of you, and to all the people of Israel, that this man is standing before you in good health by the name of Jesus Christ of Nazareth,[d] whom you crucified, whom God raised from the dead. [11]This Jesus[e] is

'the stone that was rejected
    by you, the builders;
it has become the
    cornerstone.'[f]

[12]There is salvation in no one else, for there is no other name under heaven given among mortals by which we must be saved."

13 Now when they saw the boldness of Peter and John and realized that they were uneducated and ordinary men, they were amazed and recognized them as companions of Jesus. [14]When they saw the man who had been cured standing beside them, they had nothing to say in opposition. [15]So they ordered them to leave the council while they discussed the matter with one another. [16]They said, "What will we do with them? For it is obvious to all who live in Jerusalem that a notable sign has been done through them; we cannot deny it. [17]But to keep it from spreading further among the people, let us warn them to speak no more to anyone in this name." [18]So they called them and ordered them not to speak or teach at all in the name of Jesus. [19]But Peter and John answered them, "Whether it is right in God's sight to listen to you rather than to God, you must judge; [20]for we cannot keep from speaking about what we have seen and heard." [21]After threatening them again, they let them go, finding no way to punish them because of the people, for all of them praised God for what had happened. [22]For the man on whom

---

[a]Gk *While they* [b]Other ancient authorities read *Jonathan* [c]Gk *them* [d]Gk *the Nazorean* [e]Gk *this* [f]Or *keystone*

this sign of healing had been performed was more than forty years old.

23 After they were released, they went to their friends[a] and reported what the chief priests and the elders had said to them. [24]When they heard it, they raised their voices together to God and said, "Sovereign Lord, who made the heaven and the earth, the sea, and everything in them, [25]it is you who said by the Holy Spirit through our ancestor David, your servant:[b]

'Why did the Gentiles rage,
    and the peoples imagine
        vain things?
26   The kings of the earth took
        their stand,
    and the rulers have
        gathered together
        against the Lord
        and against his
        Messiah.'[c]

[27]For in this city, in fact, both Herod and Pontius Pilate, with the Gentiles and the peoples of Israel, gathered together against your holy servant[d] Jesus, whom you anointed, [28]to do whatever your hand and your plan had predestined to take place. [29]And now, Lord, look at their threats, and grant to your servants[d] to speak your word with all boldness, [30]while you stretch out your hand to heal, and signs and wonders are performed through the name of your holy servant[b] Jesus." [31]When they had prayed, the place in which they were gathered together was shaken; and they were all filled with the Holy Spirit and spoke the word of God with boldness.

32 Now the whole group of those who believed were of one heart and soul, and no one claimed private ownership of any possessions, but everything they owned was held in common. [33]With great power the apostles gave their testimony to the resurrection of the Lord Jesus, and great grace was upon them all. [34]There was not a needy person among them, for as many as owned lands or houses sold them and brought the proceeds of what was sold. [35]They laid it at the apostles' feet, and it was distributed to each as any had need. [36]There was a Levite, a native of Cyprus, Joseph, to whom the apostles gave the name Barnabas (which means "son of encouragement"). [37]He sold a field that belonged to him, then brought the money, and laid it at the apostles' feet.

5 But a man named Ananias, with the consent of his wife Sapphira, sold a piece of property; [2]with his wife's knowledge, he kept back some of the proceeds, and brought only a part and laid it at the apostles' feet. [3]"Ananias," Peter asked, "why has Satan filled your heart to lie to the Holy Spirit and to keep back part of the proceeds of the land? [4]While it remained unsold, did it not remain your own? And after it was sold, were not the proceeds at your disposal? How

[a]Gk *their own* [b]Or *child* [c]Or *his Christ* [d]Gk *slaves*

is it that you have contrived this deed in your heart? You did not lie to us[a] but to God!" [5]Now when Ananias heard these words, he fell down and died. And great fear seized all who heard of it. [6]The young men came and wrapped up his body,[b] then carried him out and buried him.

[7] After an interval of about three hours his wife came in, not knowing what had happened. [8]Peter said to her, "Tell me whether you and your husband sold the land for such and such a price." And she said, "Yes, that was the price." [9]Then Peter said to her, "How is it that you have agreed together to put the Spirit of the Lord to the test? Look, the feet of those who have buried your husband are at the door, and they will carry you out." [10]Immediately she fell down at his feet and died. When the young men came in they found her dead, so they carried her out and buried her beside her husband. [11]And great fear seized the whole church and all who heard of these things.

[12] Now many signs and wonders were done among the people through the apostles. And they were all together in Solomon's Portico. [13]None of the rest dared to join them, but the people held them in high esteem. [14]Yet more than ever believers were added to the Lord, great numbers of both men and women, [15]so that they even carried out the sick into the streets, and laid them on cots and mats, in order that Peter's shadow might fall on some of them as he came by. [16]A great number of people would also gather from the towns around Jerusalem, bringing the sick and those tormented by unclean spirits, and they were all cured.

[17] Then the high priest took action; he and all who were with him (that is, the sect of the Sadducees), being filled with jealousy, [18]arrested the apostles and put them in the public prison. [19]But during the night an angel of the Lord opened the prison doors, brought them out, and said, [20]"Go, stand in the temple and tell the people the whole message about this life." [21]When they heard this, they entered the temple at daybreak and went on with their teaching.

When the high priest and those with him arrived, they called together the council and the whole body of the elders of Israel, and sent to the prison to have them brought. [22]But when the temple police went there, they did not find them in the prison; so they returned and reported, [23]"We found the prison securely locked and the guards standing at the doors, but when we opened them, we found no one inside." [24]Now when the captain of the temple and the chief priests heard these words, they were perplexed about them, wondering what might be going on. [25]Then someone arrived and announced, "Look, the men

[a] Gk to men [b] Meaning of Gk uncertain

whom you put in prison are standing in the temple and teaching the people!" [26]Then the captain went with the temple police and brought them, but without violence, for they were afraid of being stoned by the people.

27 When they had brought them, they had them stand before the council. The high priest questioned them, [28]saying, "We gave you strict orders not to teach in this name,[a] yet here you have filled Jerusalem with your teaching and you are determined to bring this man's blood on us." [29]But Peter and the apostles answered, "We must obey God rather than any human authority.[b] [30]The God of our ancestors raised up Jesus, whom you had killed by hanging him on a tree. [31]God exalted him at his right hand as Leader and Savior that he might give repentance to Israel and forgiveness of sins. [32]And we are witnesses to these things, and so is the Holy Spirit whom God has given to those who obey him."

33 When they heard this, they were enraged and wanted to kill them. [34]But a Pharisee in the council named Gamaliel, a teacher of the law, respected by all the people, stood up and ordered the men to be put outside for a short time. [35]Then he said to them, "Fellow Israelites,[c] consider carefully what you propose to do to these men. [36]For some time ago Theudas rose up, claiming to be somebody, and a number of men, about four hundred, joined him; but he was killed, and all

who followed him were dispersed and disappeared. [37]After him Judas the Galilean rose up at the time of the census and got people to follow him; he also perished, and all who followed him were scattered. [38]So in the present case, I tell you, keep away from these men and let them alone; because if this plan or this undertaking is of human origin, it will fail; [39]but if it is of God, you will not be able to overthrow them—in that case you may even be found fighting against God!"

They were convinced by him, [40]and when they had called in the apostles, they had them flogged. Then they ordered them not to speak in the name of Jesus, and let them go. [41]As they left the council, they rejoiced that they were considered worthy to suffer dishonor for the sake of the name. [42]And every day in the temple and at home[d] they did not cease to teach and proclaim Jesus as the Messiah.[e]

6 Now during those days, when the disciples were increasing in number, the Hellenists complained against the Hebrews because their widows were being neglected in the daily distribution of food. [2]And the twelve called together the whole community of the disciples and said, "It is not right that we should neglect the word of God

---

[a]Other ancient authorities read *Did we not give you strict orders not to teach in this name?* [b]Gk *than men* [c]Gk *Men, Israelites* [d]Or *from house to house* [e]Or *the Christ*

in order to wait on tables.[a] [3]Therefore, friends,[b] select from among yourselves seven men of good standing, full of the Spirit and of wisdom, whom we may appoint to this task, [4]while we, for our part, will devote ourselves to prayer and to serving the word." [5]What they said pleased the whole community, and they chose Stephen, a man full of faith and the Holy Spirit, together with Philip, Prochorus, Nicanor, Timon, Parmenas, and Nicolaus, a proselyte of Antioch. [6]They had these men stand before the apostles, who prayed and laid their hands on them.

7 The word of God continued to spread; the number of the disciples increased greatly in Jerusalem, and a great many of the priests became obedient to the faith.

8 Stephen, full of grace and power, did great wonders and signs among the people. [9]Then some of those who belonged to the synagogue of the Freedmen (as it was called), Cyrenians, Alexandrians, and others of those from Cilicia and Asia, stood up and argued with Stephen. [10]But they could not withstand the wisdom and the Spirit[c] with which he spoke. [11]Then they secretly instigated some men to say, "We have heard him speak blasphemous words against Moses and God." [12]They stirred up the people as well as the elders and the scribes; then they suddenly confronted him, seized him, and brought him

before the council. [13]They set up false witnesses who said, "This man never stops saying things against this holy place and the law; [14]for we have heard him say that this Jesus of Nazareth[d] will destroy this place and will change the customs that Moses handed on to us." [15]And all who sat in the council looked intently at him, and they saw that his face was like the face of an angel.

7 Then the high priest asked him, "Are these things so?" [2]And Stephen replied: "Brothers[e] and fathers, listen to me. The God of glory appeared to our ancestor Abraham when he was in Mesopotamia, before he lived in Haran, [3]and said to him, 'Leave your country and your relatives and go to the land that I will show you.' [4]Then he left the country of the Chaldeans and settled in Haran. After his father died, God had him move from there to this country in which you are now living. [5]He did not give him any of it as a heritage, not even a foot's length, but promised to give it to him as his possession and to his descendants after him, even though he had no child. [6]And God spoke in these terms, that his descendants would be resident aliens in a country belonging to others, who would enslave them and mistreat them during four hundred years. [7]'But I will judge the nation that they serve,' said God, 'and after that

[a]Or keep accounts [b]Gk brothers [c]Or spirit [d]Gk the Nazorean [e]Gk Men, brothers

they shall come out and worship me in this place.' 8Then he gave him the covenant of circumcision. And so Abraham*a* became the father of Isaac and circumcised him on the eighth day; and Isaac became the father of Jacob, and Jacob of the twelve patriarchs.

9 "The patriarchs, jealous of Joseph, sold him into Egypt; but God was with him, 10and rescued him from all his afflictions, and enabled him to win favor and to show wisdom when he stood before Pharaoh, king of Egypt, who appointed him ruler over Egypt and over all his household. 11Now there came a famine throughout Egypt and Canaan, and great suffering, and our ancestors could find no food. 12But when Jacob heard that there was grain in Egypt, he sent our ancestors there on their first visit. 13On the second visit Joseph made himself known to his brothers, and Joseph's family became known to Pharaoh. 14Then Joseph sent and invited his father Jacob and all his relatives to come to him, seventy-five in all; 15so Jacob went down to Egypt. He himself died there as well as our ancestors, 16and their bodies*b* were brought back to Shechem and laid in the tomb that Abraham had bought for a sum of silver from the sons of Hamor in Shechem.

17 "But as the time drew near for the fulfillment of the promise that God had made to Abraham, our people in Egypt increased and multiplied 18until another king who had not known Joseph ruled over Egypt. 19He dealt craftily with our race and forced our ancestors to abandon their infants so that they would die. 20At this time Moses was born, and he was beautiful before God. For three months he was brought up in his father's house; 21and when he was abandoned, Pharaoh's daughter adopted him and brought him up as her own son. 22So Moses was instructed in all the wisdom of the Egyptians and was powerful in his words and deeds.

23 "When he was forty years old, it came into his heart to visit his relatives, the Israelites.*c* 24When he saw one of them being wronged, he defended the oppressed man and avenged him by striking down the Egyptian. 25He supposed that his kinsfolk would understand that God through him was rescuing them, but they did not understand. 26The next day he came to some of them as they were quarreling and tried to reconcile them, saying, 'Men, you are brothers; why do you wrong each other?' 27But the man who was wronging his neighbor pushed Moses*d* aside, saying, 'Who made you a ruler and a judge over us? 28Do you want to kill me as you killed the Egyptian yesterday?' 29When he heard this, Moses fled and became a resident alien in the land of Midian. There he became the father of two sons.

30 "Now when forty years had

*a*Gk he *b*Gk they *c*Gk his brothers, the sons of Israel *d*Gk him passed, an angel appeared to him in the wilderness of Mount Sinai, in the flame of a burning bush. [31]When Moses saw it, he was amazed at the sight; and as he approached to look, there came the voice of the Lord: [32]'I am the God of your ancestors, the God of Abraham, Isaac, and Jacob.' Moses began to tremble and did not dare to look. [33]Then the Lord said to him, 'Take off the sandals from your feet, for the place where you are standing is holy ground. [34]I have surely seen the mistreatment of my people who are in Egypt and have heard their groaning, and I have come down to rescue them. Come now, I will send you to Egypt.'

[35] "It was this Moses whom they rejected when they said, 'Who made you a ruler and a judge?' and whom God now sent as both ruler and liberator through the angel who appeared to him in the bush. [36]He led them out, having performed wonders and signs in Egypt, at the Red Sea, and in the wilderness for forty years. [37]This is the Moses who said to the Israelites, 'God will raise up a prophet for you from your own people[a] as he raised me up.' [38]He is the one who was in the congregation in the wilderness with the angel who spoke to him at Mount Sinai, and with our ancestors; and he received living oracles to give to us. [39]Our ancestors were unwilling to obey him; instead, they pushed him aside, and in their hearts they turned back to Egypt, [40]saying to Aaron, 'Make gods for us who will lead the way for us; as for this Moses who led us out from the land of Egypt, we do not know what has happened to him.' [41]At that time they made a calf, offered a sacrifice to the idol, and reveled in the works of their hands. [42]But God turned away from them and handed them over to worship the host of heaven, as it is written in the book of the prophets:

'Did you offer to me slain
　　victims and sacrifices
　forty years in the
　　　wilderness, O house
　　　of Israel?
[43]　No; you took along the tent
　　　of Moloch,
　and the star of your god
　　　Rephan,
　　　the images that you
　　　made to worship;
　so I will remove
　　　you beyond Babylon.'

[44] "Our ancestors had the tent of testimony in the wilderness, as God[b] directed when he spoke to Moses, ordering him to make it according to the pattern he had seen. [45]Our ancestors in turn brought it in with Joshua when they dispossessed the nations that God drove out before our ancestors. And it was there until the time of David, [46]who found favor with God and asked that he might find a dwelling place for the house of Jacob.[c] [47]But it was Solomon who built a house

---

[a]Gk *your brothers*　[b]Gk *he*　[c]Other ancient authorities read *for the God of Jacob*

for him. [48]Yet the Most High does not dwell in houses made with human hands;[a] as the prophet says,

[49] 'Heaven is my throne,
　　and the earth is my footstool.
What kind of house will
　　you build for me,
　　　says the Lord,
　or what is the place of
　　my rest?
[50] 　Did not my hand make all
　　these things?'

[51] "You stiff-necked people, uncircumcised in heart and ears, you are forever opposing the Holy Spirit, just as your ancestors used to do. [52]Which of the prophets did your ancestors not persecute? They killed those who foretold the coming of the Righteous One, and now you have become his betrayers and murderers. [53]You are the ones that received the law as ordained by angels, and yet you have not kept it."

[54] When they heard these things, they became enraged and ground their teeth at Stephen.[b] [55]But filled with the Holy Spirit, he gazed into heaven and saw the glory of God and Jesus standing at the right hand of God. [56]"Look," he said, "I see the heavens opened and the Son of Man standing at the right hand of God!" [57]But they covered their ears, and with a loud shout all rushed together against him. [58]Then they dragged him out of the city and began to stone him; and the witnesses laid their coats at the feet of a young man named

Saul. [59]While they were stoning Stephen, he prayed, "Lord Jesus, receive my spirit." [60]Then he knelt down and cried out in a loud voice, "Lord, do not hold this sin against them."

8 When he had said this, he died.[c] [1]And Saul approved of their killing him.

That day a severe persecution began against the church in Jerusalem, and all except the apostles were scattered throughout the countryside of Judea and Samaria. [2]Devout men buried Stephen and made loud lamentation over him. [3]But Saul was ravaging the church by entering house after house; dragging off both men and women, he committed them to prison.

[4] Now those who were scattered went from place to place, proclaiming the word. [5]Philip went down to the city[d] of Samaria and proclaimed the Messiah[e] to them. [6]The crowds with one accord listened eagerly to what was said by Philip, hearing and seeing the signs that he did, [7]for unclean spirits, crying with loud shrieks, came out of many who were possessed; and many others who were paralyzed or lame were cured. [8]So there was great joy in that city.

[9] Now a certain man named Simon had previously practiced magic in the city and amazed the people of Samaria, saying that he was someone great. [10]All of them,

---

[a]Gk with hands [b]Gk him [c]Gk fell asleep [d]Other ancient authorities read a city [e]Or the Christ

from the least to the greatest, listened to him eagerly, saying, "This man is the power of God that is called Great." [11]And they listened eagerly to him because for a long time he had amazed them with his magic. [12]But when they believed Philip, who was proclaiming the good news about the kingdom of God and the name of Jesus Christ, they were baptized, both men and women. [13]Even Simon himself believed. After being baptized, he stayed constantly with Philip and was amazed when he saw the signs and great miracles that took place.

14 Now when the apostles at Jerusalem heard that Samaria had accepted the word of God, they sent Peter and John to them. [15]The two went down and prayed for them that they might receive the Holy Spirit [16](for as yet the Spirit had not come[a] upon any of them; they had only been baptized in the name of the Lord Jesus). [17]Then Peter and John[b] laid their hands on them, and they received the Holy Spirit. [18]Now when Simon saw that the Spirit was given through the laying on of the apostles' hands, he offered them money, [19]saying, "Give me also this power so that anyone on whom I lay my hands may receive the Holy Spirit." [20]But Peter said to him, "May your silver perish with you, because you thought you could obtain God's gift with money! [21]You have no part or share in this, for your heart is not right before God. [22]Repent therefore of

this wickedness of yours, and pray to the Lord that, if possible, the intent of your heart may be forgiven you. [23]For I see that you are in the gall of bitterness and the chains of wickedness." [24]Simon answered, "Pray for me to the Lord, that nothing of what you[c] have said may happen to me."

25 Now after Peter and John[d] had testified and spoken the word of the Lord, they returned to Jerusalem, proclaiming the good news to many villages of the Samaritans.

26 Then an angel of the Lord said to Philip, "Get up and go toward the south[e] to the road that goes down from Jerusalem to Gaza." (This is a wilderness road.) [27]So he got up and went. Now there was an Ethiopian eunuch, a court official of the Candace, queen of the Ethiopians, in charge of her entire treasury. He had come to Jerusalem to worship [28]and was returning home; seated in his chariot, he was reading the prophet Isaiah. [29]Then the Spirit said to Philip, "Go over to this chariot and join it." [30]So Philip ran up to it and heard him reading the prophet Isaiah. He asked, "Do you understand what you are reading?" [31]He replied, "How can I, unless someone guides me?" And he invited Philip to get in and sit beside him. [32]Now the passage of the scripture that he was reading was this:

---

[a]Gk *fallen* [b]Gk *they* [c]The Greek word for *you* and the verb *pray* are plural [d]Gk *after they* [e]Or *go at noon*

"Like a sheep he was led to
the slaughter,
and like a lamb silent
before its shearer,
so he does not open
his mouth.

[33] In his humiliation justice
was denied him.
Who can describe his
generation?
For his life is taken
away from the earth."

[34]The eunuch asked Philip, "About whom, may I ask you, does the prophet say this, about himself or about someone else?" [35]Then Philip began to speak, and starting with this scripture, he proclaimed to him the good news about Jesus. [36]As they were going along the road, they came to some water; and the eunuch said, "Look, here is water! What is to prevent me from being baptized?"[a] [38]He commanded the chariot to stop, and both of them, Philip and the eunuch, went down into the water, and Philip[b] baptized him. [39]When they came up out of the water, the Spirit of the Lord snatched Philip away; the eunuch saw him no more, and went on his way rejoicing. [40]But Philip found himself at Azotus, and as he was passing through the region, he proclaimed the good news to all the towns until he came to Caesarea.

9 Meanwhile Saul, still breathing threats and murder against the disciples of the Lord, went to the high priest [2]and asked him for letters to the synagogues at Damascus, so that if he found any who belonged to the Way, men or women, he might bring them bound to Jerusalem. [3]Now as he was going along and approaching Damascus, suddenly a light from heaven flashed around him. [4]He fell to the ground and heard a voice saying to him, "Saul, Saul, why do you persecute me?" [5]He asked, "Who are you, Lord?" The reply came, "I am Jesus, whom you are persecuting. [6]But get up and enter the city, and you will be told what you are to do." [7]The men who were traveling with him stood speechless because they heard the voice but saw no one. [8]Saul got up from the ground, and though his eyes were open, he could see nothing; so they led him by the hand and brought him into Damascus. [9]For three days he was without sight, and neither ate nor drank.

10 Now there was a disciple in Damascus named Ananias. The Lord said to him in a vision, "Ananias." He answered, "Here I am, Lord." [11]The Lord said to him, "Get up and go to the street called Straight, and at the house of Judas look for a man of Tarsus named Saul. At this moment he is praying, [12]and he has seen in a vision[c] a man named Ananias come in and lay his hands on him so that he might regain his

[a]Other ancient authorities add all or most of verse 37, *And Philip said, "If you believe with all your heart, you may." And he replied, "I believe that Jesus Christ is the Son of God."* [b]Gk *he* [c]Other ancient authorities lack *in a vision*

sight." ¹³But Ananias answered, "Lord, I have heard from many about this man, how much evil he has done to your saints in Jerusalem; ¹⁴and here he has authority from the chief priests to bind all who invoke your name." ¹⁵But the Lord said to him, "Go, for he is an instrument whom I have chosen to bring my name before Gentiles and kings and before the people of Israel; ¹⁶I myself will show him how much he must suffer for the sake of my name." ¹⁷So Ananias went and entered the house. He laid his hands on Saul*a* and said, "Brother Saul, the Lord Jesus, who appeared to you on your way here, has sent me so that you may regain your sight and be filled with the Holy Spirit." ¹⁸And immediately something like scales fell from his eyes, and his sight was restored. Then he got up and was baptized, ¹⁹and after taking some food, he regained his strength.

For several days he was with the disciples in Damascus, ²⁰and immediately he began to proclaim Jesus in the synagogues, saying, "He is the Son of God." ²¹All who heard him were amazed and said, "Is not this the man who made havoc in Jerusalem among those who invoked this name? And has he not come here for the purpose of bringing them bound before the chief priests?" ²²Saul became increasingly more powerful and confounded the Jews who lived in Damascus by proving that Jesus*b* was the Messiah.*c*

23 After some time had passed, the Jews plotted to kill him, ²⁴but their plot became known to Saul. They were watching the gates day and night so that they might kill him; ²⁵but his disciples took him by night and let him down through an opening in the wall,*d* lowering him in a basket.

26 When he had come to Jerusalem, he attempted to join the disciples; and they were all afraid of him, for they did not believe that he was a disciple. ²⁷But Barnabas took him, brought him to the apostles, and described for them how on the road he had seen the Lord, who had spoken to him, and how in Damascus he had spoken boldly in the name of Jesus. ²⁸So he went in and out among them in Jerusalem, speaking boldly in the name of the Lord. ²⁹He spoke and argued with the Hellenists; but they were attempting to kill him. ³⁰When the believers*e* learned of it, they brought him down to Caesarea and sent him off to Tarsus.

31 Meanwhile the church throughout Judea, Galilee, and Samaria had peace and was built up. Living in the fear of the Lord and in the comfort of the Holy Spirit, it increased in numbers.

32 Now as Peter went here and there among all the believers,*f* he came down also to the saints living in Lydda. ³³There he found

*a*Gk him *b*Gk that this *c*Or the Christ *d*Gk through the wall *e*Gk brothers *f*Gk all of them

a man named Aeneas, who had been bedridden for eight years, for he was paralyzed. [34]Peter said to him, "Aeneas, Jesus Christ heals you; get up and make your bed!" And immediately he got up. [35]And all the residents of Lydda and Sharon saw him and turned to the Lord.

[36] Now in Joppa there was a disciple whose name was Tabitha, which in Greek is Dorcas.[a] She was devoted to good works and acts of charity. [37]At that time she became ill and died. When they had washed her, they laid her in a room upstairs. [38]Since Lydda was near Joppa, the disciples, who heard that Peter was there, sent two men to him with the request, "Please come to us without delay." [39]So Peter got up and went with them; and when he arrived, they took him to the room upstairs. All the widows stood beside him, weeping and showing tunics and other clothing that Dorcas had made while she was with them. [40]Peter put all of them outside, and then he knelt down and prayed. He turned to the body and said, "Tabitha, get up." Then she opened her eyes, and seeing Peter, she sat up. [41]He gave her his hand and helped her up. Then calling the saints and widows, he showed her to be alive. [42]This became known throughout Joppa, and many believed in the Lord. [43]Meanwhile he stayed in Joppa for some time with a certain Simon, a tanner.

10 In Caesarea there was a man named Cornelius, a centurion of the Italian Cohort, as it was called. [2]He was a devout man who feared God with all his household; he gave alms generously to the people and prayed constantly to God. [3]One afternoon at about three o'clock he had a vision in which he clearly saw an angel of God coming in and saying to him, "Cornelius." [4]He stared at him in terror and said, "What is it, Lord?" He answered, "Your prayers and your alms have ascended as a memorial before God. [5]Now send men to Joppa for a certain Simon who is called Peter; [6]he is lodging with Simon, a tanner, whose house is by the seaside." [7]When the angel who spoke to him had left, he called two of his slaves and a devout soldier from the ranks of those who served him, [8]and after telling them everything, he sent them to Joppa.

[9] About noon the next day, as they were on their journey and approaching the city, Peter went up on the roof to pray. [10]He became hungry and wanted something to eat; and while it was being prepared, he fell into a trance. [11]He saw the heaven opened and something like a large sheet coming down, being lowered to the ground by its four corners. [12]In it were all kinds of four-footed creatures and reptiles and birds of the air. [13]Then he

[a]The name Tabitha in Aramaic and the name Dorcas in Greek mean *a gazelle*

heard a voice saying, "Get up, Peter; kill and eat." [14]But Peter said, "By no means, Lord; for I have never eaten anything that is profane or unclean." [15]The voice said to him again, a second time, "What God has made clean, you must not call profane." [16]This happened three times, and the thing was suddenly taken up to heaven.

17 Now while Peter was greatly puzzled about what to make of the vision that he had seen, suddenly the men sent by Cornelius appeared. They were asking for Simon's house and were standing by the gate. [18]They called out to ask whether Simon, who was called Peter, was staying there. [19]While Peter was still thinking about the vision, the Spirit said to him, "Look, three[a] men are searching for you. [20]Now get up, go down, and go with them without hesitation; for I have sent them." [21]So Peter went down to the men and said, "I am the one you are looking for; what is the reason for your coming?" [22]They answered, "Cornelius, a centurion, an upright and God-fearing man, who is well spoken of by the whole Jewish nation, was directed by a holy angel to send for you to come to his house and to hear what you have to say." [23]So Peter[b] invited them in and gave them lodging.

The next day he got up and went with them, and some of the believers[c] from Joppa accompanied him. [24]The following day they came to Caesarea. Cornelius was expecting them and had called together his relatives and close friends. [25]On Peter's arrival Cornelius met him, and falling at his feet, worshiped him. [26]But Peter made him get up, saying, "Stand up; I am only a mortal." [27]And as he talked with him, he went in and found that many had assembled; [28]and he said to them, "You yourselves know that it is unlawful for a Jew to associate with or to visit a Gentile; but God has shown me that I should not call anyone profane or unclean. [29]So when I was sent for, I came without objection. Now may I ask why you sent for me?"

30 Cornelius replied, "Four days ago at this very hour, at three o'clock, I was praying in my house when suddenly a man in dazzling clothes stood before me. [31]He said, 'Cornelius, your prayer has been heard and your alms have been remembered before God. [32]Send therefore to Joppa and ask for Simon, who is called Peter; he is staying in the home of Simon, a tanner, by the sea.' [33]Therefore I sent for you immediately, and you have been kind enough to come. So now all of us are here in the presence of God to listen to all that the Lord has commanded you to say."

34 Then Peter began to speak to them: "I truly understand that God shows no partiality, [35]but in every nation anyone who fears him and does what is right is ac-

---

[a]One ancient authority reads *two*; others lack the word
[b]Gk *he* [c]Gk *brothers*

ceptable to him. [36]You know the message he sent to the people of Israel, preaching peace by Jesus Christ—he is Lord of all. [37]That message spread throughout Judea, beginning in Galilee after the baptism that John announced: [38]how God anointed Jesus of Nazareth with the Holy Spirit and with power; how he went about doing good and healing all who were oppressed by the devil, for God was with him. [39]We are witnesses to all that he did both in Judea and in Jerusalem. They put him to death by hanging him on a tree; [40]but God raised him on the third day and allowed him to appear, [41]not to all the people but to us who were chosen by God as witnesses, and who ate and drank with him after he rose from the dead. [42]He commanded us to preach to the people and to testify that he is the one ordained by God as judge of the living and the dead. [43]All the prophets testify about him that everyone who believes in him receives forgiveness of sins through his name."

44 While Peter was still speaking, the Holy Spirit fell upon all who heard the word. [45]The circumcised believers who had come with Peter were astounded that the gift of the Holy Spirit had been poured out even on the Gentiles, [46]for they heard them speaking in tongues and extolling God. Then Peter said, [47]"Can anyone withhold the water for baptizing these people who have received the Holy Spirit just as we have?" [48]So he ordered them to be baptized in the name of Jesus Christ. Then they invited him to stay for several days.

11 Now the apostles and the believers[a] who were in Judea heard that the Gentiles had also accepted the word of God. [2]So when Peter went up to Jerusalem, the circumcised believers[b] criticized him, [3]saying, "Why did you go to uncircumcised men and eat with them?" [4]Then Peter began to explain it to them, step by step, saying, [5]"I was in the city of Joppa praying, and in a trance I saw a vision. There was something like a large sheet coming down from heaven, being lowered by its four corners; and it came close to me. [6]As I looked at it closely I saw four-footed animals, beasts of prey, reptiles, and birds of the air. [7]I also heard a voice saying to me, 'Get up, Peter; kill and eat.' [8]But I replied, 'By no means, Lord; for nothing profane or unclean has ever entered my mouth.' [9]But a second time the voice answered from heaven, 'What God has made clean, you must not call profane.' [10]This happened three times; then everything was pulled up again to heaven. [11]At that very moment three men, sent to me from Caesarea, arrived at the house where we were. [12]The Spirit told me to go with them and not to make a distinction between them and us.[c] These six brothers also accompanied me, and we entered the man's house.

[a]Gk brothers [b]Gk lacks believers [c]Or not to hesitate

185

[13]He told us how he had seen the angel standing in his house and saying, 'Send to Joppa and bring Simon, who is called Peter; [14]he will give you a message by which you and your entire household will be saved.' [15]And as I began to speak, the Holy Spirit fell upon them just as it had upon us at the beginning. [16]And I remembered the word of the Lord, how he had said, 'John baptized with water, but you will be baptized with the Holy Spirit.' [17]If then God gave them the same gift that he gave us when we believed in the Lord Jesus Christ, who was I that I could hinder God?" [18]When they heard this, they were silenced. And they praised God, saying, "Then God has given even to the Gentiles the repentance that leads to life."

[19]Now those who were scattered because of the persecution that took place over Stephen traveled as far as Phoenicia, Cyprus, and Antioch, and they spoke the word to no one except Jews. [20]But among them were some men of Cyprus and Cyrene who, on coming to Antioch, spoke to the Hellenists[a] also, proclaiming the Lord Jesus. [21]The hand of the Lord was with them, and a great number became believers and turned to the Lord. [22]News of this came to the ears of the church in Jerusalem, and they sent Barnabas to Antioch. [23]When he came and saw the grace of God, he rejoiced, and he exhorted them all to remain faithful to the Lord with steadfast devotion; [24]for he was a good man, full of the Holy Spirit and of faith. And a great many people were brought to the Lord. [25]Then Barnabas went to Tarsus to look for Saul, [26]and when he had found him, he brought him to Antioch. So it was that for an entire year they met with[b] the church and taught a great many people, and it was in Antioch that the disciples were first called "Christians."

[27]At that time prophets came down from Jerusalem to Antioch. [28]One of them named Agabus stood up and predicted by the Spirit that there would be a severe famine over all the world; and this took place during the reign of Claudius. [29]The disciples determined that according to their ability, each would send relief to the believers living in Judea; [30]this they did, sending it to the elders by Barnabas and Saul.

12 About that time King Herod laid violent hands upon some who belonged to the church. [2]He had James, the brother of John, killed with the sword. [3]After he saw that it pleased the Jews, he proceeded to arrest Peter also. (This was during the festival of Unleavened Bread.) [4]When he had seized him, he put him in prison and handed him over to four squads of soldiers to guard him, intending to bring him out to the people after the Passover. [5]While Peter was kept

[a]Other ancient authorities read *Greeks* [b]Or *were guests of*

in prison, the church prayed fervently to God for him.

6 The very night before Herod was going to bring him out, Peter, bound with two chains, was sleeping between two soldiers, while guards in front of the door were keeping watch over the prison. [7]Suddenly an angel of the Lord appeared and a light shone in the cell. He tapped Peter on the side and woke him, saying, "Get up quickly." And the chains fell off his wrists. [8]The angel said to him, "Fasten your belt and put on your sandals." He did so. Then he said to him, "Wrap your cloak around you and follow me." [9]Peter[a] went out and followed him; he did not realize that what was happening with the angel's help was real; he thought he was seeing a vision. [10]After they had passed the first and the second guard, they came before the iron gate leading into the city. It opened for them of its own accord, and they went outside and walked along a lane, when suddenly the angel left him. [11]Then Peter came to himself and said, "Now I am sure that the Lord has sent his angel and rescued me from the hands of Herod and from all that the Jewish people were expecting."

12 As soon as he realized this, he went to the house of Mary, the mother of John whose other name was Mark, where many had gathered and were praying. [13]When he knocked at the outer gate, a maid named Rhoda came to answer. [14]On recognizing Peter's voice, she was so overjoyed that, instead of opening the gate, she ran in and announced that Peter was standing at the gate. [15]They said to her, "You are out of your mind!" But she insisted that it was so. They said, "It is his angel." [16]Meanwhile Peter continued knocking; and when they opened the gate, they saw him and were amazed. [17]He motioned to them with his hand to be silent, and described for them how the Lord had brought him out of the prison. And he added, "Tell this to James and to the believers."[b] Then he left and went to another place.

18 When morning came, there was no small commotion among the soldiers over what had become of Peter. [19]When Herod had searched for him and could not find him, he examined the guards and ordered them to be put to death. Then Peter went down from Judea to Caesarea and stayed there.

20 Now Herod[c] was angry with the people of Tyre and Sidon. So they came to him in a body; and after winning over Blastus, the king's chamberlain, they asked for a reconciliation, because their country depended on the king's country for food. [21]On an appointed day Herod put on his royal robes, took his seat on the platform, and delivered a public address to them. [22]The people kept shouting, "The voice of a god, and not of a mortal!" [23]And

[a]Gk He [b]Gk brothers [c]Gk he

immediately, because he had not given the glory to God, an angel of the Lord struck him down, and he was eaten by worms and died.

24 But the word of God continued to advance and gain adherents. 25Then after completing their mission Barnabas and Saul returned to*a* Jerusalem and brought with them John, whose other name was Mark.

13 Now in the church at Antioch there were prophets and teachers: Barnabas, Simeon who was called Niger, Lucius of Cyrene, Manaen a member of the court of Herod the ruler,*b* and Saul. 2While they were worshiping the Lord and fasting, the Holy Spirit said, "Set apart for me Barnabas and Saul for the work to which I have called them." 3Then after fasting and praying they laid their hands on them and sent them off.

4 So, being sent out by the Holy Spirit, they went down to Seleucia; and from there they sailed to Cyprus. 5When they arrived at Salamis, they proclaimed the word of God in the synagogues of the Jews. And they had John also to assist them. 6When they had gone through the whole island as far as Paphos, they met a certain magician, a Jewish false prophet, named Bar-Jesus. 7He was with the proconsul, Sergius Paulus, an intelligent man, who summoned Barnabas and Saul and wanted to hear the word of God. 8But the magician Elymas (for that is the translation of his name) opposed them and tried to turn the proconsul away from the faith. 9But Saul, also known as Paul, filled with the Holy Spirit, looked intently at him 10and said, "You son of the devil, you enemy of all righteousness, full of all deceit and villainy, will you not stop making crooked the straight paths of the Lord? 11And now listen—the hand of the Lord is against you, and you will be blind for a while, unable to see the sun." Immediately mist and darkness came over him, and he went about groping for someone to lead him by the hand. 12When the proconsul saw what had happened, he believed, for he was astonished at the teaching about the Lord.

13 Then Paul and his companions set sail from Paphos and came to Perga in Pamphylia. John, however, left them and returned to Jerusalem; 14but they went on from Perga and came to Antioch in Pisidia. And on the sabbath day they went into the synagogue and sat down. 15After the reading of the law and the prophets, the officials of the synagogue sent them a message, saying, "Brothers, if you have any word of exhortation for the people, give it." 16So Paul stood up and with a gesture began to speak:

"You Israelites,*c* and others who fear God, listen. 17The God of this people Israel chose our ancestors and made the people

---

*a*Other ancient authorities read *from* *b*Gk *tetrarch* *c*Gk *Men, Israelites*

great during their stay in the land of Egypt, and with uplifted arm he led them out of it. [18]For about forty years he put up with[a] them in the wilderness. [19]After he had destroyed seven nations in the land of Canaan, he gave them their land as an inheritance [20]for about four hundred fifty years. After that he gave them judges until the time of the prophet Samuel. [21]Then they asked for a king; and God gave them Saul son of Kish, a man of the tribe of Benjamin, who reigned for forty years. [22]When he had removed him, he made David their king. In his testimony about him he said, 'I have found David, son of Jesse, to be a man after my heart, who will carry out all my wishes.' [23]Of this man's posterity God has brought to Israel a Savior, Jesus, as he promised; [24]before his coming John had already proclaimed a baptism of repentance to all the people of Israel. [25]And as John was finishing his work, he said, 'What do you suppose that I am? I am not he. No, but one is coming after me; I am not worthy to untie the thong of the sandals[b] on his feet."

26 "My brothers, you descendants of Abraham's family, and others who fear God, to us[c] the message of this salvation has been sent. [27]Because the residents of Jerusalem and their leaders did not recognize him or understand the words of the prophets that are read every sabbath, they fulfilled those words by condemning him. [28]Even

though they found no cause for a sentence of death, they asked Pilate to have him killed. [29]When they had carried out everything that was written about him, they took him down from the tree and laid him in a tomb. [30]But God raised him from the dead; [31]and for many days he appeared to those who came up with him from Galilee to Jerusalem, and they are now his witnesses to the people. [32]And we bring you the good news that what God promised to our ancestors [33]he has fulfilled for us, their children, by raising Jesus; as also it is written in the second psalm,

'You are my Son;
    today I have begotten
        you.'

[34]As to his raising him from the dead, no more to return to corruption, he has spoken in this way,

'I will give you the holy
    promises made to
        David.'

[35]Therefore he has also said in another psalm,

'You will not let your Holy
    One experience
        corruption.'

[36]For David, after he had served the purpose of God in his own generation, died,[d] was laid beside his ancestors, and experienced corruption; [37]but he whom God raised up experienced no corruption. [38]Let it be known to

---

[a]Other ancient authorities read *cared for* [b]Gk *untie the sandals* [c]Other ancient authorities read *you* [d]Gk *fell asleep*

you therefore, my brothers, that through this man forgiveness of sins is proclaimed to you; [39]by this Jesus[a] everyone who believes is set free from all those sins[b] from which you could not be freed by the law of Moses. [40]Beware, therefore, that what the prophets said does not happen to you:

[41]   'Look, you scoffers!
      Be amazed and perish,
   for in your days I am doing
      a work,
  a work that you will
      never believe, even if
      someone tells you.'"

[42] As Paul and Barnabas[c] were going out, the people urged them to speak about these things again the next sabbath. [43]When the meeting of the synagogue broke up, many Jews and devout converts to Judaism followed Paul and Barnabas, who spoke to them and urged them to continue in the grace of God.

[44] The next sabbath almost the whole city gathered to hear the word of the Lord.[d] [45]But when the Jews saw the crowds, they were filled with jealousy; and blaspheming, they contradicted what was spoken by Paul. [46]Then both Paul and Barnabas spoke out boldly, saying, "It was necessary that the word of God should be spoken first to you. Since you reject it and judge yourselves to be unworthy of eternal life, we are now turning to the Gentiles. [47]For so the Lord has commanded us, saying,

   'I have set you to be a light
      for the Gentiles,

   so that you may bring
      salvation to the ends
      of the earth.'"

[48] When the Gentiles heard this, they were glad and praised the word of the Lord; and as many as had been destined for eternal life became believers. [49]Thus the word of the Lord spread throughout the region. [50]But the Jews incited the devout women of high standing and the leading men of the city, and stirred up persecution against Paul and Barnabas, and drove them out of their region. [51]So they shook the dust off their feet in protest against them, and went to Iconium. [52]And the disciples were filled with joy and with the Holy Spirit.

14

The same thing occurred in Iconium, where Paul and Barnabas[c] went into the Jewish synagogue and spoke in such a way that a great number of both Jews and Greeks became believers. [2]But the unbelieving Jews stirred up the Gentiles and poisoned their minds against the brothers. [3]So they remained for a long time, speaking boldly for the Lord, who testified to the word of his grace by granting signs and wonders to be done through them. [4]But the residents of the city were divided; some sided with the Jews, and some with the apostles. [5]And when an attempt was made by both Gentiles and Jews, with their rulers, to mistreat

---

[a]Gk *this* [b]Gk *all* [c]Gk *they* [d]Other ancient authorities read *God*

them and to stone them, [6]the apostles learned of it and fled to Lystra and Derbe, cities of Lycaonia, and to the surrounding country; [7]and there they continued proclaiming the good news.

8 In Lystra there was a man sitting who could not use his feet and had never walked, for he had been crippled from birth. [9]He listened to Paul as he was speaking. And Paul, looking at him intently and seeing that he had faith to be healed, [10]said in a loud voice, "Stand upright on your feet." And the man[a] sprang up and began to walk. [11]When the crowds saw what Paul had done, they shouted in the Lycaonian language, "The gods have come down to us in human form!" [12]Barnabas they called Zeus, and Paul they called Hermes, because he was the chief speaker. [13]The priest of Zeus, whose temple was just outside the city,[b] brought oxen and garlands to the gates; he and the crowds wanted to offer sacrifice. [14]When the apostles Barnabas and Paul heard of it, they tore their clothes and rushed out into the crowd, shouting, [15]"Friends,[c] why are you doing this? We are mortals just like you, and we bring you good news, that you should turn from these worthless things to the living God, who made the heaven and the earth and the sea and all that is in them. [16]In past generations he allowed all the nations to follow their own ways; [17]yet he has not left himself without a witness in doing good—giving you rains from heaven and fruitful seasons, and filling you with food and your hearts with joy." [18]Even with these words, they scarcely restrained the crowds from offering sacrifice to them.

19 But Jews came there from Antioch and Iconium and won over the crowds. Then they stoned Paul and dragged him out of the city, supposing that he was dead. [20]But when the disciples surrounded him, he got up and went into the city. The next day he went on with Barnabas to Derbe.

21 After they had proclaimed the good news to that city and had made many disciples, they returned to Lystra, then on to Iconium and Antioch. [22]There they strengthened the souls of the disciples and encouraged them to continue in the faith, saying, "It is through many persecutions that we must enter the kingdom of God." [23]And after they had appointed elders for them in each church, with prayer and fasting they entrusted them to the Lord in whom they had come to believe.

24 Then they passed through Pisidia and came to Pamphylia. [25]When they had spoken the word in Perga, they went down to Attalia. [26]From there they sailed back to Antioch, where they had been commended to the grace of God for the work[d] that they had completed. [27]When they

---

[a]Gk he [b]Or The priest of Zeus-Outside-the-City [c]Gk Men [d]Or committed in the grace of God to the work

arrived, they called the church together and related all that God had done with them, and how he had opened a door of faith for the Gentiles. [28]And they stayed there with the disciples for some time.

15 Then certain individuals came down from Judea and were teaching the brothers, "Unless you are circumcised according to the custom of Moses, you cannot be saved." [2]And after Paul and Barnabas had no small dissension and debate with them, Paul and Barnabas and some of the others were appointed to go up to Jerusalem to discuss this question with the apostles and the elders. [3]So they were sent on their way by the church, and as they passed through both Phoenicia and Samaria, they reported the conversion of the Gentiles, and brought great joy to all the believers.[a] [4]When they came to Jerusalem, they were welcomed by the church and the apostles and the elders, and they reported all that God had done with them. [5]But some believers who belonged to the sect of the Pharisees stood up and said, "It is necessary for them to be circumcised and ordered to keep the law of Moses."

6 The apostles and the elders met together to consider this matter. [7]After there had been much debate, Peter stood up and said to them, "My brothers,[b] you know that in the early days God made a choice among you, that I should be the one through whom the Gentiles would hear the message of the good news and become believers. [8]And God, who knows the human heart, testified to them by giving them the Holy Spirit, just as he did to us; [9]and in cleansing their hearts by faith he has made no distinction between them and us. [10]Now therefore why are you putting God to the test by placing on the neck of the disciples a yoke that neither our ancestors nor we have been able to bear? [11]On the contrary, we believe that we will be saved through the grace of the Lord Jesus, just as they will."

12 The whole assembly kept silence, and listened to Barnabas and Paul as they told of all the signs and wonders that God had done through them among the Gentiles. [13]After they finished speaking, James replied, "My brothers,[b] listen to me. [14]Simeon has related how God first looked favorably on the Gentiles, to take from among them a people for his name. [15]This agrees with the words of the prophets, as it is written,

16 'After this I will return,
      and I will rebuild the
         dwelling of David,
            which has fallen;
      from its ruins I will
         rebuild it,
      and I will set it up,
17   so that all other peoples
         may seek the Lord—
      even all the Gentiles over
         whom my name has
         been called.

[a]Gk brothers [b]Gk Men, brothers

Thus says the Lord,
who has been
making these things
[18]known from long
ago.'[a]

[19]Therefore I have reached the decision that we should not trouble those Gentiles who are turning to God, [20]but we should write to them to abstain only from things polluted by idols and from fornication and from whatever has been strangled[b] and from blood. [21]For in every city, for generations past, Moses has had those who proclaim him, for he has been read aloud every sabbath in the synagogues."

22 Then the apostles and the elders, with the consent of the whole church, decided to choose men from among their members[c] and to send them to Antioch with Paul and Barnabas. They sent Judas called Barsabbas, and Silas, leaders among the brothers, [23]with the following letter: "The brothers, both the apostles and the elders, to the believers[d] of Gentile origin in Antioch and Syria and Cilicia, greetings. [24]Since we have heard that certain persons who have gone out from us, though with no instructions from us, have said things to disturb you and have unsettled your minds,[e] [25]we have decided unanimously to choose representatives[f] and send them to you, along with our beloved Barnabas and Paul, [26]who have risked their lives for the sake of our Lord Jesus Christ. [27]We have therefore sent Judas and Silas, who themselves will tell you the same things by word of mouth. [28]For it has seemed good to the Holy Spirit and to us to impose on you no further burden than these essentials: [29]that you abstain from what has been sacrificed to idols and from blood and from what is strangled[g] and from fornication. If you keep yourselves from these, you will do well. Farewell."

30 So they were sent off and went down to Antioch. When they gathered the congregation together, they delivered the letter. [31]When its members[h] read it, they rejoiced at the exhortation. [32]Judas and Silas, who were themselves prophets, said much to encourage and strengthen the believers.[d] [33]After they had been there for some time, they were sent off in peace by the believers to those who had sent them.[i] [35]But Paul and Barnabas remained in Antioch, and there, with many others, they taught and proclaimed the word of the Lord.

36 After some days Paul said to Barnabas, "Come, let us return and visit the believers[d] in every city where we proclaimed the word of the Lord and see how they are doing." [37]Barnabas wanted to take with them John called

---

[a]Other ancient authorities read things [18]Known to God from of old are all his works.' [b]Other ancient authorities lack and from whatever has been strangled [c]Gk from among them [d]Gk brothers [e]Other ancient authorities lack saying, 'You must be circumcised and keep the law,' [f]Gk men [g]Other ancient authorities lack and from what is strangled [h]Gk When they [i]Other ancient authorities add verse 34, But it seemed good to Silas to remain there

Mark. [38]But Paul decided not to take with them one who had deserted them in Pamphylia and had not accompanied them in the work. [39]The disagreement became so sharp that they parted company; Barnabas took Mark with him and sailed away to Cyprus. [40]But Paul chose Silas and set out, the believers commending him to the grace of the Lord. [41]He went through Syria and Cilicia, strengthening the churches.

16 Paul[a] went on also to Derbe and to Lystra, where there was a disciple named Timothy, the son of a Jewish woman who was a believer; but his father was a Greek. [2]He was well spoken of by the believers[b] in Lystra and Iconium. [3]Paul wanted Timothy to accompany him; and he took him and had him circumcised because of the Jews who were in those places, for they all knew that his father was a Greek. [4]As they went from town to town, they delivered to them for observance the decisions that had been reached by the apostles and elders who were in Jerusalem. [5]So the churches were strengthened in the faith and increased in numbers daily.

[6] They went through the region of Phrygia and Galatia, having been forbidden by the Holy Spirit to speak the word in Asia. [7]When they had come opposite Mysia, they attempted to go into Bithynia, but the Spirit of Jesus did not allow them; [8]so, passing by Mysia, they went down to Troas. [9]During the night Paul had a vision: there stood a man of Macedonia pleading with him and saying, "Come over to Macedonia and help us." [10]When he had seen the vision, we immediately tried to cross over to Macedonia, being convinced that God had called us to proclaim the good news to them.

[11] We set sail from Troas and took a straight course to Samothrace, the following day to Neapolis, [12]and from there to Philippi, which is a leading city of the district[c] of Macedonia and a Roman colony. We remained in this city for some days. [13]On the sabbath day we went outside the gate by the river, where we supposed there was a place of prayer; and we sat down and spoke to the women who had gathered there. [14]A certain woman named Lydia, a worshiper of God, was listening to us; she was from the city of Thyatira and a dealer in purple cloth. The Lord opened her heart to listen eagerly to what was said by Paul. [15]When she and her household were baptized, she urged us, saying, "If you have judged me to be faithful to the Lord, come and stay at my home." And she prevailed upon us.

[16] One day, as we were going to the place of prayer, we met a slave-girl who had a spirit of divination and brought her owners a great deal of money by fortune-telling. [17]While she followed Paul

[a]Gk He [b]Gk brothers [c]Other authorities read *a city of the first district*

and us, she would cry out, "These men are slaves of the Most High God, who proclaim to you[a] a way of salvation." [18]She kept doing this for many days. But Paul, very much annoyed, turned and said to the spirit, "I order you in the name of Jesus Christ to come out of her." And it came out that very hour.

19 But when her owners saw that their hope of making money was gone, they seized Paul and Silas and dragged them into the marketplace before the authorities. [20]When they had brought them before the magistrates, they said, "These men are disturbing our city; they are Jews [21]and are advocating customs that are not lawful for us as Romans to adopt or observe." [22]The crowd joined in attacking them, and the magistrates had them stripped of their clothing and ordered them to be beaten with rods. [23]After they had given them a severe flogging, they threw them into prison and ordered the jailer to keep them securely. [24]Following these instructions, he put them in the innermost cell and fastened their feet in the stocks.

25 About midnight Paul and Silas were praying and singing hymns to God, and the prisoners were listening to them. [26]Suddenly there was an earthquake, so violent that the foundations of the prison were shaken; and immediately all the doors were opened and everyone's chains were unfastened. [27]When the jailer woke up and saw the prison doors wide open, he drew his sword and was about to kill himself, since he supposed that the prisoners had escaped. [28]But Paul shouted in a loud voice, "Do not harm yourself, for we are all here." [29]The jailer[b] called for lights, and rushing in, he fell down trembling before Paul and Silas. [30]Then he brought them outside and said, "Sirs, what must I do to be saved?" [31]They answered, "Believe on the Lord Jesus, and you will be saved, you and your household." [32]They spoke the word of the Lord[c] to him and to all who were in his house. [33]At the same hour of the night he took them and washed their wounds; then he and his entire family were baptized without delay. [34]He brought them up into the house and set food before them; and he and his entire household rejoiced that he had become a believer in God.

35 When morning came, the magistrates sent the police, saying, "Let those men go." [36]And the jailer reported the message to Paul, saying, "The magistrates sent word to let you go; therefore come out now and go in peace." [37]But Paul replied, "They have beaten us in public, uncondemned, men who are Roman citizens, and have thrown us into prison; and now are they going to discharge us in secret? Certainly not! Let them come and take us out themselves." [38]The police

---

[a]Other ancient authorities read *to us* [b]Gk *He* [c]Other ancient authorities read *word of God*

reported these words to the magistrates, and they were afraid when they heard that they were Roman citizens; [39]so they came and apologized to them. And they took them out and asked them to leave the city. [40]After leaving the prison they went to Lydia's home; and when they had seen and encouraged the brothers and sisters[a] there, they departed.

17 After Paul and Silas[b] had passed through Amphipolis and Apollonia, they came to Thessalonica, where there was a synagogue of the Jews. [2]And Paul went in, as was his custom, and on three sabbath days argued with them from the scriptures, [3]explaining and proving that it was necessary for the Messiah[c] to suffer and to rise from the dead, and saying, "This is the Messiah,[c] Jesus whom I am proclaiming to you." [4]Some of them were persuaded and joined Paul and Silas, as did a great many of the devout Greeks and not a few of the leading women. [5]But the Jews became jealous, and with the help of some ruffians in the marketplaces they formed a mob and set the city in an uproar. While they were searching for Paul and Silas to bring them out to the assembly, they attacked Jason's house. [6]When they could not find them, they dragged Jason and some believers[a] before the city authorities,[d] shouting, "These people who have been turning the world upside down have come here also, [7]and Jason has entertained them as guests. They are all acting contrary to the decrees of the emperor, saying that there is another king named Jesus." [8]The people and the city officials were disturbed when they heard this, [9]and after they had taken bail from Jason and the others, they let them go.

[10] That very night the believers[a] sent Paul and Silas off to Beroea; and when they arrived, they went to the Jewish synagogue. [11]These Jews were more receptive than those in Thessalonica, for they welcomed the message very eagerly and examined the scriptures every day to see whether these things were so. [12]Many of them therefore believed, including not a few Greek women and men of high standing. [13]But when the Jews of Thessalonica learned that the word of God had been proclaimed by Paul in Beroea as well, they came there too, to stir up and incite the crowds. [14]Then the believers[a] immediately sent Paul away to the coast, but Silas and Timothy remained behind. [15]Those who conducted Paul brought him as far as Athens; and after receiving instructions to have Silas and Timothy join him as soon as possible, they left him.

[16] While Paul was waiting for them in Athens, he was deeply distressed to see that the city was full of idols. [17]So he argued in the synagogue with the Jews and the devout persons, and also in the

[a]Gk brothers [b]Gk they [c]Or the Christ [d]Gk politarchs

marketplace[a] every day with those who happened to be there. [18]Also some Epicurean and Stoic philosophers debated with him. Some said, "What does this babbler want to say?" Others said, "He seems to be a proclaimer of foreign divinities." (This was because he was telling the good news about Jesus and the resurrection.) [19]So they took him and brought him to the Areopagus and asked him, "May we know what this new teaching is that you are presenting? [20]It sounds rather strange to us, so we would like to know what it means." [21]Now all the Athenians and the foreigners living there would spend their time in nothing but telling or hearing something new.

22 Then Paul stood in front of the Areopagus and said, "Athenians, I see how extremely religious you are in every way. [23]For as I went through the city and looked carefully at the objects of your worship, I found among them an altar with the inscription, 'To an unknown god.' What therefore you worship as unknown, this I proclaim to you. [24]The God who made the world and everything in it, he who is Lord of heaven and earth, does not live in shrines made by human hands, [25]nor is he served by human hands, as though he needed anything, since he himself gives to all mortals life and breath and all things. [26]From one ancestor[b] he made all nations to inhabit the whole earth, and he allotted the times of their exis-

tence and the boundaries of the places where they would live, [27]so that they would search for God[c] and perhaps grope for him and find him—though indeed he is not far from each one of us. [28]For 'In him we live and move and have our being'; as even some of your own poets have said,

'For we too are his
offspring.'

[29]Since we are God's offspring, we ought not to think that the deity is like gold, or silver, or stone, an image formed by the art and imagination of mortals. [30]While God has overlooked the times of human ignorance, now he commands all people everywhere to repent, [31]because he has fixed a day on which he will have the world judged in righteousness by a man whom he has appointed, and of this he has given assurance to all by raising him from the dead."

32 When they heard of the resurrection of the dead, some scoffed; but others said, "We will hear you again about this." [33]At that point Paul left them. [34]But some of them joined him and became believers, including Dionysius the Areopagite and a woman named Damaris, and others with them.

18 After this Paul[d] left Athens and went to Corinth. [2]There he found a Jew named Aquila, a native of Pontus, who had recently

---

[a]Or *civic center;* Gk *agora* [b]Gk *From one;* other ancient authorities read *From one blood* [c]Other ancient authorities read *the Lord* [d]Gk *he*

come from Italy with his wife Priscilla, because Claudius had ordered all Jews to leave Rome. Paul[a] went to see them, [3]and, because he was of the same trade, he stayed with them, and they worked together—by trade they were tentmakers. [4]Every sabbath he would argue in the synagogue and would try to convince Jews and Greeks.

[5] When Silas and Timothy arrived from Macedonia, Paul was occupied with proclaiming the word,[b] testifying to the Jews that the Messiah[c] was Jesus. [6]When they opposed and reviled him, in protest he shook the dust from his clothes[d] and said to them, "Your blood be on your own heads! I am innocent. From now on I will go to the Gentiles." [7]Then he left the synagogue[e] and went to the house of a man named Titius[f] Justus, a worshiper of God; his house was next door to the synagogue. [8]Crispus, the official of the synagogue, became a believer in the Lord, together with all his household; and many of the Corinthians who heard Paul became believers and were baptized. [9]One night the Lord said to Paul in a vision, "Do not be afraid, but speak and do not be silent; [10]for I am with you, and no one will lay a hand on you to harm you, for there are many in this city who are my people." [11]He stayed there a year and six months, teaching the word of God among them.

[12] But when Gallio was proconsul of Achaia, the Jews made a united attack on Paul and brought him before the tribunal. [13]They said, "This man is persuading people to worship God in ways that are contrary to the law." [14]Just as Paul was about to speak, Gallio said to the Jews, "If it were a matter of crime or serious villainy, I would be justified in accepting the complaint of you Jews; [15]but since it is a matter of questions about words and names and your own law, see to it yourselves; I do not wish to be a judge of these matters." [16]And he dismissed them from the tribunal. [17]Then all of them[g] seized Sosthenes, the official of the synagogue, and beat him in front of the tribunal. But Gallio paid no attention to any of these things.

[18] After staying there for a considerable time, Paul said farewell to the believers[h] and sailed for Syria, accompanied by Priscilla and Aquila. At Cenchreae he had his hair cut, for he was under a vow. [19]When they reached Ephesus, he left them there, but first he himself went into the synagogue and had a discussion with the Jews. [20]When they asked him to stay longer, he declined; [21]but on taking leave of them, he said, "I[i] will return to you, if God wills." Then he set sail from Ephesus.

[22] When he had landed at Caesarea, he went up to Jerusalem[j] and greeted the church, and

[a]Gk He [b]Gk with the word [c]Or the Christ [d]Gk reviled him, he shook out his clothes [e]Gk left there [f]Other ancient authorities read Titus [g]Other ancient authorities read all the Greeks [h]Gk brothers [i]Other ancient authorities read I must at all costs keep the approaching festival in Jerusalem, but I [j]Gk went up

then went down to Antioch. [23]After spending some time there he departed and went from place to place through the region of Galatia[a] and Phrygia, strengthening all the disciples.

24 Now there came to Ephesus a Jew named Apollos, a native of Alexandria. He was an eloquent man, well-versed in the scriptures. [25]He had been instructed in the Way of the Lord; and he spoke with burning enthusiasm and taught accurately the things concerning Jesus, though he knew only the baptism of John. [26]He began to speak boldly in the synagogue; but when Priscilla and Aquila heard him, they took him aside and explained the Way of God to him more accurately. [27]And when he wished to cross over to Achaia, the believers encouraged him and wrote to the disciples to welcome him. On his arrival he greatly helped those who through grace had become believers, [28]for he powerfully refuted the Jews in public, showing by the scriptures that the Messiah is Jesus.

19 While Apollos was in Corinth, Paul passed through the interior regions and came to Ephesus, where he found some disciples. [2]He said to them, "Did you receive the Holy Spirit when you became believers?" They replied, "No, we have not even heard that there is a Holy Spirit." [3]Then he said, "Into what then were you baptized?" They answered, "Into John's baptism." [4]Paul said, "John baptized with the baptism of repentance, telling the people to believe in the one who was to come after him, that is, in Jesus." [5]On hearing this, they were baptized in the name of the Lord Jesus. [6]When Paul had laid his hands on them, the Holy Spirit came upon them, and they spoke in tongues and prophesied— [7]altogether there were about twelve of them.

8 He entered the synagogue and for three months spoke out boldly, and argued persuasively about the kingdom of God. [9]When some stubbornly refused to believe and spoke evil of the Way before the congregation, he left them, taking the disciples with him, and argued daily in the lecture hall of Tyrannus.[b] [10]This continued for two years, so that all the residents of Asia, both Jews and Greeks, heard the word of the Lord.

11 God did extraordinary miracles through Paul, [12]so that when the handkerchiefs or aprons that had touched his skin were brought to the sick, their diseases left them, and the evil spirits came out of them. [13]Then some itinerant Jewish exorcists tried to use the name of the Lord Jesus over those who had evil spirits, saying, "I adjure you by the Jesus whom Paul proclaims." [14]Seven sons of a Jewish high priest named Sceva were doing this. [15]But the evil spirit said to them in reply, "Jesus I know, and

[a]Gk *the Galatian region* [b]Other ancient authorities read *of a certain Tyrannus, from eleven o' clock in the morning to four in the afternoon*

Paul I know; but who are you?" [16]Then the man with the evil spirit leaped on them, mastered them all, and so overpowered them that they fled out of the house naked and wounded. [17]When this became known to all residents of Ephesus, both Jews and Greeks, everyone was awestruck; and the name of the Lord Jesus was praised. [18]Also many of those who became believers confessed and disclosed their practices. [19]A number of those who practiced magic collected their books and burned them publicly; when the value of these books[a] was calculated, it was found to come to fifty thousand silver coins. [20]So the word of the Lord grew mightily and prevailed.

21 Now after these things had been accomplished, Paul resolved in the Spirit to go through Macedonia and Achaia, and then to go on to Jerusalem. He said, "After I have gone there, I must also see Rome." [22]So he sent two of his helpers, Timothy and Erastus, to Macedonia, while he himself stayed for some time longer in Asia.

23 About that time no little disturbance broke out concerning the Way. [24]A man named Demetrius, a silversmith who made silver shrines of Artemis, brought no little business to the artisans. [25]These he gathered together, with the workers of the same trade, and said, "Men, you know that we get our wealth from this business. [26]You also see and hear that not only in Ephesus but in almost the whole of Asia this Paul has persuaded and drawn away a considerable number of people by saying that gods made with hands are not gods. [27]And there is danger not only that this trade of ours may come into disrepute but also that the temple of the great goddess Artemis will be scorned, and she will be deprived of her majesty that brought all Asia and the world to worship her."

28 When they heard this, they were enraged and shouted, "Great is Artemis of the Ephesians!" [29]The city was filled with the confusion; and people[b] rushed together to the theater, dragging with them Gaius and Aristarchus, Macedonians who were Paul's travel companions. [30]Paul wished to go into the crowd, but the disciples would not let him; [31]even some officials of the province of Asia,[c] who were friendly to him, sent him a message urging him not to venture into the theater. [32]Meanwhile, some were shouting one thing, some another; for the assembly was in confusion, and most of them did not know why they had come together. [33]Some of the crowd gave instructions to Alexander, whom the Jews had pushed forward. And Alexander motioned for silence and tried to make a defense before the people. [34]But when they recognized

---

[a]Gk them [b]Gk they [c]Gk some of the Asiarchs

that he was a Jew, for about two hours all of them shouted in unison, "Great is Artemis of the Ephesians!" [35]But when the town clerk had quieted the crowd, he said, "Citizens of Ephesus, who is there that does not know that the city of the Ephesians is the temple keeper of the great Artemis and of the statue that fell from heaven?[a] [36]Since these things cannot be denied, you ought to be quiet and do nothing rash. [37]You have brought these men here who are neither temple robbers nor blasphemers of[b] our goddess. [38]If therefore Demetrius and the artisans with him have a complaint against anyone, the courts are open, and there are proconsuls; let them bring charges there against one another. [39]If there is anything further[c] you want to know, it must be settled in the regular assembly. [40]For we are in danger of being charged with rioting today, since there is no cause that we can give to justify this commotion." [41]When he had said this, he dismissed the assembly.

20 After the uproar had ceased, Paul sent for the disciples; and after encouraging them and saying farewell, he left for Macedonia. [2]When he had gone through those regions and had given the believers[d] much encouragement, he came to Greece, [3]where he stayed for three months. He was about to set sail for Syria when a plot was made against him by the Jews, and so he decided to return through Macedonia. [4]He was

accompanied by Sopater son of Pyrrhus from Beroea, by Aristarchus and Secundus from Thessalonica, by Gaius from Derbe, and by Timothy, as well as by Tychicus and Trophimus from Asia. [5]They went ahead and were waiting for us in Troas; [6]but we sailed from Philippi after the days of Unleavened Bread, and in five days we joined them in Troas, where we stayed for seven days.

7 On the first day of the week, when we met to break bread, Paul was holding a discussion with them; since he intended to leave the next day, he continued speaking until midnight. [8]There were many lamps in the room upstairs where we were meeting. [9]A young man named Eutychus, who was sitting in the window, began to sink off into a deep sleep while Paul talked still longer. Overcome by sleep, he fell to the ground three floors below and was picked up dead. [10]But Paul went down, and bending over him took him in his arms, and said, "Do not be alarmed, for his life is in him." [11]Then Paul went upstairs, and after he had broken bread and eaten, he continued to converse with them until dawn; then he left. [12]Meanwhile they had taken the boy away alive and were not a little comforted.

13 We went ahead to the ship and set sail for Assos, intending to take Paul on board there; for he

[a]Meaning of Gk uncertain [b]Other ancient authorities read *your* [c]Other ancient authorities read *about other matters* [d]Gk *given them*

had made this arrangement, intending to go by land himself. [14]When he met us in Assos, we took him on board and went to Mitylene. [15]We sailed from there, and on the following day we arrived opposite Chios. The next day we touched at Samos, and[a] the day after that we came to Miletus. [16]For Paul had decided to sail past Ephesus, so that he might not have to spend time in Asia; he was eager to be in Jerusalem, if possible, on the day of Pentecost.

[17] From Miletus he sent a message to Ephesus, asking the elders of the church to meet him. [18]When they came to him, he said to them:

"You yourselves know how I lived among you the entire time from the first day that I set foot in Asia, [19]serving the Lord with all humility and with tears, enduring the trials that came to me through the plots of the Jews. [20]I did not shrink from doing anything helpful, proclaiming the message to you and teaching you publicly and from house to house, [21]as I testified to both Jews and Greeks about repentance toward God and faith toward our Lord Jesus. [22]And now, as a captive to the Spirit,[b] I am on my way to Jerusalem, not knowing what will happen to me there, [23]except that the Holy Spirit testifies to me in every city that imprisonment and persecutions are waiting for me. [24]But I do not count my life of any value to myself, if only I may finish my course and the ministry that I received from the Lord Jesus, to testify to the good news of God's grace.

[25] "And now I know that none of you, among whom I have gone about proclaiming the kingdom, will ever see my face again. [26]Therefore I declare to you this day that I am not responsible for the blood of any of you, [27]for I did not shrink from declaring to you the whole purpose of God. [28]Keep watch over yourselves and over all the flock, of which the Holy Spirit has made you overseers, to shepherd the church of God[c] that he obtained with the blood of his own Son.[d] [29]I know that after I have gone, savage wolves will come in among you, not sparing the flock. [30]Some even from your own group will come distorting the truth in order to entice the disciples to follow them. [31]Therefore be alert, remembering that for three years I did not cease night or day to warn everyone with tears. [32]And now I commend you to God and to the message of his grace, a message that is able to build you up and to give you the inheritance among all who are sanctified. [33]I coveted no one's silver or gold or clothing. [34]You know for yourselves that I worked with my own hands to support myself and my companions. [35]In all this I have given you an example that by such work we must support the weak, remembering

[a]Other ancient authorities add *after remaining at Trogyllium* [b]Or *And now, bound in the spirit* [c]Other ancient authorities read *of the Lord* [d]Or *with his own blood;* Gk *with the blood of his Own*

the words of the Lord Jesus, for he himself said, 'It is more blessed to give than to receive.'"

36 When he had finished speaking, he knelt down with them all and prayed. [37]There was much weeping among them all; they embraced Paul and kissed him, [38]grieving especially because of what he had said, that they would not see him again. Then they brought him to the ship.

21 When we had parted from them and set sail, we came by a straight course to Cos, and the next day to Rhodes, and from there to Patara.[a] [2]When we found a ship bound for Phoenicia, we went on board and set sail. [3]We came in sight of Cyprus; and leaving it on our left, we sailed to Syria and landed at Tyre, because the ship was to unload its cargo there. [4]We looked up the disciples and stayed there for seven days. Through the Spirit they told Paul not to go on to Jerusalem. [5]When our days there were ended, we left and proceeded on our journey; and all of them, with wives and children, escorted us outside the city. There we knelt down on the beach and prayed [6]and said farewell to one another. Then we went on board the ship, and they returned home.

7 When we had finished[b] the voyage from Tyre, we arrived at Ptolemais; and we greeted the believers[c] and stayed with them for one day. [8]The next day we left and came to Caesarea; and we went into the house of Philip the evangelist, one of the seven, and stayed with him. [9]He had four unmarried daughters[d] who had the gift of prophecy. [10]While we were staying there for several days, a prophet named Agabus came down from Judea. [11]He came to us and took Paul's belt, bound his own feet and hands with it, and said, "Thus says the Holy Spirit, 'This is the way the Jews in Jerusalem will bind the man who owns this belt and will hand him over to the Gentiles.'" [12]When we heard this, we and the people there urged him not to go up to Jerusalem. [13]Then Paul answered, "What are you doing, weeping and breaking my heart? For I am ready not only to be bound but even to die in Jerusalem for the name of the Lord Jesus." [14]Since he would not be persuaded, we remained silent except to say, "The Lord's will be done."

15 After these days we got ready and started to go up to Jerusalem. [16]Some of the disciples from Caesarea also came along and brought us to the house of Mnason of Cyprus, an early disciple, with whom we were to stay.

17 When we arrived in Jerusalem, the brothers welcomed us warmly. [18]The next day Paul went with us to visit James; and all the elders were present. [19]After greeting them, he related one by one the things that God had done among the Gentiles through his ministry. [20]When they

---

[a]Other ancient authorities add *and Myra* [b]Or *continued* [c]Gk *brothers* [d]Gk *four daughters, virgins,*

heard it, they praised God. Then they said to him, "You see, brother, how many thousands of believers there are among the Jews, and they are all zealous for the law. [21]They have been told about you that you teach all the Jews living among the Gentiles to forsake Moses, and that you tell them not to circumcise their children or observe the customs. [22]What then is to be done? They will certainly hear that you have come. [23]So do what we tell you. We have four men who are under a vow. [24]Join these men, go through the rite of purification with them, and pay for the shaving of their heads. Thus all will know that there is nothing in what they have been told about you, but that you yourself observe and guard the law. [25]But as for the Gentiles who have become believers, we have sent a letter with our judgment that they should abstain from what has been sacrificed to idols and from blood and from what is strangled[a] and from fornication." [26]Then Paul took the men, and the next day, having purified himself, he entered the temple with them, making public the completion of the days of purification when the sacrifice would be made for each of them.

27 When the seven days were almost completed, the Jews from Asia, who had seen him in the temple, stirred up the whole crowd. They seized him, [28]shouting, "Fellow Israelites, help! This is the man who is teaching every-

one everywhere against our people, our law, and this place; more than that, he has actually brought Greeks into the temple and has defiled this holy place." [29]For they had previously seen Trophimus the Ephesian with him in the city, and they supposed that Paul had brought him into the temple. [30]Then all the city was aroused, and the people rushed together. They seized Paul and dragged him out of the temple, and immediately the doors were shut. [31]While they were trying to kill him, word came to the tribune of the cohort that all Jerusalem was in an uproar. [32]Immediately he took soldiers and centurions and ran down to them. When they saw the tribune and the soldiers, they stopped beating Paul. [33]Then the tribune came, arrested him, and ordered him to be bound with two chains; he inquired who he was and what he had done. [34]Some in the crowd shouted one thing, some another; and as he could not learn the facts because of the uproar, he ordered him to be brought into the barracks. [35]When Paul[b] came to the steps, the violence of the mob was so great that he had to be carried by the soldiers. [36]The crowd that followed kept shouting, "Away with him!"

37 Just as Paul was about to be brought into the barracks, he said to the tribune, "May I say something to you?" The tribune[c]

---

[a]Other ancient authorities lack *and from what is strangled* [b]Gk *he* [c]Gk *He*

replied, "Do you know Greek? ³⁸Then you are not the Egyptian who recently stirred up a revolt and led the four thousand assassins out into the wilderness?" ³⁹Paul replied, "I am a Jew, from Tarsus in Cilicia, a citizen of an important city; I beg you, let me speak to the people." ⁴⁰When he had given him permission, Paul stood on the steps and motioned to the people for silence; and when there was a great hush, he addressed them in the Hebrew*a* language, saying:

22 "Brothers and fathers, listen to the defense that I now make before you."

2 When they heard him addressing them in Hebrew,*a* they became even more quiet. Then he said:

3 "I am a Jew, born in Tarsus in Cilicia, but brought up in this city at the feet of Gamaliel, educated strictly according to our ancestral law, being zealous for God, just as all of you are today. ⁴I persecuted this Way up to the point of death by binding both men and women and putting them in prison, ⁵as the high priest and the whole council of elders can testify about me. From them I also received letters to the brothers in Damascus, and I went there in order to bind those who were there and to bring them back to Jerusalem for punishment.

6 "While I was on my way and approaching Damascus, about noon a great light from heaven suddenly shone about me. ⁷I fell to the ground and heard a voice saying to me, 'Saul, Saul, why are you persecuting me?' ⁸I answered, 'Who are you, Lord?' Then he said to me, 'I am Jesus of Nazareth*b* whom you are persecuting.' ⁹Now those who were with me saw the light but did not hear the voice of the one who was speaking to me. ¹⁰I asked, 'What am I to do, Lord?' The Lord said to me, 'Get up and go to Damascus; there you will be told everything that has been assigned to you to do.' ¹¹Since I could not see because of the brightness of that light, those who were with me took my hand and led me to Damascus.

12 "A certain Ananias, who was a devout man according to the law and well spoken of by all the Jews living there, ¹³came to me; and standing beside me, he said, 'Brother Saul, regain your sight!' In that very hour I regained my sight and saw him. ¹⁴Then he said, 'The God of our ancestors has chosen you to know his will, to see the Righteous One and to hear his own voice; ¹⁵for you will be his witness to all the world of what you have seen and heard. ¹⁶And now why do you delay? Get up, be baptized, and have your sins washed away, calling on his name.'

17 "After I had returned to Jerusalem and while I was praying in the temple, I fell into a trance ¹⁸and saw Jesus*c* saying to

---

*a*That is, *Aramaic* *b*Gk *the Nazorean* *c*Gk *him*

me, 'Hurry and get out of Jerusalem quickly, because they will not accept your testimony about me.' [19]And I said, 'Lord, they themselves know that in every synagogue I imprisoned and beat those who believed in you. [20]And while the blood of your witness Stephen was shed, I myself was standing by, approving and keeping the coats of those who killed him.' [21]Then he said to me, 'Go, for I will send you far away to the Gentiles.'"

22 Up to this point they listened to him, but then they shouted, "Away with such a fellow from the earth! For he should not be allowed to live." [23]And while they were shouting, throwing off their cloaks, and tossing dust into the air, [24]the tribune directed that he was to be brought into the barracks, and ordered him to be examined by flogging, to find out the reason for this outcry against him. [25]But when they had tied him up with thongs,[a] Paul said to the centurion who was standing by, "Is it legal for you to flog a Roman citizen who is uncondemned?" [26]When the centurion heard that, he went to the tribune and said to him, "What are you about to do? This man is a Roman citizen." [27]The tribune came and asked Paul, "Tell me, are you a Roman citizen?" And he said, "Yes." [28]The tribune answered, "It cost me a large sum of money to get my citizenship." Paul said, "But I was born a citizen." [29]Immediately those who were about to

examine him drew back from him; and the tribune also was afraid, for he realized that Paul was a Roman citizen and that he had bound him.

30 Since he wanted to find out what Paul[b] was being accused of by the Jews, the next day he released him and ordered the chief priests and the entire council to meet. He brought Paul down and had him stand before them.

23 While Paul was looking intently at the council he said, "Brothers,[c] up to this day I have lived my life with a clear conscience before God." [2]Then the high priest Ananias ordered those standing near him to strike him on the mouth. [3]At this Paul said to him, "God will strike you, you whitewashed wall! Are you sitting there to judge me according to the law, and yet in violation of the law you order me to be struck?" [4]Those standing nearby said, "Do you dare to insult God's high priest?" [5]And Paul said, "I did not realize, brothers, that he was high priest; for it is written, 'You shall not speak evil of a leader of your people.'"

6 When Paul noticed that some were Sadducees and others were Pharisees, he called out in the council, "Brothers, I am a Pharisee, a son of Pharisees. I am on trial concerning the hope of the resurrection[d] of the dead." [7]When he said this, a dissension began between the Pharisees and

[a]Or *up for the lashes* [b]Gk *he* [c]Gk *Men, brothers* [d]Gk *concerning hope and resurrection*

the Sadducees, and the assembly was divided. 8(The Sadducees say that there is no resurrection, or angel, or spirit; but the Pharisees acknowledge all three.) 9Then a great clamor arose, and certain scribes of the Pharisees' group stood up and contended, "We find nothing wrong with this man. What if a spirit or an angel has spoken to him?" 10When the dissension became violent, the tribune, fearing that they would tear Paul to pieces, ordered the soldiers to go down, take him by force, and bring him into the barracks.

11 That night the Lord stood near him and said, "Keep up your courage! For just as you have testified for me in Jerusalem, so you must bear witness also in Rome."

12 In the morning the Jews joined in a conspiracy and bound themselves by an oath neither to eat nor drink until they had killed Paul. 13There were more than forty who joined in this conspiracy. 14They went to the chief priests and elders and said, "We have strictly bound ourselves by an oath to taste no food until we have killed Paul. 15Now then, you and the council must notify the tribune to bring him down to you, on the pretext that you want to make a more thorough examination of his case. And we are ready to do away with him before he arrives."

16 Now the son of Paul's sister heard about the ambush; so he went and gained entrance to the barracks and told Paul. 17Paul called one of the centurions and said, "Take this young man to the tribune, for he has something to report to him." 18So he took him, brought him to the tribune, and said, "The prisoner Paul called me and asked me to bring this young man to you; he has something to tell you." 19The tribune took him by the hand, drew him aside privately, and asked, "What is it that you have to report to me?" 20He answered, "The Jews have agreed to ask you to bring Paul down to the council tomorrow, as though they were going to inquire more thoroughly into his case. 21But do not be persuaded by them, for more than forty of their men are lying in ambush for him. They have bound themselves by an oath neither to eat nor drink until they kill him. They are ready now and are waiting for your consent." 22So the tribune dismissed the young man, ordering him, "Tell no one that you have informed me of this."

23 Then he summoned two of the centurions and said, "Get ready to leave by nine o'clock tonight for Caesarea with two hundred soldiers, seventy horsemen, and two hundred spearmen. 24Also provide mounts for Paul to ride, and take him safely to Felix the governor." 25He wrote a letter to this effect:

26 "Claudius Lysias to his Excellency the governor Felix, greetings. 27This man was seized by the Jews and was about to be

killed by them, but when I had learned that he was a Roman citizen, I came with the guard and rescued him. [28]Since I wanted to know the charge for which they accused him, I had him brought to their council. [29]I found that he was accused concerning questions of their law, but was charged with nothing deserving death or imprisonment. [30]When I was informed that there would be a plot against the man, I sent him to you at once, ordering his accusers also to state before you what they have against him.[a]

31 So the soldiers, according to their instructions, took Paul and brought him during the night to Antipatris. [32]The next day they let the horsemen go on with him, while they returned to the barracks. [33]When they came to Caesarea and delivered the letter to the governor, they presented Paul also before him. [34]On reading the letter, he asked what province he belonged to, and when he learned that he was from Cilicia, [35]he said, "I will give you a hearing when your accusers arrive." Then he ordered that he be kept under guard in Herod's headquarters.[b]

24 Five days later the high priest Ananias came down with some elders and an attorney, a certain Tertullus, and they reported their case against Paul to the governor. [2]When Paul[c] had been summoned, Tertullus began to accuse him, saying:

"Your Excellency,[d] because of you we have long enjoyed peace, and reforms have been made for this people because of your foresight. [3]We welcome this in every way and everywhere with utmost gratitude. [4]But, to detain you no further, I beg you to hear us briefly with your customary graciousness. [5]We have, in fact, found this man a pestilent fellow, an agitator among all the Jews throughout the world, and a ringleader of the sect of the Nazarenes.[e] [6]He even tried to profane the temple, and so we seized him.[f] [8]By examining him yourself you will be able to learn from him concerning everything of which we accuse him."

9 The Jews also joined in the charge by asserting that all this was true.

10 When the governor motioned to him to speak, Paul replied:

"I cheerfully make my defense, knowing that for many years you have been a judge over this nation. [11]As you can find out, it is not more than twelve days since I went up to worship in Jerusalem. [12]They did not find me disputing with anyone in the temple or stirring up a crowd either in the synagogues or throughout the city. [13]Neither can they prove to you the charge that they now bring against me. [14]But

[a]Other ancient authorities add *Farewell* [b]Gk *praetorium* [c]Gk *he* [d]Gk lacks *Your Excellency* [e]Gk *Nazoreans* [f]Other ancient authorities add *and we would have judged him according to our law.* [7]*But the chief captain Lysias came and with great violence took him out of our hands,* [8]*commanding his accusers to come before you.*

this I admit to you, that according to the Way, which they call a sect, I worship the God of our ancestors, believing everything laid down according to the law or written in the prophets. [15]I have a hope in God—a hope that they themselves also accept—that there will be a resurrection of both[a] the righteous and the unrighteous. [16]Therefore I do my best always to have a clear conscience toward God and all people. [17]Now after some years I came to bring alms to my nation and to offer sacrifices. [18]While I was doing this, they found me in the temple, completing the rite of purification, without any crowd or disturbance. [19]But there were some Jews from Asia—they ought to be here before you to make an accusation, if they have anything against me. [20]Or let these men here tell what crime they had found when I stood before the council, [21]unless it was this one sentence that I called out while standing before them, 'It is about the resurrection of the dead that I am on trial before you today.'"

22 But Felix, who was rather well informed about the Way, adjourned the hearing with the comment, "When Lysias the tribune comes down, I will decide your case." [23]Then he ordered the centurion to keep him in custody, but to let him have some liberty and not to prevent any of his friends from taking care of his needs.

24 Some days later when Felix came with his wife Drusilla, who was Jewish, he sent for Paul and heard him speak concerning faith in Christ Jesus. [25]And as he discussed justice, self-control, and the coming judgment, Felix became frightened and said, "Go away for the present; when I have an opportunity, I will send for you." [26]At the same time he hoped that money would be given him by Paul, and for that reason he used to send for him very often and converse with him.

27 After two years had passed, Felix was succeeded by Porcius Festus; and since he wanted to grant the Jews a favor, Felix left Paul in prison.

25 Three days after Festus had arrived in the province, he went up from Caesarea to Jerusalem [2]where the chief priests and the leaders of the Jews gave him a report against Paul. They appealed to him [3]and requested, as a favor to them against Paul,[b] to have him transferred to Jerusalem. They were, in fact, planning an ambush to kill him along the way. [4]Festus replied that Paul was being kept at Caesarea, and that he himself intended to go there shortly. [5]"So," he said, "let those of you who have the authority come down with me, and if there is anything wrong about the man, let them accuse him."

6 After he had stayed among them not more than eight or ten days, he went down to Caesarea;

[a]Other ancient authorities read *of the dead, both of*
[b]Gk *him*

the next day he took his seat on the tribunal and ordered Paul to be brought. [7]When he arrived, the Jews who had gone down from Jerusalem surrounded him, bringing many serious charges against him, which they could not prove. [8]Paul said in his defense, "I have in no way committed an offense against the law of the Jews, or against the temple, or against the emperor." [9]But Festus, wishing to do the Jews a favor, asked Paul, "Do you wish to go up to Jerusalem and be tried there before me on these charges?" [10]Paul said, "I am appealing to the emperor's tribunal; this is where I should be tried. I have done no wrong to the Jews, as you very well know. [11]Now if I am in the wrong and have committed something for which I deserve to die, I am not trying to escape death; but if there is nothing to their charges against me, no one can turn me over to them. I appeal to the emperor." [12]Then Festus, after he had conferred with his council, replied, "You have appealed to the emperor; to the emperor you will go."

13 After several days had passed, King Agrippa and Bernice arrived at Caesarea to welcome Festus. [14]Since they were staying there several days, Festus laid Paul's case before the king, saying, "There is a man here who was left in prison by Felix. [15]When I was in Jerusalem, the chief priests and the elders of the Jews informed me about him and asked for a sentence against him.

[16]I told them that it was not the custom of the Romans to hand over anyone before the accused had met the accusers face to face and had been given an opportunity to make a defense against the charge. [17]So when they met here, I lost no time, but on the next day took my seat on the tribunal and ordered the man to be brought. [18]When the accusers stood up, they did not charge him with any of the crimes[a] that I was expecting. [19]Instead they had certain points of disagreement with him about their own religion and about a certain Jesus, who had died, but whom Paul asserted to be alive. [20]Since I was at a loss how to investigate these questions, I asked whether he wished to go to Jerusalem and be tried there on these charges.[b] [21]But when Paul had appealed to be kept in custody for the decision of his Imperial Majesty, I ordered him to be held until I could send him to the emperor. [22]Agrippa said to Festus, "I would like to hear the man myself." "Tomorrow," he said, "you will hear him."

23 So on the next day Agrippa and Bernice came with great pomp, and they entered the audience hall with the military tribunes and the prominent men of the city. Then Festus gave the order and Paul was brought in. [24]And Festus said, "King Agrippa and all here present with us, you

---

[a]Other ancient authorities read *with anything* [b]Gk *on them*

see this man about whom the whole Jewish community petitioned me, both in Jerusalem and here, shouting that he ought not to live any longer. ²⁵But I found that he had done nothing deserving death; and when he appealed to his Imperial Majesty, I decided to send him. ²⁶But I have nothing definite to write to our sovereign about him. Therefore I have brought him before all of you, and especially before you, King Agrippa, so that, after we have examined him, I may have something to write— ²⁷for it seems to me unreasonable to send a prisoner without indicating the charges against him."

26 Agrippa said to Paul, "You have permission to speak for yourself." Then Paul stretched out his hand and began to defend himself:

2 "I consider myself fortunate that it is before you, King Agrippa, I am to make my defense today against all the accusations of the Jews, ³because you are especially familiar with all the customs and controversies of the Jews; therefore I beg of you to listen to me patiently.

4 "All the Jews know my way of life from my youth, a life spent from the beginning among my own people and in Jerusalem. ⁵They have known for a long time, if they are willing to testify, that I have belonged to the strictest sect of our religion and lived as a Pharisee. ⁶And now I stand here on trial on account of my hope in the promise made by God to our ancestors, ⁷a promise that our twelve tribes hope to attain, as they earnestly worship day and night. It is for this hope, your Excellency,ᵃ that I am accused by Jews! ⁸Why is it thought incredible by any of you that God raises the dead?

9 "Indeed, I myself was convinced that I ought to do many things against the name of Jesus of Nazareth.ᵇ ¹⁰And that is what I did in Jerusalem; with authority received from the chief priests, I not only locked up many of the saints in prison, but I also cast my vote against them when they were being condemned to death. ¹¹By punishing them often in all the synagogues I tried to force them to blaspheme; and since I was so furiously enraged at them, I pursued them even to foreign cities.

12 "With this in mind, I was traveling to Damascus with the authority and commission of the chief priests, ¹³when at midday along the road, your Excellency,ᵃ I saw a light from heaven, brighter than the sun, shining around me and my companions. ¹⁴When we had all fallen to the ground, I heard a voice saying to me in the Hebrewᶜ language, 'Saul, Saul, why are you persecuting me? It hurts you to kick against the goads.' ¹⁵I asked, 'Who are you, Lord?' The Lord answered, 'I am Jesus whom you are persecuting. ¹⁶But get up and stand on your feet; for I have appeared to you for this purpose,

---

ᵃGk O king ᵇGk the Nazorean ᶜThat is, Aramaic

to appoint you to serve and testify to the things in which you have seen me[a] and to those in which I will appear to you. [17]I will rescue you from your people and from the Gentiles—to whom I am sending you [18]to open their eyes so that they may turn from darkness to light and from the power of Satan to God, so that they may receive forgiveness of sins and a place among those who are sanctified by faith in me.'

[19] "After that, King Agrippa, I was not disobedient to the heavenly vision, [20]but declared first to those in Damascus, then in Jerusalem and throughout the countryside of Judea, and also to the Gentiles, that they should repent and turn to God and do deeds consistent with repentance. [21]For this reason the Jews seized me in the temple and tried to kill me. [22]To this day I have had help from God, and so I stand here, testifying to both small and great, saying nothing but what the prophets and Moses said would take place: [23]that the Messiah[b] must suffer, and that, by being the first to rise from the dead, he would proclaim light both to our people and to the Gentiles."

[24] While he was making this defense, Festus exclaimed, "You are out of your mind, Paul! Too much learning is driving you *insane!*" [25]But Paul said, "I am not out of my mind, most excellent Festus, but I am speaking the sober truth. [26]Indeed the king knows about these things, and to him I speak freely; for I am certain that none of these things has escaped his notice, for this was not done in a corner. [27]King Agrippa, do you believe the prophets? I know that you believe." [28]Agrippa said to Paul, "Are you so quickly persuading me to become a Christian?"[c] [29]Paul replied, "Whether quickly or not, I pray to God that not only you but also all who are listening to me today might become such as I am—except for these chains."

[30] Then the king got up, and with him the governor and Bernice and those who had been seated with them; [31]and as they were leaving, they said to one another, "This man is doing nothing to deserve death or imprisonment." [32]Agrippa said to Festus, "This man could have been set free if he had not appealed to the emperor."

27 When it was decided that we were to sail for Italy, they transferred Paul and some other prisoners to a centurion of the Augustan Cohort, named Julius. [2]Embarking on a ship of Adramyttium that was about to set sail to the ports along the coast of Asia, we put to sea, accompanied by Aristarchus, a Macedonian from Thessalonica. [3]The next day we put in at Sidon; and Julius treated Paul kindly, and allowed him to go to his friends to be cared for. [4]Putting out to sea from there, we sailed

[a]Other ancient authorities read *the things that you have seen* [b]Or *the Christ* [c]Or *Quickly you will persuade me to play the Christian*

under the lee of Cyprus, because the winds were against us. [5]After we had sailed across the sea that is off Cilicia and Pamphylia, we came to Myra in Lycia. [6]There the centurion found an Alexandrian ship bound for Italy and put us on board. [7]We sailed slowly for a number of days and arrived with difficulty off Cnidus, and as the wind was against us, we sailed under the lee of Crete off Salmone. [8]Sailing past it with difficulty, we came to a place called Fair Havens, near the city of Lasea.

9 Since much time had been lost and sailing was now dangerous, because even the Fast had already gone by, Paul advised them, [10]saying, "Sirs, I can see that the voyage will be with danger and much heavy loss, not only of the cargo and the ship, but also of our lives." [11]But the centurion paid more attention to the pilot and to the owner of the ship than to what Paul said. [12]Since the harbor was not suitable for spending the winter, the majority was in favor of putting to sea from there, on the chance that somehow they could reach Phoenix, where they could spend the winter. It was a harbor of Crete, facing southwest and northwest.

13 When a moderate south wind began to blow, they thought they could achieve their purpose; so they weighed anchor and began to sail past Crete, close to the shore. [14]But soon a violent wind, called the northeaster, rushed down from Crete.[a] [15]Since

the ship was caught and could not be turned head-on into the wind, we gave way to it and were driven. [16]By running under the lee of a small island called Cauda[b] we were scarcely able to get the ship's boat under control. [17]After hoisting it up they took measures[c] to undergird the ship; then, fearing that they would run on the Syrtis, they lowered the sea anchor and so were driven. [18]We were being pounded by the storm so violently that on the next day they began to throw the cargo overboard, [19]and on the third day with their own hands they threw the ship's tackle overboard. [20]When neither sun nor stars appeared for many days, and no small tempest raged, all hope of our being saved was at last abandoned.

21 Since they had been without food for a long time, Paul then stood up among them and said, "Men, you should have listened to me and not have set sail from Crete and thereby avoided this damage and loss. [22]I urge you now to keep up your courage, for there will be no loss of life among you, but only of the ship. [23]For last night there stood by me an angel of the God to whom I belong and whom I worship, [24]and he said, 'Do not be afraid, Paul; you must stand before the emperor; and indeed, God has granted safety to all those who are sailing with you.' [25]So keep up your courage, men, for I have

---

[a]Gk *it* [b]Other ancient authorities read *Clauda* [c]Gk *helps*

faith in God that it will be exactly as I have been told. [26]But we will have to run aground on some island."

27 When the fourteenth night had come, as we were drifting across the sea of Adria, about midnight the sailors suspected that they were nearing land. [28]So they took soundings and found twenty fathoms; a little farther on they took soundings again and found fifteen fathoms. [29]Fearing that we might run on the rocks, they let down four anchors from the stern and prayed for day to come. [30]But when the sailors tried to escape from the ship and had lowered the boat into the sea, on the pretext of putting out anchors from the bow, [31]Paul said to the centurion and the soldiers, "Unless these men stay in the ship, you cannot be saved." [32]Then the soldiers cut away the ropes of the boat and set it adrift.

33 Just before daybreak, Paul urged all of them to take some food, saying, "Today is the fourteenth day that you have been in suspense and remaining without food, having eaten nothing. [34]Therefore I urge you to take some food, for it will help you survive; for none of you will lose a hair from your heads." [35]After he had said this, he took bread; and giving thanks to God in the presence of all, he broke it and began to eat. [36]Then all of them were encouraged and took food for themselves. [37](We were in all two hundred seventy-six[a] persons in the ship.) [38]After they had satisfied their hunger, they lightened the ship by throwing the wheat into the sea.

39 In the morning they did not recognize the land, but they noticed a bay with a beach, on which they planned to run the ship ashore, if they could. [40]So they cast off the anchors and left them in the sea. At the same time they loosened the ropes that tied the steering-oars; then hoisting the foresail to the wind, they made for the beach. [41]But striking a reef,[b] they ran the ship aground; the bow stuck and remained immovable, but the stern was being broken up by the force of the waves. [42]The soldiers' plan was to kill the prisoners, so that none might swim away and escape; [43]but the centurion, wishing to save Paul, kept them from carrying out their plan. He ordered those who could swim to jump overboard first and make for the land, [44]and the rest to follow, some on planks and others on pieces of the ship. And so it was that all were brought safely to land.

28 After we had reached safety, we then learned that the island was called Malta. [2]The natives showed us unusual kindness. Since it had begun to rain and was cold, they kindled a fire and welcomed all of us around it. [3]Paul had gathered a bundle of brushwood and was putting it on the fire, when a viper, driven out

---

[a]Other ancient authorities read *seventy-six;* others, *about seventy-six* [b]Gk *place of two seas*

by the heat, fastened itself on his hand. [4]When the natives saw the creature hanging from his hand, they said to one another, "This man must be a murderer; though he has escaped from the sea, justice has not allowed him to live." [5]He, however, shook off the creature into the fire and suffered no harm. [6]They were expecting him to swell up or drop dead, but after they had waited a long time and saw that nothing unusual had happened to him, they changed their minds and began to say that he was a god.

7 Now in the neighborhood of that place were lands belonging to the leading man of the island, named Publius, who received us and entertained us hospitably for three days. [8]It so happened that the father of Publius lay sick in bed with fever and dysentery. Paul visited him and cured him by praying and putting his hands on him. [9]After this happened, the rest of the people on the island who had diseases also came and were cured. [10]They bestowed many honors on us, and when we were about to sail, they put on board all the provisions we needed.

11 Three months later we set sail on a ship that had wintered at the island, an Alexandrian ship with the Twin Brothers as its figurehead. [12]We put in at Syracuse and stayed there for three days; [13]then we weighed anchor and came to Rhegium. After one day there a south wind sprang up, and on the second day

we came to Puteoli. [14]There we found believers[a] and were invited to stay with them for seven days. And so we came to Rome. [15]The believers[a] from there, when they heard of us, came as far as the Forum of Appius and Three Taverns to meet us. On seeing them, Paul thanked God and took courage. [16]When we came into Rome, Paul was allowed to live by himself, with the soldier who was guarding him.

17 Three days later he called together the local leaders of the Jews. When they had assembled, he said to them, "Brothers, though I had done nothing against our people or the customs of our ancestors, yet I was arrested in Jerusalem and handed over to the Romans. [18]When they had examined me, the Romans[b] wanted to release me, because there was no reason for the death penalty in my case. [19]But when the Jews objected, I was compelled to appeal to the emperor—even though I had no charge to bring against my nation. [20]For this reason therefore I have asked to see you and speak with you,[c] since it is for the sake of the hope of Israel that I am bound with this chain." [21]They replied, "We have received no letters from Judea about you, and none of the brothers coming here has reported or spoken anything evil about you.[22]But we would like to hear from you what

---

[a]Gk brothers [b]Gk they [c]Or I have asked to see me and speak with me

you think, for with regard to this sect we know that everywhere it is spoken against."

23 After they had set a day to meet with him, they came to him at his lodgings in great numbers. From morning until evening he explained the matter to them, testifying to the kingdom of God and trying to convince them about Jesus both from the law of Moses and from the prophets. 24Some were convinced by what he had said, while others refused to believe. 25So they disagreed with each other; and as they were leaving, Paul made one further statement: "The Holy Spirit was right in saying to your ancestors through the prophet Isaiah,

26 'Go to this people and say,
  You will indeed listen, but
      never understand,
  and you will indeed look,
      but never perceive.
27 For this people's heart has
      grown dull,

and their ears are hard
    of hearing,
and they have shut
    their eyes;
so that they might not
    look with their eyes,
and listen with their
    ears,
and understand with their
    heart and turn—
and I would heal them.'

28Let it be known to you then that this salvation of God has been sent to the Gentiles; they will listen."[a]

30 He lived there two whole years at his own expense[b] and welcomed all who came to him, 31proclaiming the kingdom of God and teaching about the Lord Jesus Christ with all boldness and without hindrance.

[a]Other ancient authorities add verse 29, *And when he had said these words, the Jews departed, arguing vigorously among themselves* [b]Or *in his own hired dwelling*

The Letter of Paul to the

ROMANS

1 Paul, a servant[a] of Jesus Christ, called to be an apostle, set apart for the gospel of God, 2which he promised beforehand through his prophets in the holy scriptures, 3the gospel concerning his Son, who was descended from David according to the flesh 4and was declared to be Son of God with power according to the spirit[b] of holiness by resurrection from the dead, Jesus Christ our Lord, 5through whom we have received grace and apos-

[a]Gk *slave* [b]Or *Spirit*

tleship to bring about the obedience of faith among all the Gentiles for the sake of his name, [6]including yourselves who are called to belong to Jesus Christ,

7 To all God's beloved in Rome, who are called to be saints:

Grace to you and peace from God our Father and the Lord Jesus Christ.

8 First, I thank my God through Jesus Christ for all of you, because your faith is proclaimed throughout the world. [9]For God, whom I serve with my spirit by announcing the gospel[a] of his Son, is my witness that without ceasing I remember you always in my prayers, [10]asking that by God's will I may somehow at last succeed in coming to you. [11]For I am longing to see you so that I may share with you some spiritual gift to strengthen you— [12]or rather so that we may be mutually encouraged by each other's faith, both yours and mine. [13]I want you to know, brothers and sisters,[b] that I have often intended to come to you (but thus far have been prevented), in order that I may reap some harvest among you as I have among the rest of the Gentiles. [14]I am a debtor both to Greeks and to barbarians, both to the wise and to the foolish [15]—hence my eagerness to proclaim the gospel to you also who are in Rome.

16 For I am not ashamed of the gospel; it is the power of God for salvation to everyone who has faith, to the Jew first and also to the Greek. [17]For in it the righteousness of God is revealed through faith for faith; as it is written, "The one who is righteous will live by faith."[c]

18 For the wrath of God is revealed from heaven against all ungodliness and wickedness of those who by their wickedness suppress the truth. [19]For what can be known about God is plain to them, because God has shown it to them. [20]Ever since the creation of the world his eternal power and divine nature, invisible though they are, have been understood and seen through the things he has made. So they are without excuse; [21]for though they knew God, they did not honor him as God or give thanks to him, but they became futile in their thinking, and their senseless minds were darkened. [22]Claiming to be wise, they became fools; [23]and they exchanged the glory of the immortal God for images resembling a mortal human being or birds or four-footed animals or reptiles.

24 Therefore God gave them up in the lusts of their hearts to impurity, to the degrading of their bodies among themselves, [25]because they exchanged the truth about God for a lie and worshiped and served the creature rather than the Creator, who is blessed forever! Amen.

26 For this reason God gave them up to degrading passions.

[a]Gk *my spirit in the gospel* [b]Gk *brothers* [c]Or *The one who is righteous through faith will live*

Their women exchanged natural intercourse for unnatural, [27]and in the same way also the men, giving up natural intercourse with women, were consumed with passion for one another. Men committed shameless acts with men and received in their own persons the due penalty for their error.

28 And since they did not see fit to acknowledge God, God gave them up to a debased mind and to things that should not be done. [29]They were filled with every kind of wickedness, evil, covetousness, malice. Full of envy, murder, strife, deceit, craftiness, they are gossips, [30]slanderers, God-haters,[a] insolent, haughty, boastful, inventors of evil, rebellious toward parents, [31]foolish, faithless, heartless, ruthless. [32]They know God's decree, that those who practice such things deserve to die—yet they not only do them but even applaud others who practice them.

2 Therefore you have no excuse, whoever you are, when you judge others; for in passing judgment on another you condemn yourself, because you, the judge, are doing the very same things. [2]You say,[b] "We know that God's judgment on those who do such things is in accordance with truth." [3]Do you imagine, whoever you are, that when you judge those who do such things and yet do them yourself, you will escape the judgment of God? [4]Or do you despise the riches of his kindness and forbearance and patience? Do you not realize that God's kindness is meant to lead you to repentance? [5]But by your hard and impenitent heart you are storing up wrath for yourself on the day of wrath, when God's righteous judgment will be revealed. [6]For he will repay according to each one's deeds: [7]to those who by patiently doing good seek for glory and honor and immortality, he will give eternal life; [8]while for those who are self-seeking and who obey not the truth but wickedness, there will be wrath and fury. [9]There will be anguish and distress for everyone who does evil, the Jew first and also the Greek, [10]but glory and honor and peace for everyone who does good, the Jew first and also the Greek. [11]For God shows no partiality.

12 All who have sinned apart from the law will also perish apart from the law, and all who have sinned under the law will be judged by the law. [13]For it is not the hearers of the law who are righteous in God's sight, but the doers of the law who will be justified. [14]When Gentiles, who do not possess the law, do instinctively what the law requires, these, though not having the law, are a law to themselves. [15]They show that what the law requires is written on their hearts, to which their own conscience also bears witness; and their conflicting thoughts will accuse or perhaps excuse them

[a]Or God-hated [b]Gk lacks You say

[16]on the day when, according to my gospel, God, through Jesus Christ, will judge the secret thoughts of all.

17 But if you call yourself a Jew and rely on the law and boast of your relation to God [18]and know his will and determine what is best because you are instructed in the law, [19]and if you are sure that you are a guide to the blind, a light to those who are in darkness, [20]a corrector of the foolish, a teacher of children, having in the law the embodiment of knowledge and truth, [21]you, then, that teach others, will you not teach yourself? While you preach against stealing, do you steal? [22]You that forbid adultery, do you commit adultery? You that abhor idols, do you rob temples? [23]You that boast in the law, do you dishonor God by breaking the law? [24]For, as it is written, "The name of God is blasphemed among the Gentiles because of you."

25 Circumcision indeed is of value if you obey the law; but if you break the law, your circumcision has become uncircumcision. [26]So, if those who are uncircumcised keep the requirements of the law, will not their uncircumcision be regarded as circumcision? [27]Then those who are physically uncircumcised but keep the law will condemn you that have the written code and circumcision but break the law. [28]For a person is not a Jew who is one outwardly, nor is true circumcision something external and physical. [29]Rather, a person is a Jew who is one inwardly, and real circumcision is a matter of the heart—it is spiritual and not literal. Such a person receives praise not from others but from God.

3 Then what advantage has the Jew? Or what is the value of circumcision? [2]Much, in every way. For in the first place the Jews[a] were entrusted with the oracles of God. [3]What if some were unfaithful? Will their faithlessness nullify the faithfulness of God? [4]By no means! Although everyone is a liar, let God be proved true, as it is written,

"So that you may be
    justified in your
        words,
    and prevail in your
        judging."[b]

[5]But if our injustice serves to confirm the justice of God, what should we say? That God is unjust to inflict wrath on us? (I speak in a human way.) [6]By no means! For then how could God judge the world? [7]But if through my falsehood God's truthfulness abounds to his glory, why am I still being condemned as a sinner? [8]And why not say (as some people slander us by saying that we say), "Let us do evil so that good may come"? Their condemnation is deserved!

9 What then? Are we any better off?[c] No, not at all; for we have already charged that all, both Jews and Greeks, are under the power of sin, [10]as it is written:

[a]Gk *they* [b]Gk *when you are being judged* [c]Or *at any disadvantage?*

"There is no one who is
   righteous, not even
   one;
11 there is no one who has
       understanding,
   there is no one who
       seeks God.
12 All have turned aside,
       together they have
       become worthless;
   there is no one who
       shows kindness,
   there is not even one."
13 "Their throats are opened
       graves;
   they use their tongues to
       deceive."
   "The venom of vipers
       is under their lips."
14 "Their mouths are full of
       cursing and
       bitterness."
15 "Their feet are swift to
       shed blood;
16 ruin and misery are in
       their paths,
17 and the way of peace they
       have not known."
18 "There is no fear of God
       before their eyes."

19 Now we know that whatever the law says, it speaks to those who are under the law, so that every mouth may be silenced, and the whole world may be held accountable to God. [20]For "no human being will be justified in his sight" by deeds prescribed by the law, for through the law comes the knowledge of sin.

21 But now, apart from law, the righteousness of God has been disclosed, and is attested by the law and the prophets, [22]the righteousness of God through faith in Jesus Christ[a] for all who believe. For there is no distinction, [23]since all have sinned and fall short of the glory of God; [24]they are now justified by his grace as a gift, through the redemption that is in Christ Jesus, [25]whom God put forward as a sacrifice of atonement[b] by his blood, effective through faith. He did this to show his righteousness, because in his divine forbearance he had passed over the sins previously committed; [26]it was to prove at the present time that he himself is righteous and that he justifies the one who has faith in Jesus.[c]

27 Then what becomes of boasting? It is excluded. By what law? By that of works? No, but by the law of faith. [28]For we hold that a person is justified by faith apart from works prescribed by the law. [29]Or is God the God of Jews only? Is he not the God of Gentiles also? Yes, of Gentiles also, [30]since God is one; and he will justify the circumcised on the ground of faith and the uncircumcised through that same faith. [31]Do we then overthrow the law by this faith? By no means! On the contrary, we uphold the law.

4 What then are we to say was gained by[d] Abraham, our ancestor according to the flesh? [2]For if Abraham was justified by works, he has something to boast

---

[a]Or *through the faith of Jesus Christ* [b]Or *a place of atonement* [c]Or *who has the faith of Jesus* [d]Other ancient authorities read *say about*

about, but not before God. [3]For what does the scripture say? "Abraham believed God, and it was reckoned to him as righteousness." [4]Now to one who works, wages are not reckoned as a gift but as something due. [5]But to one who without works trusts him who justifies the ungodly, such faith is reckoned as righteousness. [6]So also David speaks of the blessedness of those to whom God reckons righteousness apart from works:

[7] "Blessed are those whose
        iniquities are forgiven,
    and whose sins are
        covered;
[8] blessed is the one against
        whom the Lord will
        not reckon sin."

[9] Is this blessedness, then, pronounced only on the circumcised, or also on the uncircumcised? We say, "Faith was reckoned to Abraham as righteousness." [10]How then was it reckoned to him? Was it before or after he had been circumcised? It was not after, but before he was circumcised. [11]He received the sign of circumcision as a seal of the righteousness that he had by faith while he was still uncircumcised. The purpose was to make him the ancestor of all who believe without being circumcised and who thus have righteousness reckoned to them, [12]and likewise the ancestor of the circumcised who are not only circumcised but who also follow the example of the faith that our ancestor Abraham had before he was circumcised.

[13] For the promise that he would inherit the world did not come to Abraham or to his descendants through the law but through the righteousness of faith. [14]If it is the adherents of the law who are to be the heirs, faith is null and the promise is void. [15]For the law brings wrath; but where there is no law, neither is there violation.

[16] For this reason it depends on faith, in order that the promise may rest on grace and be guaranteed to all his descendants, not only to the adherents of the law but also to those who share the faith of Abraham (for he is the father of all of us, [17]as it is written, "I have made you the father of many nations")—in the presence of the God in whom he believed, who gives life to the dead and calls into existence the things that do not exist. [18]Hoping against hope, he believed that he would become "the father of many nations," according to what was said, "So numerous shall your descendants be." [19]He did not weaken in faith when he considered his own body, which was already[a] as good as dead (for he was about a hundred years old), or when he considered the barrenness of Sarah's womb. [20]No distrust made him waver concerning the promise of God, but he grew strong in his faith as he gave glory to God, [21]being fully convinced that God was able to do what he had promised.

[a]Other ancient athorities lack *already*

[22]Therefore his faith[a] "was reckoned to him as righteousness." [23]Now the words, "it was reckoned to him," were written not for his sake alone, [24]but for ours also. It will be reckoned to us who believe in him who raised Jesus our Lord from the dead, [25]who was handed over to death for our trespasses and was raised for our justification.

5 Therefore, since we are justified by faith, we[b] have peace with God through our Lord Jesus Christ, [2]through whom we have obtained access[c] to this grace in which we stand; and we[d] boast in our hope of sharing the glory of God. [3]And not only that, but we also boast in our sufferings, knowing that suffering produces endurance, [4]and endurance produces character, and character produces hope, [5]and hope does not disappoint us, because God's love has been poured into our hearts through the Holy Spirit that has been given to us.

6 For while we were still weak, at the right time Christ died for the ungodly. [7]Indeed, rarely will anyone die for a righteous person—though perhaps for a good person someone might actually dare to die. [8]But God proves his love for us in that while we still were sinners Christ died for us. [9]Much more surely then, now that we have been justified by his blood, will we be saved through him from the wrath of God.[e] [10]For if while we were enemies, we were reconciled to God through the death of his Son, much more surely, having been reconciled, will we be saved by his life. [11]But more than that, we even boast in God through our Lord Jesus Christ, through whom we have now received reconciliation.

12 Therefore, just as sin came into the world through one man, and death came through sin, and so death spread to all because all have sinned— [13]sin was indeed in the world before the law, but sin is not reckoned when there is no law. [14]Yet death exercised dominion from Adam to Moses, even over those whose sins were not like the transgression of Adam, who is a type of the one who was to come.

15 But the free gift is not like the trespass. For if the many died through the one man's trespass, much more surely have the grace of God and the free gift in the grace of the one man, Jesus Christ, abounded for the many. [16]And the free gift is not like the effect of the one man's sin. For the judgment following one trespass brought condemnation, but the free gift following many trespasses brings justification. [17]If, because of the one man's trespass, death exercised dominion through that one, much more surely will those who receive the abundance of grace and the free gift of righteousness exercise

[a]Gk *Therefore it* [b]Other ancient authorities read *let us* [c]Other ancient authorities add *by faith* [d]Or *let us* [e]Gk *the wrath*

dominion in life through the one man, Jesus Christ.

18 Therefore just as one man's trespass led to condemnation for all, so one man's act of righteousness leads to justification and life for all. [19]For just as by the one man's disobedience the many were made sinners, so by the one man's obedience the many will be made righteous. [20]But law came in, with the result that the trespass multiplied; but where sin increased, grace abounded all the more, [21]so that, just as sin exercised dominion in death, so grace might also exercise dominion through justification[a] leading to eternal life through Jesus Christ our Lord.

6 What then are we to say? Should we continue in sin in order that grace may abound? [2]By no means! How can we who died to sin go on living in it? [3]Do you not know that all of us who have been baptized into Christ Jesus were baptized into his death? [4]Therefore we have been buried with him by baptism into death, so that, just as Christ was raised from the dead by the glory of the Father, so we too might walk in newness of life.

5 For if we have been united with him in a death like his, we will certainly be united with him in a resurrection like his. [6]We know that our old self was crucified with him so that the body of sin might be destroyed, and we might no longer be enslaved to sin. [7]For whoever has died is freed from sin. [8]But if we have died with Christ, we believe that we will also live with him. [9]We know that Christ, being raised from the dead, will never die again; death no longer has dominion over him. [10]The death he died, he died to sin, once for all; but the life he lives, he lives to God. [11]So you also must consider yourselves dead to sin and alive to God in Christ Jesus.

12 Therefore, do not let sin exercise dominion in your mortal bodies, to make you obey their passions. [13]No longer present your members to sin as instruments[b] of wickedness, but present yourselves to God as those who have been brought from death to life, and present your members to God as instruments[b] of righteousness. [14]For sin will have no dominion over you, since you are not under law but under grace.

15 What then? Should we sin because we are not under law but under grace? By no means! [16]Do you not know that if you present yourselves to anyone as obedient slaves, you are slaves of the one whom you obey, either of sin, which leads to death, or of obedience, which leads to righteousness? [17]But thanks be to God that you, having once been slaves of sin, have become obedient from the heart to the form of teaching to which you were entrusted, [18]and that you, having been set free from sin, have become slaves

[a] Or *righteousness* [b] Or *weapons*

of righteousness. [19]I am speaking in human terms because of your natural limitations.[a] For just as you once presented your members as slaves to impurity and to greater and greater iniquity, so now present your members as slaves to righteousness for sanctification.

20 When you were slaves of sin, you were free in regard to righteousness. [21]So what advantage did you then get from the things of which you now are ashamed? The end of those things is death. [22]But now that you have been freed from sin and enslaved to God, the advantage you get is sanctification. The end is eternal life. [23]For the wages of sin is death, but the free gift of God is eternal life in Christ Jesus our Lord.

7 Do you not know, brothers and sisters[b]—for I am speaking to those who know the law— that the law is binding on a person only during that person's lifetime? [2]Thus a married woman is bound by the law to her husband as long as he lives; but if her husband dies, she is discharged from the law concerning the husband. [3]Accordingly, she will be called an adulteress if she lives with another man while her husband is alive. But if her husband dies, she is free from that law, and if she marries another man, she is not an adulteress.

4 In the same way, my friends,[b] you have died to the law through the body of Christ, so that you may belong to another, to him who has been raised from the dead in order that we may bear fruit for God. [5]While we were living in the flesh, our sinful passions, aroused by the law, were at work in our members to bear fruit for death. [6]But now we are discharged from the law, dead to that which held us captive, so that we are slaves not under the old written code but in the new life of the Spirit.

7 What then should we say? That the law is sin? By no means! Yet, if it had not been for the law, I would not have known sin. I would not have known what it is to covet if the law had not said, "You shall not covet." [8]But sin, seizing an opportunity in the commandment, produced in me all kinds of covetousness. Apart from the law sin lies dead. [9]I was once alive apart from the law, but when the commandment came, sin revived [10]and I died, and the very commandment that promised life proved to be death to me. [11]For sin, seizing an opportunity in the commandment, deceived me and through it killed me. [12]So the law is holy, and the commandment is holy and just and good.

13 Did what is good, then, bring death to me? By no means! It was sin, working death in me through what is good, in order that sin might be shown to be sin, and through the commandment might become sinful beyond measure.

14 For we know that the law is spiritual; but I am of the flesh, sold

[a]Gk the weakness of your flesh [b]Gk brothers

224

into slavery under sin.[a] [15]I do not understand my own actions. For I do not do what I want, but I do the very thing I hate. [16]Now if I do what I do not want, I agree that the law is good. [17]But in fact it is no longer I that do it, but sin that dwells within me. [18]For I know that nothing good dwells within me, that is, in my flesh. I can will what is right, but I cannot do it. [19]For I do not do the good I want, but the evil I do not want is what I do. [20]Now if I do what I do not want, it is no longer I that do it, but sin that dwells within me.

[21] So I find it to be a law that when I want to do what is good, evil lies close at hand. [22]For I delight in the law of God in my inmost self, [23]but I see in my members another law at war with the law of my mind, making me captive to the law of sin that dwells in my members. [24]Wretched man that I am! Who will rescue me from this body of death? [25]Thanks be to God through Jesus Christ our Lord!

So then, with my mind I am a slave to the law of God, but with my flesh I am a slave to the law of sin.

8 There is therefore now no condemnation for those who are in Christ Jesus. [2]For the law of the Spirit[b] of life in Christ Jesus has set you[c] free from the law of sin and of death. [3]For God has done what the law, weakened by the flesh, could not do: by sending his own Son in the likeness of sinful flesh, and to deal with sin,[d] he condemned sin in the flesh, [4]so that the just requirement of the law might be fulfilled in us, who walk not according to the flesh but according to the Spirit.[b] [5]For those who live according to the flesh set their minds on the things of the flesh, but those who live according to the Spirit[b] set their minds on the things of the Spirit.[b] [6]To set the mind on the flesh is death, but to set the mind on the Spirit is life and peace. [7]For this reason the mind that is set on the flesh is hostile to God; it does not submit to God's law—indeed it cannot, [8]and those who are in the flesh cannot please God.

[9] But you are not in the flesh; you are in the Spirit,[b] since the Spirit of God dwells in you. Anyone who does not have the Spirit of Christ does not belong to him. [10]But if Christ is in you, though the body is dead because of sin, the Spirit[b] is life because of righteousness. [11]If the Spirit of him who raised Jesus from the dead dwells in you, he who raised Christ[e] from the dead will give life to your mortal bodies also through[f] his Spirit that dwells in you.

[12] So then, brothers and sisters,[g] we are debtors, not to the flesh, to live according to the flesh— [13]for if you live according

---

[a]Gk sold under sin [b]Or spirit [c]Here the Greek word you is singular number; other ancient authorities read me or us [d]Or and as a sin offering [e]Other ancient authorities read the Christ or Christ Jesus or Jesus Christ [f]Other ancient authorities read on account of [g]Gk brothers

to the flesh, you will die; but if by the Spirit you put to death the deeds of the body, you will live. [14]For all who are led by the Spirit of God are children of God. [15]For you did not receive a spirit of slavery to fall back into fear, but you have received a spirit of adoption. When we cry, "Abba![a] Father!" [16]it is that very Spirit bearing witness[b] with our spirit that we are children of God, [17]and if children, then heirs, heirs of God and joint heirs with Christ—if, in fact, we suffer with him so that we may also be glorified with him.

18 I consider that the sufferings of this present time are not worth comparing with the glory about to be revealed to us. [19]For the creation waits with eager longing for the revealing of the children of God; [20]for the creation was subjected to futility, not of its own will but by the will of the one who subjected it, in hope [21]that the creation itself will be set free from its bondage to decay and will obtain the freedom of the glory of the children of God. [22]We know that the whole creation has been groaning in labor pains until now; [23]and not only the creation, but we ourselves, who have the first fruits of the Spirit, groan inwardly while we wait for adoption, the redemption of our bodies. [24]For in[c] hope we were saved. Now hope that is seen is not hope. For who hopes[d] for what is seen? [25]But if we hope for what we do not see, we wait for it with patience.

26 Likewise the Spirit helps us in our weakness; for we do not know how to pray as we ought, but that very Spirit intercedes[e] with sighs too deep for words. [27]And God,[f] who searches the heart, knows what is the mind of the Spirit, because the Spirit[g] intercedes for the saints according to the will of God.[h]

28 We know that all things work together for good[i] for those who love God, who are called according to his purpose. [29]For those whom he foreknew he also predestined to be conformed to the image of his Son, in order that he might be the firstborn within a large family.[j] [30]And those whom he predestined he also called; and those whom he called he also justified; and those whom he justified he also glorified.

31 What then are we to say about these things? If God is for us, who is against us? [32]He who did not withhold his own Son, but gave him up for all of us, will he not with him also give us everything else? [33]Who will bring any charge against God's elect? It is God who justifies. [34]Who is to condemn? It is Christ Jesus, who died, yes, who was raised, who is at the right hand of God, who indeed intercedes for us.[k] [35]Who will separate us from the love of

[a]Aramaic for *Father* [b]Or [15]*a spirit of adoption, by which we cry, "Abba! Father!"* [16]*The Spirit itself bears witness* [c]Or *by* [d]Other ancient authorities read *awaits* [e]Other ancient authorities add *for us* [f]Gk *the one* [g]Gk *he* or *it* [h]Gk *according to God* [i]Other authorities read *God makes all things work together for good,* or *in all things God works for good* [j]Gk *among many brothers* [k]Or *Is it Christ Jesus . . . for us?*

Christ? Will hardship, or distress, or persecution, or famine, or nakedness, or peril, or sword? [36]As it is written,

"For your sake we are
being killed all day
long;
we are accounted as
sheep to be
slaughtered."

[37]No, in all these things we are more than conquerors through him who loved us. [38]For I am convinced that neither death, nor life, nor angels, nor rulers, nor things present, nor things to come, nor powers, [39]nor height, nor depth, nor anything else in all creation, will be able to separate us from the love of God in Christ Jesus our Lord.

9 I am speaking the truth in Christ—I am not lying; my conscience confirms it by the Holy Spirit— [2]I have great sorrow and unceasing anguish in my heart. [3]For I could wish that I myself were accursed and cut off from Christ for the sake of my own people,[a] my kindred according to the flesh. [4]They are Israelites, and to them belong the adoption, the glory, the covenants, the giving of the law, the worship, and the promises; [5]to them belong the patriarchs, and from them, according to the flesh, comes the Messiah,[b] who is over all, God blessed forever.[c] Amen.

6 It is not as though the word of God had failed. For not all Israelites truly belong to Israel, [7]and not all of Abraham's chil-

dren are his true descendants; but "It is through Isaac that descendants shall be named for you." [8]This means that it is not the children of the flesh who are the children of God, but the children of the promise are counted as descendants. [9]For this is what the promise said, "About this time I will return and Sarah shall have a son." [10]Nor is that all; something similar happened to Rebecca when she had conceived children by one husband, our ancestor Isaac. [11]Even before they had been born or had done anything good or bad (so that God's purpose of election might continue, [12]not by works but by his call) she was told, "The elder shall serve the younger." [13]As it is written,

"I have loved Jacob,
but I have hated Esau."

14 What then are we to say? Is there injustice on God's part? By no means! [15]For he says to Moses,

"I will have mercy on
whom I have mercy,
and I will have
compassion on whom
I have compassion."

[16]So it depends not on human will or exertion, but on God who shows mercy. [17]For the scripture says to Pharaoh, "I have raised you up for the very purpose of showing my power in you, so that my name may be proclaimed

[a]Gk *my brothers* [b]Or *the Christ* [c]Or *Messiah, who is God over all, blessed forever;* or *Messiah. May he who is God over all be blessed forever*

in all the earth." [18]So then he has mercy on whomever he chooses, and he hardens the heart of whomever he chooses.

19 You will say to me then, "Why then does he still find fault? For who can resist his will?" [20]But who indeed are you, a human being, to argue with God? Will what is molded say to the one who molds it, "Why have you made me like this?" [21]Has the potter no right over the clay, to make out of the same lump one object for special use and another for ordinary use? [22]What if God, desiring to show his wrath and to make known his power, has endured with much patience the objects of wrath that are made for destruction; [23]and what if he has done so in order to make known the riches of his glory for the objects of mercy, which he has prepared beforehand for glory— [24]including us whom he has called, not from the Jews only but also from the Gentiles? [25]As indeed he says in Hosea,

"Those who were not my
        people I will call 'my
        people,'"
    and her who was not
        beloved I will call
        'beloved.'"
[26]   "And in the very place
        where it was said to
        them, 'You are not
        my people,'
    there they shall be called
        children of the living
        God."

27 And Isaiah cries out concerning Israel, "Though the num-ber of the children of Israel were like the sand of the sea, only a remnant of them will be saved; [28]for the Lord will execute his sentence on the earth quickly and decisively."[a] [29]And as Isaiah predicted,

"If the Lord of hosts had
        not left survivors[b] to us,
    we would have fared like
        Sodom
    and been made like
        Gomorrah."

30 What then are we to say? Gentiles, who did not strive for righteousness, have attained it, that is, righteousness through faith; [31]but Israel, who did strive for the righteousness that is based on the law, did not suc-ceed in fulfilling that law. [32]Why not? Because they did not strive for it on the basis of faith, but as if it were based on works. They have stumbled over the stum-bling stone, [33]as it is written,

"See, I am laying in Zion a
        stone that will make
        people stumble, a
        rock that will make
        them fall,
    and whoever believes in
        him[c] will not be put
        to shame."

10 Brothers and sisters,[d] my heart's desire and prayer to God for them is that they may be saved. [2]I can testify that they have a zeal for God, but it is not enlightened. [3]For, being ignorant

---

[a]Other ancient authorities read *for he will finish his work and cut it short in righteousness, because the Lord will make the sentence shortened on the earth* [b]Or *descendants*; Gk *seed* [c]Or *trusts in it* [d]Gk *Brothers*

of the righteousness that comes from God, and seeking to establish their own, they have not submitted to God's righteousness. [4]For Christ is the end of the law so that there may be righteousness for everyone who believes.

5 Moses writes concerning the righteousness that comes from the law, that "the person who does these things will live by them." [6]But the righteousness that comes from faith says, "Do not say in your heart, 'Who will ascend into heaven?'" (that is, to bring Christ down) [7]"or 'Who will descend into the abyss?'" (that is, to bring Christ up from the dead?) [8]But what does it say?

"The word is near you,
     on your lips and in
     your heart"

(that is, the word of faith that we proclaim); [9]because[a] if you confess with your lips that Jesus is Lord and believe in your heart that God raised him from the dead, you will be saved. [10]For one believes with the heart and so is justified, and one confesses with the mouth and so is saved. [11]The scripture says, "No one who believes in him will be put to shame." [12]For there is no distinction between Jew and Greek; the same Lord is Lord of all and is generous to all who call on him. [13]For, "Everyone who calls on the name of the Lord shall be saved."

14 But how are they to call on one in whom they have not believed? And how are they to believe in one of whom they have never heard? And how are they to hear without someone to proclaim him? [15]And how are they to proclaim him unless they are sent? As it is written, "How beautiful are the feet of those who bring good news!" [16]But not all have obeyed the good news;[b] for Isaiah says, "Lord, who has believed our message?" [17]So faith comes from what is heard, and what is heard comes through the word of Christ.[c]

18 But I ask, have they not heard? Indeed they have; for

"Their voice has gone out
     to all the earth,
and their words to the
     ends of the world."

[19]Again I ask, did Israel not understand? First Moses says,

"I will make you jealous of
     those who are not a
     nation;
with a foolish nation I
     will make you angry."

[20]Then Isaiah is so bold as to say,

"I have been found by
     those who did not
     seek me;
I have shown myself to
     those who did not
     ask for me."

[21]But of Israel he says, "All day long I have held out my hands to a disobedient and contrary people."

11

I ask, then, has God rejected his people? By no means! I myself am an Israelite, a descendant of Abraham, a member of the tribe of Benjamin. [2]God

---

[a]Or *namely, that* [b]Or *gospel* [c]Or *about Christ;* other ancient authorities read *of God*

has not rejected his people whom he foreknew. Do you not know what the scripture says of Elijah, how he pleads with God against Israel? 3"Lord, they have killed your prophets, they have demolished your altars; I alone am left, and they are seeking my life." 4But what is the divine reply to him? "I have kept for myself seven thousand who have not bowed the knee to Baal." 5So too at the present time there is a remnant, chosen by grace. 6But if it is by grace, it is no longer on the basis of works, otherwise grace would no longer be grace.*a*

7 What then? Israel failed to obtain what it was seeking. The elect obtained it, but the rest were hardened, 8as it is written,

"God gave them a sluggish
     spirit,
  eyes that would not see
  and ears that would not
     hear,
  down to this very day."
9And David says,
  "Let their table become a
     snare and a trap,
  a stumbling block and a
     retribution for them;
10 let their eyes be darkened
     so that they cannot
        see,
  and keep their backs
     forever bent."

11 So I ask, have they stumbled so as to fall? By no means! But through their stumbling*b* salvation has come to the Gentiles, so as to make Israel*c* jealous. 12Now if their stumbling*b* means riches for the world, and if their defeat means riches for Gentiles, how much more will their full inclusion mean!

13 Now I am speaking to you Gentiles. Inasmuch then as I am an apostle to the Gentiles, I glorify my ministry 14in order to make my own people*d* jealous, and thus save some of them. 15For if their rejection is the reconciliation of the world, what will their acceptance be but life from the dead! 16If the part of the dough offered as first fruits is holy, then the whole batch is holy; and if the root is holy, then the branches also are holy.

17 But if some of the branches were broken off, and you, a wild olive shoot, were grafted in their place to share the rich root*e* of the olive tree, 18do not boast over the branches. If you do boast, remember that it is not you that support the root, but the root that supports you. 19You will say, "Branches were broken off so that I might be grafted in." 20That is true. They were broken off because of their unbelief, but you stand only through faith. So do not become proud, but stand in awe. 21For if God did not spare the natural branches, perhaps he will not spare you.*f* 22Note then the kindness and the severity of God: severity toward those who have fallen, but God's kindness

---

*a*Other ancient authorities add *But if it is by works, it is no longer on the basis of grace, otherwise work would no longer be work* *b*Gk *transgression* *c*Gk *them* *d*Gk *my flesh* *e*Other ancient authorities read *the richness* *f*Other ancient authorities read *neither will he spare you*

toward you, provided you continue in his kindness; otherwise you also will be cut off. [23]And even those of Israel,[a] if they do not persist in unbelief, will be grafted in, for God has the power to graft them in again. [24]For if you have been cut from what is by nature a wild olive tree and grafted, contrary to nature, into a cultivated olive tree, how much more will these natural branches be grafted back into their own olive tree.

25 So that you may not claim to be wiser than you are, brothers and sisters,[b] I want you to understand this mystery: a hardening has come upon part of Israel, until the full number of the Gentiles has come in. [26]And so all Israel will be saved; as it is written,

"Out of Zion will come the
    Deliverer;
he will banish
    ungodliness from
    Jacob."
[27] "And this is my covenant
    with them,
when I take away their
    sins."

[28]As regards the gospel they are enemies of God[c] for your sake; but as regards election they are beloved, for the sake of their ancestors; [29]for the gifts and the calling of God are irrevocable. [30]Just as you were once disobedient to God but have now received mercy because of their disobedience, [31]so they have now been disobedient in order that, by the mercy shown to you, they too may now[d] receive mercy. [32]For God has imprisoned all in disobedience so that he may be merciful to all.

33 O the depth of the riches and wisdom and knowledge of God! How unsearchable are his judgments and how inscrutable his ways!
[34] "For who has known the
    mind of the Lord?
Or who has been his
    counselor?"
[35] "Or who has given a gift to
    him, to receive a gift in
    return?"
[36]For from him and through him and to him are all things. To him be the glory forever. Amen.

12 I appeal to you therefore, brothers and sisters,[b] by the mercies of God, to present your bodies as a living sacrifice, holy and acceptable to God, which is your spiritual[e] worship. [2]Do not be conformed to this world,[f] but be transformed by the renewing of your minds, so that you may discern what is the will of God— what is good and acceptable and perfect.[g]

3 For by the grace given to me I say to everyone among you not to think of yourself more highly than you ought to think, but to think with sober judgment, each according to the measure of faith that God has assigned. [4]For as in one body we have many members, and not all the members have

[a]Gk lacks *of Israel* [b]Gk *brothers* [c]Gk lacks *of God* [d]Other ancient authorities lack *now* [e]Or *reasonable* [f]Gk *age* [g]Or *what is the good and acceptable and perfect will of God*

the same function, [5]so we, who are many, are one body in Christ, and individually we are members one of another. [6]We have gifts that differ according to the grace given to us: prophecy, in proportion to faith; [7]ministry, in ministering; the teacher, in teaching; [8]the exhorter, in exhortation; the giver, in generosity; the leader, in diligence; the compassionate, in cheerfulness.

9 Let love be genuine; hate what is evil, hold fast to what is good; [10]love one another with mutual affection; outdo one another in showing honor. [11]Do not lag in zeal, be ardent in spirit, serve the Lord.[a] [12]Rejoice in hope, be patient in suffering, persevere in prayer. [13]Contribute to the needs of the saints; extend hospitality to strangers.

14 Bless those who persecute you; bless and do not curse them. [15]Rejoice with those who rejoice, weep with those who weep. [16]Live in harmony with one another; do not be haughty, but associate with the lowly;[b] do not claim to be wiser than you are. [17]Do not repay anyone evil for evil, but take thought for what is noble in the sight of all. [18]If it is possible, so far as it depends on you, live peaceably with all. [19]Beloved, never avenge yourselves, but leave room for the wrath of God;[c] for it is written, "Vengeance is mine, I will repay, says the Lord." [20]No, "if your enemies are hungry, feed them; if they are thirsty, give them something to drink; for by doing this

you will heap burning coals on their heads." [21]Do not be overcome by evil, but overcome evil with good.

13 Let every person be subject to the governing authorities; for there is no authority except from God, and those authorities that exist have been instituted by God. [2]Therefore whoever resists authority resists what God has appointed, and those who resist will incur judgment. [3]For rulers are not a terror to good conduct, but to bad. Do you wish to have no fear of the authority? Then do what is good, and you will receive its approval; [4]for it is God's servant for your good. But if you do what is wrong, you should be afraid, for the authority[d] does not bear the sword in vain! It is the servant of God to execute wrath on the wrongdoer. [5]Therefore one must be subject, not only because of wrath but also because of conscience. [6]For the same reason you also pay taxes, for the authorities are God's servants, busy with this very thing. [7]Pay to all what is due them—taxes to whom taxes are due, revenue to whom revenue is due, respect to whom respect is due, honor to whom honor is due.

8 Owe no one anything, except to love one another; for the one who loves another has fulfilled the law. [9]The commandments, "You

---

[a]Other ancient authorities read *serve the opportune time* [b]Or *give yourselves to humble tasks* [c]Gk *the wrath* [d]Gk *it*

shall not commit adultery; You shall not murder; You shall not steal; You shall not covet"; and any other commandment, are summed up in this word, "Love your neighbor as yourself." [10]Love does no wrong to a neighbor; therefore, love is the fulfilling of the law.

11 Besides this, you know what time it is, how it is now the moment for you to wake from sleep. For salvation is nearer to us now than when we became believers; [12]the night is far gone, the day is near. Let us then lay aside the works of darkness and put on the armor of light; [13]let us live honorably as in the day, not in reveling and drunkenness, not in debauchery and licentiousness, not in quarreling and jealousy. [14]Instead, put on the Lord Jesus Christ, and make no provision for the flesh, to gratify its desires.

14 Welcome those who are weak in faith,[a] but not for the purpose of quarreling over opinions. [2]Some believe in eating anything, while the weak eat only vegetables. [3]Those who eat must not despise those who abstain, and those who abstain must not pass judgment on those who eat; for God has welcomed them. [4]Who are you to pass judgment on servants of another? It is before their own lord that they stand or fall. And they will be upheld, for the Lord[b] is able to make them stand.

5 Some judge one day to be better than another, while others judge all days to be alike. Let all be fully convinced in their own minds. [6]Those who observe the day, observe it in honor of the Lord. Also those who eat, eat in honor of the Lord, since they give thanks to God; while those who abstain, abstain in honor of the Lord and give thanks to God.

7 We do not live to ourselves, and we do not die to ourselves. [8]If we live, we live to the Lord, and if we die, we die to the Lord; so then, whether we live or whether we die, we are the Lord's. [9]For to this end Christ died and lived again, so that he might be Lord of both the dead and the living.

10 Why do you pass judgment on your brother or sister?[c] Or you, why do you despise your brother or sister? For we will all stand before the judgment seat of God.[d] [11]For it is written,

"As I live, says the Lord,
    every knee shall bow
        to me,
    and every tongue shall
        give praise to[e] God."
[12]So then, each of us will be accountable to God.[f]

13 Let us therefore no longer pass judgment on one another, but resolve instead never to put a stumbling block or hindrance in the way of another.[g] [14]I know and am persuaded in the Lord Jesus that nothing is unclean in itself; but it is unclean for anyone who thinks it unclean. [15]If your brother

---

[a]Or *conviction* [b]Other ancient authorities read *for God* [c]Gk *brother* [d]Other ancient authorities read *of Christ* [e]Or *confess* [f]Other ancient authorities lack *to God* [g]Gk *of a brother*

or sister[a] is being injured by what you eat, you are no longer walking in love. Do not let what you eat cause the ruin of one for whom Christ died. [16]So do not let your good be spoken of as evil. [17]For the kingdom of God is not food and drink but righteousness and peace and joy in the Holy Spirit. [18]The one who thus serves Christ is acceptable to God and has human approval. [19]Let us then pursue what makes for peace and for mutual upbuilding. [20]Do not, for the sake of food, destroy the work of God. Everything is indeed clean, but it is wrong for you to make others fall by what you eat; [21]it is good not to eat meat or drink wine or do anything that makes your brother or sister[a] stumble.[b] [22]The faith that you have, have as your own conviction before God. Blessed are those who have no reason to condemn themselves because of what they approve. [23]But those who have doubts are condemned if they eat, because they do not act from faith;[c] for whatever does not proceed from faith[c] is sin.[d]

15 We who are strong ought to put up with the failings of the weak, and not to please ourselves. [2]Each of us must please our neighbor for the good purpose of building up the neighbor. [3]For Christ did not please himself; but, as it is written, "The insults of those who insult you have fallen on me." [4]For whatever was written in former days was written for our instruction, so that by steadfastness and by the encouragement of the scriptures we might have hope. [5]May the God of steadfastness and encouragement grant you to live in harmony with one another, in accordance with Christ Jesus, [6]so that together you may with one voice glorify the God and Father of our Lord Jesus Christ.

7 Welcome one another, therefore, just as Christ has welcomed you, for the glory of God. [8]For I tell you that Christ has become a servant of the circumcised on behalf of the truth of God in order that he might confirm the promises given to the patriarchs, [9]and in order that the Gentiles might glorify God for his mercy. As it is written,

"Therefore I will confesse
  you among the
  Gentiles,
 and sing praises to your
  name";

[10]and again he says,

"Rejoice, O Gentiles, with
  his people";

[11]and again,

"Praise the Lord, all you
  Gentiles,
 and let all the peoples
  praise him";

[12]and again Isaiah says,

"The root of Jesse shall
  come,
 the one who rises to rule
  the Gentiles;
 in him the Gentiles shall
  hope."

[a]Gk *brother* [b]Other ancient authorities add *or be upset or be weakened* [c]Or *conviction* [d]Other authorities, some ancient, add here 16.25-27 [e]Or *thank*

¹³May the God of hope fill you with all joy and peace in believing, so that you may abound in hope by the power of the Holy Spirit.

14 I myself feel confident about you, my brothers and sisters,ᵃ that you yourselves are full of goodness, filled with all knowledge, and able to instruct one another. ¹⁵Nevertheless on some points I have written to you rather boldly by way of reminder, because of the grace given me by God ¹⁶to be a minister of Christ Jesus to the Gentiles in the priestly service of the gospel of God, so that the offering of the Gentiles may be acceptable, sanctified by the Holy Spirit. ¹⁷In Christ Jesus, then, I have reason to boast of my work for God. ¹⁸For I will not venture to speak of anything except what Christ has accomplishedᵇ through me to win obedience from the Gentiles, by word and deed, ¹⁹by the power of signs and wonders, by the power of the Spirit of God,ᶜ so that from Jerusalem and as far around as Illyricum I have fully proclaimed the good newsᵈ of Christ. ²⁰Thus I make it my ambition to proclaim the good news,ᵈ not where Christ has already been named, so that I do not build on someone else's foundation, ²¹but as it is written,

"Those who have never
    been told of him shall
    see,
and those who have
    never heard of him
    shall understand."

22 This is the reason that I have so often been hindered from coming to you. ²³But now, with no further place for me in these regions, I desire, as I have for many years, to come to you ²⁴when I go to Spain. For I do hope to see you on my journey and to be sent on by you, once I have enjoyed your company for a little while. ²⁵At present, however, I am going to Jerusalem in a ministry to the saints; ²⁶for Macedonia and Achaia have been pleased to share their resources with the poor among the saints at Jerusalem. ²⁷They were pleased to do this, and indeed they owe it to them; for if the Gentiles have come to share in their spiritual blessings, they ought also to be of service to them in material things. ²⁸So, when I have completed this, and have delivered to them what has been collected,ᵉ I will set out by way of you to Spain; ²⁹and I know that when I come to you, I will come in the fullness of the blessingᶠ of Christ.

30 I appeal to you, brothers and sisters,ᵍ by our Lord Jesus Christ and by the love of the Spirit, to join me in earnest prayer to God on my behalf, ³¹that I may be rescued from the unbelievers in Judea, and that my ministryʰ to Jerusalem may be

---

ᵃGk brothers ᵇGk speak of those things that Christ has not accomplished ᶜOther ancient authorities read of the Spirit or of the Holy Spirit ᵈOr gospel ᵉGk have sealed to them this fruit ᶠOther ancient authorities add of the gospel ᵍGk brothers ʰOther ancient authorities read my bringing of a gift

acceptable to the saints, [32]so that by God's will I may come to you with joy and be refreshed in your company. [33]The God of peace be with all of you.[a] Amen.

16 I commend to you our sister Phoebe, a deacon[b] of the church at Cenchreae, [2]so that you may welcome her in the Lord as is fitting for the saints, and help her in whatever she may require from you, for she has been a benefactor of many and of myself as well.

3 Greet Prisca and Aquila, who work with me in Christ Jesus, [4]and who risked their necks for my life, to whom not only I give thanks, but also all the churches of the Gentiles. [5]Greet also the church in their house. Greet my beloved Epaenetus, who was the first convert[c] in Asia for Christ. [6]Greet Mary, who has worked very hard among you. [7]Greet Andronicus and Junia,[d] my relatives[e] who were in prison with me; they are prominent among the apostles, and they were in Christ before I was. [8]Greet Ampliatus, my beloved in the Lord. [9]Greet Urbanus, our co-worker in Christ, and my beloved Stachys. [10]Greet Apelles, who is approved in Christ. Greet those who belong to the family of Aristobulus. [11]Greet my relative[f] Herodion. Greet those in the Lord who belong to the family of Narcissus. [12]Greet those workers in the Lord, Tryphaena and Tryphosa. Greet the beloved Persis, who has worked hard in

the Lord. [13]Greet Rufus, chosen in the Lord; and greet his mother—a mother to me also. [14]Greet Asyncritus, Phlegon, Hermes, Patrobas, Hermas, and the brothers and sisters who are with them. [15]Greet Philologus, Julia, Nereus and his sister, and Olympas, and all the saints who are with them. [16]Greet one another with a holy kiss. All the churches of Christ greet you.

17 I urge you, brothers and sisters, to keep an eye on those who cause dissensions and offenses, in opposition to the teaching that you have learned; avoid them. [18]For such people do not serve our Lord Christ, but their own appetites,[g] and by smooth talk and flattery they deceive the hearts of the simple-minded. [19]For while your obedience is known to all, so that I rejoice over you, I want you to be wise in what is good and guileless in what is evil. [20]The God of peace will shortly crush Satan under your feet. The grace of our Lord Jesus Christ be with you.[h]

21 Timothy, my co-worker, greets you; so do Lucius and Jason and Sosipater, my relatives.[e]

22 I Tertius, the writer of this letter, greet you in the Lord.[i]

23 Gaius, who is host to me and to the whole church, greets

---

[a]One ancient authority adds 16.25-27 here [b]Or minister [c]Gk first fruits [d]Or Junias; other ancient authorities read Julia [e]Or compatriots [f]Or compatriot [g]Gk their own belly [h]Other ancient authorities lack this sentence [i]Or I Tertius, writing this letter in the Lord, greet you

you. Erastus, the city treasurer, and our brother Quartus, greet you.[a]

25 Now to God[b] who is able to strengthen you according to my gospel and the proclamation of Jesus Christ, according to the revelation of the mystery that was kept secret for long ages [26]but is now disclosed, and through the prophetic writings is made known to all the Gentiles, accord-ing to the command of the eternal God, to bring about the obedience of faith— [27]to the only wise God, through Jesus Christ, to whom[c] be the glory forever! Amen.[d]

[a]Other ancient authorities add verse 24, *The grace of our Lord Jesus Christ be with all of you. Amen.* [b]Gk *the one* [c]Other ancient authorities lack *to whom.* The verse then reads, *to the only wise God be the glory through Jesus Christ forever. Amen.* [d]Other ancient authorities lack 16.25-27 or include it after 14.23 or 15.33; others put verse 24 after verse 27

The First Letter of Paul to the

CORINTHIANS

1 Paul, called to be an apostle of Christ Jesus by the will of God, and our brother Sosthenes,

2 To the church of God that is in Corinth, to those who are sanctified in Christ Jesus, called to be saints, together with all those who in every place call on the name of our Lord Jesus Christ, both their Lord[a] and ours:

3 Grace to you and peace from God our Father and the Lord Jesus Christ.

4 I give thanks to my[b] God always for you because of the grace of God that has been given you in Christ Jesus, 5 for in every way you have been enriched in him, in speech and knowledge of every kind— [6]just as the testimony of[c] Christ has been strength-ened among you— [7]so that you are not lacking in any spiritual gift as you wait for the revealing of our Lord Jesus Christ. [8]He will also strengthen you to the end, so that you may be blameless on the day of our Lord Jesus Christ. [9]God is faithful; by him you were called into the fellowship of his Son, Jesus Christ our Lord.

10 Now I appeal to you, broth-ers and sisters,[d] by the name of our Lord Jesus Christ, that all of you be in agreement and that there be no divisions among you, but that you be united in the same mind and the same purpose. [11]For it has been reported to me by Chloe's people that there are quarrels among you, my brothers and sisters.[e] [12]What I mean is that

[a]Gk *theirs* [b]Other ancient authorities lack *my* [c]Or *to* [d]Gk *brothers* [e]Gk *my brothers*

each of you says, "I belong to Paul," or "I belong to Apollos," or "I belong to Cephas," or "I belong to Christ." [13]Has Christ been divided? Was Paul crucified for you? Or were you baptized in the name of Paul? [14]I thank God[a] that I baptized none of you except Crispus and Gaius, [15]so that no one can say that you were baptized in my name. [16](I did baptize also the household of Stephanas; beyond that, I do not know whether I baptized anyone else.) [17]For Christ did not send me to baptize but to proclaim the gospel, and not with eloquent wisdom, so that the cross of Christ might not be emptied of its power.

[18] For the message about the cross is foolishness to those who are perishing, but to us who are being saved it is the power of God. [19]For it is written,

"I will destroy the wisdom
    of the wise,
and the discernment of
    the discerning
    I will thwart."

[20]Where is the one who is wise? Where is the scribe? Where is the debater of this age? Has not God made foolish the wisdom of the world? [21]For since, in the wisdom of God, the world did not know God through wisdom, God decided, through the foolishness of our proclamation, to save those who believe. [22]For Jews demand signs and Greeks desire wisdom, [23]but we proclaim Christ crucified, a stumbling block to Jews and foolishness to Gentiles, [24]but to those who are the called,

both Jews and Greeks, Christ the power of God and the wisdom of God. [25]For God's foolishness is wiser than human wisdom, and God's weakness is stronger than human strength.

[26] Consider your own call, brothers and sisters:[b] not many of you were wise by human standards,[c] not many were powerful, not many were of noble birth. [27]But God chose what is foolish in the world to shame the wise; God chose what is weak in the world to shame the strong; [28]God chose what is low and despised in the world, things that are not, to reduce to nothing things that are, [29]so that no one[d] might boast in the presence of God. [30]He is the source of your life in Christ Jesus, who became for us wisdom from God, and righteousness and sanctification and redemption, [31] in order that, as it is written, "Let the one who boasts, boast in[e] the Lord."

2 When I came to you, brothers and sisters,[b] I did not come proclaiming the mystery[f] of God to you in lofty words or wisdom. [2]For I decided to know nothing among you except Jesus Christ, and him crucified. [3]And I came to you in weakness and in fear and in much trembling. [4]My speech and my proclamation were not with plausible words of wisdom,[g] but with a demonstration of the Spirit and of power,

---

[a]Other ancient authorities read *I am thankful* [b]Gk *brothers* [c]Gk *according to the flesh* [d]Gk *no flesh* [e]Or *of* [f]Other ancient authorities read *testimony* [g]Other ancient authorities read *the persuasiveness of wisdom*

[5]so that your faith might rest not on human wisdom but on the power of God.

6 Yet among the mature we do speak wisdom, though it is not a wisdom of this age or of the rulers of this age, who are doomed to perish. [7]But we speak God's wisdom, secret and hidden, which God decreed before the ages for our glory. [8]None of the rulers of this age understood this; for if they had, they would not have crucified the Lord of glory. [9]But, as it is written,

"What no eye has seen, nor
       ear heard,
    nor the human heart
       conceived,
  what God has prepared for
       those who love
       him"—

[10]these things God has revealed to us through the Spirit; for the Spirit searches everything, even the depths of God. [11]For what human being knows what is truly human except the human spirit that is within? So also no one comprehends what is truly God's except the Spirit of God. [12]Now we have received not the spirit of the world, but the Spirit that is from God, so that we may understand the gifts bestowed on us by God. [13]And we speak of these things in words not taught by human wisdom but taught by the Spirit, interpreting spiritual things to those who are spiritual.[a]

14 Those who are unspiritual[b] do not receive the gifts of God's Spirit, for they are foolishness to them, and they are unable to understand them because they are spiritually discerned. [15]Those who are spiritual discern all things, and they are themselves subject to no one else's scrutiny.

[16] "For who has known the
          mind of the Lord
       so as to instruct him?"

But we have the mind of Christ.

3 And so, brothers and sisters, I could not speak to you as spiritual people, but rather as people of the flesh, as infants in Christ. [2] I fed you with milk, not solid food, for you were not ready for solid food. Even now you are still not ready, [3]for you are still of the flesh. For as long as there is jealousy and quarreling among you, are you not of the flesh, and behaving according to human inclinations? [4]For when one says, "I belong to Paul," and another, "I belong to Apollos," are you not merely human?

5 What then is Apollos? What is Paul? Servants through whom you came to believe, as the Lord assigned to each. [6]I planted, Apollos watered, but God gave the growth. [7]So neither the one who plants nor the one who waters is anything, but only God who gives the growth. [8]The one who plants and the one who waters have a common purpose, and each will receive wages according to the labor of each. [9]For we are God's servants, working together; you are God's field, God's building.

---

[a]Or *interpreting spiritual things in spiritual language, or comparing spiritual things with spiritual* [b]Or *natural*

10 According to the grace of God given to me, like a skilled master builder I laid a foundation, and someone else is building on it. Each builder must choose with care how to build on it. ¹¹For no one can lay any foundation other than the one that has been laid; that foundation is Jesus Christ. ¹²Now if anyone builds on the foundation with gold, silver, precious stones, wood, hay, straw— ¹³the work of each builder will become visible, for the Day will disclose it, because it will be revealed with fire, and the fire will test what sort of work each has done. ¹⁴If what has been built on the foundation survives, the builder will receive a reward. ¹⁵If the work is burned up, the builder will suffer loss; the builder will be saved, but only as through fire.

16 Do you not know that you are God's temple and that God's Spirit dwells in you?^a ¹⁷If anyone destroys God's temple, God will destroy that person. For God's temple is holy, and you are that temple.

18 Do not deceive yourselves. If you think that you are wise in this age, you should become fools so that you may become wise. ¹⁹For the wisdom of this world is foolishness with God. For it is written,

"He catches the wise in
    their craftiness,"

²⁰and again,

"The Lord knows the
    thoughts of the wise,
    that they are futile."

²¹So let no one boast about human leaders. For all things are yours, ²²whether Paul or Apollos or Cephas or the world or life or death or the present or the future—all belong to you, ²³and you belong to Christ, and Christ belongs to God.

4 Think of us in this way, as servants of Christ and stewards of God's mysteries. ²Moreover, it is required of stewards that they be found trustworthy. ³But with me it is a very small thing that I should be judged by you or by any human court. I do not even judge myself. ⁴I am not aware of anything against myself, but I am not thereby acquitted. It is the Lord who judges me. ⁵Therefore do not pronounce judgment before the time, before the Lord comes, who will bring to light the things now hidden in darkness and will disclose the purposes of the heart. Then each one will receive commendation from God.

6 I have applied all this to Apollos and myself for your benefit, brothers and sisters,^b so that you may learn through us the meaning of the saying, "Nothing beyond what is written," so that none of you will be puffed up in favor of one against another. ⁷For who sees anything different in you?^c What do you have that you did not receive? And if you received it, why do you boast as if it were not a gift?

---

^aIn verses 16 and 17 the Greek word for *you* is plural *^b*Gk *brothers* *^c*Or *Who makes you different from another?*

8 Already you have all you want! Already you have become rich! Quite apart from us you have become kings! Indeed, I wish that you had become kings, so that we might be kings with you! [9]For I think that God has exhibited us apostles as last of all, as though sentenced to death, because we have become a spectacle to the world, to angels and to mortals. [10]We are fools for the sake of Christ, but you are wise in Christ. We are weak, but you are strong. You are held in honor, but we in disrepute. [11]To the present hour we are hungry and thirsty, we are poorly clothed and beaten and homeless, [12]and we grow weary from the work of our own hands. When reviled, we bless; when persecuted, we endure; [13]when slandered, we speak kindly. We have become like the rubbish of the world, the dregs of all things, to this very day.

14 I am not writing this to make you ashamed, but to admonish you as my beloved children. [15]For though you might have ten thousand guardians in Christ, you do not have many fathers. Indeed, in Christ Jesus I became your father through the gospel. [16]I appeal to you, then, be imitators of me. [17]For this reason I sent[a] you Timothy, who is my beloved and faithful child in the Lord, to remind you of my ways in Christ Jesus, as I teach them everywhere in every church. [18]But some of you, thinking that I am not coming to you, have become arrogant. [19]But I will come to you soon, if the Lord wills, and I will find out not the talk of these arrogant people but their power. [20]For the kingdom of God depends not on talk but on power. [21]What would you prefer? Am I to come to you with a stick, or with love in a spirit of gentleness?

5 It is actually reported that there is sexual immorality among you, and of a kind that is not found even among pagans; for a man is living with his father's wife. [2]And you are arrogant! Should you not rather have mourned, so that he who has done this would have been removed from among you?

3 For though absent in body, I am present in spirit; and as if present I have already pronounced judgment [4]in the name of the Lord Jesus on the man who has done such a thing.[b] When you are assembled, and my spirit is present with the power of our Lord Jesus, [5] you are to hand this man over to Satan for the destruction of the flesh, so that his spirit may be saved in the day of the Lord.[c]

6 Your boasting is not a good thing. Do you not know that a little yeast leavens the whole batch of dough? [7]Clean out the old yeast so that you may be a new batch, as you really are unleavened. For our paschal lamb, Christ, has been sacrificed. [8]Therefore, let us celebrate the festival,

[a]*Or am sending* [b]*Or on the man who has done such a thing in the name of the Lord Jesus* [c]*Other ancient authorities add Jesus*

not with the old yeast, the yeast of malice and evil, but with the unleavened bread of sincerity and truth.

9 I wrote to you in my letter not to associate with sexually immoral persons— [10]not at all meaning the immoral of this world, or the greedy and robbers, or idolaters, since you would then need to go out of the world. [11]But now I am writing to you not to associate with anyone who bears the name of brother or sister[a] who is sexually immoral or greedy, or is an idolater, reviler, drunkard, or robber. Do not even eat with such a one. [12]For what have I to do with judging those outside? Is it not those who are inside that you are to judge? [13]God will judge those outside. "Drive out the wicked person from among you."

6 When any of you has a grievance against another, do you dare to take it to court before the unrighteous, instead of taking it before the saints? [2]Do you not know that the saints will judge the world? And if the world is to be judged by you, are you incompetent to try trivial cases? [3]Do you not know that we are to judge angels—to say nothing of ordinary matters? [4]If you have ordinary cases, then do you appoint as judges those who have no standing in the church? [5]I say this to your shame. Can it be that there is no one among you wise enough to decide between one believer[a] and another, [6]but a believer[a] goes to court against a believer[a]—and before unbelievers at that?

7 In fact, to have lawsuits at all with one another is already a defeat for you. Why not rather be wronged? Why not rather be defrauded? [8]But you yourselves wrong and defraud—and believers[b] at that.

9 Do you not know that wrongdoers will not inherit the kingdom of God? Do not be deceived! Fornicators, idolaters, adulterers, male prostitutes, sodomites, [10]thieves, the greedy, drunkards, revilers, robbers— none of these will inherit the kingdom of God. [11]And this is what some of you used to be. But you were washed, you were sanctified, you were justified in the name of the Lord Jesus Christ and in the Spirit of our God.

12 "All things are lawful for me," but not all things are beneficial. "All things are lawful for me," but I will not be dominated by anything. [13] "Food is meant for the stomach and the stomach for food,"[c] and God will destroy both one and the other. The body is meant not for fornication but for the Lord, and the Lord for the body. [14]And God raised the Lord and will also raise us by his power. [15]Do you not know that your bodies are members of Christ? Should I therefore take the members of Christ and make them members of a prostitute? Never! [16]Do you not know that

---

[a]Gk *brother* [b]Gk *brothers* [c]The quotation may extend to the word *other*

whoever is united to a prostitute becomes one body with her? For it is said, "The two shall be one flesh." [17]But anyone united to the Lord becomes one spirit with him. [18]Shun fornication! Every sin that a person commits is outside the body; but the fornicator sins against the body itself. [19]Or do you not know that your body is a temple[d] of the Holy Spirit within you, which you have from God, and that you are not your own? [20]For you were bought with a price; therefore glorify God in your body.

7 Now concerning the matters about which you wrote: "It is well for a man not to touch a woman." [2]But because of cases of sexual immorality, each man should have his own wife and each woman her own husband. [3]The husband should give to his wife her conjugal rights, and likewise the wife to her husband. [4]For the wife does not have authority over her own body, but the husband does; likewise the husband does not have authority over his own body, but the wife does. [5]Do not deprive one another *except* perhaps by agreement for a set time, to devote yourselves to prayer, and then come together again, so that Satan may not tempt you because of your lack of self-control. [6]This I say by way of concession, not of command. [7]I wish that all were as I myself am. But each has a particular gift from God, one having one kind and another a different kind.

[8]To the unmarried and the widows I say that it is well for them to remain unmarried as I am. [9]But if they are not practicing self-control, they should marry. For it is better to marry than to be aflame with passion.

[10]To the married I give this command—not I but the Lord—that the wife should not separate from her husband [11](but if she does separate, let her remain unmarried or else be reconciled to her husband), and that the husband should not divorce his wife.

[12]To the rest I say—I and not the Lord—that if any believer[b] has a wife who is an unbeliever, and she consents to live with him, he should not divorce her. [13]And if any woman has a husband who is an unbeliever, and he consents to live with her, she should not divorce him. [14]For the unbelieving husband is made holy through his wife, and the unbelieving wife is made holy through her husband. Otherwise, your children would be unclean, but as it is, they are holy. [15]But if the unbelieving partner separates, let it be so; in such a case the brother or sister is not bound. It is to peace that God has called you.[c] [16]Wife, for all you know, you might save your husband. Husband, for all you know, you might save your wife.

[17]However that may be, let each of you lead the life that the Lord has assigned, to which God

---

[d]Or *sanctuary* [b]Gk *brother* [c]Other ancient authorities read *us*

called you. This is my rule in all the churches. [18]Was anyone at the time of his call already circumcised? Let him not seek to remove the marks of circumcision. Was anyone at the time of his call uncircumcised? Let him not seek circumcision. [19]Circumcision is nothing, and uncircumcision is nothing; but obeying the commandments of God is everything. [20]Let each of you remain in the condition in which you were called.

21 Were you a slave when called? Do not be concerned about it. Even if you can gain your freedom, make use of your present condition now more than ever.[a] [22]For whoever was called in the Lord as a slave is a freed person belonging to the Lord, just as whoever was free when called is a slave of Christ. [23]You were bought with a price; do not become slaves of human masters. [24]In whatever condition you were called, brothers and sisters,[b] there remain with God.

25 Now concerning virgins, I have no command of the Lord, but I give my opinion as one who by the Lord's mercy is trustworthy. [26]I think that, in view of the impending[c] crisis, it is well for you to remain as you are. [27]Are you bound to a wife? Do not seek to be free. Are you free from a wife? Do not seek a wife. [28]But if you marry, you do not sin, and if a virgin marries, she does not sin. Yet those who marry will experience distress in this life,[d] and I would spare you that. [29]I mean,

brothers and sisters,[b] the appointed time has grown short; from now on, let even those who have wives be as though they had none, [30]and those who mourn as though they were not mourning, and those who rejoice as though they were not rejoicing, and those who buy as though they had no possessions, [31]and those who deal with the world as though they had no dealings with it. For the present form of this world is passing away.

32 I want you to be free from anxieties. The unmarried man is anxious about the affairs of the Lord, how to please the Lord; [33]but the married man is anxious about the affairs of the world, how to please his wife, [34]and his interests are divided. And the unmarried woman and the virgin are anxious about the affairs of the Lord, so that they may be holy in body and spirit; but the married woman is anxious about the affairs of the world, how to please her husband. [35]I say this for your own benefit, not to put any restraint upon you, but to promote good order and unhindered devotion to the Lord.

36 If anyone thinks that he is not behaving properly toward his fiancée,[e] if his passions are strong, and so it has to be, let him marry as he wishes; it is no sin. Let them marry. [37]But if someone stands firm in his resolve, being under no necessity but having his

---

[a]Or *avail yourself of the opportunity* [b]Gk *brothers* [c]Or *present* [d]Gk *in the flesh* [e]Gk *virgin*

own desire under control, and has determined in his own mind to keep her as his fiancée, he will do well. [38]So then, he who marries his fiancee does well; and he who refrains from marriage will do better.

39 A wife is bound as long as her husband lives. But if the husband dies,[a] she is free to marry anyone she wishes, only in the Lord. [40]But in my judgment she is more blessed if she remains as she is. And I think that I too have the Spirit of God.

8 Now concerning food sacrificed to idols: we know that "all of us possess knowledge." Knowledge puffs up, but love builds up. [2]Anyone who claims to know something does not yet have the necessary knowledge; [3]but anyone who loves God is known by him.

4 Hence, as to the eating of food offered to idols, we know that "no idol in the world really exists," and that "there is no God but one." [5]Indeed, even though there may be so-called gods in heaven or on earth—as in fact there are many gods and many lords— [6]yet for us there is one God, the Father, from whom are all things and for whom we exist, and one Lord, Jesus Christ, through whom are all things and through whom we exist.

7 It is not everyone, however, who has this knowledge. Since some have become so accustomed to idols until now, they still think of the food they eat as food offered to an idol; and their conscience, being weak, is defiled. [8]"Food will not bring us close to God."[b] We are no worse off if we do not eat, and no better off if we do. [9]But take care that this liberty of yours does not somehow become a stumbling block to the weak. [10]For if others see you, who possess knowledge, eating in the temple of an idol, might they not, since their conscience is weak, be encouraged to the point of eating food sacrificed to idols? [11]So by your knowledge those weak believers for whom Christ died are destroyed.[c] [12]But when you thus sin against members of your family,[d] and wound their conscience when it is weak, you sin against Christ. [13]Therefore, if food is a cause of their falling,[e] I will never eat meat, so that I may not cause one of them[f] to fall.

9 Am I not free? Am I not an apostle? Have I not seen Jesus our Lord? Are you not my work in the Lord? [2]If I am not an apostle to others, at least I am to you; for you are the seal of my apostleship in the Lord.

3 This is my defense to those who would examine me. [4]Do we not have the right to our food and drink? [5]Do we not have the right to be accompanied by a believing wife,[g] as do the other apostles and the brothers of the Lord and Cephas? [6]Or is it only Barnabas

---

[a]Gk *falls asleep* [b]The quotation may extend to the end of the verse [c]Gk *the weak brother . . . is destroyed* [d]Gk *against the brothers* [e]Gk *my brother's falling* [f]Gk *cause my brother* [g]Gk *a sister as wife*

and I who have no right to refrain from working for a living? [7]Who at any time pays the expenses for doing military service? Who plants a vineyard and does not eat any of its fruit? Or who tends a flock and does not get any of its milk?

8 Do I say this on human authority? Does not the law also say the same? [9]For it is written in the law of Moses, "You shall not muzzle an ox while it is treading out the grain." Is it for oxen that God is concerned? [10]Or does he not speak entirely for our sake? It was indeed written for our sake, for whoever plows should plow in hope and whoever threshes should thresh in hope of a share in the crop. [11]If we have sown spiritual good among you, is it too much if we reap your material benefits? [12]If others share this rightful claim on you, do not we still more?

Nevertheless, we have not made use of this right, but we endure anything rather than put an obstacle in the way of the gospel of Christ. [13]Do you not know that those who are employed in the temple service get their food from the temple, and those who serve at the altar share in what is sacrificed on the altar? [14]In the same way, the Lord commanded that those who pro-claim the gospel should get their living by the gospel.

15 But I have made no use of any of these rights, nor am I writing this so that they may be applied in my case. Indeed, I would rather die than that—no one will deprive me of my ground for boasting! [16]If I proclaim the gospel, this gives me no ground for boasting, for an obligation is laid on me, and woe to me if I do not proclaim the gospel! [17]For if I do this of my own will, I have a reward; but if not of my own will, I am entrusted with a commission. [18]What then is my reward? Just this: that in my proclamation I may make the gospel free of charge, so as not to make full use of my rights in the gospel.

19 For though I am free with respect to all, I have made myself a slave to all, so that I might win more of them. [20]To the Jews I became as a Jew, in order to win Jews. To those under the law I became as one under the law (though I myself am not under the law) so that I might win those under the law. [21]To those outside the law I became as one outside the law (though I am not free from God's law but am under Christ's law) so that I might win those outside the law. [22]To the weak I became weak, so that I might win the weak. I have become all things to all people, that I might by all means save some. [23]I do it all for the sake of the gospel, so that I may share in its blessings.

24 Do you not know that in a race the runners all compete, but only one receives the prize? Run in such a way that you may win it. [25]Athletes exercise self-control in all things; they do it to receive a perishable wreath, but we an

imperishable one. [26]So I do not run aimlessly, nor do I box as though beating the air; [27]but I punish my body and enslave it, so that after proclaiming to others I myself should not be disqualified.

10 I do not want you to be unaware, brothers and sisters,[a] that our ancestors were all under the cloud, and all passed through the sea, [2]and all were baptized into Moses in the cloud and in the sea, [3]and all ate the same spiritual food, [4]and all drank the same spiritual drink. For they drank from the spiritual rock that followed them, and the rock was Christ. [5]Nevertheless, God was not pleased with most of them, and they were struck down in the wilderness.

[6] Now these things occurred as examples for us, so that we might not desire evil as they did. [7]Do not become idolaters as some of them did; as it is written, "The people sat down to eat and drink, and they rose up to play." [8]We must not indulge in sexual immorality as some of them did, and twenty-three thousand fell in a single day. [9]We must not put Christ[b] to the test, as some of them did, and were destroyed by serpents. [10]And do not complain as some of them did, and were destroyed by the destroyer. [11]These things happened to them to serve as an example, and they were written down to instruct us, on whom the ends of the ages have come. [12]So if you think you are standing, watch out that you do not fall.

[13]No testing has overtaken you that is not common to everyone. God is faithful, and he will not let you be tested beyond your strength, but with the testing he will also provide the way out so that you may be able to endure it.

[14] Therefore, my dear friends,[c] flee from the worship of idols. [15]I speak as to sensible people; judge for yourselves what I say. [16]The cup of blessing that we bless, is it not a sharing in the blood of Christ? The bread that we break, is it not a sharing in the body of Christ? [17]Because there is one bread, we who are many are one body, for we all partake of the one bread. [18]Consider the people of Israel;[d] are not those who eat the sacrifices partners in the altar? [19]What do I imply then? That food sacrificed to idols is anything, or that an idol is anything? [20]No, I imply that what pagans sacrifice, they sacrifice to demons and not to God. I do not want you to be partners with demons. [21]You cannot drink the cup of the Lord and the cup of demons. You cannot partake of the table of the Lord and the table of demons. [22]Or are we provoking the Lord to jealousy? Are we stronger than he?

[23] "All things are lawful," but not all things are beneficial. "All things are lawful," but not all things build up. [24]Do not seek your own advantage, but that of the other. [25]Eat whatever is sold in the meat market without raising

[a]Gk *brothers* [b]Other ancient authorities read *the Lord* [c]Gk *my beloved* [d]Gk *Israel according to the flesh*

any question on the ground of conscience, [26]for "the earth and its fullness are the Lord's." [27]If an unbeliever invites you to a meal and you are disposed to go, eat whatever is set before you without raising any question on the ground of conscience. [28]But if someone says to you, "This has been offered in sacrifice," then do not eat it, out of consideration for the one who informed you, and for the sake of conscience— [29]I mean the other's conscience, not your own. For why should my liberty be subject to the judgment of someone else's conscience? [30]If I partake with thankfulness, why should I be denounced because of that for which I give thanks?

31 So, whether you eat or drink, or whatever you do, do everything for the glory of God. [32]Give no offense to Jews or to Greeks or to the church of God, [33] just as I try to please everyone in everything I do, not seeking my own advantage, but that of many, so that they may be saved.

11 Be imitators of me, as I am of Christ.

2 I commend you because you remember me in everything and maintain the traditions just as I handed them on to you. [3]But I want you to understand that Christ is the head of every man, and the husband[a] is the head of his wife,[b] and God is the head of Christ. [4]Any man who prays or prophesies with something on his head disgraces his head, [5]but any woman who prays or proph-

esies with her head unveiled disgraces her head—it is one and the same thing as having her head shaved. [6]For if a woman will not veil herself, then she should cut off her hair; but if it is disgraceful for a woman to have her hair cut off or to be shaved, she should wear a veil. [7]For a man ought not to have his head veiled, since he is the image and reflection[c] of God; but woman is the reflection[c] of man. [8]Indeed, man was not made from woman, but woman from man. [9]Neither was man created for the sake of woman, but woman for the sake of man. [10]For this reason a woman ought to have a symbol of[d] authority on her head,[e] because of the angels. [11]Nevertheless, in the Lord woman is not independent of man or man independent of woman. [12]For just as woman came from man, so man comes through woman; but all things come from God. [13]Judge for yourselves: is it proper for a woman to pray to God with her head unveiled? [14]Does not nature itself teach you that if a man wears long hair, it is degrading to him, [15]but if a woman has long hair, it is her glory? For her hair is given to her for a covering. [16]But if anyone is disposed to be contentious—we have no such custom, nor do the churches of God.

17 Now in the following instructions I do not commend you,

[a]The same Greek word means *man* or *husband* [b]Or *head of the woman* [c]Or *glory* [d]Gk lacks *a symbol of* [e]Or *have freedom of choice regarding her head*

because when you come together it is not for the better but for the worse. [18]For, to begin with, when you come together as a church, I hear that there are divisions among you; and to some extent I believe it. [19]Indeed, there have to be factions among you, for only so will it become clear who among you are genuine. [20]When you come together, it is not really to eat the Lord's supper. [21]For when the time comes to eat, each of you goes ahead with your own supper, and one goes hungry and another becomes drunk. [22]What! Do you not have homes to eat and drink in? Or do you show contempt for the church of God and humiliate those who have nothing? What should I say to you? Should I commend you? In this matter I do not commend you!

23 For I received from the Lord what I also handed on to you, that the Lord Jesus on the night when he was betrayed took a loaf of bread, [24]and when he had given thanks, he broke it and said, "This is my body that is for[a] you. Do this in remembrance of me." [25]In the same way he took the cup also, after supper, saying, "This cup is the new covenant in my blood. Do this, as often as you drink it, in remembrance of me." [26]For as often as you eat this bread and drink the cup, you proclaim the Lord's death until he comes.

27 Whoever, therefore, eats the bread or drinks the cup of the Lord in an unworthy manner will be answerable for the body and blood of the Lord. [28]Examine yourselves, and only then eat of the bread and drink of the cup. [29]For all who eat and drink[b] without discerning the body,[c] eat and drink judgment against themselves. [30]For this reason many of you are weak and ill, and some have died.[d] [31]But if we judged ourselves, we would not be judged. [32]But when we are judged by the Lord, we are disciplined[e] so that we may not be condemned along with the world.

33 So then, my brothers and sisters,[f] when you come together to eat, wait for one another. [34]If you are hungry, eat at home, so that when you come together, it will not be for your condemnation. About the other things I will give instructions when I come.

12 Now concerning spiritual gifts,[g] brothers and sisters,[f] I do not want you to be uninformed. [2]You know that when you were pagans, you were enticed and led astray to idols that could not speak. [3]Therefore I want you to understand that no one speaking by the Spirit of God ever says "Let Jesus be cursed!" and no one can say "Jesus is Lord" except by the Holy Spirit.

4 Now there are varieties of gifts, but the same Spirit; [5]and there are varieties of services, but the same Lord; [6]and there are varieties of activities, but it is the

---

[a]Other ancient authorities read *is broken for* [b]Other ancient authorities add *in an unworthy manner.* [c]Other ancient authorities read *the Lord's body* [d]Gk *fallen asleep* [e]Or *When we are judged, we are being disciplined by the Lord* [f]Gk *brothers* [g]Or *spiritual persons*

same God who activates all of them in everyone. [7]To each is given the manifestation of the Spirit for the common good. [8]To one is given through the Spirit the utterance of wisdom, and to another the utterance of knowledge according to the same Spirit, [9]to another faith by the same Spirit, to another gifts of healing by the one Spirit, [10]to another the working of miracles, to another prophecy, to another the discernment of spirits, to another various kinds of tongues, to another the interpretation of tongues. [11]All these are activated by one and the same Spirit, who allots to each one individually just as the Spirit chooses.

[12] For just as the body is one and has many members, and all the members of the body, though many, are one body, so it is with Christ. [13]For in the one Spirit we were all baptized into one body—Jews or Greeks, slaves or free—and we were all made to drink of one Spirit.

[14] Indeed, the body does not consist of one member but of many. [15]If the foot would say, "Because I am not a hand, I do not belong to the body," that would not make it any less a part of the body. [16]And if the ear would say, "Because I am not an eye, I do not belong to the body," that would not make it any less a part of the body. [17]If the whole body were an eye, where would the hearing be? If the whole body were hearing, where would the sense of smell be? [18]But as it is,

God arranged the members in the body, each one of them, as he chose. [19]If all were a single member, where would the body be? [20]As it is, there are many members, yet one body. [21]The eye cannot say to the hand, "I have no need of you," nor again the head to the feet, "I have no need of you." [22]On the contrary, the members of the body that seem to be weaker are indispensable, [23]and those members of the body that we think less honorable we clothe with greater honor, and our less respectable members are treated with greater respect; [24]whereas our more respectable members do not need this. But God has so arranged the body, giving the greater honor to the inferior member, [25]that there may be no dissension within the body, but the members may have the same care for one another. [26]If one member suffers, all suffer together with it; if one member is honored, all rejoice together with it.

[27] Now you are the body of Christ and individually members of it. [28]And God has appointed in the church first apostles, second prophets, third teachers; then deeds of power, then gifts of healing, forms of assistance, forms of leadership, various kinds of tongues. [29]Are all apostles? Are all prophets? Are all teachers? Do all work miracles? [30]Do all possess gifts of healing? Do all speak in tongues? Do all interpret? [31]But strive for the greater gifts. And I will show you a still more excellent way.

13 If I speak in the tongues of mortals and of angels, but do not have love, I am a noisy gong or a clanging cymbal. [2]And if I have prophetic powers, and understand all mysteries and all knowledge, and if I have all faith, so as to remove mountains, but do not have love, I am nothing. [3]If I give away all my possessions, and if I hand over my body so that I may boast,[a] but do not have love, I gain nothing.

4 Love is patient; love is kind; love is not envious or boastful or arrogant [5]or rude. It does not insist on its own way; it is not irritable or resentful; [6]it does not rejoice in wrongdoing, but rejoices in the truth. [7]It bears all things, believes all things, hopes all things, endures all things.

8 Love never ends. But as for prophecies, they will come to an end; as for tongues, they will cease; as for knowledge, it will come to an end. [9]For we know only in part, and we prophesy only in part; [10]but when the complete comes, the partial will come to an end. [11]When I was a child, I spoke like a child, I thought like a child, I reasoned like a child; when I became an adult, I put an end to childish ways. [12]For now we see in a mirror, dimly,[b] but then we will see face to face. Now I know only in part; then I will know fully, even as I have been fully known. [13]And now faith, hope, and love abide, these three; and the greatest of these is love.

14 Pursue love and strive for the spiritual gifts, and especially that you may prophesy. [2]For those who speak in a tongue do not speak to other people but to God; for nobody understands them, since they are speaking mysteries in the Spirit. [3]On the other hand, those who prophesy speak to other people for their upbuilding and encouragement and consolation. [4]Those who speak in a tongue build up themselves, but those who prophesy build up the church. [5]Now I would like all of you to speak in tongues, but even more to prophesy. One who prophesies is greater than one who speaks in tongues, unless someone interprets, so that the church may be built up.

6 Now, brothers and sisters,[c] if I come to you speaking in tongues, how will I benefit you unless I speak to you in some revelation or knowledge or prophecy or teaching? [7]It is the same way with lifeless instruments that produce sound, such as the flute or the harp. If they do not give distinct notes, how will anyone know what is being played? [8]And if the bugle gives an indistinct sound, who will get ready for battle? [9]So with yourselves; if in a tongue you utter speech that is not intelligible, how will anyone know what is being said? For you will be speaking into the air. [10]There are doubtless many different kinds of

[a]Other ancient authorities read *body to be burned* [b]Gk *in a riddle* [c]Gk *brothers*

sounds in the world, and nothing is without sound. ¹¹If then I do not know the meaning of a sound, I will be a foreigner to the speaker and the speaker a foreigner to me. ¹²So with yourselves; since you are eager for spiritual gifts, strive to excel in them for building up the church.

13 Therefore, one who speaks in a tongue should pray for the power to interpret. ¹⁴For if I pray in a tongue, my spirit prays but my mind is unproductive. ¹⁵What should I do then? I will pray with the spirit, but I will pray with the mind also; I will sing praise with the spirit, but I will sing praise with the mind also. ¹⁶Otherwise, if you say a blessing with the spirit, how can anyone in the position of an outsider say the "Amen" to your thanksgiving, since the outsider does not know what you are saying? ¹⁷For you may give thanks well enough, but the other person is not built up. ¹⁸I thank God that I speak in tongues more than all of you; ¹⁹nevertheless, in church I would rather speak five words with my mind, in order to instruct others also, than ten thousand words in a tongue.

20 Brothers and sisters,ᵃ do not be children in your thinking; rather, be infants in evil, but in thinking be adults. ²¹In the law it is written,

"By people of strange tongues
and by the lips of foreigners
I will speak to this people;

yet even then they will
not listen to me,"

says the Lord. ²²Tongues, then, are a sign not for believers but for unbelievers, while prophecy is not for unbelievers but for believers. ²³If, therefore, the whole church comes together and all speak in tongues, and outsiders or unbelievers enter, will they not say that you are out of your mind? ²⁴But if all prophesy, an unbeliever or outsider who enters is reproved by all and called to account by all. ²⁵After the secrets of the unbeliever's heart are disclosed, that person will bow down before God and worship him, declaring, "God is really among you."

26 What should be done then, my friends?ᵃ When you come together, each one has a hymn, a lesson, a revelation, a tongue, or an interpretation. Let all things be done for building up. ²⁷If anyone speaks in a tongue, let there be only two or at most three, and each in turn; and let one interpret. ²⁸But if there is no one to interpret, let them be silent in church and speak to themselves and to God. ²⁹Let two or three prophets speak, and let the others weigh what was said. ³⁰If a revelation is made to someone else sitting nearby, let the first person be silent. ³¹For you can all prophesy one by one, so that all may learn and all be encouraged. ³²And the spirits of prophets are subject to the prophets, ³³for God

ᵃGk brothers

is a God not of disorder but of peace.

(As in all the churches of the saints, [34]women should be silent in the churches. For they are not permitted to speak, but should be subordinate, as the law also says. [35]If there is anything they desire to know, let them ask their husbands at home. For it is shameful for a woman to speak in church.[a] [36]Or did the word of God originate with you? Or are you the only ones it has reached?)

37 Anyone who claims to be a prophet, or to have spiritual powers, must acknowledge that what I am writing to you is a command of the Lord. [38]Anyone who does not recognize this is not to be recognized. [39]So, my friends,[b] be eager to prophesy, and do not forbid speaking in tongues; [40]but all things should be done decently and in order.

15 Now I would remind you, brothers and sisters, of the good news[c] that I proclaimed to you, which you in turn received, in which also you stand, [2]through which also you are being saved, if you hold firmly to the message that I proclaimed to you—unless you have come to believe in vain.

3 For I handed on to you as of first importance what I in turn had received: that Christ died for our sins in accordance with the scriptures, [4]and that he was buried, and that he was raised on the third day in accordance with the scriptures, [5]and that he appeared to Cephas, then to the twelve. [6]Then he appeared to more than five hundred brothers and sisters at one time, most of whom are still alive, though some have died.[d] [7]Then he appeared to James, then to all the apostles. [8]Last of all, as to one untimely born, he appeared also to me. [9]For I am the least of the apostles, unfit to be called an apostle, because I persecuted the church of God. [10]But by the grace of God I am what I am, and his grace toward me has not been in vain. On the contrary, I worked harder than any of them—though it was not I, but the grace of God that is with me. [11]Whether then it was I or they, so we proclaim and so you have come to believe.

12 Now if Christ is proclaimed as raised from the dead, how can some of you say there is no resurrection of the dead? [13]If there is no resurrection of the dead, then Christ has not been raised; [14]and if Christ has not been raised, then our proclamation has been in vain and your faith has been in vain. [15]We are even found to be misrepresenting God, because we testified of God that he raised Christ—whom he did not raise if it is true that the dead are not raised. [16]For if the dead are not raised, then Christ has not been raised. [17]If Christ has not been raised, your faith is futile and you are still in your sins. [18]Then those also who have died[d] in Christ have perished. [19]If for

[a]Other ancient authorities put verses 34-35 after verse 40 [b]Gk my brothers [c]Or gospel [d]Gk fallen asleep

253

life only we have hoped in Christ, we are of all people most to be pitied.

20 But in fact Christ has been raised from the dead, the first fruits of those who have died.*a* *21*For since death came through a human being, the resurrection of the dead has also come through a human being; *22*for as all die in Adam, so all will be made alive in Christ. *23*But each in his own order: Christ the first fruits, then at his coming those who belong to Christ. *24*Then comes the end,*b* when he hands over the kingdom to God the Father, after he has destroyed every ruler and every authority and power. *25*For he must reign until he has put all his enemies under his feet. *26*The last enemy to be destroyed is death. *27*For "God*c* has put all things in subjection under his feet." But when it says, "All things are put in subjection," it is plain that this does not include the one who put all things in subjection under him. *28*When all things are subjected to him, then the Son himself will also be subjected to the one who put all things in subjection under him, so that God may be all in all.

29 Otherwise, what will those people do who receive baptism on behalf of the dead? If the dead are not raised at all, why are people baptized on their behalf?

30 And why are we putting ourselves in danger every hour? *31*I die every day! That is as certain, brothers and sisters,*d* as my boasting of you—a boast that I

make in Christ Jesus our Lord. *32*If with merely human hopes I fought with wild animals at Ephesus, what would I have gained by it? If the dead are not raised,

"Let us eat and drink,
    for tomorrow we die."

33   Do not be deceived:
    "Bad company ruins good
        morals."

*34*Come to a sober and right mind, and sin no more; for some people have no knowledge of God. I say this to your shame.

35 But someone will ask, "How are the dead raised? With what kind of body do they come?" *36*Fool! What you sow does not come to life unless it dies. *37*And as for what you sow, you do not sow the body that is to be, but a bare seed, perhaps of wheat or of some other grain. *38*But God gives it a body as he has chosen, and to each kind of seed its own body. *39*Not all flesh is alike, but there is one flesh for human beings, another for animals, another for birds, and another for fish. *40*There are both heavenly bodies and earthly bodies, but the glory of the heavenly is one thing, and that of the earthly is another. *41*There is one glory of the sun, and another glory of the moon, and another glory of the stars; indeed, star differs from star in glory.

42 So it is with the resurrection of the dead. What is sown is perishable, what is raised is

Gk fallen asleep *bOr Then come the rest* *cGk he* *dGk brothers*

imperishable. ⁴³It is sown in dishonor, it is raised in glory. It is sown in weakness, it is raised in power. ⁴⁴It is sown a physical body, it is raised a spiritual body. If there is a physical body, there is also a spiritual body. ⁴⁵Thus it is written, "The first man, Adam, became a living being"; the last Adam became a life-giving spirit. ⁴⁶But it is not the spiritual that is first, but the physical, and then the spiritual. ⁴⁷The first man was from the earth, a man of dust; the second man is*ᵃ* from heaven. ⁴⁸As was the man of dust, so are those who are of the dust; and as is the man of heaven, so are those who are of heaven. ⁴⁹Just as we have borne the image of the man of dust, we will*ᵇ* also bear the image of the man of heaven.

50 What I am saying, brothers and sisters,*ᶜ* is this: flesh and blood cannot inherit the kingdom of God, nor does the perishable inherit the imperishable. ⁵¹Listen, I will tell you a mystery! We will not all die,*ᵈ* but we will all be changed, ⁵²in a moment, in the twinkling of an eye, at the last trumpet. For the trumpet will sound, and the dead will be raised imperishable, and we will be changed. ⁵³For this perishable body must put on imperishability, and this mortal body must put on immortality. ⁵⁴When this perishable body puts on imperishability, and this mortal body puts on immortality, then the saying that is written will be fulfilled:

"Death has been swallowed
up in victory."

⁵⁵ "Where, O death, is your
victory?
Where, O death, is your
sting?"
⁵⁶The sting of death is sin, and the power of sin is the law. ⁵⁷But thanks be to God, who gives us the victory through our Lord Jesus Christ.

58 Therefore, my beloved,*ᵉ* be steadfast, immovable, always excelling in the work of the Lord, because you know that in the Lord your labor is not in vain.

16 Now concerning the collection for the saints: you should follow the directions I gave to the churches of Galatia. ²On the first day of every week, each of you is to put aside and save whatever extra you earn, so that collections need not be taken when I come. ³And when I arrive, I will send any whom you approve with letters to take your gift to Jerusalem. ⁴If it seems advisable that I should go also, they will accompany me.

5 I will visit you after passing through Macedonia—for I intend to pass through Macedonia— ⁶and perhaps I will stay with you or even spend the winter, so that you may send me on my way, wherever I go. ⁷I do not want to see you now just in passing, for I hope to spend some time with you, if the Lord permits. ⁸But I will stay in Ephesus until Pentecost,

*ᵃ*Other ancient authorities add *the Lord* *ᵇ*Other ancient authorities read *let us* *ᶜ*Gk *brothers* *ᵈ*Gk *fall asleep* *ᵉ*Gk *beloved brothers*

9for a wide door for effective work has opened to me, and there are many adversaries.

10 If Timothy comes, see that he has nothing to fear among you, for he is doing the work of the Lord just as I am; 11therefore let no one despise him. Send him on his way in peace, so that he may come to me; for I am expecting him with the brothers.

12 Now concerning our brother Apollos, I strongly urged him to visit you with the other brothers, but he was not at all willing*a* to come now. He will come when he has the opportunity.

13 Keep alert, stand firm in your faith, be courageous, be strong. 14Let all that you do be done in love.

15 Now, brothers and sisters,*b* you know that members of the household of Stephanas were the first converts in Achaia, and they have devoted themselves to the service of the saints; 16I urge you to put yourselves at the service of such people, and of everyone who works and toils with them. 17I rejoice at the coming of Stephanas and Fortunatus and Achaicus, because they have made up for your absence; 18for they refreshed my spirit as well as yours. So give recognition to such persons.

19 The churches of Asia send greetings. Aquila and Prisca, together with the church in their house, greet you warmly in the Lord. 20All the brothers and sisters*b* send greetings. Greet one another with a holy kiss.

21 I, Paul, write this greeting with my own hand. 22Let anyone be accursed who has no love for the Lord. Our Lord, come!*c* 23The grace of the Lord Jesus be with you. 24My love be with all of you in Christ Jesus.*d*

*a*Or *it was not at all God's will for him* *b*Gk *brothers* *c*Gk *Marana tha.* These Aramaic words can also be read *Maran atha,* meaning *Our Lord has come* *d*Other ancient authorities add *Amen*

The Second Letter of Paul to the
CORINTHIANS

1 Paul, an apostle of Christ Jesus by the will of God, and Timothy our brother,

To the church of God that is in Corinth, including all the saints throughout Achaia:

2 Grace to you and peace from God our Father and the Lord Jesus Christ.

3 Blessed be the God and Father of our Lord Jesus Christ,

the Father of mercies and the God of all consolation, [4]who consoles us in all our affliction, so that we may be able to console those who are in any affliction with the consolation with which we ourselves are consoled by God. [5]For just as the sufferings of Christ are abundant for us, so also our consolation is abundant through Christ. [6]If we are being afflicted, it is for your consolation and salvation; if we are being consoled, it is for your consolation, which you experience when you patiently endure the same sufferings that we are also suffering. [7]Our hope for you is unshaken; for we know that as you share in our sufferings, so also you share in our consolation.

8 We do not want you to be unaware, brothers and sisters,[a] of the affliction we experienced in Asia; for we were so utterly, unbearably crushed that we despaired of life itself. [9]Indeed, we felt that we had received the sentence of death so that we would rely not on ourselves but on God who raises the dead. [10]He who rescued us from so deadly a peril will continue to rescue us; on him we have set our hope that he will rescue us again, [11]as you also join in helping us by your prayers, so that many will give thanks on our[b] behalf for the blessing granted us through the prayers of many.

12 Indeed, this is our boast, the testimony of our conscience: we have behaved in the world with frankness[c] and godly sincer-

ity, not by earthly wisdom but by the grace of God—and all the more toward you. [13]For we write you nothing other than what you can read and also understand; I hope you will understand until the end— [14]as you have already understood us in part—that on the day of the Lord Jesus we are your boast even as you are our boast.

15 Since I was sure of this, I wanted to come to you first, so that you might have a double favor;[d] [16]I wanted to visit you on my way to Macedonia, and to come back to you from Macedonia and have you send me on to Judea. [17]Was I vacillating when I wanted to do this? Do I make my plans according to ordinary human standards,[e] ready to say "Yes, yes" and "No, no" at the same time? [18]As surely as God is faithful, our word to you has not been "Yes and No." [19]For the Son of God, Jesus Christ, whom we proclaimed among you, Silvanus and Timothy and I, was not "Yes and No"; but in him it is always "Yes." [20]For in him every one of God's promises is a "Yes." For this reason it is through him that we say the "Amen," to the glory of God. [21]But it is God who establishes us with you in Christ and has anointed us, [22]by putting his seal on us and giving us his Spirit in our hearts as a first installment.

23 But I call on God as witness against me: it was to spare you

---

[a]Gk *brothers* [b]Other ancient authorities read *your* [c]Other ancient authorities read *holiness* [d]Other ancient authorities read *pleasure* [e]Gk *according to the flesh*

that I did not come again to Corinth. 24I do not mean to imply that we lord it over your faith; rather, we are workers with you for your joy, because you stand firm in the faith. 1So I made up my mind not to make you another painful visit. 2For if I cause you pain, who is there to make me glad but the one whom I have pained? 3And I wrote as I did, so that when I came, I might not suffer pain from those who should have made me rejoice; for I am confident about all of you, that my joy would be the joy of all of you. 4For I wrote you out of much distress and anguish of heart and with many tears, not to cause you pain, but to let you know the abundant love that I have for you.

5 But if anyone has caused pain, he has caused it not to me, but to some extent—not to exaggerate it—to all of you. 6This punishment by the majority is enough for such a person; 7so now instead you should forgive and console him, so that he may not be overwhelmed by excessive sorrow. 8So I urge you to reaffirm your love for him. 9I wrote for this reason: to test you and to know whether you are obedient in everything. 10Anyone whom you forgive, I also forgive. What I have forgiven, if I have forgiven anything, has been for your sake in the presence of Christ. 11And we do this so that we may not be outwitted by Satan; for we are not ignorant of his designs.

12 When I came to Troas to proclaim the good news of Christ, a door was opened for me in the Lord; 13but my mind could not rest because I did not find my brother Titus there. So I said farewell to them and went on to Macedonia.

14 But thanks be to God, who in Christ always leads us in triumphal procession, and through us spreads in every place the fragrance that comes from knowing him. 15For we are the aroma of Christ to God among those who are being saved and among those who are perishing; 16to the one a fragrance from death to death, to the other a fragrance from life to life. Who is sufficient for these things? 17For we are not peddlers of God's word like so many;[a] but in Christ we speak as persons of sincerity, as persons sent from God and standing in his presence.

3 Are we beginning to commend ourselves again? Surely we do not need, as some do, letters of recommendation to you or from you, do we? 2You yourselves are our letter, written on our[b] hearts, to be known and read by all; 3and you show that you are a letter of Christ, prepared by us, written not with ink but with the Spirit of the living God, not on tablets of stone but on tablets of human hearts.

4 Such is the confidence that we have through Christ toward God. 5Not that we are competent of ourselves to claim anything as coming from us; our competence

---

[a]Other ancient authorities read *like the others* [b]Other ancient authorities read *your*

is from God, [6]who has made us competent to be ministers of a new covenant, not of letter but of spirit; for the letter kills, but the Spirit gives life.

7 Now if the ministry of death, chiseled in letters on stone tablets,[a] came in glory so that the people of Israel could not gaze at Moses' face because of the glory of his face, a glory now set aside, [8]how much more will the ministry of the Spirit come in glory? [9]For if there was glory in the ministry of condemnation, much more does the ministry of justification abound in glory! [10]Indeed, what once had glory has lost its glory because of the greater glory; [11]for if what was set aside came through glory, much more has the permanent come in glory!

12 Since, then, we have such a hope, we act with great boldness, [13]not like Moses, who put a veil over his face to keep the people of Israel from gazing at the end of the glory that[b] was being set aside. [14]But their minds were hardened. Indeed, to this very day, when they hear the reading of the old covenant, that same veil is still there, since only in Christ is it set aside. [15]Indeed, to this very day whenever Moses is read, a veil lies over their minds; [16]but when one turns to the Lord, the veil is removed. [17]Now the Lord is the Spirit, and where the Spirit of the Lord is, there is freedom. [18]And all of us, with unveiled faces, seeing the glory of the Lord as though reflected in a mirror, are being transformed into the same image from one degree of glory to another; for this comes from the Lord, the Spirit.

4 Therefore, since it is by God's mercy that we are engaged in this ministry, we do not lose heart. [2]We have renounced the shameful things that one hides; we refuse to practice cunning or to falsify God's word; but by the open statement of the truth we commend ourselves to the conscience of everyone in the sight of God. [3]And even if our gospel is veiled, it is veiled to those who are perishing. [4]In their case the god of this world has blinded the minds of the unbelievers, to keep them from seeing the light of the gospel of the glory of Christ, who is the image of God. [5]For we do not proclaim ourselves; we proclaim Jesus Christ as Lord and ourselves as your slaves for Jesus' sake. [6]For it is the God who said, "Let light shine out of darkness," who has shone in our hearts to give the light of the knowledge of the glory of God in the face of Jesus Christ.

7 But we have this treasure in clay jars, so that it may be made clear that this extraordinary power belongs to God and does not come from us. [8]We are afflicted in every way, but not crushed; perplexed, but not driven to despair; [9]persecuted, but not forsaken; struck down, but not destroyed; [10]always carrying in the body the death of Jesus, so that that the life of Jesus may also be

[a]Gk on stones [b]Gk of what

259

made visible in our bodies. [11]For while we live, we are always being given up to death for Jesus' sake, so that the life of Jesus may be made visible in our mortal flesh. [12]So death is at work in us, but life in you.

13 But just as we have the same spirit of faith that is in accordance with scripture—"I believed, and so I spoke"—we also believe, and so we speak, [14]because we know that the one who raised the Lord Jesus will raise us also with Jesus, and will bring us with you into his presence. [15]Yes, everything is for your sake, so that grace, as it extends to more and more people, may increase thanksgiving, to the glory of God.

16 So we do not lose heart. Even though our outer nature is wasting away, our inner nature is being renewed day by day. [17]For this slight momentary affliction is preparing us for an eternal weight of glory beyond all measure, [18]because we look not at what can be seen but at what cannot be seen; for what can be seen is temporary, but what cannot be seen is eternal.

5 For we know that if the earthly tent we live in is destroyed, we have a building from God, a house not made with hands, eternal in the heavens. [2]For in this tent we groan, longing to be clothed with our heavenly dwelling— [3]if indeed, when we have taken it off[a] we will not be found naked. [4]For while we are still in this tent, we groan

under our burden, because we wish not to be unclothed but to be further clothed, so that what is mortal may be swallowed up by life. [5]He who has prepared us for this very thing is God, who has given us the Spirit as a guarantee.

6 So we are always confident; even though we know that while we are at home in the body we are away from the Lord— [7]for we walk by faith, not by sight. [8]Yes, we do have confidence, and we would rather be away from the body and at home with the Lord. [9]So whether we are at home or away, we make it our aim to please him. [10]For all of us must appear before the judgment seat of Christ, so that each may receive recompense for what has been done in the body, whether good or evil.

11 Therefore, knowing the fear of the Lord, we try to persuade others; but we ourselves are well known to God, and I hope that we are also well known to your consciences. [12]We are not commending ourselves to you again, but giving you an opportunity to boast about us, so that you may be able to answer those who boast in outward appearance and not in the heart. [13]For if we are beside ourselves, it is for God; if we are in our right mind, it is for you. [14]For the love of Christ urges us on, because we are convinced that one has died for all; therefore all have died. [15]And he died for all, so that those who live might

[a]Other ancient authorities read *put it on*

live no longer for themselves, but for him who died and was raised for them.

16 From now on, therefore, we regard no one from a human point of view;[a] even though we once knew Christ from a human point of view,[a] we know him no longer in that way. 17So if anyone is in Christ, there is a new creation: everything old has passed away; see, everything has become new! 18All this is from God, who reconciled us to himself through Christ, and has given us the ministry of reconciliation; 19that is, in Christ God was reconciling the world to himself,[b] not counting their trespasses against them, and entrusting the message of reconciliation to us. 20So we are ambassadors for Christ, since God is making his appeal through us; we entreat you on behalf of Christ, be reconciled to God. 21For our sake he made him to be sin who knew no sin, so that in him we might become the righteousness of God.

6 As we work together with him,[c] we urge you also not to accept the grace of God in vain. 2For he says,

"At an acceptable time I
    have listened to you,
and on a day of salvation
    I have helped you."

See, now is the acceptable time; see, now is the day of salvation! 3We are putting no obstacle in anyone's way, so that no fault may be found with our ministry, 4but as servants of God we have commended ourselves in every way: through great endurance, in afflictions, hardships, calamities, 5beatings, imprisonments, riots, labors, sleepless nights, hunger; 6by purity, knowledge, patience, kindness, holiness of spirit, genuine love, 7truthful speech, and the power of God; with the weapons of righteousness for the right hand and for the left; 8in honor and dishonor, in ill repute and good repute. We are treated as impostors, and yet are true; 9as unknown, and yet are well known; as dying, and see—we are alive; as punished, and yet not killed; 10as sorrowful, yet always rejoicing; as poor, yet making many rich; as having nothing, and yet possessing everything.

11 We have spoken frankly to you Corinthians; our heart is wide open to you. 12There is no restriction in our affections, but only in yours. 13In return—I speak as to children—open wide your hearts also.

14 Do not be mismatched with unbelievers. For what partnership is there between righteousness and lawlessness? Or what fellowship is there between light and darkness? 15What agreement does Christ have with Beliar? Or what does a believer share with an unbeliever? 16What agreement has the temple of God with idols? For we[d] are the temple of the living God; as God said,

---

[a] Gk *according to the flesh* [b] Or *God was in Christ reconciling the world to himself* [c] Gk *As we work together* [d] Other ancient authorities read *you*

"I will live in them and
　　walk among them,
　and I will be their God,
　and they shall be my
　　people.
17 Therefore come out from
　　them,
　and be separate from
　　them, says the Lord,
　and touch nothing unclean;
　then I will welcome you,
18 and I will be your father,
　and you shall be my sons
　　and daughters,
says the Lord Almighty."

7 Since we have these promises, beloved, let us cleanse
ourselves from every defilement
of body and of spirit, making holiness perfect in the fear of God.

2 Make room in your hearts[a]
for us; we have wronged no one,
we have corrupted no one, we
have taken advantage of no one. 3I
do not say this to condemn you,
for I said before that you are in
our hearts, to die together and to
live together. 4I often boast about
you; I have great pride in you; I
am filled with consolation; I am
overjoyed in all our affliction.

5 For even when we came into
Macedonia, our bodies had no
rest, but we were afflicted in
every way—disputes without
and fears within. 6But God, who
consoles the downcast, consoled
us by the arrival of Titus, 7and
not only by his coming, but also
by the consolation with which he
was consoled about you, as he
told us of your longing, your
mourning, your zeal for me, so

that I rejoiced still more. 8For
even if I made you sorry with my
letter, I do not regret it (though I
did regret it, for I see that I grieved
you with that letter, though only
briefly). 9Now I rejoice, not
because you were grieved, but
because your grief led to repentance; for you felt a godly grief, so
that you were not harmed in any
way by us. 10For godly grief produces a repentance that leads to
salvation and brings no regret,
but worldly grief produces death.
11For see what earnestness this
godly grief has produced in you,
what eagerness to clear yourselves, what indignation, what
alarm, what longing, what zeal,
what punishment! At every point
you have proved yourselves
guiltless in the matter. 12So
although I wrote to you, it was
not on account of the one who
did the wrong, nor on account of
the one who was wronged, but in
order that your zeal for us might
be made known to you before
God. 13In this we find comfort.

In addition to our own consolation, we rejoiced still more at
the joy of Titus, because his mind
has been set at rest by all of you.
14For if I have been somewhat
boastful about you to him, I was
not disgraced; but just as everything we said to you was true, so
our boasting to Titus has proved
true as well. 15And his heart goes
out all the more to you, as he
remembers the obedience of all
of you, and how you welcomed

---

[a]Gk lacks in your hearts

him with fear and trembling. [16]I rejoice, because I have complete confidence in you.

8 We want you to know, brothers and sisters,[a] about the grace of God that has been granted to the churches of Macedonia; [2]for during a severe ordeal of affliction, their abundant joy and their extreme poverty have overflowed in a wealth of generosity on their part. [3]For, as I can testify, they voluntarily gave according to their means, and even beyond their means, [4]begging us earnestly for the privilege[b] of sharing in this ministry to the saints— [5]and this, not merely as we expected; they gave themselves first to the Lord and, by the will of God, to us, [6]so that we might urge Titus that, as he had already made a beginning, so he should also complete this generous undertaking[c] among you. [7]Now as you excel in everything—in faith, in speech, in knowledge, in utmost eagerness, and in our love for you[d]—so we want you to excel also in this generous undertaking.

[8] I do not say this as a command, but I am testing the genuineness of your love against the earnestness of others. [9]For you know the generous act[e] of our Lord Jesus Christ, that though he was rich, yet for your sakes he became poor, so that by his poverty you might become rich. [10]And in this matter I am giving my advice: it is appropriate for you who began last year not only

to do something but even to desire to do something— [11]now finish doing it, so that your eagerness may be matched by completing it according to your means. [12]For if the eagerness is there, the gift is acceptable according to what one has—not according to what one does not have. [13]I do not mean that there should be relief for others and pressure on you, but it is a question of a fair balance between [14]your present abundance and their need, so that their abundance may be for your need, in order that there may be a fair balance. [15]As it is written,

"The one who had much
did not have too
much,
and the one who had
little did not have too
little."

[16] But thanks be to God who put in the heart of Titus the same eagerness for you that I myself have. [17]For he not only accepted our appeal, but since he is more eager than ever, he is going to you of his own accord. [18]With him we are sending the brother who is famous among all the churches for his proclaiming the good news;[f] [19]and not only that, but he has also been appointed by the churches to travel with us while we are administering this generous undertaking[c] for the glory of the Lord himself[g] and to show our goodwill. [20]We intend

---

[a]Gk brothers [b]Gk grace [c]Gk this grace [d]Other ancient authorities read your love for us [e]Gk the grace [f]Or the gospel [g]Other ancient authorities lack himself

that no one should blame us about this generous gift that we are administering, [21]for we intend to do what is right not only in the Lord's sight but also in the sight of others. [22]And with them we are sending our brother whom we have often tested and found eager in many matters, but who is now more eager than ever because of his great confidence in you. [23]As for Titus, he is my partner and co-worker in your service; as for our brothers, they are messengers[a] of the churches, the glory of Christ. [24]Therefore openly before the churches, show them the proof of your love and of our reason for boasting about you.

9 Now it is not necessary for me to write you about the ministry to the saints, [2]for I know your eagerness, which is the subject of my boasting about you to the people of Macedonia, saying that Achaia has been ready since last year; and your zeal has stirred up most of them. [3]But I am sending the brothers in order that our boasting about you may not prove to have been empty in this case, so that you may be ready, as I said you would be; [4]otherwise, if some Macedonians come with me and find that you are not ready, we would be humiliated—to say nothing of you—in this undertaking.[b] [5]So I thought it necessary to urge the brothers to go on ahead to you, and arrange in advance for this bountiful gift that you have promised, so that it may be ready as a voluntary gift and not as an extortion.

[6] The point is this: the one who sows sparingly will also reap sparingly, and the one who sows bountifully will also reap bountifully. [7]Each of you must give as you have made up your mind, not reluctantly or under compulsion, for God loves a cheerful giver. [8]And God is able to provide you with every blessing in abundance, so that by always having enough of everything, you may share abundantly in every good work. [9]As it is written,

"He scatters abroad, he
     gives to the poor;
   his righteousness[c]
     endures forever."

[10]He who supplies seed to the sower and bread for food will supply and multiply your seed for sowing and increase the harvest of your righteousness.[c] [11]You will be enriched in every way for your great generosity, which will produce thanksgiving to God through us; [12]for the rendering of this ministry not only supplies the needs of the saints but also overflows with many thanksgivings to God. [13]Through the testing of this ministry you glorify God by your obedience to the confession of the gospel of Christ and by the generosity of your sharing with them and with all others, [14]while they long for you and pray for you because of the surpassing grace of God that he has given you. [15]Thanks be to God for his indescribable gift!

---

[a]Gk apostles [b]Other ancient authorities add of boasting [c]Or benevolence

10 I myself, Paul, appeal to you by the meekness and gentleness of Christ—I who am humble when face to face with you, but bold toward you when I am away!— [2]I ask that when I am present I need not show boldness by daring to oppose those who think we are acting according to human standards.[a] [3]Indeed, we live as human beings,[b] but we do not wage war according to human standards;[a] [4]for the weapons of our warfare are not merely human,[c] but they have divine power to destroy strongholds. We destroy arguments [5]and every proud obstacle raised up against the knowledge of God, and we take every thought captive to obey Christ. [6]We are ready to punish every disobedience when your obedience is complete.

[7]Look at what is before your eyes. If you are confident that you belong to Christ, remind yourself of this, that just as you belong to Christ, so also do we. [8]Now, even if I boast a little too much of our authority, which the Lord gave for building you up and not for tearing you down, I will not be ashamed of it. [9]I do not want to seem as though I am trying to frighten you with my letters. [10]For they say, "His letters are weighty and strong, but his bodily presence is weak, and his speech contemptible." [11]Let such people understand that what we say by letter when absent, we will also do when present.

[12]We do not dare to classify or compare ourselves with some of those who commend themselves. But when they measure themselves by one another, and compare themselves with one another, they do not show good sense. [13]We, however, will not boast beyond limits, but will keep within the field that God has assigned to us, to reach out even as far as you. [14]For we were not overstepping our limits when we reached you; we were the first to come all the way to you with the good news[d] of Christ. [15]We do not boast beyond limits, that is, in the labors of others; but our hope is that, as your faith increases, our sphere of action among you may be greatly enlarged, [16]so that we may proclaim the good news[d] in lands beyond you, without boasting of work already done in someone else's sphere of action. [17]"Let the one who boasts, boast in the Lord." [18]For it is not those who commend themselves that are approved, but those whom the Lord commends.

11 I wish you would bear with me in a little foolishness. Do bear with me! [2]I feel a divine jealousy for you, for I promised you in marriage to one husband, to present you as a chaste virgin to Christ. [3]But I am afraid that as the serpent deceived Eve by its cunning, your thoughts will be led astray from a sincere and pure[e] devotion to Christ. [4]For if someone comes and proclaims another Jesus than

[a]Gk *according to the flesh* [b]Gk *in the flesh* [c]Gk *fleshly*
[d]Or *the gospel* [e]Other ancient authorities lack *and pure*

the one we proclaimed, or if you receive a different spirit from the one you received, or a different gospel from the one you accepted, you submit to it readily enough. [5]I think that I am not in the least inferior to these super-apostles. [6]I may be untrained in speech, but not in knowledge; certainly in every way and in all things we have made this evident to you.

7 Did I commit a sin by humbling myself so that you might be exalted, because I proclaimed God's good news[a] to you free of charge? [8]I robbed other churches by accepting support from them in order to serve you. [9]And when I was with you and was in need, I did not burden anyone, for my needs were supplied by the friends[b] who came from Macedonia. So I refrained and will continue to refrain from burdening you in any way. [10]As the truth of Christ is in me, this boast of mine will not be silenced in the regions of Achaia. [11]And why? Because I do not love you? God knows I do!

12 And what I do I will also continue to do, in order to deny an opportunity to those who want an opportunity to be recognized as our equals in what they boast about. [13]For such boasters are false apostles, deceitful workers, disguising themselves as apostles of Christ. [14]And no wonder! Even Satan disguises himself as an angel of light. [15]So it is not strange if his ministers also disguise themselves as ministers of righteousness. Their end will match their deeds.

16 I repeat, let no one think that I am a fool; but if you do, then accept me as a fool, so that I too may boast a little. [17] What I am saying in regard to this boastful confidence, I am saying not with the Lord's authority, but as a fool; [18] since many boast according to human standards,[c] I will also boast. [19] For you gladly put up with fools, being wise yourselves! [20] For you put up with it when someone makes slaves of you, or preys upon you, or takes advantage of you, or puts on airs, or gives you a slap in the face. [21] To my shame, I must say, we were too weak for that!

But whatever anyone dares to boast of—I am speaking as a fool—I also dare to boast of that. [22]Are they Hebrews? So am I. Are they Israelites? So am I. Are they descendants of Abraham? So am I. [23]Are they ministers of Christ? I am talking like a madman—I am a better one: with far greater labors, far more imprisonments, with countless floggings, and often near death. [24]Five times I have received from the Jews the forty lashes minus one. [25]Three times I was beaten with rods. Once I received a stoning. Three times I was shipwrecked; for a night and a day I was adrift at sea; [26]on frequent journeys, in danger from rivers, danger from bandits, danger from my own

[a]Gk *the gospel of God* [b]Gk *brothers* [c]Gk *according to the flesh*

people, danger from Gentiles, danger in the city, danger in the wilderness, danger at sea, danger from false brothers and sisters; [27]in toil and hardship, through many a sleepless night, hungry and thirsty, often without food, cold and naked. [28]And, besides other things, I am under daily pressure because of my anxiety for all the churches. [29]Who is weak, and I am not weak? Who is made to stumble, and I am not indignant?

30 If I must boast, I will boast of the things that show my weakness. [31]The God and Father of the Lord Jesus (blessed be he forever!) knows that I do not lie. [32]In Damascus, the governor[a] under King Aretas guarded the city of Damascus in order to[b] seize me, [33]but I was let down in a basket through a window in the wall,[c] and escaped from his hands.

12 It is necessary to boast; nothing is to be gained by it, but I will go on to visions and revelations of the Lord. [2]I know a person in Christ who fourteen years ago was caught up to the third heaven—whether in the body or out of the body I do not know; God knows. [3]And I know that such a person—whether in the body or out of the body I do not know; God knows— [4]was caught up into Paradise and heard things that are not to be told, that no mortal is permitted to repeat. [5]On behalf of such a one I will boast, but on my own behalf I will not boast, except of my weaknesses. [6]But if I wish to boast, I will not be a fool, for I will be speaking the truth. But I refrain from it, so that no one may think better of me than what is seen in me or heard from me, [7]even considering the exceptional character of the revelations. Therefore, to keep[d] me from being too elated, a thorn was given me in the flesh, a messenger of Satan to torment me, to keep me from being too elated.[e] [8]Three times I appealed to the Lord about this, that it would leave me, [9]but he said to me, "My grace is sufficient for you, for power[f] is made perfect in weakness." So, I will boast all the more gladly of my weaknesses, so that the power of Christ may dwell in me. [10]Therefore I am content with weaknesses, insults, hardships, persecutions, and calamities for the sake of Christ; for whenever I am weak, then I am strong.

11 I have been a fool! You forced me to it. Indeed you should have been the ones commending me, for I am not at all inferior to these super-apostles, even though I am nothing. [12]The signs of a true apostle were performed among you with utmost patience, signs and wonders and mighty works. [13]How have you been worse off than the other churches, except that I myself did not burden you? Forgive me this wrong!

[a]Gk *ethnarch* [b]Other ancient authorities read *and wanted to* [c]Gk *through the wall* [d]Other ancient authorities read *To keep* [e]Other ancient authorities lack *to keep me from being too elated* [f]Other ancient authorities read *my power*

14 Here I am, ready to come to you this third time. And I will not be a burden, because I do not want what is yours but you; for children ought not to lay up for their parents, but parents for their children. [15]I will most gladly spend and be spent for you. If I love you more, am I to be loved less? [16]Let it be assumed that I did not burden you. Nevertheless (you say) since I was crafty, I took you in by deceit. [17]Did I take advantage of you through any of those whom I sent to you? [18]I urged Titus to go, and sent the brother with him. Titus did not take advantage of you, did he? Did we not conduct ourselves with the same spirit? Did we not take the same steps?

19 Have you been thinking all along that we have been defending ourselves before you? We are speaking in Christ before God. Everything we do, beloved, is for the sake of building you up. [20]For I fear that when I come, I may find you not as I wish, and that you may find me not as you wish; I fear that there may perhaps be quarreling, jealousy, anger, selfishness, slander, gossip, conceit, and disorder. [21]I fear that when I come again, my God may humble me before you, and that I may have to mourn over many who previously sinned and have not repented of the impurity, sexual immorality, and licentiousness that they have practiced.

13 This is the third time I am coming to you. "Any charge must be sustained by the evidence of two or three witnesses." [2]I warned those who sinned previously and all the others, and I warn them now while absent, as I did when present on my second visit, that if I come again, I will not be lenient— [3]since you desire proof that Christ is speaking in me. He is not weak in dealing with you, but is powerful in you. [4]For he was crucified in weakness, but lives by the power of God. For we are weak in him,[a] but in dealing with you we will live with him by the power of God.

5 Examine yourselves to see whether you are living in the faith. Test yourselves. Do you not realize that Jesus Christ is in you?—unless, indeed, you fail to meet the test! [6]I hope you will find out that we have not failed. [7]But we pray to God that you may not do anything wrong—not that we may appear to have met the test, but that you may do what is right, though we may seem to have failed. [8]For we cannot do anything against the truth, but only for the truth. [9]For we rejoice when we are weak and you are strong. This is what we pray for, that you may become perfect. [10]So I write these things while I am away from you, so that when I come, I may not have to be severe in using the authority that the Lord has given me for building up and not for tearing down.

11 Finally, brothers and sisters,[b]

---

[a]Other ancient authorities read *with him* [b]Gk *brothers*

farewell.[a] Put things in order, listen to my appeal,[b] agree with one another, live in peace; and the God of love and peace will be with you. [12]Greet one another with a holy kiss. All the saints greet you.

13 The grace of the Lord Jesus Christ, the love of God, and the communion of[c] the Holy Spirit be with all of you.

[a]Or *rejoice* [b]Or *encourage one another* [c]Or *and the sharing in*

The Letter of Paul to the

GALATIANS

1 Paul an apostle—sent neither by human commission nor from human authorities, but through Jesus Christ and God the Father, who raised him from the dead— [2]and all the members of God's family[a] who are with me,

To the churches of Galatia:

3 Grace to you and peace from God our Father and the Lord Jesus Christ, [4]who gave himself for our sins to set us free from the present evil age, according to the will of our God and Father, [5]to whom be the glory forever and ever. Amen.

6 I am astonished that you are so quickly deserting the one who called you in the grace of Christ and are turning to a different gospel— [7]not that there is another gospel, but there are some who are confusing you and want to pervert the gospel of Christ. [8]But even if we or an angel[b] from heaven should proclaim to you a gospel contrary to what we proclaimed to you, let that one be accursed! [9]As we have said before, so now I repeat, if anyone proclaims to you a gospel contrary to what you received, let that one be accursed!

10 Am I now seeking human approval, or God's approval? Or am I trying to please people? If I were still pleasing people, I would not be a servant[c] of Christ.

11 For I want you to know, brothers and sisters,[d] that the gospel that was proclaimed by me is not of human origin; [12]for I did not receive it from a human source, nor was I taught it, but I received it through a revelation of Jesus Christ.

13 You have heard, no doubt, of my earlier life in Judaism. I was violently persecuting the church of God and was trying to destroy it. [14]I advanced in Judaism beyond many among my people of the same age, for I was far more

[a]Gk *all the brothers* [b]Or *a messenger* [c]Gk *slave* [d]Gk *brothers*

zealous for the traditions of my ancestors. [15]But when God, who had set me apart before I was born and called me through his grace, was pleased [16]to reveal his Son to me,[a] so that I might proclaim him among the Gentiles, I did not confer with any human being, [17]nor did I go up to Jerusalem to those who were already apostles before me, but I went away at once into Arabia, and afterwards I returned to Damascus.

18 Then after three years I did go up to Jerusalem to visit Cephas and stayed with him fifteen days; [19]but I did not see any other apostle except James the Lord's brother. [20]In what I am writing to you, before God, I do not lie! [21]Then I went into the regions of Syria and Cilicia, [22]and I was still unknown by sight to the churches of Judea that are in Christ; [23]they only heard it said, "The one who formerly was persecuting us is now proclaiming the faith he once tried to destroy." [24]And they glorified God because of me.

2 Then after fourteen years I went up again to Jerusalem with Barnabas, taking Titus along with me. [2]I went up in response to a revelation. Then I laid before them (though only in a private meeting with the acknowledged leaders) the gospel that I proclaim among the Gentiles, in order to make sure that I was not running, or had not run, in vain. [3]But even Titus, who was with me, was not compelled to be circumcised, though he was a Greek. [4]But because of false

believers[b] secretly brought in, who slipped in to spy on the freedom we have in Christ Jesus, so that they might enslave us— [5]we did not submit to them even for a moment, so that the truth of the gospel might always remain with you. [6]And from those who were supposed to be acknowledged leaders (what they actually were makes no difference to me; God shows no partiality)—those leaders contributed nothing to me. [7]On the contrary, when they saw that I had been entrusted with the gospel for the uncircumcised, just as Peter had been entrusted with the gospel for the circumcised [8](for he who worked through Peter making him an apostle to the circumcised also worked through me in sending me to the Gentiles), [9]and when James and Cephas and John, who were acknowledged pillars, recognized the grace that had been given to me, they gave to Barnabas and me the right hand of fellowship, agreeing that we should go to the Gentiles and they to the circumcised. [10]They asked only one thing, that we remember the poor, which was actually what I was[c] eager to do.

11 But when Cephas came to Antioch, I opposed him to his face, because he stood self-condemned; [12]for until certain people came from James, he used to eat with the Gentiles. But after they came, he drew back and kept himself separate for fear of

[a]Gk in me [b]Gk false brothers [c]Or had been

the circumcision faction. [13]And the other Jews joined him in this hypocrisy, so that even Barnabas was led astray by their hypocrisy. [14]But when I saw that they were not acting consistently with the truth of the gospel, I said to Cephas before them all, "If you, though a Jew, live like a Gentile and not like a Jew, how can you compel the Gentiles to live like Jews?"[a]

15 We ourselves are Jews by birth and not Gentile sinners; [16]yet we know that a person is justified[b] not by the works of the law but through faith in Jesus Christ.[c] And we have come to believe in Christ Jesus, so that we might be justified by faith in Christ,[d] and not by doing the works of the law, because no one will be justified by the works of the law. [17]But if, in our effort to be justified in Christ, we ourselves have been found to be sinners, is Christ then a servant of sin? Certainly not! [18]But if I build up again the very things that I once tore down, then I demonstrate that I am a transgressor. [19]For through the law I died to the law, so that I might live to God. I have been crucified with Christ; [20]and it is no longer I who live, but it is Christ who lives in me. And the life I now live in the flesh I live by faith in the Son of God,[e] who loved me and gave himself for me. [21]I do not nullify the grace of God; for if justification[f] comes through the law, then Christ died for nothing.

3 You foolish Galatians! Who has bewitched you? It was

before your eyes that Jesus Christ was publicly exhibited as crucified! [2]The only thing I want to learn from you is this: Did you receive the Spirit by doing the works of the law or by believing what you heard? [3]Are you so foolish? Having started with the Spirit, are you now ending with the flesh? [4]Did you experience so much for nothing?—if it really was for nothing. [5]Well then, does God[g] supply you with the Spirit and work miracles among you by your doing the works of the law, or by your believing what you heard?

6 Just as Abraham "believed God, and it was reckoned to him as righteousness," [7]so, you see, those who believe are the descendants of Abraham. [8]And the scripture, foreseeing that God would justify the Gentiles by faith, declared the gospel beforehand to Abraham, saying, "All the Gentiles shall be blessed in you." [9]For this reason, those who believe are blessed with Abraham who believed.

10 For all who rely on the works of the law are under a curse; for it is written, "Cursed is everyone who does not observe and obey all the things written in the book of the law." [11]Now it is evident that no one is justified before God by the law; for "The one who is righteous will live by

---

[a]Some interpreters hold that the quotation extends into the following paragraph [b]Or *reckoned as righteous;* and so elsewhere [c]Or *the faith of Jesus Christ* [d]Or *the faith of Christ* [e]Or *by the faith of the Son of God* [f]Or *righteousness* [g]Gk *he*

faith."[a] [12]But the law does not rest on faith; on the contrary, "Whoever does the works of the law[b] will live by them." [13]Christ redeemed us from the curse of the law by becoming a curse for us—for it is written, "Cursed is everyone who hangs on a tree"— [14]in order that in Christ Jesus the blessing of Abraham might come to the Gentiles, so that we might receive the promise of the Spirit through faith.

[15] Brothers and sisters,[c] I give an example from daily life: once a person's will[d] has been ratified, no one adds to it or annuls it. [16]Now the promises were made to Abraham and to his offspring;[e] it does not say, "And to offsprings,"[f] as of many; but it says, "And to your offspring,"[e] that is, to one person, who is Christ. [17]My point is this: the law, which came four hundred thirty years later, does not annul a covenant previously ratified by God, so as to nullify the promise. [18]For if the inheritance comes from the law, it no longer comes from the promise; but God granted it to Abraham through the promise.

[19] Why then the law? It was added because of transgressions, until the offspring[e] would come to whom the promise had been made; and it was ordained through angels by a mediator. [20]Now a mediator involves more than one party; but God is one.

[21] Is the law then opposed to the promises of God? Certainly not! For if a law had been given that could make alive, then right-eousness would indeed come through the law. [22]But the scripture has imprisoned all things under the power of sin, so that what was promised through faith in Jesus Christ[g] might be given to those who believe.

[23] Now before faith came, we were imprisoned and guarded under the law until faith would be revealed. [24]Therefore the law was our disciplinarian until Christ came, so that we might be justified by faith. [25]But now that faith has come, we are no longer subject to a disciplinarian, [26]for in Christ Jesus you are all children of God through faith. [27]As many of you as were baptized into Christ have clothed your-selves with Christ. [28]There is no longer Jew or Greek, there is no longer slave or free, there is no longer male and female; for all of you are one in Christ Jesus. [29]And if you belong to Christ, then you are Abraham's offspring, heirs according to the promise.

4 My point is this: heirs, as long as they are minors, are no better than slaves, though they are the owners of all the property; [2]but they remain under guardians and trustees until the date set by the father. [3]So with us; while we were minors, we were enslaved to the elemental spirits[h] of the world. [4]But when the fullness of time had come, God sent his Son, born of a woman,

[a]Or *The one who is righteous through faith will live* [b]Gk *does them* [c]Gk *Brothers* [d]Or *covenant* (as in verse 17) [e]Gk *seed* [f]Gk *seeds* [g]Or *through the faith of Jesus Christ* [h]Or *the rudiments*

born under the law, [5]in order to redeem those who were under the law, so that we might receive adoption as children. [6]And because you are children, God has sent the Spirit of his Son into our[a] hearts, crying, "Abba![b] Father!" [7]So you are no longer a slave but a child, and if a child then also an heir, through God.[c]

8 Formerly, when you did not know God, you were enslaved to beings that by nature are not gods. [9]Now, however, that you have come to know God, or rather to be known by God, how can you turn back again to the weak and beggarly elemental spirits?[d] How can you want to be enslaved to them again? [10]You are observing special days, and months, and seasons, and years. [11]I am afraid that my work for you may have been wasted.

12 Friends,[e] I beg you, become as I am, for I also have become as you are. You have done me no wrong. [13]You know that it was because of a physical infirmity that I first announced the gospel to you; [14]though my condition put you to the test, you did not scorn or despise me, but welcomed me as an angel of God, as Christ Jesus. [15]What has become of the goodwill you felt? For I testify that, had it been possible, you would have torn out your eyes and given them to me. [16]Have I now become your enemy by telling you the truth? [17]They make much of you, but for no good purpose; they want to exclude you, so that you may make much of them. [18]It is good to be made much of for a good purpose at all times, and not only when I am present with you. [19]My little children, for whom I am again in the pain of childbirth until Christ is formed in you, [20]I wish I were present with you now and could change my tone, for I am perplexed about you.

21 Tell me, you who desire to be subject to the law, will you not listen to the law? [22]For it is written that Abraham had two sons, one by a slave woman and the other by a free woman. [23]One, the child of the slave, was born according to the flesh; the other, the child of the free woman, was born through the promise. [24]Now this is an allegory: these women are two covenants. One woman, in fact, is Hagar, from Mount Sinai, bearing children for slavery. [25]Now Hagar is Mount Sinai in Arabia[f] and corresponds to the present Jerusalem, for she is in slavery with her children. [26]But the other woman corresponds to the Jerusalem above; she is free, and she is our mother. [27]For it is written,

> "Rejoice, you childless one,
>   you who bear no
>   children,
> burst into song and
>   shout, you who
>   endure no
>   birth pangs;

[a]Other ancient authorities read *your* [b]Aramaic for *Father* [c]Other ancient authorities read *an heir of God through Christ* [d]Or *beggarly rudiments* [e]Gk *Brothers* [f]Other ancient authorities read *For Sinai is a mountain in Arabia*

for the children of the
    desolate woman are
    more numerous
than the children of the
    one who is married."
28Now you,[a] my friends,[b] are children of the promise, like Isaac.
29But just as at that time the child who was born according to the flesh persecuted the child who was born according to the Spirit, so it is now also. 30But what does the scripture say? "Drive out the slave and her child; for the child of the slave will not share the inheritance with the child of the free woman." 31So then, friends,[b] we are children, not of the slave but of the free woman.

5 1For freedom Christ has set us free. Stand firm, therefore, and do not submit again to a yoke of slavery.

2 Listen! I, Paul, am telling you that if you let yourselves be circumcised, Christ will be of no benefit to you. 3Once again I testify to every man who lets himself be circumcised that he is obliged to obey the entire law. 4You who want to be justified by the law have cut yourselves off from Christ; you have fallen away from grace. 5For through the Spirit, by faith, we eagerly wait for the hope of righteousness. 6For in Christ Jesus neither circumcision nor uncircumcision counts for anything; the only thing that counts is faith working[c] through love.

7 You were running well; who prevented you from obeying the truth? 8Such persuasion does not come from the one who calls you. 9A little yeast leavens the whole batch of dough. 10I am confident about you in the Lord that you will not think otherwise. But whoever it is that is confusing you will pay the penalty. 11But my friends,[b] why am I still being persecuted if I am still preaching circumcision? In that case the offense of the cross has been removed. 12I wish those who unsettle you would castrate themselves!

13 For you were called to freedom, brothers and sisters;[b] only do not use your freedom as an opportunity for self-indulgence,[d] but through love become slaves to one another. 14For the whole law is summed up in a single commandment, "You shall love your neighbor as yourself." 15If, however, you bite and devour one another, take care that you are not consumed by one another.

16 Live by the Spirit, I say, and do not gratify the desires of the flesh. 17For what the flesh desires is opposed to the Spirit, and what the Spirit desires is opposed to the flesh; for these are opposed to each other, to prevent you from doing what you want. 18But if you are led by the Spirit, you are not subject to the law. 19Now the works of the flesh are obvious: fornication, impurity, licentiousness, 20idolatry, sorcery, enmities, strife, jealousy, anger, quarrels, dissensions, factions, 21envy,[e]

---

[a]Other ancient authorities read we [b]Gk brothers [c]Or made effective [d]Gk the flesh [e]Other ancient authorities add murder

drunkenness, carousing, and things like these. I am warning you, as I warned you before: those who do such things will not inherit the kingdom of God.

22 By contrast, the fruit of the Spirit is love, joy, peace, patience, kindness, generosity, faithfulness, [23]gentleness, and self-control. There is no law against such things. [24]And those who belong to Christ Jesus have crucified the flesh with its passions and desires. [25]If we live by the Spirit, let us also be guided by the Spirit. [26]Let us not become conceited, competing against one another, envying one another.

6 My friends,[a] if anyone is detected in a transgression, you who have received the Spirit should restore such a one in a spirit of gentleness. Take care that you yourselves are not tempted. [2]Bear one another's burdens, and in this way you will fulfill[b] the law of Christ. [3]For if those who are nothing think they are something, they deceive themselves. [4]All must test their own work; then that work, rather than their neighbor's work, will become a cause for pride. [5]For all must carry their own loads.

6 Those who are taught the word must share in all good things with their teacher.

7 Do not be deceived; God is not mocked, for you reap whatever you sow. [8]If you sow to your own flesh, you will reap corruption from the flesh; but if you sow to the Spirit, you will reap eternal life from the Spirit. [9]So let us not grow weary in doing what is right, for we will reap at harvest time, if we do not give up. [10]So then, whenever we have an opportunity, let us work for the good of all, and especially for those of the family of faith.

11 See what large letters I make when I am writing in my own hand! [12]It is those who want to make a good showing in the flesh that try to compel you to be circumcised—only that they may not be persecuted for the cross of Christ. [13]Even the circumcised do not themselves obey the law, but they want you to be circumcised so that they may boast about your flesh. [14]May I never boast of anything except the cross of our Lord Jesus Christ, by which[c] the world has been crucified to me, and I to the world. [15]For[d] neither circumcision nor uncircumcision is anything; but a new creation is everything! [16]As for those who will follow this rule—peace be upon them, and mercy, and upon the Israel of God.

17 From now on, let no one make trouble for me; for I carry the marks of Jesus branded on my body.

18 May the grace of our Lord Jesus Christ be with your spirit, brothers and sisters.[e] Amen.

---

[a]Gk *Brothers* [b]Other ancient authorities read *in this way fulfill* [c]Or *through whom* [d]Other ancient authorities add *in Christ Jesus* [e]Gk *brothers*

The Letter of Paul to the

EPHESIANS

1 Paul, an apostle of Christ Jesus by the will of God,

To the saints who are in Ephesus and are faithful[a] in Christ Jesus:

2 Grace to you and peace from God our Father and the Lord Jesus Christ.

3 Blessed be the God and Father of our Lord Jesus Christ, who has blessed us in Christ with every spiritual blessing in the heavenly places, [4]just as he chose us in Christ[b] before the foundation of the world to be holy and blameless before him in love. [5]He destined us for adoption as his children through Jesus Christ, according to the good pleasure of his will, [6]to the praise of his glorious grace that he freely bestowed on us in the Beloved. [7]In him we have redemption through his blood, the forgiveness of our trespasses, according to the riches of his grace [8]that he lavished on us. With all wisdom and insight [9]he has made known to us the mystery of his will, according to his good pleasure that he set forth in Christ, [10]as a plan for the fullness of time, to gather up all things in him, things in heaven and things on earth. [11]In Christ we have also obtained an inheritance,[c] having been destined according to the purpose of him who accomplishes all things according to his counsel and will, [12]so that we, who were the first to set our hope on Christ, might live for the praise of his glory. [13]In him you also, when you had heard the word of truth, the gospel of your salvation, and had believed in him, were marked with the seal of the promised Holy Spirit; [14]this[d] is the pledge of our inheritance toward redemption as God's own people, to the praise of his glory.

15 I have heard of your faith in the Lord Jesus and your love[e] toward all the saints, and for this reason [16]I do not cease to give thanks for you as I remember you in my prayers. [17]I pray that the God of our Lord Jesus Christ, the Father of glory, may give you a spirit of wisdom and revelation as you come to know him, [18]so that, with the eyes of your heart enlightened, you may know what is the hope to which he has called you, what are the riches of his glorious inheritance among the saints, [19]and what is the immeasurable greatness of his power for us who believe, according to the working of his great power. [20]God[f] put this power

---

[a]Other ancient authorities lack *in Ephesus,* reading *saints who are also faithful* [b]Gk *in him* [c]Or *been made a heritage* [d]Other ancient authorities read *who* [e]Other ancient authorities lack *and your love* [f]Gk *He*

to work in Christ when he raised him from the dead and seated him at his right hand in the heavenly places, [21]far above all rule and authority and power and dominion, and above every name that is named, not only in this age but also in the age to come. [22]And he has put all things under his feet and has made him the head over all things for the church, [23]which is his body, the fullness of him who fills all in all.

2 You were dead through the trespasses and sins [2]in which you once lived, following the course of this world, following the ruler of the power of the air, the spirit that is now at work among those who are disobedient. [3]All of us once lived among them in the passions of our flesh, following the desires of flesh and senses, and we were by nature children of wrath, like everyone else. [4]But God, who is rich in mercy, out of the great love with which he loved us [5]even when we were dead through our trespasses, made us alive together with Christ[a]—by grace you have been saved— [6]and raised us up with him and seated us with him in the heavenly places in Christ Jesus, [7]so that in the ages to come he might show the immeasurable riches of his grace in kindness toward us in Christ Jesus. [8]For by grace you have been saved through faith, and this is not your own doing; it is the gift of God— [9]not the result of works, so that no one may boast. [10]For we are what he has made us, created

in Christ Jesus for good works, which God prepared beforehand to be our way of life.

11 So then, remember that at one time you Gentiles by birth,[b] called "the uncircumcision" by those who are called "the circumcision"—a physical circumcision made in the flesh by human hands— [12]remember that you were at that time without Christ, being aliens from the commonwealth of Israel, and strangers to the covenants of promise, having no hope and without God in the world. [13]But now in Christ Jesus you who once were far off have been brought near by the blood of Christ. [14]For he is our peace; in his flesh he has made both groups into one and has broken down the dividing wall, that is, the hostility between us. [15]He has abolished the law with its commandments and ordinances, that he might create in himself one new humanity in place of the two, thus making peace, [16]and might reconcile both groups to God in one body[c] through the cross, thus putting to death that hostility through it.[d] [17]So he came and proclaimed peace to you who were far off and peace to those who were near; [18]for through him both of us have access in one Spirit to the Father. [19]So then you are no longer strangers and aliens, but you are citizens with the saints and also

[a]Other ancient authorities read *in Christ* [b]Gk *in the flesh* [c]Or *reconcile both of us in one body for God* [d]Or *in him,* or *in himself*

members of the household of God, [20]built upon the foundation of the apostles and prophets, with Christ Jesus himself as the cornerstone.[a] [21]In him the whole structure is joined together and grows into a holy temple in the Lord; [22]in whom you also are built together spiritually[b] into a dwelling place for God.

3 This is the reason that I Paul am a prisoner for[c] Christ Jesus for the sake of you Gentiles— [2]for surely you have already heard of the commission of God's grace that was given me for you, [3]and how the mystery was made known to me by revelation, as I wrote above in a few words, [4]a reading of which will enable you to perceive my understanding of the mystery of Christ. [5]In former generations this mystery[d] was not made known to humankind, as it has now been revealed to his holy apostles and prophets by the Spirit: [6]that is, the Gentiles have become fellow heirs, members of the same body, and sharers in the promise in Christ Jesus through the gospel.

[7] Of this gospel I have become a servant according to the gift of God's grace that was given me by the working of his power. [8]Although I am the very least of all the saints, this grace was given to me to bring to the Gentiles the news of the boundless riches of Christ, [9]and to make everyone see[e] what is the plan of the mystery hidden for ages in[f] God who created all things; [10]so that

through the church the wisdom of God in its rich variety might now be made known to the rulers and authorities in the heavenly places. [11]This was in accordance with the eternal purpose that he has carried out in Christ Jesus our Lord, [12]in whom we have access to God in boldness and confidence through faith in him.[g] [13]I pray therefore that you[h] may not lose heart over my sufferings for you; they are your glory.

[14] For this reason I bow my knees before the Father,[i] [15]from whom every family[j] in heaven and on earth takes its name. [16]I pray that, according to the riches of his glory, he may grant that you may be strengthened in your inner being with power through his Spirit, [17]and that Christ may dwell in your hearts through faith, as you are being rooted and grounded in love. [18]I pray that you may have the power to comprehend, with all the saints, what is the breadth and length and height and depth, [19]and to know the love of Christ that surpasses knowledge, so that you may be filled with all the fullness of God.

[20] Now to him who by the power at work within us is able to accomplish abundantly far more than all we can ask or imagine, [21]to him be glory in the church and in Christ Jesus to all generations, forever and ever. Amen.

[a]Or keystone [b]Gk in the Spirit. [c]Or of [d]Gk it [e]Other ancient authorities read to bring to light [f]Or by [g]Or the faith of him [h]Or I [i]Other ancient authorities add of our Lord Jesus Christ [j]Gk fatherhood

4 I therefore, the prisoner in the Lord, beg you to lead a life worthy of the calling to which you have been called, [2]with all humility and gentleness, with patience, bearing with one another in love, [3]making every effort to maintain the unity of the Spirit in the bond of peace. [4]There is one body and one Spirit, just as you were called to the one hope of your calling, [5]one Lord, one faith, one baptism, [6]one God and Father of all, who is above all and through all and in all.

7 But each of us was given grace according to the measure of Christ's gift. [8]Therefore it is said,

"When he ascended on
 high he made
 captivity itself a
 captive;
he gave gifts to his
 people."

[9](When it says, "He ascended," what does it mean but that he had also descended[a] into the lower parts of the earth? [10]He who descended is the same one who ascended far above all the heavens, so that he might fill all things.) [11]The gifts he gave were that some would be apostles, some prophets, some evangelists, some pastors and teachers, [12]to equip the saints for the work of ministry, for building up the body of Christ, [13]until all of us come to the unity of the faith and of the knowledge of the Son of God, to maturity, to the measure of the full stature of Christ. [14]We must no longer be children, tossed to and fro and blown about by every wind of doctrine, by people's trickery, by their craftiness in deceitful scheming. [15]But speaking the truth in love, we must grow up in every way into him who is the head, into Christ, [16]from whom the whole body, joined and knit together by every ligament with which it is equipped, as each part is working properly, promotes the body's growth in building itself up in love.

17 Now this I affirm and insist on in the Lord: you must no longer live as the Gentiles live, in the futility of their minds. [18]They are darkened in their understanding, alienated from the life of God because of their ignorance and hardness of heart. [19]They have lost all sensitivity and have abandoned themselves to licentiousness, greedy to practice every kind of impurity. [20]That is not the way you learned Christ! [21]For surely you have heard about him and were taught in him, as truth is in Jesus. [22]You were taught to put away your former way of life, your old self, corrupt and deluded by its lusts, [23]and to be renewed in the spirit of your minds, [24]and to clothe yourselves with the new self, created according to the likeness of God in true righteousness and holiness.

25 So then, putting away falsehood, let all of us speak the truth to our neighbors, for we are members of one another. [26]Be angry but do not sin; do not let

---

[a]Other ancient authorities add *first*

the sun go down on your anger, [27]and do not make room for the devil. [28]Thieves must give up stealing; rather let them labor and work honestly with their own hands, so as to have something to share with the needy. [29]Let no evil talk come out of your mouths, but only what is useful for building up,[a] as there is need, so that your words may give grace to those who hear. [30]And do not grieve the Holy Spirit of God, with which you were marked with a seal for the day of redemption. [31]Put away from you all bitterness and wrath and anger and wrangling and slander, together with all malice, [32]and be kind to one another, tenderhearted, forgiving one another, as God in Christ has forgiven you.[b]

5 [1]Therefore be imitators of God, as beloved children, [2]and live in love, as Christ loved us[c] and gave himself up for us, a fragrant offering and sacrifice to God.

3 But fornication and impurity of any kind, or greed, must not even be mentioned among you, as is proper among saints. [4]Entirely out of place is obscene, silly, and vulgar talk; but instead, let there be thanksgiving. [5]Be sure of this, that no fornicator or impure person, or one who is greedy (that is, an idolater), has any inheritance in the kingdom of Christ and of God.

6 Let no one deceive you with empty words, for because of these things the wrath of God comes on those who are disobedient. [7]Therefore do not be associated with them. [8]For once you were darkness, but now in the Lord you are light. Live as children of light— [9]for the fruit of the light is found in all that is good and right and true. [10]Try to find out what is pleasing to the Lord. [11]Take no part in the unfruitful works of darkness, but instead expose them. [12]For it is shameful even to mention what such people do secretly; [13]but everything exposed by the light becomes visible, [14]for everything that becomes visible is light. Therefore it says,

"Sleeper, awake!
  Rise from the dead,
    and Christ will shine
      on you."

15 Be careful then how you live, not as unwise people but as wise, [16]making the most of the time, because the days are evil. [17]So do not be foolish, but understand what the will of the Lord is. [18]Do not get drunk with wine, for that is debauchery; but be filled with the Spirit, [19]as you sing psalms and hymns and spiritual songs among yourselves, singing and making melody to the Lord in your hearts, [20]giving thanks to God the Father at all times and for everything in the name of our Lord Jesus Christ.

21 Be subject to one another out of reverence for Christ.

22 Wives, be subject to your husbands as you are to the Lord. [23]For the husband is the head of

[a]Other ancient authorities read *building up faith* [b]Other ancient authorities read *us* [c]Other ancient authorities read *you*

the wife just as Christ is the head of the church, the body of which he is the Savior. [24]Just as the church is subject to Christ, so also wives ought to be, in everything, to their husbands.

25 Husbands, love your wives, just as Christ loved the church and gave himself up for her, [26]in order to make her holy by cleansing her with the washing of water by the word, [27]so as to present the church to himself in splendor, without a spot or wrinkle or anything of the kind—yes, so that she may be holy and without blemish. [28]In the same way, husbands should love their wives as they do their own bodies. He who loves his wife loves himself. [29]For no one ever hates his own body, but he nourishes and tenderly cares for it, just as Christ does for the church, [30]because we are members of his body.[a] [31]"For this reason a man will leave his father and mother and be joined to his wife, and the two will become one flesh." [32]This is a great mystery, and I am applying it to Christ and the church. [33]Each of you, however, should love his wife as himself, and a wife should respect her husband.

6 Children, obey your parents in the Lord,[b] for this is right. [2]"Honor your father and mother"—this is the first commandment with a promise: [3]"so that it may be well with you and you may live long on the earth."

4 And, fathers, do not provoke your children to anger, but bring them up in the discipline and instruction of the Lord.

5 Slaves, obey your earthly masters with fear and trembling, in singleness of heart, as you obey Christ; [6]not only while being watched, and in order to please them, but as slaves of Christ, doing the will of God from the heart. [7]Render service with enthusiasm, as to the Lord and not to men and women, [8]knowing that whatever good we do, we will receive the same again from the Lord, whether we are slaves or free.

9 And, masters, do the same to them. Stop threatening them, for you know that both of you have the same Master in heaven, and with him there is no partiality.

10 Finally, be strong in the Lord and in the strength of his power. [11]Put on the whole armor of God, so that you may be able to stand against the wiles of the devil. [12]For our[c] struggle is not against enemies of blood and flesh, but against the rulers, against the authorities, against the cosmic powers of this present darkness, against the spiritual forces of evil in the heavenly places. [13]Therefore take up the whole armor of God, so that you may be able to withstand on that evil day, and having done everything, to stand firm. [14]Stand therefore, and fasten the belt of truth around your waist, and put on the breastplate of righteousness. [15]As shoes for your feet put

---

[a]Other ancient authorities add *of his flesh and of his bones* [b]Other ancient authorities lack *in the Lord* [c]Other ancient authorities read *your*

on whatever will make you ready to proclaim the gospel of peace. [16]With all of these,[a] take the shield of faith, with which you will be able to quench all the flaming arrows of the evil one. [17]Take the helmet of salvation, and the sword of the Spirit, which is the word of God.

18 Pray in the Spirit at all times in every prayer and supplication. To that end keep alert and always persevere in supplication for all the saints. [19]Pray also for me, so that when I speak, a message may be given to me to make known with boldness the mystery of the gospel,[b] [20]for which I am an ambassador in chains. Pray that I may declare it boldly, as I must speak.

21 So that you also may know how I am and what I am doing, Tychicus will tell you everything. He is a dear brother and a faithful minister in the Lord. [22]I am sending him to you for this very purpose, to let you know how we are, and to encourage your hearts.

23 Peace be to the whole community,[c] and love with faith, from God the Father and the Lord Jesus Christ. [24]Grace be with all who have an undying love for our Lord Jesus Christ.[d]

[a]Or *In all circumstances* [b]Other ancient authorities lack *of the gospel* [c]Gk *to the brothers* [d]Other ancient authorities add *Amen*

The Letter of Paul to the

PHILIPPIANS

1 Paul and Timothy, servants[a] of Christ Jesus,

To all the saints in Christ Jesus who are in Philippi, with the bishops[b] and deacons:[c]

2 Grace to you and peace from God our Father and the Lord Jesus Christ.

3 I thank my God every time I remember you, [4]constantly praying with joy in every one of my prayers for all of you, [5]because of your sharing in the gospel from the first day until now. [6]I am confident of this, that the one who began a good work among you will bring it to completion by the day of Jesus Christ. [7]It is right for me to think this way about all of you, because you hold me in your heart,[d] for all of you share in God's grace[e] with me, both in my imprisonment and in the defense and confirmation of the

[a]Gk *slaves* [b]Or *overseers* [c]Or *overseers and helpers* [d]Or *because I hold you in my heart* [e]Gk *in grace*

gospel. [8]For God is my witness, how I long for all of you with the compassion of Christ Jesus. [9]And this is my prayer, that your love may overflow more and more with knowledge and full insight [10]to help you to determine what is best, so that in the day of Christ you may be pure and blameless, [11]having produced the harvest of righteousness that comes through Jesus Christ for the glory and praise of God.

12 I want you to know, beloved[a] that what has happened to me has actually helped to spread the gospel, [13]so that it has become known throughout the whole imperial guard[b] and to everyone else that my imprisonment is for Christ; [14]and most of the brothers and sisters,[a] having been made confident in the Lord by my imprisonment, dare to speak the word[c] with greater boldness and without fear.

15 Some proclaim Christ from envy and rivalry, but others from goodwill. [16]These proclaim Christ out of love, knowing that I have been put here for the defense of the gospel; [17]the others proclaim Christ out of selfish ambition, not sincerely but intending to increase my suffering in my imprisonment. [18]What does it matter? Just this, that Christ is proclaimed in every way, whether out of false motives or true; and in that I rejoice.

Yes, and I will continue to rejoice, [19]for I know that through your prayers and the help of the Spirit of Jesus Christ this will turn out for my deliverance. [20]It is my eager expectation and hope that I will not be put to shame in any way, but that by my speaking with all boldness, Christ will be exalted now as always in my body, whether by life or by death. [21]For to me, living is Christ and dying is gain. [22]If I am to live in the flesh, that means fruitful labor for me; and I do not know which I prefer. [23]I am hard pressed between the two: my desire is to depart and be with Christ, for that is far better; [24]but to remain in the flesh is more necessary for you. [25]Since I am convinced of this, I know that I will remain and continue with all of you for your progress and joy in faith, [26]so that I may share abundantly in your boasting in Christ Jesus when I come to you again.

27 Only, live your life in a manner worthy of the gospel of Christ, so that, whether I come and see you or am absent and hear about you, I will know that you are standing firm in one spirit, striving side by side with one mind for the faith of the gospel, [28]and are in no way intimidated by your opponents. For them this is evidence of their destruction, but of your salvation. And this is God's doing. [29]For he has graciously granted you the privilege not only of believing in Christ, but of suffering for him as well— [30]since you are having the same struggle that you saw I had and now hear that I still have.

[a]Gk brothers [b]Gk whole praetorium [c]Other ancient authorities read word of God

2 If then there is any encouragement in Christ, any consolation from love, any sharing in the Spirit, any compassion and sympathy, [2]make my joy complete: be of the same mind, having the same love, being in full accord and of one mind. [3]Do nothing from selfish ambition or conceit, but in humility regard others as better than yourselves. [4]Let each of you look not to your own interests, but to the interests of others. [5]Let the same mind be in you that was[a] in Christ Jesus,

[6] who, though he was in the
form of God,
did not regard equality
with God
as something to be
exploited,

[7] but emptied himself,
taking the form of a slave,
being born in human
likeness.
And being found in human
form,

[8] he humbled himself
and became obedient to
the point of death—
even death on a cross.

[9] Therefore God also highly
exalted him
and gave him the name
that is above every name,

[10] so that at the name of
Jesus
every knee should bend,
in heaven and on earth
and under the earth,

[11] and every tongue should
confess
that Jesus Christ is Lord,

to the glory of God the
Father.

12 Therefore, my beloved, just as you have always obeyed me, not only in my presence, but much more now in my absence, work out your own salvation with fear and trembling; [13]for it is God who is at work in you, enabling you both to will and to work for his good pleasure.

14 Do all things without murmuring and arguing, [15]so that you may be blameless and innocent, children of God without blemish in the midst of a crooked and perverse generation, in which you shine like stars in the world. [16]It is by your holding fast to the word of life that I can boast on the day of Christ that I did not run in vain or labor in vain. [17]But even if I am being poured out as a libation over the sacrifice and the offering of your faith, I am glad and rejoice with all of you— [18]and in the same way you also must be glad and rejoice with me.

19 I hope in the Lord Jesus to send Timothy to you soon, so that I may be cheered by news of you. [20]I have no one like him who will be genuinely concerned for your welfare. [21]All of them are seeking their own interests, not those of Jesus Christ. [22]But Timothy's worth[b] you know, how like a son with a father he has served with me in the work of the gospel. [23]I hope therefore to send him as soon as I see how things

[a]Or *that you have* [b]Gk *his*

go with me; [24]and I trust in the Lord that I will also come soon.

25 Still, I think it necessary to send to you Epaphroditus—my brother and co-worker and fellow soldier, your messenger[a] and minister to my need; [26]for he has been longing for[b] all of you, and has been distressed because you heard that he was ill. [27]He was indeed so ill that he nearly died. But God had mercy on him, and not only on him but on me also, so that I would not have one sorrow after another. [28]I am the more eager to send him, therefore, in order that you may rejoice at seeing him again, and that I may be less anxious. [29]Welcome him then in the Lord with all joy, and honor such people, [30]because he came close to death for the work of Christ,[c] risking his life to make up for those services that you could not give me.

3 Finally, my brothers and sisters,[d] rejoice[e] in the Lord.

To write the same things to you is not troublesome to me, and for you it is a safeguard.

2 Beware of the dogs, beware of the evil workers, beware of those who mutilate the flesh![f] [3]For it is we who are the circumcision, who worship in the Spirit of God[g] and boast in Christ Jesus and have no confidence in the flesh— [4]even though I, too, have reason for confidence in the flesh.

If anyone else has reason to be confident in the flesh, I have more: [5]circumcised on the eighth day, a member of the people of Israel, of the tribe of Benjamin, a Hebrew born of Hebrews; as to the law, a Pharisee; [6]as to zeal, a persecutor of the church; as to righteousness under the law, blameless.

7 Yet whatever gains I had, these I have come to regard as loss because of Christ. [8]More than that, I regard everything as loss because of the surpassing value of knowing Christ Jesus my Lord. For his sake I have suffered the loss of all things, and I regard them as rubbish, in order that I may gain Christ [9]and be found in him, not having a righteousness of my own that comes from the law, but one that comes through faith in Christ,[h] the righteousness from God based on faith. [10]I want to know Christ[i] and the power of his resurrection and the sharing of his sufferings by becoming like him in his death, [11]if somehow I may attain the resurrection from the dead.

12 Not that I have already obtained this or have already reached the goal;[j] but I press on to make it my own, because Christ Jesus has made me his own. [13]Beloved,[k] I do not consider that I have made it my own;[l] but this one thing I do: forgetting what lies behind and straining forward to what lies ahead, [14]I

---

[a]Gk apostle [b]Other ancient authorities read longing to see [c]Other ancient authorities read of the Lord [d]Gk my brothers [e]Or farewell [f]Gk the mutilation [g]Other ancient authorities read worship God in spirit [h]Or through the faith of Christ [i]Gk him [j]Or have already been made perfect [k]Gk Brothers [l]Other ancient authorities read my own yet

press on toward the goal for the prize of the heavenly[a] call of God in Christ Jesus. [15]Let those of us then who are mature be of the same mind; and if you think differently about anything, this too God will reveal to you. [16]Only let us hold fast to what we have attained.

17 Brothers and sisters, join in imitating me, and observe those who live according to the example you have in us. [18]For many live as enemies of the cross of Christ; I have often told you of them, and now I tell you even with tears. [19]Their end is destruction; their god is the belly; and their glory is in their shame; their minds are set on earthly things. [20]But our citizenship[b] is in heaven, and it is from there that we are expecting a Savior, the Lord Jesus Christ. [21]He will transform the body of our humiliation[c] that it may be conformed to the body of his glory,[d] by the power that also enables him to make all things subject to himself.

4 [1]Therefore, my brothers and sisters,[e] whom I love and long for, my joy and crown, stand firm in the Lord in this way, my beloved.

2 I urge Euodia and I urge Syntyche to be of the same mind in the Lord. [3]Yes, and I ask you also, my loyal companion,[f] help these women, for they have struggled beside me in the work of the gospel, together with Clement and the rest of my co-workers, whose names are in the book of life.

4 Rejoice[g] in the Lord always;

again I will say, Rejoice.[g] [5]Let your gentleness be known to everyone. The Lord is near. [6]Do not worry about anything, but in everything by prayer and supplication with thanksgiving let your requests be made known to God. [7]And the peace of God, which surpasses all understanding, will guard your hearts and your minds in Christ Jesus.

8 Finally, beloved,[h] whatever is true, whatever is honorable, whatever is just, whatever is pure, whatever is pleasing, whatever is commendable, if there is any excellence and if there is anything worthy of praise, think about[i] these things. [9]Keep on doing the things that you have learned and received and heard and seen in me, and the God of peace will be with you.

10 I rejoice[j] in the Lord greatly that now at last you have revived your concern for me; indeed, you were concerned for me, but had no opportunity to show it.[k] [11]Not that I am referring to being in need; for I have learned to be content with whatever I have. [12]I know what it is to have little, and I know what it is to have plenty. In any and all circumstances I have learned the secret of being well-fed and of going hungry, of having plenty and of being in need. [13]I can do all things through him who strengthens me.

[a]Gk *upward* [b]Or *commonwealth* [c]Or *our humble bodies* [d]Or *his glorious body* [e]Gk *my brothers* [f]Or *loyal Syzygus* [g]Or *Farewell* [h]Gk *brothers* [i]Gk *take account of* [j]Gk *I rejoiced* [k]Gk lacks *to show it*

[14]In any case, it was kind of you to share my distress.

15 You Philippians indeed know that in the early days of the gospel, when I left Macedonia, no church shared with me in the matter of giving and receiving, except you alone. [16]For even when I was in Thessalonica, you sent me help for my needs more than once. [17]Not that I seek the gift, but I seek the profit that accumulates to your account. [18]I have been paid in full and have more than enough; I am fully satisfied, now that I have received from Epaphroditus the gifts you sent, a fragrant offering, a sacrifice acceptable and pleasing to God. [19]And my God will fully satisfy every need of yours according to his riches in glory in Christ Jesus. [20]To our God and Father be glory forever and ever. Amen.

21 Greet every saint in Christ Jesus. The friends[a] who are with me greet you. [22]All the saints greet you, especially those of the emperor's household.
23 The grace of the Lord Jesus Christ be with your spirit.[b]

---

[a]Gk brothers [b]Other ancient authorities add Amen

The Letter of Paul to the

COLOSSIANS

1 Paul, an apostle of Christ Jesus by the will of God, and Timothy our brother,
2 To the saints and faithful brothers and sisters[a] in Christ in Colossae:
Grace to you and peace from God our Father.

3 In our prayers for you we always thank God, the Father of our Lord Jesus Christ, [4]for we have heard of your faith in Christ Jesus and of the love that you have for all the saints, [5]because of the hope laid up for you in heaven. You have heard of this hope before in the word of the truth, the gospel [6]that has come to you. Just as it is bearing fruit and growing in the whole world, so it has been bearing fruit among yourselves from the day you heard it and truly comprehended the grace of God. [7]This you learned from Epaphras, our beloved fellow servant.[b] He is a faithful minister of Christ on your[c] behalf, [8]and he has made known to us your love in the Spirit.
9 For this reason, since the day

---

[a]Gk brothers [b]Gk slave [c]Other ancient authorities read our

we heard it, we have not ceased praying for you and asking that you may be filled with the knowledge of God's[a] will in all spiritual wisdom and understanding, [10]so that you may lead lives worthy of the Lord, fully pleasing to him, as you bear fruit in every good work and as you grow in the knowledge of God. [11]May you be made strong with all the strength that comes from his glorious power, and may you be prepared to endure everything with patience, while joyfully [12]giving thanks to the Father, who has enabled[b] you[c] to share in the inheritance of the saints in the light. [13]He has rescued us from the power of darkness and transferred us into the kingdom of his beloved Son, [14]in whom we have redemption, the forgiveness of sins.[d]

15 He is the image of the invisible God, the firstborn of all creation; [16]for in[e] him all things in heaven and on earth were created, things visible and invisible, whether thrones or dominions or rulers or powers—all things have been created through him and for him. [17]He himself is before all things, and in[e] him all things hold together. [18]He is the head of the body, the church; he is the beginning, the firstborn from the dead, so that he might come to have first place in everything. [19]For in him all the fullness of God was pleased to dwell, [20]and through him God was pleased to reconcile to himself all things, whether on earth or in heaven, by making peace through the blood of his cross. [21]And you who were once

estranged and hostile in mind, doing evil deeds, [22]he has now reconciled[f] in his fleshly body[g] through death, so as to present you holy and blameless and irreproachable before him— [23]provided that you continue securely established and steadfast in the faith, without shifting from the hope promised by the gospel that you heard, which has been proclaimed to every creature under heaven. I, Paul, became a servant of this gospel.

24 I am now rejoicing in my sufferings for your sake, and in my flesh I am completing what is lacking in Christ's afflictions for the sake of his body, that is, the church. [25]I became its servant according to God's commission that was given to me for you, to make the word of God fully known, [26]the mystery that has been hidden throughout the ages and generations but has now been revealed to his saints. [27]To them God chose to make known how great among the Gentiles are the riches of the glory of this mystery, which is Christ in you, the hope of glory. [28]It is he whom we proclaim, warning everyone and teaching everyone in all wisdom, so that we may present everyone mature in Christ. [29]For this I toil and struggle with all the energy that he powerfully inspires within me.

[a]Gk *his* [b]Other ancient authorities read *called* [c]Other ancient authorities read *us* [d]Other ancient authorities add *through his blood* [e]Or *by* [f]Other ancient authorities read *you have now been reconciled* [g]Gk *in the body of his flesh*

2 For I want you to know how much I am struggling for you, and for those in Laodicea, and for all who have not seen me face to face. ²I want their hearts to be encouraged and united in love, so that they may have all the riches of assured understanding and have the knowledge of God's mystery, that is, Christ himself,ᵃ ³in whom are hidden all the treasures of wisdom and knowledge. ⁴I am saying this so that no one may deceive you with plausible arguments. ⁵For though I am absent in body, yet I am with you in spirit, and I rejoice to see your morale and the firmness of your faith in Christ.

6 As you therefore have received Christ Jesus the Lord, continue to live your livesᵇ in him, ⁷rooted and built up in him and established in the faith, just as you were taught, abounding in thanksgiving.

8 See to it that no one takes you captive through philosophy and empty deceit, according to human tradition, according to the elemental spirits of the universe,ᶜ and not according to Christ. ⁹For in him the whole fullness of deity dwells bodily, ¹⁰and you have come to fullness in him, who is the head of every ruler and authority. ¹¹In him also you were circumcised with a spiritual circumcision,ᵈ by putting off the body of the flesh in the circumcision of Christ; ¹²when you were buried with him in baptism, you were also raised with him through faith in the power of God, who raised him from the dead. ¹³And when you were dead in trespasses and the uncircumcision of your flesh, Godᵉ made youᶠ alive together with him, when he forgave us all our trespasses, ¹⁴erasing the record that stood against us with its legal demands. He set this aside, nailing it to the cross. ¹⁵He disarmedᵍ the rulers and authorities and made a public example of them, triumphing over them in it.

16 Therefore do not let anyone condemn you in matters of food and drink or of observing festivals, new moons, or sabbaths. ¹⁷These are only a shadow of what is to come, but the substance belongs to Christ. ¹⁸Do not let anyone disqualify you, insisting on self-abasement and worship of angels, dwellingʰ on visions,ⁱ puffed up without cause by a human way of thinking,ʲ ¹⁹and not holding fast to the head, from whom the whole body, nourished and held together by its ligaments and sinews, grows with a growth that is from God.

20 If with Christ you died to the elemental spirits of the universe,ᶜ why do you live as if you still belonged to the world? Why do you submit to regulations, ²¹"Do not handle, Do not taste, Do

---

ᵃOther ancient authorities read *of the mystery of God, both of the Father and of Christ* ᵇGk *to walk* ᶜOr *the rudiments of the world* ᵈGk *a circumcision made without hands* ᵉGk *he* ᶠOther ancient authorities read *made us*; others, *made* ᵍOr *divested himself of* ʰOther ancient authorities read *not dwelling* ⁱMeaning of Gk uncertain ʲGk *by the mind of his flesh*

not touch"? [22]All these regulations refer to things that perish with use; they are simply human commands and teachings. [23]These have indeed an appearance of wisdom in promoting self-imposed piety, humility, and severe treatment of the body, but they are of no value in checking self-indulgence.[a]

3 So if you have been raised with Christ, seek the things that are above, where Christ is, seated at the right hand of God. [2]Set your minds on things that are above, not on things that are on earth, [3]for you have died, and your life is hidden with Christ in God. [4]When Christ who is your[b] life is revealed, then you also will be revealed with him in glory.

[5] Put to death, therefore, whatever in you is earthly: fornication, impurity, passion, evil desire, and greed (which is idolatry). [6]On account of these the wrath of God is coming on those who are disobedient.[c] [7]These are the ways you also once followed, when you were living that life.[d] [8]But now you must get rid of all such things—anger, wrath, malice, slander, and abusive[e] language from your mouth. [9]Do not lie to one another, seeing that you have stripped off the old self with its practices [10]and have clothed yourselves with the new self, which is being renewed in knowledge according to the image of its creator. [11]In that renewal[f] there is no longer Greek and Jew, circumcised and uncir-cumcised, barbarian, Scythian, slave and free; but Christ is all and in all!

[12] As God's chosen ones, holy and beloved, clothe yourselves with compassion, kindness, humility, meekness, and patience. [13]Bear with one another and, if anyone has a complaint against another, forgive each other; just as the Lord[g] has forgiven you, so you also must forgive. [14]Above all, clothe yourselves with love, which binds everything together in perfect harmony. [15]And let the peace of Christ rule in your hearts, to which indeed you were called in the one body. And be thankful. [16]Let the word of Christ[h] dwell in you richly; teach and admonish one another in all wisdom; and with gratitude in your hearts sing psalms, hymns, and spiritual songs to God.[i] [17]And whatever you do, in word or deed, do everything in the name of the Lord Jesus, giving thanks to God the Father through him.

[18] Wives, be subject to your husbands, as is fitting in the Lord. [19]Husbands, love your wives and never treat them harshly. [20]Children, obey your parents in everything, for this is your acceptable duty in the Lord. [21]Fathers, do not provoke your children, or they may lose heart. [22]Slaves, obey

[a]Or are of no value, serving only to indulge the flesh [b]Other authorities read our [c]Other ancient authorities lack on those who are disobedient (Gk the children of disobedience) [d]Or living among such people [e]Or filthy [f]Gk its creator, [11]where [g]Other ancient authorities read just as Christ [h]Other ancient authorities read of God, or of the Lord [i]Other ancient authorities read to the Lord

your earthly masters[a] in everything, not only while being watched and in order to please them, but wholeheartedly, fearing the Lord.[a] 23Whatever your task, put yourselves into it, as done for the Lord and not for your masters,[b] 24since you know that from the Lord you will receive the inheritance as your reward; you serve[c] the Lord Christ. 25For the wrongdoer will be paid back for whatever wrong has been done, and there is no partiality.

4 1Masters, treat your slaves justly and fairly, for you know that you also have a Master in heaven.

2 Devote yourselves to prayer, keeping alert in it with thanksgiving. 3At the same time pray for us as well that God will open to us a door for the word, that we may declare the mystery of Christ, for which I am in prison, 4so that I may reveal it clearly, as I should. 5 Conduct yourselves wisely toward outsiders, making the most of the time.[d] 6Let your speech always be gracious, seasoned with salt, so that you may know how you ought to answer everyone.

7 Tychicus will tell you all the news about me; he is a beloved brother, a faithful minister, and a fellow servant[e] in the Lord. 8I have sent him to you for this very purpose, so that you may know how we are[f] and that he may encourage your hearts; 9he is coming with Onesimus, the faithful and beloved brother,

who is one of you. They will tell you about everything here.

10 Aristarchus my fellow prisoner greets you, as does Mark the cousin of Barnabas, concerning whom you have received instructions—if he comes to you, welcome him. 11And Jesus who is called Justus greets you. These are the only ones of the circumcision among my co-workers for the kingdom of God, and they have been a comfort to me. 12Epaphras, who is one of you, a servant[e] of Christ Jesus, greets you. He is always wrestling in his prayers on your behalf, so that you may stand mature and fully assured in everything that God wills. 13For I testify for him that he has worked hard for you and for those in Laodicea and in Hierapolis. 14Luke, the beloved physician, and Demas greet you. 15Give my greetings to the brothers and sisters[g] in Laodicea, and to Nympha and the church in her house. 16And when this letter has been read among you, have it read also in the church of the Laodiceans; and see that you read also the letter from Laodicea. 17And say to Archippus, "See that you complete the task that you have received in the Lord."

18 I, Paul, write this greeting with my own hand. Remember my chains. Grace be with you.[h]

---

[a]In Greek the same word is used for *master* and *Lord* [b]Gk *not for men* [c]Or *You are slaves of,* or *be slaves of* [d]Or *opportunity* [e]Gk *slave* [f]Other authorities read *that I may know how you are* [g]Gk *brothers* [h]Other ancient authorities add *Amen*

The First Letter of Paul to the

THESSALONIANS

1 Paul, Silvanus, and Timothy,

To the church of the Thessalonians in God the Father and the Lord Jesus Christ:

Grace to you and peace.

2 We always give thanks to God for all of you and mention you in our prayers, constantly [3]remembering before our God and Father your work of faith and labor of love and steadfastness of hope in our Lord Jesus Christ. [4]For we know, brothers and sisters[a] beloved by God, that he has chosen you, [5]because our message of the gospel came to you not in word only, but also in power and in the Holy Spirit and with full conviction; just as you know what kind of persons we proved to be among you for your sake. [6]And you became imitators of us and of the Lord, for in spite of persecution you received the word with joy inspired by the Holy Spirit, [7]so that you became an example to all the believers in Macedonia and in Achaia. [8]For the word of the Lord has sounded forth from you not only in Macedonia and Achaia, but in every place your faith in God has become known, so that we have no need to speak about it. [9]For the people of those regions[b] report about us what kind of welcome we had among you, and how you turned to God from idols, to serve a living and true God, [10]and to wait for his Son from heaven, whom he raised from the dead— Jesus, who rescues us from the wrath that is coming.

2 You yourselves know, brothers and sisters,[a] that our coming to you was not in vain, [2]but though we had already suffered and been shamefully mistreated at Philippi, as you know, we had courage in our God to declare to you the gospel of God in spite of great opposition. [3]For our appeal does not spring from deceit or impure motives or trickery, [4]but just as we have been approved by God to be entrusted with the message of the gospel, even so we speak, not to please mortals, but to please God who tests our hearts. [5]As you know and as God is our witness, we never came with words of flattery or with a pretext for greed; [6]nor did we seek praise from mortals, whether from you or from others, [7]though we might have made demands as apostles of Christ. But we were gentle[c] among you, like a nurse tenderly caring for her own children. [8]So deeply do we care for you that we are determined to share with you not only the gospel of God but also our own selves, because you have become very dear to us.

[a]Gk brothers [b]Gk For they [c]Other ancient authorities read infants

9 You remember our labor and toil, brothers and sisters; we worked night and day, so that we might not burden any of you while we proclaimed to you the gospel of God. [10]You are witnesses, and God also, how pure, upright, and blameless our conduct was toward you believers. [11]As you know, we dealt with each one of you like a father with his children, [12]urging and encouraging you and pleading that you lead a life worthy of God, who calls you into his own kingdom and glory.

13 We also constantly give thanks to God for this, that when you received the word of God that you heard from us, you accepted it not as a human word but as what it really is, God's word, which is also at work in you believers. [14]For you, brothers and sisters,[a] became imitators of the churches of God in Christ Jesus that are in Judea, for you suffered the same things from your own compatriots as they did from the Jews, [15]who killed both the Lord Jesus and the prophets,[b] and drove us out; they displease God and oppose everyone [16]by hindering us from speaking to the Gentiles so that they may be saved. Thus they have constantly been filling up the measure of their sins; but God's wrath has overtaken them at last.[c]

17 As for us, brothers and sisters, when, for a short time, we were made orphans by being separated from you—in person, not ⸰ ⸰eart—we longed with great ⸰ ⸰ess to see you face to face.

[18]For we wanted to come to you—certainly I, Paul, wanted to again and again—but Satan blocked our way. [19]For what is our hope or joy or crown of boasting before our Lord Jesus at his coming? Is it not you? [20]Yes, you are our glory and joy!

3 Therefore when we could bear it no longer, we decided to be left alone in Athens; [2]and we sent Timothy, our brother and co-worker for God in proclaiming[d] the gospel of Christ, to strengthen and encourage you for the sake of your faith, [3]so that no one would be shaken by these persecutions. Indeed, you yourselves know that this is what we are destined for. [4]In fact, when we were with you, we told you beforehand that we were to suffer persecution; so it turned out, as you know. [5]For this reason, when I could bear it no longer, I sent to find out about your faith; I was afraid that somehow the tempter had tempted you and that our labor had been in vain.

6 But Timothy has just now come to us from you, and has brought us the good news of your faith and love. He has told us also that you always remember us kindly and long to see us—just as we long to see you. [7]For this reason, brothers and sisters,[a] during all our distress and persecution we have been encouraged about you through your faith. [8]For

---

[a]Gk brothers [b]Other ancient authorities read their own prophets [c]Or completely or forever [d]Gk lacks proclaiming

we now live, if you continue to stand firm in the Lord. 9How can we thank God enough for you in return for all the joy that we feel before our God because of you? 10Night and day we pray most earnestly that we may see you face to face and restore whatever is lacking in your faith.

11 Now may our God and Father himself and our Lord Jesus direct our way to you. 12And may the Lord make you increase and abound in love for one another and for all, just as we abound in love for you. 13And may he so strengthen your hearts in holiness that you may be blameless before our God and Father at the coming of our Lord Jesus with all his saints.

4 Finally, brothers and sisters, we ask and urge you in the Lord Jesus that, as you learned from us how you ought to live and to please God (as, in fact, you are doing), you should do so more and more. 2For you know what instructions we gave you through the Lord Jesus. 3For this is the will of God, your sanctification: that you abstain from fornication; 4that each one of you know how to control your own body*a* in holiness and honor, 5not with lustful passion, like the Gentiles who do not know God; 6that no one wrong or exploit a brother or sister*b* in this matter, because the Lord is an avenger in all these things, just as we have already told you beforehand and solemnly warned you. 7For God

did not call us to impurity but in holiness. 8Therefore whoever rejects this rejects not human authority but God, who also gives his Holy Spirit to you.

9 Now concerning love of the brothers and sisters,*c* you do not need to have anyone write to you, for you yourselves have been taught by God to love one another; 10and indeed you do love all the brothers and sisters throughout Macedonia. But we urge you, beloved, to do so more and more, 11to aspire to live quietly, to mind your own affairs, and to work with your hands, as we directed you, 12so that you may behave properly toward outsiders and be dependent on no one.

13 But we do not want you to be uninformed, brothers and sisters,*c* about those who have died,*d* so that you may not grieve as others do who have no hope. 14For since we believe that Jesus died and rose again, even so, through Jesus, God will bring with him those who have died.*d* 15For this we declare to you by the word of the Lord, that we who are alive, who are left until the coming of the Lord, will by no means precede those who have died.*d* 16For the Lord himself, with a cry of command, with the archangel's call and with the sound of God's trumpet, will descend from heaven, and the dead in Christ will rise first. 17Then we who are alive,

*a*Or how to take a wife for himself *b*Gk brother *c*Gk brothers *d*Gk fallen asleep

who are left, will be caught up in the clouds together with them to meet the Lord in the air; and so we will be with the Lord forever. [18]Therefore encourage one another with these words.

5 Now concerning the times and the seasons, brothers and sisters,[a] you do not need to have anything written to you. [2]For you yourselves know very well that the day of the Lord will come like a thief in the night. [3]When they say, "There is peace and security," then sudden destruction will come upon them, as labor pains come upon a pregnant woman, and there will be no escape! [4]But you, beloved,[a] are not in darkness, for that day to surprise you like a thief; [5]for you are all children of light and children of the day; we are not of the night or of darkness. [6]So then let us not fall asleep as others do, but let us keep awake and be sober; [7]for those who sleep sleep at night, and those who are drunk get drunk at night. [8]But since we belong to the day, let us be sober, and put on the breastplate of faith and love, and for a helmet the hope of salvation. [9]For God has destined us not for wrath but for obtaining salvation through our Lord Jesus Christ, [10]who died for us, so that whether we are awake or asleep we may live with him. [11]Therefore encourage one another and build up each other, as indeed you are doing.

12 But we appeal to you, brothers and sisters,[a] to respect those who labor among you, and have charge of you in the Lord and admonish you; [13]esteem them very highly in love because of their work. Be at peace among yourselves. [14]And we urge you, beloved,[a] to admonish the idlers, encourage the faint hearted, help the weak, be patient with all of them. [15]See that none of you repays evil for evil, but always seek to do good to one another and to all. [16]Rejoice always, [17]pray without ceasing, [18]give thanks in all circumstances; for this is the will of God in Christ Jesus for you. [19]Do not quench the Spirit. [20]Do not despise the words of prophets,[b] [21]but test everything; hold fast to what is good; [22]abstain from every form of evil.

23 May the God of peace himself sanctify you entirely; and may your spirit and soul and body be kept sound[c] and blameless at the coming of our Lord Jesus Christ. [24]The one who calls you is faithful, and he will do this.

25 Beloved,[d] pray for us.

26 Greet all the brothers and sisters[a] with a holy kiss. [27]I solemnly command you by the Lord that this letter be read to all of them.[e]

28 The grace of our Lord Jesus Christ be with you.[f]

---

[a]Gk brothers [b]Gk despise prophecies [c]Or complete
[d]Gk Brothers [e]Gk to all the brothers [f]Other ancient
authorities add Amen

The Second Letter of Paul to the

THESSALONIANS

1 Paul, Silvanus, and Timothy,
To the church of the
Thessalonians in God our Father
and the Lord Jesus Christ:

2 Grace to you and peace from
God our[a] Father and the Lord
Jesus Christ.

3 We must always give thanks
to God for you, brothers and sisters,[b] as is right, because your
faith is growing abundantly, and
the love of everyone of you for
one another is increasing. [4]Therefore we ourselves boast of you
among the churches of God for
your steadfastness and faith during all your persecutions and the
afflictions that you are enduring.

5 This is evidence of the righteous judgment of God, and is
intended to make you worthy of
the kingdom of God, for which
you are also suffering. [6]For it is
indeed just of God to repay with
affliction those who afflict you,
[7]and to give relief to the afflicted
as well as to us, when the Lord
Jesus is revealed from heaven
with his mighty angels [8]in flaming fire, inflicting vengeance on
those who do not know God and
on those who do not obey the
gospel of our Lord Jesus. [9]These
will suffer the punishment of
eternal destruction, separated
from the presence of the Lord
and from the glory of his might,
[10]when he comes to be glorified
by his saints and to be marveled

at on that day among all who
have believed, because our testimony to you was believed. [11]To
this end we always pray for you,
asking that our God will make
you worthy of his call and will
fulfill by his power every good
resolve and work of faith, [12]so
that the name of our Lord Jesus
may be glorified in you, and you
in him, according to the grace of
our God and the Lord Jesus Christ.

2 As to the coming of our Lord
Jesus Christ and our being
gathered together to him, we beg
you, brothers and sisters,[b] [2]not to
be quickly shaken in mind or
alarmed, either by spirit or by
word or by letter, as though from
us, to the effect that the day of
the Lord is already here. [3]Let no
one deceive you in any way; for
that day will not come unless
the rebellion comes first and the
lawless one[c] is revealed, the one
destined for destruction.[d] [4]He
opposes and exalts himself above
every so-called god or object of
worship, so that he takes his seat
in the temple of God, declaring
himself to be God. [5]Do you not
remember that I told you these
things when I was still with you?
[6]And you know what is now
restraining him, so that he may be

---

[a]Other ancient authorities read *the* [b]Gk *brothers* [c]Gk
the man of lawlessness; other ancient authorities read
the man of sin [d]Gk *the son of destruction*

296

revealed when his time comes. [7]For the mystery of lawlessness is already at work, but only until the one who now restrains it is removed. [8]And then the lawless one will be revealed, whom the Lord Jesus[a] will destroy[b] with the breath of his mouth, annihilating him by the manifestation of his coming. [9]The coming of the lawless one is apparent in the working of Satan, who uses all power, signs, lying wonders, [10]and every kind of wicked deception for those who are perishing, because they refused to love the truth and so be saved. [11]For this reason God sends them a powerful delusion, leading them to believe what is false, [12]so that all who have not believed the truth but took pleasure in unrighteousness will be condemned.

[13] But we must always give thanks to God for you, brothers and sisters[c] beloved by the Lord, because God chose you as the first fruits[d] for salvation through sanctification by the Spirit and through belief in the truth. [14]For this purpose he called you through our proclamation of the good news,[e] so that you may obtain the glory of our Lord Jesus Christ. [15]So then, brothers and sisters,[c] stand firm and hold fast to the traditions that you were taught by us, either by word of mouth or by our letter.

[16] Now may our Lord Jesus Christ himself and God our Father, who loved us and through grace gave us eternal comfort and good hope, [17]comfort your hearts

and strengthen them in every good work and word.

3 Finally, brothers and sisters,[c] pray for us, so that the word of the Lord may spread rapidly and be glorified everywhere, just as it is among you, [2]and that we may be rescued from wicked and evil people; for not all have faith. [3]But the Lord is faithful; he will strengthen you and guard you from the evil one.[f] [4]And we have confidence in the Lord concerning you, that you are doing and will go on doing the things that we command. [5]May the Lord direct your hearts to the love of God and to the steadfastness of Christ.

[6] Now we command you, beloved,[c] in the name of our Lord Jesus Christ, to keep away from believers who are[g] living in idleness and not according to the tradition that they[h] received from us. [7]For you yourselves know how you ought to imitate us; we were not idle when we were with you, [8]and we did not eat anyone's bread without paying for it; but with toil and labor we worked night and day, so that we might not burden any of you. [9]This was not because we do not have that right, but in order to give you an example to imitate. [10]For even when we were with you, we gave you this command: Anyone unwilling to work should

---

[a]Other ancient authorities lack *Jesus* [b]Other ancient authorities read *consume* [c]Gk *brothers* [d]Other ancient authorities read *from the beginning* [e]Or *through our gospel* [f]Or *from evil* [g]Gk *from every brother who is* [h]Other ancient authorities read *you*

not eat. ¹¹For we hear that some of you are living in idleness, mere busybodies, not doing any work. ¹²Now such persons we command and exhort in the Lord Jesus Christ to do their work quietly and to earn their own living. ¹³Brothers and sisters,[a] do not be weary in doing what is right.

14 Take note of those who do not obey what we say in this letter; have nothing to do with them, so that they may be ashamed. ¹⁵Do not regard them as enemies, but warn them as believers.[b]

16 Now may the Lord of peace himself give you peace at all times in all ways. The Lord be with all of you.

17 I, Paul, write this greeting with my own hand. This is the mark in every letter of mine; it is the way I write. ¹⁸The grace of our Lord Jesus Christ be with all of you.[c]

[a]Gk Brothers [b]Gk a brother [c]Other ancient authorities add Amen

The First Letter of Paul to
TIMOTHY

1 Paul, an apostle of Christ Jesus by the command of God our Savior and of Christ Jesus our hope,

2 To Timothy, my loyal child in the faith: Grace, mercy, and peace from God the Father and Christ Jesus our Lord.

3 I urge you, as I did when I was on my way to Macedonia, to remain in Ephesus so that you may instruct certain people not to teach any different doctrine, ⁴and not to occupy themselves with myths and endless genealogies that promote speculations rather than the divine training[a] that is known by faith. ⁵But the aim of such instruction is love that comes from a pure heart, a good conscience, and sincere faith. ⁶Some people have deviated from these and turned to meaningless talk, ⁷desiring to be teachers of the law, without understanding either what they are saying or the things about which they make assertions.

8 Now we know that the law is good, if one uses it legitimately. ⁹This means understanding that the law is laid down not for the innocent but for the lawless and disobedient, for the godless and sinful, for the unholy and profane, for those who kill their father or mother, for murderers,

[a]Or plan

298

[10]fornicators, sodomites, slave traders, liars, perjurers, and whatever else is contrary to the sound teaching [11]that conforms to the glorious gospel of the blessed God, which he entrusted for me.

12 I am grateful to Christ Jesus our Lord, who has strengthened me, because he judged me faithful and appointed me to his service, [13]even though I was formerly a blasphemer, a persecutor, and a man of violence. But I received mercy because I had acted ignorantly in unbelief, [14]and the grace of our Lord overflowed for me with the faith and love that are in Christ Jesus. [15]The saying is sure and worthy of full acceptance, that Christ Jesus came into the world to save sinners—of whom I am the foremost. [16]But for that very reason I received mercy, so that in me, as the foremost, Jesus Christ might display the utmost patience, making me an example to those who would come to believe in him for eternal life. [17]To the King of the ages, immortal, invisible, the only God, be honor and glory forever and ever.[a] Amen.

18 I am giving you these instructions, Timothy, my child, in accordance with the prophecies made earlier about you, so that by following them you may fight the good fight, [19]having faith and a good conscience. By rejecting conscience, certain persons have suffered shipwreck in the faith; [20]among them are Hymenaeus and Alexander, whom I have turned over to Satan, so that they may learn not to blaspheme.

2 First of all, then, I urge that supplications, prayers, intercessions, and thanksgivings be made for everyone, [2]for kings and all who are in high positions, so that we may lead a quiet and peaceable life in all godliness and dignity. [3]This is right and is acceptable in the sight of God our Savior, [4]who desires everyone to be saved and to come to the knowledge of the truth. [5]For

there is one God;
there is also one
mediator between
God and humankind,
Christ Jesus, himself
human,
[6] who gave himself a
ransom for all

—this was attested at the right time. [7]For this I was appointed a herald and an apostle (I am telling the truth,[b] I am not lying), a teacher of the Gentiles in faith and truth.

8 I desire, then, that in every place the men should pray, lifting up holy hands without anger or argument; [9]also that the women should dress themselves modestly and decently in suitable clothing, not with their hair braided, or with gold, pearls, or expensive clothes, [10]but with good works, as is proper for women who profess reverence for God. [11]Let a woman[c] learn in

[a]Gk to the ages of the ages [b]Other ancient authorities add in Christ [c]Or wife

299

silence with full submission. [12]I permit no woman[a] to teach or to have authority over a man;[b] she is to keep silent. [13]For Adam was formed first, then Eve; [14]and Adam was not deceived, but the woman was deceived and became a transgressor. [15]Yet she will be saved through childbearing, provided they continue in faith and love and holiness, with modesty.

3 The saying is sure:[c] whoever aspires to the office of bishop[d] desires a noble task. [2]Now a bishop[e] must be above reproach, married only once,[f] temperate, sensible, respectable, hospitable, an apt teacher, [3]not a drunkard, not violent but gentle, not quarrelsome, and not a lover of money. [4]He must manage his own household well, keeping his children submissive and respectful in every way— [5]for if someone does not know how to manage his own household, how can he take care of God's church? [6]He must not be a recent convert, or he may be puffed up with conceit and fall into the condemnation of the devil. [7]Moreover, he must be well thought of by outsiders, so that he may not fall into disgrace and the snare of the devil.

[8] Deacons likewise must be serious, not double-tongued, not indulging in much wine, not greedy for money; [9]they must hold fast to the mystery of the faith with a clear conscience. [10]And let them first be tested; then, if they prove themselves blameless, let them serve as deacons. [11]Women[g] likewise must be

serious, not slanderers, but temperate, faithful in all things. [12]Let deacons be married only once,[h] and let them manage their children and their households well; [13]for those who serve well as deacons gain a good standing for themselves and great boldness in the faith that is in Christ Jesus.

14 I hope to come to you soon, but I am writing these instructions to you so that, [15]if I am delayed, you may know how one ought to behave in the household of God, which is the church of the living God, the pillar and bulwark of the truth. [16]Without any doubt, the mystery of our religion is great:

He[i] was revealed in flesh,
vindicated[j] in spirit,[k]
seen by angels,
proclaimed among
Gentiles,
believed in throughout
the world,
taken up in glory.

4 Now the Spirit expressly says that in later[l] times some will renounce the faith by paying attention to deceitful spirits and teachings of demons, [2]through the hypocrisy of liars whose consciences are seared with a hot iron. [3]They forbid marriage and demand abstinence from foods, which God created to

[a]Or *wife* [b]Or *husband* [c]Some interpreters place these words at the end of the previous paragraph. Other ancient authorities read *The saying is commonly accepted* [d]Or *overseer* [e]Or *an overseer* [f]Gk *the husband of one wife* [g]Or *Their wives,* or *Women deacons* [h]Gk *be husbands of one wife* [i]Gk *Who;* other ancient authorities read *God;* others, *Which* [j]Or *justified* [k]Or *by the Spirit* [l]Or *the last*

be received with thanksgiving by those who believe and know the truth. [4]For everything created by God is good, and nothing is to be rejected, provided it is received with thanksgiving; [5]for it is sanctified by God's word and by prayer.

6 If you put these instructions before the brothers and sisters,[a] you will be a good servant[b] of Christ Jesus, nourished on the words of the faith and of the sound teaching that you have followed. [7]Have nothing to do with profane myths and old wives' tales. Train yourself in godliness, [8]for, while physical training is of some value, godliness is valuable in every way, holding promise for both the present life and the life to come. [9]The saying is sure and worthy of full acceptance. [10]For to this end we toil and struggle,[c] because we have our hope set on the living God, who is the Savior of all people, especially of those who believe.

11 These are the things you must insist on and teach. [12]Let no one despise your youth, but set the believers an example in speech and conduct, in love, in faith, in purity. [13]Until I arrive, give attention to the public reading of scripture,[d] to exhorting, to teaching. [14]Do not neglect the gift that is in you, which was given to you through prophecy with the laying on of hands by the council of elders.[e] [15]Put these things into practice, devote yourself to them, so that all may see your progress. [16]Pay close attention to yourself and to your teaching; continue in these things, for in doing this you will save both yourself and your hearers.

5 Do not speak harshly to an older man,[f] but speak to him as to a father, to younger men as brothers, [2]to older women as mothers, to younger women as sisters—with absolute purity.

3 Honor widows who are really widows. [4]If a widow has children or grandchildren, they should first learn their religious duty to their own family and make some repayment to their parents; for this is pleasing in God's sight. [5]The real widow, left alone, has set her hope on God and continues in supplications and prayers night and day; [6]but the widow[g] who lives for pleasure is dead even while she lives. [7]Give these commands as well, so that they may be above reproach. [8]And whoever does not provide for relatives, and especially for family members, has denied the faith and is worse than an unbeliever.

9 Let a widow be put on the list if she is not less than sixty years old and has been married only once;[h] [10]she must be well attested for her good works, as one who has brought up children, shown hospitality, washed the saints' feet, helped the afflicted, and devoted herself to doing good in every way. [11]But refuse to put younger widows on the list;

---

[a]Gk brothers [b]Or deacon [c]Other ancient authorities read suffer reproach [d]Gk to the reading [e]Gk by the presbytery [f]Or an elder, or a presbyter [g]Gk she [h]Gk the wife of one husband

for when their sensual desires alienate them from Christ, they want to marry, ¹²and so they incur condemnation for having violated their first pledge. ¹³Besides that, they learn to be idle, gadding about from house to house; and they are not merely idle, but also gossips and busybodies, saying what they should not say. ¹⁴So I would have younger widows marry, bear children, and manage their households, so as to give the adversary no occasion to revile us. ¹⁵For some have already turned away to follow Satan. ¹⁶If any believing woman*ᵃ* has relatives who are really widows, let her assist them; let the church not be burdened, so that it can assist those who are real widows.

17 Let the elders who rule well be considered worthy of double honor,*ᵇ* especially those who labor in preaching and teaching; ¹⁸for the scripture says, "You shall not muzzle an ox while it is treading out the grain," and, "The laborer deserves to be paid." ¹⁹Never accept any accusation against an elder except on the evidence of two or three witnesses. ²⁰As for those who persist in sin, rebuke them in the presence of all, so that the rest also may stand in fear. ²¹In the presence of God and of Christ Jesus and of the elect angels, I warn you to keep these instructions without prejudice, doing nothing on the basis of partiality. ²²Do not ordain*ᶜ* anyone hastily, and do not participate in the sins of others; keep yourself pure.

23 No longer drink only water, but take a little wine for the sake of your stomach and your frequent ailments.

24 The sins of some people are conspicuous and precede them to judgment, while the sins of others follow them there. ²⁵So also good works are conspicuous; and even when they are not, they cannot remain hidden.

6 Let all who are under the yoke of slavery regard their masters as worthy of all honor, so that the name of God and the teaching may not be blasphemed. ²Those who have believing masters must not be disrespectful to them on the ground that they are members of the church;*ᵈ* rather they must serve them all the more, since those who benefit by their service are believers and beloved.*ᵉ*

Teach and urge these duties. ³Whoever teaches otherwise and does not agree with the sound words of our Lord Jesus Christ and the teaching that is in accordance with godliness, ⁴is conceited, understanding nothing, and has a morbid craving for controversy and for disputes about words. From these come envy, dissension, slander, base suspicions, ⁵and wrangling among those who are depraved in mind and bereft of the truth, imagining that godliness is a means of

---

*ᵃ*Other ancient authorities read *believing man or woman;* others, *believing man* *ᵇ*Or *compensation* *ᶜ*Gk *Do not lay hands on* *ᵈ*Gk *are brothers* *ᵉ*Or *since they are believers and beloved, who devote themselves to good deeds*

gain.[a] [6]Of course, there is great gain in godliness combined with contentment; [7]for we brought nothing into the world, so that[b] we can take nothing out of it; [8]but if we have food and clothing, we will be content with these. [9]But those who want to be rich fall into temptation and are trapped by many senseless and harmful desires that plunge people into ruin and destruction. [10]For the love of money is a root of all kinds of evil, and in their eagerness to be rich some have wandered away from the faith and pierced themselves with many pains.

[11] But as for you, man of God, shun all this; pursue righteousness, godliness, faith, love, endurance, gentleness. [12]Fight the good fight of the faith; take hold of the eternal life, to which you were called and for which you made[c] the good confession in the presence of many witnesses. [13]In the presence of God, who gives life to all things, and of Christ Jesus, who in his testimony before Pontius Pilate made the good confession, I charge you [14]to keep the commandment without spot or blame until the manifestation of our Lord Jesus Christ,

[15]which he will bring about at the right time—he who is the blessed and only Sovereign, the King of kings and Lord of lords. [16]It is he alone who has immortality and dwells in unapproachable light, whom no one has ever seen or can see; to him be honor and eternal dominion. Amen.

17 As for those who in the present age are rich, command them not to be haughty, or to set their hopes on the uncertainty of riches, but rather on God who richly provides us with everything for our enjoyment. [18]They are to do good, to be rich in good works, generous, and ready to share, [19]thus storing up for themselves the treasure of a good foundation for the future, so that they may take hold of the life that really is life.

20 Timothy, guard what has been entrusted to you. Avoid the profane chatter and contradictions of what is falsely called knowledge; [21]by professing it some have missed the mark as regards the faith.

Grace be with you.[d]

[a]Other ancient authorities add *Withdraw yourself from such people* [b]Other ancient authorities read *world—it is certain that* [c]Gk *confessed* [d]The Greek word for *you* here is plural; in other ancient authorities it is singular. Other ancient authorities add *Amen*

The Second Letter of Paul to

TIMOTHY

1 Paul, an apostle of Christ Jesus by the will of God, for the sake of the promise of life that is in Christ Jesus,

2 To Timothy, my beloved child:

Grace, mercy, and peace from God the Father and Christ Jesus our Lord.

3 I am grateful to God—whom I worship with a clear conscience, as my ancestors did—when I remember you constantly in my prayers night and day. [4]Recalling your tears, I long to see you so that I may be filled with joy. [5]I am reminded of your sincere faith, a faith that lived first in your grandmother Lois and your mother Eunice and now, I am sure, lives in you. [6]For this reason I remind you to rekindle the gift of God that is within you through the laying on of my hands; [7]for God did not give us a spirit of cowardice, but rather a spirit of power and of love and of self-discipline.

8 Do not be ashamed, then, of the testimony about our Lord or of me his prisoner, but join with me in suffering for the gospel, relying on the power of God, [9]who saved us and called us with a holy calling, not according to our works but according to his own purpose and grace. This grace was given to us in Christ Jesus before the ages began, [10]but

it has now been revealed through the appearing of our Savior Christ Jesus, who abolished death and brought life and immortality to light through the gospel. [11]For this gospel I was appointed a herald and an apostle and a teacher,[a] [12]and for this reason I suffer as I do. But I am not ashamed, for I know the one in whom I have put my trust, and I am sure that he is able to guard until that day what I have entrusted to him.[b] [13]Hold to the standard of sound teaching that you have heard from me, in the faith and love that are in Christ Jesus. [14]Guard the good treasure entrusted to you, with the help of the Holy Spirit living in us.

15 You are aware that all who are in Asia have turned away from me, including Phygelus and Hermogenes. [16]May the Lord grant mercy to the household of Onesiphorus, because he often refreshed me and was not ashamed of my chain; [17]when he arrived in Rome, he eagerly[c] searched for me and found me [18]—may the Lord grant that he will find mercy from the Lord on that day! And you know very well how much service he rendered in Ephesus.

---

[a]Other ancient authorities add *of the Gentiles* [b]Or *what has been entrusted to me* [c]Or *promptly*

2 You then, my child, be strong in the grace that is in Christ Jesus; [2]and what you have heard from me through many witnesses entrust to faithful people who will be able to teach others as well. [3]Share in suffering like a good soldier of Christ Jesus. [4]No one serving in the army gets entangled in everyday affairs; the soldier's aim is to please the enlisting officer. [5]And in the case of an athlete, no one is crowned without competing according to the rules. [6]It is the farmer who does the work who ought to have the first share of the crops. [7]Think over what I say, for the Lord will give you understanding in all things.

8 Remember Jesus Christ, raised from the dead, a descendant of David—that is my gospel, [9]for which I suffer hardship, even to the point of being chained like a criminal. But the word of God is not chained. [10]Therefore I endure everything for the sake of the elect, so that they may also obtain the salvation that is in Christ Jesus, with eternal glory. [11]The saying is sure:

If we have died with him,
we will also live with
him;
[12] if we endure, we will also
reign with him;
if we deny him, he will
also deny us;
[13] if we are faithless, he
remains faithful—
for he cannot deny himself.

14 Remind them of this, and warn them before God[a] that they are to avoid wrangling over words, which does no good but only ruins those who are listening. [15]Do your best to present yourself to God as one approved by him, a worker who has no need to be ashamed, rightly explaining the word of truth. [16]Avoid profane chatter, for it will lead people into more and more impiety, [17]and their talk will spread like gangrene. Among them are Hymenaeus and Philetus, [18]who have swerved from the truth by claiming that the resurrection has already taken place. They are upsetting the faith of some. [19]But God's firm foundation stands, bearing this inscription: "The Lord knows those who are his," and, "Let everyone who calls on the name of the Lord turn away from wickedness."

20 In a large house there are utensils not only of gold and silver but also of wood and clay, some for special use, some for ordinary. [21]All who cleanse themselves of the things I have mentioned[b] will become special utensils, dedicated and useful to the owner of the house, ready for every good work. [22]Shun youthful passions and pursue righteousness, faith, love, and peace, along with those who call on the Lord from a pure heart. [23]Have nothing to do with stupid and senseless controversies; you know that they breed quarrels. [24]And the Lord's servant[c] must not be quarrelsome but kindly to everyone, an apt teacher, patient,

[a]Other ancient authorities read *the Lord* [b]Gk *of these things* [c]Gk *slave*

[25]correcting opponents with gentleness. God may perhaps grant that they will repent and come to know the truth, [26]and that they may escape from the snare of the devil, having been held captive by him to do his will.[a]

3 You must understand this, that in the last days distressing times will come. [2]For people will be lovers of themselves, lovers of money, boasters, arrogant, abusive, disobedient to their parents, ungrateful, unholy, [3]inhuman, implacable, slanderers, profligates, brutes, haters of good, [4]treacherous, reckless, swollen with conceit, lovers of pleasure rather than lovers of God, [5]holding to the outward form of godliness but denying its power. Avoid them! [6]For among them are those who make their way into households and captivate silly women, overwhelmed by their sins and swayed by all kinds of desires, [7]who are always being instructed and can never arrive at a knowledge of the truth. [8]As Jannes and Jambres opposed Moses, so these people, of corrupt mind and counterfeit faith, also oppose the truth. [9]But they will not make much progress, because, as in the case of those two men,[b] their folly will become plain to everyone.

[10] Now you have observed my teaching, my conduct, my aim in life, my faith, my patience, my love, my steadfastness, [11]my persecutions and suffering the things that happened to me in Antioch, Iconium, and Lystra. What persecutions I endured! Yet the Lord rescued me from all of them. [12]Indeed, all who want to live a godly life in Christ Jesus will be persecuted. [13]But wicked people and impostors will go from bad to worse, deceiving others and being deceived. [14]But as for you, continue in what you have learned and firmly believed, knowing from whom you learned it, [15]and how from childhood you have known the sacred writings that are able to instruct you for salvation through faith in Christ Jesus. [16]All scripture is inspired by God and is[c] useful for teaching, for reproof, for correction, and for training in righteousness, [17]so that everyone who belongs to God may be proficient, equipped for every good work.

4 In the presence of God and of Christ Jesus, who is to judge the living and the dead, and in view of his appearing and his kingdom, I solemnly urge you: [2]proclaim the message; be persistent whether the time is favorable or unfavorable; convince, rebuke, and encourage, with the utmost patience in teaching. [3]For the time is coming when people will not put up with sound doctrine, but having itching ears, they will accumulate for themselves teachers to suit their own desires, [4]and will turn away from listening to the truth and wander away to myths.

[a]Or *by him, to do his* (that is, God's) *will* [b]Gk lacks *two men* [c]Or *Every scripture inspired by God is also*

[5]As for you, always be sober, endure suffering, do the work of an evangelist, carry out your ministry fully.

6 As for me, I am already being poured out as a libation, and the time of my departure has come. [7]I have fought the good fight, I have finished the race, I have kept the faith. [8]From now on there is reserved for me the crown of righteousness, which the Lord, the righteous judge, will give me on that day, and not only to me but also to all who have longed for his appearing.

9 Do your best to come to me soon, [10]for Demas, in love with this present world, has deserted me and gone to Thessalonica; Crescens has gone to Galatia,[a] Titus to Dalmatia. [11]Only Luke is with me. Get Mark and bring him with you, for he is useful in my ministry. [12]I have sent Tychicus to Ephesus. [13]When you come, bring the cloak that I left with Carpus at Troas, also the books, and above all the parchments. [14]Alexander the coppersmith did me great harm; the Lord will pay him back for his deeds. [15]You also must beware of him, for he strongly opposed our message.

16 At my first defense no one came to my support, but all deserted me. May it not be counted against them! [17]But the Lord stood by me and gave me strength, so that through me the message might be fully proclaimed and all the Gentiles might hear it. So I was rescued from the lion's mouth. [18]The Lord will rescue me from every evil attack and save me for his heavenly kingdom. To him be the glory forever and ever. Amen.

19 Greet Prisca and Aquila, and the household of Onesiphorus. [20]Erastus remained in Corinth; Trophimus I left ill in Miletus. [21]Do your best to come before winter. Eubulus sends greetings to you, as do Pudens and Linus and Claudia and all the brothers and sisters.[b]

22 The Lord be with your spirit. Grace be with you.[c]

[a]Other ancient authorities read *Gaul* [b]Gk *all the brothers* [c]The Greek word for *you* here is plural. Other ancient authorities add *Amen*

The Letter of Paul to
TITUS

1 Paul, a servant[a] of God and an apostle of Jesus Christ, for the sake of the faith of God's elect and the knowledge of the truth that is in accordance with godliness, [2]in the hope of eternal life that God, who never lies, promised before the ages began—[3]in due time he revealed his word through the proclamation with which I have been entrusted by the command of God our Savior,

4 To Titus, my loyal child in the faith we share:

Grace[b] and peace from God the Father and Christ Jesus our Savior.

5 I left you behind in Crete for this reason, so that you should put in order what remained to be done, and should appoint elders in every town, as I directed you: [6]someone who is blameless, married only once,[c] whose children are believers, not accused of debauchery and not rebellious. [7]For a bishop,[d] as God's steward, must be blameless; he must not be arrogant or quick-tempered or addicted to wine or violent or greedy for gain; [8]but he must be hospitable, a lover of goodness, prudent, upright, devout, and self-controlled. [9]He must have a firm grasp of the word that is trustworthy in accordance with the teaching, so that he may be able both to preach with sound doctrine and to refute those who contradict it.

10 There are also many rebellious people, idle talkers and deceivers, especially those of the circumcision; [11]they must be silenced, since they are upsetting whole families by teaching for sordid gain what it is not right to teach. [12]It was one of them, their very own prophet, who said,

> "Cretans are always liars,
>   vicious brutes, lazy
>   gluttons."

[13]That testimony is true. For this reason rebuke them sharply, so that they may become sound in the faith, [14]not paying attention to Jewish myths or to commandments of those who reject the truth. [15]To the pure all things are pure, but to the corrupt and unbelieving nothing is pure. Their very minds and consciences are corrupted. [16]They profess to know God, but they deny him by their actions. They are detestable, disobedient, unfit for any good work.

2 But as for you, teach what is consistent with sound doctrine. [2]Tell the older men to be

[a]Gk *slave* [b]Other ancient authorities read *Grace, mercy,* [c]Gk *husband of one wife* [d]Or *an overseer*

temperate, serious, prudent, and sound in faith, in love, and in endurance.

3 Likewise, tell the older women to be reverent in behavior, not to be slanderers or slaves to drink; they are to teach what is good, [4]so that they may encourage the young women to love their husbands, to love their children, [5]to be self-controlled, chaste, good managers of the household, kind, being submissive to their husbands, so that the word of God may not be discredited.

6 Likewise, urge the younger men to be self-controlled. [7]Show yourself in all respects a model of good works, and in your teaching show integrity, gravity, [8]and sound speech that cannot be censured; then any opponent will be put to shame, having nothing evil to say of us.

9 Tell slaves to be submissive to their masters and to give satisfaction in every respect; they are not to talk back, [10]not to pilfer, but to show complete and perfect fidelity, so that in everything they may be an ornament to the doctrine of God our Savior.

11 For the grace of God has appeared, bringing salvation to all,[a] [12]training us to renounce impiety and worldly passions, and in the present age to live lives that are self-controlled, upright, and godly, [13]while we wait for the blessed hope and the manifestation of the glory of our great God and Savior,[b] Jesus Christ. [14]He it is who gave himself for us that he might redeem us from all iniquity and purify for himself a people of his own who are zealous for good deeds.

15 Declare these things; exhort and reprove with all authority.[c] Let no one look down on you.

3 Remind them to be subject to rulers and authorities, to be obedient, to be ready for every good work, [2]to speak evil of no one, to avoid quarreling, to be gentle, and to show every courtesy to everyone. [3]For we ourselves were once foolish, disobedient, led astray, slaves to various passions and pleasures, passing our days in malice and envy, despicable, hating one another. [4]But when the goodness and loving kindness of God our Savior appeared, [5]he saved us, not because of any works of righteousness that we had done, but according to his mercy, through the water[d] of rebirth and renewal by the Holy Spirit. [6]This Spirit he poured out on us richly through Jesus Christ our Savior, [7]so that, having been justified by his grace, we might become heirs according to the hope of eternal life. [8]The saying is sure.

I desire that you insist on these things, so that those who have come to believe in God may be careful to devote themselves to good works; these things are excellent and profitable to everyone. [9]But avoid stupid controversies, genealogies, dissensions, and

---

[a]Or *has appeared to all, bringing salvation* [b]Or *of the great God and our Savior* [c]Gk *commandment* [d]Gk *washing*

quarrels about the law, for they are unprofitable and worthless. [10]After a first and second admonition, have nothing more to do with anyone who causes divisions, [11]since you know that such a person is perverted and sinful, being self-condemned.

12 When I send Artemas to you, or Tychicus, do your best to come to me at Nicopolis, for I have decided to spend the winter there. [13]Make every effort to send Zenas the lawyer and Apollos on their way, and see that they lack nothing. [14]And let people learn to devote themselves to good works in order to meet urgent needs, so that they may not be unproductive.

15 All who are with me send greetings to you. Greet those who love us in the faith.

Grace be with all of you.[a]

[a]Other ancient authorities add *Amen*

The Letter of Paul to

PHILEMON

1 Paul, a prisoner of Christ Jesus, and Timothy our brother,[a]

To Philemon our dear friend and co-worker, [2]to Apphia our sister,[b] to Archippus our fellow soldier, and to the church in your house:

3 Grace to you and peace from God our Father and the Lord Jesus Christ.

4 When I remember you[c] in my prayers, I always thank my God [5]because I hear of your love for all the saints and your faith toward the Lord Jesus. [6]I pray that the sharing of your faith may become effective when you perceive all the good that we[d] may do for Christ. [7]I have indeed received much joy and encouragement from your love, because the hearts of the saints have been refreshed through you, my brother.

8 For this reason, though I am bold enough in Christ to command you to do your duty, [9]yet I would rather appeal to you on the basis of love—and I, Paul, do this as an old man, and now also as a prisoner of Christ Jesus.[e] [10]I am appealing to you for my child, Onesimus, whose father I have become during my imprisonment. [11]Formerly he was useless to you, but now he is indeed useful[f] both to you and to me. [12]I am sending him, that is, my own

[a]Gk *the brother* [b]Gk *the sister* [c]From verse 4 through verse 21, *you* is singular [d]Other ancient authorities read *you* (plural) [e]Or *as an ambassador of Christ Jesus, and now also his prisoner* [f]The name Onesimus means *useful* or (compare verse 20) *beneficial*

heart, back to you. [13]I wanted to keep him with me, so that he might be of service to me in your place during my imprisonment for the gospel; [14]but I preferred to do nothing without your consent, in order that your good deed might be voluntary and not something forced. [15]Perhaps this is the reason he was separated from you for a while, so that you might have him back forever, [16]no longer as a slave but more than a slave, a beloved brother—especially to me but how much more to you, both in the flesh and in the Lord.

17 So if you consider me your partner, welcome him as you would welcome me. [18]If he has wronged you in any way, or owes you anything, charge that to my account. [19]I, Paul, am writing this with my own hand: I will repay it. I say nothing about your owing me even your own self. [20]Yes, brother, let me have this benefit from you in the Lord! Refresh my heart in Christ. [21]Confident of your obedience, I am writing to you, knowing that you will do even more than I say.

22 One thing more—prepare a guest room for me, for I am hoping through your prayers to be restored to you.

23 Epaphras, my fellow prisoner in Christ Jesus, sends greetings to you,[a] [24]and so do Mark, Aristarchus, Demas, and Luke, my fellow workers.

25 The grace of the Lord Jesus Christ be with your spirit.[b]

[a]Here *you* is singular. [b]Other ancient authorities add *Amen*

The Letter to the

HEBREWS

1 Long ago God spoke to our ancestors in many and various ways by the prophets, [2]but in these last days he has spoken to us by a Son,[a] whom he appointed heir of all things, through whom he also created the worlds. [3]He is the reflection of God's glory and the exact imprint of God's very being, and he sustains[b] all things by his powerful word. When he had made purification for sins, he sat down at the right hand of the Majesty on high, [4]having become as much superior to angels as the name he has inherited is more excellent than theirs.

5 For to which of the angels did God ever say,

"You are my Son;
today I have begotten you"?

Or again,

[a]Or *the Son* [b]Or *bears along*

"I will be his Father,
   and he will be my Son"?
[6]And again, when he brings the firstborn into the world, he says,
"Let all God's angels
   worship him."
[7]Of the angels he says,
"He makes his angels
   winds,
and his servants flames
   of fire."
[8]But of the Son he says,
"Your throne, O God, is[a]
   forever and ever,
and the righteous scepter
   is the scepter of
   your[b] kingdom.
[9] You have loved
   righteousness and
   hated wickedness;
therefore God, your God,
   has anointed you
with the oil of gladness
   beyond your
   companions."
[10]And,
"In the beginning, Lord,
   you founded the earth,
and the heavens are the
   work of your hands;
[11] they will perish, but you
   remain;
they will all wear out
   like clothing;
[12] like a cloak you will roll
   them up,
   and like clothing[c] they
   will be changed.
But you are the same,
   and your years will
   never end."
[13]But to which of the angels has he ever said,

"Sit at my right hand
   until I make your
   enemies a footstool
   for your feet"?
[14]Are not all angels[d] spirits in the divine service, sent to serve for the sake of those who are to inherit salvation?

2 Therefore we must pay greater attention to what we have heard, so that we do not drift away from it. [2]For if the message declared through angels was valid, and every transgression or disobedience received a just penalty, [3]how can we escape if we neglect so great a salvation? It was declared at first through the Lord, and it was attested to us by those who heard him, [4]while God added his testimony by signs and wonders and various miracles, and by gifts of the Holy Spirit, distributed according to his will.

5 Now God[e] did not subject the coming world, about which we are speaking, to angels. [6]But someone has testified somewhere,

"What are human beings
   that you are mindful
   of them,[f]
or mortals, that you care
   for them?[g]
[7] You have made them for a
   little while lower[h]
   than the angels;

---

[a]Or *God is your throne* [b]Other ancient authorities read *his* [c]Other ancient authorities lack *like clothing* [d]Gk *all of them* [e]Gk *he* [f]Gk *What is man that you are mindful of him?* [g]Gk *or the son of man that you care for him?* In the Hebrew of Psalm 8.4-6 both *man* and *son of man* refer to all humankind [h]Or *them only a little lower*

you have crowned them
with glory and honor,[a]
8   subjecting all things
under their feet."
Now in subjecting all things to
them, God left nothing outside
their control. As it is, we do not
yet see everything in subjection
to them, [9]but we do see Jesus,
who for a little while was made
lower[b] than the angels, now
crowned with glory and honor
because of the suffering of death,
so that by the grace of God[c] he
might taste death for everyone.

10 It was fitting that God,[d] for
whom and through whom all
things exist, in bringing many
children to glory, should make
the pioneer of their salvation perfect through sufferings. [11]For the
one who sanctifies and those
who are sanctified all have one
Father.[e] For this reason Jesus is
not ashamed to call them brothers and sisters,[f] [12]saying,
"I will proclaim your name
to my brothers and
sisters,[f]
in the midst of the
congregation I will
praise you."
[13]And again,
"I will put my trust in him."
And again,
"Here am I and the
children whom God
has given me."

14 Since, therefore, the children share flesh and blood, he
himself likewise shared the same
things, so that through death he
might destroy the one who has
the power of death, that is, the
devil, [15]and free those who all
their lives were held in slavery
by the fear of death. [16]For it is
clear that he did not come to help
angels, but the descendants of
Abraham. [17]Therefore he had to
become like his brothers and sisters[f] in every respect, so that he
might be a merciful and faithful
high priest in the service of God,
to make a sacrifice of atonement
for the sins of the people.
[18]Because he himself was tested
by what he suffered, he is able to
help those who are being tested.

3 Therefore, brothers and sisters,[f] holy partners in a
heavenly calling, consider that
Jesus, the apostle and high priest
of our confession, [2]was faithful to
the one who appointed him, just
as Moses also "was faithful in all[g]
God's[h] house." [3]Yet Jesus[i] is worthy of more glory than Moses,
just as the builder of a house has
more honor than the house itself.
[4](For every house is built by
someone, but the builder of all
things is God.) [5]Now Moses was
faithful in all God's[h] house as a
servant, to testify to the things
that would be spoken later.
[6]Christ, however, was faithful
over God's[h] house as a son, and
we are his house if we hold firm[j]
the confidence and the pride that
belong to hope.

[a]Other ancient authorities add *and set them over the
works of your hands* [b]Or *who was made a little lower*
[c]Other ancient authorities read *apart from God* [d]Gk *he*
[e]Gk *are all of one* [f]Gk *brothers* [g]Other ancient authorities lack *all* [h]Gk *his* [i]Gk *this one* [j]Other ancient
authorities add *to the end*

7 Therefore, as the Holy Spirit says,

"Today, if you hear his
    voice,
8 do not harden your hearts
        as in the rebellion,
    as on the day of testing
        in the wilderness,
9 where your ancestors put
        me to the test,
    though they had seen my
        works ¹⁰for forty
        years.
    Therefore I was angry with
        that generation,
    and I said, 'They always go
        astray in their hearts,
    and they have not known
        my ways.'
11 As in my anger I swore,
    'They will not enter my
        rest.'"

¹²Take care, brothers and sisters,[a] that none of you may have an evil, unbelieving heart that turns away from the living God. ¹³But exhort one another every day, as long as it is called "today," so that none of you may be hardened by the deceitfulness of sin. ¹⁴For we have become partners of Christ, if only we hold our first confidence firm to the end. ¹⁵As it is said,

"Today, if you hear his
    voice,
    do not harden your hearts
        as in the rebellion."

¹⁶Now who were they who heard and yet were rebellious? Was it not all those who left Egypt under the leadership of Moses? ¹⁷But with whom was he angry forty years? Was it not those who sinned, whose bodies fell in the wilderness? ¹⁸And to whom did he swear that they would not enter his rest, if not to those who were disobedient? ¹⁹So we see that they were unable to enter because of unbelief.

4 Therefore, while the promise of entering his rest is still open, let us take care that none of you should seem to have failed to reach it. ²For indeed the good news came to us just as to them; but the message they heard did not benefit them, because they were not united by faith with those who listened.[b] ³For we who have believed enter that rest, just as God has said,

"As in my anger I swore,
    'They shall not enter my
        rest,'"

though his works were finished at the foundation of the world. ⁴For in one place it speaks about the seventh day as follows, "And God rested on the seventh day from all his works." ⁵And again in this place it says, "They shall not enter my rest." ⁶Since therefore it remains open for some to enter it, and those who formerly received the good news failed to enter because of disobedience, ⁷again he sets a certain day—"today"— saying through David much later, in the words already quoted,

"Today, if you hear his
    voice,
    do not harden your hearts."

⁸For if Joshua had given them rest, God[c] would not speak later

---

[a]Gk *brothers* [b]Other ancient authorities read *it did not meet with faith in those who listened* [c]Gk *he*

about another day. [9]So then, a sabbath rest still remains for the people of God; [10]for those who enter God's rest also cease from their labors as God did from his. [11]Let us therefore make every effort to enter that rest, so that no one may fall through such disobedience as theirs.

[12]Indeed, the word of God is living and active, sharper than any two-edged sword, piercing until it divides soul from spirit, joints from marrow; it is able to judge the thoughts and intentions of the heart. [13]And before him no creature is hidden, but all are naked and laid bare to the eyes of the one to whom we must render an account.

[14]Since, then, we have a great high priest who has passed through the heavens, Jesus, the Son of God, let us hold fast to our confession. [15]For we do not have a high priest who is unable to sympathize with our weaknesses, but we have one who in every respect has been tested[a] as we are, yet without sin. [16]Let us therefore approach the throne of grace with boldness, so that we may receive mercy and find grace to help in time of need.

5 Every high priest chosen from among mortals is put in charge of things pertaining to God on their behalf, to offer gifts and sacrifices for sins. [2]He is able to deal gently with the ignorant and wayward, since he himself is subject to weakness; [3]and because of this he must offer sacrifice for his own sins as well as for those of the people. [4]And one does not presume to take this honor, but takes it only when called by God, just as Aaron was.

[5]So also Christ did not glorify himself in becoming a high priest, but was appointed by the one who said to him,

"You are my Son,
   today I have begotten you";

[6]as he says also in another place,

"You are a priest forever,
   according to the order of
      Melchizedek."

[7]In the days of his flesh, Jesus[b] offered up prayers and supplications, with loud cries and tears, to the one who was able to save him from death, and he was heard because of his reverent submission. [8]Although he was a Son, he learned obedience through what he suffered; [9]and having been made perfect, he became the source of eternal salvation for all who obey him, [10]having been designated by God a high priest according to the order of Melchizedek.

[11]About this[c] we have much to say that is hard to explain, since you have become dull in understanding. [12]For though by this time you ought to be teachers, you need someone to teach you again the basic elements of the oracles of God. You need milk, not solid food; [13]for everyone who lives on milk, being still an infant, is unskilled in the word of righteousness. [14]But solid

[a]Or tempted [b]Gk he [c]Or him

food is for the mature, for those whose faculties have been trained by practice to distinguish good from evil.

6 Therefore let us go on toward perfection,[a] leaving behind the basic teaching about Christ, and not laying again the foundation: repentance from dead works and faith toward God, [2]instruction about baptisms, laying on of hands, resurrection of the dead, and eternal judgment. [3]And we will do[b] this, if God permits. [4]For it is impossible to restore again to repentance those who have once been enlightened, and have tasted the heavenly gift, and have shared in the Holy Spirit, [5]and have tasted the goodness of the word of God and the powers of the age to come, [6]and then have fallen away, since on their own they are crucifying again the Son of God and are holding him up to contempt. [7]Ground that drinks up the rain falling on it repeatedly, and that produces a crop useful to those for whom it is cultivated, receives a blessing from God. [8]But if it produces thorns and thistles, it is worthless and on the verge of being cursed; its end is to be burned over.

[9] Even though we speak in this way, beloved, we are confident of better things in your case, things that belong to salvation. [10]For God is not unjust; he will not overlook your work and the love that you showed for his sake[c] in serving the saints, as you still do. [11]And we want each one of you to show the same diligence so as to realize the full assurance of hope to the very end, [12]so that you may not become sluggish, but imitators of those who through faith and patience inherit the promises.

[13] When God made a promise to Abraham, because he had no one greater by whom to swear, he swore by himself, [14]saying, "I will surely bless you and multiply you." [15]And thus Abraham, having patiently endured, obtained the promise. [16]Human beings, of course, swear by someone greater than themselves, and an oath given as confirmation puts an end to all dispute. [17]In the same way, when God desired to show even more clearly to the heirs of the promise the unchangeable character of his purpose, he guaranteed it by an oath, [18]so that through two unchangeable things, in which it is impossible that God would prove false, we who have taken refuge might be strongly encouraged to seize the hope set before us. [19]We have this hope, a sure and steadfast anchor of the soul, a hope that enters the inner shrine behind the curtain, [20]where Jesus, a forerunner on our behalf, has entered, having become a high priest forever according to the order of Melchizedek.

7 This "King Melchizedek of Salem, priest of the Most High God, met Abraham as he was returning from defeating the

[a]Or *toward maturity* [b]Other ancient authorities read *let us do* [c]Gk *for his name*

316

kings and blessed him"; [2]and to him Abraham apportioned "one-tenth of everything." His name, in the first place, means "king of righteousness"; next he is also king of Salem, that is, "king of peace." [3]Without father, without mother, without genealogy, having neither beginning of days nor end of life, but resembling the Son of God, he remains a priest forever.

4 See how great he is! Even[a] Abraham the patriarch gave him a tenth of the spoils. [5]And those descendants of Levi who receive the priestly office have a command-ment in the law to collect tithes[b] from the people, that is, from their kindred,[c] though these also are descended from Abraham. [6]But this man, who does not belong to their ancestry, collected tithes[b] from Abraham and blessed him who had received the prom-ises. [7]It is beyond dispute that the inferior is blessed by the superior. [8]In the one case, tithes are received by those who are mortal; in the other, by one of whom it is testified that he lives. [9]One might even say that Levi himself, who receives tithes, paid tithes through Abraham, [10]for he was still in the loins of his ancestor when Melchizedek met him. [11]Now if perfection had been attainable through the levitical priesthood—for the people received the law under this priest-hood—what further need would there have been to speak of anoth-er priest arising according to the order of Melchizedek, rather than one according to the order of Aaron? [12]For when there is a change in the priesthood, there is necessarily a change in the law as well. [13]Now the one of whom these things are spoken belonged to another tribe, from which no one has ever served at the altar. [14]For it is evident that our Lord was descended from Judah, and in connection with that tribe Moses said nothing about priests.

15 It is even more obvious when another priest arises, resem-bling Melchizedek, [16]one who has become a priest, not through a legal requirement concerning physical descent, but through the power of an indestructible life. [17]For it is attested of him,

"You are a priest forever,
    according to the order of
        Melchizedek."

[18]There is, on the one hand, the abrogation of an earlier com-mandment because it was weak and ineffectual [19](for the law made nothing perfect); there is, on the other hand, the introduc-tion of a better hope, through which we approach God.

20 This was confirmed with an oath; for others who became priests took their office without an oath, [21]but this one became a priest with an oath, because of the one who said to him,

"The Lord has sworn
    and will not change his
        mind,
'You are a priest
        forever'"—

[a]Other ancient authorities lack *Even* [b]Or *a tenth* [c]Gk *brothers*

[22]accordingly Jesus has also become the guarantee of a better covenant.

23 Furthermore, the former priests were many in number, because they were prevented by death from continuing in office; [24]but he holds his priesthood permanently, because he continues forever. [25]Consequently he is able for all time to save[a] those who approach God through him, since he always lives to make intercession for them.

26 For it was fitting that we should have such a high priest, holy, blameless, undefiled, separated from sinners, and exalted above the heavens. [27]Unlike the other[b] high priests, he has no need to offer sacrifices day after day, first for his own sins, and then for those of the people; this he did once for all when he offered himself. [28]For the law appoints as high priests those who are subject to weakness, but the word of the oath, which came later than the law, appoints a Son who has been made perfect forever.

8 Now the main point in what we are saying is this: we have such a high priest, one who is seated at the right hand of the throne of the Majesty in the heavens, [2]a minister in the sanctuary and the true tent[c] that the Lord, and not any mortal, has set up. [3]For every high priest is appointed to offer gifts and sacrifices; hence it is necessary for this priest also to have something to offer. [4]Now if he were on earth, he would not be a priest at all, since there are priests who offer gifts according to the law. [5]They offer worship in a sanctuary that is a sketch and shadow of the heavenly one; for Moses, when he was about to erect the tent,[c] was warned, "See that you make everything according to the pattern that was shown you on the mountain." [6]But Jesus[d] has now obtained a more excellent ministry, and to that degree he is the mediator of a better covenant, which has been enacted through better promises. [7]For if that first covenant had been faultless, there would have been no need to look for a second one.

8 God[e] finds fault with them when he says:

"The days are surely
    coming, says the
    Lord,
when I will establish a
    new covenant with
    the house of Israel
and with the house of
    Judah;
[9] not like the covenant that I
    made with their
    ancestors,
on the day when I took
    them by the hand to
    lead them out of the
    land of Egypt;
for they did not continue in
    my covenant,
and so I had no concern
    for them, says the
    Lord.

[a]Or *able to save completely* [b]Gk lacks *other* [c]Or *tabernacle* [d]Gk *he* [e]Gk *He*

[10] This is the covenant that I
will make with the
house of Israel
after those days, says the
Lord:
I will put my laws in their
minds,
and write them on their
hearts,
and I will be their God,
and they shall be my
people.
[11] And they shall not teach
one another
or say to each other,
'Know the Lord,'
for they shall all know me,
from the least of them to
the greatest.
[12] For I will be merciful
toward their iniquities,
and I will remember
their sins no more."
[13]In speaking of "a new covenant,"
he has made the first one obsolete. And what is obsolete and
growing old will soon disappear.

9 Now even the first covenant
had regulations for worship
and an earthly sanctuary. [2]For a
tent[a] was constructed, the first
one, in which were the lampstand, the table, and the bread of
the Presence;[b] this is called the
Holy Place. [3]Behind the second
curtain was a tent called the Holy
of Holies. [4]In it stood the golden
altar of incense and the ark of the
covenant overlaid on all sides
with gold, in which there were a
golden urn holding the manna,
and Aaron's rod that budded,
and the tablets of the covenant;
[5]above it were the cherubim of

glory overshadowing the mercy
seat.[c] Of these things we cannot
speak now in detail.

6 Such preparations having
been made, the priests go continually into the first tent to carry out
their ritual duties; [7]but only the
high priest goes into the second,
and he but once a year, and not
without taking the blood that he
offers for himself and for the sins
committed unintentionally by the
people. [8]By this the Holy Spirit
indicates that the way into the
sanctuary has not yet been disclosed as long as the first tent is
still standing. [9]This is a symbol[d]
of the present time, during which
gifts and sacrifices are offered
that cannot perfect the conscience of the worshiper, [10]but
deal only with food and drink
and various baptisms, regulations
for the body imposed until the
time comes to set things right.

11 But when Christ came as a
high priest of the good things
that have come,[e] then through
the greater and perfect[f] tent (not
made with hands, that is, not of
this creation), [12]he entered once
for all into the Holy Place, not
with the blood of goats and
calves, but with his own blood,
thus obtaining eternal redemption. [13]For if the blood of goats
and bulls, with the sprinkling of
the ashes of a heifer, sanctifies
those who have been defiled so
that their flesh is purified, [14]how

---

[a]Or *tabernacle* [b]Gk *the presentation of the loaves* [c]Or
the place of atonement [d]Gk *parable* [e]Other ancient
authorities read *good things to come* [f]Gk *more perfect*

much more will the blood of Christ, who through the eternal Spirit[a] offered himself without blemish to God, purify our[b] conscience from dead works to worship the living God!

15 For this reason he is the mediator of a new covenant,[c] so that those who are called may receive the promised eternal inheritance, because a death has occurred that redeems them from the transgressions under the first covenant.[c] [16]Where a will[c] is involved, the death of the one who made it must be established. [17]For a will takes effect only at death, since it is not in force as long as the one who made it is alive. [18]Hence not even the first covenant was inaugurated without blood. [19]For when every commandment had been told to all the people by Moses in accordance with the law, he took the blood of calves and goats,[d] with water and scarlet wool and hyssop, and sprinkled both the scroll itself and all the people, [20]saying, "This is the blood of the covenant that God has ordained for you." [21]And in the same way he sprinkled with the blood both the tent[e] and all the vessels used in worship. [22]Indeed, under the law almost everything is purified with blood, and without the shedding of blood there is no forgiveness of sins.

23 Thus it was necessary for the sketches of the heavenly things to be purified with these rites, but the heavenly things themselves need better sacrifices than these. [24]For Christ did not enter a sanctuary made by human hands, a mere copy of the true one, but he entered into heaven itself, now to appear in the presence of God on our behalf. [25]Nor was it to offer himself again and again, as the high priest enters the Holy Place year after year with blood that is not his own; [26]for then he would have had to suffer again and again since the foundation of the world. But as it is, he has appeared once for all at the end of the age to remove sin by the sacrifice of himself. [27]And just as it is appointed for mortals to die once, and after that the judgment, [28]so Christ, having been offered once to bear the sins of many, will appear a second time, not to deal with sin, but to save those who are eagerly waiting for him.

10 Since the law has only a shadow of the good things to come and not the true form of these realities, it[f] can never, by the same sacrifices that are continually offered year after year, make perfect those who approach. [2]Otherwise, would they not have ceased being offered, since the worshipers, cleansed once for all, would no longer have any consciousness of sin? [3]But in these sacrifices there is a reminder of sin year after year. [4]For it is impossible for the blood of bulls and goats to take away sins.

[a]Other ancient authorities read *Holy Spirit* [b]Other ancient authorities read *your* [c]The Greek word used here means both *covenant* and *will* [d]Other ancient authorities lack *and goats* [e]Or *tabernacle* [f]Other ancient authorities read *they*

[5]Consequently, when Christ[a] came into the world, he said,

"Sacrifices and offerings
    you have not desired,
but a body you have
    prepared for me;
[6] in burnt offerings and sin
    offerings
you have taken no
    pleasure.
[7] Then I said, 'See, God, I
    have come to do your
    will, O God'
    (in the scroll of the
      book[b] it is written of
      me)."

[8]When he said above, "You have neither desired nor taken pleasure in sacrifices and offerings and burnt offerings and sin offerings" (these are offered according to the law), [9]then he added, "See, I have come to do your will." He abolishes the first in order to establish the second. [10]And it is by God's will[c] that we have been sanctified through the offering of the body of Jesus Christ once for all.

11 And every priest stands day after day at his service, offering again and again the same sacrifices that can never take away sins. [12]But when Christ[d] had offered for all time a single sacrifice for sins, "he sat down at the right hand of God," [13]and since then has been waiting "until his enemies would be made a footstool for his feet." [14]For by a single offering he has perfected for all time those who are sanctified. [15]And the Holy Spirit also testifies to us, for after saying,

[16] "This is the covenant that I
    will make with them
    after those days, says the
      Lord:
I will put my laws in their
    hearts,
    and I will write them on
      their minds,"
[17]he also adds,

"I will remember their
    sins and their lawless
    deeds no more."

[18]Where there is forgiveness of these, there is no longer any offering for sin.

19 Therefore, my friends,[f] since we have confidence to enter the sanctuary by the blood of Jesus, [20]by the new and living way that he opened for us through the curtain (that is, through his flesh), [21]and since we have a great priest over the house of God, [22]let us approach with a true heart in full assurance of faith, with our hearts sprinkled clean from an evil conscience and our bodies washed with pure water. [23]Let us hold fast to the confession of our hope without wavering, for he who has promised is faithful. [24]And let us consider how to provoke one another to love and good deeds, [25]not neglecting to meet together, as is the habit of some, but encouraging one another, and all the more as you see the Day approaching.

26 For if we willfully persist in sin after having received the

[a]Gk *he* [b]Meaning of Gk uncertain [c]Gk *by that will* [d]Gk *this one* [e]Gk *on their minds and I will remember* [f]Gk *Therefore, brothers*

321

knowledge of the truth, there no longer remains a sacrifice for sins, 27but a fearful prospect of judgment, and a fury of fire that will consume the adversaries. 28Anyone who has violated the law of Moses dies without mercy "on the testimony of two or three witnesses." 29How much worse punishment do you think will be deserved by those who have spurned the Son of God, profaned the blood of the covenant by which they were sanctified, and outraged the Spirit of grace? 30For we know the one who said, "Vengeance is mine, I will repay." And again, "The Lord will judge his people." 31It is a fearful thing to fall into the hands of the living God.

32 But recall those earlier days when, after you had been enlightened, you endured a hard struggle with sufferings, 33sometimes being publicly exposed to abuse and persecution, and sometimes being partners with those so treated. 34For you had compassion for those who were in prison, and you cheerfully accepted the plundering of your possessions, knowing that you yourselves possessed something better and more lasting. 35Do not, therefore, abandon that confidence of yours; it brings a great reward. 36For you need endurance, so that when you have done the will of God, you may receive what was promised. 37For yet

"in a very little while,
    the one who is coming
        will come and will
            not delay;
38 but my righteous one will
        live by faith.
    My soul takes no
        pleasure in anyone
            who shrinks back."

39But we are not among those who shrink back and so are lost, but among those who have faith and so are saved.

11 Now faith is the assurance of things hoped for, the conviction of things not seen. 2Indeed, by faith[a] our ancestors received approval. 3By faith we understand that the worlds were prepared by the word of God, so that what is seen was made from things that are not visible.[b]

4 By faith Abel offered to God a more acceptable[c] sacrifice than Cain's. Through this he received approval as righteous, God himself giving approval to his gifts; he died, but through his faith[d] he still speaks. 5By faith Enoch was taken so that he did not experience death; and "he was not found, because God had taken him." For it was attested before he was taken away that "he had pleased God." 6And without faith it is impossible to please God, for whoever would approach him must believe that he exists and that he rewards those who seek him. 7By faith Noah, warned by God about events as yet unseen, respected the warning and built an ark to save his household; by this he condemned the world and

---

[a]Gk by this [b]Or was not made out of visible things [c]Gk greater [d]Gk through it

became an heir to the righteousness that is in accordance with faith.

8 By faith Abraham obeyed when he was called to set out for a place that he was to receive as an inheritance; and he set out, not knowing where he was going. [9]By faith he stayed for a time in the land he had been promised, as in a foreign land, living in tents, as did Isaac and Jacob, who were heirs with him of the same promise. [10]For he looked forward to the city that has foundations, whose architect and builder is God. [11]By faith he received power of procreation, even though he was too old—and Sarah herself was barren—because he considered him faithful who had promised.[a] [12]Therefore from one person, and this one as good as dead, descendants were born, "as many as the stars of heaven and as the innumerable grains of sand by the seashore."

13 All of these died in faith without having received the promises, but from a distance they saw and greeted them. They confessed that they were strangers and foreigners on the earth, [14]for people who speak in this way make it clear that they are seeking a homeland. [15]If they had been thinking of the land that they had left behind, they would have had opportunity to return. [16]But as it is, they desire a better country, that is, a heavenly one. Therefore God is not ashamed to be called their God; indeed, he has prepared a city for them.

17 By faith Abraham, when put to the test, offered up Isaac. He who had received the promises was ready to offer up his only son, [18]of whom he had been told, "It is through Isaac that descendants shall be named for you." [19]He considered the fact that God is able even to raise someone from the dead—and figuratively speaking, he did receive him back. [20]By faith Isaac invoked blessings for the future on Jacob and Esau. [21]By faith Jacob, when dying, blessed each of the sons of Joseph, "bowing in worship over the top of his staff." [22]By faith Joseph, at the end of his life, made mention of the exodus of the Israelites and gave instructions about his burial.[b]

23 By faith Moses was hidden by his parents for three months after his birth, because they saw that the child was beautiful; and they were not afraid of the king's edict.[c] [24]By faith Moses, when he was grown up, refused to be called a son of Pharaoh's daughter, [25]choosing rather to share ill-treatment with the people of God than to enjoy the fleeting pleasures of sin. [26]He considered abuse suffered for the Christ[d] to be greater wealth than the treasures of Egypt, for he was looking ahead to the reward. [27]By faith he left Egypt, unafraid of the king's

---

[a]Or By faith Sarah herself, though barren, received power to conceive, even when she was too old, because she considered him faithful who had promised. [b]Gk his bones [c]Other ancient authorities add By faith Moses, when he was grown up, killed the Egyptian, because he observed the humiliation of his people (Gk brothers) [d]Or the Messiah

anger; for he persevered as though[a] he saw him who is invisible. [28]By faith he kept the Passover and the sprinkling of blood, so that the destroyer of the firstborn would not touch the firstborn of Israel.[b]

29 By faith the people passed through the Red Sea as if it were dry land, but when the Egyptians attempted to do so they were drowned. [30]By faith the walls of Jericho fell after they had been encircled for seven days. [31]By faith Rahab the prostitute did not perish with those who were disobedient,[c] because she had received the spies in peace.

32 And what more should I say? For time would fail me to tell of Gideon, Barak, Samson, Jephthah, of David and Samuel and the prophets— [33]who through faith conquered kingdoms, administered justice, obtained promises, shut the mouths of lions, [34]quenched raging fire, escaped the edge of the sword, won strength out of weakness, became mighty in war, put foreign armies to flight. [35]Women received their dead by resurrection. Others were tortured, refusing to accept release, in order to obtain a better resurrection. [36]Others suffered mocking and flogging, and even chains and imprisonment. [37]They were stoned to death, they were sawn in two,[d] they were killed by the sword; they went about in skins of sheep and goats, destitute, persecuted, tormented— [38]of whom the world was not worthy. They wandered in deserts and mountains, and in caves and holes in the ground.

39 Yet all these, though they were commended for their faith, did not receive what was promised, [40]since God had provided something better so that they would not, apart from us, be made perfect.

12 Therefore, since we are surrounded by so great a cloud of witnesses, let us also lay aside every weight and the sin that clings so closely,[e] and let us run with perseverance the race that is set before us, [2]looking to Jesus the pioneer and perfecter of our faith, who for the sake of[f] the joy that was set before him endured the cross, disregarding its shame, and has taken his seat at the right hand of the throne of God.

3 Consider him who endured such hostility against himself from sinners,[g] so that you may not grow weary or lose heart. [4]In your struggle against sin you have not yet resisted to the point of shedding your blood. [5]And you have forgotten the exhortation that addresses you as children—

"My child, do not regard
　　lightly the discipline
　　　　of the Lord,
　or lose heart when you
　　are punished by him;
[6]　for the Lord disciplines
　　those whom he loves,

---

[a]Or because [b]Gk would not touch them [c]Or unbelieving [d]Other ancient authorities add they were tempted [e]Other ancient authorities read sin that easily distracts [f]Or who instead of [g]Other ancient authorities read such hostility from sinners against themselves

and chastises every child
whom he accepts."

7 Endure trials for the sake of discipline. God is treating you as children; for what child is there whom a parent does not discipline? [8]If you do not have that discipline in which all children share, then you are illegitimate and not his children. [9]Moreover, we had human parents to discipline us, and we respected them. Should we not be even more willing to be subject to the Father of spirits and live? [10]For they disciplined us for a short time as seemed best to them, but he disciplines us for our good, in order that we may share his holiness. [11]Now, discipline always seems painful rather than pleasant at the time, but later it yields the peaceful fruit of righteousness to those who have been trained by it.

12 Therefore lift your drooping hands and strengthen your weak knees, [13]and make straight paths for your feet, so that what is lame may not be put out of joint, but rather be healed.

14 Pursue peace with everyone, and the holiness without which no one will see the Lord. [15]See to it that no one fails to obtain the grace of God; that no root of bitterness springs up and causes trouble, and through it many become defiled. [16]See to it that no one becomes like Esau, an immoral and godless person, who sold his birthright for a single meal. [17]You know that later, when he wanted to inherit the blessing, he was rejected, for he found no chance to repent,[a] even though he sought the blessing[b] with tears.

18 You have not come to something[c] that can be touched, a blazing fire, and darkness, and gloom, and a tempest, [19]and the sound of a trumpet, and a voice whose words made the hearers beg that not another word be spoken to them. [20](For they could not endure the order that was given, "If even an animal touches the mountain, it shall be stoned to death." [21]Indeed, so terrifying was the sight that Moses said, "I tremble with fear.") [22]But you have come to Mount Zion and to the city of the living God, the heavenly Jerusalem, and to innumerable angels in festal gathering, [23]and to the assembly[d] of the firstborn who are enrolled in heaven, and to God the judge of all, and to the spirits of the righteous made perfect, [24]and to Jesus, the mediator of a new covenant, and to the sprinkled blood that speaks a better word than the blood of Abel.

25 See that you do not refuse the one who is speaking; for if they did not escape when they refused the one who warned them on earth, how much less will we escape if we reject the one who warns from heaven! [26]At that time his voice shook the earth; but now he has promised, "Yet once more I will shake not only the earth but also the heaven." [27]This phrase, "Yet once more,"

---

[a]Or *no chance to change his father's mind* [b]Gk *it*
[c]Other ancient authorities read *a mountain* [d]Or *angels, and to the festal gathering* [23]*and assembly*

indicates the removal of what is shaken—that is, created things—so that what cannot be shaken may remain. ²⁸Therefore, since we are receiving a kingdom that cannot be shaken, let us give thanks, by which we offer to God an acceptable worship with reverence and awe; ²⁹for indeed our God is a consuming fire.

13 Let mutual love continue. ²Do not neglect to show hospitality to strangers, for by doing that some have entertained angels without knowing it. ³Remember those who are in prison, as though you were in prison with them; those who are being tortured, as though you yourselves were being tortured.[a] ⁴Let marriage be held in honor by all, and let the marriage bed be kept undefiled; for God will judge fornicators and adulterers. ⁵Keep your lives free from the love of money, and be content with what you have; for he has said, "I will never leave you or forsake you." ⁶So we can say with confidence,

"The Lord is my helper;
    I will not be afraid.
What can anyone do to me?"

7 Remember your leaders, those who spoke the word of God to you; consider the outcome of their way of life, and imitate their faith. ⁸Jesus Christ is the same yesterday and today and forever. ⁹Do not be carried away by all kinds of strange teachings; for it is well for the heart to be strengthened by grace, not by regulations about food,[b] which have not benefited those who observe them. ¹⁰We have an altar from which those who officiate in the tent[c] have no right to eat. ¹¹For the bodies of those animals whose blood is brought into the sanctuary by the high priest as a sacrifice for sin are burned outside the camp. ¹²Therefore Jesus also suffered outside the city gate in order to sanctify the people by his own blood. ¹³Let us then go to him outside the camp and bear the abuse he endured. ¹⁴For here we have no lasting city, but we are looking for the city that is to come. ¹⁵Through him, then, let us continually offer a sacrifice of praise to God, that is, the fruit of lips that confess his name. ¹⁶Do not neglect to do good and to share what you have, for such sacrifices are pleasing to God.

17 Obey your leaders and submit to them, for they are keeping watch over your souls and will give an account. Let them do this with joy and not with sighing—for that would be harmful to you.

18 Pray for us; we are sure that we have a clear conscience, desiring to act honorably in all things. ¹⁹I urge you all the more to do this, so that I may be restored to you very soon.

20 Now may the God of peace, who brought back from the dead our Lord Jesus, the great shepherd of the sheep, by the blood of the eternal covenant, ²¹make you complete in everything good so

---

[a]Gk were in the body [b]Gk not by foods [c]Or tabernacle

that you may do his will, working among us[a] that which is pleasing in his sight, through Jesus Christ, to whom be the glory forever and ever. Amen.

22 I appeal to you, brothers and sisters,[b] bear with my word of exhortation, for I have written to you briefly. [23]I want you to know that our brother Timothy has been set free; and if he comes in time, he will be with me when I see you. [24]Greet all your leaders and all the saints. Those from Italy send you greetings. [25]Grace be with all of you.[c]

[a]Other ancient authorities read *you* [b]Gk *brothers*
[c]Other ancient authorities add *Amen*

The Letter of

JAMES

1 James, a servant[a] of God and of the Lord Jesus Christ,
To the twelve tribes in the Dispersion:
Greetings.

2 My brothers and sisters,[b] whenever you face trials of any kind, consider it nothing but joy, [3]because you know that the testing of your faith produces endurance; [4]and let endurance have its full effect, so that you may be mature and complete, lacking in nothing.

5 If any of you is lacking in wisdom, ask God, who gives to all generously and ungrudgingly, and it will be given you. [6]But ask in faith, never doubting, for the one who doubts is like a wave of the sea, driven and tossed by the wind; [7,8]for the doubter, being double-minded and unstable in every way, must not expect to receive anything from the Lord.

9 Let the believer[c] who is lowly boast in being raised up, [10]and the rich in being brought low, because the rich will disappear like a flower in the field. [11]For the sun rises with its scorching heat and withers the field; its flower falls, and its beauty perishes. It is the same way with the rich; in the midst of a busy life, they will wither away.

12 Blessed is anyone who endures temptation. Such a one has stood the test and will receive the crown of life that the Lord[d] has promised to those who love him. [13]No one, when tempted, should say, "I am being tempted by God"; for God cannot be tempted by evil and he himself

[a]Gk *slave* [b]Gk *brothers* [c]Gk *brother* [d]Gk *he;* other ancient authorities read *God*

tempts no one. [14]But one is tempted by one's own desire, being lured and enticed by it; [15]then, when that desire has conceived, it gives birth to sin, and that sin, when it is fully grown, gives birth to death. [16]Do not be deceived, my beloved.[a]

17 Every generous act of giving, with every perfect gift, is from above, coming down from the Father of lights, with whom there is no variation or shadow due to change.[b] [18]In fulfillment of his own purpose he gave us birth by the word of truth, so that we would become a kind of first fruits of his creatures.

19 You must understand this, my beloved:[a] let everyone be quick to listen, slow to speak, slow to anger; [20]for your anger does not produce God's righteousness. [21]Therefore rid yourselves of all sordidness and rank growth of wickedness, and welcome with meekness the implanted word that has the power to save your souls.

22 But be doers of the word, and not merely hearers who deceive themselves. [23]For if any are hearers of the word and not doers, they are like those who look at themselves[c] in a mirror; [24]for they look at themselves and, on going away, immediately forget what they were like. [25]But those who look into the perfect law, the law of liberty, and persevere, being not hearers who forget but doers who act—they will be blessed in their doing.

26 If any think they are religious, and do not bridle their tongues but deceive their hearts, their religion is worthless. [27]Religion that is pure and undefiled before God, the Father, is this: to care for orphans and widows in their distress, and to keep oneself unstained by the world.

2 My brothers and sisters,[d] do you with your acts of favoritism really believe in our glorious Lord Jesus Christ?[e] [2]For if a person with gold rings and in fine clothes comes into your assembly, and if a poor person in dirty clothes also comes in, [3]and if you take notice of the one wearing the fine clothes and say, "Have a seat here, please," while to the one who is poor you say, "Stand there," or, "Sit at my feet,"[f] [4]have you not made distinctions among yourselves, and become judges with evil thoughts? [5]Listen, my beloved brothers and sisters. Has not God chosen the poor in the world to be rich in faith and to be heirs of the kingdom that he has promised to those who love him? [6]But you have dishonored the poor. Is it not the rich who oppress you? Is it not they who drag you into court? [7]Is it not they who blaspheme the excellent name that was invoked over you?

8 You do well if you really fulfill the royal law according to the scripture, "You shall love your neighbor as yourself." [9]But if you

---

[a]Gk *my beloved brothers* [b]Other ancient authorities read *variation due to a shadow of turning* [c]Gk *at the face of his birth* [d]Gk *My brothers* [e]Or *hold the faith of our glorious Lord Jesus Christ without acts of favoritism* [f]Gk *Sit under my footstool*

show partiality, you commit sin and are convicted by the law as transgressors. [10]For whoever keeps the whole law but fails in one point has become accountable for all of it. [11]For the one who said, "You shall not commit adultery," also said, "You shall not murder." Now if you do not commit adultery but if you murder, you have become a transgressor of the law. [12]So speak and so act as those who are to be judged by the law of liberty. [13]For judgment will be without mercy to anyone who has shown no mercy; mercy triumphs over judgment.

14 What good is it, my brothers and sisters,[a] if you say you have faith but do not have works? Can faith save you? [15]If a brother or sister is naked and lacks daily food, [16]and one of you says to them, "Go in peace; keep warm and eat your fill," and yet you do not supply their bodily needs, what is the good of that? [17]So faith by itself, if it has no works, is dead.

18 But someone will say, "You have faith and I have works." Show me your faith apart from your works, and I by my works will show you my faith. [19]You believe that God is one; you do well. Even the demons believe— and shudder. [20]Do you want to be shown, you senseless person, that faith apart from works is barren? [21]Was not our ancestor Abraham justified by works when he offered his son Isaac on the altar? [22]You see that faith was active along with his works, and

faith was brought to completion by the works. [23]Thus the scripture was fulfilled that says, "Abraham believed God, and it was reckoned to him as righteousness," and he was called the friend of God. [24]You see that a person is justified by works and not by faith alone. [25]Likewise, was not Rahab the prostitute also justified by works when she welcomed the messengers and sent them out by another road? [26]For just as the body without the spirit is dead, so faith without works is also dead.

3 Not many of you should become teachers, my brothers and sisters,[a] for you know that we who teach will be judged with greater strictness. [2]For all of us make many mistakes. Anyone who makes no mistakes in speaking is perfect, able to keep the whole body in check with a bridle. [3]If we put bits into the mouths of horses to make them obey us, we guide their whole bodies. [4]Or look at ships: though they are so large that it takes strong winds to drive them, yet they are guided by a very small rudder wherever the will of the pilot directs. [5]So also the tongue is a small member, yet it boasts of great exploits.

How great a forest is set ablaze by a small fire! [6]And the tongue is a fire. The tongue is placed among our members as a world of iniquity; it stains the whole body, sets on fire the cycle of nature,[b] and is itself set on fire by

[a]Gk brothers [b]Or wheel of birth

hell.[a] [7]For every species of beast and bird, of reptile and sea creature, can be tamed and has been tamed by the human species, [8]but no one can tame the tongue—a restless evil, full of deadly poison. [9]With it we bless the Lord and Father, and with it we curse those who are made in the likeness of God. [10]From the same mouth come blessing and cursing. My brothers and sisters,[b] this ought not to be so. [11]Does a spring pour forth from the same opening both fresh and brackish water? [12]Can a fig tree, my brothers and sisters,[c] yield olives, or a grapevine figs? No more can salt water yield fresh.

[13] Who is wise and understanding among you? Show by your good life that your works are done with gentleness born of wisdom. [14]But if you have bitter envy and selfish ambition in your hearts, do not be boastful and false to the truth. [15]Such wisdom does not come down from above, but is earthly, unspiritual, devilish. [16]For where there is envy and selfish ambition, there will also be disorder and wickedness of every kind. [17]But the wisdom from above is first pure, then peaceable, gentle, willing to yield, full of mercy and good fruits, without a trace of partiality or hypocrisy. [18]And a harvest of righteousness is sown in peace for[d] those who make peace.

[4] Those conflicts and disputes among you, where do they come from? Do they not come from your cravings that are at war within you? [2]You want something and do not have it; so you commit murder. And you covet[e] something and cannot obtain it; so you engage in disputes and conflicts. You do not have, because you do not ask. [3]You ask and do not receive, because you ask wrongly, in order to spend what you get on your pleasures. [4]Adulterers! Do you not know that friendship with the world is enmity with God? Therefore whoever wishes to be a friend of the world becomes an enemy of God. [5]Or do you suppose that it is for nothing that the scripture says, "God[f] yearns jealously for the spirit that he has made to dwell in us"? [6]But he gives all the more grace; therefore it says,

"God opposes the proud,
    but gives grace to the
        humble."

[7]Submit yourselves therefore to God. Resist the devil, and he will flee from you. [8]Draw near to God, and he will draw near to you. Cleanse your hands, you sinners, and purify your hearts, you double-minded. [9]Lament and mourn and weep. Let your laughter be turned into mourning and your joy into dejection. [10]Humble yourselves before the Lord, and he will exalt you.

[11] Do not speak evil against one another, brothers and sisters.[g] Whoever speaks evil against another or judges another, speaks evil against the law and judges the

[a]Gk Gehenna [b]Gk My brothers [c]Gk my brothers [d]Or by [e]Or you murder and you covet [f]Gk He [g]Gk brothers

law; but if you judge the law, you are not a doer of the law but a judge. [12]There is one lawgiver and judge who is able to save and to destroy. So who, then, are you to judge your neighbor?

13 Come now, you who say, "Today or tomorrow we will go to such and such a town and spend a year there, doing business and making money." [14]Yet you do not even know what tomorrow will bring. What is your life? For you are a mist that appears for a little while and then vanishes. [15]Instead you ought to say, "If the Lord wishes, we will live and do this or that." [16]As it is, you boast in your arrogance; all such boasting is evil. [17]Anyone, then, who knows the right thing to do and fails to do it, commits sin.

5 Come now, you rich people, weep and wail for the miseries that are coming to you. [2]Your riches have rotted, and your clothes are moth-eaten. [3]Your gold and silver have rusted, and their rust will be evidence against you, and it will eat your flesh like fire. You have laid up treasure[a] for the last days. [4]Listen! The wages of the laborers who mowed your fields, which you kept back by fraud, cry out, and the cries of the harvesters have reached the ears of the Lord of hosts. [5]You have lived on the earth in luxury and in pleasure; you have fattened your hearts in a day of slaughter. [6]You have condemned and mur-

dered the righteous one, who does not resist you.

7 Be patient, therefore, beloved,[b] until the coming of the Lord. The farmer waits for the precious crop from the earth, being patient with it until it receives the early and the late rains. [8]You also must be patient. Strengthen your hearts, for the coming of the Lord is near.[c] [9]Beloved,[d] do not grumble against one another, so that you may not be judged. See, the Judge is standing at the doors! [10]As an example of suffering and patience, beloved,[b] take the prophets who spoke in the name of the Lord. [11]Indeed we call blessed those who showed endurance. You have heard of the endurance of Job, and you have seen the purpose of the Lord, how the Lord is compassionate and merciful.

12 Above all, my beloved,[b] do not swear, either by heaven or by earth or by any other oath, but let your "Yes" be yes and your "No" be no, so that you may not fall under condemnation.

13 Are any among you suffering? They should pray. Are any cheerful? They should sing songs of praise. [14]Are any among you sick? They should call for the elders of the church and have them pray over them, anointing them with oil in the name of the Lord. [15]The prayer of faith will save the sick, and the Lord will

---

[a]*Or will eat your flesh, since you have stored up fire*
[b]*Gk brothers* [c]*Or is at hand* [d]*Gk Brothers*

raise them up; and anyone who has committed sins will be forgiven. [16]Therefore confess your sins to one another, and pray for one another, so that you may be healed. The prayer of the righteous is powerful and effective. [17]Elijah was a human being like us, and he prayed fervently that it might not rain, and for three years and six months it did not rain on the earth. [18]Then he prayed again, and the heaven gave rain and the earth yielded its harvest.

[19] My brothers and sisters,[a] if anyone among you wanders from the truth and is brought back by another, [20]you should know that whoever brings back a sinner from wandering will save the sinner's[b] soul from death and will cover a multitude of sins.

[a]Gk My brothers [b]Gk his

The First Letter of

PETER

1 Peter, an apostle of Jesus Christ,

To the exiles of the Dispersion in Pontus, Galatia, Cappadocia, Asia, and Bithynia, [2]who have been chosen and destined by God the Father and sanctified by the Spirit to be obedient to Jesus Christ and to be sprinkled with his blood:

May grace and peace be yours in abundance.

3 Blessed be the God and Father of our Lord Jesus Christ! By his great mercy he has given us a new birth into a living hope through the resurrection of Jesus Christ from the dead, [4]and into an inheritance that is imperishable, undefiled, and unfading, kept in heaven for you, [5]who are being protected by the power of God through faith for a salvation ready to be revealed in the last time. [6]In this you rejoice,[a] even if now for a little while you have had to suffer various trials, [7]so that the genuineness of your faith—being more precious than gold that, though perishable, is tested by fire—may be found to result in praise and glory and honor when Jesus Christ is revealed. [8]Although you have not seen[b] him, you love him; and even though you do not see him now, you believe in him and rejoice with an indescribable and glorious joy, [9]for you are receiving the outcome of your faith, the salvation of your souls.

10 Concerning this salvation, the prophets who prophesied of

[a]Or Rejoice in this [b]Other ancient authorities read known

332

the grace that was to be yours made careful search and inquiry, [11]inquiring about the person or time that the Spirit of Christ within them indicated when it testified in advance to the sufferings destined for Christ and the subsequent glory. [12]It was revealed to them that they were serving not themselves but you, in regard to the things that have now been announced to you through those who brought you good news by the Holy Spirit sent from heaven—things into which angels long to look!

[13] Therefore prepare your minds for action;[a] discipline yourselves; set all your hope on the grace that Jesus Christ will bring you when he is revealed. [14]Like obedient children, do not be conformed to the desires that you formerly had in ignorance. [15]Instead, as he who called you is holy, be holy yourselves in all your conduct; [16]for it is written, "You shall be holy, for I am holy."

[17] If you invoke as Father the one who judges all people impartially according to their deeds, live in reverent fear during the time of your exile. [18]You know that you were ransomed from the futile ways inherited from your ancestors, not with perishable things like silver or gold, [19]but with the precious blood of Christ, like that of a lamb without defect or blemish. [20]He was destined before the foundation of the world, but was revealed at the end of the ages for your sake. [21]Through him you have come to trust in God, who raised him from the dead and gave him glory, so that your faith and hope are set on God.

[22] Now that you have purified your souls by your obedience to the truth[b] so that you have genuine mutual love, love one another deeply[c] from the heart.[d] [23]You have been born anew, not of perishable but of imperishable seed, through the living and enduring word of God.[e] [24]For

"All flesh is like grass
    and all its glory like the flower of grass.
The grass withers,
    and the flower falls,
25 but the word of the Lord
    endures forever."

That word is the good news that was announced to you.

2 Rid yourselves, therefore, of all malice, and all guile, insincerity, envy, and all slander. [2]Like newborn infants, long for the pure, spiritual milk, so that by it you may grow into salvation— [3]if indeed you have tasted that the Lord is good.

[4] Come to him, a living stone, though rejected by mortals yet chosen and precious in God's sight, and [5]like living stones, let yourselves be built[f] into a spiritual house, to be a holy priesthood, to offer spiritual sacrifices acceptable to God through Jesus Christ. [6]For it stands in scripture:

[a]Gk *gird up the loins of your mind* [b]Other ancient authorities add *through the Spirit* [c]Or *constantly* [d]Other ancient authorities read *a pure heart* [e]Or *through the word of the living and enduring God* [f]Or *you yourselves are being built*

"See, I am laying in Zion a
    stone,
    a cornerstone chosen
      and precious;
    and whoever believes in
      him[a] will not be put
      to shame."

[7]To you then who believe, he is precious; but for those who do not believe,

"The stone that the
    builders rejected
  has become the very
    head of the corner,"

[8]and

"A stone that makes them
    stumble,
  and a rock that makes them
    fall."

They stumble because they disobey the word, as they were destined to do.

[9] But you are a chosen race, a royal priesthood, a holy nation, God's own people,[b] in order that you may proclaim the mighty acts of him who called you out of darkness into his marvelous light.

[10]   Once you were not a
    people,
  but now you are God's
    people;
  once you had not received
    mercy,
  but now you have
    received mercy.

[11] Beloved, I urge you as aliens and exiles to abstain from the desires of the flesh that wage war against the soul. [12]Conduct yourselves honorably among the Gentiles, so that, though they malign you as evildoers, they may see your honorable deeds and glorify God when he comes to judge.[c]

[13] For the Lord's sake accept the authority of every human institution,[d] whether of the emperor as supreme, [14]or of governors, as sent by him to punish those who do wrong and to praise those who do right. [15]For it is God's will that by doing right you should silence the ignorance of the foolish. [16]As servants[e] of God, live as free people, yet do not use your freedom as a pretext for evil. [17]Honor everyone. Love the family of believers.[f] Fear God. Honor the emperor.

[18] Slaves, accept the authority of your masters with all deference, not only those who are kind and gentle but also those who are harsh. [19]For it is a credit to you if, being aware of God, you endure pain while suffering unjustly. [20]If you endure when you are beaten for doing wrong, what credit is that? But if you endure when you do right and suffer for it, you have God's approval. [21]For to this you have been called, because Christ also suffered for you, leaving you an example, so that you should follow in his steps.

[22]   "He committed no sin,
    and no deceit was found
      in his mouth."

[23]When he was abused, he did not return abuse; when he suffered, he did not threaten; but he

---

[a]Or it [b]Gk a people for his possession [c]Gk God on the day of visitation [d]Or every institution ordained for human beings [e]Gk slaves [f]Gk Love the brotherhood

entrusted himself to the one who judges justly. [24]He himself bore our sins in his body on the cross,[a] so that, free from sins, we might live for righteousness; by his wounds[b] you have been healed. [25]For you were going astray like sheep, but now you have returned to the shepherd and guardian of your souls.

3 Wives, in[j] the same way, accept the authority of your husbands, so that, even if some of them do not obey the word, they may be won over without a word by their wives' conduct, [2]when they see the purity and reverence of your lives. [3]Do not adorn yourselves outwardly by braiding your hair, and by wearing gold ornaments or fine clothing; [4]rather, let your adornment be the inner self with the lasting beauty of a gentle and quiet spirit, which is very precious in God's sight. [5]It was in this way long ago that the holy women who hoped in God used to adorn themselves by accepting the authority of their husbands. [6]Thus Sarah obeyed Abraham and called him lord. You have become her daughters as long as you do what is good and never let fears alarm you.

7 Husbands, in the same way, show consideration for your wives in your life together, paying honor to the woman as the weaker sex,[c] since they too are also heirs of the gracious gift of life—so that nothing may hinder your prayers.

8 Finally, all of you, have unity of spirit, sympathy, love for one another, a tender heart, and a humble mind. [9]Do not repay evil for evil or abuse for abuse; but, on the contrary, repay with a blessing. It is for this that you were called—that you might inherit a blessing. [10]For

"Those who desire life
   and desire to see good
     days,
let them keep their tongues
   from evil
   and their lips from
     speaking deceit;
[11] let them turn away from
    evil and do good;
   let them seek peace and
    pursue it.
[12] For the eyes of the Lord
   are on the righteous,
   and his ears are open to
    their prayer.
But the face of the Lord is
    against those who do
    evil."

13 Now who will harm you if you are eager to do what is good? [14]But even if you do suffer for doing what is right, you are blessed. Do not fear what they fear,[d] and do not be intimidated, [15]but in your hearts sanctify Christ as Lord. Always be ready to make your defense to anyone who demands from you an accounting for the hope that is in you; [16]yet do it with gentleness and reverence.[e] Keep your conscience clear, so that, when you are maligned, those who abuse you for your good conduct in Christ may be put to shame. [17]For

[a]Or *carried up our sins in his body to the tree* [b]Gk *bruise* [c]Gk *vessel* [d]Gk *their fear* [e]Or *respect*

it is better to suffer for doing good, if suffering should be God's will, than to suffer for doing evil. [18]For Christ also suffered[a] for sins once for all, the righteous for the unrighteous, in order to bring you[b] to God. He was put to death in the flesh, but made alive in the spirit, [19]in which also he went and made a proclamation to the spirits in prison, [20]who in former times did not obey, when God waited patiently in the days of Noah, during the building of the ark, in which a few, that is, eight persons, were saved through water. [21]And baptism, which this prefigured, now saves you—not as a removal of dirt from the body, but as an appeal to God for[c] a good conscience, through the resurrection of Jesus Christ, [22]who has gone into heaven and is at the right hand of God, with angels, authorities, and powers made subject to him.

4 Since therefore Christ suffered in the flesh,[d] arm yourselves also with the same intention (for whoever has suffered in the flesh has finished with sin), [2]so as to live for the rest of your earthly life[e] no longer by human desires but by the will of God. [3]You have already spent enough time in doing what the Gentiles like to do, living in licentiousness, passions, drunkenness, revels, carousing, and lawless idolatry. [4]They are surprised that you no longer join them in the same excesses of dissipation, and so they blaspheme.[f] [5]But they will have to give an accounting to him who stands ready to judge the living and the dead. [6]For this is the reason the gospel was proclaimed even to the dead, so that, though they had been judged in the flesh as everyone is judged, they might live in the spirit as God does.

7 The end of all things is near;[g] therefore be serious and discipline yourselves for the sake of your prayers. [8]Above all, maintain constant love for one another, for love covers a multitude of sins. [9]Be hospitable to one another without complaining. [10]Like good stewards of the manifold grace of God, serve one another with whatever gift each of you has received. [11]Whoever speaks must do so as one speaking the very words of God; whoever serves must do so with the strength that God supplies, so that God may be glorified in all things through Jesus Christ. To him belong the glory and the power forever and ever. Amen.

12 Beloved, do not be surprised at the fiery ordeal that is taking place among you to test you, as though something strange were happening to you. [13]But rejoice insofar as you are sharing Christ's sufferings, so that you may also be glad and shout for joy when his glory is revealed. [14]If you are reviled for the name

[a]Other ancient authorities read *died* [b]Other ancient authorities read *us* [c]Or *a pledge to God from* [d]Other ancient authorities add *for us*; others, *for you* [e]Gk *rest of the time in the flesh* [f]Or *they malign you* [g]Or is at hand

of Christ, you are blessed, because the spirit of glory,[a] which is the Spirit of God, is resting on you.[b] 15But let none of you suffer as a murderer, a thief, a criminal, or even as a mischief maker. 16Yet if any of you suffers as a Christian, do not consider it a disgrace, but glorify God because you bear this name. 17For the time has come for judgment to begin with the household of God; if it begins with us, what will be the end for those who do not obey the gospel of God? 18And

> "If it is hard for the
> righteous to be saved,
> what will become of the
> ungodly and the
> sinners?"

19Therefore, let those suffering in accordance with God's will entrust themselves to a faithful Creator, while continuing to do good.

5 Now as an elder myself and a witness of the sufferings of Christ, as well as one who shares in the glory to be revealed, I exhort the elders among you 2to tend the flock of God that is in your charge, exercising the oversight,[c] not under compulsion but willingly, as God would have you do it[d]—not for sordid gain but eagerly. 3Do not lord it over those in your charge, but be examples to the flock. 4And when the chief shepherd appears, you will win the crown of glory that never fades away. 5In the same way, you who are younger must accept the authority of the elders.[e] And all of you must clothe yourselves with humility in your dealings with one another, for

> "God opposes the proud,
> but gives grace to the
> humble."

6 Humble yourselves therefore under the mighty hand of God, so that he may exalt you in due time. 7Cast all your anxiety on him, because he cares for you. 8Discipline yourselves, keep alert.[f] Like a roaring lion your adversary the devil prowls around, looking for someone to devour. 9Resist him, steadfast in your faith, for you know that your brothers and sisters[g] in all the world are undergoing the same kinds of suffering. 10And after you have suffered for a little while, the God of all grace, who has called you to his eternal glory in Christ, will himself restore, support, strengthen, and establish you. 11To him be the power forever and ever. Amen.

12 Through Silvanus, whom I consider a faithful brother, I have written this short letter to encourage you and to testify that this is the true grace of God. Stand fast in it. 13Your sister church[h] in Babylon, chosen together with you, sends you greetings; and so does my son Mark. 14Greet one another with a kiss of love.

Peace to all of you who are in Christ.[i]

---

[a]Other ancient authorities add *and of power* [b]Other ancient authorities add *On their part he is blasphemed, but on your part he is glorified* [c]Other ancient authorities lack *exercising the oversight* [d]Other ancient authorities lack *as God would have you do it* [e]Or *of those who are older* [f]Or *be vigilant* [g]Gk *your brotherhood* [h]Gk *She who is* [i]Other ancient authorities add *Amen*

The Second Letter of
PETER

1 Simeon[a] Peter, a servant[b] and apostle of Jesus Christ,

To those who have received a faith as precious as ours through the righteousness of our God and Savior Jesus Christ:[c]

2 May grace and peace be yours in abundance in the knowledge of God and of Jesus our Lord.

3 His divine power has given us everything needed for life and godliness, through the knowledge of him who called us by[d] his own glory and goodness. [4]Thus he has given us, through these things, his precious and very great promises, so that through them you may escape from the corruption that is in the world because of lust, and may become participants of the divine nature. [5]For this very reason, you must make every effort to support your faith with goodness, and goodness with knowledge, [6]and knowledge with self-control, and self-control with endurance, and endurance with godliness, [7]and godliness with mutual[e] affection, and mutual[e] affection with love. [8]For if these things are yours and are increasing among you, they keep you from being ineffective and unfruitful in the knowledge of our Lord Jesus Christ. [9]For anyone who lacks these things is nearsighted and blind, and is forgetful of the cleansing of past sins.

[10]Therefore, brothers and sisters,[f] be all the more eager to confirm your call and election, for if you do this, you will never stumble. [11]For in this way, entry into the eternal kingdom of our Lord and Savior Jesus Christ will be richly provided for you.

12 Therefore I intend to keep on reminding you of these things, though you know them already and are established in the truth that has come to you. [13]I think it right, as long as I am in this body,[g] to refresh your memory, [14]since I know that my death[h] will come soon, as indeed our Lord Jesus Christ has made clear to me. [15]And I will make every effort so that after my departure you may be able at any time to recall these things.

16 For we did not follow cleverly devised myths when we made known to you the power and coming of our Lord Jesus Christ, but we had been eyewitnesses of his majesty. [17]For he received honor and glory from God the Father when that voice was conveyed to him by the Majestic Glory, saying, "This is my Son, my Beloved,[i] with whom I am well pleased." [18]We ourselves

---

[a]Other ancient authorities read *Simon* [b]Gk *slave* [c]*Or of our God and the Savior Jesus Christ* [d]Other ancient authorities read *through* [e]Gk *brotherly* [f]Gk *brothers* [g]Gk *tent* [h]Gk *the putting off of my tent* [i]Other ancient authorities read *my beloved Son*

heard this voice come from heaven, while we were with him on the holy mountain.

19 So we have the prophetic message more fully confirmed. You will do well to be attentive to this as to a lamp shining in a dark place, until the day dawns and the morning star rises in your hearts. [20]First of all you must understand this, that no prophecy of scripture is a matter of one's own interpretation, [21]because no prophecy ever came by human will, but men and women moved by the Holy Spirit spoke from God.[a]

2 But false prophets also arose among the people, just as there will be false teachers among you, who will secretly bring in destructive opinions. They will even deny the Master who bought them—bringing swift destruction on themselves. [2]Even so, many will follow their licentious ways, and because of these teachers[b] the way of truth will be maligned. [3]And in their greed they will exploit you with deceptive words. Their condemnation, pronounced against them long ago, has not been idle, and their destruction is not asleep.

4 For if God did not spare the angels when they sinned, but cast them into hell[c] and committed them to chains[d] of deepest darkness to be kept until the judgment; [5]and if he did not spare the ancient world, even though he saved Noah, a herald of righteousness, with seven others, when he brought a flood on a world of the ungodly; [6]and if by

turning the cities of Sodom and Gomorrah to ashes he condemned them to extinction[e] and made them an example of what is coming to the ungodly;[f] [7]and if he rescued Lot, a righteous man greatly distressed by the licentiousness of the lawless [8](for that righteous man, living among them day after day, was tormented in his righteous soul by their lawless deeds that he saw and heard), [9]then the Lord knows how to rescue the godly from trial, and to keep the unrighteous under punishment until the day of judgment [10]—especially those who indulge their flesh in depraved lust, and who despise authority.

Bold and willful, they are not afraid to slander the glorious ones,[g] [11]whereas angels, though greater in might and power, do not bring against them a slanderous judgment from the Lord.[h] [12]These people, however, are like irrational animals, mere creatures of instinct, born to be caught and killed. They slander what they do not understand, and when those creatures are destroyed,[i] they also will be destroyed, [13]suffering[j] the penalty for doing wrong. They count it a pleasure to revel in the daytime. They are blots and blemishes, reveling in

---

[a]Other ancient authorities read *but moved by the Holy Spirit saints of God spoke* [b]Gk *because of them* [c]Gk *Tartaros* [d]Other ancient authorities read *pits* [e]Other ancient authorities lack *to extinction* [f]Other ancient authorities read *an example 'to those who were to be ungodly* [g]Or *angels;* Gk *glories* [h]Other ancient authorities read *before the Lord;* others lack the phrase [i]Gk *in their destruction* [j]Other ancient authorities read *receiving*

their dissipation[a] while they feast with you. [14]They have eyes full of adultery, insatiable for sin. They entice unsteady souls. They have hearts trained in greed. Accursed children! [15]They have left the straight road and have gone astray, following the road of Balaam son of Bosor,[b] who loved the wages of doing wrong, [16]but was rebuked for his own transgression; a speechless donkey spoke with a human voice and restrained the prophet's madness.

17 These are waterless springs and mists driven by a storm; for them the deepest darkness has been reserved. [18]For they speak bombastic nonsense, and with licentious desires of the flesh they entice people who have just[c] escaped from those who live in error. [19]They promise them freedom, but they themselves are slaves of corruption; for people are slaves to whatever masters them. [20]For if, after they have escaped the defilements of the world through the knowledge of our Lord and Savior Jesus Christ, they are again entangled in them and overpowered, the last state has become worse for them than the first. [21]For it would have been better for them never to have known the way of righteousness than, after knowing it, to turn back from the holy commandment that was passed on to them. [22]It has happened to them according to the true proverb,

> "The dog turns back to its own vomit,"

and,

> "The sow is washed only to wallow in the mud."

3 This is now, beloved, the second letter I am writing to you; in them I am trying to arouse your sincere intention by reminding you [2]that you should remember the words spoken in the past by the holy prophets, and the commandment of the Lord and Savior spoken through your apostles. [3]First of all you must understand this, that in the last days scoffers will come, scoffing and indulging their own lusts [4]and saying, "Where is the promise of his coming? For ever since our ancestors died,[d] all things continue as they were from the beginning of creation!" [5]They deliberately ignore this fact, that by the word of God heavens existed long ago and an earth was formed out of water and by means of water, [6]through which the world of that time was deluged with water and perished. [7]But by the same word the present heavens and earth have been reserved for fire, being kept until the day of judgment and destruction of the godless.

8 But do not ignore this one fact, beloved, that with the Lord one day is like a thousand years, and a thousand years are like one day. [9]The Lord is not slow about his promise, as some think of slowness, but is patient with

---

[a]Other ancient authorities read *love-feasts* [b]Other ancient authorities read *Beor* [c]Other ancient authorities read *actually* [d]Gk *our fathers fell asleep*

you,[a] not wanting any to perish, but all to come to repentance. [10]But the day of the Lord will come like a thief, and then the heavens will pass away with a loud noise, and the elements will be dissolved with fire, and the earth and everything that is done on it will be disclosed.[b]

11 Since all these things are to be dissolved in this way, what sort of persons ought you to be in leading lives of holiness and godliness, [12]waiting for and hastening[c] the coming of the day of God, because of which the heavens will be set ablaze and dissolved, and the elements will melt with fire? [13]But, in accordance with his promise, we wait for new heavens and a new earth, where righteousness is at home.

14 Therefore, beloved, while you are waiting for these things, strive to be found by him at peace, without spot or blemish; [15]and regard the patience of our Lord as salvation. So also our beloved brother Paul wrote to you according to the wisdom given him, [16]speaking of this as he does in all his letters. There are some things in them hard to understand, which the ignorant and unstable twist to their own destruction, as they do the other scriptures. [17]You therefore, beloved, since you are forewarned, beware that you are not carried away with the error of the lawless and lose your own stability. [18]But grow in the grace and knowledge of our Lord and Savior Jesus Christ. To him be the glory both now and to the day of eternity. Amen.[d]

[a]Other ancient authorities read *on your account* [b]Other ancient authorities read *will be burned up* [c]Or *earnestly desiring* [d]Other ancient authorities lack *Amen*

The First Letter of

JOHN

1 We declare to you what was from the beginning, what we have heard, what we have seen with our eyes, what we have looked at and touched with our hands, concerning the word of life— [2]this life was revealed, and we have seen it and testify to it, and declare to you the eternal life that was with the Father and was revealed to us— [3]we declare to you what we have seen and heard so that you also may have fellowship with us; and truly our fellowship is with the Father and with his Son Jesus Christ. [4]We are writing these things so that our[a] joy may be complete.

[a]Other ancient authorities read *your*

5 This is the message we have heard from him and proclaim to you, that God is light and in him there is no darkness at all. [6]If we say that we have fellowship with him while we are walking in darkness, we lie and do not do what is true; [7]but if we walk in the light as he himself is in the light, we have fellowship with one another, and the blood of Jesus his Son cleanses us from all sin. [8]If we say that we have no sin, we deceive ourselves, and the truth is not in us. [9]If we confess our sins, he who is faithful and just will forgive us our sins and cleanse us from all unrighteousness. [10]If we say that we have not sinned, we make him a liar, and his word is not in us.

2 My little children, I am writing these things to you so that you may not sin. But if anyone does sin, we have an advocate with the Father, Jesus Christ the righteous; [2]and he is the atoning sacrifice for our sins, and not for ours only but also for the sins of the whole world.

3 Now by this we may be sure that we know him, if we obey his commandments. [4]Whoever says, "I have come to know him," but does not obey his commandments, is a liar, and in such a person the truth does not exist; [5]but whoever obeys his word, truly in this person the love of God has reached perfection. By this we may be sure that we are in him: [6]whoever says, "I abide in him," ought to walk just as he walked.

7 Beloved, I am writing you no new commandment, but an old commandment that you have had from the beginning; the old commandment is the word that you have heard. [8]Yet I am writing you a new commandment that is true in him and in you, because[a] the darkness is passing away and the true light is already shining. [9]Whoever says, "I am in the light," while hating a brother or sister,[b] is still in the darkness. [10]Whoever loves a brother or sister[c] lives in the light, and in such a person[d] there is no cause for stumbling. [11]But whoever hates another believer[e] is in the darkness, walks in the darkness, and does not know the way to go, because the darkness has brought on blindness.

[12] I am writing to you, little children,
  because your sins are forgiven on account of his name.
[13] I am writing to you, fathers,
  because you know him who is from the beginning.
  I am writing to you, young people,
  because you have conquered the evil one.
[14] I write to you, children,
  because you know the Father.
  I write to you, fathers,
  because you know him who is from the beginning.

[a]Or that [b]Gk hating a brother [c]Gk loves a brother [d]Or in it [e]Gk hates a brother

I write to you, young
people,
because you are strong
and the word of God
abides in you,
and you have
overcome the evil one.

15 Do not love the world or
the things in the world. The love
of the Father is not in those who
love the world; [16]for all that is in
the world—the desire of the
flesh, the desire of the eyes, the
pride in riches—comes not from
the Father but from the world.
[17]And the world and its desire[a]
are passing away, but those who
do the will of God live forever.

18 Children, it is the last hour!
As you have heard that antichrist
is coming, so now many anti-
christs have come. From this we
know that it is the last hour.
[19]They went out from us, but they
did not belong to us; for if they
had belonged to us, they would
have remained with us. But by
going out they made it plain that
none of them belongs to us. [20]But
you have been anointed by the
Holy One, and all of you have
knowledge.[b] [21]I write to you, not
because you do not know the
truth, but because you know it,
and you know that no lie comes
from the truth. [22]Who is the liar
but the one who denies that Jesus
is the Christ?[c] This is the
antichrist, the one who denies the
Father and the Son. [23]No one who
denies the Son has the Father;
everyone who confesses the Son
has the Father also. [24]Let what you
heard from the beginning abide in

you. If what you heard from the
beginning abides in you, then
you will abide in the Son and in
the Father. [25]And this is what he
has promised[d] us, eternal life.

26 I write these things to you
concerning those who would
deceive you. [27]As for you, the
anointing that you received from
him abides in you, and so you do
not need anyone to teach you.
But as his anointing teaches you
about all things, and is true and
is not a lie, and just as it has
taught you, abide in him.[e]

28 And now, little children,
abide in him, so that when he is
revealed we may have confidence and not be put to shame
before him at his coming.

29 If you know that he is righteous, you may be sure that everyone who does right has

3 been born of him. [1]See what
love the Father has given us,
that we should be called children
of God; and that is what we are.
The reason the world does not
know us is that it did not know
him. [2]Beloved, we are God's children now; what we will be has
not yet been revealed. What we
do know is this: when he[e] is
revealed, we will be like him, for
we will see him as he is. [3]And all
who have this hope in him purify themselves, just as he is pure.

4 Everyone who commits sin
is guilty of lawlessness; sin is lawlessness. [5]You know that he was

---

[a]Or the desire for it [b]Other ancient authorities read
you know all things [c]Or the Messiah [d]Other ancient
authorities read you [e]Or it

revealed to take away sins, and in him there is no sin. [6]No one who abides in him sins; no one who sins has either seen him or known him. [7]Little children, let no one deceive you. Everyone who does what is right is righteous, just as he is righteous. [8]Everyone who commits sin is a child of the devil; for the devil has been sinning from the beginning. The Son of God was revealed for this purpose, to destroy the works of the devil. [9]Those who have been born of God do not sin, because God's seed abides in them;[a] they cannot sin, because they have been born of God. [10]The children of God and the children of the devil are revealed in this way: all who do not do what is right are not from God, nor are those who do not love their brothers and sisters.[b]

[11] For this is the message you have heard from the beginning, that we should love one another. [12]We must not be like Cain who was from the evil one and murdered his brother. And why did he murder him? Because his own deeds were evil and his brother's righteous. [13]Do not be astonished, brothers and sisters,[c] that the world hates you. [14]We know that we have passed from death to life because we love one another. Whoever does not love abides in death. [15]All who hate a brother or sister[b] are murderers, and you know that murderers do not have eternal life abiding in them. [16]We know love by this, that he laid down his life for us—and we ought to lay down our lives for one another. [17]How does God's love abide in anyone who has the world's goods and sees a brother or sister[d] in need and yet refuses help?

[18] Little children, let us love, not in word or speech, but in truth and action. [19]And by this we will know that we are from the truth and will reassure our hearts before him [20]whenever our hearts condemn us; for God is greater than our hearts, and he knows everything. [21]Beloved, if our hearts do not condemn us, we have boldness before God; [22]and we receive from him whatever we ask, because we obey his commandments and do what pleases him.

[23] And this is his commandment, that we should believe in the name of his Son Jesus Christ and love one another, just as he has commanded us. [24]All who obey his commandments abide in him, and he abides in them. And by this we know that he abides in us, by the Spirit that he has given us.

4 Beloved, do not believe every spirit, but test the spirits to see whether they are from God; for many false prophets have gone out into the world. [2]By this you know the Spirit of God: every spirit that confesses that Jesus Christ has come in the flesh is from God, [3]and every spirit that does not confess Jesus[e] is not from God.

[a]Or *because the children of God abide in him* [b]Gk *his brother* [c]Gk *brothers* [d]Gk *brother* [e]Other ancient authorities read *does away with Jesus* (Gk *dissolves Jesus*)

And this is the spirit of the antichrist, of which you have heard that it is coming; and now it is already in the world. [4]Little children, you are from God, and have conquered them; for the one who is in you is greater than the one who is in the world. [5]They are from the world; therefore what they say is from the world, and the world listens to them. [6]We are from God. Whoever knows God listens to us, and whoever is not from God does not listen to us. From this we know the spirit of truth and the spirit of error.

7 Beloved, let us love one another, because love is from God; everyone who loves is born of God and knows God. [8]Whoever does not love does not know God, for God is love. [9]God's love was revealed among us in this way: God sent his only Son into the world so that we might live through him. [10]In this is love, not that we loved God but that he loved us and sent his Son to be the atoning sacrifice for our sins. [11]Beloved, since God loved us so much, we also ought to love one another. [12]No one has ever seen God; if we love one another, God lives in us, and his love is perfected in us.

13 By this we know that we abide in him and he in us, because he has given us of his Spirit. [14]And we have seen and do testify that the Father has sent his Son as the Savior of the world. [15]God abides in those who confess that Jesus is the Son of God, and they abide in God. [16]So we have known and believe the love that God has for us.

God is love, and those who abide in love abide in God, and God abides in them. [17]Love has been perfected among us in this: that we may have boldness on the day of judgment, because as he is, so are we in this world. [18]There is no fear in love, but perfect love casts out fear; for fear has to do with punishment, and whoever fears has not reached perfection in love. [19]We love[a] because he first loved us. [20]Those who say, "I love God," and hate their brothers or sisters,[b] are liars; for those who do not love a brother or sister[c] whom they have seen, cannot love God whom they have not seen. [21]The commandment we have from him is this: those who love God must love their brothers and sisters[b] also.

5 Everyone who believes that Jesus is the Christ[d] has been born of God, and everyone who loves the parent loves the child. [2]By this we know that we love the children of God, when we love God and obey his commandments. [3]For the love of God is this, that we obey his commandments. And his commandments are not burdensome, [4]for whatever is born of God conquers the world. And this is the victory that conquers the world, our faith. [5]Who is it that conquers the world but the one who believes that Jesus is the Son of God?

---

[a]Other ancient authorities add *him;* others add *God*
[b]Gk *brothers* [c]Gk *brother* [d]Or *the Messiah*

6 This is the one who came by water and blood, Jesus Christ, not with the water only but with the water and the blood. And the Spirit is the one that testifies, for the Spirit is the truth. ⁷There are three that testify:ᵃ ⁸the Spirit and the water and the blood, and these three agree. ⁹If we receive human testimony, the testimony of God is greater; for this is the testimony of God that he has testified to his Son. ¹⁰Those who believe in the Son of God have the testimony in their hearts. Those who do not believe in Godᵇ have made him a liar by not believing in the testimony that God has given concerning his Son. ¹¹And this is the testimony: God gave us eternal life, and this life is in his Son. ¹²Whoever has the Son has life; whoever does not have the Son of God does not have life.

13 I write these things to you who believe in the name of the Son of God, so that you may know that you have eternal life.

14 And this is the boldness we have in him, that if we ask anything according to his will, he hears us. ¹⁵And if we know that he hears us in whatever we ask, we know that we have obtained the requests made of him. ¹⁶If you see your brother or sisterᶜ committing what is not a mortal sin, you will ask, and Godᵈ will give life to such a one—to those whose sin is not mortal. There is sin that is mortal; I do not say that you should pray about that. ¹⁷All wrongdoing is sin, but there is sin that is not mortal.

18 We know that those who are born of God do not sin, but the one who was born of God protects them, and the evil one does not touch them. ¹⁹We know that we are God's children, and that the whole world lies under the power of the evil one. ²⁰And we know that the Son of God has come and has given us understanding so that we may know him who is true;ᵉ and we are in him who is true, in his Son Jesus Christ. He is the true God and eternal life.

21 Little children, keep yourselves from idols.ᶠ

ᵃ A few other authorities read (with variations) ⁷There are three that testify in heaven, the Father, the Word, and the Holy Spirit, and these three are one. ⁸And there are three that testify on earth: ᵇOther ancient authorities read in the Son ᶜGk your brother ᵈGk he ᵉOther ancient authorities read know the true God ᶠOther ancient authorities add Amen

The Second Letter of

JOHN

1 The elder to the elect lady and her children, whom I love in the truth, and not only I but also all who know the truth, ²because of the truth that abides in us and will be with us forever:

3 Grace, mercy, and peace will be with us from God the Father and from*a* Jesus Christ, the Father's Son, in truth and love.

4 I was overjoyed to find some of your children walking in the truth, just as we have been commanded by the Father. ⁵But now, dear lady, I ask you, not as though I were writing you a new commandment, but one we have had from the beginning, let us love one another. ⁶And this is love, that we walk according to his commandments; this is the commandment just as you have heard it from the beginning—you must walk in it.

7 Many deceivers have gone out into the world, those who do not confess that Jesus Christ has come in the flesh; any such person is the deceiver and the antichrist! ⁸Be on your guard, so that you do not lose what we*b* have worked for, but may receive a full reward. ⁹Everyone who does not abide in the teaching of Christ, but goes beyond it, does not have God; whoever abides in the teaching has both the Father and the Son. ¹⁰Do not receive into the house or welcome anyone who comes to you and does not bring this teaching; ¹¹for to welcome is to participate in the evil deeds of such a person.

12 Although I have much to write to you, I would rather not use paper and ink; instead I hope to come to you and talk with you face to face, so that our joy may be complete.

13 The children of your elect sister send you their greetings.*c*

*a*Other ancient authorities add *the Lord* *b*Other ancient authorities read *you* *c*Other ancient authorities add *Amen*

The Third Letter of

JOHN

1 The elder to the beloved Gaius, whom I love in truth.

2 Beloved, I pray that all may go well with you and that you may be in good health, just as it is well with your soul. ³I was

overjoyed when some of the friends[a] arrived and testified to your faithfulness to the truth, namely how you walk in the truth. [4]I have no greater joy than this, to hear that my children are walking in the truth.

5 Beloved, you do faithfully whatever you do for the friends,[a] even though they are strangers to you; [6]they have testified to your love before the church. You will do well to send them on in a manner worthy of God; [7]for they began their journey for the sake of Christ,[b] accepting no support from non-believers.[c] [8]Therefore we ought to support such people, so that we may become co-workers with the truth.

9 I have written something to the church; but Diotrephes, who likes to put himself first, does not acknowledge our authority. [10]So if I come, I will call attention to what he is doing in spreading false charges against us. And not content with those charges, he refuses to welcome the friends,[a] and even prevents those who want to do so and expels them from the church.

11 Beloved, do not imitate what is evil but imitate what is good. Whoever does good is from God; whoever does evil has not seen God. [12]Everyone has testified favorably about Demetrius, and so has the truth itself. We also testify for him,[d] and you know that our testimony is true.

13 I have much to write to you, but I would rather not write with pen and ink; [14]instead I hope to see you soon, and we will talk together face to face.

15 Peace to you. The friends send you their greetings. Greet the friends there, each by name.

[a]Gk brothers [b]Gk for the sake of the name [c]Gk the Gentiles [d]Gk lacks for him

The Letter of

JUDE

1 Jude,[a] a servant[b] of Jesus Christ and brother of James,

To those who are called, who are beloved[c] in[d] God the Father and kept safe for[d] Jesus Christ:

2 May mercy, peace, and love be yours in abundance.

3 Beloved, while eagerly preparing to write to you about the salvation we share, I find it necessary to write and appeal to you to contend for the faith that was once for all entrusted to the saints. [4]For certain intruders have stolen in among you, people

[a]Gk Judas [b]Gk slave [c]Other ancient authorities read sanctified [d]Or by

who long ago were designated for this condemnation as ungodly, who pervert the grace of our God into licentiousness and deny our only Master and Lord, Jesus Christ.[a]

5 Now I desire to remind you, though you are fully informed, that the Lord, who once for all saved[b] people out of the land of Egypt, afterward destroyed those who did not believe. [6]And the angels who did not keep their own position, but left their proper dwelling, he has kept in eternal chains in deepest darkness for the judgment of the great Day. [7]Likewise, Sodom and Gomorrah and the surrounding cities, which, in the same manner as they, indulged in sexual immorality and pursued unnatural lust,[c]serve as an example by undergoing a punishment of eternal fire.

8 Yet in the same way these dreamers also defile the flesh, reject authority, and slander the glorious ones.[d] [9]But when the archangel Michael contended with the devil and disputed about the body of Moses, he did not dare to bring a condemnation of slander[e] against him, but said, "The Lord rebuke you!" [10]But these people slander whatever they do not understand, and they are destroyed by those things that, like irrational animals, they know by instinct. [11]Woe to them! For they go the way of Cain, and abandon themselves to Balaam's error for the sake of gain, and perish in Korah's rebellion. [12]These are blemishes[f] on your love-feasts, while they feast with you without fear, feeding themselves.[g] They are waterless clouds carried along by the winds; autumn trees without fruit, twice dead, uprooted; [13]wild waves of the sea, casting up the foam of their own shame; wandering stars, for whom the deepest darkness has been reserved forever.

14 It was also about these that Enoch, in the seventh generation from Adam, prophesied, saying, "See, the Lord is coming[h] with ten thousands of his holy ones, [15]to execute judgment on all, and to convict everyone of all the deeds of ungodliness that they have committed in such an ungodly way, and of all the harsh things that ungodly sinners have spoken against him." [16]These are grumblers and malcontents; they indulge their own lusts; they are bombastic in speech, flattering people to their own advantage.

17 But you, beloved, must remember the predictions of the apostles of our Lord Jesus Christ; [18]for they said to you, "In the last time there will be scoffers, indulging their own ungodly lusts." [19]It is these worldly people, devoid of the Spirit, who are causing divisions. [20]But you, beloved, build yourselves up on your most holy faith; pray in the

---

[a]Or *the only Master and our Lord Jesus Christ* [b]Other ancient authorities read *though you were once for all fully informed, that Jesus* (or *Joshua*) *who saved* [c]Gk *went after other flesh* [d]Or *angels;* Gk *glories* [e]Or *condemnation for blasphemy* [f]Or *reefs.* [g]Or *without fear. They are shepherds who care only for themselves* [h]Gk *came*

Holy Spirit; [21]keep yourselves in the love of God; look forward to the mercy of our Lord Jesus Christ that leads to[a] eternal life. [22]And have mercy on some who are wavering; [23]save others by snatching them out of the fire; and have mercy on still others with fear, hating even the tunic defiled by their bodies.[b]

24 Now to him who is able to keep you from falling, and to make you stand without blemish in the presence of his glory with rejoicing, [25]to the only God our Savior, through Jesus Christ our Lord, be glory, majesty, power, and authority, before all time and now and forever. Amen.

[a]Gk *Christ to* [b]Gk *by the flesh.* The Greek text of verses 22-23 is uncertain at several points

The
REVELATION
to John

1 The revelation of Jesus Christ, which God gave him to show his servants[a] what must soon take place; he made[b] it known by sending his angel to his servant[c] John, [2]who testified to the word of God and to the testimony of Jesus Christ, even to all that he saw.

3 Blessed is the one who reads aloud the words of the prophecy, and blessed are those who hear and who keep what is written in it; for the time is near.

4 John to the seven churches that are in Asia:

Grace to you and peace from him who is and who was and who is to come, and from the seven spirits who are before his throne, [5]and from Jesus Christ, the faithful witness, the firstborn of the dead, and the ruler of the kings of the earth.

To him who loves us and freed[d] us from our sins by his blood, [6]and made[b] us to be a kingdom, priests serving[e] his God and Father, to him be glory and dominion forever and ever. Amen.

7　Look! He is coming with
　　　the clouds;
　every eye will see him,
　even those who pierced
　　　him;
　and on his account all
　　　the tribes of the earth
　　　will wail.
So it is to be. Amen.

8 "I am the Alpha and the Omega," says the Lord God, who

[a]Gk *slaves* [b]Gk *and he made* [c]Gk *slave* [d]Other ancient authorities read *washed* [e]Gk *priests to*

is and who was and who is to come, the Almighty.

9 I, John, your brother who share with you in Jesus the persecution and the kingdom and the patient endurance, was on the island called Patmos because of the word of God and the testimony of Jesus.[a] [10]I was in the spirit[b] on the Lord's day, and I heard behind me a loud voice like a trumpet [11]saying, "Write in a book what you see and send it to the seven churches, to Ephesus, to Smyrna, to Pergamum, to Thyatira, to Sardis, to Philadelphia, and to Laodicea."

12 Then I turned to see whose voice it was that spoke to me, and on turning I saw seven golden lampstands, [13]and in the midst of the lampstands I saw one like the Son of Man, clothed with a long robe and with a golden sash across his chest. [14]His head and his hair were white as white wool, white as snow; his eyes were like a flame of fire, [15]his feet were like burnished bronze, refined as in a furnace, and his voice was like the sound of many waters. [16]In his right hand he held seven stars, and from his mouth came a sharp, two-edged sword, and his face was like the sun shining with full force.

17 When I saw him, I fell at his feet as though dead. But he placed his right hand on me, saying, "Do not be afraid; I am the first and the last, [18]and the living one. I was dead, and see, I am alive forever and ever; and I have the keys of Death and of Hades. [19]Now write what you have seen, what is, and what is to take place after this. [20]As for the mystery of the seven stars that you saw in my right hand, and the seven golden lampstands: the seven stars are the angels of the seven churches, and the seven lampstands are the seven churches.

2 "To the angel of the church in Ephesus write: These are the words of him who holds the seven stars in his right hand, who walks among the seven golden lampstands:

2 "I know your works, your toil and your patient endurance. I know that you cannot tolerate evildoers; you have tested those who claim to be apostles but are not, and have found them to be false. [3]I also know that you are enduring patiently and bearing up for the sake of my name, and that you have not grown weary. [4]But I have this against you, that you have abandoned the love you had at first. [5]Remember then from what you have fallen; repent, and do the works you did at first. If not, I will come to you and remove your lampstand from its place, unless you repent. [6]Yet this is to your credit: you hate the works of the Nicolaitans, which I also hate. [7]Let anyone who has an ear listen to what the Spirit is saying to the churches. To everyone who conquers, I will give permission to eat from the tree of life that is in the paradise of God.

[a]Or testimony to Jesus [b]Or in the Spirit

8 "And to the angel of the church in Smyrna write: These are the words of the first and the last, who was dead and came to life:

9 "I know your affliction and your poverty, even though you are rich. I know the slander on the part of those who say that they are Jews and are not, but are a synagogue of Satan. [10]Do not fear what you are about to suffer. Beware, the devil is about to throw some of you into prison so that you may be tested, and for ten days you will have affliction. Be faithful until death, and I will give you the crown of life. [11]Let anyone who has an ear listen to what the Spirit is saying to the churches. Whoever conquers will not be harmed by the second death.

12 "And to the angel of the church in Pergamum write: These are the words of him who has the sharp two-edged sword:

13 "I know where you are living, where Satan's throne is. Yet you are holding fast to my name, and you did not deny your faith in me[a] even in the days of Antipas my witness, my faithful one, who was killed among you, where Satan lives. [14]But I have a few things against you: you have some there who hold to the teaching of Balaam, who taught Balak to put a stumbling block before the people of Israel, so that they would eat food sacrificed to idols and practice fornication. [15]So you also have some who hold to the teaching of the Nicolaitans. [16]Repent then. If not, I will come to you soon and make war against them with the sword of my mouth. [17]Let anyone who has an ear listen to what the Spirit is saying to the churches. To everyone who conquers I will give some of the hidden manna, and I will give a white stone, and on the white stone is written a new name that no one knows except the one who receives it.

18 "And to the angel of the church in Thyatira write: These are the words of the Son of God, who has eyes like a flame of fire, and whose feet are like burnished bronze:

19 "I know your works—your love, faith, service, and patient endurance. I know that your last works are greater than the first. [20]But I have this against you: you tolerate that woman Jezebel, who calls herself a prophet and is teaching and beguiling my servants[b] to practice fornication and to eat food sacrificed to idols. [21]I gave her time to repent, but she refuses to repent of her fornication. [22]Beware, I am throwing her on a bed, and those who commit adultery with her I am throwing into great distress, unless they repent of her doings; [23]and I will strike her children dead. And all the churches will know that I am the one who searches minds and hearts, and I will give to each of you as your works deserve. [24]But to the rest of you in Thyatira, who do not hold this teaching, who have not learned what some

[a]Or deny my faith [b]Gk slaves

call 'the deep things of Satan,' to you I say, I do not lay on you any other burden; ²⁵only hold fast to what you have until I come. ²⁶To everyone who conquers and continues to do my works to the end,

I will give authority over
the nations;
²⁷ to rule*a* them with an iron
rod,
as when clay pots are
shattered—

²⁸even as I also received authority from my Father. To the one who conquers I will also give the morning star. ²⁹Let anyone who has an ear listen to what the Spirit is saying to the churches.

3 "And to the angel of the church in Sardis write: These are the words of him who has the seven spirits of God and the seven stars:

"I know your works; you have a name of being alive, but you are dead. ²Wake up, and strengthen what remains and is on the point of death, for I have not found your works perfect in the sight of my God. ³Remember then what you received and heard; obey it, and repent. If you do not wake up, I will come like a thief, and you will not know at what hour I will come to you. ⁴Yet you have still a few persons in Sardis who have not soiled their clothes; they will walk with me, dressed in white, for they are worthy. ⁵If you conquer, you will be clothed like them in white robes, and I will not blot your name out of the book of life; I will confess your

name before my Father and before his angels. ⁶Let anyone who has an ear listen to what the Spirit is saying to the churches.

7 "And to the angel of the church in Philadelphia write:
These are the words of the
holy one,
the true one,
who has the key of David,
who opens and no one
will shut,
who shuts and no one
opens:

8 "I know your works. Look, I have set before you an open door, which no one is able to shut. I know that you have but little power, and yet you have kept my word and have not denied my name. ⁹I will make those of the synagogue of Satan who say that they are Jews and are not, but are lying—I will make them come and bow down before your feet, and they will learn that I have loved you. ¹⁰Because you have kept my word of patient endurance, I will keep you from the hour of trial that is coming on the whole world to test the inhabitants of the earth. ¹¹I am coming soon; hold fast to what you have, so that no one may seize your crown. ¹²If you conquer, I will make you a pillar in the temple of my God; you will never go out of it. I will write on you the name of my God, and the name of the city of my God, the new Jerusalem that comes down

---

*a*Or *to shepherd*

from my God out of heaven, and my own new name. [13]Let anyone who has an ear listen to what the Spirit is saying to the churches.

14 "And to the angel of the church in Laodicea write: The words of the Amen, the faithful and true witness, the origin[a] of God's creation:

15 "I know your works; you are neither cold nor hot. I wish that you were either cold or hot. [16]So, because you are lukewarm, and neither cold nor hot, I am about to spit you out of my mouth. [17]For you say, 'I am rich, I have prospered, and I need nothing.' You do not realize that you are wretched, pitiable, poor, blind, and naked. [18]Therefore I counsel you to buy from me gold refined by fire so that you may be rich; and white robes to clothe you and to keep the shame of your nakedness from being seen; and salve to anoint your eyes so that you may see. [19]I reprove and discipline those whom I love. Be earnest, therefore, and repent. [20]Listen! I am standing at the door, knocking; if you hear my voice and open the door, I will come in to you and eat with you, and you with me. [21]To the one who conquers I will give a place with me on my throne, just as I myself conquered and sat down with my Father on his throne. [22]Let anyone who has an ear listen to what the Spirit is saying to the churches."

4 After this I looked, and there in heaven a door stood open! And the first voice, which I had heard speaking to me like a trumpet, said, "Come up here, and I will show you what must take place after this." [2]At once I was in the spirit,[b] and there in heaven stood a throne, with one seated on the throne! [3]And the one seated there looks like jasper and carnelian, and around the throne is a rainbow that looks like an emerald. [4]Around the throne are twenty-four thrones, and seated on the thrones are twenty-four elders, dressed in white robes, with golden crowns on their heads. [5]Coming from the throne are flashes of lightning, and rumblings and peals of thunder, and in front of the throne burn seven flaming torches, which are the seven spirits of God; [6]and in front of the throne there is something like a sea of glass, like crystal.

Around the throne, and on each side of the throne, are four living creatures, full of eyes in front and behind: [7]the first living creature like a lion, the second living creature like an ox, the third living creature with a face like a human face, and the fourth living creature like a flying eagle. [8]And the four living creatures, each of them with six wings, are full of eyes all around and inside. Day and night without ceasing they sing,

"Holy, holy, holy,
   the Lord God the Almighty,
      who was and is and is to
         come."

[9]And whenever the living crea-

[a]Or beginning [b]Or in the Spirit

tures give glory and honor and thanks to the one who is seated on the throne, who lives forever and ever, [10]the twenty-four elders fall before the one who is seated on the throne and worship the one who lives forever and ever; they cast their crowns before the throne, singing,

[11] "You are worthy, our Lord
        and God,
    to receive glory and
        honor and power,
for you created all things,
    and by your will they
        existed and were
        created."   .

5 Then I saw in the right hand of the one seated on the throne a scroll written on the inside and on the back, sealed[a] with seven seals; [2]and I saw a mighty angel proclaiming with a loud voice, "Who is worthy to open the scroll and break its seals?" [3]And no one in heaven or on earth or under the earth was able to open the scroll or to look into it. [4]And I began to weep bitterly because no one was found worthy to open the scroll or to look into it. [5]Then one of the elders said to me, "Do not weep. See, the Lion of the tribe of Judah, the Root of David, has conquered, so that he can open the scroll and its seven seals."

6 Then I saw between the throne and the four living creatures and among the elders a Lamb standing as if it had been slaughtered, having seven horns and seven eyes, which are the seven spirits of God sent out into all the earth. [7]He went and took the scroll from the right hand of the one who was seated on the throne. [8]When he had taken the scroll, the four living creatures and the twenty-four elders fell before the Lamb, each holding a harp and golden bowls full of incense, which are the prayers of the saints. [9]They sing a new song:

    "You are worthy to take
        the scroll
    and to open its seals,
for you were slaughtered
    and by your blood
        you ransomed for God
    saints from[b] every tribe
    and language and
        people and nation;
[10] you have made them to be
    a kingdom and priests
        serving[c] our God,
    and they will reign on
        earth."

11 Then I looked, and I heard the voice of many angels surrounding the throne and the living creatures and the elders; they numbered myriads of myriads and thousands of thousands, [12]singing with full voice,

    "Worthy is the Lamb that
        was slaughtered
    to receive power and
        wealth and wisdom
        and might
    and honor and glory and
        blessing!"

[13]Then I heard every creature in heaven and on earth and under

[a]Or written on the inside, and sealed on the back [b]Gk ransomed for God from [c]Gk priests to

the earth and in the sea, and all that is in them, singing,

"To the one seated on the
  throne and to the
  Lamb
be blessing and honor and
  glory and might
  forever and ever!"

¹⁴And the four living creatures said, "Amen!" And the elders fell down and worshiped.

6 Then I saw the Lamb open one of the seven seals, and I heard one of the four living creatures call out, as with a voice of thunder, "Come!"ᵃ ²I looked, and there was a white horse! Its rider had a bow; a crown was given to him, and he came out conquering and to conquer.

3 When he opened the second seal, I heard the second living creature call out, "Come!"ᵃ ⁴And out cameᵇ another horse, bright red; its rider was permitted to take peace from the earth, so that people would slaughter one another; and he was given a great sword.

5 When he opened the third seal, I heard the third living creature call out, "Come!"ᵃ I looked, and there was a black horse! Its rider held a pair of scales in his hand, ⁶and I heard what seemed to be a voice in the midst of the four living creatures saying, "A quart of wheat for a day's pay,ᶜ and three quarts of barley for a day's pay,ᶜ but do not damage the olive oil and the wine!"

7 When he opened the fourth seal, I heard the voice of the fourth living creature call out,

"Come!"ᵃ ⁸I looked and there was a pale green horse! Its rider's name was Death, and Hades followed with him; they were given authority over a fourth of the earth, to kill with sword, famine, and pestilence, and by the wild animals of the earth.

9 When he opened the fifth seal, I saw under the altar the souls of those who had been slaughtered for the word of God and for the testimony they had given; ¹⁰they cried out with a loud voice, "Sovereign Lord, holy and true, how long will it be before you judge and avenge our blood on the inhabitants of the earth?" ¹¹They were each given a white robe and told to rest a little longer, until the number would be complete both of their fellow servantsᵈ and of their brothers and sisters,ᵉ who were soon to be killed as they themselves had been killed.

12 When he opened the sixth seal, I looked, and there came a great earthquake; the sun became black as sackcloth, the full moon became like blood, ¹³and the stars of the sky fell to the earth as the fig tree drops its winter fruit when shaken by a gale. ¹⁴The sky vanished like a scroll rolling itself up, and every mountain and island was removed from its place. ¹⁵Then the kings of the earth and the magnates and the generals and the rich and the powerful, and everyone, slave and free, hid in the caves and among

ᵃOr "*Go!*" ᵇOr went ᶜGk *a denarius* ᵈGk *slaves* ᵉGk *brothers* the rocks of the mountains, [16]calling to the mountains and rocks, "Fall on us and hide us from the face of the one seated on the throne and from the wrath of the Lamb; [17]for the great day of their wrath has come, and who is able to stand?"

7 After this I saw four angels standing at the four corners of the earth, holding back the four winds of the earth so that no wind could blow on earth or sea or against any tree. [2]I saw another angel ascending from the rising of the sun, having the seal of the living God, and he called with a loud voice to the four angels who had been given power to damage earth and sea, [3]saying, "Do not damage the earth or the sea or the trees, until we have marked the servants of our God with a seal on their foreheads."

4 And I heard the number of those who were sealed, one hundred forty-four thousand, sealed out of every tribe of the people of Israel:

5 From the tribe of Judah
   twelve thousand sealed,
   from the tribe of Reuben
   twelve thousand,
   from the tribe of Gad twelve
   thousand,
6 from the tribe of Asher
   twelve thousand,
   from the tribe of Naphtali
   twelve thousand,
   from the tribe of Manasseh
   twelve thousand,
7 from the tribe of Simeon
   twelve thousand,

from the tribe of Levi twelve
   thousand,
from the tribe of Issachar
   twelve thousand,
8 from the tribe of Zebulun
   twelve thousand,
from the tribe of Joseph
   twelve thousand,
from the tribe of Benjamin
   twelve thousand sealed.

9 After this I looked, and there was a great multitude that no one could count, from every nation, from all tribes and peoples and languages, standing before the throne and before the Lamb, robed in white, with palm branches in their hands. [10]They cried out in a loud voice, saying,

"Salvation belongs to our
   God who is seated on
   the throne, and to the
   Lamb!"

[11]And all the angels stood around the throne and around the elders and the four living creatures, and they fell on their faces before the throne and worshiped God, [12]singing,

"Amen! Blessing and glory
   and wisdom
   and thanksgiving and
   honor
   and power and might
   be to our God forever and
   ever! Amen."

13 Then one of the elders addressed me, saying, "Who are these, robed in white, and where have they come from?" [14]I said to him, "Sir, you are the one that knows." Then he said to me, "These are they who have come out of the great ordeal; they have

washed their robes and made them white in the blood of the Lamb.

15 For this reason they are
　　before the throne of
　　　God,
　and worship him day
　　　and night within his
　　　temple,
　and the one who is
　　seated on the throne
　will shelter them.

16 They will hunger no more,
　　and thirst no more;
　the sun will not strike
　　them,
　nor any scorching heat;

17 for the Lamb at the center
　　of the throne will be
　　their shepherd,
　and he will guide them
　　to springs of the
　　water of life,
　and God will wipe away
　　every tear from their eyes."

8 When the Lamb opened the seventh seal, there was silence in heaven for about half an hour. 2And I saw the seven angels who stand before God, and seven trumpets were given to them.

3 Another angel with a golden censer came and stood at the altar; he was given a great quantity of incense to offer with the prayers of all the saints on the golden altar that is before the throne. 4And the smoke of the incense, with the prayers of the saints, rose before God from the hand of the angel. 5Then the angel took the censer and filled it with fire from the altar and threw it on the earth; and there were peals of thunder, rumblings, flashes of lightning, and an earthquake.

6 Now the seven angels who had the seven trumpets made ready to blow them.

7 The first angel blew his trumpet, and there came hail and fire, mixed with blood, and they were hurled to the earth; and a third of the earth was burned up, and a third of the trees were burned up, and all green grass was burned up.

8 The second angel blew his trumpet, and something like a great mountain, burning with fire, was thrown into the sea. 9A third of the sea became blood, a third of the living creatures in the sea died, and a third of the ships were destroyed.

10 The third angel blew his trumpet, and a great star fell from heaven, blazing like a torch, and it fell on a third of the rivers and on the springs of water. 11The name of the star is Wormwood. A third of the waters became wormwood, and many died from the water, because it was made bitter.

12 The fourth angel blew his trumpet, and a third of the sun was struck, and a third of the moon, and a third of the stars, so that a third of their light was darkened; a third of the day was kept from shining, and likewise the night.

13 Then I looked, and I heard an eagle crying with a loud voice as it flew in midheaven, "Woe, woe, woe to the inhabitants of the earth, at the blasts of the other trumpets that the three angels are about to blow!"

9 And the fifth angel blew his trumpet, and I saw a star that had fallen from heaven to earth, and he was given the key to the shaft of the bottomless pit; [2]he opened the shaft of the bottomless pit, and from the shaft rose smoke like the smoke of a great furnace, and the sun and the air were darkened with the smoke from the shaft. [3]Then from the smoke came locusts on the earth, and they were given authority like the authority of scorpions of the earth. [4]They were told not to damage the grass of the earth or any green growth or any tree, but only those people who do not have the seal of God on their foreheads. [5]They were allowed to torture them for five months, but not to kill them, and their torture was like the torture of a scorpion when it stings someone. [6]And in those days people will seek death but will not find it; they will long to die, but death will flee from them.

7 In appearance the locusts were like horses equipped for battle. On their heads were what looked like crowns of gold; their faces were like human faces, [8]their hair like women's hair, and their teeth were like lions' teeth; [9]they had scales like iron breastplates, and the noise of their wings was like the noise of many chariots with horses rushing into battle. [10]They have tails like scorpions, with stingers, and in their tails is their power to harm people for five months. [11]They have as king over them the angel of the bottomless pit; his name in Hebrew is Abaddon,[a] and in Greek he is called Apollyon.[b]

12 The first woe has passed. There are still two woes to come.

13 Then the sixth angel blew his trumpet, and I heard a voice from the four[c] horns of the golden altar before God, [14]saying to the sixth angel who had the trumpet, "Release the four angels who are bound at the great river Euphrates." [15]So the four angels were released, who had been held ready for the hour, the day, the month, and the year, to kill a third of humankind. [16]The number of the troops of cavalry was two hundred million; I heard their number. [17]And this was how I saw the horses in my vision: the riders wore breastplates the color of fire and of sapphire[d] and of sulfur; the heads of the horses were like lions' heads, and fire and smoke and sulfur came out of their mouths. [18]By these three plagues a third of humankind was killed, by the fire and smoke and sulfur coming out of their mouths. [19]For the power of the horses is in their mouths and in their tails; their tails are like serpents, having heads; and with them they inflict harm.

20 The rest of humankind, who were not killed by these plagues, did not repent of the works of their hands or give up worshiping demons and idols of gold and silver and bronze and stone and wood, which cannot see

---

[a]That is, *Destruction* [b]That is, *Destroyer* [c]Other ancient authorities lack *four* [d]Gk *hyacinth*

or hear or walk. ²¹And they did not repent of their murders or their sorceries or their fornication or their thefts.

10

And I saw another mighty angel coming down from heaven, wrapped in a cloud, with a rainbow over his head; his face was like the sun, and his legs like pillars of fire. ²He held a little scroll open in his hand. Setting his right foot on the sea and his left foot on the land, ³he gave a great shout, like a lion roaring. And when he shouted, the seven thunders sounded. ⁴And when the seven thunders had sounded, I was about to write, but I heard a voice from heaven saying, "Seal up what the seven thunders have said, and do not write it down." ⁵Then the angel whom I saw standing on the sea and the land

raised his right hand to
heaven
⁶   and swore by him who
lives forever and
ever,

who created heaven and what is in it, the earth and what is in it, and the sea and what is in it: "There will be no more delay, ⁷but in the days when the seventh angel is to blow his trumpet, the mystery of God will be fulfilled, as he announced to his servants[a] the prophets."

8 Then the voice that I had heard from heaven spoke to me again, saying, "Go, take the scroll that is open in the hand of the angel who is standing on the sea and on the land." ⁹So I went to the angel and told him to give me the little scroll; and he said to me, "Take it, and eat; it will be bitter to your stomach, but sweet as honey in your mouth." ¹⁰So I took the little scroll from the hand of the angel and ate it; it was sweet as honey in my mouth, but when I had eaten it, my stomach was made bitter.

11 Then they said to me, "You must prophesy again about many peoples and nations and languages and kings."

11

Then I was given a measuring rod like a staff, and I was told, "Come and measure the temple of God and the altar and those who worship there, ²but do not measure the court outside the temple; leave that out, for it is given over to the nations, and they will trample over the holy city for forty-two months. ³And I will grant my two witnesses authority to prophesy for one thousand two hundred sixty days, wearing sackcloth."

4 These are the two olive trees and the two lampstands that stand before the Lord of the earth. ⁵And if anyone wants to harm them, fire pours from their mouth and consumes their foes; anyone who wants to harm them must be killed in this manner. ⁶They have authority to shut the sky, so that no rain may fall during the days of their prophesying, and they have authority over the waters to turn them into blood, and to strike the earth with

―――――――――――――――
[a]Gk slaves

every kind of plague, as often as they desire.

7 When they have finished their testimony, the beast that comes up from the bottomless pit will make war on them and conquer them and kill them, [8]and their dead bodies will lie in the street of the great city that is prophetically[a] called Sodom and Egypt, where also their Lord was crucified. [9]For three and a half days members of the peoples and tribes and languages and nations will gaze at their dead bodies and refuse to let them be placed in a tomb; [10]and the inhabitants of the earth will gloat over them and celebrate and exchange presents, because these two prophets had been a torment to the inhabitants of the earth.

11 But after the three and a half days, the breath[b] of life from God entered them, and they stood on their feet, and those who saw them were terrified. [12]Then they[c] heard a loud voice from heaven saying to them, "Come up here!" And they went up to heaven in a cloud while their enemies watched them. [13]At that moment there was a great earthquake, and a tenth of the city fell; seven thousand people were killed in the earthquake, and the rest were terrified and gave glory to the God of heaven.

14 The second woe has passed. The third woe is coming very soon.

15 Then the seventh angel blew his trumpet, and there were loud voices in heaven, saying,

"The kingdom of the world
    has become the
    kingdom of our Lord
    and of his Messiah,[d]
and he will reign forever
    and ever."

16 Then the twenty-four elders who sit on their thrones before God fell on their faces and worshiped God, [17]singing,

"We give you thanks, Lord
    God Almighty,
who are and who were,
for you have taken your
    great power
    and begun to reign.
[18]   The nations raged,
    but your wrath has come,
    and the time for judging
        the dead,
for rewarding your
    servants,[e] the
        prophets
    and saints and all who
        fear your name,
    both small and great,
and for destroying those
    who destroy the earth."

19 Then God's temple in heaven was opened, and the ark of his covenant was seen within his temple; and there were flashes of lightning, rumblings, peals of thunder, an earthquake, and heavy hail.

12 A great portent appeared in heaven: a woman clothed with the sun, with the moon under her feet, and on her head a crown of twelve stars. [2]She

[a]Or *allegorically;* Gk *spiritually* [b]Or *the spirit* [c]Other ancient authorities read *I* [d]Gk *Christ* [e]Gk *slaves*

was pregnant and was crying out in birth pangs, in the agony of giving birth. [3]Then another portent appeared in heaven: a great red dragon, with seven heads and ten horns, and seven diadems on his heads. [4]His tail swept down a third of the stars of heaven and threw them to the earth. Then the dragon stood before the woman who was about to bear a child, so that he might devour her child as soon as it was born. [5]And she gave birth to a son, a male child, who is to rule[a] all the nations with a rod of iron. But her child was snatched away and taken to God and to his throne; [6]and the woman fled into the wilderness, where she has a place prepared by God, so that there she can be nourished for one thousand two hundred sixty days.

7 And war broke out in heaven; Michael and his angels fought against the dragon. The dragon and his angels fought back, [8]but they were defeated, and there was no longer any place for them in heaven. [9]The great dragon was thrown down, that ancient serpent, who is called the Devil and Satan, the deceiver of the whole world—he was thrown down to the earth, and his angels were thrown down with him.

10 Then I heard a loud voice in heaven, proclaiming,

"Now have come the
     salvation and the
     power
and the kingdom of our
     God
and the authority of his
     Messiah,[b]
for the accuser of our
     comrades[c] has been
     thrown down,
who accuses them day
     and night before our
     God.
[11] But they have conquered
     him by the blood of
     the Lamb
and by the word of their
     testimony,
for they did not cling to life
     even in the face of
     death.
[12] Rejoice then, you heavens
     and those who dwell in
     them!
But woe to the earth and
     the sea,
for the devil has come
     down to you
with great wrath,
because he knows that
     his time is short!"

13 So when the dragon saw that he had been thrown down to the earth, he pursued[d] the woman who had given birth to the male child. [14]But the woman was given the two wings of the great eagle, so that she could fly from the serpent into the wilderness, to her place where she is nourished for a time, and times, and half a time. [15]Then from his mouth the serpent poured water like a river after the woman, to sweep her away with the flood. [16]But the earth came to the help of the woman; it opened its mouth

---

[a]Or to shepherd [b]Gk Christ [c]Gk brothers [d]Or persecuted

and swallowed the river that the dragon had poured from his mouth. [17]Then the dragon was angry with the woman, and went off to make war on the rest of her children, those who keep the commandments of God and hold the testimony of Jesus.

18 Then the dragon[a] took his stand on the sand of the seashore.

13 [1]And I saw a beast rising out of the sea, having ten horns and seven heads; and on its horns were ten diadems, and on its heads were blasphemous names. [2]And the beast that I saw was like a leopard, its feet were like a bear's, and its mouth was like a lion's mouth. And the dragon gave it his power and his throne and great authority. [3]One of its heads seemed to have received a death-blow, but its mortal wound[b] had been healed. In amazement the whole earth followed the beast. [4]They worshiped the dragon, for he had given his authority to the beast, and they worshiped the beast, saying, "Who is like the beast, and who can fight against it?"

5 The beast was given a mouth uttering haughty and blasphemous words, and it was allowed to exercise authority for forty-two months. [6]It opened its mouth to utter blasphemies against God, blaspheming his name and his dwelling, that is, those who dwell in heaven. [7]Also it was allowed to make war on the saints and to conquer them.[c] It was given authority over every tribe and people and language

and nation, [8]and all the inhabitants of the earth will worship it, everyone whose name has not been written from the foundation of the world in the book of life of the Lamb that was slaughtered.[d]

9 Let anyone who has an ear listen:

10 If you are to be taken
        captive,
      into captivity you go;
    if you kill with the sword,
      with the sword you must
        be killed.

Here is a call for the endurance and faith of the saints.

11 Then I saw another beast that rose out of the earth; it had two horns like a lamb and it spoke like a dragon. [12]It exercises all the authority of the first beast on its behalf, and it makes the earth and its inhabitants worship the first beast, whose mortal wound[e] had been healed. [13]It performs great signs, even making fire come down from heaven to earth in the sight of all; [14]and by the signs that it is allowed to perform on behalf of the beast, it deceives the inhabitants of earth, telling them to make an image for the beast that had been wounded by the sword[f] and yet lived; [15]and it was allowed to give breath[g] to the image of the beast so that the image of the beast could even speak and cause those who would

[a]Gk *Then he;* other ancient authorities read *Then I stood* [b]Gk *the plague of its death* [c]Other ancient authorities lack this sentence [d]Or *written in the book of life of the Lamb that was slaughtered from the foundation of the world* [e]Gk *whose plague of its death* [f]Or *that had received the plague of the sword* [g]Or *spirit*

not worship the image of the beast to be killed. [16]Also it causes all, both small and great, both rich and poor, both free and slave, to be marked on the right hand or the forehead, [17]so that no one can buy or sell who does not have the mark, that is, the name of the beast or the number of its name. [18]This calls for wisdom: let anyone with understanding calculate the number of the beast, for it is the number of a person. Its number is six hundred sixty-six.[a]

14 Then I looked, and there was the Lamb, standing on Mount Zion! And with him were one hundred forty-four thousand who had his name and his Father's name written on their foreheads. [2]And I heard a voice from heaven like the sound of many waters and like the sound of loud thunder; the voice I heard was like the sound of harpists playing on their harps, [3]and they sing a new song before the throne and before the four living creatures and before the elders. No one could learn that song except the one hundred forty-four thousand who have been redeemed from the earth. [4]It is these who have not defiled themselves with women, for they are virgins; these follow the Lamb wherever he goes. They have been redeemed from humankind as first fruits for God and the Lamb, [5]and in their mouth no lie was found; they are blameless.

[6]Then I saw another angel flying in midheaven, with an eternal gospel to proclaim to those who live[b] on the earth—to every nation and tribe and language and people. [7]He said in a loud voice, "Fear God and give him glory, for the hour of his judgment has come; and worship him who made heaven and earth, the sea and the springs of water."

[8]Then another angel, a second, followed, saying, "Fallen, fallen is Babylon the great! She has made all nations drink of the wine of the wrath of her fornication."

[9]Then another angel, a third, followed them, crying with a loud voice, "Those who worship the beast and its image, and receive a mark on their foreheads or on their hands, [10]they will also drink the wine of God's wrath, poured unmixed into the cup of his anger, and they will be tormented with fire and sulfur in the presence of the holy angels and in the presence of the Lamb. [11]And the smoke of their torment goes up forever and ever. There is no rest day or night for those who worship the beast and its image and for anyone who receives the mark of its name."

[12]Here is a call for the endurance of the saints, those who keep the commandments of God and hold fast to the faith of[c] Jesus.

[13]And I heard a voice from heaven saying, "Write this: Blessed are the dead who from now on die in the Lord." "Yes," says the Spirit, "they will rest from their labors, for their deeds follow them."

---

[a]Other ancient authorities read *six hundred sixteen*
[b]Gk *sit* [c]Or *to their faith in*

14 Then I looked, and there was a white cloud, and seated on the cloud was one like the Son of Man, with a golden crown on his head, and a sharp sickle in his hand! [15]Another angel came out of the temple, calling with a loud voice to the one who sat on the cloud, "Use your sickle and reap, for the hour to reap has come, because the harvest of the earth is fully ripe." [16]So the one who sat on the cloud swung his sickle over the earth, and the earth was reaped.

17 Then another angel came out of the temple in heaven, and he too had a sharp sickle. [18]Then another angel came out from the altar, the angel who has authority over fire, and he called with a loud voice to him who had the sharp sickle, "Use your sharp sickle and gather the clusters of the vine of the earth, for its grapes are ripe." [19]So the angel swung his sickle over the earth and gathered the vintage of the earth, and he threw it into the great wine press of the wrath of God. [20]And the wine press was trodden outside the city, and blood flowed from the wine press, as high as a horse's bridle, for a distance of about two hundred miles.[a]

15 Then I saw another portent in heaven, great and amazing: seven angels with seven plagues, which are the last, for with them the wrath of God is ended.

2 And I saw what appeared to be a sea of glass mixed with fire, and those who had conquered the beast and its image and the number of its name, standing beside the sea of glass with harps of God in their hands. [3]And they sing the song of Moses, the servant[b] of God, and the song of the Lamb:

"Great and amazing are
    your deeds,
  Lord God the Almighty!
Just and true are your ways,
  King of the nations![c]
4 Lord, who will not fear
  and glorify your name?
For you alone are holy.
  All nations will come
  and worship before you,
for your judgments have
    been revealed."

5 After this I looked, and the temple of the tent[d] of witness in heaven was opened, [6]and out of the temple came the seven angels with the seven plagues, robed in pure bright linen,[e] with golden sashes across their chests. [7]Then one of the four living creatures gave the seven angels seven golden bowls full of the wrath of God, who lives forever and ever; [8]and the temple was filled with smoke from the glory of God and from his power, and no one could enter the temple until the seven plagues of the seven angels were ended.

16 Then I heard a loud voice from the temple telling the seven angels, "Go and pour out on the earth the seven bowls of the wrath of God."

---

[a]Gk *one thousand six hundred stadia* [b]Gk *slave* [c]Other ancient authorities read *the ages* [d]Or *tabernacle* [e]Other ancient authorities read *stone*

2 So the first angel went and poured his bowl on the earth, and a foul and painful sore came on those who had the mark of the beast and who worshiped its image.

3 The second angel poured his bowl into the sea, and it became like the blood of a corpse, and every living thing in the sea died.

4 The third angel poured his bowl into the rivers and the springs of water, and they became blood. [5]And I heard the angel of the waters say,

"You are just, O Holy One,
    who are and were,
for you have judged
    these things;
[6] because they shed the
    blood of saints and
    prophets,
you have given them
    blood to drink.
It is what they deserve!"
[7]And I heard the altar respond,
"Yes, O Lord God, the
    Almighty,
your judgments are true
    and just!"

8 The fourth angel poured his bowl on the sun, and it was allowed to scorch them with fire; [9]they were scorched by the fierce heat, but they cursed the name of God, who had authority over these plagues, and they did not repent and give him glory.

10 The fifth angel poured his bowl on the throne of the beast, and its kingdom was plunged into darkness; people gnawed their tongues in agony, [11]and cursed the God of heaven because of their pains and sores, and they did not repent of their deeds.

12 The sixth angel poured his bowl on the great river Euphrates, and its water was dried up in order to prepare the way for the kings from the east. [13]And I saw three foul spirits like frogs coming from the mouth of the dragon, from the mouth of the beast, and from the mouth of the false prophet. [14]These are demonic spirits, performing signs, who go abroad to the kings of the whole world, to assemble them for battle on the great day of God the Almighty. [15]("See, I am coming like a thief! Blessed is the one who stays awake and is clothed[a], not going about naked and exposed to shame.") [16]And they assembled them at the place that in Hebrew is called Harmagedon.

17 The seventh angel poured his bowl into the air, and a loud voice came out of the temple, from the throne, saying, "It is done!" [18]And there came flashes of lightning, rumblings, peals of thunder, and a violent earthquake, such as had not occurred since people were upon the earth, so violent was that earthquake. [19]The great city was split into three parts, and the cities of the nations fell. God remembered great Babylon and gave her the wine-cup of the fury of his wrath. [20]And every island fled away, and no mountains were to be found; [21]and huge hailstones, each weighing about a hundred pounds,[b]

---

[a]Gk and keeps his robes [b]Gk weighing about a talent

dropped from heaven on people, until they cursed God for the plague of the hail, so fearful was that plague.

17 Then one of the seven angels who had the seven bowls came and said to me, "Come, I will show you the judgment of the great whore who is seated on many waters, ²with whom the kings of the earth have committed fornication, and with the wine of whose fornication the inhabitants of the earth have become drunk." ³So he carried me away in the spirit*ᵃ* into a wilderness, and I saw a woman sitting on a scarlet beast that was full of blasphemous names, and it had seven heads and ten horns. ⁴The woman was clothed in purple and scarlet, and adorned with gold and jewels and pearls, holding in her hand a golden cup full of abominations and the impurities of her fornication; ⁵and on her forehead was written a name, a mystery: "Babylon the great, mother of whores and of earth's abominations." ⁶And I saw that the woman was drunk with the blood of the saints and the blood of the witnesses to Jesus.

When I saw her, I was greatly amazed. ⁷But the angel said to me, "Why are you so amazed? I will tell you the mystery of the woman, and of the beast with seven heads and ten horns that carries her. ⁸The beast that you saw was, and is not, and is about to ascend from the bottomless pit and go to destruction. And the inhabitants of the earth, whose names have not been written in the book of life from the foundation of the world, will be amazed when they see the beast, because it was and is not and is to come.

9 "This calls for a mind that has wisdom: the seven heads are seven mountains on which the woman is seated; also, they are seven kings, ¹⁰of whom five have fallen, one is living, and the other has not yet come; and when he comes, he must remain only a little while. ¹¹As for the beast that was and is not, it is an eighth but it belongs to the seven, and it goes to destruction. ¹²And the ten horns that you saw are ten kings who have not yet received a kingdom, but they are to receive authority as kings for one hour, together with the beast. ¹³These are united in yielding their power and authority to the beast; ¹⁴they will make war on the Lamb, and the Lamb will conquer them, for he is Lord of lords and King of kings, and those with him are called and chosen and faithful."

15 And he said to me, "The waters that you saw, where the whore is seated, are peoples and multitudes and nations and languages. ¹⁶And the ten horns that you saw, they and the beast will hate the whore; they will make her desolate and naked; they will devour her flesh and burn her up with fire. ¹⁷For God has put it into their hearts to carry out his

ᵃOr in the Spirit

purpose by agreeing to give their kingdom to the beast, until the words of God will be fulfilled. [18]The woman you saw is the great city that rules over the kings of the earth."

18

After this I saw another angel coming down from heaven, having great authority; and the earth was made bright with his splendor. [2]He called out with a mighty voice,

"Fallen, fallen is Babylon
　　the great!
It has become a dwelling
　　place of demons,
a haunt of every foul spirit,
a haunt of every foul bird,
a haunt of every foul and
　　hateful beast.[a]
[3]For all the nations have
　　drunk[b]
of the wine of the wrath
　　of her fornication,
and the kings of the earth
　　have committed
　　fornication with her,
and the merchants of the
　　earth have grown
　　rich from the power[c]
　　of her luxury."

[4]Then I heard another voice from heaven saying,

"Come out of her, my
　　people,
so that you do not take
　　part in her sins,
and so that you do not
　　share in her plagues;
[5]for her sins are heaped
　　high as heaven,
and God has
　　remembered her
　　iniquities.

[6]Render to her as she
　　herself has rendered,
and repay her double for
　　her deeds;
mix a double draught for
　　her in the cup she
　　mixed.
[7]As she glorified herself and
　　lived luxuriously,
so give her a like
　　measure of torment
　　and grief.
Since in her heart she says,
'I rule as a queen;
I am no widow,
and I will never see grief,'
[8]therefore her plagues will
　　come in a single day—
pestilence and mourning
　　and famine—
and she will be burned
　　with fire;
for mighty is the Lord
　　God who judges her."

[9]And the kings of the earth, who committed fornication and lived in luxury with her, will weep and wail over her when they see the smoke of her burning; [10]they will stand far off, in fear of her torment, and say,

"Alas, alas, the great city,
　　Babylon, the mighty city!
For in one hour your
　　judgment has come."

[11]And the merchants of the earth weep and mourn for her, since no one buys their cargo anymore, [12]cargo of gold, silver,

---

[a]Other ancient authorities lack the words *a haunt of every foul beast* and attach the words *and hateful* to the previous line so as to read *a haunt of every foul and hateful bird* [b]Other ancient authorities read *She has made all nations drink* [c]Or *resources*

jewels and pearls, fine linen, purple, silk and scarlet, all kinds of scented wood, all articles of ivory, all articles of costly wood, bronze, iron, and marble, [13]cinnamon, spice, incense, myrrh, frankincense, wine, olive oil, choice flour and wheat, cattle and sheep, horses and chariots, slaves—and human lives.[a]

[14] "The fruit for which your
soul longed
has gone from you,
and all your dainties and
your splendor
are lost to you,
never to be found again!"

[15]The merchants of these wares, who gained wealth from her, will stand far off, in fear of her torment, weeping and mourning aloud,

[16] "Alas, alas, the great city,
clothed in fine linen,
in purple and scarlet,
adorned with gold,
with jewels, and with
pearls!

[17] For in one hour all this
wealth has been laid
waste!"

And all shipmasters and seafarers, sailors and all whose trade is on the sea, stood far off [18]and cried out as they saw the smoke of her burning,

"What city was like the
great city?"

[19]And they threw dust on their heads, as they wept and mourned, crying out,

"Alas, alas, the great city,
where all who had ships
at sea
grew rich by her wealth!

For in one hour she has
been laid waste.

[20] Rejoice over her, O heaven,
you saints and apostles
and prophets!
For God has given
judgment for you
against her."

[21] Then a mighty angel took up a stone like a great millstone and threw it into the sea, saying,

"With such violence
Babylon the great city
will be thrown down,
and will be found no more;

[22] and the sound of harpists
and minstrels and of
flutists and trumpeters
will be heard in you no
more;
and an artisan of any trade
will be found in you no
more;
and the sound of the
millstone
will be heard in you no
more;

[23] and the light of a lamp
will shine in you no more;
and the voice of
bridegroom and bride
will be heard in you no
more;
for your merchants were
the magnates of the
earth,
and all nations were
deceived by your
sorcery.

[24] And in you[b] was found the
blood of prophets
and of saints,

---

[a]Or chariots, and human bodies and souls [b]Gk her

and of all who have been
    slaughtered on earth."

19 After this I heard what
seemed to be the loud
voice of a great multitude in heav-
en, saying,
    "Hallelujah!
    Salvation and glory and
        power to our God,
2   for his judgments are
        true and just;
    he has judged the great
        whore
    who corrupted the earth
        with her fornication,
    and he has avenged on her
        the blood of his
        servants."[a]
3Once more they said,
    "Hallelujah!
    The smoke goes up from
        her forever and ever."
4And the twenty-four elders and
the four living creatures fell
down and worshiped God who is
seated on the throne, saying,
    "Amen. Hallelujah!"
    5 And from the throne came a
voice saying,
    "Praise our God,
    all you his servants,[a]
    and all who fear him,
        small and great."
6Then I heard what seemed to be
the voice of a great multitude,
like the sound of many waters
and like the sound of mighty
thunderpeals, crying out,
    "Hallelujah!
    For the Lord our God
        the Almighty reigns.
7   Let us rejoice and exult
        and give him the glory,
    for the marriage of the

Lamb has come,
    and his bride has made
        herself ready;
8   to her it has been granted
        to be clothed
    with fine linen, bright
        and pure"—
for the fine linen is the righteous
deeds of the saints.

9 And the angel said[b] to me,
"Write this: Blessed are those
who are invited to the marriage
supper of the Lamb." And he
said to me, "These are true words
of God." 10Then I fell down at his
feet to worship him, but he said
to me, "You must not do that! I
am a fellow servant[c] with you
and your comrades[d] who hold
the testimony of Jesus.[e] Worship
God! For the testimony of Jesus[e]
is the spirit of prophecy."

11 Then I saw heaven opened,
and there was a white horse! Its
rider is called Faithful and True,
and in righteousness he judges
and makes war. 12His eyes are
like a flame of fire, and on his
head are many diadems; and he
has a name inscribed that no one
knows but himself. 13He is
clothed in a robe dipped in[f]
blood, and his name is called
The Word of God. 14And the
armies of heaven, wearing fine
linen, white and pure, were following him on white horses.
15From his mouth comes a sharp
sword with which to strike down

---

[a]Gk slaves [b]Gk he said [c]Gk slave [d]Gk brothers [e]Or
to Jesus [f]Other ancient authorities read sprinkled
with

the nations, and he will rule[a] them with a rod of iron; he will tread the wine press of the fury of the wrath of God the Almighty. [16]On his robe and on his thigh he has a name inscribed, "King of kings and Lord of lords."

17 Then I saw an angel standing in the sun, and with a loud voice he called to all the birds that fly in midheaven, "Come, gather for the great supper of God, [18]to eat the flesh of kings, the flesh of captains, the flesh of the mighty, the flesh of horses and their riders—flesh of all, both free and slave, both small and great." [19]Then I saw the beast and the kings of the earth with their armies gathered to make war against the rider on the horse and against his army. [20]And the beast was captured, and with it the false prophet who had performed in its presence the signs by which he deceived those who had received the mark of the beast and those who worshiped its image. These two were thrown alive into the lake of fire that burns with sulfur. [21]And the rest were killed by the sword of the rider on the horse, the sword that came from his mouth; and all the birds were gorged with their flesh.

20 Then I saw an angel coming down from heaven, holding in his hand the key to the bottomless pit and a great chain. [2]He seized the dragon, that ancient serpent, who is the Devil and Satan, and bound him for a thousand years, [3]and threw him into the pit, and locked and sealed it over him, so that he would deceive the nations no more, until the thousand years were ended. After that he must be let out for a little while.

4 Then I saw thrones, and those seated on them were given authority to judge. I also saw the souls of those who had been beheaded for their testimony to Jesus[b] and for the word of God. They had not worshiped the beast or its image and had not received its mark on their foreheads or their hands. They came to life and reigned with Christ a thousand years. [5](The rest of the dead did not come to life until the thousand years were ended.) This is the first resurrection. [6]Blessed and holy are those who share in the first resurrection. Over these the second death has no power, but they will be priests of God and of Christ, and they will reign with him a thousand years.

7 When the thousand years are ended, Satan will be released from his prison [8]and will come out to deceive the nations at the four corners of the earth, Gog and Magog, in order to gather them for battle; they are as numerous as the sands of the sea. [9]They marched up over the breadth of the earth and surrounded the camp of the saints and the beloved city. And fire came down from heaven[c] and consumed them. [10]And the devil who had deceived them was thrown into

[a]Or will shepherd [b]Or for the testimony of Jesus [c]Other ancient authorities read from God, out of heaven, or out of heaven from God

the lake of fire and sulfur, where the beast and the false prophet were, and they will be tormented day and night forever and ever.

11 Then I saw a great white throne and the one who sat on it; the earth and the heaven fled from his presence, and no place was found for them. [12]And I saw the dead, great and small, standing before the throne, and books were opened. Also another book was opened, the book of life. And the dead were judged according to their works, as recorded in the books. [13]And the sea gave up the dead that were in it, Death and Hades gave up the dead that were in them, and all were judged according to what they had done. [14]Then Death and Hades were thrown into the lake of fire. This is the second death, the lake of fire; [15]and anyone whose name was not found written in the book of life was thrown into the lake of fire.

21 Then I saw a new heaven and a new earth; for the first heaven and the first earth had passed away, and the sea was no more. [2]And I saw the holy city, the new Jerusalem, coming down out of heaven from God, prepared as a bride adorned for her husband. [3]And I heard a loud voice from the throne saying,

"See, the home[a] of God is
    among mortals.
He will dwell[b] with them
    as their God;
they will be his peoples,[c]
and God himself will be
    with them;[d]

4 he will wipe every tear
       from their eyes.
Death will be no more;
    mourning and crying and
       pain will be no more,
    for the first things have
       passed away."

5 And the one who was seated on the throne said, "See, I am making all things new." Also he said, "Write this, for these words are trustworthy and true." [6]Then he said to me, "It is done! I am the Alpha and the Omega, the beginning and the end. To the thirsty I will give water as a gift from the spring of the water of life. [7]Those who conquer will inherit these things, and I will be their God and they will be my children. [8]But as for the cowardly, the faithless,[e] the polluted, the murderers, the fornicators, the sorcerers, the idolaters, and all liars, their place will be in the lake that burns with fire and sulfur, which is the second death."

9 Then one of the seven angels who had the seven bowls full of the seven last plagues came and said to me, "Come, I will show you the bride, the wife of the Lamb." [10]And in the spirit[f] he carried me away to a great, high mountain and showed me the holy city Jerusalem coming down out of heaven from God. [11]It has the glory of God and a radiance like a very rare jewel, like jasper, clear as crystal. [12]It has

---

[a]Gk the tabernacle [b]Gk will tabernacle [c]Other ancient authorities read people [d]Other ancient authorities add and be their God [e]Or the unbelieving [f]Or in the Spirit

a great, high wall with twelve gates, and at the gates twelve angels, and on the gates are inscribed the names of the twelve tribes of the Israelites; [13]on the east three gates, on the north three gates, on the south three gates, and on the west three gates. [14]And the wall of the city has twelve foundations, and on them are the twelve names of the twelve apostles of the Lamb.

15 The angel[a] who talked to me had a measuring rod of gold to measure the city and its gates and walls. [16]The city lies foursquare, its length the same as its width; and he measured the city with his rod, fifteen hundred miles;[b] its length and width and height are equal. [17]He also measured its wall, one hundred forty-four cubits[c] by human measurement, which the angel was using. [18]The wall is built of jasper, while the city is pure gold, clear as glass. [19]The foundations of the wall of the city are adorned with every jewel; the first was jasper, the second sapphire, the third agate, the fourth emerald, [20]the fifth onyx, the sixth carnelian, the seventh chrysolite, the eighth beryl, the ninth topaz, the tenth chrysoprase, the eleventh jacinth, the twelfth amethyst. [21]And the twelve gates are twelve pearls, each of the gates is a single pearl, and the street of the city is pure gold, transparent as glass. [22]I saw no temple in the city, for its temple is the Lord God the Almighty and the Lamb. [23]And the city has no need of sun or moon to shine on it, for the glory of God is its light, and its lamp is the Lamb. [24]The nations will walk by its light, and the kings of the earth will bring their glory into it. [25]Its gates will never be shut by day—and there will be no night there. [26]People will bring into it the glory and the honor of the nations. [27]But nothing unclean will enter it, nor anyone who practices abomination or falsehood, but only those who are written in the Lamb's book of life.

22 Then the angel[d] showed me the river of the water of life, bright as crystal, flowing from the throne of God and of the Lamb [2]through the middle of the street of the city. On either side of the river is the tree of life[e] with its twelve kinds of fruit, producing its fruit each month; and the leaves of the tree are for the healing of the nations. [3]Nothing accursed will be found there any more. But the throne of God and of the Lamb will be in it, and his servants[f] will worship him; [4]they will see his face, and his name will be on their foreheads. [5]And there will be no more night; they need no light of lamp or sun, for the Lord God will be their light, and they will reign forever and ever.

6 And he said to me, "These words are trustworthy and true, for the Lord, the God of the spirits of the prophets, has sent his angel to show his servants[f] what must soon take place."

---

[a]Gk *He* [b]Gk *twelve thousand stadia* [c]*That is, almost seventy-five yards* [d]Gk *he* [e]*Or the Lamb.* [2]*In the middle of the street of the city, and on either side of the river, is the tree of life* [f]Gk *slaves*

7 "See, I am coming soon! Blessed is the one who keeps the words of the prophecy of this book."

8 I, John, am the one who heard and saw these things. And when I heard and saw them, I fell down to worship at the feet of the angel who showed them to me; [9]but he said to me, "You must not do that! I am a fellow servant[a] with you and your comrades[b] the prophets, and with those who keep the words of this book. Worship God!"

10 And he said to me, "Do not seal up the words of the prophecy of this book, for the time is near. [11]Let the evildoer still do evil, and the filthy still be filthy, and the righteous still do right, and the holy still be holy."

12 "See, I am coming soon; my reward is with me, to repay according to everyone's work. [13]I am the Alpha and the Omega, the first and the last, the beginning and the end."

14 Blessed are those who wash their robes,[c] so that they will have the right to the tree of life and may enter the city by the gates. [15]Outside are the dogs and sorcerers and fornicators and murderers and idolaters, and everyone who loves and practices falsehood.

16 "It is I, Jesus, who sent my angel to you with this testimony for the churches. I am the root and the descendant of David, the bright morning star."

17   The Spirit and the bride
       say, "Come."
   And let everyone who
       hears say, "Come."
   And let everyone who is
       thirsty come.
   Let anyone who wishes
       take the water of life
       as a gift.

18 I warn everyone who hears the words of the prophecy of this book: if anyone adds to them, God will add to that person the plagues described in this book; [19]if anyone takes away from the words of the book of this prophecy, God will take away that person's share in the tree of life and in the holy city, which are described in this book.

20 The one who testifies to these things says, "Surely I am coming soon." Amen. Come, Lord Jesus!

21 The grace of the Lord Jesus be with all the saints. Amen.[d]

[a]Gk slave [b]Gk brothers [c]Other ancient authorities read do his commandments [d]Other ancient authorities lack all; others lack the saints; others lack Amen

THE PSALMS

BOOK I

(Psalms 1-41)

Psalm 1

1 Happy are those
who do not follow the
advice of the wicked,
or take the path that
sinners tread,
or sit in the seat of scoffers;
2 but their delight is in the
law of the LORD,
and on his law they
meditate day and
night.
3 They are like trees
planted by streams of
water,
which yield their fruit in its
season,
and their leaves do not
wither.
In all that they do, they
prosper.

4 The wicked are not so,
but are like chaff that
the wind drives away.
5 Therefore the wicked will
not stand in
the judgment,
nor sinners in the
congregation of
the righteous;
6 for the LORD watches over
the way of the
righteous,
but the way of the
wicked will perish.

Psalm 2

1 Why do the nations
conspire,
and the peoples plot in
vain?
2 The kings of the earth set
themselves,
and the rulers take
counsel together,
against the LORD and his
anointed, saying,
3 "Let us burst their bonds
asunder,
and cast their cords
from us."

4 He who sits in the heavens
laughs;
the LORD has them in
derision.
5 Then he will speak to them
in his wrath,
and terrify them in his
fury, saying,
6 "I have set my king on
Zion, my holy hill."

7 I will tell of the decree of
the LORD:
He said to me, "You are
my son;
today I have begotten
you.
8 Ask of me, and I will make
the nations your
heritage,
and the ends of the earth
your possession.
9 You shall break them with a
rod of iron,

and dash them in pieces
   like a potter's vessel."

[10] Now therefore, O kings,
   be wise;
  be warned, O rulers of
   the earth.
[11] Serve the LORD with fear,
  with trembling [12]kiss
   his feet,[a]
or he will be angry,
  and you will
   perish in the way;
for his wrath is
   quickly kindled.

Happy are all who take
  refuge in him.

Psalm 3

*A Psalm of David, when he fled
from his son Absalom.*

[1] O LORD, how many are my
   foes!
  Many are rising against me;
[2] many are saying to me,
  "There is no help for
   you[b] in God."   *Selah*

[3] But you, O Lord, are a shield
   around me,
  my glory, and the one
   who lifts up my head.
[4] I cry aloud to the Lord,
  and he answers me from
   his holy hill.   *Selah*

[5] I lie down and sleep;
  I wake again, for the
   LORD sustains me.
[6] I am not afraid of ten
   thousands of people
  who have set themselves
   against me all around.

[7] Rise up, O LORD!
  Deliver me, O my God!
For you strike all my
   enemies on the cheek;
  you break the teeth
   of the wicked.

[8] Deliverance belongs to the
   LORD;
  may your blessing be on
   your people!   *Selah*

Psalm 4

*To the leader: with stringed
instruments. A Psalm of David.*

[1] Answer me when I call,
   O God of my right!
  You gave me room when
   I was in distress.
  Be gracious to me, and
   hear my prayer.

[2] How long, you people, shall
   my honor suffer
   shame?
  How long will you love
   vain words, and seek
   after lies?   *Selah*

[3] But know that the LORD
   has set apart the
   faithful for himself;
  the LORD hears when
   I call to him.

[4] When you are disturbed,[c]
   do not sin;
  ponder it on your beds,
   and be silent.   *Selah*
[5] Offer right sacrifices,

---

[a]Cn: Meaning of Heb of verses 11b and 12a is uncertain [b] Syr: Heb *him* [c] Or *are angry*

and put your trust in the
LORD.

⁶ There are many who say,
"O that we might see
some good!
Let the light of your face
shine on us, O Lord!"
⁷ You have put gladness
in my heart
more than when their
grain and wine abound.

⁸ I will both lie down and
sleep in peace;
for you alone, O LORD,
make me lie down
in safety.

Psalm 5

*To the leader: for the flutes.
A Psalm of David.*

¹ Give ear to my words,
O LORD;
give heed to my sighing.
² Listen to the sound of my
cry,
my King and my God,
for to you I pray.
³ O LORD, in the morning
you hear my voice;
in the morning I plead
my case to you, and
watch.

⁴ For you are not a God who
delights in
wickedness;
evil will not sojourn
with you.
⁵ The boastful will not stand
before your eyes;
you hate all evildoers.

⁶ You destroy those who
speak lies;
the LORD abhors the
bloodthirsty and
deceitful.

⁷ But I, through the abundance
of your steadfast love,
will enter your house,
I will bow down toward
your holy temple
in awe of you.
⁸ Lead me, O LORD, in your
righteousness
because of my enemies;
make your way straight
before me.

⁹ For there is no truth in
their mouths;
their hearts are destruction;
their throats are open graves;
they flatter with their
tongues.
¹⁰ Make them bear their guilt,
O God;
let them fall by their
own counsels;
because of their many
transgressions
cast them out,
for they have rebelled
against you.

¹¹ But let all who take refuge
in you rejoice;
let them ever sing for joy.
Spread your protection
over them,
so that those who love
your name
may exult in you.
¹² For you bless the righteous,
O LORD;

you cover them with
    favor as with a
    shield.

Psalm 6

*To the leader: with stringed
instruments; according to The
Sheminith. A Psalm of David.*

1 O LORD, do not rebuke me
    in your anger,
    or discipline me in your
      wrath.
2 Be gracious to me, O LORD,
    for I am languishing;
    O LORD, heal me, for my
      bones are shaking
      with terror.
3 My soul also is struck with
    terror,
    while you, O LORD—how
      long?

4 Turn, O LORD, save my life;
    deliver me for the sake
      of your steadfast love.
5 For in death there is no
    remembrance of you;
    in Sheol who can give
      you praise?

6 I am weary with my
    moaning;
    every night I flood my
      bed with tears;
    I drench my couch with
      my weeping.
7 My eyes waste away
    because of grief;
    they grow weak because
      of all my foes.

8 Depart from me, all you
    workers of evil,

for the LORD has heard
    the sound of my
    weeping.
9 The LORD has heard my
    supplication;
    the LORD accepts my
      prayer.
10 All my enemies shall be
    ashamed and struck
    with terror;
    they shall turn back, and
      in a moment be put
      to shame.

Psalm 7

*A Shiggaion of David, which he
sang to the LORD concerning
Cush, a Benjaminite.*

1 O LORD my God, in you I
    take refuge;
    save me from all my
      pursuers, and deliver
      me,
2 or like a lion they will tear
    me apart;
    they will drag me away,
      with no one to rescue.

3 O LORD my God, if I have
    done this,
    if there is wrong in my
      hands,
4 if I have repaid my ally
    with harm
    or plundered my foe
      without cause,
5 then let the enemy pursue
    and overtake me,
    trample my life to the
      ground,
    and lay my soul in the
      dust.   *Selah*

⁶ Rise up, O LORD, in your
    anger;
  lift yourself up against
    the fury of my enemies;
  awake, O my God;*a* you
    have appointed a
    judgment.
⁷ Let the assembly of the
    peoples be gathered
    around you,
  and over it take your
    seat*b* on high.
⁸ The LORD judges the
    peoples;
  judge me, O LORD,
    according to my
    righteousness
  and according to the
    integrity that is in me.

⁹ O let the evil of the wicked
    come to an end,
  but establish the righteous,
  you who test the minds
    and hearts,
  O righteous God.
¹⁰ God is my shield,
  who saves the upright in
    heart.
¹¹ God is a righteous judge,
  and a God who has
    indignation every day.

¹² If one does not repent,
    God*c* will whet his
    sword;
  he has bent and strung
    his bow;
¹³ he has prepared his deadly
    weapons,
  making his arrows fiery
    shafts.
¹⁴ See how they conceive
    evil,

and are pregnant with
    mischief,
  and bring forth lies.
¹⁵ They make a pit, digging it
    out,
  and fall into the hole that
    they have made.
¹⁶ Their mischief returns
    upon their own heads,
  and on their own heads
    their violence
    descends.

¹⁷ I will give to the LORD
    the thanks due to his
    righteousness,
  and sing praise to the
    name of the LORD,
    the Most High.

Psalm 8

To the leader: according to The
Gittith. A Psalm of David.

¹ O LORD, our Sovereign,
  how majestic is your
    name in all the earth!

  You have set your glory
    above the heavens.
² Out of the mouths of
    babes and infants
  you have founded a
    bulwark because of
    your foes,
  to silence the enemy and
    the avenger.

³ When I look at your
    heavens, the work of
    your fingers,
  the moon and the stars

aOr awake for me bCn: Heb return cHeb he

that you have
established;
4 what are human beings
that you are mindful
of them,
mortals[a] that you care
for them?

5 Yet you have made them a
little lower than
God,[b]
and crowned them with
glory and honor.
6 You have given them
dominion over the
works of your hands;
you have put all things
under their feet,
7 all sheep and oxen,
and also the beasts of
the field,
8 the birds of the air, and
the fish of the sea,
whatever passes along
the paths of the seas.

9 O LORD, our Sovereign,
how majestic is your
name in all the earth!

Psalm 9

*To the leader: according to
Muth-labben. A Psalm of David.*

1 I will give thanks to the
LORD with my whole
heart;
I will tell of all your
wonderful deeds.
2 I will be glad and exult in
you;
I will sing praise to your
name, O Most High.

3 When my enemies turned
back,
they stumbled and
perished before you.
4 For you have maintained
my just cause;
you have sat on the
throne giving
righteous judgment.

5 You have rebuked the
nations, you have
destroyed the wicked;
you have blotted out
their name forever
and ever.
6 The enemies have vanished
in everlasting ruins;
their cities you have
rooted out;
the very memory of them
has perished.

7 But the LORD sits
enthroned forever,
he has established his
throne for judgment.
8 He judges the world with
righteousness;
he judges the peoples
with equity.

9 The LORD is a stronghold
for the oppressed,
a stronghold in times of
trouble.

10 And those who know your
name put their trust
in you,
for you, O LORD, have

---

[a]Heb *ben adam*, lit. *son of man*   [b]Or *than the divine
beings* or *angels*: Heb *elohim*

not forsaken those
who seek you.

11 Sing praises to the LORD,
who dwells in Zion.
Declare his deeds among
the peoples.
12 For he who avenges blood
is mindful of them;
he does not forget the
cry of the afflicted.

13 Be gracious to me, O LORD.
See what I suffer from
those who hate me;
you are the one who lifts
me up from the gates
of death,
14 so that I may recount all
your praises,
and, in the gates of
daughter Zion,
rejoice in your deliverance.

15 The nations have sunk in
the pit that they made;
in the net that they hid
has their own foot
been caught.
16 The LORD has made
himself known, he has
executed judgment;
the wicked are snared in
the work of their
own hands.
Higgaion. Selah

17 The wicked shall depart to
Sheol,
all the nations that forget
God.

18 For the needy shall not
always be forgotten,

nor the hope of the poor
perish forever.

19 Rise up, O LORD! Do not
let mortals prevail;
let the nations be judged
before you.
20 Put them in fear, O LORD;
let the nations know that
they are only human.
Selah

Psalm 10

1 Why, O LORD, do you
stand far off?
Why do you hide
yourself in times of
trouble?
2 In arrogance the wicked
persecute the poor—
let them be caught in the
schemes they have
devised.

3 For the wicked boast of the
desires of their heart,
those greedy for gain
curse and renounce
the LORD.
4 In the pride of their
countenance the
wicked say, "God will
not seek it out";
all their thoughts are,
"There is no God."

5 Their ways prosper at all
times;
your judgments are on
high, out of their sight;
as for their foes, they
scoff at them.
6 They think in their heart,
"We shall not be
moved;

throughout all
generations we shall
not meet adversity."

7 Their mouths are filled
with cursing
and deceit and
oppression;
under their tongues are
mischief and iniquity.
8 They sit in ambush in the
villages;
in hiding places they
murder the innocent.

Their eyes stealthily watch
for the helpless;
9 they lurk in secret like a
lion in its covert;
they lurk that they may
seize the poor;
they seize the poor and
drag them off in their
net.

10 They stoop, they crouch,
and the helpless fall by
their might.
11 They think in their heart,
"God has forgotten,
he has hidden his face,
he will never see it."

12 Rise up, O LORD; O God,
lift up your hand;
do not forget the oppressed.
13 Why do the wicked
renounce God,
and say in their hearts,
"You will not call us
to account"?

14 But you do see! Indeed you
note trouble and grief,

that you may take it into
your hands;
the helpless commit
themselves to you;
you have been the helper
of the orphan.

15 Break the arm of the
wicked and evildoers;
seek out their
wickedness until you
find none.
16 The LORD is king forever
and ever;
the nations shall perish
from his land.

17 O LORD, you will hear the
desire of the meek;
you will strengthen their
heart, you will incline
your ear
18 to do justice for the orphan
and the oppressed,
so that those from earth
may strike terror no
more.[a]

Psalm 11

To the leader. Of David.

1 In the LORD I take refuge;
how can you say to me,
"Flee like a bird to the
mountains;[b]
2 for look, the wicked bend
the bow,
they have fitted their
arrow to the string,
to shoot in the dark at
the upright in heart.

---

[a]Meaning of Heb uncertain [b]Gk Syr Jerome Tg: Heb
flee to your mountain, O bird

³ If the foundations are
   destroyed,
      what can the righteous do?"

⁴ The LORD is in his holy temple;
   the LORD's throne is in
      heaven.
   His eyes behold, his gaze
      examines humankind.
⁵ The LORD tests the
      righteous and the
      wicked,
   and his soul hates the
      lover of violence.
⁶ On the wicked he will rain
      coals of fire and sulfur;
   a scorching wind shall
      be the portion of
      their cup.
⁷ For the LORD is righteous;
   he loves righteous deeds;
      the upright shall behold
      his face.

Psalm 12

*To the leader: according to The
Sheminith. A Psalm of David.*

¹ Help, O LORD, for there is
      no longer anyone
      who is godly;
   the faithful have
      disappeared from
      humankind.
² They utter lies to each other;
   with flattering lips and a
      double heart they
      speak.

³ May the LORD cut off all
      flattering lips,
   the tongue that makes
      great boasts,

⁴ those who say, "With our
      tongues we will prevail;
   our lips are our own—
      who is our master?"

⁵ "Because the poor are
      despoiled, because
      the needy groan,
   I will now rise up," says
      the LORD;
   "I will place them in the
      safety for which they
      long."
⁶ The promises of the LORD
      are promises that are
      pure,
   silver refined in a
      furnace on the ground,
      purified seven times.

⁷ You, O LORD, will protect us;
   you will guard us from
      this generation
      forever.
⁸ On every side the wicked
      prowl,
   as vileness is exalted
      among humankind.

Psalm 13

To the leader. A Psalm of David.

¹ How long, O LORD? Will
      you forget me
      forever?
   How long will you hide
      your face from me?
² How long must I bear
      painᵃ in my soul,
   and have sorrow in my
      heart all day long?
   How long shall my enemy
      be exalted over me?

ᵃSyr: Heb *hold counsels*

3 Consider and answer me,
       O LORD my God!
    Give light to my eyes, or
       I will sleep the sleep
       of death,
4 and my enemy will say, "I
       have prevailed";
    my foes will rejoice
       because I am shaken.

5 But I trusted in your
       steadfast love;
    my heart shall rejoice in
       your salvation.
6 I will sing to the LORD,
    because he has dealt
       bountifully with me.

Psalm 14

To the leader. Of David.

1 Fools say in their hearts,
       "There is no God."
    They are corrupt, they
       do abominable deeds;
    there is no one who does
       good.

2 The LORD looks down from
       heaven on humankind
    to see if there are any
       who are wise,
    who seek after God.

3 They have all gone astray,
       they are all alike
       perverse;
    there is no one who does
       good,
    no, not one.

4 Have they no knowledge,
       all the evildoers

who eat up my people as
       they eat bread,
    and do not call upon the
       LORD?

5 There they shall be in great
       terror,
    for God is with the
       company of the
       righteous.
6 You would confound the
       plans of the poor,
    but the LORD is their refuge.

7 O that deliverance for
       Israel would come
       from Zion!
    When the LORD restores
       the fortunes of his
       people,
    Jacob will rejoice; Israel
       will be glad.

Psalm 15

A Psalm of David.

1 O LORD, who may abide in
       your tent?
    Who may dwell on your
       holy hill?

2 Those who walk
       blamelessly, and do
       what is right,
    and speak the truth from
       their heart;
3 who do not slander with
       their tongue,
    and do no evil to their
       friends,
    nor take up a reproach
       against their neighbors;
4 in whose eyes the wicked
       are despised,

but who honor those
    who fear the LORD;
    who stand by their oath
    even to their hurt;
5 who do not lend money at
    interest,
    and do not take a bribe
    against the innocent.

Those who do these things
    shall never be moved.

Psalm 16

A Miktam of David.

1 Protect me, O God, for in
    you I take refuge.
2 I say to the LORD, "You are
    my Lord;
    I have no good apart
    from you."[a]

3 As for the holy ones in the
    land, they are the noble,
    in whom is all my delight.

4 Those who choose another
    god multiply their
    sorrows;[b]
    their drink offerings of
    blood I will not pour
    out
    or take their names upon
    my lips.

5 The LORD is my chosen
    portion and my cup;
    you hold my lot.
6 The boundary lines have
    fallen for me in
    pleasant places;
    I have a goodly heritage.

7 I bless the LORD who gives
    me counsel;

in the night also my
    heart instructs me.
8 I keep the LORD always
    before me;
    because he is at my right
    hand, I shall not be
    moved.

9 Therefore my heart is glad,
    and my soul rejoices;
    my body also rests secure.

10 For you do not give me up
    to Sheol,
    or let your faithful one
    see the Pit.

11 You show me the path of life.
    In your presence there is
    fullness of joy;
    in your right hand are
    pleasures forevermore.

Psalm 17

A Prayer of David.

1 Hear a just cause, O LORD;
    attend to my cry;
    give ear to my prayer
    from lips free of deceit.
2 From you let my
    vindication come;
    let your eyes see the right.

3 If you try my heart, if you
    visit me by night,
    if you test me, you will
    find no wickedness in
    me;
    my mouth does not
    transgress.
4 As for what others do, by the
    word of your lips

[a]Jerome Tg: Meaning of Heb uncertain [b]Cn: Meaning
of Heb uncertain

385

I have avoided the ways
   of the violent.
5 My steps have held fast to
   your paths;
   my feet have not slipped.

6 I call upon you, for you
   will answer me, O God;
   incline your ear to me,
   hear my words.
7 Wondrously show your
   steadfast love,
   O savior of those who
   seek refuge
   from their adversaries at
   your right hand.

8 Guard me as the apple of
   the eye;
   hide me in the shadow of
   your wings,
9 from the wicked who
   despoil me,
   my deadly enemies who
   surround me.
10 They close their hearts to pity;
   with their mouths they
   speak arrogantly.
11 They track me down;[a]
   now they surround me;
   they set their eyes to cast
   me to the ground.
12 They are like a lion eager
   to tear,
   like a young lion lurking
   in ambush.

13 Rise up, O LORD, confront
   them, overthrow
   them!
   By your sword deliver
   my life from the wicked,
14 from mortals—by your hand,
   O LORD—

from mortals whose portion
   in life is in this world.
May their bellies be filled
   with what you have
   stored up for them;
   may their children have
   more than enough;
   may they leave
   something over to
   their little ones.

15 As for me, I shall behold
   your face in
   righteousness;
   when I awake I shall be
   satisfied, beholding
   your likeness.

Psalm 18

*To the leader. A Psalm of David
the servant of the LORD, who
addressed the words of this
song to the LORD on the day
when the LORD delivered him
from the hand of all his enemies, and from the hand of
Saul. He said:*

1 I love you, O LORD, my
   strength.
2 The LORD is my rock, my
   fortress, and my
   deliverer,
   my God, my rock in
   whom I take refuge,
   my shield, and the horn
   of my salvation, my
   stronghold.
3 I call upon the LORD, who
   is worthy to be praised,
   so I shall be saved from
   my enemies.

[a]One Ms Compare Syr: MT *Our steps*

⁴ The cords of death
        encompassed me;
    the torrents of perdition
        assailed me;
⁵ the cords of Sheol
        entangled me;
    the snares of death
        confronted me.

⁶ In my distress I called upon
        the LORD;
    to my God I cried for help.
    From his temple he heard
        my voice,
    and my cry to him
        reached his ears.

⁷ Then the earth reeled and
        rocked;
    the foundations also of
        the mountains trembled
    and quaked, because he
        was angry.
⁸ Smoke went up from his
        nostrils,
    and devouring fire from
        his mouth;
    glowing coals flamed
        forth from him.
⁹ He bowed the heavens, and
        came down;
    thick darkness was
        under his feet.
¹⁰ He rode on a cherub, and flew;
    he came swiftly upon the
        wings of the wind.
¹¹ He made darkness his
        covering around him,
    his canopy thick clouds
        dark with water.
¹² Out of the brightness
        before him
    there broke through his
        clouds

    hailstones and coals
        of fire.
¹³ The LORD also thundered
        in the heavens,
    and the Most High
        uttered his voice.ᵃ
¹⁴ And he sent out his arrows,
        and scattered them;
    he flashed forth lightnings,
        and routed them.
¹⁵ Then the channels of the
        sea were seen,
    and the foundations of
        the world were laid bare
    at your rebuke, O LORD,
        at the blast of the breath
        of your nostrils.

¹⁶ He reached down from on
        high, he took me;
    he drew me out of
        mighty waters.
¹⁷ He delivered me from my
        strong enemy,
    and from those who
        hated me;
    for they were too mighty
        for me.
¹⁸ They confronted me in the
        day of my calamity;
    but the LORD was my
        support.
¹⁹ He brought me out into a
        broad place;
    he delivered me, because
        he delighted in me.

²⁰ The LORD rewarded me
        according to my
        righteousness;
    according to the cleanness

ᵃGk See 2 Sam 22.14: Heb adds *hailstones and coals of fire*

387

of my hands he
　　recompensed me.
21 For I have kept the ways of
　　　the LORD,
　　and have not wickedly
　　　departed from my God.
22 For all his ordinances were
　　　before me,
　　and his statutes I did not
　　　put away from me.
23 I was blameless before him,
　　and I kept myself from
　　　guilt.
24 Therefore the LORD has
　　　recompensed me
　　according to my
　　　righteousness,
　　according to the
　　　cleanness of my
　　　hands in his sight.

25 With the loyal you show
　　　yourself loyal;
　　with the blameless you
　　　show yourself
　　　blameless;
26 with the pure you show
　　　yourself pure;
　　and with the crooked
　　　you show yourself
　　　perverse.
27 For you deliver a humble
　　　people,
　　but the haughty eyes you
　　　bring down.
28 It is you who light my lamp;
　　the LORD, my God, lights
　　　up my darkness.
29 By you I can crush a troop,
　　and by my God I can
　　　leap over a wall.
30 This God—his way is perfect;
　　the promise of the LORD
　　　proves true;

he is a shield for all who
　　take refuge in him.

31 For who is God except the
　　　LORD?
　　And who is a rock
　　　besides our God?—
32 the God who girded me
　　　with strength,
　　and made my way safe.
33 He made my feet like the
　　　feet of a deer,
　　and set me secure on the
　　　heights.
34 He trains my hands for war,
　　so that my arms can
　　　bend a bow of bronze.
35 You have given me the
　　　shield of your salvation,
　　and your right hand has
　　　supported me;
　　your help*a* has made me
　　　great.
36 You gave me a wide place
　　　for my steps under me,
　　and my feet did not slip.
37 I pursued my enemies and
　　　overtook them;
　　and did not turn back
　　　until they were
　　　consumed.
38 I struck them down, so that
　　　they were not able to
　　　rise;
　　they fell under my feet.
39 For you girded me with
　　　strength for the
　　　battle;
　　you made my assailants
　　　sink under me.
40 You made my enemies turn
　　　their backs to me,

*a*Or *gentleness*

388

and those who hated me
    I destroyed.
[41] They cried for help, but
        there was no one to
        save them;
    they cried to the LORD,
        but he did not
        answer them.
[42] I beat them fine, like dust
        before the wind;
    I cast them out like the
        mire of the streets.

[43] You delivered me from
        strife with the peoples;[a]
    you made me head of the
        nations;
    people whom I had not
        known served me.
[44] As soon as they heard of
        me they obeyed me;
    foreigners came cringing
        to me.
[45] Foreigners lost heart,
    and came trembling out
        of their strongholds.

[46] The LORD lives! Blessed be
        my rock,
    and exalted be the God
        of my salvation,
[47] the God who gave me
        vengeance
    and subdued peoples
        under me;
[48] who delivered me from my
        enemies;
    indeed, you exalted me
        above my adversaries;
    you delivered me from
        the violent.

[49] For this I will extol you,
        O LORD, among the
        nations,

and sing praises to your
        name.
[50] Great triumphs he gives to
        his king,
    and shows steadfast love
        to his anointed,
    to David and his
        descendants forever.

Psalm 19

To the leader. A Psalm of David.

[1] The heavens are telling the
        glory of God;
    and the firmament[b]
        proclaims his
        handiwork.
[2] Day to day pours forth speech,
    and night to night declares
        knowledge.
[3] There is no speech, nor are
        there words;
    their voice is not heard;
[4] yet their voice[c] goes out
        through all the earth,
    and their words to the
        end of the world.

In the heavens[d] he has set
    a tent for the sun,
[5] which comes out like a
        bridegroom from his
        wedding canopy,
    and like a strong man
        runs its course with joy.
[6] Its rising is from the end of
        the heavens,
    and its circuit to the end
        of them;
    and nothing is hid from
        its heat.

---

[a]Gk Tg: Heb *people* [b]Or *dome* [c]Gk Jerome Compare
Syr: Heb *line* [d]Heb *In them*

7 The law of the LORD is perfect,
　　reviving the soul;
　the decrees of the LORD are
　　　sure,
　　making wise the simple;
8 the precepts of the LORD
　　　are right,
　rejoicing the heart;
　the commandment of the
　　　LORD is clear,
　　enlightening the eyes;
9 the fear of the LORD is pure,
　　enduring forever;
　the ordinances of the LORD
　　　are true
　　and righteous altogether.
10 More to be desired are
　　　they than gold,
　　even much fine gold;
　sweeter also than honey,
　　and drippings of the
　　　honeycomb.

11 Moreover by them is your
　　　servant warned;
　in keeping them there is
　　　great reward.
12 But who can detect their
　　　errors?
　Clear me from hidden faults.
13 Keep back your servant
　　　also from the insolent;[a]
　do not let them have
　　　dominion over me.
　Then I shall be blameless,
　　and innocent of great
　　　transgression.

14 Let the words of my mouth
　　　and the meditation of
　　　my heart
　be acceptable to you,
　O LORD, my rock and my
　　　redeemer.

Psalm 20

To the leader. A Psalm of David.

1 The LORD answer you in
　　　the day of trouble!
　The name of the God of
　　　Jacob protect you!
2 May he send you help from
　　　the sanctuary,
　and give you support
　　　from Zion.
3 May he remember all your
　　　offerings,
　and regard with favor
　　　your burnt sacrifices.
　　　　　　　Selah

4 May he grant you your
　　　heart's desire,
　and fulfill all your plans.
5 May we shout for joy over
　　　your victory,
　and in the name of our
　　　God set up our banners.
　May the LORD fulfill all
　　　your petitions.

6 Now I know that the LORD
　　　will help his
　　　anointed;
　he will answer him from
　　　his holy heaven
　with mighty victories by
　　　his right hand.
7 Some take pride in
　　　chariots, and some in
　　　horses,
　but our pride is in the
　　　name of the LORD
　　　our God.
8 They will collapse and fall,
　　but we shall rise and
　　　stand upright.

a Or *from proud thoughts*

9 Give victory to the king,
    O LORD;
  answer us when we call.[a]

Psalm 21

To the leader. A Psalm of David.

1 In your strength the king
      rejoices, O LORD,
  and in your help how
      greatly he exults!
2 You have given him his
      heart's desire,
  and have not withheld
      the request of his lips.
                              Selah
3 For you meet him with rich
      blessings;
  you set a crown of fine gold
      on his head.
4 He asked you for life;
      you gave it to him—
  length of days forever
      and ever.
5 His glory is great through
      your help;
  splendor and majesty you
      bestow on him.
6 You bestow on him
      blessings forever;
  you make him glad with
      the joy of your presence.
7 For the king trusts in the LORD,
      and through the
      steadfast love of the
      Most High he shall
      not be moved.

8 Your hand will find out all
      your enemies;
  your right hand will find
      out those who hate you.
9 You will make them like a
      fiery furnace

when you appear.
The LORD will swallow them
      up in his wrath,
  and fire will consume them.
10 You will destroy their
      offspring from the earth,
  and their children from
      among humankind.
11 If they plan evil against you,
  if they devise mischief,
      they will not succeed.
12 For you will put them to
      flight;
  you will aim at their
      faces with your bows.

13 Be exalted, O LORD, in
      your strength!
  We will sing and praise
      your power.

Psalm 22

*To the leader: according to The
Deer of the Dawn. A Psalm of
David.*

1 My God, my God, why
      have you forsaken me?
  Why are you so far from
      helping me, from the
      words of my groaning?
2 O my God, I cry by day,
      but you do not answer;
  and by night, but find no
      rest.

3 Yet you are holy,
      enthroned on the praises
      of Israel.
4 In you our ancestors trusted;
  they trusted, and you
      delivered them.

[a]Gk: Heb *give victory, O LORD; let the King answer us
when we call*

5 To you they cried,
    and were saved;
  in you they trusted, and
      were not put to shame.

6 But I am a worm, and not
    human;
  scorned by others, and
    despised by the people.
7 All who see me mock at me;
  they make mouths at me,
    they shake their heads;
8 "Commit your cause to the
    LORD; let him deliver—
  let him rescue the one in
    whom he delights!"

9 Yet it was you who took
    me from the womb;
  you kept me safe on my
    mother's breast.
10 On you I was cast from my
    birth,
  and since my mother
    bore me you have
    been my God.
11 Do not be far from me,
  for trouble is near
  and there is no one to help.

12 Many bulls encircle me,
  strong bulls of Bashan
    surround me;
13 they open wide their
    mouths at me,
  like a ravening and
    roaring lion.

14 I am poured out like water,
  and all my bones are out
    of joint;
  my heart is like wax;
    it is melted within my
    breast;

15 my mouth[a] is dried up like
    a potsherd,
  and my tongue sticks to
    my jaws;
  you lay me in the dust of
    death.

16 For dogs are all around me;
  a company of evildoers
    encircles me.
My hands and feet have
    shriveled;[b]
17 I can count all my bones.
  They stare and gloat over
    me;
18 they divide my clothes
    among themselves,
  and for my clothing they
    cast lots.

19 But you, O LORD, do not be
    far away!
  O my help, come quickly
    to my aid!
20 Deliver my soul from the
    sword,
  my life[c] from the power
    of the dog!
21 Save me from the mouth
    of the lion!

From the horns of the wild
    oxen you have
    rescued[d] me.
22 I will tell of your name to
    my brothers and sisters;[e]
  in the midst of the
    congregation I will
    praise you:
23 You who fear the LORD,
    praise him!

[a] Cn: Heb *strength* [b] Meaning of Heb uncertain [c] Heb *my only one* [d] Heb *answered* [e] Or *kindred*

All you offspring of
Jacob, glorify him;
stand in awe of him, all
you offspring of
Israel!
24 For he did not despise or
abhor
the affliction of the afflicted;
he did not hide his face
from me,[a]
but heard when I[b] cried
to him.

25 From you comes my praise
in the great
congregation;
my vows I will pay
before those who fear
him.
26 The poor[c] shall eat and be
satisfied;
those who seek him shall
praise the LORD.
May your hearts live
forever!

27 All the ends of the earth
shall remember
and turn to the LORD;
and all the families of the
nations
shall worship before him.[d]
28 For dominion belongs to
the LORD,
and he rules over the
nations.

29 To him,[e] indeed, shall all
who sleep in[f] the
earth bow down;
before him shall bow all
who go down to the
dust,
and I shall live for him.[g]

30 Posterity will serve him;
future generations will
be told about the Lord,
31 and[h] proclaim his
deliverance to a
people yet unborn,
saying that he has done it.

Psalm 23
A Psalm of David.

1 The LORD is my shepherd,
I shall not want.
2   He makes me lie down
in green pastures;
he leads me beside still
waters;[i]
3   he restores my soul.[j]
He leads me in right paths[k]
for his name's sake.

4 Even though I walk
through the darkest
valley,[l]
I fear no evil;
for you are with me;
your rod and your staff—
they comfort me.

5 You prepare a table before me
in the presence of my
enemies;
you anoint my head with
oil;
my cup overflows.
6 Surely[m] goodness and mercy[n]
shall follow me

---

[a]Heb *him* [b]Heb *he* [c]Or *afflicted* [d]Gk Syr Jerome: Heb *you* [e]Cn: Heb *They have eaten and* [f]Cn: Heb *all the fat ones* [g]Compare Gk Syr Vg: Heb *and he who cannot keep himself alive* [h] Compare Gk: Heb *it will be told about the Lord to the generation,* [31]*they will come and* [i]Heb *waters of rest* [j]Or *life* [k]Or *paths of righteousness* [l]Or *the valley of the shadow of death* [m]Or *Only* [n]Or *kindness*

all the days of my life,
and I shall dwell in the
house of the LORD
my whole life long.*a*

Psalm 24

Of David. A Psalm.

[1] The earth is the LORD's and
all that is in it,
the world, and those who
live in it;
[2] for he has founded it on
the seas,
and established it on
the rivers.

[3] Who shall ascend the hill
of the LORD?
And who shall stand in
his holy place?
[4] Those who have clean hands
and pure hearts,
who do not lift up their
souls to what is false,
and do not swear
deceitfully.
[5] They will receive blessing
from the LORD,
and vindication from the
God of their salvation.
[6] Such is the company of
those who seek him,
who seek the face of the
God of Jacob.*b*   *Selah*

[7] Lift up your heads,
O gates!
and be lifted up,
O ancient doors!
that the King of glory
may come in.
[8] Who is the King of glory?

The LORD, strong and
mighty,
the LORD, mighty in battle.
[9] Lift up your heads, O gates!
and be lifted up,
O ancient doors!
that the King of glory
may come in.
[10] Who is this King of glory?
The LORD of hosts,
he is the King of glory.
                              Selah

Psalm 25

Of David.

[1] To you, O LORD, I lift up
my soul.
[2] O my God, in you I trust;
do not let me be put to
shame;
do not let my enemies
exult over me.
[3] Do not let those who wait
for you be put to
shame;
let them be ashamed
who are wantonly
treacherous.

[4] Make me to know your
ways, O LORD;
teach me your paths.
[5] Lead me in your truth, and
teach me,
for you are the God of
my salvation;
for you I wait all day long.

[6] Be mindful of your mercy,
O LORD, and of your
steadfast love,

---

*a*Heb *for length of days* *b*Gk Syr: Heb *your face, O
Jacob*

for they have been from
of old.
7 Do not remember the sins
of my youth or my
transgressions;
according to your
steadfast love
remember me,
for your goodness' sake,
O LORD!

8 Good and upright is the LORD;
therefore he instructs
sinners in the way.
9 He leads the humble in
what is right,
and teaches the humble
his way.
10 All the paths of the LORD
are steadfast love
and faithfulness,
for those who keep his
covenant and his
decrees.

11 For your name's sake, O LORD,
pardon my guilt, for it is
great.
12 Who are they that fear the
LORD?
He will teach them the way
that they should choose.

13 They will abide in prosperity,
and their children shall
possess the land.
14 The friendship of the LORD is
for those who fear him,
and he makes his covenant
known to them.
15 My eyes are ever toward
the LORD,
for he will pluck my feet
out of the net.

16 Turn to me and be
gracious to me,
for I am lonely and afflicted.
17 Relieve the troubles of my
heart,
and bring me*a* out of my
distress.
18 Consider my affliction and
my trouble,
and forgive all my sins.

19 Consider how many are
my foes,
and with what violent
hatred they hate me.
20 O guard my life, and
deliver me;
do not let me be put to
shame, for I take
refuge in you.
21 May integrity and
uprightness preserve
me,
for I wait for you.

22 Redeem Israel, O God,
out of all its troubles.

Psalm 26

Of David.

1 Vindicate me, O LORD,
for I have walked in my
integrity,
and I have trusted in the
LORD without wavering.
2 Prove me, O LORD, and try me;
test my heart and mind.
3 For your steadfast love is
before my eyes,
and I walk in
faithfulness to you.*b*

*a*Or *The troubles of my heart are enlarged; bring me*
*b*Or *in your faithfulness*

⁴ I do not sit with the worthless,
    nor do I consort with
      hypocrites;
⁵ I hate the company of
    evildoers,
    and will not sit with the
      wicked.

⁶ I wash my hands in
    innocence,
    and go around your altar,
      O LORD,
⁷ singing aloud a song of
    thanksgiving,
    and telling all your
      wondrous deeds.

⁸ O LORD, I love the house in
    which you dwell,
    and the place where your
      glory abides.
⁹ Do not sweep me away
    with sinners,
    nor my life with the
      bloodthirsty,
¹⁰ those in whose hands are
    evil devices,
    and whose right hands
      are full of bribes.

¹¹ But as for me, I walk in my
    integrity;
    redeem me, and be
      gracious to me.
¹² My foot stands on level
    ground;
    in the great congregation
      I will bless the LORD.

Psalm 27

Of David.

¹ The LORD is my light and
    my salvation;
    whom shall I fear?

The LORD is the
    strongholdᵃ of my life;
    of whom shall I be afraid?

² When evildoers assail me
    to devour my flesh—
    my adversaries and foes—
    they shall stumble and fall.

³ Though an army encamp
    against me,
    my heart shall not fear;
    though war rise up against
      me,
    yet I will be confident.

⁴ One thing I asked of the LORD,
    that will I seek after:
    to live in the house of the
      LORD
    all the days of my life,
    to behold the beauty of the
      LORD,
    and to inquire in his temple.

⁵ For he will hide me in his
    shelter
    in the day of trouble;
    he will conceal me under
      the cover of his tent;
    he will set me high on a
      rock.

⁶ Now my head is lifted up
    above my enemies all
      around me,
    and I will offer in his tent
      sacrifices with shouts of joy;
    I will sing and make
      melody to the LORD.

⁷ Hear, O LORD, when I cry
aloud,

ᵃOr *refuge*

be gracious to me and
answer me!
⁸ "Come," my heart says,
"seek his face!"
Your face, LORD, do I seek.
⁹   Do not hide your face
from me.

Do not turn your servant
away in anger,
you who have been my help.
Do not cast me off, do not
forsake me,
O God of my salvation!
¹⁰ If my father and mother
forsake me,
the LORD will take me up.

¹¹ Teach me your way, O LORD,
and lead me on a level path
because of my enemies.
¹² Do not give me up to the
will of my adversaries,
for false witnesses have
risen against me,
and they are breathing
out violence.

¹³ I believe that I shall see the
goodness of the LORD
in the land of the living.
¹⁴ Wait for the LORD;
be strong, and let your
heart take courage;
wait for the LORD!

Psalm 28
Of David.

¹ To you, O LORD, I call;
my rock, do not refuse to
hear me,
for if you are silent to me,
I shall be like those who
go down to the Pit.

² Hear the voice of my
supplication,
as I cry to you for help,
as I lift up my hands
toward your most holy
sanctuary.ᵃ

³ Do not drag me away with
the wicked,
with those who are
workers of evil,
who speak peace with their
neighbors,
while mischief is in their
hearts.
⁴ Repay them according to
their work,
and according to the evil
of their deeds;
repay them according to
the work of their hands;
render them their due
reward.
⁵ Because they do not regard
the works of the LORD,
or the work of his hands,
he will break them down
and build them up no
more.

⁶ Blessed be the LORD,
for he has heard the
sound of my pleadings.
⁷ The LORD is my strength
and my shield;
in him my heart trusts;
so I am helped, and my
heart exults,
and with my song I give
thanks to him.

⁸ The LORD is the strength of
his people;

ᵃHeb *your innermost sanctuary*

397

he is the saving refuge of
his anointed.
9 O save your people, and bless
your heritage;
be their shepherd, and carry
them forever.

Psalm 29

A Psalm of David.

1 Ascribe to the LORD,
O heavenly beings,[a]
ascribe to the LORD glory
and strength.
2 Ascribe to the LORD the
glory of his name;
worship the LORD in
holy splendor.

3 The voice of the LORD is
over the waters;
the God of glory thunders,
the LORD, over mighty
waters.
4 The voice of the LORD is
powerful;
the voice of the LORD is
full of majesty.

5 The voice of the LORD
breaks the cedars;
the LORD breaks the cedars
of Lebanon.
6 He makes Lebanon skip
like a calf,
and Sirion like a young
wild ox.

7 The voice of the LORD
flashes forth flames
of fire.
8 The voice of the LORD
shakes the wilderness;

the LORD shakes the
wilderness of Kadesh.

9 The voice of the LORD
causes the oaks to
whirl,[b]
and strips the forest bare;
and in his temple all say,
"Glory!"

10 The LORD sits enthroned
over the flood;
the LORD sits enthroned
as king forever.
11 May the LORD give strength
to his people!
May the LORD bless his
people with peace!

Psalm 30

*A Psalm. A Song at the
dedication of the temple. Of
David.*

1 I will extol you, O LORD,
for you have drawn
me up,
and did not let my foes
rejoice over me.
2 O LORD my God, I cried to
you for help,
and you have healed me.
3 O LORD, you brought up
my soul from Sheol,
restored me to life from
among those gone
down to the Pit.[c]

4 Sing praises to the LORD,
O you his faithful ones,
and give thanks to his
holy name.

[a]Heb *sons of gods* [b]Or *causes the deer to calve* [c]Or
that I should not go down to the Pit

398

⁵ For his anger is but for a
        moment;
    his favor is for a lifetime.
Weeping may linger for the
        night,
    but joy comes with the
        morning.

⁶ As for me, I said in my
        prosperity,
    "I shall never be moved."
⁷ By your favor, O LORD,
    you had established me
        as a strong mountain;
    you hid your face;
        I was dismayed.

⁸ To you, O LORD, I cried,
    and to the LORD I made
        supplication:
⁹ "What profit is there in my
        death,
    if I go down to the Pit?
Will the dust praise you?
    Will it tell of your
        faithfulness?
¹⁰ Hear, O LORD, and be
        gracious to me!
    O LORD, be my helper!"

¹¹ You have turned my
        mourning into dancing;
    you have taken off my
        sackcloth
    and clothed me with joy,
¹² so that my soul[a] may praise
        you and not be silent.
    O LORD my God, I will give
        thanks to you forever.

Psalm 31

To the leader. A Psalm of David.

¹ In you, O LORD, I seek refuge;

do not let me ever be put
        to shame;
    in your righteousness
        deliver me.
² Incline your ear to me;
    rescue me speedily.
Be a rock of refuge for me,
    a strong fortress to save
        me.

³ You are indeed my rock
        and my fortress;
    for your name's sake
        lead me and guide me,
⁴ take me out of the net that
        is hidden for me,
    for you are my refuge.
⁵ Into your hand I commit
        my spirit;
    you have redeemed me,
        O LORD, faithful God.

⁶ You hate[b] those who pay regard
        to worthless idols,
    but I trust in the LORD.
⁷ I will exult and rejoice in
        your steadfast love,
    because you have seen
        my affliction;
    you have taken heed of
        my adversities,
⁸ and have not delivered me
        into the hand of the
        enemy;
    you have set my feet in a
        broad place.

⁹ Be gracious to me, O LORD,
    for I am in distress;
    my eye wastes away
        from grief,
    my soul and body also.

[a]Heb *that glory* [b]One Heb Ms Gk Syr Jerome: MT *I hate*

399

¹⁰ For my life is spent with
      sorrow,
   and my years with sighing;
   my strength fails because
      of my misery,[a]
   and my bones waste away.

¹¹ I am the scorn of all my
      adversaries,
   a horror[b] to my neighbors,
   an object of dread to my
      acquaintances;
   those who see me in the
      street flee from me.
¹² I have passed out of mind
      like one who is dead;
   I have become like a
      broken vessel.
¹³ For I hear the whispering
      of many—
   terror all around!—
   as they scheme together
      against me,
   as they plot to take my life.

¹⁴ But I trust in you, O LORD;
   I say, "You are my God."
¹⁵ My times are in your hand;
   deliver me from the hand
      of my enemies and
      persecutors.
¹⁶ Let your face shine upon
      your servant;
   save me in your steadfast
      love.
¹⁷ Do not let me be put to
      shame, O LORD,
   for I call on you;
   let the wicked be put to
      shame;
   let them go dumbfounded
      to Sheol.
¹⁸ Let the lying lips be stilled
   that speak insolently

against the righteous
   with pride and contempt.

¹⁹ O how abundant is your
      goodness
   that you have laid up for
      those who fear you,
   and accomplished for those
      who take refuge in you,
   in the sight of everyone!
²⁰ In the shelter of your
      presence you hide them
      from human plots;
   you hold them safe under
      your shelter
   from contentious tongues.

²¹ Blessed be the LORD,
   for he has wondrously
      shown his steadfast
      love to me
   when I was beset as a
      city under siege.
²² I had said in my alarm,
   "I am driven far[c] from
      your sight."
   But you heard my
      supplications
   when I cried out to you
      for help.

²³ Love the LORD, all you his
      saints.
   The LORD preserves the
      faithful,
   but abundantly repays
      the one who acts
      haughtily.
²⁴ Be strong, and let your
      heart take courage,
   all you who wait for the
      LORD.

[a]Gk Syr: Heb *my iniquity*   [b]Cn: Heb *exceedingly*
[c]Another reading is *cut off*

Psalm 32

Of David. A Maskil.

[1] Happy are those whose
  transgression is
  forgiven,
  whose sin is covered.
[2] Happy are those to whom
  the LORD imputes no
  iniquity,
  and in whose spirit there
  is no deceit.

[3] While I kept silence, my
  body wasted away
  through my groaning all
  day long.
[4] For day and night your
  hand was heavy
  upon me;
  my strength was dried
  up[a] as by the heat of
  summer.   *Selah*

[5] Then I acknowledged my
  sin to you,
  and I did not hide my
  iniquity;
  I said, "I will confess my
  transgressions to the
  LORD,"
  and you forgave the guilt
  of my sin.   *Selah*

[6] Therefore let all who are
  faithful
  offer prayer to you;
  at a time of distress,[b] the
  rush of mighty waters
  shall not reach them.
[7] You are a hiding place for me;
  you preserve me from
  trouble;

you surround me with
  glad cries of
  deliverance.   *Selah*

[8] I will instruct you and
  teach you the way
  you should go;
  I will counsel you with
  my eye upon you.
[9] Do not be like a horse or a
  mule, without
  understanding,
  whose temper must be
  curbed with bit and
  bridle,
  else it will not stay near you.

[10] Many are the torments of
  the wicked,
  but steadfast love
  surrounds those who
  trust in the LORD.
[11] Be glad in the LORD and
  rejoice, O righteous,
  and shout for joy, all you
  upright in heart.

Psalm 33

[1] Rejoice in the LORD, O you
  righteous.
  Praise befits the upright.
[2] Praise the LORD with the lyre;
  make melody to him
  with the harp of ten
  strings.
[3] Sing to him a new song;
  play skillfully on the strings,
  with loud shouts.

[4] For the word of the LORD
  is upright,

[a]Meaning of Heb uncertain [b]Cn: Heb *at a time of finding only*

and all his work is done
  in faithfulness.
⁵ He loves righteousness and
    justice;
  the earth is full of the
    steadfast love of the
    LORD.

⁶ By the word of the LORD the
    heavens were made,
  and all their host by the
    breath of his mouth.
⁷ He gathered the waters of
    the sea as in a
    bottle;
  he put the deeps in
    storehouses.

⁸ Let all the earth fear the LORD;
  let all the inhabitants of
    the world stand in
    awe of him.
⁹ For he spoke, and it came to be;
  he commanded, and it
    stood firm.

¹⁰ The LORD brings the
    counsel of the
    nations to nothing;
  he frustrates the plans of
    the peoples.
¹¹ The counsel of the LORD
    stands forever,
  the thoughts of his heart
    to all generations.
¹² Happy is the nation whose
    God is the LORD,
  the people whom he has
    chosen as his heritage.

¹³ The LORD looks down from
    heaven;
  he sees all humankind.

¹⁴ From where he sits
    enthroned he watches
  all the inhabitants of the
    earth—
¹⁵ he who fashions the hearts
    of them all,
  and observes all their deeds.
¹⁶ A king is not saved by his
    great army;
  a warrior is not delivered
    by his great strength.
¹⁷ The war horse is a vain
    hope for victory,
  and by its great might it
    cannot save.

¹⁸ Truly the eye of the LORD
    is on those who fear
    him,
  on those who hope in his
    steadfast love,
¹⁹ to deliver their soul from
    death,
  and to keep them alive in
    famine.

²⁰ Our soul waits for the LORD;
  he is our help and shield.
²¹ Our heart is glad in him,
  because we trust in his
    holy name.
²² Let your steadfast love,
    O LORD, be upon us,
  even as we hope in you.

Psalm 34

*Of David, when he feigned
madness before Abimelech, so
that he drove him out, and he
went away.*

¹ I will bless the LORD
  at all times;

his praise shall continually
be in my mouth.
2 My soul makes its boast in
the LORD;
let the humble hear and
be glad.
3 O magnify the LORD with me,
and let us exalt his name
together.

4 I sought the LORD, and he
answered me,
and delivered me from
all my fears.
5 Look to him, and be radiant;
so your[a] faces shall
never be ashamed.
6 This poor soul cried, and
was heard by the LORD,
and was saved from
every trouble.
7 The angel of the LORD encamps
around those who fear him,
and delivers them.
8 O taste and see that the
LORD is good;
happy are those who
take refuge in him.
9 O fear the LORD, you his
holy ones,
for those who fear him
have no want.
10 The young lions suffer
want and hunger,
but those who seek the
LORD lack no good thing.

11 Come, O children, listen to
me;
I will teach you the fear
of the LORD.
12 Which of you desires life,
and covets many days to
enjoy good?

13 Keep your tongue from
evil,
and your lips from
speaking deceit.
14 Depart from evil, and do good;
seek peace, and pursue it.

15 The eyes of the LORD are
on the righteous,
and his ears are open to
their cry.
16 The face of the LORD is
against evildoers,
to cut off the
remembrance of them
from the earth.
17 When the righteous cry for
help, the LORD hears,
and rescues them from
all their troubles.
18 The LORD is near to the
brokenhearted,
and saves the crushed in
spirit.

19 Many are the afflictions of
the righteous,
but the LORD rescues
them from them all.
20 He keeps all their bones;
not one of them will be
broken.
21 Evil brings death to the
wicked,
and those who hate the
righteous will be
condemned.
22 The LORD redeems the life
of his servants;
none of those who take
refuge in him will be
condemned.

[a] Gk Syr Jerome: Heb *their*

403

Psalm 35

Of David.

[1] Contend, O LORD, with those
    who contend with me;
  fight against those who
    fight against me!
[2] Take hold of shield and
    buckler,
  and rise up to help me!
[3] Draw the spear and javelin
    against my pursuers;
  say to my soul,
    "I am your salvation."

[4] Let them be put to shame
    and dishonor
  who seek after my life.
  Let them be turned back
    and confounded
  who devise evil against me.
[5] Let them be like chaff
    before the wind,
  with the angel of the LORD
    driving them on.
[6] Let their way be dark and
    slippery,
  with the angel of the LORD
    pursuing them.

[7] For without cause they hid
    their net[a] for me;
  without cause they dug a
    pit[b] for my life.
[8] Let ruin come on them
    unawares.
  And let the net that they
    hid ensnare them;
  let them fall in it—to
    their ruin.

[9] Then my soul shall rejoice
    in the LORD,
  exulting in his deliverance.

[10] All my bones shall say,
    "O LORD, who is like you?
  You deliver the weak
    from those too strong for
      them,
  the weak and needy
    from those who
      despoil them."

[11] Malicious witnesses rise up;
  they ask me about things
    I do not know.
[12] They repay me evil for good;
  my soul is forlorn.
[13] But as for me, when they
      were sick,
  I wore sackcloth;
  I afflicted myself with
    fasting.
  I prayed with head bowed[c]
    on my bosom,

[14] as though I grieved for a
      friend or a brother;
  I went about as one who
    laments for a mother,
  bowed down and in
    mourning.

[15] But at my stumbling they
    gathered in glee,
  they gathered together
    against me;
  ruffians whom I did not
    know
  tore at me without ceasing;
[16] they impiously mocked
    more and more,[d]
  gnashing at me with their
    teeth.

---

[a] Heb *a pit, their net* [b] The word *pit* is transposed from
the preceding line [c] Or *My prayer turned back* [d] Cn
Compare Gk: Heb *like the profanest of mockers of a
cake*

17 How long, O LORD, will
      you look on?
   Rescue me from their
      ravages,
   my life from the lions!
18 Then I will thank you in
      the great congregation;
   in the mighty throng I
      will praise you.

19 Do not let my treacherous
      enemies rejoice over me,
   or those who hate me
      without cause wink
      the eye.
20 For they do not speak peace,
      but they conceive
      deceitful words
   against those who are
      quiet in the land.
21 They open wide their
      mouths against me;
   they say, "Aha, Aha,
      our eyes have seen it."

22 You have seen, O LORD; do
      not be silent!
   O LORD, do not be far
      from me!
23 Wake up! Bestir yourself
      for my defense,
   for my cause, my God
      and my Lord!
24 Vindicate me, O LORD, my
      God,
   according to your
      righteousness,
   and do not let them
      rejoice over me.
25 Do not let them say to
      themselves,
   "Aha, we have our
      heart's desire."
   Do not let them say,

"We have swallowed
      you*a* up."

26 Let all those who rejoice at
      my calamity
   be put to shame and
      confusion;
   let those who exalt
      themselves against me
   be clothed with shame
      and dishonor.

27 Let those who desire my
      vindication
   shout for joy and be glad,
      and say evermore,
   "Great is the LORD,
      who delights in the welfare
      of his servant."
28 Then my tongue shall tell
      of your righteousness
   and of your praise all
      day long.

Psalm 36

*To the leader. Of David,
the servant of the LORD.*

1 Transgression speaks to
      the wicked
   deep in their hearts;
   there is no fear of God
      before their eyes.
2 For they flatter themselves
      in their own eyes
   that their iniquity cannot
      be found out and hated.
3 The words of their mouths are
      mischief and deceit;
   they have ceased to act
      wisely and do good.
4 They plot mischief while on
      their beds;

---

a Heb *him*

405

they are set on a way that is
not good;
they do not reject evil.

5 Your steadfast love, O Lord,
extends to the heavens,
your faithfulness to the
clouds.
6 Your righteousness is like the
mighty mountains,
your judgments are like
the great deep;
you save humans and
animals alike,
O Lord.

7 How precious is your steadfast
love, O God!
All people may take
refuge in the shadow
of your wings.
8 They feast on the abundance
of your house,
and you give them drink
from the river of your
delights.
9 For with you is the
fountain of life;
in your light we see light.

10 O continue your steadfast
love to those who
know you,
and your salvation to the
upright of heart!
11 Do not let the foot of the
arrogant tread on me,
or the hand of the wicked
drive me away.
12 There the evildoers lie
prostrate;
they are thrust down,
unable to rise.

Psalm 37
Of David.

1 Do not fret because of the
wicked;
do not be envious of
wrongdoers,
2 for they will soon fade like
the grass,
and wither like the green
herb.

3 Trust in the Lord, and do good;
so you will live in the land,
and enjoy security.
4 Take delight in the Lord,
and he will give you the
desires of your heart.

5 Commit your way to the Lord;
trust in him, and he will act.
6 He will make your vindication
shine like the light,
and the justice of your cause
like the noonday.

7 Be still before the Lord, and
wait patiently for him;
do not fret over those who
prosper in their way,
over those who carry out
evil devices.

8 Refrain from anger,
and forsake wrath.
Do not fret—it leads only
to evil.
9 For the wicked shall be cut off,
but those who wait for
the Lord shall inherit
the land.

10 Yet a little while, and the
wicked will be no more;

though you look diligently
for their place, they will
not be there.
¹¹ But the meek shall inherit
the land,
and delight themselves in
abundant prosperity.

¹² The wicked plot against
the righteous,
and gnash their teeth at
them;
¹³ but the LORD laughs at the
wicked,
for he sees that their day
is coming.

¹⁴ The wicked draw the sword
and bend their bows
to bring down the poor
and needy,
to kill those who walk
uprightly;
¹⁵ their sword shall enter their
own heart,
and their bows shall be
broken.

¹⁶ Better is a little that the
righteous person has
than the abundance of
many wicked.
¹⁷ For the arms of the wicked
shall be broken,
but the LORD upholds the
righteous.

¹⁸ The LORD knows the days
of the blameless,
and their heritage will
abide forever;
¹⁹ they are not put to shame
in evil times,
in the days of famine
they have abundance.

²⁰ But the wicked perish,
and the enemies of the
LORD are like the glory of
the pastures;
they vanish—like smoke
they vanish away.

²¹ The wicked borrow, and do
not pay back,
but the righteous are
generous and keep
giving;
²² for those blessed by the LORD
shall inherit the land,
but those cursed by him
shall be cut off.

²³ Our steps^a are made firm
by the LORD,
when he delights in our^b
way;
²⁴ though we stumble,^c we^d shall
not fall headlong,
for the LORD holds us^e
by the hand.

²⁵ I have been young,
and now am old,
yet I have not seen the
righteous forsaken
or their children begging
bread.
²⁶ They are ever giving
liberally and lending,
and their children
become a blessing.

²⁷ Depart from evil, and do good;
so you shall abide forever.
²⁸ For the LORD loves justice;
he will not forsake his
faithful ones.

^aHeb *A man's steps* ^bHeb *his* ^cHeb *he stumbles* ^dHeb
he ^eHeb *him*

The righteous shall be kept
  safe forever,
but the children of the
  wicked shall be cut off.
29 The righteous shall inherit
  the land,
  and live in it forever.

30 The mouths of the righteous
  utter wisdom,
  and their tongues speak
  justice.
31 The law of their God is in
  their hearts;
  their steps do not slip.

32 The wicked watch for the
  righteous,
  and seek to kill them.
33 The LORD will not abandon
  them to their power,
  or let them be condemned
  when they are brought
  to trial.

34 Wait for the LORD, and keep
  to his way,
  and he will exalt you to
  inherit the land;
  you will look on the
  destruction of the
  wicked.

35 I have seen the wicked
  oppressing,
  and towering like a
  cedar of Lebanon.[a]
36 Again I[b] passed by, and
  they were no more;
  though I sought them, they
  could not be found.

37 Mark the blameless, and
  behold the upright,

for there is posterity for
  the peaceable.
38 But transgressors shall be
  altogether destroyed;
  the posterity of the wicked
  shall be cut off.

39 The salvation of the righteous
  is from the LORD;
  he is their refuge in the
  time of trouble.
40 The LORD helps them and
  rescues them;
  he rescues them from the
  wicked, and saves them,
  because they take refuge
  in him.

Psalm 38

*A Psalm of David, for the
memorial offering.*

1 O Lord, do not rebuke me
  in your anger,
  or discipline me in your
  wrath.
2 For your arrows have sunk
  into me,
  and your hand has come
  down on me.

3 There is no soundness in
  my flesh
  because of your indignation;
  there is no health in my
  bones
  because of my sin.
4 For my iniquities have
  gone over my head;
  they weigh like a burden
  too heavy for me.

[a]Gk: Meaning of Heb uncertain [b]Gk Syr Jerome: Heb
he

408

⁵ My wounds grow foul and
      fester
   because of my foolishness;
⁶ I am utterly bowed down
         and prostrate;
   all day long I go around
      mourning.
⁷ For my loins are filled with
      burning,
   and there is no soundness
      in my flesh.
⁸ I am utterly spent and crushed;
   I groan because of the
      tumult of my heart.

⁹ O Lord, all my longing is
      known to you;
   my sighing is not hidden
      from you.
¹⁰ My heart throbs, my
      strength fails me;
   as for the light of my eyes—
      it also has gone from
      me.
¹¹ My friends and companions
      stand aloof from my
      affliction,
   and my neighbors stand
      far off.

¹² Those who seek my life lay
      their snares;
   those who seek to hurt
      me speak of ruin,
   and meditate treachery
      all day long.

¹³ But I am like the deaf,
      I do not hear;
   like the mute, who
      cannot speak.
¹⁴ Truly, I am like one who
      does not hear,
   and in whose mouth is
      no retort.

¹⁵ But it is for you, O Lord,
      that I wait;
   it is you, O Lord my God,
      who will answer.
¹⁶ For I pray, "Only do not let
      them rejoice over me,
   those who boast against me
      when my foot slips."

¹⁷ For I am ready to fall,
   and my pain is ever with
      me.
¹⁸ I confess my iniquity;
   I am sorry for my sin.
¹⁹ Those who are my foes
      without cause*a* are
      mighty,
   and many are those who
      hate me wrongfully.
²⁰ Those who render me evil
      for good
   are my adversaries because
      I follow after good.

²¹ Do not forsake me, O Lord;
   O my God, do not be far
      from me;
²² make haste to help me,
   O Lord, my salvation.

Psalm 39

*To the leader: to Jeduthun. A
Psalm of David.*

¹ I said, "I will guard my ways
   that I may not sin with my
      tongue;
   I will keep a muzzle on my
      mouth
   as long as the wicked are in
      my presence."
² I was silent and still;

*a*Q Ms: MT *my living foes*

I held my peace to no avail;
my distress grew worse,
3   my heart became hot
        within me.
While I mused, the fire
        burned;
    then I spoke with my
        tongue:

4 "LORD, let me know my end,
    and what is the measure of
        my days;
    let me know how fleeting
        my life is.
5 You have made my days a few
        handbreadths,
    and my lifetime is as
        nothing in your sight.
Surely everyone stands as a
        mere breath.   *Selah*
6   Surely everyone goes about
        like a shadow.
Surely for nothing they are
        in turmoil;
    they heap up, and do not
        know who will gather.

7 "And now, O LORD, what do I
        wait for?
My hope is in you.
8 Deliver me from all my
        transgressions.
    Do not make me the scorn
        of the fool.
9 I am silent; I do not open my
        mouth,
    for it is you who have
        done it.
10 Remove your stroke from me;
    I am worn down by the
        blows[a] of your hand.

11 "You chastise mortals
    in punishment for sin,

consuming like a moth what
        is dear to them;
    surely everyone is a mere
        breath.   *Selah*

12 "Hear my prayer, O LORD,
    and give ear to my cry;
    do not hold your peace
        at my tears.
For I am your passing guest,
    an alien, like all my
        forebears.
13 Turn your gaze away from me,
    that I may smile again,
    before I depart and am
        no more."

Psalm 40

*To the leader. Of David. A
Psalm.*

1 I waited patiently for the Lord;
    he inclined to me and heard
        my cry.
2 He drew me up from the
        desolate pit,[b]
    out of the miry bog,
    and set my feet upon a rock,
        making my steps secure.
3 He put a new song in my
        mouth,
    a song of praise to our God.
Many will see and fear,
    and put their trust in the
        LORD.

4 Happy are those who make
    the LORD their trust,
who do not turn to the proud,
    to those who go astray after
        false gods.
5 You have multiplied,
    O LORD my God,

---

[a]Heb *hostility* [b]Cn: Heb *pit of tumult*

your wondrous deeds and
   your thoughts toward
   us;
      none can compare with you.
Were I to proclaim and tell of
   them,
      they would be more than
      can be counted.

6 Sacrifice and offering you do
   not desire,
      but you have given me an
      open ear.[a]
Burnt offering and sin
   offering
      you have not required.
7 Then I said, "Here I am;
   in the scroll of the book it is
   written of me.[b]
8 I delight to do your will, O my
   God;
      your law is within my
      heart."

9 I have told the glad news of
   deliverance
   in the great congregation;
      see, I have not restrained my
      lips,
         as you know, O LORD.
10 I have not hidden your saving
   help within my heart,
   I have spoken of your
   faithfulness and your
   salvation;
      I have not concealed your
      steadfast love and your
      faithfulness
         from the great congregation.

11 Do not, O LORD, withhold
   your mercy from me;
      let your steadfast love and
      your faithfulness
         keep me safe forever.

12 For evils have
      encompassed me
      without number;
   my iniquities have
      overtaken me,
      until I cannot see;
   they are more than the hairs of
   my head,
      and my heart fails me.

13 Be pleased, O LORD, to deliver
   me;
      O LORD, make haste to help
      me.
14 Let all those be put to shame
   and confusion
      who seek to snatch away my
      life;
   let those be turned back and
   brought to dishonor
      who desire my hurt.
15 Let those be appalled
      because of their
      shame
   who say to me, "Aha,
   Aha!"

16 But may all who seek you
   rejoice and be glad in
   you;
      may those who love your
      salvation
         say continually, "Great is the
         LORD!"
17 As for me, I am poor and
   needy,
      but the Lord takes thought
      for me.
   You are my help and my
   deliverer;
      do not delay, O my God.

---

[a]Heb *ears you have dug for me* [b]Meaning of Heb uncertain

411

Psalm 41

To the leader. A Psalm of David.

[1] Happy are those who consider
    the poor;[a]
  the LORD delivers them in
    the day of trouble.
[2] The LORD protects them and
    keeps them alive;
  they are called happy in the
    land.
  You do not give them up to
    the will of their
    enemies.
[3] The LORD sustains them on
    their sickbed;
  in their illness you heal all
    their infirmities.[b]

[4] As for me, I said, "O LORD, be
    gracious to me;
  heal me, for I have sinned
    against you."
[5] My enemies wonder in malice
    when I will die, and my
    name perish.
[6] And when they come to see
    me, they utter empty
    words,
  while their hearts gather
    mischief;
  when they go out, they tell it
    abroad.
[7] All who hate me whisper
    together about me;
  they imagine the worst for
    me.

[8] They think that a deadly thing
    has fastened on me,
  that I will not rise again
    from where I lie.
[9] Even my bosom friend in
    whom I trusted,
  who ate of my bread, has
    lifted the heel against
    me.
[10] But you, O LORD, be gracious
    to me,
  and raise me up, that I may
    repay them.

[11] By this I know that you are
    pleased with me;
  because my enemy has not
    triumphed over me.
[12] But you have upheld me
    because of my integrity,
  and set me in your presence
    forever.

[13] Blessed be the LORD, the God
    of Israel,
  from everlasting to
    everlasting.
  Amen and Amen.

BOOK II

(Psalms 42–72)

Psalm 42

*To the leader. A Maskil of the
Korahites.*

[1] As a deer longs for flowing
    streams,
  so my soul longs for you,
    O God.
[2] My soul thirsts for God,
    for the living God.
  When shall I come and
    behold the face of God?

[3] My tears have been my food
    day and night,

---

[a]Or *weak* [b]Heb *you change all his bed*

while people say to me
  continually,
  "Where is your God?"

⁴ These things I remember,
  as I pour out my soul:
how I went with the throng,ᵃ
  and led them in procession
    to the house of God,
with glad shouts and songs
    of thanksgiving,
  a multitude keeping festival.
⁵ Why are you cast down,
    O my soul,
  and why are you disquieted
    within me?
Hope in God; for I shall
    again praise him,
  my help ⁶and my God.

My soul is cast down within
    me;
  therefore I remember you
from the land of Jordan and
    of Hermon,
  from Mount Mizar.
⁷ Deep calls to deep
  at the thunder of your
    cataracts;
  all your waves and your
    billows
  have gone over me.
⁸ By day the LORD commands
    his steadfast love,
  and at night his song is
    with me,
  a prayer to the God of my
    life.

⁹ I say to God, my rock,
  "Why have you forgotten
    me?
Why must I walk about
    mournfully

because the enemy
  oppresses me?"
¹⁰ As with a deadly wound in
    my body,
  my adversaries taunt me,
while they say to me
  continually,
  "Where is your God?"

¹¹ Why are you cast down,
    O my soul,
  and why are you disquieted
    within me?
Hope in God; for I shall again
    praise him,
  my help and my God.

Psalm 43

¹ Vindicate me, O God, and
    defend my cause
  against an ungodly people;
from those who are deceitful
    and unjust
  deliver me!
² For you are the God in whom I
    take refuge;
  why have you cast me off?
Why must I walk about
    mournfully
  because of the oppression of
    the enemy?

³ O send out your light and your
    truth;
  let them lead me;
  let them bring me to your
    holy hill
  and to your dwelling.
⁴ Then I will go to the altar of
    God,
  to God my exceeding joy;
and I will praise you with
    the harp,
  O God, my God.

ᵃMeaning of Heb uncertain

413

⁵ Why are you cast down,
      O my soul,
   and why are you disquieted
      within me?
   Hope in God; for I shall again
      praise him,
   my help and my God.

Psalm 44

*To the leader. Of the Korahites.
A Maskil.*

¹ We have heard with our ears,
      O God,
   our ancestors have told us,
what deeds you performed
      in their days,
   in the days of old:
² you with your own hand drove
      out the nations,
   but them you planted;
you afflicted the peoples,
   but them you set free;
³ for not by their own sword
   did they win the land,
   nor did their own arm give
      them victory;
but your right hand, and
      your arm,
   and the light of your
      countenance,
   for you delighted in them.

⁴ You are my King and my God;
   you command^a victories
      for Jacob.
⁵ Through you we push down
      our foes;
   through your name we tread
      down our assailants.
⁶ For not in my bow do I trust,
   nor can my sword save me.
⁷ But you have saved us from our
      foes,

   and have put to confusion
      those who hate us.
⁸ In God we have boasted
      continually,
   and we will give thanks to
      your name forever.
                        Selah

⁹ Yet you have rejected us and
      abased us,
   and have not gone out with
      our armies.
¹⁰ You made us turn back from
      the foe,
   and our enemies have gotten
      spoil.
¹¹ You have made us like sheep
      for slaughter,
   and have scattered us among
      the nations.
¹² You have sold your people for
      a trifle,
   demanding no high price for
      them.

¹³ You have made us the taunt of
      our neighbors,
   the derision and scorn of
      those around us.
¹⁴ You have made us a byword
      among the nations,
   a laughingstock^b among the
      peoples.

¹⁵ All day long my disgrace is
      before me,
   and shame has covered my
      face
¹⁶ at the words of the taunters
      and revilers,
   at the sight of the enemy and
      the avenger.

^{a}Gk Syr: Heb *You are my King, O God; command*
^{b}Heb *a shaking of the head*

¹⁷ All this has come upon us,
yet we have not forgotten
you,
or been false to your
covenant.
¹⁸ Our heart has not turned back,
nor have our steps departed
from your way,
¹⁹ yet you have broken us in the
haunt of jackals,
and covered us with deep
darkness.

²⁰ If we had forgotten the name
of our God,
or spread out our hands to a
strange god,
²¹ would not God discover
this?
For he knows the secrets of
the heart.
²² Because of you we are
being killed all day
long,
and accounted as sheep for
the slaughter.

²³ Rouse yourself! Why do you
sleep, O Lord?
Awake, do not cast us off
forever!
²⁴ Why do you hide your
face?
Why do you forget our
affliction and
oppression?
²⁵ For we sink down to the
dust;
our bodies cling to the
ground.
²⁶ Rise up, come to our help.
Redeem us for the sake of
your steadfast love.

Psalm 45

*To the leader: according to
Lilies. Of the Korahites. A
Maskil. A love song.*

¹ My heart overflows with a
goodly theme;
I address my verses to the
king;
my tongue is like the pen of
a ready scribe.

² You are the most handsome of
men;
grace is poured upon your
lips;
therefore God has blessed
you forever.
³ Gird your sword on your thigh,
O mighty one,
in your glory and majesty.

⁴ In your majesty ride on
victoriously
for the cause of truth and to
defend^a the right;
let your right hand teach
you dread deeds.
⁵ Your arrows are sharp
in the heart of the king's
enemies;
the peoples fall under you.

⁶ Your throne, O God,^b endures
forever and ever.
Your royal scepter is a
scepter of equity;
⁷ you love righteousness and
hate wickedness.
Therefore God, your God,
has anointed you

---

^aCn: Heb *and the meekness of* ^bOr *Your throne is a
throne of God, it*

with the oil of gladness
beyond your
companions;
8　your robes are all fragrant
with myrrh and aloes
and cassia.
From ivory palaces stringed
instruments make you
glad;
9　daughters of kings are among
your ladies of honor;
at your right hand stands the
queen in gold of Ophir.

10 Hear, O daughter, consider
and incline your ear;
forget your people and your
father's house,
11　and the king will desire your
beauty.
Since he is your Lord, bow
to him;
12　the people[a] of Tyre will seek
your favor with gifts,
the richest of the people
13with all kinds of
wealth.

The princess is decked in
her chamber with
gold-woven robes;[b]
14　in many-colored robes she is
led to the king;
behind her the virgins, her
companions, follow.
15 With joy and gladness they are
led along
as they enter the palace of
the king.

16 In the place of ancestors you,
O king,[c] shall have sons;
you will make them princes
in all the earth.

17 I will cause your name to be
celebrated in all
generations;
therefore the peoples will
praise you forever and
ever.

Psalm 46

*To the leader. Of the Korahites.
According to Alamoth. A Song.*

1 God is our refuge and strength,
a very present[d] help in
trouble.
2 Therefore we will not fear,
though the earth should
change,
though the mountains shake
in the heart of the sea;
3 though its waters roar and
foam,
though the mountains
tremble with its tumult.
Selah

4 There is a river whose streams
make glad the city of
God,
the holy habitation of the
Most High.
5 God is in the midst of the city;[e]
it shall not be moved;
God will help it when the
morning dawns.
6 The nations are in an uproar,
the kingdoms totter;
he utters his voice, the earth
melts.
7 The LORD of hosts is with us;
the God of Jacob is our
refuge.[f]　　　*Selah*

---

*[a]Heb daughter　[b]Or people.　13All glorious is the
princess within, gold embroidery is her clothing　[c]Heb
lacks O king　[d]Or well proved　[e]Heb of it　[f]Or fortress*

416

8 Come, behold the works of
the LORD;
see what desolations he has
brought on the earth.
9 He makes wars cease to the
end of the earth;
he breaks the bow, and
shatters the spear;
he burns the shields with
fire.
10 "Be still, and know that I am
God!
I am exalted among the
nations,
I am exalted in the earth."
11 The LORD of hosts is with us;
the God of Jacob is our
refuge.[a]   Selah

Psalm 47

*To the leader. Of the Korahites.
A Psalm.*

1 Clap your hands, all you
peoples;
shout to God with loud
songs of joy.
2 For the LORD, the Most High, is
awesome,
a great king over all the
earth.
3 He subdued peoples under us,
and nations under our feet.
4 He chose our heritage for us,
the pride of Jacob whom he
loves.   Selah

5 God has gone up with a shout,
the LORD with the sound of a
trumpet.
6 Sing praises to God, sing
praises;
sing praises to our King, sing
praises.

7 For God is the king of all the
earth;
sing praises with a psalm.[b]

8 God is king over the nations;
God sits on his holy throne.
9 The princes of the peoples
gather
as the people of the God of
Abraham.
For the shields of the earth
belong to God;
he is highly exalted.

Psalm 48

*A Song. A Psalm of the
Korahites.*

1 Great is the LORD and greatly to
be praised
in the city of our God.
His holy mountain,
2beautiful in elevation,
is the joy of all the earth,
Mount Zion, in the far north,
the city of the great King.
3 Within its citadels God
has shown himself a
sure defense.

4 Then the kings assembled,
they came on together.
5 As soon as they saw it, they
were astounded;
they were in panic, they
took to flight;
6 trembling took hold of them
there,
pains as of a woman in
labor,
7 as when an east wind shatters
the ships of Tarshish.

[a]Or *fortress* [b]Heb *Maskil*

⁸ As we have heard, so have
    we seen
  in the city of the LORD of
      hosts,
  in the city of our God,
    which God establishes
      forever.   *Selah*

⁹ We ponder your steadfast love,
    O God,
  in the midst of your temple.
¹⁰ Your name, O God, like your
      praise,
  reaches to the ends of the
      earth.
  Your right hand is filled
      with victory.
¹¹   Let Mount Zion be glad,
  let the towns*ᵃ* of Judah
      rejoice
  because of your judgments.

¹² Walk about Zion, go all
      around it,
  count its towers,
¹³ consider well its ramparts;
  go through its citadels,
  that you may tell the next
      generation
¹³   that this is God,
  our God forever and ever.
    He will be our guide forever.

Psalm 49

To the leader. Of the Korahites.
A Psalm.

¹ Hear this, all you peoples;
  give ear, all inhabitants of
      the world,
² both low and high,
  rich and poor together.
³ My mouth shall speak wisdom;

  the meditation of my heart
    shall be understanding.
⁴ I will incline my ear to a
      proverb;
  I will solve my riddle to the
    music of the harp.

⁵ Why should I fear in times of
      trouble,
  when the iniquity of
    my persecutors
      surrounds me,
⁶ those who trust in their wealth
  and boast of the
      abundance of their
        riches?
⁷ Truly, no ransom avails for
      one's life,*ᵇ*
  there is no price one can
    give to God for it.
⁸ For the ransom of life is costly,
  and can never suffice,
⁹ that one should live on forever
  and never see the grave.*ᶜ*

¹⁰ When we look at the wise,
      they die;
  fool and dolt perish together
  and leave their wealth to
      others.
¹¹ Their graves*ᵈ* are their homes
      forever,
  their dwelling places to all
      generations,
  though they named lands
    their own.
¹² Mortals cannot abide in their
      pomp;
  they are like the animals
    that perish.

---

*ᵃ*Heb *daughters* *ᵇ*Another reading is *no one can ran-*
som a brother *ᶜ*Heb *the pit* *ᵈ*Gk Syr Compare Tg: Heb
their inward (thought)

¹³ Such is the fate of the
foolhardy,
the end of those*a* who are
pleased with their lot.
Selah

¹⁴ Like sheep they are
appointed for Sheol
Death shall be their
shepherd;
straight to the grave they
descend,*b*
and their form shall
waste away;
Sheol shall be their
home.*c*

¹⁵ But God will ransom my soul
from the power of
Sheol,
for he will receive me.
Selah

¹⁶ Do not be afraid when some
become rich,
when the wealth of their
houses increases.

¹⁷ For when they die they will
carry nothing away;
their wealth will not go
down after them.

¹⁸ Though in their lifetime
they count
themselves happy
—for you are praised
when you do well for
yourself—

¹⁹ they*d* will go to the
company of their
ancestors,
who will never again see the
light.

²⁰ Mortals cannot abide in their
pomp;
they are like the animals
that perish.

Psalm 50

A Psalm of Asaph.

¹ The mighty one, God the LORD,
speaks and summons the
earth
from the rising of the sun to
its setting.

² Out of Zion, the perfection of
beauty,
God shines forth.

³ Our God comes and does not
keep silence,
before him is a devouring
fire,
and a mighty tempest all
around him.

⁴ He calls to the heavens above
and to the earth, that he may
judge his people:

⁵ "Gather to me my faithful ones,
who made a covenant with
me by sacrifice!"

⁶ The heavens declare his
righteousness,
for God himself is judge.
Selah

⁷ "Hear, O my people, and I will
speak,
O Israel, I will testify against
you.
I am God, your God.

⁸ Not for your sacrifices do I
rebuke you;
your burnt offerings are
continually before me.

⁹ I will not accept a bull from
your house,
or goats from your folds.

*a*Tg: Heb *after them* *b*Cn: Heb *the upright shall have dominion over them in the morning* *c*Meaning of Heb uncertain *d*Cn: Heb *you*

419

10 For every wild animal of the
      forest is mine,
   the cattle on a thousand
      hills.
11 I know all the birds of the air,[a]
   and all that moves in the
      field is mine.

12 "If I were hungry, I would not
      tell you,
   for the world and all that is
      in it is mine.
13 Do I eat the flesh of bulls,
   or drink the blood of goats?
14 Offer to God a sacrifice of
      thanksgiving,[b]
   and pay your vows to the
      Most High.
15 Call on me in the day of
      trouble;
   I will deliver you, and you
      shall glorify me."

16 But to the wicked God says:
   "What right have you to
      recite my statutes,
   or take my covenant on your
      lips?
17 For you hate discipline,
   and you cast my words
      behind you.
18 You make friends with a thief
      when you see one,
   and you keep company with
      adulterers.

19 "You give your mouth free
      rein for evil,
   and your tongue frames
      deceit.
20 You sit and speak against your
      kin;
   you slander your own
      mother's child.

21 These things you have done
      and I have been silent;
   you thought that I was one
      just like yourself.
   But now I rebuke you, and
      lay the charge before
      you.

22 "Mark this, then, you who
      forget God,
   or I will tear you apart, and
      there will be no one to
      deliver.
23 Those who bring
      thanksgiving as their
      sacrifice honor me;
   to those who go the right
      way[c]
   I will show the salvation of
      God."

Psalm 51

*To the leader. A Psalm of David,
when the prophet Nathan came
to him, after he had gone in to
Bathsheba.*

1 Have mercy on me, O God,
      according to your steadfast
      love;
   according to your abundant
      mercy
   blot out my transgressions.
2 Wash me thoroughly from my
      iniquity,
   and cleanse me from my sin.

3 For I know my transgressions,
   and my sin is ever
      before me.
4 Against you, you alone, have I
      sinned,

[a]Gk Syr Tg: Heb *mountains* [b]Or *make thanksgiving
your sacrifice to God* [c]Heb *who set a way*

and done what is evil in
   your sight,
so that you are justified in
   your sentence
   and blameless when you
   pass judgment.
⁵ Indeed, I was born guilty,
   a sinner when my mother
   conceived me.

⁶ You desire truth in the inward
   being;*a*
   therefore teach me wisdom
   in my secret heart.
⁷ Purge me with hyssop, and I
   shall be clean;
   wash me, and I shall be
   whiter than snow.
⁸ Let me hear joy and gladness;
   let the bones that you have
   crushed rejoice.
⁹ Hide your face from my sins,
   and blot out all my
   iniquities.

¹⁰ Create in me a clean heart,
   O God,
   and put a new and right*b*
   spirit within me.
¹¹ Do not cast me away from
   your presence,
   and do not take your holy
   spirit from me.
¹² Restore to me the joy of your
   salvation,
   and sustain in me a willing*c*
   spirit.

¹³ Then I will teach transgressors
   your ways,
   and sinners will return to
   you.
¹⁴ Deliver me from bloodshed,
   O God,

O God of my salvation,
   and my tongue will sing
   aloud of your
   deliverance.

¹⁵ O Lord, open my lips,
   and my mouth will declare
   your praise.
¹⁶ For you have no delight in
   sacrifice;
   if I were to give a burnt
   offering, you would not
   be pleased.
¹⁷ The sacrifice acceptable to
   God*d* is a broken spirit;
   a broken and contrite heart,
   O God, you will not
   despise.

¹⁸ Do good to Zion in your good
   pleasure;
   rebuild the walls of
   Jerusalem,
¹⁹ then you will delight in right
   sacrifices,
   in burnt offerings and whole
   burnt offerings;
   then bulls will be offered on
   your altar.

Psalm 52

*To the leader. A Maskil of
David, when Doeg the Edomite
came to Saul and said to him,
"David has come to the house
of Ahimelech."*

¹ Why do you boast, O mighty
   one,
   of mischief done against the
   godly?*e*

---

*a*Meaning of Heb uncertain *b*Or *steadfast* *c*Or *generous* *d*Or *My sacrifice, O God,* *e*Cn Compare Syr: Heb
the kindness of God

All day long [2]you are
    plotting destruction.
Your tongue is like a sharp
    razor,
  you worker of treachery.
[3] You love evil more than good,
  and lying more than
    speaking the truth.
                            Selah
[4] You love all words that devour,
  O deceitful tongue.

[5] But God will break you down
    forever;
  he will snatch and tear you
    from your tent;
  he will uproot you from the
    land of the living.
                            Selah
[6] The righteous will see, and
    fear,
  and will laugh at the
    evildoer,[a] saying,
[7] "See the one who would not
    take
  refuge in God,
but trusted in abundant
    riches,
  and sought refuge in
    wealth!"[b]

[8] But I am like a green olive
    tree
  in the house of God.
I trust in the steadfast love
    of God
  forever and ever.
[9] I will thank you forever,
    because of what you have
    done.
In the presence of the
    faithful
  I will proclaim[c] your name,
    for it is good.

Psalm 53

*To the leader: according to
Mahalath. A Maskil of David.*

[1] Fools say in their hearts,
    "There is no God."
  They are corrupt, they
    commit abominable
    acts;
  there is no one who does
    good.

[2] God looks down from heaven
    on humankind
  to see if there are any who
    are wise,
  who seek after God.

[3] They have all fallen away, they
    are all alike perverse;
  there is no one who does
    good, no, not one.

[4] Have they no knowledge, those
    evildoers,
  who eat up my people as
    they eat bread,
  and do not call upon God?

[5] There they shall be in great
    terror,
  in terror such as has not
    been.
  For God will scatter the
    bones of the ungodly;[d]
  they will be put to shame,[e]
    for God has rejected
    them.

[6] O that deliverance for Israel
    would come from Zion!

---

[a]Heb *him* [b]Syr Tg: Heb *in his destruction* [c]Cn: Heb
wait for [d]Cn Compare Gk Syr: Heb *him who encamps
against you* [e]Gk: Heb *you have put (them) to shame*

When God restores the
fortunes of his people,
Jacob will rejoice; Israel will
be glad.

Psalm 54

*To the leader: with stringed
instruments. A Maskil of David,
when the Ziphites went and
told Saul, "David is in hiding
among us."*

[1] Save me, O God, by your name,
and vindicate me by your
might.
[2] Hear my prayer, O God;
give ear to the words of my
mouth.

[3] For the insolent have risen
against me,
the ruthless seek my life;
they do not set God before
them.

Selah

[4] But surely, God is my helper;
the Lord is the upholder of[a]
my life.
[5] He will repay my enemies for
their evil.
In your faithfulness, put an
end to them.

[6] With a freewill offering I will
sacrifice to you;
I will give thanks to your
name, O LORD, for it is
good.
[7] For he has delivered me from
every trouble,
and my eye has looked in
triumph on my enemies.

Psalm 55

*To the leader: with stringed
instruments. A Maskil of David.*

[1] Give ear to my prayer, O God;
do not hide yourself from
my supplication.
[2] Attend to me, and answer me;
I am troubled in my
complaint.
I am distraught [3]by the noise
of the enemy,
because of the clamor of the
wicked.
For they bring[b] trouble upon
me,
and in anger they cherish
enmity against me.

[4] My heart is in anguish within
me,
the terrors of death have
fallen upon me.
[5] Fear and trembling come upon
me,
and horror overwhelms me.
[6] And I say, "O that I had wings
like a dove!
I would fly away and be at
rest;
[7] truly, I would flee far away;
I would lodge in the
wilderness;   *Selah*
[8] I would hurry to find a shelter
for myself
from the raging wind and
tempest."

[9] Confuse, O LORD, confound
their speech;

---

[a]Gk Syr Jerome: Heb *is of those who uphold* or *is with
those who uphold* [b]Cn Compare Gk: Heb *they cause
to totter*

for I see violence and strife
    in the city.
10 Day and night they go
    around it
on its walls,
and iniquity and trouble
    are within it;
11   ruin is in its midst;
oppression and fraud
    do not depart from
    its marketplace.

12 It is not enemies who taunt
    me—
    I could bear that;
it is not adversaries who
    deal insolently with
    me—
    I could hide from them.
13 But it is you, my equal,
    my companion, my familiar
    friend,
14 with whom I kept pleasant
    company;
    we walked in the house
    of God with the throng.
15 Let death come upon them;
    let them go down alive
    to Sheol;
for evil is in their homes and
    in their hearts.

16 But I call upon God,
    and the LORD will save me.
17 Evening and morning and
    at noon
    I utter my complaint
    and moan,
and he will hear my voice.
18 He will redeem me unharmed
    from the battle that I wage,
    for many are arrayed
    against me.

19 God, who is enthroned from
    of old,   *Selah*
will hear, and will humble
    them—
because they do not change,
    and do not fear God.

20 My companion laid hands on
    a friend
    and violated a covenant
    with me*a*
21 with speech smoother than
    butter,
    but with a heart set on war;
with words that were softer
    than oil,
    but in fact were drawn
    swords.

22 Cast your burden*b* on the
    LORD,
    and he will sustain you;
he will never permit
    the righteous to be moved.

23 But you, O God, will cast them
    down
    into the lowest pit;
the bloodthirsty and
    treacherous
    shall not live out half their
    days.
But I will trust in you.

Psalm 56

*To the leader: according to The
Dove on Far-off Terebinths. Of
David. A Miktam, when the
Philistines seized him in Gath.*

1 Be gracious to me, O God, for
    people trample on me;

*a*Heb lacks *with me* *b*Or *Cast what he has given you*

424

all day long foes oppress me;
² my enemies trample on me all
    day long,
for many fight against me.
O Most High, ³when I am
    afraid,
I put my trust in you.
⁴ In God, whose word I praise,
    in God I trust; I am not
    afraid;
what can flesh do to me?

⁵ All day long they seek to
    injure my cause;
all their thoughts are against
    me for evil.
⁶ They stir up strife, they lurk,
    they watch my steps.
As they hoped to have my
    life,
⁷   so repay*a* them for their
    crime;
in wrath cast down the
    peoples, O God!

⁸ You have kept count of my
    tossings;
put my tears in your bottle.
Are they not in your record?
⁹ Then my enemies will retreat
    in the day when I call.
This I know, that*b* God is
    for me.
¹⁰ In God, whose word I praise,
    in the LORD, whose word I
    praise,
¹¹ in God I trust; I am not afraid.
What can a mere mortal do
    to me?

¹² My vows to you I must
    perform, O God;
I will render thank offerings
    to you.

¹³ For you have delivered my
    soul from death,
and my feet from falling,
so that I may walk before
    God
in the light of life.

Psalm 57

*To the leader: Do Not Destroy.
Of David. A Miktam, when he
fled from Saul, in the cave.*

¹ Be merciful to me, O God, be
    merciful to me,
for in you my soul takes
    refuge;
in the shadow of your wings
    I will take refuge,
until the destroying storms
    pass by.
² I cry to God Most High,
to God who fulfills his
    purpose for me.
³ He will send from heaven and
    save me,
he will put to shame those
    who trample on me.
              Selah
God will send forth his
    steadfast love and his
    faithfulness.

⁴ I lie down among lions
    that greedily devour*c*
    human prey;
their teeth are spears and
    arrows,
their tongues sharp swords.

⁵ Be exalted, O God, above the
    heavens.
Let your glory be over all the
    earth.

*a*Cn: Heb *rescue* *b*Or *because* *c*Cn: Heb *are aflame for*

425

⁶ They set a net for my steps;
  my soul was bowed down.
They dug a pit in my path,
  but they have fallen into it
    themselves.   *Selah*
⁷ My heart is steadfast, O God,
  my heart is steadfast.
I will sing and make melody.
⁸ Awake, my soul!
Awake, O harp and lyre!
  I will awake the dawn.
⁹ I will give thanks to you,
    O Lord, among the
    peoples;
  I will sing praises to you
    among the nations.
¹⁰ For your steadfast love is
    as high as the
    heavens;
  your faithfulness extends
    to the clouds.

¹¹ Be exalted, O God, above the
    heavens.
  Let your glory be over all the
    earth.

Psalm 58

To the leader: Do Not Destroy.
Of David. A Miktam.

¹ Do you indeed decree what
    is right, you gods?[a]
Do you judge people
    fairly?
² No, in your hearts you devise
    wrongs;
  your hands deal out
    violence on earth.

³ The wicked go astray from the
    womb;
  they err from their birth,
    speaking lies.

⁴ They have venom like the
    venom of a serpent,
  like the deaf adder that stops
    its ear,
⁵ so that it does not hear the
    voice of charmers
  or of the cunning
    enchanter.

⁶ O God, break the teeth in their
    mouths;
  tear out the fangs of the
    young lions, O LORD!
⁷ Let them vanish like water that
    runs away;
  like grass let them be
    trodden down[b] and
    wither.
⁸ Let them be like the snail
    that dissolves into
    slime;
  like the untimely birth
    that never sees the
    sun.
⁹ Sooner than your pots can
    feel the heat of thorns,
  whether green or ablaze,
    may he sweep them
    away!

¹⁰ The righteous will rejoice
    when they see
    vengeance done;
  they will bathe their feet
    in the blood of the
    wicked.
¹¹ People will say, "Surely
    there is a reward for
    the righteous;
  surely there is a God
    who judges on
    earth."

---

[a]Or *mighty lords* [b]Cn: Meaning of Heb uncertain

Psalm 59

To the leader: Do Not Destroy.
Of David. A Miktam, when Saul
ordered his house to be watched
in order to kill him.

[1] Deliver me from my enemies,
O my God;
  protect me from those who
  rise up against me.
[2] Deliver me from those who
  work evil;
  from the bloodthirsty
  save me.

[3] Even now they lie in wait for
  my life;
  the mighty stir up strife
  against me.
For no transgression or sin
  of mine, O LORD,
[4]   for no fault of mine, they run
  and make ready.
  Rouse yourself, come to my
  help and see!
[5]   You, LORD God of hosts, are
  God of Israel.
Awake to punish all the
  nations;
  spare none of those who
  treacherously plot evil.
  Selah

[6] Each evening they come back,
  howling like dogs
  and prowling about the city.
[7] There they are, bellowing with
  their mouths,
  with sharp words[a] on their
  lips—
  for "Who," they think,[b] "will
  hear us?"

[8] But you laugh at them, O LORD;

you hold all the nations
  in derision.
[9] O my strength, I will watch for
  you;
  for you, O God, are my
  fortress.
[10] My God in his steadfast love
  will meet me;
  my God will let me look in
  triumph on my enemies.

[11] Do not kill them, or my people
  may forget;
  make them totter by your
  power, and bring them
  down,
  O Lord, our shield.
[12] For the sin of their mouths,
  the words of their lips,
  let them be trapped in their
  pride.
For the cursing and lies that
  they utter,
[13]   consume them in wrath;
  consume them until they are
  no more.
Then it will be known to the
  ends of the earth
  that God rules over Jacob.
  Selah

[14] Each evening they come back,
  howling like dogs
  and prowling about the city.
[15] They roam about for food,
  and growl if they do not get
  their fill.

[16] But I will sing of your might;
  I will sing aloud of your
  steadfast love in the
  morning.

[a]Heb *with swords* [b]Heb lacks *they think*

427

For you have been a fortress
    for me
  and a refuge in the day of my
    distress.
[17] O my strength, I will sing
    praises to you,
  for you, O God, are my
    fortress,
  the God who shows me
    steadfast love.

Psalm 60

*To the leader: according to the
Lily of the Covenant. A Miktam
of David; for instruction; when
he struggled with
Aramnaharaim and with Aram-
zobah, and when Joab on his
return killed twelve thousand
Edomites in the Valley of Salt.*

[1] O God, you have rejected us,
    broken our defenses;
  you have been angry; now
    restore us!
[2] You have caused the land to
    quake; you have torn it
    open;
  repair the cracks in it, for it
    is tottering.
[3] You have made your people
    suffer hard things;
  you have given us wine to
    drink that made us reel.

[4] You have set up a banner for
    those who fear you,
  to rally to it out of bowshot.[a]
        Selah
[5] Give victory with your right
    hand, and answer us,[b]
  so that those whom you love
    may be rescued.

[6] God has promised in his
    sanctuary:[c]
  "With exultation I will
    divide up Shechem,
  and portion out the Vale of
    Succoth.
[7] Gilead is mine, and Manasseh
    is mine;
  Ephraim is my helmet;
    Judah is my scepter.
[8] Moab is my washbasin;
  on Edom I hurl my shoe;
  over Philistia I shout in
    triumph."

[9] Who will bring me to the
    fortified city?
  Who will lead me to Edom?
[10] Have you not rejected us,
    O God?
  You do not go out, O God,
    with our armies.
[11] O grant us help against the foe,
    for human help is worthless.
[12] With God we shall do
    valiantly;
  it is he who will tread down
    our foes.

Psalm 61

*To the leader: with stringed
instruments. Of David.*

[1] Hear my cry, O God;
  listen to my prayer.
[2] From the end of the earth I call
    to you,
  when my heart is faint.

Lead me to the rock
  that is higher than I;

---

[a]Gk Syr Jerome: Heb *because of the truth* [b]Another
reading is *me* [c]Or *by his holiness*

428

³ for you are my refuge,
  a strong tower against
    the enemy.

⁴ Let me abide in your tent
    forever,
  find refuge under the shelter
    of your wings.   *Selah*
⁵ For you, O God, have heard
    my vows;
  you have given me the
    heritage of those who
    fear your name.

⁶ Prolong the life of the king;
  may his years endure to al
    generations!
⁷ May he be enthroned forever
    before God;
  appoint steadfast love and
    faithfulness to watch
    over him!

⁸ So I will always sing praises to
    your name,
  as I pay my vows day after
    day.

Psalm 62

*To the leader: according to
Jeduthun. A Psalm of David.*

¹ For God alone my soul waits
    in silence;
  from him comes my
    salvation.
² He alone is my rock and my
    salvation,
  my fortress; I shall never
    be shaken.

³ How long will you assail a
    person,

will you batter your victim,
    all of you,
  as you would a leaning wall,
    a tottering fence?
⁴ Their only plan is to bring
    down a person of
    prominence.
  They take pleasure in
    falsehood;
they bless with their
    mouths,
  but inwardly they curse.
                    Selah

⁵ For God alone my soul waits
    in silence,
  for my hope is from him.
⁶ He alone is my rock and my
    salvation,
  my fortress; I shall not be
    shaken.
⁷ On God rests my deliverance
    and my honor;
  my mighty rock, my refuge
    is in God.

⁸ Trust in him at all times,
    O people;
  pour out your heart before
    him;
  God is a refuge for us.
                    Selah

⁹ Those of low estate are but
    a breath,
  those of high estate are a
    delusion;
in the balances they go up;
  they are together lighter
    than a breath.
¹⁰ Put no confidence in
    extortion,
  and set no vain hopes on
    robbery;

if riches increase, do not set
    your heart on them.

11 Once God has spoken;
    twice have I heard this:
that power belongs to God,
12   and steadfast love belongs to
    you, O LORD.
For you repay to all
    according to their work.

Psalm 63

*A Psalm of David, when he
was in the Wilderness of Judah.*

1 O God, you are my God, I
    seek you,
    my soul thirsts for you;
my flesh faints for you,
    as in a dry and weary land
    where there is no water.
2 So I have looked upon you in
    the sanctuary,
    beholding your power and
    glory.
3 Because your steadfast love is
    better than life,
    my lips will praise you.
4 So I will bless you as long as
    I live;
    I will lift up my hands and
    call on your name.

5 My soul is satisfied as with
    a rich feast,[a]
    and my mouth praises you
    with joyful lips
6 when I think of you on my bed,
    and meditate on you in the
    watches of the night;
7 for you have been my help,
    and in the shadow of your
    wings I sing for joy.

8 My soul clings to you;
    your right hand upholds me.

9 But those who seek to destroy
    my life
    shall go down into the
    depths of the earth;
10 they shall be given over to the
    power of the sword,
    they shall be prey for
    jackals.
11 But the king shall rejoice in
    God;
    all who swear by him shall
    exult,
    for the mouths of liars will
    be stopped.

Psalm 64

To the leader. A Psalm of David.

1 Hear my voice, O God, in my
    complaint;
    preserve my life from the
    dread enemy.
2 Hide me from the secret plots
    of the wicked,
    from the scheming of
    evildoers,
3 who whet their tongues like
    swords,
    who aim bitter words like
    arrows,
4 shooting from ambush at the
    blameless;
    they shoot suddenly and
    without fear.
5 They hold fast to their evil
    purpose;
    they talk of laying snares
    secretly,
    thinking, "Who can see us?[b]

[a]Heb *with fat and fatness* [b]Syr: Heb *them*

430

6   Who can search out our
       crimes?[a]
   We have thought out a
       cunningly conceived
       plot."
   For the human heart and
       mind are deep.

7 But God will shoot his arrow
       at them;
   they will be wounded
       suddenly.
8 Because of their tongue he will
       bring them to ruin;[b]
   all who see them will shake
       with horror.
9 Then everyone will fear;
   they will tell what God
       has brought about,
   and ponder what he has
       done.

10 Let the righteous rejoice in
       the LORD
   and take refuge in him.
   Let all the upright in heart
       glory.

Psalm 65

*To the leader. A Psalm of David.
   A Song.*

1 Praise is due to you,
   O God, in Zion;
   and to you shall vows
       be performed,
2   O you who answer prayer!
   To you all flesh shall come.
3 When deeds of iniquity
       overwhelm us,
   you forgive our
       transgressions.
4 Happy are those whom you
       choose and bring near

   to live in your courts.
   We shall be satisfied with
       the goodness of your
       house,
   your holy temple.

5 By awesome deeds you answer
       us with deliverance,
   O God of our salvation;
   you are the hope of all the
       ends of the earth
   and of the farthest seas.
6 By your[c] strength you
       established the
       mountains;
   you are girded with might.
7 You silence the roaring of
       the seas,
   the roaring of their waves,
   the tumult of the peoples.
8 Those who live at earth's
       farthest bounds are
       awed by your signs;
   you make the gateways of
       the morning and the
       evening shout for joy.

9 You visit the earth and water it,
   you greatly enrich it;
   the river of God is full of
       water;
   you provide the people with
       grain,
   for so you have prepared it.
10 You water its furrows
       abundantly,
   settling its ridges,
   softening it with showers,
   and blessing its growth.
11 You crown the year with your
       bounty;

---

[a]Cn: Heb *They search out crimes* [b]Cn: Heb *They will
bring him to ruin, their tongue being against them*
[c]Gk Jerome: Heb *his*

431

your wagon tracks overflow
with richness.
12 The pastures of the
wilderness overflow,
the hills gird themselves
with joy,
13 the meadows clothe
themselves with flocks,
the valleys deck themselves
with grain,
they shout and sing together
for joy.

Psalm 66

To the leader. A Song. A Psalm.

1 Make a joyful noise to God,
all the earth;
2   sing the glory of his name;
give to him glorious praise.
3 Say to God, "How awesome are
your deeds!
Because of your great power,
your enemies cringe
before you.
4 All the earth worships you;
they sing praises to you,
sing praises to your name."
Selah

5 Come and see what God has
done:
he is awesome in his deeds
among mortals.
6 He turned the sea into dry land;
they passed through the
river on foot.
There we rejoiced in him,
7   who rules by his might
forever,
whose eyes keep watch on
the nations—
let the rebellious not exalt
themselves.   *Selah*

8 Bless our God, O peoples,
let the sound of his praise
be heard,
9 who has kept us among the
living,
and has not let our feet slip.
10 For you, O God, have
tested us;
you have tried us as silver
is tried.
11 You brought us into the net;
you laid burdens on our
backs;
12 you let people ride over our
heads;
we went through fire and
through water;
yet you have brought us out
to a spacious place.*ᵃ*

13 I will come into your house
with burnt offerings;
I will pay you my vows,
14 those that my lips uttered
and my mouth promised
when I was in trouble.
15 I will offer to you burnt
offerings of fatlings,
with the smoke of the
sacrifice of rams;
I will make an offering of
bulls and goats.
Selah

16 Come and hear, all you who
fear God,
and I will tell what he has
done for me.
17 I cried aloud to him,
and he was extolled with
my tongue.
18 If I had cherished iniquity in
my heart,

---

*ᵃ*Cn Compare Gk Syr Jerome Tg: Heb *to a saturation*

the LORD would not have
listened.
[19] But truly God has listened;
he has given heed to the
words of my prayer.

[20] Blessed be God,
because he has not rejected
my prayer
or removed his steadfast
love from me.

Psalm 67

*To the leader: with stringed
instruments. A Psalm. A Song.*

[1] May God be gracious to us and
bless us
and make his face to shine
upon us,   *Selah*
[2] that your way may be known
upon earth,
your saving power among
all nations.
[3] Let the peoples praise you,
O God;
let all the peoples
praise you.

[4] Let the nations be glad and sing
for joy,
for you judge the peoples
with equity
and guide the nations upon
earth.   *Selah*
[5] Let the peoples praise you,
O God;
let all the peoples praise
you.

[6] The earth has yielded its
increase;
God, our God, has blessed us.

[7] May God continue to bless us;
let all the ends of the earth
revere him.

Psalm 68

*To the leader. Of David.
A Psalm. A Song.*

[1] Let God rise up, let his enemies
be scattered;
let those who hate him flee
before him.
[2] As smoke is driven away,
so drive them away;
as wax melts before the fire,
let the wicked perish before
God.
[3] But let the righteous be joyful;
let them exult before God;
let them be jubilant with joy.

[4] Sing to God, sing praises to his
name;
lift up a song to him who
rides upon the clouds[a]—
his name is the LORD—
be exultant before him.

[5] Father of orphans and
protector of widows
is God in his holy
habitation.
[6] God gives the desolate a home
to live in;
he leads out the prisoners to
prosperity,
but the rebellious live in
a parched land.

[7] O God, when you went out
before your people,

---

[a]Or *cast up a highway for him who rides through the
deserts*

433

when you marched through
    the wilderness,   *Selah*
8 the earth quaked, the heavens
    poured down rain
  at the presence of God, the
    God of Sinai,
  at the presence of God, the
    God of Israel.
9 Rain in abundance, O God, you
    showered abroad;
  you restored your heritage
    when it languished;
10 your flock found a dwelling
    in it;
  in your goodness, O God,
    you provided for the
    needy.

11 The LORD gives the command;
  great is the company of
    those*a* who bore the
    tidings:
12   "The kings of the armies,
    they flee, they flee!"
  The women at home divide
    the spoil,
13   though they stay among the
    sheepfolds—
  the wings of a dove covered
    with silver,
  its pinions with green gold.
14 When the Almighty*b*
    scattered kings there,
  snow fell on Zalmon.

15 O mighty mountain,
    mountain of Bashan;
  O many-peaked mountain,
    mountain of Bashan!
16 Why do you look with envy,
    O many-peaked
    mountain,
  at the mount that God
    desired for his abode,

where the LORD will reside
    forever?

17 With mighty chariotry, twice
    ten thousand,
  thousands upon thousands,
    the Lord came from Sinai
    into the holy place.*c*
18 You ascended the high mount,
    leading captives in your
    train
  and receiving gifts from
    people,
  even from those who rebel
    against the LORD God's
    abiding there.
19 Blessed be the Lord,
    who daily bears us up;
    God is our salvation.
                              Selah
20 Our God is a God of salvation,
    and to God, the Lord,
    belongs escape from
    death.

21 But God will shatter the heads
    of his enemies,
  the hairy crown of those
    who walk in their guilty
    ways.
22 The Lord said,
    "I will bring them back from
    Bashan,
  I will bring them back from
    the depths of the sea,
23 so that you may bathe*d* your
    feet in blood,
  so that the tongues of your
    dogs may have their
    share from the foe."

*a*Or *company of the women* *b*Traditional rendering of
Heb *Shaddai* *c*Cn: Heb *The Lord among them Sinai in
the holy* (place) *d*Gk Syr Tg: Heb *shatter*

24 Your solemn processions are
        seen,[a] O God,
    the processions of my God,
        my King, into the
        sanctuary—
25 the singers in front, the
        musicians last,
    between them girls playing
        tambourines:
26 "Bless God in the great
        congregation,
    the LORD, O you who are of
        Israel's fountain!"
27 There is Benjamin, the least of
        them, in the lead,
    the princes of Judah in a
        body,
    the princes of Zebulun, the
        princes of Naphtali.

28 Summon your might,
        O God;
    show your strength, O God,
        as you have done for us
        before.
29 Because of your temple at
        Jerusalem
    kings bear gifts to you.
30 Rebuke the wild animals
        that live among
        the reeds,
    the herd of bulls with
        the calves of the
        peoples.
    Trample[b] under foot
        those who lust after
        tribute;
    scatter the peoples who
        delight in war.[c]
31 Let bronze be brought from
        Egypt;
    let Ethiopia[d] hasten to
        stretch out its hands
        to God.

32 Sing to God, O kingdoms of
        the earth;
    sing praises to the LORD,
                        Selah
33 O rider in the heavens, the
        ancient heavens;
    listen, he sends out his
        voice, his mighty voice.
34 Ascribe power to God,
    whose majesty is over Israel;
    and whose power is in the
        skies.
35 Awesome is God in his[e]
        sanctuary,
    the God of Israel;
    he gives power and strength
        to his people.

    Blessed be God!

Psalm 69

*To the leader: according to
Lilies. Of David.*

1 Save me, O God,
    for the waters have come
        up to my neck.
2 I sink in deep mire,
    where there is no foothold;
    I have come into deep
        waters,
    and the flood sweeps
        over me.
3 I am weary with my crying;
    my throat is parched.
    My eyes grow dim
        with waiting for my God.

4 More in number than the hairs
        of my head

[a] Or *have been seen* [b] Cn: Heb *Trampling* [c] Meaning of
Heb of verse 30 is uncertain [d] Or *Nubia;* Heb *Cush*
[e] Gk: Heb *from your*

are those who hate me
    without cause;
many are those who would
    destroy me,
    my enemies who accuse
        me falsely.
What I did not steal
    must I now restore?
[5] O God, you know my folly;
    the wrongs I have done are
        not hidden from you.

[6] Do not let those who hope in
        you be put to shame
        because of me,
    O LORD God of hosts;
do not let those who seek
        you be dishonored
        because of me,
    O God of Israel.
[7] It is for your sake that I have
        borne reproach,
    that shame has covered
        my face.
[8] I have become a stranger to
        my kindred,
    an alien to my mother's
        children.

[9] It is zeal for your house that
        has consumed me;
    the insults of those who
        insult you have fallen
        on me.
[10] When I humbled my soul with
    fasting,[a]
    they insulted me for
        doing so.
[11] When I made sackcloth my
    clothing,
    I became a byword to them.
[12] I am the subject of gossip for
        those who sit in the
        gate,

and the drunkards make
    songs about me.

[13] But as for me, my prayer is to
        you, O LORD.
At an acceptable time,
    O God,
in the abundance of your
        steadfast love, answer
        me.
With your faithful help
    [14]rescue me
    from sinking in the mire;
let me be delivered from
        my enemies
and from the deep waters.
[15] Do not let the flood sweep
        over me,
    or the deep swallow me up,
    or the Pit close its mouth
        over me.

[16] Answer me, O LORD, for your
        steadfast love is good;
    according to your abundant
        mercy, turn to me.
[17] Do not hide your face from
        your servant,
    for I am in distress—make
        haste to answer me.
[18] Draw near to me, redeem me,
    set me free because of my
        enemies.

[19] You know the insults I receive,
    and my shame and
        dishonor;
    my foes are all known
        to you.
[20] Insults have broken my heart,
    so that I am in despair.

[a]Gk Syr: Heb *I wept, with fasting my soul,* or *I made my soul mourn with fasting*

I looked for pity, but there
was none;
and for comforters, but I
found none.
21 They gave me poison for food,
and for my thirst they gave
me vinegar to drink.

22 Let their table be a trap for
them,
a snare for their allies.
23 Let their eyes be darkened
so that they cannot
see,
and make their loins
tremble continually.
24 Pour out your indignation
upon them,
and let your burning anger
overtake them.
25 May their camp be a
desolation;
let no one live in their tents.
26 For they persecute those
whom you have struck
down,
and those whom you have
wounded, they attack
still more.[a]
27 Add guilt to their guilt;
may they have no acquittal
from you.
28 Let them be blotted out of the
book of the living;
let them not be enrolled
among the righteous.
29 But I am lowly and in pain;
let your salvation, O God,
protect me.

30 I will praise the name of God
with a song;
I will magnify him with
thanksgiving.

31 This will please the LORD more
than an ox
or a bull with horns and
hoofs.
32 Let the oppressed see it and
be glad;
you who seek God, let your
hearts revive.
33 For the LORD hears the needy,
and does not despise his
own that are in bonds.

34 Let heaven and earth praise
him,
the seas and everything that
moves in them.
35 For God will save Zion
and rebuild the cities of
Judah;
and his servants shall live[b]
there and possess it;
36 the children of his
servants shall inherit
it,
and those who love his
name shall live in it.

Psalm 70

*To the leader. Of David, for the
memorial offering.*

1 Be pleased, O God, to
deliver me.
O LORD, make haste
to help me!
2 Let those be put to shame
and confusion
who seek my life.
Let those be turned back and
brought to dishonor
who desire to hurt me.

[a]Gk Syr: Heb *recount the pain of* [b]Syr: Heb *and they
shall live*

437

³ Let those who say, "Aha, Aha!"
    turn back because of
      their shame.

⁴ Let all who seek you
    rejoice and be glad in you.
Let those who love your
      salvation
    say evermore, "God is
      great!"
⁵ But I am poor and needy;
    hasten to me, O God!
You are my help and
      my deliverer;
    O Lord, do not delay!

Psalm 71

¹ In you, O Lord, I take refuge;
    let me never be put to
      shame.
² In your righteousness deliver
      me and rescue me;
    incline your ear to me and
      save me.
³ Be to me a rock of refuge,
    a strong fortress,ᵃ to
      save me,
    for you are my rock and
      my fortress.

⁴ Rescue me, O my God,
    from the hand of the
      wicked,
    from the grasp of the
      unjust and cruel.
⁵ For you, O Lord, are my hope,
    my trust, O Lord, from
      my youth.
⁶ Upon you I have leaned from
      my birth;
    it was you who took me
      from my mother's
      womb.

My praise is continually
    of you.

⁷ I have been like a portent
    to many,
    but you are my strong
      refuge.
⁸ My mouth is filled with
    your praise,
    and with your glory all day
      long.
⁹ Do not cast me off in the time
    of old age;
    do not forsake me when my
      strength is spent.
¹⁰ For my enemies speak
      concerning me,
    and those who watch for my
      life consult together.
¹¹ They say, "Pursue and seize
      that person
    whom God has forsaken,
    for there is no one to
      deliver."

¹² O God, do not be far from me;
    O my God, make haste to
      help me!
¹³ Let my accusers be put to
      shame and consumed;
    let those who seek to
      hurt me
    be covered with scorn and
      disgrace.
¹⁴ But I will hope continually,
    and will praise you yet
      more and more.
¹⁵ My mouth will tell of your
      righteous acts,
    of your deeds of salvation
      all day long,

ᵃGk Compare 31.3: Heb *to come continually you have commanded*

though their number is
  past my knowledge.
[16] I will come praising
    the mighty deeds of the
      Lord GOD,
  I will praise your
    righteousness, yours
      alone.

[17] O God, from my youth you
    have taught me,
  and I still proclaim your
    wondrous deeds.
[18] So even to old age and
    gray hairs,
  O God, do not forsake me,
until I proclaim your might
  to all the generations to
    come.[a]
Your power [19]and your
    righteousness, O God,
  reach the high heavens.

You who have done great
  things,
  O God, who is like you?
[20] You who have made me
    see many troubles and
      calamities
  will revive me again;
from the depths of the earth
  you will bring me up again.
[21] You will increase my honor,
  and comfort me once again.

[22] I will also praise you with
    the harp
  for your faithfulness, O my
    God;
  I will sing praises to you
    with the lyre,
  O Holy One of Israel.
[23] My lips will shout for joy
    when I sing praises to you;

my soul also, which you
  have rescued.
[24] All day long my tongue will
    talk of your righteous
      help,
  for those who tried to do
    me harm
  have been put to shame, and
    disgraced.

Psalm 72

Of Solomon.

[1] Give the king your justice,
    O God,
  and your righteousness to
    a king's son.
[2] May he judge your people
    with righteousness,
  and your poor with justice.
[3] May the mountains yield
    prosperity for the
      people,
  and the hills, in
    righteousness.
[4] May he defend the cause of
    the poor of the people,
  give deliverance to the
    needy,
  and crush the oppressor.

[5] May he live[b] while the sun
    endures,
  and as long as the moon,
    throughout all
      generations.
[6] May he be like rain that falls
    on the mown grass,
  like showers that water
    the earth.
[7] In his days may righteousness
    flourish

---

[a]Gk Compare Syr: Heb *to a generation, to all that come* [b]Gk: Heb *may they fear you*

and peace abound, until the
    moon is no more.

⁸ May he have dominion from
    sea to sea,
    and from the River to the
      ends of the earth.
⁹ May his foes*ᵃ* bow down
    before him,
    and his enemies lick
      the dust.
¹⁰ May the kings of Tarshish and
    of the isles
    render him tribute,
    may the kings of Sheba
      and Seba
    bring gifts.
¹¹ May all kings fall down
    before him,
    all nations give him service.

¹² For he delivers the needy
    when they call,
    the poor and those who have
      no helper.
¹³ He has pity on the weak and
    the needy,
    and saves the lives of the
      needy.
¹⁴ From oppression and
    violence he redeems
    their life;
    and precious is their
      blood in his sight.

¹⁵ Long may he live!
    May gold of Sheba be given
      to him.
    May prayer be made for him
      continually,
    and blessings invoked for
      him all day long.
¹⁶ May there be abundance of
    grain in the land;

may it wave on the tops of
    the mountains;
    may its fruit be like
      Lebanon;
and may people blossom in
    the cities
    like the grass of the field.
¹⁷ May his name endure forever,
    his fame continue as long as
      the sun.
May all nations be blessed
    in him;*ᵇ*
    may they pronounce him
      happy.

¹⁸ Blessed be the Lᴏʀᴅ, the God
    of Israel,
    who alone does wondrous
      things.
¹⁹ Blessed be his glorious name
    forever;
    may his glory fill the
      whole earth.
    Amen and Amen.

²⁰ The prayers of David son of
    Jesse are ended.

BOOK III

(Psalms 73-89)

Psalm 73
A Psalm of Asaph.

¹ Truly God is good to the
    upright,*ᶜ*
    to those who are pure
      in heart.
² But as for me, my feet had
    almost stumbled;
    my steps had nearly slipped.

---

*ᵃCn: Heb those who live in the wilderness ᵇOr bless
themselves by him ᶜOr good to Israel*

³ For I was envious of the
   arrogant;
   I saw the prosperity of the
      wicked.

⁴ For they have no pain;
   their bodies are sound and
      sleek.
⁵ They are not in trouble as
      others are;
   they are not plagued like
      other people.
⁶ Therefore pride is their
      necklace;
   violence covers them like
      a garment.
⁷ Their eyes swell out with
      fatness;
   their hearts overflow with
      follies.
⁸ They scoff and speak with
      malice;
   loftily they threaten
      oppression.
⁹ They set their mouths against
      heaven,
   and their tongues range over
      the earth.

¹⁰ Therefore the people turn
      and praise them,ᵃ
   and find no fault in
      them.ᵇ
¹¹ And they say, "How can God
      know?
   Is there knowledge in the
      Most High?"
¹² Such are the wicked;
   always at ease, they increase
      in riches.
¹³ All in vain I have kept my
      heart clean
   and washed my hands in
      innocence.

¹⁴ For all day long I have been
      plagued,
   and am punished every
      morning.

¹⁵ If I had said, "I will talk on
      in this way,"
   I would have been untrue
      to the circle of your
      children.
¹⁶ But when I thought how to
      understand this,
   it seemed to me a
      wearisome task,
¹⁷ until I went into the sanctuary
      of God;
   then I perceived their end.
¹⁸ Truly you set them in slippery
      places;
   you make them fall to ruin.
¹⁹ How they are destroyed in
      a moment,
   swept away utterly by
      terrors!
²⁰ They areᶜ like a dream when
      one awakes;
   on awaking you despise
      their phantoms.

²¹ When my soul was
      embittered,
   when I was pricked in heart,
²² I was stupid and ignorant;
   I was like a brute beast
      toward you.
²³ Nevertheless I am continually
      with you;
   you hold my right hand.
²⁴ You guide me with your
      counsel,

ᵃCn: Heb *his people return here* ᵇCn: Heb *abundant
waters are drained by them* ᶜCn: Heb LORD

and afterward you will
   receive me with honor.[a]
25 Whom have I in heaven
      but you?
   And there is nothing on
      earth that I desire other
      than you.
26 My flesh and my heart may
      fail,
   but God is the strength[b] of
      my heart and my
      portion forever.

27 Indeed, those who are far
      from you will perish;
   you put an end to those
      who are false to you.
28 But for me it is good to be
      near God;
   I have made the LORD God
      my refuge,
   to tell of all your works.

Psalm 74

A Maskil of Asaph.

1 O God, why do you cast us off
      forever?
   Why does your anger
      smoke against the
      sheep of your
      pasture?
2 Remember your congregation,
      which you acquired
      long ago,
   which you redeemed to be
      the tribe of your
      heritage.
   Remember Mount Zion,
      where you came to
      dwell.
3 Direct your steps to the
      perpetual ruins;

the enemy has destroyed
      everything in the
      sanctuary.

4 Your foes have roared
      within your holy
      place;
   they set up their
      emblems there.
5 At the upper entrance they
      hacked
   the wooden trellis with
      axes.[c]
6 And then, with hatchets and
      hammers,
   they smashed all its
      carved work.
7 They set your sanctuary on fire;
   they desecrated the dwelling
      place of your name,
   bringing it to the ground.
8 They said to themselves, "We
      will utterly subdue
      them";
   they burned all the meeting
      places of God in the
      land.

9 We do not see our
      emblems;
   there is no longer any
      prophet,
   and there is no one
      among us who knows
      how long.
10 How long, O God, is the foe
      to scoff?
   Is the enemy to revile your
      name forever?
11 Why do you hold back your
      hand;

---

[a] Or *to glory* [b] Heb *rock* [c] Cn Compare Gk Syr:
Meaning of Heb uncertain

why do you keep your hand
in[a] your bosom?
12 Yet God my King is from
of old,
working salvation in the
earth.
13 You divided the sea by
your might;
you broke the heads of the
dragons in the waters.
14 You crushed the heads of
Leviathan;
you gave him as food[b] for
the creatures of the
wilderness.
15 You cut openings for springs
and torrents;
you dried up ever-flowing
streams.
16 Yours is the day, yours also
the night;
you established the
luminaries[c] and the sun.
17 You have fixed all the bounds
of the earth;
you made summer and
winter.

18 Remember this, O LORD,
how the enemy
scoffs,
and an impious people
reviles your name.
19 Do not deliver the soul of
your dove to the wild
animals;
do not forget the life of
your poor forever.

20 Have regard for your[d]
covenant,
for the dark places of
the land are full of the
haunts of violence.

21 Do not let the downtrodden be
put to shame;
let the poor and needy
praise your name.
22 Rise up, O God, plead your
cause;
remember how the
impious scoff at you
all day long.
23 Do not forget the clamor of
your foes,
the uproar of your
adversaries that goes up
continually.

Psalm 75

To the leader: Do Not Destroy.
A Psalm of Asaph. A Song.

1 We give thanks to you,
O God;
we give thanks; your name
is near.
People tell of your
wondrous deeds.

2 At the set time that I appoint
I will judge with equity.
3 When the earth totters, with
all its inhabitants,
it is I who keep its pillars
steady.   *Selah*
4 I say to the boastful, "Do not
boast,"
and to the wicked, "Do not
lift up your horn;
5 do not lift up your horn on
high,
or speak with insolent
neck."

---

[a]Cn: Heb *do you consume your right hand from* [b]Heb *food for the people* [c]Or *moon;* Heb *light* [d]Gk Syr: Heb *the*

443

6 For not from the east or from
        the west
    and not from the wilderness
        comes lifting up;
7 but it is God who executes
        judgment,
    putting down one and
        lifting up another.
8 For in the hand of the LORD
        there is a cup
    with foaming wine, well
        mixed;
    he will pour a draught
        from it,
    and all the wicked of the
        earth
    shall drain it down to the
        dregs.

9 But I will rejoice[a] forever;
    I will sing praises to the
        God of Jacob.

10 All the horns of the wicked
        I will cut off,
    but the horns of the
        righteous shall be
        exalted.

Psalm 76

*To the leader: with stringed
instruments. A Psalm of Asaph.
A Song.*

1 In Judah God is known,
    his name is great in Israel.
2 His abode has been established
        in Salem,
    his dwelling place in Zion.
3 There he broke the
        flashing arrows,
    the shield, the sword, and
        the weapons of war.
                            Selah

4 Glorious are you, more
        majestic
    than the everlasting
        mountains.[b]
5 The stouthearted were
        stripped of their spoil;
    they sank into sleep;
    none of the troops
        was able to lift a hand.
6 At your rebuke, O God of Jacob,
    both rider and horse lay
        stunned.

7 But you indeed are
        awesome!
    Who can stand before you
    when once your anger is
        roused?
8 From the heavens you
        uttered judgment;
    the earth feared and was still
9 when God rose up to establish
        judgment,
    to save all the oppressed of
        the earth.   *Selah*

10 Human wrath serves only to
        praise you,
    when you bind the last bit of
        your[c] wrath around
        you.
11 Make vows to the LORD
        your God, and perform
        them;
    let all who are around him
        bring gifts
    to the one who is awesome,
12 who cuts off the spirit of
        princes,
    who inspires fear in the
        kings of the earth.

[a]Gk: Heb *declare* [b]Gk: Heb *the mountains of prey*
[c]Heb lacks *your*

Psalm 77

*To the leader: according to
Jeduthun. Of Asaph. A Psalm.*

1 I cry aloud to God,
     aloud to God, that he may
          hear me.
2 In the day of my trouble I
          seek the Lord;
     in the night my hand is
          stretched out without
          wearying;
     my soul refuses to be
          comforted.
3 I think of God, and I moan;
     I meditate, and my spirit
          faints.   *Selah*

4 You keep my eyelids from
          closing;
     I am so troubled that I
          cannot speak.
5 I consider the days of old,
     and remember the years of
          long ago.
6 I commune[a] with my heart in
          the night;
     I meditate and search my
          spirit:[b]
7 "Will the LORD spurn forever,
     and never again be
          favorable?
8 Has his steadfast love ceased
          forever?
     Are his promises at an end
          for all time?
9 Has God forgotten to be
          gracious?
     Has he in anger shut up his
          compassion?"
                                   Selah
10 And I say, "It is my grief
     that the right hand of the

Most High has
     changed."

11 I will call to mind the deeds of
          the LORD;
     I will remember your
          wonders of old.
12 I will meditate on all your
          work,
     and muse on your mighty
          deeds.
13 Your way, O God, is holy.
     What god is so great as
          our God?
14 You are the God who works
          wonders;
     you have displayed your
          might among the
          peoples.
15 With your strong arm you
          redeemed your people,
     the descendants of Jacob
          and Joseph.   *Selah*

16 When the waters saw you,
          O God,
     when the waters saw
          you,they were
          afraid;
     the very deep trembled.
17 The clouds poured out
          water;
     the skies thundered;
     your arrows flashed on
          every side.
18 The crash of your thunder was
          in the whirlwind;
     your lightnings lit up the
          world;
     the earth trembled and
          shook.

[a]Gk Syr: Heb *My music* [b]Syr Jerome: Heb *my spirit
searches*

445

19 Your way was through the sea,
      your path, through the
         mighty waters;
   yet your footprints were
      unseen.
20 You led your people like a
      flock
   by the hand of Moses and
      Aaron.

Psalm 78

A Maskil of Asaph.

1 Give ear, O my people, to
      my teaching;
   incline your ears to the
      words of my mouth.
2 I will open my mouth in a
      parable;
   I will utter dark sayings
      from of old,
3 things that we have heard
      and known,
   that our ancestors have
      told us.
4 We will not hide them from
      their children;
   we will tell to the coming
      generation
   the glorious deeds of the
      LORD, and his might,
   and the wonders that he
      has done.

5 He established a decree in
      Jacob,
   and appointed a law in
      Israel,
   which he commanded our
      ancestors
   to teach to their children;
6 that the next generation
      might know them,

the children yet unborn,
   and rise up and tell them
      to their children,
7   so that they should set their
         hope in God,
   and not forget the works
      of God,
   but keep his
      commandments;
8 and that they should not be
      like their ancestors,
   a stubborn and rebellious
      generation,
   a generation whose heart
      was not steadfast,
   whose spirit was not
      faithful to God.

9 The Ephraimites, armed with[a]
      the bow,
   turned back on the day of
      battle.
10 They did not keep God's
      covenant,
   but refused to walk
      according to his law.
11 They forgot what he had
      done,
   and the miracles that he had
      shown them.
12 In the sight of their ancestors
      he worked marvels
   in the land of Egypt, in the
      fields of Zoan.
13 He divided the sea and let
      them pass through it,
   and made the waters stand
      like a heap.
14 In the daytime he led them
      with a cloud,
   and all night long with a
      fiery light.

[a] Heb *armed with shooting*

¹⁵ He split rocks open in the
    wilderness,
    and gave them drink
        abundantly as from the
        deep.
¹⁶ He made streams come out
    of the rock,
    and caused waters to flow
        down like rivers.

¹⁷ Yet they sinned still more
    against him,
    rebelling against the Most
        High in the desert.
¹⁸ They tested God in their heart
    by demanding the food
        they craved.
¹⁹ They spoke against God,
    saying,
    "Can God spread a table
        in the wilderness?
²⁰ Even though he struck the
    rock so that water
        gushed out
    and torrents overflowed,
    can he also give bread,
    or provide meat for his
        people?"

²¹ Therefore, when the LORD
    heard, he was full of
        rage;
    a fire was kindled against
        Jacob,
    his anger mounted against
        Israel,
²² because they had no faith in
    God,
    and did not trust his saving
        power.
²³ Yet he commanded the
    skies above,
    and opened the doors of
        heaven;

²⁴ he rained down on them
    manna to eat,
    and gave them the grain of
        heaven.
²⁵ Mortals ate of the bread of
    angels;
    he sent them food in
        abundance.
²⁶ He caused the east wind to
    blow in the heavens,
    and by his power he led
        out the south wind;
²⁷ he rained flesh upon them
    like dust,
    winged birds like the sand
        of the seas;
²⁸ he let them fall within
    their camp,
    all around their dwellings.
²⁹ And they ate and were well
    filled,
    for he gave them what they
        craved.
³⁰ But before they had
    satisfied their
        craving,
    while the food was still
        in their mouths,
³¹ the anger of God rose against
    them
    and he killed the strongest
        of them,
    and laid low the flower of
        Israel.

³² In spite of all this they still
    sinned;
    they did not believe in his
        wonders.
³³ So he made their days vanish
    like a breath,
    and their years in terror.
³⁴ When he killed them, they
    sought for him;

they repented and sought
    God earnestly.
35 They remembered that God
        was their rock,
    the Most High God their
        redeemer.
36 But they flattered him with
        their mouths;
    they lied to him with
        their tongues.
37 Their heart was not steadfast
        toward him;
    they were not true to his
        covenant.
38 Yet he, being
        compassionate,
    forgave their iniquity,
    and did not destroy them;
    often he restrained his
        anger,
    and did not stir up all
        his wrath.
39 He remembered that they
        were but flesh,
    a wind that passes and does
        not come again.
40 How often they rebelled
        against him in the
        wilderness
    and grieved him in the
        desert!
41 They tested God again and
        again,
    and provoked the Holy One
        of Israel.
42 They did not keep in mind
        his power,
    or the day when he
        redeemed them from
        the foe;
43 when he displayed his signs
        in Egypt,
    and his miracles in the
        fields of Zoan.

44 He turned their rivers
        to blood,
    so that they could not drink
        of their streams.
45 He sent among them
        swarms of flies, which
        devoured them,
    and frogs, which destroyed
        them.
46 He gave their crops to the
        caterpillar,
    and the fruit of their labor
        to the locust.
47 He destroyed their vines
        with hail,
    and their sycamores with
        frost.
48 He gave over their cattle to
        the hail,
    and their flocks to
        thunderbolts.
49 He let loose on them his
        fierce anger,
    wrath, indignation, and
        distress,
    a company of destroying
        angels.
50 He made a path for his anger;
    he did not spare them from
        death,
    but gave their lives over to
        the plague.
51 He struck all the firstborn
        in Egypt,
    the first issue of their
        strength in the tents of
        Ham.
52 Then he led out his people
        like sheep,
    and guided them in the
        wilderness like a flock.
53 He led them in safety, so
        that they were not
        afraid;

448

but the sea overwhelmed
their enemies.
54 And he brought them to his
holy hill,
to the mountain that his
right hand had won.
55 He drove out nations before
them;
he apportioned them for a
possession
and settled the tribes of
Israel in their tents.

56 Yet they tested the Most High
God,
and rebelled against him.
They did not observe his
decrees,
57 but turned away and were
faithless like their
ancestors;
they twisted like a
treacherous bow.
58 For they provoked him to
anger with their high
places;
they moved him to jealousy
with their idols.
59 When God heard, he was full
of wrath,
and he utterly rejected
Israel.
60 He abandoned his dwelling
at Shiloh,
the tent where he dwelt
among mortals,
61 and delivered his power to
captivity,
his glory to the hand of the
foe.
62 He gave his people to the
sword,
and vented his wrath on
his heritage.

63 Fire devoured their young
men,
and their girls had no
marriage song.
64 Their priests fell by the sword,
and their widows made no
lamentation.
65 Then the Lord awoke as from
sleep,
like a warrior shouting
because of wine.
66 He put his adversaries to rout;
he put them to everlasting
disgrace.

67 He rejected the tent of Joseph,
he did not choose the tribe
of Ephraim;
68 but he chose the tribe of
Judah,
Mount Zion, which he loves.
69 He built his sanctuary like
the high heavens,
like the earth, which he has
founded forever.
70 He chose his servant David,
and took him from the
sheepfolds;
71 from tending the nursing
ewes he brought him
to be the shepherd of his
people Jacob,
of Israel, his inheritance.
72 With upright heart he
tended them,
and guided them with
skillful hand.

Psalm 79

A Psalm of Asaph.

1 O God, the nations have come
into your inheritance;

449

they have defiled your holy
temple;
they have laid Jerusalem in
ruins.
2 They have given the bodies of
your servants
to the birds of the air for
food,
the flesh of your faithful
to the wild animals of
the earth.
3 They have poured out their
blood like water
all around Jerusalem,
and there was no one to
bury them.
4 We have become a taunt to
our neighbors,
mocked and derided by
those around us.

5 How long, O LORD? Will you
be angry forever?
Will your jealous wrath
burn like fire?
6 Pour out your anger on the
nations
that do not know you,
and on the kingdoms
that do not call on your
name.
7 For they have devoured Jacob
and laid waste his
habitation.

8 Do not remember against
us the iniquities of
our ancestors;
let your compassion come
speedily to meet us,
for we are brought very low.
9 Help us, O God of our
salvation,
for the glory of your name;

deliver us, and forgive our
sins,
for your name's sake.
10 Why should the nations say,
"Where is their God?"
Let the avenging of the
outpoured blood of your
servants
be known among the nations
before our eyes.

11 Let the groans of the prisoners
come before you;
according to your great
power preserve those
doomed to die.
12 Return sevenfold into the
bosom of our neighbors
the taunts with which they
taunted you, O Lord!
13 Then we your people, the
flock of your pasture,
will give thanks to you
forever;
from generation to
generation we will
recount your praise.

Psalm 80

*To the leader: on Lilies, a
Covenant. Of Asaph. A Psalm.*

1 Give ear, O Shepherd of Israel,
you who lead Joseph like
a flock!
You who are enthroned
upon the cherubim,
shine forth
2   before Ephraim and
Benjamin and
Manasseh.
Stir up your might,
and come to save us!

³ Restore us, O God;
  let your face shine, that we
    may be saved.

⁴ O Lord God of hosts,
  how long will you be angry
    with your people's
      prayers?
⁵ You have fed them with the
    bread of tears,
  and given them tears to
    drink in full measure.
⁶ You make us the scorn*a* of
    our neighbors;
  our enemies laugh among
    themselves.

⁷ Restore us, O God of hosts;
  let your face shine, that we
    may be saved.

⁸ You brought a vine out of
    Egypt;
  you drove out the nations
    and planted it.
⁹ You cleared the ground for it;
  it took deep root and filled
    the land.
¹⁰ The mountains were covered
    with its shade,
  the mighty cedars with its
    branches;
¹¹ it sent out its branches to
    the sea,
  and its shoots to the River.
¹² Why then have you broken
    down its walls,
  so that all who pass
    along the way pluck
      its fruit?
¹³ The boar from the forest
    ravages it,
  and all that move in the
    field feed on it.

¹⁴ Turn again, O God of hosts;
  look down from heaven,
    and see;
  have regard for this vine,
¹⁵ the stock that your right hand
    planted.*b*
¹⁶ They have burned it with fire,
  they have cut it
    down;*c*
  may they perish at the
    rebuke of your
      countenance.
¹⁷ But let your hand be upon the
    one at your right hand,
  the one whom you made
    strong for yourself.
¹⁸ Then we will never turn
    back from you;
  give us life, and we will
    call on your name.

¹⁹ Restore us, O Lord God of
    hosts;
  let your face shine, that we
    may be saved.

Psalm 81

*To the leader: according to
The Gittith. Of Asaph.*

¹ Sing aloud to God our strength;
  shout for joy to the God of
    Jacob.
² Raise a song, sound the
    tambourine,
  the sweet lyre with the harp.
³ Blow the trumpet at the
    new moon,
  at the full moon, on our
    festal day.

*a*Syr: Heb *strife* *b*Heb adds from verse 17 *and upon
the one whom you made strong for yourself* *c*Cn: Heb
it is cut down

451

⁴ For it is a statute for Israel,
    an ordinance of the God
        of Jacob.
⁵ He made it a decree in Joseph,
    when he went out over[a] the
        land of Egypt.

I hear a voice I had not
        known:
⁶ "I relieved your[b] shoulder of
        the burden;
    your[b] hands were freed
        from the basket.
⁷ In distress you called, and I
        rescued you;
    I answered you in the
        secret place of
        thunder;
    I tested you at the waters
        of Meribah.   *Selah*
⁸ Hear, O my people, while
        I admonish you;
    O Israel, if you would
        but listen to me!
⁹ There shall be no strange
        god among you;
    you shall not bow down to
        a foreign god.
¹⁰ I am the LORD your God,
    who brought you up out
        of the land of Egypt.
    Open your mouth wide and
        I will fill it.

¹¹ "But my people did not listen
        to my voice;
    Israel would not submit
        to me.
¹² So I gave them over to their
        stubborn hearts,
    to follow their own
        counsels.
¹³ O that my people would listen
        to me,

that Israel would walk in
        my ways!
¹⁴ Then I would quickly subdue
        their enemies,
    and turn my hand against
        their foes.
¹⁵ Those who hate the LORD
        would cringe before
        him,
    and their doom would last
        forever.
¹⁶ I would feed you[b] with the
        finest of the wheat,
    and with honey from the
        rock I would satisfy
        you."

Psalm 82

A Psalm of Asaph.

¹ God has taken his place in
        the divine council;
    in the midst of the gods
        he holds judgment:
² "How long will you judge
        unjustly
    and show partiality to the
        wicked?   *Selah*
³ Give justice to the weak and
        the orphan;
    maintain the right of the
        lowly and the destitute.
⁴ Rescue the weak and the
        needy;
    deliver them from the hand
        of the wicked."

⁵ They have neither knowledge
        nor understanding,
    they walk around in
        darkness;

[a]Or *against* [b]Heb *his* [b]Cn Compare verse 16b: Heb *he would feed him*

all the foundations of the
earth are shaken.

[6] I say, "You are gods,
children of the Most High,
all of you;
[7] nevertheless, you shall die
like mortals,
and fall like any prince."[a]

[8] Rise up, O God, judge the earth;
for all the nations belong
to you!

Psalm 83

A Song. A Psalm of Asaph.

[1] O God, do not keep silence;
do not hold your peace or
be still, O God!
[2] Even now your enemies are
in tumult;
those who hate you have
raised their heads.
[3] They lay crafty plans against
your people;
they consult together against
those you protect.
[4] They say, "Come, let us wipe
them out as a nation;
let the name of Israel be
remembered no more."
[5] They conspire with one
accord;
against you they make a
covenant—
[6] the tents of Edom and the
Ishmaelites,
Moab and the Hagrites,
[7] Gebal and Ammon and
Amalek,
Philistia with the
inhabitants of Tyre;

[8] Assyria also has joined them;
they are the strong arm of
the children of Lot.
Selah

[9] Do to them as you did to
Midian,
as to Sisera and Jabin at
the Wadi Kishon,
[10] who were destroyed at Endor,
who became dung for the
ground.
[11] Make their nobles like Oreb
and Zeeb,
all their princes like Zebah
and Zalmunna,
[12] who said, "Let us take the
pastures of God
for our own possession."

[13] O my God, make them like
whirling dust,[b]
like chaff before the wind.
[14] As fire consumes the forest,
as the flame sets the
mountains ablaze,
[15] so pursue them with your
tempest
and terrify them with your
hurricane.
[16] Fill their faces with shame,
so that they may seek
your name, O LORD.
[17] Let them be put to shame
and dismayed
forever;
let them perish in disgrace.
[18] Let them know that you
alone,
whose name is the LORD,
are the Most High over
all the earth.

[a]Or *fall as one man, O princes* [b]Or *a tumbleweed*

453

Psalm 84

*To the leader: according to The
Gittith. Of the Korahites.
A Psalm.*

1 How lovely is your
dwelling place,
O LORD of hosts!
2 My soul longs, indeed it
faints
for the courts of the LORD;
my heart and my flesh sing
for joy
to the living God.

3 Even the sparrow finds a
home,
and the swallow a nest
for herself,
where she may lay her
young,
at your altars, O LORD of
hosts,
my King and my God.
4 Happy are those who live
in your house,
ever singing your praise.
Selah

5 Happy are those whose
strength is in you,
in whose heart are the
highways to Zion.[a]
6 As they go through the
valley of Baca
they make it a place of
springs;
the early rain also covers
it with pools.
7 They go from strength to
strength;
the God of gods will be seen
in Zion.

8 O LORD God of hosts, hear
my prayer;
give ear, O God of Jacob!
Selah
9 Behold our shield, O God;
look on the face of your
anointed.

10 For a day in your courts is
better
than a thousand elsewhere.
I would rather be a
doorkeeper in the house
of my God
than live in the tents of
wickedness.
11 For the LORD God is a sun
and shield;
he bestows favor and honor.
No good thing does the
LORD withhold
from those who walk
uprightly.
12 O LORD of hosts,
happy is everyone who
trusts in you.

Psalm 85

*To the leader. Of the Korahites.
A Psalm.*

1 LORD, you were favorable to
your land;
you restored the fortunes
of Jacob.
2 You forgave the iniquity of
your people;
you pardoned all their sin.
Selah
3 You withdrew all your wrath;
you turned from your hot
anger.

[a]Heb lacks *to Zion*

4 Restore us again, O God of
       our salvation,
    and put away your
       indignation toward us.
5 Will you be angry with us
       forever?
    Will you prolong your
       anger to all generations?
6 Will you not revive us again,
    so that your people may
       rejoice in you?
7 Show us your steadfast love,
       O LORD,
    and grant us your salvation.

8 Let me hear what God the LORD
       will speak,
    for he will speak peace to
       his people,
    to his faithful, to those who
       turn to him in their
       hearts.[a]
9 Surely his salvation is at hand
       for those who fear him,
    that his glory may dwell in
       our land.

10 Steadfast love and faithfulness
       will meet;
    righteousness and peace
       will kiss each other.
11 Faithfulness will spring up
       from the ground,
    and righteousness will
       look down from the
       sky.
12 The LORD will give what is
       good,
    and our land will yield its
       increase.
13 Righteousness will go
       before him,
    and will make a path for
       his steps.

Psalm 86

A Prayer of David.

1 Incline your ear, O LORD, and
       answer me,
    for I am poor and needy.
2 Preserve my life, for I am
       devoted to you;
    save your servant who
       trusts in you.
    You are my God; 3be
       gracious to me,
       O Lord,
    for to you do I cry all
       day long.
4 Gladden the soul of your
       servant,
    for to you, O Lord, I lift up
       my soul.
5 For you, O Lord, are good
       and forgiving,
    abounding in steadfast
       love to all who call
       on you.
6 Give ear, O LORD, to my prayer;
    listen to my cry of
       supplication.
7 In the day of my trouble I call
       on you,
    for you will answer me.

8 There is none like you
       among the gods,
       O Lord,
    nor are there any works
       like yours.
9 All the nations you have
       made shall come
    and bow down before
       you, O Lord,
    and shall glorify your
       name.

[a]Gk: Heb *but let them not turn back to folly*

10 For you are great and do
     wondrous things;
   you alone are God.
11 Teach me your way,
     O LORD,
   that I may walk in
     your truth;
   give me an undivided heart
     to revere your name.
12 I give thanks to you, O Lord
     my God, with my
     whole heart,
   and I will glorify your
     name forever.
13 For great is your steadfast love
     toward me;
   you have delivered my soul
     from the depths of
     Sheol.

14 O God, the insolent rise up
     against me;
   a band of ruffians seeks
     my life,
   and they do not set you
     before them.
15 But you, O Lord, are a God
     merciful and
     gracious,
   slow to anger and
     abounding in
     steadfast love and
     faithfulness.
16 Turn to me and be gracious
     to me;
   give your strength to your
     servant;
   save the child of your
     serving girl.
17 Show me a sign of your
     favor,
   so that those who hate
     me may see it and be
     put to shame,

because you, LORD, have
   helped me and
   comforted me.

Psalm 87

Of the Korahites. A Psalm.
A Song.

1 On the holy mount stands the
     city he founded;
2   the LORD loves the gates
       of Zion
   more than all the
     dwellings of Jacob.
3 Glorious things are spoken
     of you,
   O city of God.   *Selah*

4 Among those who know me
     I mention Rahab and
     Babylon;
   Philistia too, and Tyre, with
     Ethiopia[a]—
   "This one was born there,"
     they say.

5 And of Zion it shall be
     said,
   "This one and that one
     were born in it";
   for the Most High
     himself will establish
     it.
6 The LORD records, as he
     registers the peoples,
   "This one was born
     there."   *Selah*

7 Singers and dancers alike
     say,
   "All my springs are in
     you."

[a]Or *Nubia;* Heb *Cush*

Psalm 88

A Song. A Psalm of the Korahites. To the leader: according to Mahalath Leannoth. A Maskil of Heman the Ezrahite.

1 O LORD, God of my salvation,
    when, at night, I cry out
        in your presence,
2 let my prayer come before you;
    incline your ear to my cry.

3 For my soul is full of troubles,
    and my life draws near to
        Sheol.
4 I am counted among those
        who go down to the Pit;
    I am like those who have
        no help,
5 like those forsaken among
        the dead,
    like the slain that lie in the
        grave,
like those whom you
        remember no more,
    for they are cut off from
        your hand.
6 You have put me in the depths
        of the Pit,
    in the regions dark and
        deep.
7 Your wrath lies heavy upon
        me,
    and you overwhelm me
        with all your waves.   *Selah*

8 You have caused my
        companions to shun me;
    you have made me a thing
        of horror to them.
    I am shut in so that I
        cannot escape;

9 my eye grows dim through
        sorrow.
Every day I call on you,
        O LORD;
    I spread out my hands
        to you.
10 Do you work wonders for
        the dead?
    Do the shades rise up to
        praise you?   *Selah*
11 Is your steadfast love declared
        in the grave,
    or your faithfulness in
        Abaddon?
12 Are your wonders known in
        the darkness,
    or your saving help in the
        land of forgetfulness?

13 But I, O LORD, cry out to you;
    in the morning my prayer
        comes before you.
14 O LORD, why do you cast me
        off?
    Why do you hide your face
        from me?
15 Wretched and close to death
        from my youth up,
    I suffer your terrors; I am
        desperate.[a]
16 Your wrath has swept over me;
    your dread assaults
        destroy me.
17 They surround me like a flood
        all day long;
    from all sides they close in
        on me.
18 You have caused friend
        and neighbor to shun
        me;
    my companions are in
        darkness.

[a]Meaning of Heb uncertain

457

Psalm 89

A Maskil of Ethan the Ezrahite.

[1] I will sing of your steadfast
love, O LORD,[a] forever;
with my mouth I will
proclaim your
faithfulness to all
generations.
[2] I declare that your steadfast
love is established
forever;
your faithfulness is as firm
as the heavens.

[3] You said, "I have made a
covenant with my
chosen one,
I have sworn to my servant
David:
[4] 'I will establish your
descendants forever,
and build your throne for all
generations.' "

Selah

[5] Let the heavens praise your
wonders, O LORD,
your faithfulness in the
assembly of the holy
ones.
[6] For who in the skies can be
compared to the LORD?
Who among the heavenly
beings is like the LORD,
[7] a God feared in the council
of the holy ones,
great and awesome[b]
above all that are
around him?
[8] O LORD God of hosts,
who is as mighty as you,
O LORD?

Your faithfulness
surrounds you.
[9] You rule the raging of the sea;
when its waves rise, you
still them.
[10] You crushed Rahab like
a carcass;
you scattered your enemies
with your mighty arm.
[11] The heavens are yours, the
earth also is yours;
the world and all that is
in it—you have founded
them.
[12] The north and the south[c]—
you created them;
Tabor and Hermon joyously
praise your name.
[13] You have a mighty arm;
strong is your hand, high
your right hand.
[14] Righteousness and justice
are the foundation of
your throne;
steadfast love and
faithfulness go before
you.
[15] Happy are the people who
know the festal
shout,
who walk, O LORD, in
the light of your
countenance;
[16] they exult in your name all
day long,
and extol[c] your
righteousness.
[17] For you are the glory of
their strength;
by your favor our horn is
exalted.

[a]Gk: Heb *the steadfast love of the LORD* [b]Gk Syr: Heb
greatly awesome [c]Or *Zaphon and Yamin* [c]Cn: Heb *are
exalted in*

18 For our shield belongs to
  the LORD,
    our king to the Holy One
    of Israel.

19 Then you spoke in a vision
    to your faithful one,
    and said:
  "I have set the crown[a] on
    one who is mighty,
  I have exalted one chosen
    from the people.
20 I have found my servant
    David;
  with my holy oil I have
    anointed him;
21 my hand shall always remain
    with him;
  my arm also shall
    strengthen him.
22 The enemy shall not
    outwit him,
  the wicked shall not
    humble him.
23 I will crush his foes before
    him
  and strike down those who
    hate him.
24 My faithfulness and steadfast
    love shall be with him;
  and in my name his horn
    shall be exalted.
25 I will set his hand on the sea
  and his right hand on
    the rivers.
26 He shall cry to me, 'You are
    my Father,
  my God, and the Rock of
    my salvation!'
27 I will make him the firstborn,
  the highest of the kings of
    the earth.
28 Forever I will keep my
    steadfast love for him,

  and my covenant with him
    will stand firm.
29 I will establish his line
    forever,
  and his throne as long as
    the heavens endure.
30 If his children forsake my
    law
  and do not walk
    according to my
    ordinances,
31 if they violate my statutes
  and do not keep my
    commandments,
32 then I will punish their
    transgression with the
    rod
  and their iniquity with
    scourges;
33 but I will not remove from
    him my steadfast love,
  or be false to my
    faithfulness.
34 I will not violate my covenant,
  or alter the word that went
    forth from my lips.
35 Once and for all I have
    sworn by my holiness;
  I will not lie to David.
36 His line shall continue forever,
  and his throne endure
    before me like the sun.
37 It shall be established forever
    like the moon,
  an enduring witness in
    the skies."   Selah

38 But now you have spurned
    and rejected him;
  you are full of wrath
    against your
    anointed.

[a]Cn: Heb help

459

39 You have renounced the
     covenant with your
     servant;
   you have defiled his
     crown in the dust.
40 You have broken through all
     his walls;
   you have laid his
     strongholds in ruins.
41 All who pass by plunder him;
   he has become the scorn of
     his neighbors.
42 You have exalted the
     right hand of his foes;
   you have made all his
     enemies rejoice.
43 Moreover, you have turned
     back the edge of his
     sword,
   and you have not supported
     him in battle.
44 You have removed the scepter
     from his hand,*a*
   and hurled his throne to
     the ground.
45 You have cut short the days
     of his youth;
   you have covered him
     with shame.   *Selah*

46 How long, O Lord? Will
     you hide yourself
     forever?
   How long will your
     wrath burn like fire?
47 Remember how short my
     time is—*b*
   for what vanity you have
     created all mortals!
48 Who can live and never
     see death?
   Who can escape the
     power of Sheol?
                         Selah

49 Lord, where is your steadfast
     love of old,
   which by your faithfulness
     you swore to David?
50 Remember, O Lord, how your
     servant is taunted;
   how I bear in my bosom the
     insults of the peoples,*c*
51 with which your enemies
     taunt, O Lord,
   with which they taunted the
     footsteps of your
     anointed.

52 Blessed be the Lord forever.
   Amen and Amen.

BOOK IV

(Psalms 90–106)

Psalm 90

*A Prayer of Moses,
the man of God.*

1 Lord, you have been our
     dwelling place*d*
   in all generations.
2 Before the mountains were
     brought forth,
   or ever you had formed the
     earth and the world,
   from everlasting to
     everlasting you are God.

3 You turn us*e* back to dust,
   and say, "Turn back, you
     mortals."
4 For a thousand years in
     your sight
   are like yesterday when it
     is past,
   or like a watch in the night.

*a*Cn: Heb *removed his cleanness* *b*Meaning of Heb
uncertain *c*Cn: Heb *bosom all of many peoples*
*d*Another reading is *our refuge* *e*Heb *humankind*

⁵ You sweep them away; they are
    like a dream,
  like grass that is renewed in
    the morning;
⁶ in the morning it flourishes
    and is renewed;
  in the evening it fades
    and withers.

⁷ For we are consumed by
    your anger;
  by your wrath we are
    overwhelmed.
⁸ You have set our iniquities
    before you,
  our secret sins in the light
    of your countenance.

⁹ For all our days pass away
    under your wrath;
  our years come to an end[a]
    like a sigh.
¹⁰ The days of our life are
    seventy years,
  or perhaps eighty, if we
    are strong;
  even then their span[b] is only
    toil and trouble;
  they are soon gone, and we
    fly away.

¹¹ Who considers the power of
    your anger?
  Your wrath is as great as the
    fear that is due you.
¹² So teach us to count our days
    that we may gain a wise
    heart.

¹³ Turn, O LORD! How long?
  Have compassion on
    your servants!
¹⁴ Satisfy us in the morning with
    your steadfast love,

so that we may rejoice and
    be glad all our days.
¹⁵ Make us glad as many days as
    you have afflicted us,
  and as many years as we
    have seen evil.
¹⁶ Let your work be manifest to
    your servants,
  and your glorious power to
    their children.
¹⁷ Let the favor of the Lord our
    God be upon us,
  and prosper for us the work
    of our hands—
  O prosper the work of our
    hands!

Psalm 91

¹ You who live in the shelter of
    the Most High,
  who abide in the shadow of
    the Almighty,[c]
² will say to the LORD, "My
    refuge and my
    fortress;
  my God, in whom I trust."
³ For he will deliver you from
    the snare of the fowler
  and from the deadly
    pestilence;
⁴ he will cover you with his
    pinions,
  and under his wings you
    will find refuge;
  his faithfulness is a
    shield and buckler.
⁵ You will not fear the terror
    of the night,
  or the arrow that flies
    by day,

[a]Syr: Heb *we bring our years to an end* [b]Cn Compare
Gk Syr Jerome Tg: Heb *pride* [c]Traditional rendering
of Heb *Shaddai*

6 or the pestilence that stalks
in darkness,
or the destruction that
wastes at noonday.

7 A thousand may fall at
your side,
ten thousand at your
right hand,
but it will not come
near you.
8 You will only look with
your eyes
and see the punishment of
the wicked.

9 Because you have made the
LORD your refuge,[a]
the Most High your
dwelling place,
10 no evil shall befall you,
no scourge come near
your tent.

11 For he will command his
angels concerning
you
to guard you in all
your ways.
12 On their hands they will
bear you up,
so that you will not dash
your foot against a
stone.
13 You will tread on the lion
and the adder,
the young lion and the
serpent you will trample
under foot.

14 Those who love me, I will
deliver;
I will protect those who
know my name.

15 When they call to me,
I will answer them;
I will be with them in
trouble,
I will rescue them and
honor them.
16 With long life I will satisfy
them,
and show them my
salvation.

Psalm 92

*A Psalm. A Song for the
Sabbath Day.*

1 It is good to give thanks to
the LORD,
to sing praises to your name,
O Most High;
2 to declare your steadfast love
in the morning,
and your faithfulness
by night,
3 to the music of the lute and
the harp,
to the melody of the lyre.
4 For you, O LORD, have
made me glad by
your work;
at the works of your hands
I sing for joy.

5 How great are your works,
O LORD!
Your thoughts are very deep!
6 The dullard cannot know,
the stupid cannot
understand this:
7 though the wicked sprout
like grass
and all evildoers flourish,

---

[a]Cn: Heb *Because you, LORD, are my refuge; you have
made*

they are doomed to
destruction forever,
8 but you, O LORD, are on
high forever.

9 For your enemies, O LORD,
for your enemies shall
perish;
all evildoers shall be
scattered.

10 But you have exalted my horn
like that of the wild ox;
you have poured over me[a]
fresh oil.
11 My eyes have seen the
downfall of my
enemies;
my ears have heard the
doom of my evil
assailants.

12 The righteous flourish like the
palm tree,
and grow like a cedar
in Lebanon.
13 They are planted in the house
of the LORD;
they flourish in the courts of
our God.
14 In old age they still produce
fruit;
they are always green and
full of sap,
15 showing that the LORD is
upright;
he is my rock, and there is
no unrighteousness
in him.

Psalm 93

1 The LORD is king, he is robed
in majesty;
the LORD is robed, he is
girded with strength.
He has established the
world; it shall never
be moved;
2 your throne is established
from of old;
you are from everlasting.

3 The floods have lifted up,
O LORD,
the floods have lifted up
their voice;
the floods lift up their
roaring.
4 More majestic than the
thunders of mighty
waters,
more majestic than the
waves[b] of the sea,
majestic on high is the LORD!

5 Your decrees are very sure;
holiness befits your house,
O LORD, forevermore.

Psalm 94

1 O LORD, you God of vengeance,
you God of vengeance,
shine forth!
2 Rise up, O judge of the earth;
give to the proud what
they deserve!
3 O LORD, how long shall
the wicked,
how long shall the
wicked exult?

4 They pour out their arrogant
words;
all the evildoers boast.

[a]Syr: Meaning of Heb uncertain [b]Cn: Heb *majestic
are the waves*

463

5 They crush your people,
    O Lord,
  and afflict your heritage.
6 They kill the widow and
    the stranger,
  they murder the orphan,
7 and they say, "The Lord does
    not see;
  the God of Jacob does
    not perceive."

8 Understand, O dullest of
    the people;
  fools, when will you be
    wise?
9 He who planted the ear, does
    he not hear?
  He who formed the eye,
    does he not see?
10 He who disciplines the
    nations,
  he who teaches knowledge
    to humankind,
  does he not chastise?
11 The Lord knows our
    thoughts,[a]
  that they are but an empty
    breath.

12 Happy are those whom
    you discipline,
    O Lord,
  and whom you teach out of
    your law,
13 giving them respite from days
    of trouble,
  until a pit is dug for the
    wicked.
14 For the Lord will not
    forsake his people;
  he will not abandon his
    heritage;
15 for justice will return to
    the righteous,

and all the upright in heart
    will follow it.

16 Who rises up for me against
    the wicked?
  Who stands up for me
    against evildoers?
17 If the Lord had not been
    my help,
  my soul would soon have
    lived in the land of
    silence.
18 When I thought, "My foot
    is slipping,"
  your steadfast love, O Lord,
    held me up.
19 When the cares of my heart
    are many,
  your consolations cheer
    my soul.
20 Can wicked rulers be allied
    with you,
  those who contrive
    mischief by statute?
21 They band together against
    the life of the
    righteous,
  and condemn the
    innocent to death.
22 But the Lord has become my
    stronghold,
  and my God the rock of
    my refuge.
23 He will repay them for
    their iniquity
  and wipe them out for their
    wickedness;
  the Lord our God will wipe
    them out.

Psalm 95

1 O come, let us sing to the Lord;

[a]Heb the thoughts of humankind

464

let us make a joyful noise to
the rock of our
salvation!
2 Let us come into his presence
with thanksgiving;
let us make a joyful noise to
him with songs of
praise!
3 For the LORD is a great God,
and a great King above all
gods.
4 In his hand are the depths of
the earth;
the heights of the mountains
are his also.
5 The sea is his, for he made it,
and the dry land, which his
hands have formed.

6 O come, let us worship and
bow down,
let us kneel before the LORD,
our Maker!
7 For he is our God,
and we are the people of
his pasture,
and the sheep of his hand.

O that today you would
listen to his voice!
8 　Do not harden your hearts,
as at Meribah,
as on the day at Massah
in the wilderness,
9 when your ancestors tested me,
and put me to the proof,
though they had seen
my work.
10 For forty years I loathed that
generation
and said, "They are a people
whose hearts go astray,
and they do not regard
my ways."

11 Therefore in my anger I swore,
"They shall not enter
my rest."

Psalm 96

1 O sing to the LORD a new
song;
sing to the LORD, all the
earth.
2 Sing to the LORD, bless his
name;
tell of his salvation from day
to day.
3 Declare his glory among the
nations,
his marvelous works among
all the peoples.
4 For great is the LORD, and
greatly to be praised;
he is to be revered above
all gods.
5 For all the gods of the
peoples are idols,
but the LORD made the
heavens.
6 Honor and majesty are
before him;
strength and beauty are
in his sanctuary.

7 Ascribe to the LORD,
O families of the
peoples,
ascribe to the LORD glory
and strength.
8 Ascribe to the LORD
the glory due his name;
bring an offering, and
come into his courts.
9 Worship the LORD in holy
splendor;
tremble before him, all
the earth.

¹⁰ Say among the nations, "The
 LORD is king!
 The world is firmly
  established; it shall
  never be moved.
 He will judge the peoples
  with equity."
¹¹ Let the heavens be glad, and
  let the earth rejoice;
 let the sea roar, and all that
  fills it;
¹² let the field exult, and
  everything in it.
 Then shall all the trees of
  the forest sing for joy
¹³ before the LORD; for he is
  coming,
 for he is coming to judge
  the earth.
 He will judge the world
  with righteousness,
 and the peoples with his
  truth.

Psalm 97

¹ The LORD is king! Let the
  earth rejoice;
 let the many coastlands be
  glad!
² Clouds and thick darkness are
  all around him;
 righteousness and justice are
  the foundation of his
  throne.
³ Fire goes before him,
 and consumes his
  adversaries on every
  side.
⁴ His lightnings light up
  the world;
 the earth sees and trembles.
⁵ The mountains melt like
  wax before the LORD,

before the LORD of all the
 earth.

⁶ The heavens proclaim his
  righteousness;
 and all the peoples behold
  his glory.
⁷ All worshipers of images are
  put to shame,
 those who make their boast
  in worthless idols;
 all gods bow down before
  him.
⁸ Zion hears and is glad,
 and the towns^a of Judah
  rejoice,
 because of your judgments,
  O God.
⁹ For you, O LORD, are most high
  over all the earth;
 you are exalted far above
  all gods.

¹⁰ The LORD loves those who
  hate^b evil;
 he guards the lives of his
  faithful;
 he rescues them from the
  hand of the wicked.
¹¹ Light dawns^c for the righteous,
 and joy for the upright in
  heart.
¹² Rejoice in the LORD,
  O you righteous,
 and give thanks to his holy
  name!

Psalm 98
A Psalm.

¹ O sing to the LORD a new song,

---

^aHeb *daughters* ^bCn: Heb *You who love the LORD hate*
^cGk Syr Jerome: Heb *is sown*

466

for he has done marvelous
    things.
His right hand and his holy
    arm
have gotten him victory.
[2] The LORD has made known
    his victory;
he has revealed his
    vindication in the sight
    of the nations.
[3] He has remembered his
    steadfast love and
    faithfulness
to the house of Israel.
All the ends of the earth
    have seen
the victory of our God.

[4] Make a joyful noise to the LORD,
    all the earth;
break forth into joyous song
    and sing praises.
[5] Sing praises to the LORD with
    the lyre,
with the lyre and the sound
    of melody.
[6] With trumpets and the sound
    of the horn
make a joyful noise before
    the King, the LORD.

[7] Let the sea roar, and all that
    fills it;
the world and those who
    live in it.
[8] Let the floods clap their hands;
    let the hills sing together
    for joy
[9] at the presence of the LORD, for
    he is coming
to judge the earth.
He will judge the world
    with righteousness,
and the peoples with equity.

Psalm 99

[1] The LORD is king; let the
    peoples tremble!
He sits enthroned upon the
    cherubim; let the earth
    quake!
[2] The LORD is great in Zion;
    he is exalted over all the
    peoples.
[3] Let them praise your great and
    awesome name.
    Holy is he!
[4] Mighty King,[a] lover of justice,
    you have established
    equity;
    you have executed justice
    and righteousness in
    Jacob.
[5] Extol the LORD our God;
    worship at his footstool.
    Holy is he!

[6] Moses and Aaron were
    among his priests,
    Samuel also was among
    those who called on
    his name.
    They cried to the LORD,
    and he answered
    them.
[7] He spoke to them in the pillar
    of cloud;
    they kept his decrees,
    and the statutes that he gave
    them.

[8] O LORD our God, you answered
    them;
    you were a forgiving God
    to them,
    but an avenger of their
    wrongdoings.

[a]Cn: Heb *And a king's strength*

467

⁹ Extol the LORD our God,
    and worship at his holy
      mountain;
    for the LORD our God is holy.

Psalm 100

A Psalm of thanksgiving.

¹ Make a joyful noise to the LORD,
    all the earth.
²   Worship the LORD with
      gladness;
    come into his presence
      with singing.
³ Know that the LORD is
      God.
    It is he that made us, and
      we are his;[a]
    we are his people, and
      the sheep of his
      pasture.

⁴ Enter his gates with
      thanksgiving,
    and his courts with praise.
    Give thanks to him, bless
      his name.

⁵ For the LORD is good;
    his steadfast love endures
      forever,
    and his faithfulness to all
      generations.

Psalm 101

Of David. A Psalm.

¹ I will sing of loyalty and of
      justice;
    to you, O LORD, I will sing.
² I will study the way that is
      blameless.
    When shall I attain it?

I will walk with integrity of
      heart
    within my house;
³ I will not set before my eyes
    anything that is base.

I hate the work of those
    who fall away;
    it shall not cling to me.
⁴ Perverseness of heart shall be
      far from me;
    I will know nothing of evil.

⁵ One who secretly slanders a
      neighbor
    I will destroy.
A haughty look and an
      arrogant heart
    I will not tolerate.

⁶ I will look with favor on the
      faithful in the land,
    so that they may live
      with me;
whoever walks in the way
      that is blameless
    shall minister to me.

⁷ No one who practices
      deceit
    shall remain in my house;
no one who utters lies
    shall continue in my
      presence.

⁸ Morning by morning I will
      destroy
    all the wicked in the
      land,
cutting off all evildoers
    from the city of the
      LORD.

[a]Another reading is *and not we ourselves*

Psalm 102

*A prayer of one afflicted,
when faint and pleading before
the Lord.*

[1] Hear my prayer, O Lord;
let my cry come to you.
[2] Do not hide your face from me
in the day of my distress.
Incline your ear to me;
answer me speedily in the
day when I call.

[3] For my days pass away like
smoke,
and my bones burn like
a furnace.
[4] My heart is stricken and
withered like grass;
I am too wasted to eat my
bread.
[5] Because of my loud groaning
my bones cling to my skin.
[6] I am like an owl of the
wilderness,
like a little owl of the waste
places.
[7] I lie awake;
I am like a lonely bird on
the housetop.
[8] All day long my enemies
taunt me;
those who deride me use my
name for a curse.
[9] For I eat ashes like bread,
and mingle tears with my
drink,
[10] because of your indignation
and anger;
for you have lifted me up
and thrown me aside.
[11] My days are like an
evening shadow;
I wither away like grass.

[12] But you, O Lord, are
enthroned forever;
your name endures to all
generations.
[13] You will rise up and have
compassion on Zion,
for it is time to favor it;
the appointed time has
come.
[14] For your servants hold its
stones dear,
and have pity on its dust.
[15] The nations will fear the name
of the Lord,
and all the kings of the earth
your glory.
[16] For the Lord will build up
Zion;
he will appear in his glory.
[17] He will regard the prayer of
the destitute,
and will not despise their
prayer.

[18] Let this be recorded for a
generation to come,
so that a people yet unborn
may praise the Lord:
[19] that he looked down from his
holy height,
from heaven the Lord
looked at the earth,
[20] to hear the groans of the
prisoners,
to set free those who were
doomed to die;
[21] so that the name of the Lord
may be declared in
Zion,
and his praise in Jerusalem,
[22] when peoples gather
together,
and kingdoms, to
worship the Lord.

23 He has broken my strength
    in midcourse;
  he has shortened my days.
24 "O my God," I say, "do not
    take me away
    at the midpoint of my life,
  you whose years endure
    throughout all generations."

25 Long ago you laid the
    foundation of the earth,
  and the heavens are the
    work of your hands.
26 They will perish, but you
    endure;
  they will all wear out like
    a garment.
  You change them like
    clothing, and they pass
    away;
27   but you are the same, and
    your years have no end.
28 The children of your servants
    shall live secure;
  their offspring shall be
    established in your
    presence.

Psalm 103

Of David.

1 Bless the LORD, O my soul,
  and all that is within me,
    bless his holy name.
2 Bless the LORD, O my soul,
  and do not forget all his
    benefits—
3 who forgives all your iniquity,
  who heals all your diseases,
4 who redeems your life from
    the Pit,
  who crowns you with
    steadfast love and
    mercy,

5 who satisfies you with good as
    long as you live*a*
  so that your youth is
    renewed like the eagle's.

6 The LORD works vindication
  and justice for all who are
    oppressed.
7 He made known his ways to
    Moses,
  his acts to the people of
    Israel.
8 The LORD is merciful and
    gracious,
  slow to anger and abounding
    in steadfast love.
9 He will not always accuse,
  nor will he keep his anger
    forever.
10 He does not deal with us
    according to our sins,
  nor repay us according to
    our iniquities.
11 For as the heavens are high
    above the earth,
  so great is his steadfast love
    toward those who fear
    him;
12 as far as the east is from
    the west,
  so far he removes our
    transgressions from
    us.
13 As a father has compassion
    for his children,
  so the LORD has
    compassion for those
    who fear him.
14 For he knows how we were
    made;
  he remembers that we are
    dust.

*a*Meaning of Heb uncertain

¹⁵ As for mortals, their days are
    like grass;
    they flourish like a flower of
    the field;
¹⁶ for the wind passes over it,
    and it is gone,
    and its place knows it
    no more.
¹⁷ But the steadfast love of the
    LORD is from everlasting
    to everlasting
    on those who fear him,
    and his righteousness to
    children's children,
¹⁸ to those who keep his
    covenant
    and remember to do his
    commandments.

¹⁹ The LORD has established his
    throne in the heavens,
    and his kingdom rules
    over all.
²⁰ Bless the LORD, O you his
    angels,
    you mighty ones who do
    his bidding,
    obedient to his spoken
    word.
²¹ Bless the LORD, all his hosts,
    his ministers that do his
    will.
²² Bless the LORD, all his works,
    in all places of his
    dominion.
    Bless the LORD, O my soul.

Psalm 104

¹ Bless the LORD, O my soul.
    O LORD my God, you are
    very great.
    You are clothed with honor
    and majesty,
² wrapped in light as with a
    garment.
    You stretch out the heavens
    like a tent,
³   you set the beams of your^a
    chambers on the
    waters,
    you make the clouds your^a
    chariot,
    you ride on the wings of
    the wind,
⁴ you make the winds your^a
    messengers,
    fire and flame your^a
    ministers.

⁵ You set the earth on its
    foundations,
    so that it shall never be
    shaken.
⁶ You cover it with the deep as
    with a garment;
    the waters stood above the
    mountains.
⁷ At your rebuke they flee;
    at the sound of your thunder
    they take to flight.
⁸ They rose up to the mountains,
    ran down to the valleys
    to the place that you
    appointed for them.
⁹ You set a boundary that they
    may not pass,
    so that they might not again
    cover the earth.

¹⁰ You make springs gush forth
    in the valleys;
    they flow between the hills,
¹¹ giving drink to every wild
    animal;

^aHeb *his*

the wild asses quench
their thirst.
12 By the streams[a] the birds of
the air have their
habitation;
they sing among the
branches.
13 From your lofty abode you
water the mountains;
the earth is satisfied with
the fruit of your work.

14 You cause the grass to grow for
the cattle,
and plants for people to
use,[b]
to bring forth food from
the earth,
15 and wine to gladden the
human heart,
oil to make the face shine,
and bread to strengthen the
human heart.
16 The trees of the LORD are
watered abundantly,
the cedars of Lebanon that
he planted.
17 In them the birds build their
nests;
the stork has its home in the
fir trees.
18 The high mountains are for
the wild goats;
the rocks are a refuge for the
coneys.
19 You have made the moon to
mark the seasons;
the sun knows its time for
setting.
20 You make darkness, and it is
night,
when all the animals of the
forest come creeping
out.

21 The young lions roar for
their prey,
seeking their food from God.
22 When the sun rises, they
withdraw
and lie down in their dens.
23 People go out to their work
and to their labor until the
evening.

24 O LORD, how manifold are
your works!
In wisdom you have made
them all;
the earth is full of your
creatures.
25 Yonder is the sea, great and
wide,
creeping things innumerable
are there,
living things both small and
great.
26 There go the ships,
and Leviathan that you
formed to sport in it.

27 These all look to you
to give them their food in
due season;
28 when you give to them, they
gather it up;
when you open your hand,
they are filled with good
things.
29 When you hide your face, they
are dismayed;
when you take away their
breath, they die
and return to their dust.
30 When you send forth your
spirit,[c] they are
created;

---

[a]Heb By them   [b]Or to cultivate   [c]Or your breath

and you renew the face of
the ground.

³¹ May the glory of the LORD
endure forever;
may the LORD rejoice in his
works—
³² who looks on the earth and
it trembles,
who touches the mountains
and they smoke.
³³ I will sing to the LORD as long
as I live;
I will sing praise to my God
while I have being.
³⁴ May my meditation be
pleasing to him,
for I rejoice in the LORD.
³⁵ Let sinners be consumed from
the earth,
and let the wicked be no
more.
Bless the LORD, O my soul.
Praise the LORD!

Psalm 105

¹ O give thanks to the LORD, call
on his name,
make known his deeds
among the peoples.
² Sing to him, sing praises to
him;
tell of all his wonderful
works.
³ Glory in his holy name;
let the hearts of those
who seek the LORD
rejoice.
⁴ Seek the LORD and his strength;
seek his presence
continually.
⁵ Remember the wonderful
works he has done,

his miracles, and the
judgments he has
uttered,
⁶ O offspring of his servant
Abraham,ᵃ
children of Jacob, his chosen
ones.

⁷ He is the LORD our God;
his judgments are in all
the earth.
⁸ He is mindful of his
covenant forever,
of the word that he
commanded, for a
thousand
generations,
⁹ the covenant that he made
with Abraham,
his sworn promise to
Isaac,
¹⁰ which he confirmed to Jacob
as a statute,
to Israel as an everlasting
covenant,
¹¹ saying, "To you I will give
the land of Canaan
as your portion for an
inheritance."

¹² When they were few in
number,
of little account, and
strangers in it,
¹³ wandering from nation to
nation,
from one kingdom to
another people,
¹⁴ he allowed no one to oppress
them;
he rebuked kings on their
account,

ᵃAnother reading is *Israel* (compare 1 Chr 16.13)

473

15 saying, "Do not touch my
      anointed ones;
   do my prophets no harm."

16 When he summoned famine
      against the land,
   and broke every staff of
      bread,
17 he had sent a man ahead of
      them,
   Joseph, who was sold as
      a slave.
18 His feet were hurt with
      fetters,
   his neck was put in a collar
      of iron;
19 until what he had said came
      to pass,
   the word of the LORD kept
      testing him.
20 The king sent and released
      him;
   the ruler of the peoples set
      him free.
21 He made him Lord of his
      house,
   and ruler of all his
      possessions,
22 to instruct[a] his officials at
      his pleasure,
   and to teach his elders
      wisdom.

23 Then Israel came to Egypt;
   Jacob lived as an alien in the
      land of Ham.
24 And the LORD made his people
      very fruitful,
   and made them stronger
      than their foes,
25 whose hearts he then turned
      to hate his people,
   to deal craftily with his
      servants.

26 He sent his servant Moses,
   and Aaron whom he had
      chosen.
27 They performed his signs
      among them,
   and miracles in the land of
      Ham.
28 He sent darkness, and made
      the land dark;
   they rebelled[b] against his
      words.
29 He turned their waters into
      blood,
   and caused their fish to die.
30 Their land swarmed with
      frogs,
   even in the chambers of
      their kings.
31 He spoke, and there came
      swarms of flies,
   and gnats throughout their
      country.
32 He gave them hail for rain,
   and lightning that flashed
      through their land.
33 He struck their vines and
      fig trees,
   and shattered the trees of
      their country.
34 He spoke, and the locusts
      came,
   and young locusts without
      number;
35 they devoured all the
      vegetation in their land,
   and ate up the fruit of their
      ground.
36 He struck down all the
      firstborn in their land,
   the first issue of all their
      strength.

---

[a]Gk Syr Jerome: Heb *to bind* [b]Cn Compare Gk Syr:
Heb *they did not rebel*

37 Then he brought Israel[a] out
    with silver and gold,
  and there was no one among
    their tribes who
    stumbled.
38 Egypt was glad when they
    departed,
  for dread of them had fallen
    upon it.
39 He spread a cloud for a
    covering,
  and fire to give light by
    night.
40 They asked, and he brought
    quails,
  and gave them food from
    heaven in abundance.
41 He opened the rock, and
    water gushed out;
  it flowed through the desert
    like a river.
42 For he remembered his holy
    promise,
  and Abraham, his servant.

43 So he brought his people out
    with joy,
  his chosen ones with
    singing.
44 He gave them the lands of
    the nations,
  and they took possession of
    the wealth of the
    peoples,
45 that they might keep his
    statutes
  and observe his laws.
  Praise the LORD!

Psalm 106

1 Praise the LORD!
  O give thanks to the LORD,
    for he is good;

for his steadfast love
    endures forever.
2 Who can utter the mighty
    doings of the LORD,
  or declare all his praise?
3 Happy are those who observe
    justice,
  who do righteousness at all
    times.

4 Remember me, O LORD,
    when you show favor
    to your people;
  help me when you
    deliver them;
5 that I may see the prosperity
    of your chosen ones,
  that I may rejoice in the
    gladness of your nation,
  that I may glory in your
    heritage.

6 Both we and our ancestors
    have sinned;
  we have committed iniquity,
    have done wickedly.
7 Our ancestors, when they were
    in Egypt,
  did not consider your
    wonderful works;
  they did not remember the
    abundance of your
    steadfast love,
  but rebelled against the
    Most High[b] at the Red
    Sea.[c]
8 Yet he saved them for his
    name's sake,
  so that he might make
    known his mighty
    power.

[a]Heb *them* [b]Cn Compare 78.17, 56: Heb *rebelled at
the sea* [c]Or *Sea of Reeds*

⁹ He rebuked the Red Sea,ᵃ and
   it became dry;
   he led them through the
      deep as through a
      desert.
¹⁰ So he saved them from the
      hand of the foe,
   and delivered them from the
      hand of the enemy.
¹¹ The waters covered their
      adversaries;
   not one of them was left.
¹² Then they believed his words;
   they sang his praise.

¹³ But they soon forgot his
      works;
   they did not wait for his
      counsel.
¹⁴ But they had a wanton craving
      in the wilderness,
   and put God to the test in
      the desert;
¹⁵ he gave them what they asked,
   but sent a wasting disease
      among them.

¹⁶ They were jealous of Moses
      in the camp,
   and of Aaron, the holy one
      of the LORD.
¹⁷ The earth opened and
      swallowed up Dathan,
   and covered the faction of
      Abiram.
¹⁸ Fire also broke out in their
      company;
   the flame burned up the
      wicked.

¹⁹ They made a calf at Horeb
   and worshiped a cast image.
²⁰ They exchanged the glory
   of Godᵇ

for the image of an ox that
   eats grass.
²¹ They forgot God, their Savior,
   who had done great things
      in Egypt,
²² wondrous works in the land
      of Ham,
   and awesome deeds by the
      Red Sea.ᶜ
²³ Therefore he said he would
      destroy them—
   had not Moses, his chosen
      one,
stood in the breach before
      him,
   to turn away his wrath from
      destroying them.

²⁴ Then they despised the
      pleasant land,
   having no faith in his
      promise.
²⁵ They grumbled in their tents,
   and did not obey the voice
      of the LORD.
²⁶ Therefore he raised his hand
      and swore to them
   that he would make them
      fall in the wilderness,
²⁷ and would disperseᵈ their
      descendants among the
      nations,
   scattering them over the
      lands.

²⁸ Then they attached
      themselves to the Baal
      of Peor,
   and ate sacrifices offered to
      the dead;

ᵃOr *Sea of Reeds* ᵇCompare Gk Mss: Heb *exchanged their glory* ᶜOr *Sea of Reeds* ᵈSyr Compare Ezek 20.23: Heb *cause to fall*

29 they provoked the LORD to
 anger with their deeds,
and a plague broke out
 among them.
30 Then Phinehas stood up
 and interceded,
and the plague was stopped.
31 And that has been reckoned
 to him as righteousness
from generation to
 generation forever.

32 They angered the LORD[a] at
 the waters of Meribah,
and it went ill with Moses
 on their account;
33 for they made his spirit bitter,
 and he spoke words that
 were rash.

34 They did not destroy the
 peoples,
as the LORD commanded
 them,
35 but they mingled with the
 nations
and learned to do as
 they did.
36 They served their idols,
 which became a snare to
 them.
37 They sacrificed their sons
 and their daughters to the
 demons;
38 they poured out innocent
 blood,
the blood of their sons and
 daughters,
whom they sacrificed to the
 idols of Canaan;
and the land was polluted
 with blood.
39 Thus they became unclean by
 their acts,

and prostituted themselves
 in their doings.

40 Then the anger of the LORD
 was kindled against his
 people,
and he abhorred his
 heritage;
41 he gave them into the hand
 of the nations,
so that those who hated
 them ruled over them.
42 Their enemies oppressed
 them,
and they were brought into
 subjection under their
 power.
43 Many times he delivered
 them,
but they were rebellious in
 their purposes,
and were brought low
 through their iniquity.
44 Nevertheless he regarded their
 distress
when he heard their cry.
45 For their sake he remembered
 his covenant,
and showed compassion
 according to the
 abundance of his
 steadfast love.
46 He caused them to be pitied
 by all who held them
 captive.

47 Save us, O LORD our God,
 and gather us from among
 the nations,
that we may give thanks to
 your holy name
and glory in your praise.

[a]Heb him

[48] Blessed be the LORD, the God
of Israel,
from everlasting to
everlasting.
And let all the people
say, "Amen."
Praise the LORD!

BOOK V

(Psalms 107–150)

Psalm 107

[1] O give thanks to the LORD,
for he is good;
for his steadfast love
endures forever.
[2] Let the redeemed of the LORD
say so,
those he redeemed from
trouble
[3] and gathered in from the lands,
from the east and from
the west,
from the north and from
the south.[a]

[4] Some wandered in desert
wastes,
finding no way to an
inhabited town;
[5] hungry and thirsty,
their soul fainted within
them.
[6] Then they cried to the LORD in
their trouble,
and he delivered them from
their distress;
[7] he led them by a straight way,
until they reached an
inhabited town.
[8] Let them thank the LORD for
his steadfast love,

for his wonderful works to
humankind.
[9] For he satisfies the thirsty,
and the hungry he fills with
good things.

[10] Some sat in darkness and in
gloom,
prisoners in misery and in
irons,
[11] for they had rebelled
against the words of
God,
and spurned the counsel
of the Most High.
[12] Their hearts were bowed
down with hard
labor;
they fell down, with no
one to help.
[13] Then they cried to the LORD in
their trouble,
and he saved them from
their distress;
[14] he brought them out of
darkness and gloom,
and broke their bonds
asunder.
[15] Let them thank the LORD
for his steadfast love,
for his wonderful works to
humankind.
[16] For he shatters the doors of
bronze,
and cuts in two the bars of
iron.

[17] Some were sick[b] through
their sinful ways,
and because of their
iniquities endured
affliction;

[a]Cn: Heb *sea* [b]Cn: Heb *fools*

¹⁸ they loathed any kind of food,
    and they drew near to the
        gates of death.
¹⁹ Then they cried to the LORD
        in their trouble,
    and he saved them from
        their distress;
²⁰ he sent out his word and
        healed them,
    and delivered them from
        destruction.
²¹ Let them thank the LORD for
        his steadfast love,
    for his wonderful works
        to humankind.
²² And let them offer
        thanksgiving sacrifices,
    and tell of his deeds with
        songs of joy.

²³ Some went down to the sea
        in ships,
    doing business on the
        mighty waters;
²⁴ they saw the deeds of the
        LORD,
    his wondrous works in the
        deep.
²⁵ For he commanded and
        raised the stormy wind,
    which lifted up the waves
        of the sea.
²⁶ They mounted up to heaven,
        they went down to the
        depths;
    their courage melted
        away in their calamity;
²⁷ they reeled and staggered
        like drunkards,
    and were at their wits' end.
²⁸ Then they cried to the LORD
        in their trouble,
    and he brought them out
        from their distress;

²⁹ he made the storm be still,
    and the waves of the sea
        were hushed.
³⁰ Then they were glad because
        they had quiet,
    and he brought them to
        their desired haven.
³¹ Let them thank the LORD
        for his steadfast love,
    for his wonderful works
        to humankind.
³² Let them extol him in the
        congregation of the
        people,
    and praise him in the
        assembly of the elders.

³³ He turns rivers into a desert,
    springs of water into
        thirsty ground,
³⁴ a fruitful land into a salty
        waste,
    because of the wickedness
        of its inhabitants.
³⁵ He turns a desert into pools
        of water,
    a parched land into springs
        of water.
³⁶ And there he lets the
        hungry live,
    and they establish a town to
        live in;
³⁷ they sow fields, and plant
        vineyards,
    and get a fruitful yield.
³⁸ By his blessing they multiply
        greatly,
    and he does not let their
        cattle decrease.

³⁹ When they are diminished
        and brought low
    through oppression, trouble,
        and sorrow,

⁴⁰ he pours contempt on princes
and makes them wander in
trackless wastes;
⁴¹ but he raises up the needy out
of distress,
and makes their families
like flocks.
⁴² The upright see it and are
glad;
and all wickedness stops
its mouth.
⁴³ Let those who are wise give
heed to these things,
and consider the steadfast
love of the LORD.

Psalm 108

A Song. A Psalm of David.

¹ My heart is steadfast, O God,
my heart is steadfast;[a]
I will sing and make
melody.
Awake, my soul![b]
² Awake, O harp and lyre!
I will awake the dawn.
³ I will give thanks to you,
O LORD, among the
peoples,
and I will sing praises to
you among the nations.
⁴ For your steadfast love is
higher than the
heavens,
and your faithfulness
reaches to the clouds.

⁵ Be exalted, O God, above the
heavens,
and let your glory be over
all the earth.
⁶ Give victory with your right
hand, and answer me,

so that those whom you
love may be rescued.

⁷ God has promised in his
sanctuary:[c]
"With exultation I will
divide up Shechem,
and portion out the Vale
of Succoth.
⁸ Gilead is mine; Manasseh
is mine;
Ephraim is my helmet;
Judah is my scepter.
⁹ Moab is my washbasin;
on Edom I hurl my shoe;
over Philistia I shout in
triumph."

¹⁰ Who will bring me to the
fortified city?
Who will lead me to
Edom?
¹¹ Have you not rejected us,
O God?
You do not go out, O God,
with our armies.
¹² O grant us help against
the foe,
for human help is
worthless.
¹³ With God we shall do
valiantly;
it is he who will tread
down our foes.

Psalm 109

*To the leader. Of David.
A Psalm.*

¹ Do not be silent, O God of my
praise.

---

[a]Heb Mss Gk Syr: MT lacks *my heart is steadfast*
[b]Compare 57.8: Heb *also my soul* [c]Or *by his holiness*

[2] For wicked and deceitful
    mouths are opened
    against me,
  speaking against me with
    lying tongues.
[3] They beset me with words
    of hate,
  and attack me without
    cause.
[4] In return for my love they
    accuse me,
  even while I make prayer
    for them.[a]
[5] So they reward me evil for
    good,
  and hatred for my love.

[6] They say,[b] "Appoint a wicked
    man against him;
  let an accuser stand on
    his right.
[7] When he is tried, let him be
    found guilty;
  let his prayer be counted
    as sin.
[8] May his days be few;
  may another seize his
    position.
[9] May his children be
    orphans,
  and his wife a widow.
[10] May his children wander
    about and beg;
  may they be driven out
    of[c] the ruins they
    inhabit.
[11] May the creditor seize all
    that he has;
  may strangers plunder the
    fruits of his toil.
[12] May there be no one to do
    him a kindness,
  nor anyone to pity his
    orphaned children.

[13] May his posterity be cut off;
  may his name be blotted
    out in the second
    generation.
[14] May the iniquity of his
    father[d] be remembered
    before the LORD,
  and do not let the sin of
    his mother be blotted
    out.
[15] Let them be before the LORD
    continually,
  and may his[e] memory be
    cut off from the earth.
[16] For he did not remember to
    show kindness,
  but pursued the poor and
    needy
  and the brokenhearted to
    their death.
[17] He loved to curse; let
    curses come on him.
  He did not like blessing;
    may it be far from
    him.
[18] He clothed himself with
    cursing as his coat,
  may it soak into his body
    like water,
  like oil into his bones.
[19] May it be like a garment
    that he wraps around
    himself,
  like a belt that he wears
    every day."

[20] May that be the reward of
    my accusers from the
    LORD,
  of those who speak evil
    against my life.

[a]Syr: Heb *I prayer* [b]Heb lacks *They say* [c]Gk: Heb *and seek* [d]Cn: Heb *fathers* [e]Gk: Heb *their*

21 But you, O LORD my Lord,
    act on my behalf for your
        name's sake;
    because your steadfast love
        is good, deliver me.
22 For I am poor and needy,
    and my heart is pierced
        within me.
23 I am gone like a shadow at
        evening;
    I am shaken off like a locust.
24 My knees are weak through
        fasting;
    my body has become gaunt.
25 I am an object of scorn to my
        accusers;
    when they see me, they
        shake their heads.

26 Help me, O LORD my God!
    Save me according to your
        steadfast love.
27 Let them know that this is
        your hand;
    you, O LORD, have done it.
28 Let them curse, but you will
        bless.
    Let my assailants be put to
        shame;[a] may your
        servant be glad.
29 May my accusers be clothed
        with dishonor;
    may they be wrapped in
        their own shame as in
        a mantle.
30 With my mouth I will give
        great thanks to the LORD;
    I will praise him in the
        midst of the throng.
31 For he stands at the right hand
        of the needy,
    to save them from those
        who would condemn
        them to death.

Psalm 110

Of David. A Psalm.

1 The LORD says to my lord,
    "Sit at my right hand
    until I make your enemies
        your footstool."

2 The LORD sends out from Zion
    your mighty scepter.
    Rule in the midst of your
        foes.
3 Your people will offer
        themselves willingly
    on the day you lead your
        forces
    on the holy mountains.[b]
From the womb of the
        morning,
    like dew, your youth[c] will
        come to you.
4 The Lord has sworn and will
        not change his mind,
    "You are a priest forever
        according to the order of
        Melchizedek."[d]

5 The LORD is at your right hand;
    he will shatter kings on the
        day of his wrath.
6 He will execute judgment
        among the nations,
    filling them with corpses;
    he will shatter heads
        over the wide earth.
7 He will drink from the stream
        by the path;
    therefore he will lift up
        his head.

[a]Gk: Heb They have risen up and have been put to shame [b]Another reading is in holy splendor [c]Cn: Heb the dew of your youth [d]Or forever, a rightful king by my edict

Psalm 111

[1] Praise the LORD!
　I will give thanks to the
　　　LORD with my whole
　　　heart,
　　in the company of the
　　　upright, in the
　　　congregation.
[2] Great are the works of the
　　　LORD,
　　studied by all who
　　　delight in them.
[3] Full of honor and majesty is
　　　his work,
　　and his righteousness
　　　endures forever.
[4] He has gained renown by his
　　　wonderful deeds;
　　the LORD is gracious and
　　　merciful.
[5] He provides food for those who
　　　fear him;
　　he is ever mindful of his
　　　covenant.
[6] He has shown his people the
　　　power of his works,
　　in giving them the heritage
　　　of the nations.
[7] The works of his hands are
　　　faithful and just;
　　all his precepts are
　　　trustworthy.
[8] They are established forever
　　　and ever,
　　to be performed with
　　　faithfulness and
　　　uprightness.
[9] He sent redemption to his
　　　people;
　　he has commanded his
　　　covenant forever.
　　Holy and awesome is his
　　　name.

[10] The fear of the LORD is the
　　　beginning of wisdom;
　　all those who practice it[a]
　　　have a good
　　　understanding.
　　His praise endures forever.

Psalm 112

[1] Praise the LORD!
　　Happy are those who fear
　　　the LORD,
　　who greatly delight in his
　　　commandments.
[2] Their descendants will be
　　　mighty in the land;
　　the generation of the
　　　upright will be blessed.
[3] Wealth and riches are in their
　　　houses,
　　and their righteousness
　　　endures forever.
[4] They rise in the darkness as
　　　a light for the upright;
　　they are gracious, merciful,
　　　and righteous.
[5] It is well with those who deal
　　　generously and lend,
　　who conduct their affairs
　　　with justice.
[6] For the righteous will never
　　　be moved;
　　they will be remembered
　　　forever.
[7] They are not afraid of evil
　　　tidings;
　　their hearts are firm, secure
　　　in the LORD.
[8] Their hearts are steady,
　　　they will not be
　　　afraid;
　　in the end they will look
　　　in triumph on their foes.

---

[a] Gk Syr: Heb *them*

483

⁹ They have distributed freely,
they have given to the
poor;
their righteousness endures
forever;
their horn is exalted in
honor.
¹⁰ The wicked see it and are
angry;
they gnash their teeth and
melt away;
the desire of the wicked
comes to nothing.

Psalm 113

¹ Praise the LORD!
Praise, O servants of the
LORD;
praise the name of the
LORD.

² Blessed be the name of the
LORD
from this time on and
forevermore.
³ From the rising of the sun to
its setting
the name of the LORD is to
be praised.
⁴ The LORD is high above all
nations,
and his glory above the
heavens.

⁵ Who is like the LORD our God,
who is seated on high,
⁶ who looks far down
on the heavens and the
earth?
⁷ He raises the poor from the
dust,
and lifts the needy from
the ash heap,

⁸ to make them sit with princes,
with the princes of his
people.
⁹ He gives the barren woman
a home,
making her the joyous
mother of children.
Praise the LORD!

Psalm 114

¹ When Israel went out from
Egypt,
the house of Jacob from a
people of strange
language,
² Judah became God'sᵃ
sanctuary,
Israel his dominion.

³ The sea looked and fled;
Jordan turned back.
⁴ The mountains skipped like
rams,
the hills like lambs.

⁵ Why is it, O sea, that you
flee?
O Jordan, that you turn
back?
⁶ O mountains, that you skip
like rams?
O hills, like lambs?

⁷ Tremble, O earth, at the
presence of the
LORD,
at the presence of the
God of Jacob,
⁸ who turns the rock into a pool
of water,
the flint into a spring of
water.

ᵃHeb *his*

484

Psalm 115

[1] Not to us, O LORD, not to
   us, but to your name
   give glory,
   for the sake of your
      steadfast love and
      your faithfulness.
[2] Why should the nations
      say,
   "Where is their God?"

[3] Our God is in the heavens;
   he does whatever he
      pleases.
[4] Their idols are silver and
      gold,
   the work of human hands.
[5] They have mouths, but do not
      speak;
   eyes, but do not see.
[6] They have ears, but do not
      hear;
   noses, but do not smell.
[7] They have hands, but do
      not feel;
   feet, but do not walk;
   they make no sound in
      their throats.
[8] Those who make them are
      like them;
   so are all who trust in them.

[9] O Israel, trust in the LORD!
   He is their help and
      their shield.
[10] O house of Aaron, trust in
      the LORD!
   He is their help and their
      shield.
[11] You who fear the LORD, trust
      in the LORD!
   He is their help and their
      shield.

[12] The LORD has been
      mindful of us; he will
      bless us;
   he will bless the house of
      Israel;
   he will bless the house of
      Aaron;
[13] he will bless those who fear
      the LORD,
   both small and great.

[14] May the LORD give you
      increase,
   both you and your children.
[15] May you be blessed by the
      LORD,
   who made heaven and earth.

[16] The heavens are the
      LORD's heavens,
   but the earth he has
      given to human
      beings.
[17] The dead do not praise the
      LORD,
   nor do any that go down
      into silence.
[18] But we will bless the LORD
   from this time on and
      forevermore.
   Praise the LORD!

Psalm 116

[1] I love the LORD, because he
      has heard
   my voice and my
      supplications.
[2] Because he inclined his ear
      to me,
   therefore I will call on him
      as long as I live.
[3] The snares of death
      encompassed me;

485

the pangs of Sheol laid hold
on me;
I suffered distress and
anguish.
4 Then I called on the name
of the LORD:
"O LORD, I pray, save my
life!"

5 Gracious is the LORD, and
righteous;
our God is merciful.
6 The LORD protects the simple;
when I was brought low,
he saved me.
7 Return, O my soul, to your rest,
for the LORD has dealt
bountifully with you.

8 For you have delivered my
soul from death,
my eyes from tears,
my feet from stumbling.
9 I walk before the LORD
in the land of the living.
10 I kept my faith, even when
I said,
"I am greatly afflicted";
11 I said in my consternation,
"Everyone is a liar."

12 What shall I return to the LORD
for all his bounty to me?
13 I will lift up the cup of
salvation
and call on the name of
the LORD,
14 I will pay my vows to the LORD
in the presence of all his
people.
15 Precious in the sight of the
LORD
is the death of his faithful
ones.

16 O LORD, I am your servant;
I am your servant, the child
of your serving girl.
You have loosed my bonds.
17 I will offer to you a
thanksgiving sacrifice
and call on the name of
the LORD.
18 I will pay my vows to the LORD
in the presence of all his
people,
19 in the courts of the house
of the LORD,
in your midst, O Jerusalem.
Praise the LORD!

Psalm 117

1 Praise the LORD, all you
nations!
Extol him, all you peoples!
2 For great is his steadfast
love toward us,
and the faithfulness of
the LORD endures
forever.
Praise the LORD!

Psalm 118

1 O give thanks to the LORD,
for he is good;
his steadfast love endures
forever!

2 Let Israel say,
"His steadfast love endures
forever."
3 Let the house of Aaron say,
"His steadfast love endures
forever."
4 Let those who fear the LORD
say,
"His steadfast love endures
forever."

5 Out of my distress I called on
  the LORD;
  the LORD answered me
  and set me in a broad
  place.
6 With the LORD on my side I
  do not fear.
  What can mortals do to me?
7 The LORD is on my side to
  help me;
  I shall look in triumph on
  those who hate me.
8 It is better to take refuge in
  the LORD
  than to put confidence in
  mortals.
9 It is better to take refuge in
  the LORD
  than to put confidence in
  princes.

10 All nations surrounded me;
  in the name of the LORD I
  cut them off!
11 They surrounded me,
  surrounded me on every
  side;
  in the name of the LORD
  I cut them off!
12 They surrounded me like bees;
  they blazed[a] like a fire
  of thorns;
  in the name of the LORD I
  cut them off!
13 I was pushed hard,[b] so that
  I was falling,
  but the LORD helped me.
14 The LORD is my strength
  and my might;
  he has become my salvation.

15 There are glad songs of
  victory in the tents of
  the righteous:

"The right hand of the LORD
  does valiantly;
16   the right hand of the LORD
  is exalted;
  the right hand of the LORD
  does valiantly."
17 I shall not die, but I shall
  live,
  and recount the deeds of
  the LORD.
18 The LORD has punished me
  severely,
  but he did not give me over
  to death.

19 Open to me the gates of
  righteousness,
  that I may enter through
  them
  and give thanks to the LORD.

20 This is the gate of the LORD;
  the righteous shall enter
  through it.

21 I thank you that you have
  answered me
  and have become my
  salvation.
22 The stone that the builders
  rejected
  has become the chief
  cornerstone.
23 This is the LORD's doing;
  it is marvelous in our eyes.
24 This is the day that the LORD
  has made;
  let us rejoice and be glad
  in it.[c]
25 Save us, we beseech you,
  O LORD!

---

[a]Gk: Heb were extinguished [b]Gk Syr Jerome: Heb You
pushed me hard [c]Or in him

O LORD, we beseech you,
  give us success!

26 Blessed is the one who
    comes in the name of
    the LORD.*a*
  We bless you from the
    house of the LORD.
27 The LORD is God,
    and he has given us
    light.
  Bind the festal procession
    with branches,
    up to the horns of the
    altar.*b*

28 You are my God, and I will
    give thanks to you;
  you are my God, I will
    extol you.

29 O give thanks to the LORD,
    for he is good,
  for his steadfast love
    endures forever.

Psalm 119

1 Happy are those whose way
    is blameless,
  who walk in the law of
    the LORD.
2 Happy are those who keep his
    decrees,
  who seek him with their
    whole heart,
3 who also do no wrong,
    but walk in his ways.
4 You have commanded your
    precepts
  to be kept diligently.
5 O that my ways may be
    steadfast
  in keeping your statutes!

6 Then I shall not be put to
    shame,
  having my eyes fixed on
    all your
    commandments.
7 I will praise you with an
    upright heart,
  when I learn your
    righteous ordinances.
8 I will observe your statutes;
  do not utterly forsake me.

9 How can young people keep
    their way pure?
  By guarding it according
    to your word.
10 With my whole heart I
    seek you;
  do not let me stray from
    your commandments.
11 I treasure your word in
    my heart,
  so that I may not sin
    against you.
12 Blessed are you, O LORD;
  teach me your statutes.
13 With my lips I declare
  all the ordinances of
    your mouth.
14 I delight in the way of your
    decrees
  as much as in all riches.
15 I will meditate on your
    precepts,
  and fix my eyes on your
    ways.
16 I will delight in your statutes;
  I will not forget your word.

17 Deal bountifully with your
    servant,

---

*a*Or *Blessed in the name of the LORD is the one who
comes* *b*Meaning of Heb uncertain

so that I may live and
observe your word.
18 Open my eyes, so that I
may behold
wondrous things out of
your law.
19 I live as an alien in the
land;
do not hide your
commandments from
me.
20 My soul is consumed with
longing
for your ordinances at all
times.
21 You rebuke the insolent,
accursed ones,
who wander from your
commandments;
22 take away from me their
scorn and contempt,
for I have kept your
decrees.
23 Even though princes sit
plotting against me,
your servant will meditate
on your statutes.
24 Your decrees are my delight,
they are my counselors.

25 My soul clings to the dust;
revive me according to
your word.
26 When I told of my ways,
you answered me;
teach me your statutes.
27 Make me understand the
way of your precepts,
and I will meditate on
your wondrous works.
28 My soul melts away for
sorrow;
strengthen me according
to your word.

29 Put false ways far from
me;
and graciously teach me
your law.
30 I have chosen the way of
faithfulness;
I set your ordinances
before me.
31 I cling to your decrees,
O LORD;
let me not be put to shame.
32 I run the way of your
commandments,
for you enlarge my
understanding.

33 Teach me, O LORD, the way
of your statutes,
and I will observe it to the
end.
34 Give me understanding, that
I may keep your law
and observe it with my
whole heart.
35 Lead me in the path of
your commandments,
for I delight in it.
36 Turn my heart to your decrees,
and not to selfish gain.
37 Turn my eyes from looking
at vanities;
give me life in your ways.
38 Confirm to your servant your
promise,
which is for those who fear
you.
39 Turn away the disgrace that
I dread,
for your ordinances are
good.
40 See, I have longed for your
precepts;
in your righteousness give
me life.

41 Let your steadfast love come
        to me, O LORD,
    your salvation according
        to your promise.
42 Then I shall have an answer
        for those who taunt me,
    for I trust in your word.
43 Do not take the word of truth
        utterly out of my mouth,
    for my hope is in your
        ordinances.
44 I will keep your law
        continually,
    forever and ever.
45 I shall walk at liberty,
    for I have sought your
        precepts.
46 I will also speak of your
        decrees before kings,
    and shall not be put to
        shame;
47 I find my delight in your
        commandments,
    because I love them.
48 I revere your commandments,
        which I love,
    and I will meditate on your
        statutes.

49 Remember your word to
        your servant,
    in which you have made
        me hope.
50 This is my comfort in my
        distress,
    that your promise gives
        me life.
51 The arrogant utterly deride
        me,
    but I do not turn away from
        your law.
52 When I think of your
        ordinances from of old,
    I take comfort, O LORD.

53 Hot indignation seizes me
        because of the
        wicked,
    those who forsake your
        law.
54 Your statutes have been
        my songs
    wherever I make my
        home.
55 I remember your name in the
        night, O LORD,
    and keep your law.
56 This blessing has fallen to me,
    for I have kept your
        precepts.

57 The LORD is my portion;
    I promise to keep your
        words.
58 I implore your favor with all
        my heart;
    be gracious to me
        according to your
        promise.
59 When I think of your ways,
    I turn my feet to your
        decrees;
60 I hurry and do not delay
    to keep your
        commandments.
61 Though the cords of the
        wicked ensnare me,
    I do not forget your law.
62 At midnight I rise to praise
        you,
    because of your righteous
        ordinances.
63 I am a companion of all who
        fear you,
    of those who keep your
        precepts.
64 The earth, O LORD, is full of
        your steadfast love;
    teach me your statutes.

⁶⁵ You have dealt well with
        your servant,
    O LORD, according to your
        word.
⁶⁶ Teach me good judgment
        and knowledge,
    for I believe in your
        commandments.
⁶⁷ Before I was humbled I
        went astray,
    but now I keep your
        word.
⁶⁸ You are good and do good;
    teach me your statutes.
⁶⁹ The arrogant smear me
        with lies,
    but with my whole heart
        I keep your precepts.
⁷⁰ Their hearts are fat and
        gross,
    but I delight in your law.
⁷¹ It is good for me that I
        was humbled,
    so that I might learn your
        statutes.
⁷² The law of your mouth is
        better to me
    than thousands of gold and
        silver pieces.

⁷³ Your hands have made and
        fashioned me;
    give me understanding that
        I may learn your
        commandments.
⁷⁴ Those who fear you shall see
        me and rejoice,
    because I have hoped in
        your word.
⁷⁵ I know, O LORD, that your
        judgments are right,
    and that in faithfulness
        you have humbled
        me.

⁷⁶ Let your steadfast love
        become my comfort
    according to your promise
        to your servant.
⁷⁷ Let your mercy come to me,
        that I may live;
    for your law is my delight.
⁷⁸ Let the arrogant be put to
        shame,
    because they have subverted
        me with guile;
    as for me, I will meditate on
        your precepts.
⁷⁹ Let those who fear you
        turn to me,
    so that they may know
        your decrees.
⁸⁰ May my heart be blameless
        in your statutes,
    so that I may not be put
        to shame.

⁸¹ My soul languishes for your
        salvation;
    I hope in your word.
⁸² My eyes fail with watching
        for your promise;
    I ask, "When will you
        comfort me?"
⁸³ For I have become like a
        wineskin in the smoke,
    yet I have not forgotten
        your statutes.
⁸⁴ How long must your servant
        endure?
    When will you judge those
        who persecute me?
⁸⁵ The arrogant have dug
        pitfalls for me;
    they flout your law.
⁸⁶ All your commandments
        are enduring;
    I am persecuted without
        cause; help me!

87 They have almost made an
        end of me on earth;
    but I have not forsaken
        your precepts.
88 In your steadfast love
        spare my life,
    so that I may keep the
        decrees of your
        mouth.

89 The LORD exists forever;
    your word is firmly fixed
        in heaven.
90 Your faithfulness endures
        to all generations;
    you have established the
        earth, and it stands
        fast.
91 By your appointment they
        stand today,
    for all things are your
        servants.
92 If your law had not been my
        delight,
    I would have perished in
        my misery.
93 I will never forget your
        precepts,
    for by them you have given
        me life.
94 I am yours; save me,
    for I have sought your
        precepts.
95 The wicked lie in wait to
        destroy me,
    but I consider your decrees.
96 I have seen a limit to all
        perfection,
    but your commandment is
        exceedingly broad.

97 Oh, how I love your law!
    It is my meditation all day
        long.

98 Your commandment makes
        me wiser than my
        enemies,
    for it is always with me.
99 I have more understanding
        than all my teachers,
    for your decrees are my
        meditation.
100 I understand more than the
        aged,
    for I keep your precepts.
101 I hold back my feet from
        every evil way,
    in order to keep your word.
102 I do not turn away from
        your ordinances,
    for you have taught me.
103 How sweet are your words
        to my taste,
    sweeter than honey to my
        mouth!
104 Through your precepts
        I get understanding;
    therefore I hate every
        false way.

105 Your word is a lamp to
        my feet
    and a light to my path.
106 I have sworn an oath and
        confirmed it,
    to observe your righteous
        ordinances.
107 I am severely afflicted;
    give me life, O LORD,
        according to your word.
108 Accept my offerings of praise,
        O LORD,
    and teach me your
        ordinances.
109 I hold my life in my hand
        continually,
    but I do not forget your
        law.

110 The wicked have laid a
snare for me,
   but I do not stray from your
precepts.
111 Your decrees are my
heritage forever;
   they are the joy of my heart.
112 I incline my heart to
perform your statutes
forever, to the end.

113 I hate the double-minded,
   but I love your law.
114 You are my hiding place
and my shield;
   I hope in your word.
115 Go away from me, you
evildoers,
   that I may keep the
commandments of my
God.
116 Uphold me according to
your promise, that I
may live,
   and let me not be put to
shame in my hope.
117 Hold me up, that I may
be safe
   and have regard for your
statutes continually.
118 You spurn all who go
astray from your
statutes;
   for their cunning is in
vain.
119 All the wicked of the
earth you count as
dross;
   therefore I love your
decrees.
120 My flesh trembles for fear
of you,
   and I am afraid of your
judgments.

121 I have done what is just
and right;
   do not leave me to my
oppressors.
122 Guarantee your servant's
well-being;
   do not let the godless
oppress me.
123 My eyes fail from watching
for your salvation,
   and for the fulfillment of
your righteous promise.
124 Deal with your servant
according to your
steadfast love,
   and teach me your statutes.
125 I am your servant; give me
understanding,
   so that I may know
your decrees.
126 It is time for the LORD to act,
   for your law has been
broken.
127 Truly I love your
commandments
   more than gold, more than
fine gold.
128 Truly I direct my steps by
all your precepts;[a]
   I hate every false way.

129 Your decrees are
wonderful;
   therefore my soul keeps
them.
130 The unfolding of your words
gives light;
   it imparts understanding
to the simple.
131 With open mouth I pant,
   because I long for your
commandments.

[a]Gk Jerome: Meaning of Heb uncertain

[132] Turn to me and be gracious
to me,
    as is your custom toward
    those who love your
    name.
[133] Keep my steps steady
according to your
promise,
    and never let iniquity have
    dominion over me.
[134] Redeem me from human
oppression,
    that I may keep your
    precepts.
[135] Make your face shine upon
your servant,
    and teach me your statutes.
[136] My eyes shed streams of tears
because your law is not
kept.

[137] You are righteous, O LORD,
and your judgments are
right.
[138] You have appointed your
decrees in righteousness
and in all faithfulness.
[139] My zeal consumes me
because my foes forget your
words.
[140] Your promise is well tried,
and your servant loves it.
[141] I am small and despised,
yet I do not forget your
precepts.
[142] Your righteousness is an
everlasting
righteousness,
and your law is the truth.
[143] Trouble and anguish have
come upon me,
    but your
    commandments are
    my delight.

[144] Your decrees are righteous
forever;
    give me understanding that
    I may live.

[145] With my whole heart I cry;
answer me, O LORD.
    I will keep your statutes.
[146] I cry to you; save me,
    that I may observe your
    decrees.
[147] I rise before dawn and cry
for help;
    I put my hope in your
    words.
[148] My eyes are awake before
each watch of the night,
    that I may meditate on
    your promise.
[149] In your steadfast love hear
my voice;
    O LORD, in your justice
    preserve my life.
[150] Those who persecute me
with evil purpose
draw near;
    they are far from your law.
[151] Yet you are near, O LORD,
and all your commandments
are true.
[152] Long ago I learned from
your decrees
    that you have
    established them
    forever.

[153] Look on my misery and
rescue me,
    for I do not forget your
    law.
[154] Plead my cause and
redeem me;
    give me life according to
    your promise.

155 Salvation is far from the
        wicked,
    for they do not seek
        your statutes.
156 Great is your mercy,
        O LORD;
    give me life according to
        your justice.
157 Many are my persecutors
        and my adversaries,
    yet I do not swerve from
        your decrees.
158 I look at the faithless with
        disgust,
    because they do not
        keep your
        commands.
159 Consider how I love your
        precepts;
    preserve my life according
        to your steadfast love.
160 The sum of your word is
        truth;
    and every one of your
        righteous ordinances
        endures forever.

161 Princes persecute me
        without cause,
    but my heart stands in awe
        of your words.
162 I rejoice at your word
    like one who finds great
        spoil.
163 I hate and abhor falsehood,
    but I love your law.
164 Seven times a day I praise
        you
    for your righteous
        ordinances.
165 Great peace have those who
        love your law;
    nothing can make them
        stumble.

166 I hope for your salvation,
        O LORD,
    and I fulfill your
        commandments.
167 My soul keeps your decrees;
    I love them exceedingly.
168 I keep your precepts and
        decrees,
    for all my ways are before
        you.

169 Let my cry come before you,
        O LORD;
    give me understanding
        according to your word.
170 Let my supplication come
        before you;
    deliver me according to
        your promise.
171 My lips will pour forth
        praise,
    because you teach me your
        statutes.
172 My tongue will sing of your
        promise,
    for all your commandments
        are right.
173 Let your hand be ready to
        help me,
    for I have chosen your
        precepts.
174 I long for your salvation,
        O LORD,
    and your law is my
        delight.
175 Let me live that I may
        praise you,
    and let your ordinances
        help me.
176 I have gone astray like a
        lost sheep; seek out
        your servant,
    for I do not forget your
        commandments.

Psalm 120

A Song of Ascents.

¹ In my distress I cry to the LORD,
    that he may answer me:
² "Deliver me, O LORD,
    from lying lips,
    from a deceitful tongue."

³ What shall be given to you?
    And what more shall be
        done to you,
    you deceitful tongue?
⁴ A warrior's sharp arrows,
    with glowing coals of the
        broom tree!

⁵ Woe is me, that I am an alien
        in Meshech,
    that I must live among the
        tents of Kedar.
⁶ Too long have I had my
        dwelling
    among those who hate
        peace.
⁷ I am for peace;
    but when I speak,
    they are for war.

Psalm 121

A Song of Ascents.

¹ I lift up my eyes to the hills—
    from where will my help
        come?
² My help comes from the LORD,
    who made heaven and
        earth.

³ He will not let your foot
        be moved;
    he who keeps you will
        not slumber.

⁴ He who keeps Israel
    will neither slumber nor
        sleep.

⁵ The LORD is your keeper;
    the LORD is your shade at
        your right hand.
⁶ The sun shall not strike you
        by day,
    nor the moon by night.

⁷ The LORD will keep you
        from all evil;
    he will keep your life.
⁸ The LORD will keep
    your going out and your
        coming in
    from this time on and
        forevermore.

Psalm 122

A Song of Ascents. Of David.

¹ I was glad when they said
        to me,
    "Let us go to the house of
        the LORD!"
² Our feet are standing
    within your gates,
        O Jerusalem.

³ Jerusalem—built as a city
    that is bound firmly
        together.
⁴ To it the tribes go up,
    the tribes of the LORD,
    as was decreed for Israel,
    to give thanks to the name
        of the LORD.
⁵ For there the thrones for
        judgment were set up,
    the thrones of the house
        of David.

⁶ Pray for the peace of Jerusalem:
"May they prosper who
love you.
⁷ Peace be within your walls,
and security within your
towers."
⁸ For the sake of my relatives
and friends
I will say, "Peace be
within you."
⁹ For the sake of the house of
the LORD our God,
I will seek your good.

Psalm 123

A Song of Ascents.

¹ To you I lift up my eyes,
O you who are
enthroned in the
heavens!
² As the eyes of servants
look to the hand of their
master,
as the eyes of a maid
to the hand of her
mistress,
so our eyes look to the
LORD our God,
until he has mercy upon
us.

³ Have mercy upon us, O LORD,
have mercy upon us,
for we have had more
than enough of
contempt.
⁴ Our soul has had more than
its fill
of the scorn of those who are
at ease,
of the contempt of the
proud.

Psalm 124

A Song of Ascents. Of David.

¹ If it had not been the LORD
who was on our side
—let Israel now say—
² if it had not been the LORD
who was on our side,
when our enemies attacked
us,
³ then they would have
swallowed us up alive,
when their anger was
kindled against us;
⁴ then the flood would have
swept us away,
the torrent would have
gone over us;
⁵ then over us would have
gone
the raging waters.

⁶ Blessed be the LORD,
who has not given us
as prey to their teeth.
⁷ We have escaped like a
bird
from the snare of the
fowlers;
the snare is broken,
and we have escaped.

⁸ Our help is in the name of
the LORD,
who made heaven and
earth.

Psalm 125

A Song of Ascents.

¹ Those who trust in the LORD
are like Mount
Zion,

which cannot be moved,
    but abides forever.
2 As the mountains surround
    Jerusalem,
  so the LORD surrounds his
    people,
  from this time on and
    forevermore.
3 For the scepter of wickedness
    shall not rest
  on the land allotted to the
    righteous,
  so that the righteous might
    not stretch out
  their hands to do wrong.
4 Do good, O LORD, to those
    who are good,
  and to those who are
    upright in their hearts.
5 But those who turn aside to
    their own crooked
    ways
  the LORD will lead away
    with evildoers.
  Peace be upon Israel!

Psalm 126

A Song of Ascents.

1 When the LORD restored
    the fortunes of
    Zion,[a]
  we were like those who
    dream.
2 Then our mouth was filled
    with laughter,
  and our tongue with
    shouts of joy;
  then it was said among the
    nations,
  "The LORD has done
    great things for
    them."

3 The LORD has done great
    things for us,
  and we rejoiced.
4 Restore our fortunes,
    O LORD,
  like the watercourses in
    the Negeb.
5 May those who sow in
    tears
  reap with shouts of
    joy.
6 Those who go out weeping,
  bearing the seed for
    sowing,
  shall come home with
    shouts of joy,
    carrying their sheaves.

Psalm 127

A Song of Ascents. Of Solomon.

1 Unless the LORD builds the
    house,
  those who build it labor
    in vain.
  Unless the LORD guards
    city,
  the guard keeps watch in
    the vain.
2 It is in vain that you rise
    up early
  and go late to rest,
  eating the bread of anxious
    toil;
  for he gives sleep to his
    beloved.[b]

3 Sons are indeed a heritage from
    the LORD,
  the fruit of the womb a
    reward.

---

[a]Or *brought back those who returned to Zion* [b]Or *for
he provides for his beloved during sleep*

4 Like arrows in the hand of
a warrior
are the sons of one's
youth.
5 Happy is the man who has
his quiver full of them.
He shall not be put to
shame
when he speaks with his
enemies in the gate.

Psalm 128
A Song of Ascents.

1 Happy is everyone who
fears the LORD,
who walks in his ways.
2 You shall eat the fruit of
the labor of your
hands;
you shall be happy,
and it shall go well
with you.

3 Your wife will be like a
fruitful vine
within your house;
your children will be like
olive shoots
around your table.
4 Thus shall the man be
blessed
who fears the LORD.

5 The LORD bless you from
Zion.
May you see the
prosperity of
Jerusalem
all the days of your life.
6 May you see your
children's children.
Peace be upon Israel!

Psalm 129
A Song of Ascents.

1 "Often have they attacked
me from my youth"
—let Israel now say—
2 "often have they attacked
me from my youth,
yet they have not
prevailed against me.
3 The plowers plowed on my
back;
they made their furrows
long."
4 The LORD is righteous;
he has cut the cords of
the wicked.
5 May all who hate Zion
be put to shame and
turned backward.
6 Let them be like the grass
on the housetops
that withers before it
grows up,
7 with which reapers do not
fill their hands
or binders of sheaves their
arms,
8 while those who pass by do
not say,
"The blessing of the LORD
be upon you!
We bless you in the name
of the LORD!"

Psalm 130
A Song of Ascents.

1 Out of the depths I cry to you,
O LORD.
2 Lord, hear my voice!
Let your ears be attentive
to the voice of my
supplications!

3 If you, O LORD, should
        mark iniquities,
    Lord, who could stand?
4 But there is forgiveness
        with you,
    so that you may be revered.

5 I wait for the LORD, my
        soul waits,
    and in his word I hope;
6 my soul waits for the Lord
        more than those who
        watch for the morning,
    more than those who
        watch for the morning.

7 O Israel, hope in the LORD!
    For with the LORD there
        is steadfast love,
    and with him is great
        power to redeem.
8 It is he who will redeem
        Israel
    from all its iniquities.

Psalm 131

A Song of Ascents. Of David.

1 O LORD, my heart is not
        lifted up,
    my eyes are not raised
        too high;
    I do not occupy myself
        with things
    too great and too
        marvelous for me.
2 But I have calmed and
        quieted my soul,
    like a weaned child with
        its mother;
    my soul is like the
        weaned child that is
        with me.[a]

3 O Israel, hope in the LORD
    from this time on and
        forevermore.

Psalm 132

A Song of Ascents.

1 O LORD, remember in
        David's favor
    all the hardships he
        endured;
2 how he swore to the LORD
    and vowed to the Mighty
        One of Jacob,
3 "I will not enter my house
    or get into my bed;
4 I will not give sleep to my
        eyes
    or slumber to my eyelids,
5 until I find a place for the LORD,
    a dwelling place for the
        Mighty One of
        Jacob."

6 We heard of it in
        Ephrathah;
    we found it in the fields
        of Jaar.
7 "Let us go to his dwelling
        place;
    let us worship at his
        footstool."

8 Rise up, O LORD, and go to
        your resting place,
    you and the ark of your
        might.
9 Let your priests be clothed
        with righteousness,
    and let your faithful
        shout for joy.

---

[a] Or *my soul within me is like a weaned child*

¹⁰ For your servant David's
sake
do not turn away the
face of your anointed
one.

¹¹ The LORD swore to David
a sure oath
from which he will not
turn back:
"One of the sons of your
body
I will set on your throne.
¹² If your sons keep my
covenant
and my decrees that I
shall teach them,
their sons also,
forevermore,
shall sit on your throne."

¹³ For the LORD has chosen
Zion;
he has desired it for his
habitation:
¹⁴ "This is my resting place
forever;
here I will reside, for I
have desired it.
¹⁵ I will abundantly bless its
provisions;
I will satisfy its poor
with bread.
¹⁶ Its priests I will clothe with
salvation,
and its faithful will shout
for joy.
¹⁷ There I will cause a horn
to sprout up for
David;
I have prepared a lamp
for my anointed one.
¹⁸ His enemies I will clothe
with disgrace,

but on him, his crown
will gleam."

Psalm 133

A Song of Ascents.

¹ How very good and
pleasant it is
when kindred live
together in unity!
² It is like the precious oil on
the head,
running down upon the
beard,
on the beard of Aaron,
running down over
the collar of his
robes.
³ It is like the dew of
Hermon,
which falls on the
mountains of Zion.
For there the LORD
ordained his
blessing,
life forevermore.

Psalm 134

A Song of Ascents.

¹ Come, bless the LORD, all
you servants of the
LORD,
who stand by night in
the house of the
LORD!
² Lift up your hands to the
holy place,
and bless the LORD.

³ May the LORD, maker of
heaven and earth,
bless you from Zion.

Psalm 135

1 Praise the LORD!
   Praise the name of the
      LORD;
      give praise, O servants of
         the LORD,
2 you that stand in the house
      of the LORD,
      in the courts of the house
         of our God.
3 Praise the LORD, for the
      LORD is good;
      sing to his name, for he
         is gracious.
4 For the LORD has chosen
      Jacob for himself,
      Israel as his own
         possession.

5 For I know that the LORD
      is great;
      our LORD is above all gods.
6 Whatever the LORD pleases
      he does,
      in heaven and on earth,
      in the seas and all deeps.
7 He it is who makes the
      clouds rise at the end
         of the earth;
      he makes lightnings for
         the rain
      and brings out the wind
         from his storehouses.

8 He it was who struck down
      the firstborn of
         Egypt,
      both human beings and
         animals;
9 he sent signs and wonders
      into your midst, O Egypt,
      against Pharaoh and all
         his servants.

10 He struck down many nations
      and killed mighty
         kings—
11 Sihon, king of the
      Amorites,
      and Og, king of Bashan,
      and all the kingdoms of
         Canaan—
12 and gave their land as a
      heritage,
      a heritage to his people
         Israel.

13 Your name, O LORD,
      endures forever,
      your renown, O LORD,
         throughout all ages.
14 For the LORD will vindicate
      his people,
      and have compassion on
         his servants.

15 The idols of the nations are
      silver and gold,
      the work of human
         hands.
16 They have mouths, but
      they do not speak;
      they have eyes, but they
         do not see;
17 they have ears, but they do
      not hear,
      and there is no breath in
         their mouths.
18 Those who make them
      and all who trust them
      shall become like them.

19 O house of Israel, bless the
      LORD!
      O house of Aaron, bless
         the LORD!
20 O house of Levi, bless the
      LORD!

You that fear the LORD,
    bless the LORD!
21 Blessed be the LORD from
        Zion,
    he who resides in
        Jerusalem.
    Praise the LORD!

Psalm 136

1 O give thanks to the LORD,
        for he is good,
    for his steadfast love
        endures forever.
2 O give thanks to the God of
        gods,
    for his steadfast love
        endures forever.
3 O give thanks to the Lord
        of lords,
    for his steadfast love
        endures forever;

4 who alone does great
        wonders,
    for his steadfast love
        endures forever;
5 who by understanding
        made the heavens,
    for his steadfast love
        endures forever;
6 who spread out the earth
        on the waters,
    for his steadfast love
        endures forever;
7 who made the great lights,
    for his steadfast love
        endures forever;
8 the sun to rule over the
        day,
    for his steadfast love
        endures forever;
9 the moon and stars to rule
        over the night,

for his steadfast love
        endures forever;

10 who struck Egypt through
        their firstborn,
    for his steadfast love
        endures forever;
11 and brought Israel out
        from among them,
    for his steadfast love
        endures forever;
12 with a strong hand and an
        outstretched arm,
    for his steadfast love
        endures forever;
13 who divided the Red Sea[a]
        in two,
    for his steadfast love
        endures forever;
14 and made Israel pass
        through the midst of
        it,
    for his steadfast love
        endures forever;
15 but overthrew Pharaoh and
        his army in the Red
        Sea,[a]
    for his steadfast love
        endures forever;
16 who led his people through
        the wilderness,
    for his steadfast love
        endures forever;
17 who struck down great
        kings,
    for his steadfast love
        endures forever;
18 and killed famous kings,
    for his steadfast love
        endures forever;
19 Sihon, king of the
        Amorites,

[a]Or Sea of Reeds

for his steadfast love
endures forever;
20 and Og, king of Bashan,
for his steadfast love
endures forever;
21 and gave their land as a
heritage,
for his steadfast love
endures forever;
22 a heritage to his servant
Israel,
for his steadfast love
endures forever.

23 It is he who remembered
us in our low estate,
for his steadfast love
endures forever;
24 and rescued us from our
foes,
for his steadfast love
endures forever;
25 who gives food to all flesh,
for his steadfast love
endures forever.

26 O give thanks to the God
of heaven,
for his steadfast love
endures forever.

Psalm 137

1 By the rivers of Babylon—
there we sat down and
there we wept
when we remembered
Zion.
2 On the willows[a] there
we hung up our harps.
3 For there our captors
asked us for songs,
and our tormentors asked
for mirth, saying,

"Sing us one of the songs
of Zion!"

4 How could we sing the
LORD's song
in a foreign land?
5 If I forget you,
O Jerusalem,
let my right hand wither!
6 Let my tongue cling to the
roof of my mouth,
if I do not remember
you,
if I do not set Jerusalem
above my highest joy.

7 Remember, O LORD,
against the
Edomites
the day of Jerusalem's
fall,
how they said, "Tear it
down! Tear it down!
Down to its
foundations!"
8 O daughter Babylon, you
devastator![b]
Happy shall they be who
pay you back
what you have done to us!
9 Happy shall they be who
take your little ones
and dash them against
the rock!

Psalm 138

Of David.

1 I give you thanks, O LORD,
with my whole heart;
before the gods I sing
your praise;

---

[a]Or *poplars* [b]Or *you who are devastated*

504

2 I bow down toward your
holy temple
and give thanks to your
name for your
steadfast love and
your faithfulness;
for you have exalted
your name and your
word
above everything.[a]
3 On the day I called, you
answered me,
you increased my
strength of soul.[b]

4 All the kings of the earth
shall praise you,
O LORD,
for they have heard the
words of your mouth.
5 They shall sing of the ways
of the LORD,
for great is the glory of
the LORD.
6 For though the LORD is
high, he regards the
lowly;
but the haughty he
perceives from far
away.

7 Though I walk in the midst
of trouble,
you preserve me against
the wrath of my
enemies;
you stretch out your hand,
and your right hand
delivers me.
8 The LORD will fulfill his
purpose for me;
your steadfast love,
O LORD, endures
forever.

Do not forsake the work
of your hands.

Psalm 139

*To the leader. Of David.
A Psalm.*

1 O LORD, you have searched
me and known me.
2 You know when I sit down
and when I rise up;
you discern my thoughts
from far away.
3 You search out my path
and my lying down,
and are acquainted with
all my ways.
4 Even before a word is on
my tongue,
O LORD, you know it
completely.
5 You hem me in, behind and
before,
and lay your hand upon me.
6 Such knowledge is too
wonderful for me;
it is so high that I cannot
attain it.

7 Where can I go from your
spirit?
Or where can I flee from
your presence?
8 If I ascend to heaven, you
are there;
if I make my bed in
Sheol, you are there.
9 If I take the wings of the
morning
and settle at the farthest
limits of the sea,

[a]Cn: Heb *you have exalted your word above all your
name* [b]Syr Compare Gk Tg: Heb *you made me arrogant in my soul with strength*

10 even there your hand shall
        lead me,
    and your right hand shall
        hold me fast.
11 If I say, "Surely the
        darkness shall cover
        me,
    and the light around me
        become night,"
12 even the darkness is not
        dark to you;
    the night is as bright as
        the day,
    for darkness is as light to
        you.

13 For it was you who formed
        my inward parts;
    you knit me together in
        my mother's womb.
14 I praise you, for I am
        fearfully and
        wonderfully made.
    Wonderful are your
        works;
    that I know very well.
15   My frame was not
        hidden from you,
    when I was being made in
        secret,
    intricately woven in the
        depths of the earth.
16 Your eyes beheld my
        unformed substance.
    In your book were written
    all the days that were
        formed for me,
    when none of them as
        yet existed.
17 How weighty to me are
        your thoughts,
        O God!
    How vast is the sum
        of them!

18 I try to count them—they
        are more than the
        sand;
    I come to the end[a]—I
        am still with you.

19 O that you would kill the
        wicked, O God,
    and that the bloodthirsty
        would depart from
        me—
20 those who speak of you
        maliciously,
    and lift themselves up
        against you for evil![b]
21 Do I not hate those who
        hate you, O LORD?
    And do I not loathe those
        who rise up against
        you?
22 I hate them with perfect
        hatred;
    I count them my
        enemies.
23 Search me, O God, and
        know my heart;
    test me and know my
        thoughts.
24 See if there is any wicked[c]
        way in me,
    and lead me in the way
        everlasting.[d]

Psalm 140

To the leader. A Psalm of David.

1 Deliver me, O LORD, from
        evildoers;
    protect me from those
        who are violent,

---

[a]Or *I awake* [b]Cn: Meaning of Heb uncertain [c]Heb
hurtful [d]Or *the ancient way.* Compare Jer 6.16

² who plan evil things in
their minds
and stir up wars
continually.
³ They make their tongue
sharp as a snake's,
and under their lips is
the venom of vipers.
Selah

⁴ Guard me, O Lᴏʀᴅ, from
the hands of the wicked;
protect me from the
violent
who have planned my
downfall.
⁵ The arrogant have hidden a
trap for me,
and with cords they have
spread a net,ᵃ
along the road they have
set snares for me.
Selah

⁶ I say to the Lᴏʀᴅ, "You are
my God;
give ear, O Lᴏʀᴅ, to the
voice of my
supplications."
⁷ O Lᴏʀᴅ, my Lord, my
strong deliverer,
you have covered my
head in the day of battle.
⁸ Do not grant, O Lᴏʀᴅ, the
desires of the wicked;
do not further their evil
plot.ᵇ   *Selah*

⁹ Those who surround me lift
up their heads;ᶜ
let the mischief of their
lips overwhelm them!
¹⁰ Let burning coals fall on
them!

Let them be flung into
pits, no more to rise!
¹¹ Do not let the slanderer
be established in the
land;
let evil speedily hunt
down the violent!

¹² I know that the Lᴏʀᴅ
maintains the cause
of the needy,
and executes justice for
the poor.
¹³ Surely the righteous shall
give thanks to your
name;
the upright shall live in
your presence.

Psalm 141

A Psalm of David.

¹ I call upon you, O Lord;
come quickly to me;
give ear to my voice
when I call to you.
² Let my prayer be counted
as incense before
you,
and the lifting up of my
hands as an evening
sacrifice.

³ Set a guard over my
mouth, O Lᴏʀᴅ;
keep watch over the door
of my lips.
⁴ Do not turn my heart to
any evil,

ᵃOr *they have spread cords as a net* ᵇHeb adds *they
are exalted* ᶜCn Compare Gk; Heb *those who surround me are uplifted in head*; Heb divides verses 8
and 9 differently

507

to busy myself with
wicked deeds
in company with those who
work iniquity;
do not let me eat of their
delicacies.

5 Let the righteous strike me;
let the faithful correct
me.
Never let the oil of the
wicked anoint my
head,[a]
for my prayer is
continually[b] against
their wicked deeds.
6 When they are given over
to those who shall
condemn them,
then they shall learn that
my words were
pleasant.
7 Like a rock that one breaks
apart and shatters on
the land,
so shall their bones be
strewn at the mouth
of Sheol.[c]

8 But my eyes are turned
toward you, O God,
my LORD;
in you I seek refuge; do
not leave me
defenseless.
9 Keep me from the trap that
they have laid for
me,
and from the snares of
evildoers.
10 Let the wicked fall into
their own nets,
while I alone escape.

Psalm 142

*A Maskil of David. When he
was in the cave. A Prayer.*

1 With my voice I cry to the
LORD;
with my voice I make
supplication to the
LORD.
2 I pour out my complaint
before him;
I tell my trouble before
him.
3 When my spirit is faint,
you know my way.

In the path where I walk
they have hidden a trap
for me.
4 Look on my right hand and
see—
there is no one who
takes notice of me;
no refuge remains to me;
no one cares for me.

5 I cry to you, O LORD;
I say, "You are my refuge,
my portion in the land of
the living."
6 Give heed to my cry,
for I am brought very low.

Save me from my
persecutors,
for they are too strong
for me.
7 Bring me out of prison,
so that I may give thanks
to your name.

[a]Gk: Meaning of Heb uncertain [b]Cn: Heb *for continually and my prayer* [c]Meaning of Heb of verses 5-7 is uncertain

The righteous will
 surround me,
for you will deal
 bountifully with me.

Psalm 143

A Psalm of David.

1 Hear my prayer, O LORD;
 give ear to my
  supplications in your
  faithfulness;
 answer me in your
  righteousness.
2 Do not enter into judgment
  with your servant,
 for no one living is
  righteous before you.

3 For the enemy has pursued me,
  crushing my life to the
  ground,
 making me sit in
  darkness like those
  long dead.
4 Therefore my spirit faints
  within me;
 my heart within me
  is appalled.

5 I remember the days of old,
 I think about all your
  deeds,
 I meditate on the works
  of your hands.
6 I stretch out my hands to you;
 my soul thirsts for you
  like a parched land.
            Selah

7 Answer me quickly,
  O LORD;
 my spirit fails.

Do not hide your face from
  me,
 or I shall be like those
  who go down to the
  Pit.
8 Let me hear of your
  steadfast love in the
  morning,
 for in you I put my trust.
Teach me the way I should
  go,
 for to you I lift up my
  soul.

9 Save me, O LORD, from my
  enemies;
 I have fled to you for
  refuge.[a]
10 Teach me to do your will,
 for you are my God.
Let your good spirit lead
  me
 on a level path.

11 For your name's sake,
  O LORD, preserve my
  life.
In your righteousness
  bring me out of
  trouble.
12 In your steadfast love cut
  off my enemies,
 and destroy all my
  adversaries,
 for I am your servant.

Psalm 144

Of David.

1 Blessed be the LORD, my
  rock,
 who trains my hands for

[a]One Heb Ms Gk: MT *to you I have hidden*

509

war, and my fingers
    for battle;
[2] my rock[a] and my fortress,
    my stronghold and my
        deliverer,
my shield, in whom I take
        refuge,
who subdues the
        peoples[b] under me.

[3] O LORD, what are human
        beings that you
        regard them,
    or mortals that you think
        of them?
[4] They are like a breath;
    their days are like a
        passing shadow.

[5] Bow your heavens,
        O LORD, and come
        down;
    touch the mountains so
        that they smoke.
[6] Make the lightning flash
        and scatter them;
    send out your arrows
        and rout them.
[7] Stretch out your hand from
        on high;
    set me free and rescue
        me from the mighty
        waters,
    from the hand of aliens,
[8] whose mouths speak lies,
    and whose right hands
        are false.

[9] I will sing a new song to
        you, O God;
    upon a ten-stringed harp
        I will play to you,
[10] the one who gives victory
        to kings,

who rescues his servant
        David.
[11] Rescue me from the cruel
        sword,
    and deliver me from
        the hand of aliens,
    whose mouths speak lies,
    and whose right hands
        are false.

[12] May our sons in their youth
        be like plants full grown,
    our daughters like corner
        pillars,
        cut for the building of a
        palace.
[13] May our barns be filled,
        with produce of every kind;
    may our sheep increase by
        thousands,
        by tens of thousands in
        our fields,
[14]   and may our cattle be
        heavy with young.
    May there be no breach in
        the walls,[c] no exile,
    and no cry of distress in
        our streets.

[15] Happy are the people to
        whom such blessings
        fall;
    happy are the people
        whose God is the LORD.

Psalm 145
Praise. Of David.

[1] I will extol you, my God
        and King,

[a]With 18.2 and 2 Sam 22.2: Heb *my steadfast love*
[b]Heb Mss Syr Aquila Jerome: MT *my people* [c]Heb
lacks *in the walls*

and bless your name
  forever and ever.
[2] Every day I will bless you,
  and praise your name
  forever and ever.
[3] Great is the LORD, and
  greatly to be praised;
  his greatness is
  unsearchable.

[4] One generation shall laud
  your works to
  another,
  and shall declare your
  mighty acts.
[5] On the glorious splendor of
  your majesty,
  and on your wondrous
  works, I will
  meditate.
[6] The might of your
  awesome deeds shall
  be proclaimed,
  and I will declare your
  greatness.
[7] They shall celebrate the
  fame of your
  abundant goodness,
  and shall sing aloud of
  your righteousness.

[8] The LORD is gracious and
  merciful,
  slow to anger and
  abounding in
  steadfast love.
[9] The LORD is good to all,
  and his compassion is
  over all that he has
  made.

[10] All your works shall give
  thanks to you,
  O LORD,

and all your faithful shall
  bless you.
[11] They shall speak of the
  glory of your
  kingdom,
  and tell of your power,
[12] to make known to all
  people your[a] mighty
  deeds,
  and the glorious splendor
  of your[b] kingdom.
[13] Your kingdom is an
  everlasting kingdom,
  and your dominion
  endures throughout
  all generations.

The LORD is faithful in all
  his words,
  and gracious in all his
  deeds.[c]
[14] The LORD upholds all who
  are falling,
  and raises up all who are
  bowed down.
[15] The eyes of all look to you,
  and you give them their
  food in due season.
[16] You open your hand,
  satisfying the desire of
  every living thing.
[17] The LORD is just in all his
  ways,
  and kind in all his
  doings.
[18] The LORD is near to all
  who call on him,
  to all who call on him in
  truth.
[19] He fulfills the desire of all
  who fear him;

---

[a]Gk Jerome Syr: Heb *his* [b]Heb *his* [c]These two lines
supplied by Q Ms Gk Syr

he also hears their cry,
and saves them.
²⁰ The LORD watches over all
who love him,
but all the wicked he will
destroy.

²¹ My mouth will speak the
praise of the LORD,
and all flesh will bless
his holy name
forever and ever.

Psalm 146

¹ Praise the LORD!
Praise the LORD,
O my soul!
² I will praise the LORD as
long as I live;
I will sing praises to my
God all my life long.

³ Do not put your trust in
princes,
in mortals, in whom
there is no help.
⁴ When their breath departs,
they return to the
earth;
on that very day their
plans perish.

⁵ Happy are those whose
help is the God of
Jacob,
whose hope is in the
LORD their God,
⁶ who made heaven and earth,
the sea, and all that is in
them;
who keeps faith forever;
⁷ who executes justice for
the oppressed;

who gives food to the
hungry.

The LORD sets the
prisoners free;
⁸ the LORD opens the eyes
of the blind.
The LORD lifts up those
who are bowed
down;
the LORD loves the
righteous.
⁹ The LORD watches over the
strangers;
he upholds the orphan
and the widow,
but the way of the
wicked he brings to
ruin.

¹⁰ The LORD will reign
forever,
your God, O Zion, for all
generations.
Praise the LORD!

Psalm 147

¹ Praise the LORD!
How good it is to sing
praises to our God;
for he is gracious, and a
song of praise is fitting.
² The LORD builds up
Jerusalem;
he gathers the outcasts
of Israel.
³ He heals the
brokenhearted,
and binds up their wounds.
⁴ He determines the number
of the stars;
he gives to all of them
their names.

⁵ Great is our Lord, and
        abundant in power;
    his understanding is
        beyond measure.
⁶ The Lord lifts up the
        downtrodden;
    he casts the wicked to
        the ground.

⁷ Sing to the Lord with
        thanksgiving;
    make melody to our God
        on the lyre.
⁸ He covers the heavens with
        clouds,
    prepares rain for the
        earth,
    makes grass grow on the
        hills.
⁹ He gives to the animals
        their food,
    and to the young ravens
        when they cry.
¹⁰ His delight is not in the
        strength of the horse,
    nor his pleasure in the
        speed of a runner;ᵃ
¹¹ but the Lord takes
        pleasure in those
        who fear him,
    in those who hope in his
        steadfast love.

¹² Praise the Lord,
        O Jerusalem!
    Praise your God, O Zion!
¹³ For he strengthens the bars
        of your gates;
    he blesses your children
        within you.
¹⁴ He grants peaceᵇ within
        your borders;
    he fills you with the
        finest of wheat.

¹⁵ He sends out his command
        to the earth;
    his word runs swiftly.
¹⁶ He gives snow like wool;
    he scatters frost like ashes.
¹⁷ He hurls down hail like
        crumbs—
    who can stand before his
        cold?
¹⁸ He sends out his word, and
        melts them;
    he makes his wind blow,
        and the waters flow.
¹⁹ He declares his word to
        Jacob,
    his statutes and
        ordinances to Israel.
²⁰ He has not dealt thus with
        any other nation;
    they do not know his
        ordinances.
    Praise the Lord!

Psalm 148

¹ Praise the Lord!
Praise the Lord from the
        heavens;
    praise him in the
        heights!
² Praise him, all his angels;
    praise him, all his host!

³ Praise him, sun and moon;
    praise him, all you
        shining stars!
⁴ Praise him, you highest
        heavens,
    and you waters above
        the heavens!

⁵ Let them praise the name
        of the Lord,

ᵃHeb legs of a person ᵇOr prosperity

for he commanded and
they were created.
⁶ He established them
forever and ever;
he fixed their bounds,
which cannot be
passed.ᵃ

⁷ Praise the LORD from the
earth,
you sea monsters and all
deeps,
⁸ fire and hail, snow and
frost,
stormy wind fulfilling his
command!

⁹ Mountains and all hills,
fruit trees and all cedars!
¹⁰ Wild animals and all cattle,
creeping things and
flying birds!

¹¹ Kings of the earth and all
peoples,
princes and all rulers of
the earth!
¹² Young men and women
alike,
old and young together!

¹³ Let them praise the name
of the LORD,
for his name alone is
exalted;
his glory is above earth
and heaven.
¹⁴ He has raised up a horn
for his people,
praise for all his
faithful,
for the people of Israel
who are close to him.
Praise the LORD!

Psalm 149

¹ Praise the LORD!
Sing to the LORD a new
song,
his praise in the
assembly of the
faithful.
² Let Israel be glad in its
Maker;
let the children of Zion
rejoice in their King.
³ Let them praise his name
with dancing,
making melody to him
with tambourine and
lyre.
⁴ For the LORD takes
pleasure in his
people;
he adorns the humble
with victory.
⁵ Let the faithful exult in
glory;
let them sing for joy on
their couches.
⁶ Let the high praises of God
be in their throats
and two-edged swords
in their hands,
⁷ to execute vengeance on
the nations
and punishment on the
peoples,
⁸ to bind their kings with
fetters
and their nobles with
chains of iron,
⁹ to execute on them the
judgment decreed.
This is glory for all his
faithful ones.
Praise the LORD!

ᵃOr *he set a law that cannot pass away*

514

Psalm 150

1 Praise the LORD!
  Praise God in his
        sanctuary;
      praise him in his mighty
        firmament![a]
2 Praise him for his mighty
        deeds;
      praise him according to
        his surpassing
        greatness!

3 Praise him with trumpet
        sound;
      praise him with lute and
        harp!

4 Praise him with tambourine
        and dance;
      praise him with strings
        and pipe!
5 Praise him with clanging
        cymbals;
      praise him with loud
        clashing cymbals!
6 Let everything that
        breathes praise the
        LORD!
      Praise the LORD!

[a]Or *dome*

THE ESSENTIALS FOR LEADING A PERSON TO CHRIST

1. What does it mean to share Christian faith with others?

Sharing Christian faith means spreading the good news of the kingdom of God by word, deed, and sign through the power of the Holy Spirit, and then waiting and watching in respectful humility and working in expectant hope.

Mark 1:15   Romans 15:18–19
Luke 9:1–2

2. Who is responsible for sharing faith with others?

Each Christian is called to be a witness to Christ in the particular situation in which he or she lives. Each disciple of Jesus Christ is called to declare the wonderful deeds of God

1 Peter 2:9–10

3. What are the primary concerns in effective witnessing?

Most persons become disciples of Christ because of the testimony, deeds, and encouragement of someone they trust. Therefore, two primary concerns of the faith-sharer are: (1) knowing and experiencing the basics and (2) building a relationship of trust with the other person.

4. What are some essential principles that guide us in witnessing?

  a. The person witnessing must be clear regarding his or her purpose. Our initial responsibility is to love the other person even as we have been loved by God. Our ultimate purpose is to share the gospel, to offer Christ out of love for the person and in obedience to the command of Christ.

b. Faith-sharing must be grounded in prayer.
   - To pray for someone is to love deeply the other person.
   - When we talk to God about persons, we will talk with persons about God.

c. In sharing faith, listening opens the door to speaking. Listening to God is an essential in prayer, and listening to others is a requirement in witnessing. Testimony begins not in our speaking, but in our hearing. Genuinely loving and caring for others and hearing their story precedes our telling our faith story. The faith-sharer prays, "O Lord, make me a good listener."

d. The witness takes both the person and the person's *environment* seriously. Faith-sharing always begins by genuinely caring for the person and, as much as possible, entering into the person's situation. This is precisely what Jesus did. He spoke to people in their language and with their symbols. He spoke of salt, soil, seeds, flowers, birds, foxes, shepherds and sheep, bread and wine. Jesus took seriously each person and used language appropriate to the individual and to the individual's situation. To fishermen, he said "Follow me and I will make you fish for people" (Mark 1:17); to the woman at the well, "Those who drink of the water that I will give them will never be thirsty" (see John 4:7–15). In witnessing, an essential principle is to start where the other person is in his or her experience.

e. In faith-sharing, it is better for the witness to make invitational statements rather than to ask questions. An invitational statement is an expression of fact or an observation that has the seed of a question within it. Although sometimes questions are helpful, they can build resistance in the other person if they are perceived as "nosey" or "pushy." For example, it is better to say, "It is difficult to be separated from loved ones." than to ask, "Are you lonely?" This is an observation that invites the other person to respond. Trust develops as the witness is invited into the other person's life. Our purpose is to develop a relationship of trust in which we can genuinely share faith. It is better to ask questions after statements of personal testimony than before them. This method is illustrated by Paul when he gives testimony and bears witness before King Agrippa (Acts 26:2–32). This method is rooted in the God of grace, who acts in graciousness toward God's creation first and invites persons to respond in faith and love.

f. To do the mission of Christ, one must have the mind of Christ. "Let the same mind be in you that was in Christ Jesus" (Philippians 2:5)

g. In sharing a testimony, it is better to expose our vulnerability than to pretend invulnerability. We do not have to pose as authorities on religion. It is okay to say, "I don't know." We need to listen with passion and not become argumentative. God is far more interested in our availability than in our ability. We do not trust the method, but the power of the Holy Spirit to use our honest sharing of faith.

h. In faith-sharing we do not tell people why or what they should believe; we share why and what we believe. Especially, we share the One in whom we trust.

i. A witness refrains from being judgmental, accusative, or defensive. A witness tells what he or she has seen, knows, or has experienced. In faith-sharing, one is committed to sharing the good news of Christ with others.

j. Witnessing is most effective when it is done in the first person. It is better to make "I" statements than "You" statements. That is, one does not say "You ought" or "You should. . . ." Instead, say "for me," or "In Christ, I have . . ." or "With Jesus, I know. . . ."

(Note: For further details and skills in these principles, read the *Faith-Sharing* text and view the *Faith-Sharing* video by Fox and Morris.)

5. What are some important points in giving a personal testimony?

- what Jesus Christ means to me

- what my life was like before accepting Jesus Christ

- how I became aware that I needed Christ and how Christ meets my basic needs

- who influenced me most to accept Christ as my Lord and Savior

- how I came to trust Christ Jesus as my Lord and Savior

- how I discovered ways of serving in the name of Jesus in the world

6. What is a *graceful* pattern of inviting a person to receive Jesus Christ as Lord and Savior?

As the Holy Spirit works in the life of the witness and also in the life of the other person, it is necessary for the person witnessing to be always alert to the opportunity to offer Christ, to share the good news, and to invite the other person to respond. The following is a *grace*ful pattern for sharing the good news and assisting persons in receiving Christ.

This **grace**ful pattern involves:

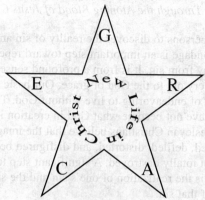

(copyright, 1995, H. Eddie Fox and George Morris)[1]

- **G** = *God's Grace in Christ Jesus for All*
  God's Grace in Creation
  God's Grace in Redemption
  God's Grace in Hope and Eternity

Helping a person become aware of God's grace for all people and God's continuing desire for a relationship of wholeness with humanity and creation is a significant step toward establishing a relationship with God.

Helping a person discover that God's grace is for all (even for me) is a major step toward "being saved."

Matthew 11:28–30   Romans 5:6–8
Luke 15   2 Corinthians 5:17
John 3:16–17   Ephesians 2:4–10
Acts 10:36–43

(Note: See "Basics," questions 9 and 10.)

- **R** = *Recognizing and Repenting of Sin*
  Receiving Salvation in Christ
  Responding in Trust
  Reconciling Grace, Being Put Right with God
  Through the Atoning Blood of Jesus Christ

Helping persons to discover the reality of sin and its resulting bondage is an important step toward repenting or turning away from sin. It is from a profound sense of need that people cry out to the God of grace. Our basic alienation is the result of endeavoring to live without God. The tragedy is that we have not become what God in creation intended us to be. Wesleyan Christians believe that the image of God was damaged, defiled, distorted, and disfigured because of sin—but not totally destroyed. A significant step to responding in trust is the realization of one's sin and the subsequent repenting of that sin.

Psalm 51
Mark 1:15
Romans 3:9–18, 23; 4:4–5; 6:23; 7:18, 24

Ephesians 2:8–9
Titus 3:5
James 4:1–3

(Note: see "Basics," questions 7 and 8.)

- **A** = *Accepting God's Forgiveness*
  Acknowledging Christ Jesus as Lord and Savior
  Assurance Through the Witness of the Holy Spirit
  Awareness of the Continuing Grace of God

Helping persons come to accept God's forgiveness is a key part of the process of being saved. Through Christ the grace of God is accessible to all. Indeed, the heart of the gospel is:

For God so loved the world that he gave his only Son, so that everyone who believes in him may not perish but may have eternal life (John 3:16).

The work of atonement (at-one-ment), made possible through the life, death, and resurrection of Jesus Christ, is for the whole world. Through acceptance of this grace, we can know forgiveness of sin and experience the restoration of the image of God in our lives.

Matthew 26:28
Acts 4:14; 16:29–31
Romans 5:1, 8; 8:31–39
2 Corinthians 5:14–18; 8:9
Colossians 2:11–15

Philippians 2:5–11
James 2:14–26
1 Peter 2:24; 3:18
1 John 2:1–2

(Note: See "Basics," questions 4 and 5.)

Closely related to helping the seeker take this step of acceptance is helping the seeker to experience the assurance of being in a right relationship with God. Here the Holy Spirit bears witness with the human heart that we are forgiven. Through the Spirit, love lives in our hearts and is reflected in our lives. Through the witness of the Holy Spirit, we can know that we are accepted by God. The sources of Christian assurance are rooted in these scriptures:

The witness of God's Word:

John 5:24; 6:37
Romans 10:9–10

Colossians 1:21–23b
1 John 1:9

The witness of the Holy Spirit:

Romans 8:14–16
2 Corinthians 1:22

Galatians 4:6
1 John 3:24

The witness of the human heart:

2 Timothy 1:12   1 John 3:18–19

In Christ, we can know the forgiveness of sin, and we are given the power to live a victorious life. Through the Spirit, love reigns in our hearts and is reflected in our lives. Through the witness of the Holy Spirit, we can know that we are accepted by God.

John 10:27–30	2 Timothy 2:11–13
Romans 8:14–17, 31–39	Hebrews 10:23–25
Galatians 5:19–23	1 John 1:5–2:6

(Note: See "Basics," question 19.)

- **C** = *Confessing Faith in Christ Jesus*
  Committing in Trust to Christ Jesus
  Commencing the Way of Christ
  Continuing the Walk with Christ

In order to appropriate the benefits of Christ's atoning work in grace, the faith-sharer helps each person by faith to confess Christ Jesus as Lord and personal Savior. Although God's saving grace is intended for all, it is not irresistible. We are created in the image of God with freedom of choice, and God will not violate our nature, even to save us. We cannot redeem ourselves, but neither can we be saved without ourselves. God alone is the giver of grace and salvation, and by the grace of God we may choose to accept the gift of salvation, or we may refuse to accept the gift when it is offered.

The faith-sharer helps a seeker confess faith in Christ. We seek to help persons put trust in Christ (John 3:6) and receive him (John 1:12).

There comes a time in the faith-sharing process when the seeker is invited to say yes to the invitation of Christ. Here is an example of a thanksgiving prayer that a faith-sharer may lead a seeker to pray in confessing faith in Jesus Christ:

Dear God, I thank you that you know me and love me. I have sinned. I have tried to live by my own strength. I have not followed your will for me. Thank you deeply that while I was still a sinner Christ Jesus died for me. By your grace I repent and turn from my sin, and by your grace I accept your forgiveness. By your grace, I confess Jesus Christ as my Lord and Savior. Through the power of the Holy Spirit, enable me to live a faithful life in your kingdom. In the name of Jesus Christ, amen.

Luke 15:17–20	2 Timothy 1:12
Romans 10:9	1 John 4:15
Philippians 2:11	Revelation 3:20

(Note: See "Basics," question 13.)

- **E** = *Entering into the Reign of God*
  Entering into the Fellowship of the Church
  Entering the Way of the Grace-filled Life
  Entering into the Mission of God

The faith-sharer yearns to enable the seeker to both see and enter the reign of God. The witness encourages and assists the seeker in the process of entering the community of faith.

When we receive Jesus Christ, we become the children of God and brothers and sisters of one another. Christian fellowship or community is not an option, but a necessity for discipleship. The church is a channel for the grace of God through worship, sacraments, fellowship, prayer, study, service, and witness.

Matthew 16:13–20;	Romans 1:6
26:26–30	1 Corinthians 1:9; 11:17–26;
Luke 22:14–23	12:12–31
John 3:1–16	Ephesians 4:7–16
Acts 1:6–8	

(Note: See "Basics," questions 21 and 22.)

7. **What are the key steps in this process of being saved by grace through faith?**

- God's grace in Christ Jesus
- Recognizing and repenting of sin
- Accepting God's forgiveness
- Confessing faith in Christ Jesus as Lord and Savior
- Entering into the reign of God and the church

The witness helps the seeker to see that he or she can enter into this new relationship with Christ now. If the seeker is not ready to say yes, the faith-sharer indicates his or her understanding and love, and assures the seeker that God will continue seeking. If the person is ready to accept the invitation, there is nothing more appropriate than prayer.

> For by grace you have been saved through faith. (Ephesians 2:8a)

8. **What are some helpful examples of prayers that may be used in the faith-sharing process?**

The following is an example of a prayer that the faith-sharer may pray with a seeker who is ready to accept the invitation of Christ.

Dear God, we thank you for the gift of your love in Jesus Christ. We praise you for taking the initiative and reaching out to us through Jesus Christ. We are grateful that you loved the world so much that you gave your only Son that whoever believes in him should not perish, but have eternal life. We praise you for making it possible for us to have our relationship with you restored. We are grateful that, through the death of your Son, you have dealt with the problem of sin, which spoiled your image in us and our relationship with you. We thank you for offering us the gifts of forgiveness and new life.

Dear God we are especially grateful that you have brought our *(brother/sister)* to this moment of commitment and decision. Surely your goodness and mercy have followed *(him/her)*, revealing your love in a very special way. We praise you. We adore you. We give you thanks that you have brought *(person's name)* to this moment of confession and surrender. We know that your Holy Spirit will make *(person's name)* become the kind of person that you want *(him/her)* to be. We thank you for your undeserved grace, and we know that you will enable *(person's name)* to continue to grow in *(his/her)* love for you and care and concern for others.

Now, we pray that you will help *(person's name)* to understand that the Christian life is a partnership. We praise you that we are not expected to struggle in our own strength and power. We praise you for the gift of your Holy Spirit, which brings us new power to live every day. We also praise you for the gift of other Christian sisters and brothers and for the support they give us in our Christian journey. Now, we pray that *(person's name)* will open *(his/her)* heart and invite you to take charge of *(his/her)* life.

At this point it is helpful to take the person by the hand (depending on the leadership of the Holy Spirit, you might lay hands upon his or her head) and pray the following prayer based on Ephesians 3:14–19:

(Person's name), may the living God strengthen you through the Holy Spirit in your inner being, that Christ may dwell in your heart through faith and that you may be filled with all the fullness of God.

9. What additional counsel is given to the faith-sharer?

- Remember that the Holy Spirit, through prevenient grace, prepares the seeker to receive the gospel in his or her own heart.
- Trust the Holy Spirit to guide you in a life and witness that conform to the mind and character of Jesus Christ (Philippians 2:5–11).
- Study the Holy Bible for a lifetime.
- Regularly worship and receive the sacrament of the Lord's Supper.
- Pray and fast. Pray and fast. Pray and fast.
- Invite the seeker to pray for you, the faith-sharer.

10. What is an important prayer for the faith-sharer to pray continually?

Lord, may I be a faithful witness in the name of God the Father, God the Son, and God the Holy Spirit. Amen

11. What is an encouraging word from the Holy Scriptures for faith-sharers?

"I pray that the sharing of your faith may become effective when you perceive all the good that we may do for Christ" (Philemon 6).

NOTES

NOTES

PRAYER LIST